Analyzing American Democracy

Politics and Political Science

Jon R. Bond
Texas A&M University

Kevin B. Smith
University of Nebraska–Lincoln

 Routledge
Taylor & Francis Group

NEW YORK AND LONDON

First published 2013
by Routledge
711 Third Avenue, New York, NY 10017

Simultaneously published in the UK
by Routledge
2 Park Square, Milton Park, Abingdon, Oxon OX14 4RN

Routledge is an imprint of the Taylor & Francis Group, an Informa business

Library of Congress Cataloging-in-Publication Data

Bond, Jon R.
Analyzing American democracy : politics and political science / by Jon Bond and Kevin Smith.
    pages cm

    1. United States—Politics and government.   2. Democracy—United States. I. Smith, Kevin B., 1963- II. Title.
JK276.B65 2013
320.473—dc23   2012044768

ISBN: 978-0-415-81051-7 (pbk)
ISBN: 978-0-203-07091-8 (ebk)
Printed in the United States of America by Courier, Kendallville, Indiana
Typeset in Minion Pro
by Apex CoVantage, LLC

CONTENTS

PART IV: CONCLUSION

PREFACE

We are political scientists. We're fascinated by politics. We seek to understand why politics works the way it does, and we believe that (political) science is the best way to achieve that understanding. Few college students are likely to share our fascination with politics. For some, politics is downright boring; others, like many Americans, are cynical and disgusted by all the partisan bickering and political infighting. Students who are interested in politics often view it as just "a matter of opinion"—it might be fun to argue about politics, but it's certainly not something that can be studied and understood scientifically. Our goal is not to convince you to share our fascination with politics. We do hope to contribute to your journey of becoming educated citizens and to show you why social science in general—and political science in particular—is an essential component of being an educated citizen.

Most of what undergraduates know and learn about politics comes from friends, family, news media, and the like, not from political science or political scientists. Indeed, most undergraduates are likely to take only one class and read only one textbook on American politics during their college career. Because our chances to contribute to their education are limited, we believe that a textbook needs to achieve three fundamental goals. First, at the most basic level, it must be comprehensive. Second, it must not only introduce students to the basic mechanics of American politics but also present in an accessible way the basics of political science and how political scientists explain why politics works the way it does. Third, and most importantly, it must provide students with some basic intellectual tools necessary to promote independent analytic thought about the often-confusing and always changing world of American politics. *Analyzing American Democracy: Politics and Political Science* seeks to achieve all three goals.

First, the book is comprehensive. It begins by providing students a historical and constitutional framework for understanding American politics. This means introducing students to the concept of democracy, the values democracy represents, and how these values are expressed in the structure and evolution of governance in America. It means a comprehensive examination of the linkage mechanisms that connect citizens to government and how those mechanisms express—or fail to express—the core democratic principles embodied in the American political system. It means systematically covering the key policymaking institutions of national government, not just the decision-making institutions established by the Constitution—legislative, executive, and judicial branches—but also bureaucracy, one of the most important and least understood institutions of American politics. Finally, it means giving an overview of how all these elements come together in making and implementing public policy. Of course, we can't cover everything, and we hope students reading this textbook might be intrigued enough by some of the topics that they will continue with additional upper-division courses in American politics. But we aim to include enough of the raw material to help students understand the workings of contemporary American politics such that they can become engaged members of the polity.

Second, this book aims not simply to cover the basics of the American political system but also to demonstrate how politics can be usefully and systematically studied generally. It is valuable for students to have the basic details down and even better for them to begin understanding how the pieces fit together. Our goal is to put into your hands a book that is about not just politics, but political *science*. We introduce students to the science and craft of political science in chapter 1 and use the frameworks and scholarship of the discipline to organize and explain all aspects of the American political system. In particular, we introduce students to three theoretical frameworks that illustrate the scientific study of politics—rational choice models, behavioral models, and evolutionary/biological models—and repeatedly return to these frameworks as explanatory aids throughout the book. Because we believe that the text used in political science courses should show students how political scientists report the results of their research, we continue to use the American Political Science Association style of in-text citations, with a comprehensive list of references. More generally, we lean heavily on political science scholarship in all of our explanatory accounts—our aim is to show students political science in action. We particularly want to do this because an introduction to American politics class may be the only political science course many students take in their undergraduate career. We want them to leave that class knowing something about what political scientists do and why it is important, just as students taking introductory economics or biology come away knowing something about the core theories and perspectives of those disciplines. In our view, too few introductory American politics textbooks achieve this, and too few members of the population see the value of political science compared to punditry and sound bites.

Third, the book seeks to be accessible but not "dumbed down." In our experience, students get the most out of this course not just by mastering the facts and theories covered, but when they further develop the tools of analytical thought. All our chapters begin with a story, written magazine-style, that provides a quick and easy introduction to the core themes of the chapter. The next section highlights the core concepts associated with the topic: What principles guide the creation and practice of a federal system? What role does public opinion, which is often ambiguous or divided, play in governance? How does political participation uphold the core principles of American democracy? What purpose does Congress serve as the national legislative institution? From there, chapters progressively build on these foundations to present the most important concepts, theories, and tools for understanding the great complexity of American politics. Undergraduate students could never hope to know everything about politics in America. Indeed, even if they did, such knowledge would quickly become outdated as new media emerge, rules change, and outcomes of public policies evolve to face new challenges among the citizenry. Students are best served by their textbook and by their undergraduate education if they also learn how to apply core principles and tools to future challenges. For example, the rapidly fragmenting and increasingly partisan media landscape feeds worries about media bias in many citizens. Understanding the core principle of political freedom puts a more partisan press into perspective—a functioning and healthy democracy does not need an unbiased press; what it needs is a *free* press. Or consider that many citizens are frustrated with the increasingly polarized nature of American politics and that elections increasingly seem to represent a choice between partisan extremes. Understanding the core principle of political equality and how the nomination process makes some more equal than others in deciding the general election ballot can help students understand why polarization exists and stimulate thinking on paths to reduce political polarization. American politics and the scholarship of political science tell an interesting and fascinating story; the task of telling that story in an engaging and accessible manner, we treated as both a challenge and an important responsibility.

PEDAGOGICAL FEATURES

We have devised a number of learning tools in this text to help students master the goals of their course. First, before students get immersed in the details of a chapter, they will find at the start a list of key questions to help frame the objectives of that chapter. These questions will help form a conceptual map of what comes next.

Next, every chapter has at least two "Politics in Practice" features that allow students to see the concepts and theories covered in the main body of the chapter in real-life terms. Here students are asked to think critically about how the practice of politics compares to the basic models presented in the text. How does the American Recovery and Reinvestment Act play out in a federal landscape? Does party alignment cause gridlock in government? How do focus groups used by political campaigns compare with random sample polls in trying to suss out what people think? Why do Americans hold their general election on Tuesdays? How does the Department of Education determine students' eligibility for financial aid?

In keeping with our focus on political science, we try to graphically illustrate researchers' findings and general concepts as much as we can. In these pages you will find a rich assortment of tables, figures, charts, and maps to present the empirical details of American politics. These are designed to support and parallel the primary themes of each chapter and help reach students with diverse learning styles.

At the end of each chapter, students might rightly ask themselves what were the most important points covered. We present the "Top 10 Takeaway Points" to answer just such questions. These lists are a handy reference for students reviewing their reading and preparing for quizzes and tests. They also further our goal of helping students see the forest through the trees, discerning the general principles that make sense of the numerous factual details.

ACKNOWLEDGMENTS

Like all books, this is a collaborative undertaking. The authors would like to extend thanks to all the good folks on the Routledge editorial team who contributed so much to what you hold in your hands. In particular, we thank Michael Kerns for his leap of faith, his patience, and his support. Thanks also to Editorial Assistant Darcy Bullock and Project Manager Denise File.

We appreciate it.

Thanks are also due to the distinguished team of teacher-scholars who reviewed the chapters. Their feedback and input was invaluable in what turned out to be an extensive set of revisions. Reviewers included Scott H. Ainsworth, Barbara Norrander, Jonathan Cole Winburn, Mark Joslyn, Richard Waterman, and additional anonymous individuals.

As always, we must also recognize Ken Meier, who made the original phone call that brought the two authors together on this project. In spite of all the hard work that phone call led to, the authors are still speaking to him—well, most of the time.

Jon Bond is grateful to numerous friends and colleagues. Rich Fleisher at Fordham University deserves special thanks. Although Rich is not a collaborator on this project, he has continued to offer cogent insights and advice that have made this a better book. Colleagues at Texas A&M University who shared their expertise on various topics include George Edwards, Roy Flemming, Bob Harmel, Kim Hill, Pat Hurley, Paul Kellstedt, Norm Luttbeg, Dave Peterson, Eric Godwin, and Jim Rogers. Several current and former graduate students helped with background research, provided technical support, and contributed in many other ways (yes, students, "many" is the appropriate adjective here). I am grateful to Lydia Andrade, Kristi Campbell, Michelle Chin, Jim Cottrill, Nathan Ilderton, Glen Krutz, Jose Villalobos, and Leslie McDonald. I am grateful to Gary Jacobson at the University of California, San Diego, and George Edwards at Texas A&M University for sharing their data that helped me update some key sections so that we can compete more effectively with their books. Larry Baum at Ohio State University, Frank Baumgartner at Pennsylvania State University, Beth Leech at Rutgers University, and John Bibby of the University of Wisconsin–Milwaukee also offered helpful comments and advice. Finally, I am most grateful for the love and support of my wife, Karon, and my daughters, Lynne, Mika, and Monika.

Kevin Smith would like to thank colleagues at the University of Nebraska–Lincoln, especially Jayme Neiman, Beth Theiss-Morse, and John Hibbing. To my family, thanks for the love and support. To my students, thanks for teaching me so much. To the Dallas Cowboys, thanks for nothing, you bunch of heartbreakers.

SUPPORT MATERIALS FOR STUDENTS AND INSTRUCTORS

Analyzing American Democracy is accompanied by a number of useful resources designed to aid in student learning and foster the instructional goals of faculty.

Classic Readings: *Perspectives on American Government*

Edited by Cal Jillson (Southern Methodist University) and David Brian Robertson (University of Missouri-St. Louis), *Perspectives on American Government: Readings in American Political Development and Institutional Change* facilitates deeper exploration of key themes in American politics. Each chapter of the reader is composed of six or seven selections, usually two or three classic readings, from Locke, the *Federalist,* Jefferson, Tocqueville, and the like, and four or five selections from the most outstanding historically oriented scholarship of recent years from top political scientists. This reader will deepen and enrich the learning experience of students using *Analyzing American Democracy.*

New Questions: *New Directions in American Politics*

Raymond J. La Raja (University of Massachusetts, Amherst) edits *New Directions in American Politics,* a stimulating and impressive collection of cutting edge puzzles in American politics. This carefully compiled volume—comprised of all original essays—builds on *Analyzing American Democracy* to show students how the American political system works as well as how political science works. The goals of La Raja's book dovetail nicely with this text in helping students build the analytical skills and critical thinking abilities necessary in college, careers, and civic life.

Online Resources

Analyzing American Democracy offers a website for both students and instructors at **www.routledge.com/cw/bond**. This site contains a wealth of useful resources to help students as they learn about American politics and instructors as they prepare their courses.

TEST BANK A full test bank, written by James Cottrill (Santa Clara University), covers each chapter with multiple choice, short answer, and essay questions. It is available in Questbank, Routledge's free online testing environment that allows instructors to build tests and quizzes using pre-loaded material, questions edited to suit individual needs, or newly crafted test items that you create. Instructors can quickly export tests as a widget on your website, an MS Word document, or a question bank that seamlessly imports into Blackboard, WebCT, Moodle, or a SCORM platform. There is no software to download, no annual fees, and unlimited access to adopters of *Analyzing American Democracy*.

POWERPOINT LECTURE SLIDES Written by Scott Granberg-Rademacker (Minnesota State University-Mankato) and Rebecca Hannagan (Northern Illinois University), these PowerPoint slides feature concise lecture outlines as well as all the figures and tables from the text.

COURSE MANAGEMENT CARTRIDGES Instructors have access to course cartridges to upload into Blackboard, Moodle, SCORM, or IMS Common Cartridge, making all the features of both the student site and instructor resources readily accessible in the platform you're already using.

STUDENT COMPANION WEBSITE Written by Byron D'Andra Orey (Jackson State University), this free online resource helps students master the main points of each chapter and develop their critical thinking skills.

- Practice Quizzes for each chapter provide students instant feedback on their answers.
- Interactive flashcards allow students to test their knowledge of the book's key concepts.
- Web exercises encourage students to explore further the themes of the book through web research.
- And links to useful websites and resources are provided here to allow for further investigation of the material.

Analyzing American Democracy

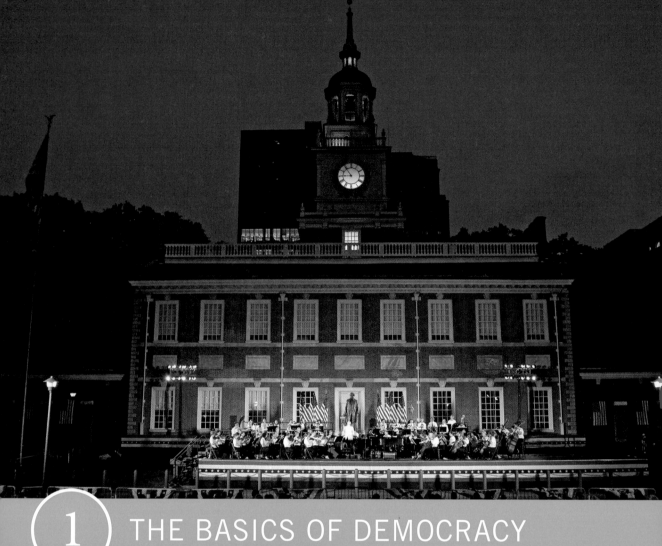

1 THE BASICS OF DEMOCRACY

KEY QUESTIONS

What is politics? What is government? What is a democracy?

What are the core principles of democracy?

How does a representative democracy uphold these core principles?

How can we make sense of democracy and politics in America?

J OHN ADAMS, second president of the United States and one of the dominant figures of the nation's founding, worried that Americans would misinterpret and misunderstand the democratic experiment he had worked so hard to set in motion. "The history of our Revolution," he wrote to his friend Benjamin Rush in 1790, "will be one continued lie from one end to the other" (Brands 2003). He thought future generations of Americans would romanticize the founders' notion of democracy rather than understand its true purpose. Adams was right.

John Adams, second president of the United States, was a native of Massachusetts. A graduate of Harvard University, where he studied law, he was a delegate to the first Constitutional Congress in 1774, where he contributed heavily to the debates on the Declaration of Independence. After serving two terms as vice president under Washington, he became president in 1796.

An overwhelming majority of Americans believe their form of government is best. Yet a similar majority mistrusts the government and gives it poor marks for job performance (Hibbing and Theiss-Morse 2003, 103). Americans express strong support for democracy, equating it with freedom, liberty, and self-determination. Yet they do not like a government that produces "uncertainty, conflicting options, long debate, competing interests, confusion, bargaining, and compromised imperfect solutions"; they want government to "do its job quietly and efficiently," without conflict and without fuss

(Hibbing and Theiss-Morse 1995, 147). Americans, in short, like the idea of democracy in the abstract, but they do not like democratic politics in practice (Slater 1991, 10).

The fundamental reason Americans hold government and politics in such disdain—and the premise of this book—is that they do not really understand what a democracy is and what a democracy does. As Adams feared, Americans' judgments of politics and government are not based on a hard-nosed assessment of the realities of democracy. Much of the frustration that Americans express about their government is anchored in a misunderstanding of what democracy is supposed to do, an unrealistic expectation of what it can do, and a failure to comprehend the dangers of pursuing undemocratic alternatives to solving problems.

KEY CONCEPTS:
POLITICS, GOVERNMENT, AND POPULAR SOVEREIGNTY

This book is about how democracy works in the United States. We examine what a democracy is, examine what it is supposed to do, and seek to explain how the institutions and processes of the American political system operate in theory and in practice. This means gaining a firm conceptual understanding of three crucial concepts—politics, government, and popular sovereignty—and what their combination means in the American context.

Politics and Government

For many people, the word "politics" is derogatory. To call others "political" is to accuse them of being manipulative and self-serving. Scholars, however, tend to view politics in more neutral terms. Following are two famous definitions of **politics**.

1. According to Harold D. Lasswell (1938), politics is "who gets what, when, and how."
2. According to David Easton (1953), politics is the "authoritative allocation of values."

politics The process of making binding decisions about who gets what or whose values everyone is going to live by.

Both definitions say the same thing: All groups must have some way to make collective decisions, and politics is the process of making those decisions. Politics is the process of coming to some definitive understanding of who is going to get what or whose values everyone is going to live by. Because individuals often disagree about who should get what or whose values should be binding on everyone, politics is a process of conflict management and resolution: it is a natural outcome of human interaction, not just something in which politicians and governments engage. Three friends in a video store arguing over what DVD to rent are engaging in a small-scale form of politics; they are figuring out whose values (in this case, taste in movies) will be binding on the group.

Although disagreements among friends over what movie to watch usually can be resolved without the group resorting to formal decision-making institutions and processes, this is not the case for large groups such as nations. How can we decide what to do as a society? Who or what gets to decide which values are binding on everyone? The institution that has the authority to make decisions that are binding on everyone is generally referred to as **government**.

Government is not the only institution that seeks to manage conflict and make authoritative decisions about who gets what. Churches, for example, make decisions about what behaviors are right and wrong and urge their members to follow church teachings. What makes government different from other decision-making institutions is coercion. Churches can coerce members of their congregation through threats of excommunication and the like, but they cannot extend that power over nonmembers and other organizations. Governments can. A church that decides that abortion or consumption of alcohol is wrong can attempt to make such values binding on its congregation. A government can make such values binding on everyone. Act in defiance of government decisions—that is, break the law—and the government can take your property, your liberty, and even your life. Government is the only institution in society that can legitimately use such coercion on all individuals and organizations, making it the ultimate decider of who gets what (Downs 1957, 23).

Popular Sovereignty

The authority to legally wield this coercive power to allocate values is called **sovereignty** (this is why monarchs are sometimes called "sovereigns," reflecting the historical role of kings and queens as absolute rulers). Governments can be categorized into three basic forms based on who wields sovereign powers. The power to authoritatively allocate values can be vested in a single person, which creates a form of government called an **autocracy**. Autocrats rule as absolute monarchs or dictators, personally deciding who gets what. Nazi Germany under Adolf Hitler and the Soviet Union under Joseph Stalin are examples of autocracies. In a second form, power can be vested in a small group of people, a government called an **oligarchy**. A military junta (a group of generals) is an example of an oligarchy. The third option is to broadly share power among all citizens, a form of government called a **democracy**. The word "democracy" is derived from two Greek roots: *demos,* which means "people," and *kratia,* which means "rule." Literally, democracy means "rule by the people."

government The institution that has the authority to make binding decisions for all of society.

sovereignty The legitimate authority in a government to wield coercive power to authoritatively allocate values.

autocracy A form of government in which the power to make authoritative decisions and allocate resources is vested in one person.

oligarchy A form of government in which the power to make authoritative decisions and allocate resources is vested in a small group of people.

democracy A form of government in which all the citizens have the opportunity to participate in the process of making authoritative decisions and allocating resources.

Thus, in an autocracy a single person is sovereign, and in an oligarchy a small elite is sovereign. In contrast, in a democracy, sovereignty belongs to *all* citizens, a distribution of political power known as **popular sovereignty**. Popular sovereignty gets to the core of what a democracy is: a form of government where all citizens have the right to participate in the process of deciding who gets what. What this means is that democracy is primarily about *process*—how decisions are made. But a democratic decision-making process does not guarantee that the *substance* of those decisions will be democratic.

Process and Substance

DEMOCRACY AS PROCESS In a democracy, how decisions are made is as important as what those decisions are. Indeed, some scholars view democracy as much more about means than ends (Schumpeter 1942). The means of democracy—the institutions and rules that organize and operate the political system—create a decision-making process that is typically slow and inefficient. Because all citizens have a right to participate, democratic decision making demands patience, tolerance of opposing viewpoints, and a willingness to compromise.

Ironically, it is this basic nature of a democratic process that Americans find most objectionable about their political system: inefficiency, gridlock, and lots of conflict (Hibbing and Theiss-Morse 1995, 147). Given its general unpopularity, it's worth asking whether a democratic decision-making process is the best approach to politics in the United States. Why opt for a form of government all but guaranteed to be slow, inefficient, and constantly embroiled in conflict? The short answer is that a system based on popular sovereignty tends to be more equitable and just. As one astute observer put it, "democracy is the worst form of government. It is the most inefficient, the most clumsy, the most unpractical. . . . Yet democracy is the only form of social order admissible because it is the only one consistent with justice" (Briffault 1930, quoted in Thomsett and Thomsett 1994, 37). A democratic process is rarely marked by efficiency, agreement, clarity, or speed. Rather than efficiency or effectiveness, the characteristics of a democratic process include the right to vote, to publicly disagree with government decisions and other citizens, to petition an elected representative, to sue, to form an organization with policy goals, to engage in a political campaign, and to support a political party.

DEMOCRATIC SUBSTANCE Though the heart of democracy is about process, substance counts too. Ironically, a democratic process can produce an undemocratic outcome. For example, in the United States, majorities historically have supported policies to deny voting rights and educational and economic opportunities to citizens based on gender, ethnicity, and race. Legislatures responded to these preferences with laws systematically denying civil rights and liberties to certain citizens. The process of making those policies could be considered democratic— elections were held, legislators debated, and the majority preference became law.

popular sovereignty The idea that the highest political authority in a democracy is the will of the people.

CHAPTER 1 THE BASICS OF DEMOCRACY

The substance of those decisions, though, systematically stripped large numbers of citizens of their ability to participate fully in political life. The end result was not just unfair, but undemocratic. By taking away the rights of certain citizens to participate in the process of deciding who gets what, the democratic process had made America less democratic.

This is one of the central problems of a democratic system: how to ensure popular sovereignty when people want to use their ability to authoritatively allocate values to limit the rights of others. As U.S. history amply demonstrates, those in power have been tempted to limit the political participation of those who disagree with them. How does democracy uphold the concept of popular sovereignty when some want to use that power to limit the rights of others?

Core Democratic Principles

In theory, popular sovereignty helps ensure a system where everyone is a political equal and free to participate in making binding decisions. In practice, popular sovereignty rests on the extent to which the process and outcomes of a political system are consistent with three core principles: majority rule, political freedom, and political equality. To be democratic, the process of making decisions *and* the outcomes of those decisions must be compatible with these core principles.

MAJORITY RULE Popular sovereignty means that in a democracy, political decisions should be responsive to the needs and demands of ordinary people. If the government does not respond to the expressed preferences of the people, citizens must be able to exercise their sovereignty and hold government accountable for its actions. The problem here is that citizens often have very different ideas of who should get what. Government cannot respond to the preferences of all citizens because citizens want government to do contradictory things. Consider differences in public opinion on issues ranging from same-sex marriage to tax cuts. The government cannot sanction same-sex unions while simultaneously outlawing them any more than it can cut taxes by raising tax rates. How can popular sovereignty be meaningful when people have such radically different notions about how values should be authoritatively allocated?

Democracies seek to exercise popular sovereignty through **majority rule**, which means that government follows the course of action preferred by most people. The preferred alternative does not necessarily have to be an **absolute majority**, defined as 50 percent plus one of all eligible citizens, or even a **simple majority**, defined as 50 percent plus one of those who actually vote. If voters' preferences are divided among three or more courses of action, so that none have more than 50 percent support, the choice with the greatest support is called a **plurality**.

Though majority rule is the basic guideline for translating popular sovereignty into political decisions in democracies, it has to be balanced with **minority rights**. A minority is any group numerically inferior to the majority, and it retains the full rights of democratic citizenship. In democracies, minority viewpoints are permitted

majority rule The principle under which government follows the course of action preferred by most people.

absolute majority Fifty percent plus one of all members or all eligible voters.

simple majority Fifty percent plus one of those participating or of those who vote.

plurality The largest percentage of a vote, when no one has a majority.

minority rights The full rights of democratic citizenship held by any group numerically inferior to the majority. These fundamental democratic rights cannot be taken away—even if a majority wishes to do so—without breaking the promise of democracy.

to be heard and to be critical of the majority's views and actions. In the theory of democracy, the rights of minorities—their political freedom—cannot be taken away, even if the majority prefers this course of action. In practice, as we shall see, majorities often have succeeded in depriving minorities of their democratic rights.

POLITICAL FREEDOM Government cannot respond to the will of the people if people are not free to express their wants and demands. To uphold the notion of popular sovereignty, minorities—even if they consist of one or two people with repugnant views—must have the right to participate and express those views. The necessary ingredients for political freedom are the right to criticize governmental leaders and policies, the right to propose new courses of government action, the right to form and join interest groups, the right to discuss political issues free from government censorship, and the right of citizens to seek and hold public office.

Note that the objects of free expression are plural. If all the people have the right to express their wants, demands, and preferences, they will rarely express the *same* wants, demands, and preferences. In the United States, political freedom means a lot of different wants, demands, and preferences, which makes it difficult for government to respond to the people. The central reason democratic governments do not respond to the will of the people is not that they fail to listen. On the contrary, it is that they are listening all too well to a set of vague, conflicting, and contradictory preferences.

Political freedom also means a basic guarantee of individual liberty. Individual citizens are free to make their own choices and to select their own goals and the means to achieve them. However, there are limits on individual liberty. Society, for example, will not sanction an individual's desire to become a skillful thief. Yet democracies keep limits on individual freedom to a minimum. Political freedom bestows on the individual the right to choose, advocate, or follow different political, social, and economic ideas, paths, and plans.

POLITICAL EQUALITY **Political equality** means individual preferences are given equal weight. Popular sovereignty means all citizens should have the same opportunities to influence the process of deciding who gets what. For example, when citizens vote, each vote should count the same. Wealth, partisanship, or ideology cannot make one person's vote count more than any other. This notion of political equality not only refers to participation in influencing governmental decisions; it also involves being subject to those decisions. Everyone is entitled to **equality under the law**. The law is applied impartially without regard to the identity or status of the individual involved. In a democracy, wealth, fame, and power are not supposed to exempt anyone from the sanction of law. Few quarrel with these notions and their importance to upholding popular sovereignty, but political equality is a complicated concept because of its relationship to social and economic equality. **Social equality** is the idea that people should be free from class or social barriers and discrimination. Many view social equality as a desirable ideal but disagree on what, if anything, the government should do to achieve it. The long battle over racial equality in the United States, for example, reflects different attitudes on race

political equality The idea that individual preferences should be given equal weight.

equality under the law The idea that the law is supposed to be applied impartially, without regard for the identity or status of the individual involved.

social equality The idea that people should be free of class or social barriers and discrimination.

as well as different views about government's responsibility to deal with racial differences in social, political, or economic opportunities or outcomes. Under its strictest interpretation, **economic equality** means each individual should receive the same amount of material goods regardless of his or her contribution to society. Equal distribution of wealth, especially as a coercive government policy, is unlikely to be considered compatible with the core principles of American democracy. Redistributing power and wealth from the well-off to the less well-off is always controversial—and for good reason: it limits the freedom of individuals to decide how to use their economic and social resources.

Yet social and economic equality are inevitably tied to political equality because social and economic resources can be translated into political influence. People with wealth and status can participate in politics more easily and effectively than others. Since democratic government responds to the preferences of those who participate—those who actually exercise the right to express their preferences—government policy tends to benefit those with wealth and status. This upper-class bias in turn gives upper-class citizens a greater ability to influence government in the future and thus brings into question the basic notion of popular sovereignty. When economic and social resources are unevenly distributed, merely giving all citizens the freedom to participate to the best of their ability may have the disturbing result of producing less political equality.

The issue of how to handle the conundrum connecting political equality with social and economic equality is largely unresolved. At a minimum, democracies must preserve political equality in the sense that everyone has an equal right to express their preferences. Yet, inequitable distribution of wealth also gives certain individuals more forceful and effective ways to express their preferences. A wealthy campaign contributor is much more likely to get the attention of a legislator than a busy single parent who can hardly find the time to vote. If accused of a crime, a rich individual can hire a top-notch attorney, a private investigator, and an independent set of experts for the defense. A poor person accused of the same crime may have to rely on a single overworked public defender.

Political equality is reconciled with social and economic equality by favoring, instead of equal distribution of wealth, **equality of opportunity**, meaning the right of all people to develop their abilities to the fullest extent. In other words, all individuals should have the opportunity to go as far in life as their desires, talents, and efforts allow. Thus, if people differ in abilities, desires, and work ethic, some will acquire more social status and economic wealth than others. In the United States, democracy aims to give individuals the paradoxical right of an equal opportunity to become unequal. This sounds good in theory, but does everyone really have the same opportunity to "become unequal" in practice? Those who are born into wealth, who live in neighborhoods with good schools, and who have nurturing parents have advantages and opportunities that those born into poverty, trapped in subpar schools, and suffering from abusive or neglectful parents do not. This disparity raises the question of whether government is required to level the playing field by guaranteeing a set of services (such as adequate nutrition, housing, education, and health care) considered essential to individual development. Equal opportunity to become unequal suggests

economic equality The idea that each individual should receive the same amount of material goods, regardless of his or her contribution to society.

equality of opportunity The idea that every individual has the right to develop to the fullest extent of his or her abilities.

that although a democratic society is not required to guarantee equality at the end of the individual's developmental process, it should ensure equality at the beginning. What constitutes equality at the beginning—what level of educational, health, and social services provides a roughly equal set of opportunities for all to develop to the fullest extent of their abilities—is a matter of constant controversy and debate.

CONFLICTING VALUES: A DELICATE BALANCING ACT To sum up, democracy is a form of government where the power to authoritatively allocate values is held by all citizens (popular sovereignty), which in turn rests on three core principles: majority rule, political freedom, and political equality. Although these have been discussed separately, one of these principles by itself is not enough to make a government democratic. At least in theory, all three must be reflected in the process and the outcomes of government decisions. In practice, though, achieving all three simultaneously is a difficult balancing act because these principles can conflict. Maximizing freedom may lead to less equality; achieving more equality may require placing limitations on someone's freedom; the majorities may use their power to rob minorities of their political freedom and their political equality.

TWO BASIC FORMS OF DEMOCRACY

All democracies share the basic traits described in the previous section, but all democracies are not the same. Democracy can take different forms depending on how popular sovereignty is put into practice. For example, consider the core principle of majority rule. Just how much control do citizens need to exercise over government decisions to uphold this principle? Is it sufficient that majorities choose decision makers, or must majorities approve specific government decisions? Do citizens need to be capable of determining for themselves what kind of policy is needed to preserve and advance liberty and equality in society, or is judging policies that are suggested by others sufficient?

These questions have no definitive answers. Reasonable people equally committed to democratic values may disagree on them. Thus, although a general theory of democracy rests on a core set of principles relating to popular sovereignty, there are different theories about the specific procedures, ideals, and assumptions associated with a democratic society. These differences can be divided into two broad categories: direct democracy and representative democracy.

Direct Democracy

direct democracy A form of democracy in which ordinary citizens, rather than representatives, collectively make government decisions.

In a **direct democracy**, citizens are the principal political decision makers. Direct democracy was first practiced in certain ancient Greek city-states, notably Athens.

DIRECT DEMOCRACY IN THE MODERN ERA

In 2008, chickens gained rights in California, and gays and lesbians lost them. Specifically, voters approved proposed amendments to the state's constitution to regulate chicken coops and to ban same-sex marriage.

This odd combination of granting rights to fowl and denying rights to people serves as a good example of the pros and cons of direct democracy, at least as it is practiced in the United States.

This form of direct democracy is the ballot initiative, which was begun a century ago by progressive reformers seeking to curb the abuses of legislatures. About half of the states have the ballot initiative, and it is popular with citizens. Supporters of the initiative process say that why is no secret: "Initiatives are fundamental to freedom," says M. Dane Waters, president of the Initiative and Referendum Institute. Opponents of initiatives—including many political scientists and other professional observers and students of politics— say they are better at making mischief than promoting freedom, and they have a damning legacy of undermining good government. Consider chickens and same-sex marriage. In the former case, direct democracy is being used to amend a constitution to deal with policy minutia. In the latter, direct democracy is being used by a majority to deny rights to a minority. In both cases, direct democracy is passing by, and perhaps undermining, representative democracy.

The contemporary popularity of the initiative is traced to 1978, when California voters triggered a nationwide tax revolt by passing Proposition 13. Proposition 13 rolled back tax assessments to their 1975 levels, mandated that property could be assessed at no more than 1 percent of its value, capped assessment increases at a maximum of 2 percent a year, and allowed reassessments only when property is sold.

To its supporters, Proposition 13 is the best-known example of the benefits of direct democracy—it let the people deal directly with an issue the legislature could not or would not satisfactorily address. To its detractors, Proposition 13 represents everything that is bad about direct democracy. Although cutting property taxes was popular, Proposition 13 clamped down on the primary revenue source of local governments, leaving them increasingly dependent on the state.

Local governments (especially schools) never fully recovered from this blow, and many remain chronically underfunded. Upset with the impact on services, California voters compensated with a raft of new initiatives (such as mandating state levels of education spending). The end result, critics point out, is what you would expect from the making of major policy decisions without full contemplation of the consequences: a mess. The "solution" to this mess has been more direct democracy and an even bigger mess. Thanks in no small part to the ballot initiative, California now has one of the longest constitutions in the world and one that severely limits the ability of representative democratic institutions to govern.

Part of the problem is that ballot initiatives are a policymaking vehicle for well-heeled interest groups as much as a genuine reflection of popular will. It is expensive to qualify a proposal for the ballot, and as a result, most ballot initiatives come from individuals or groups with very narrow agendas that are painted over with a populist ad campaign. Even genuine populism, though, is sometimes no substitute for deliberation. Voters in initiative states typically fail the basic requisites of a successful direct democracy—that is, to be very involved in public life and highly knowledgeable about the voting issues and informed about their potential consequences. Voters are often presented with propositions that are couched in lengthy legalese or have multibillion-dollar consequences, and they may be confused about what the initiatives mean. Rather than viewing it as a vehicle to exercise individual liberty, critics of the initiative process see it as doing little more than breeding bad policy, frustration, and resentment.

The founders explicitly rejected direct democracy as a basis of government for just such reasons. As James Madison put it in *Federalist* Number 10, direct democracies "have ever been spectacles of turbulence and contention; have ever been found incompatible with personal security or the rights of property; and have in general been as short in their lives as they have been violent in their deaths."

Critics suggest that supporters of the ballot initiative should pay a little less attention to populist public relations and a little more to the arguments of the founders. The solution to unresponsive and ineffective government lies in the hands of the voters every election day. If you do not like what government is doing, vote the rascals out. The problem with direct democracy is that rather than a government of laws, it produces laws without government (Broder 2000, 243).

SOURCES Broder, David S. 2000. *Democracy Derailed*. New York: Harcourt.

The Economist. 2009. "The Tyranny of the Majority." December 19, 47–48.

Quinn, Andrew. 2002. "From Cockfights to Pig Pens, Vote Sets Agenda." Reuters News Service. http://story.news.yahoo.com/news?tmpl_story2&ncid_584&e_4&u_/nm/20021103/pl_nm_/election_initiatives_dc (accessed November 3, 2002).

The Rothenberg Political Report. 2005 "Statewide Ballot Initiative Results." http://rothenbergpoliticalreport.blogspot.com/2005/11/2005-statewide-ballot-initiative.html (accessed May 5, 2006).

In limited forms, direct democracy is also currently used in the United States. The New England town meeting, where all citizens in the community are eligible to participate in making local government policy decisions, is a form of direct democracy. Direct democracy is also evident in states that allow ballot **initiative**s and **referendum**s, elections where citizens vote on policy decisions. About half of the states allow ballot initiatives, which in the past 30 years have increasingly been used to make major policy decisions on everything from setting tax rates to approving—or rejecting—same-sex marriage.

Historically, successful direct democratic systems have been rare because of a number of inherent problems that lead to instability and poor policy decisions. Part of the difficulty is the unwieldy decision-making machinery of direct democracy (imagine setting tuition rates by inviting all taxpayers in the state to a series of meetings to decide what a college education should cost). More serious are the demands that direct democracy places on the individual. Sound decision making in a direct democracy requires a huge commitment to public life on the part of average citizens. At a minimum, it requires citizens to understand the nuts and bolts of government and politics, to be fully informed of the issues on which they vote, and to be actively and continuously engaged in public life. Citizens lacking these traits cannot grasp the consequences of their decisions for the government or society, and they can be misled or manipulated by well-funded groups with a stake in seeing one side prevail. When this happens, direct democracy is prone to producing bad policy decisions. Critics argue that this is the problem with modern forms of direct democracy such as the ballot initiative (see the Politics in Practice feature "Direct Democracy in the Modern Era").

initiative An election in which ordinary citizens circulate a petition to put a proposed law on the ballot for the voters to approve.

referendum An election in which a state legislature refers a proposed law to the voters for their approval.

Even with well-informed and fully engaged citizens, direct democracies are vulnerable to tyranny of the majority or mob rule, situations where the core values of political equality and political freedom are readily violated. Policy can quickly be shaped by whatever passions incite a majority of the citizens. Those who advocate unpopular minority viewpoints in a direct democracy and incur the displeasure of the majority may face some unpleasant consequences. These risks are acute in a large and diverse society with social fault lines—such as race, religion, and ideology—separating the majority from the minority. In a direct democracy, abiding by the core principles of democracy is the majority's responsibility. Thus, to live up to the promise of democracy, the majority must consist of individuals who understand and are deeply committed to all those principles, not just the principle of majority rule. Yet a constant temptation for the majority is to abandon those principles and benefit themselves by using democratic processes to make decisions that are undemocratic in substance, since those decisions discriminate or persecute a minority. For these reasons, the history of direct democracies is often one of instability and failure (Broder 2000).

Representative Democracy

Because direct democracy is simply not a stable or practical basis for government in large, diverse societies, an alternate form of democracy developed in Western nations during the past three centuries. The form of democracy practiced in nations such as Great Britain and the United States is called **representative democracy**, defined as a system of government where ordinary citizens do not make governmental decisions themselves but choose public officials—representatives of the people—to make decisions for them. Representative democracy is based on popular sovereignty, but it is achieved indirectly by the people's representatives rather than by the people themselves, as in a direct democracy. Representative democracies such as Great Britain and the United States are sometimes called **liberal democracies**[1] because of their concern for individual liberty. In liberal democracies, the rule of law and a constitution constrain elected representatives and the will of the majority from using their power to take away the rights of minorities. Thus, liberal representative democracies embody the three basic principles of democracy, but they use different institutions and slightly different ideals to accomplish these goals. In representative democracies, only a tiny fraction of citizens hold policymaking positions. For example, each member of the U.S. House of Representatives has a constituency of about 700,000 people, which means a single individual represents the interests of nearly three-quarters of a million citizens.

The form of liberal representative democracy we know today first developed in three Western nations: Great Britain, Switzerland, and the United States. In the

> **representative democracy** Defined as a system of government where ordinary citizens do not make governmental decisions themselves but choose public officials—representatives of the people—to make decisions for them.

> **liberal democracy** A representative democracy, such as Great Britain or the United States, that has a particular concern for individual liberty. The rule of law and a constitution constrain elected representatives and the will of the majority from using their power to take away the rights of minorities.

---

[1] Keep in mind that the term "liberal" is used here in the traditional sense, meaning a concern for individual liberty. It does not refer to the contemporary political label. We discuss ideology and contemporary usage of "liberal" and "conservative" later in the chapter.

late eighteenth and early nineteenth centuries, a large number of people in these countries began to select their own political leaders. From this narrow base, liberal democracy spread to other nations of Western Europe and the British Commonwealth. Thus, liberal representative democracy is a relatively new form of government, originally practiced by just a handful of nations. In fact, if genuine democracy requires that *all* citizens have the right to affect governmental decisions by choosing the government's leaders, then this type of government is a modern phenomenon. In the United States, male citizens did not gain universal voting rights until the latter part of the nineteenth century, and women had to wait until the 1920s. Ethnic minorities were systematically excluded from political participation up until the early 1960s. One can reasonably argue that the core principles of democracy were not securely embedded in representative democratic systems until the past half-century.

REPRESENTATIVE SYSTEMS AND CORE DEMOCRATIC PRINCIPLES

Because citizens do not govern directly in a representative democracy, ensuring that basic democratic principles are protected and advanced rests on a set of political techniques and institutions different from those used in a direct democracy. Representative democracy means the many watching the few, but it is not just the few who rule who are important. The many who select and hold those rulers accountable are where we find out whether popular sovereignty is actually practiced. At a minimum, the many must be able to implement their observations through political action, and there must be an incentive for representatives to be responsive to the wishes of the people. To make this happen, representative democracy is heavily dependent on the institutions used to organize the political system and the values that underpin its operation. A number of democratic institutions are common in representative democracies. Some of the most familiar ones are elections, political parties, and interest groups.

In 2012 voters for the first time used ballot initiatives to approve same-sex marriage laws. Same-sex marriage proposals were approved in Maine and Maryland, making them the first states to adopt such laws through a popular ballot.

© AP Photo/Joel Page

Elections

The most obvious mechanism that representative democracies employ to incorporate democratic principles into the political system is elections. Through elections, representative democracies deliberately create job insecurity for major officeholders. Those who hold office exercise power for a fixed term, so that citizens have periodic opportunities to determine whether the officeholders should continue exercising power. If citizens are displeased with the performance of those in public office, the remedy is to replace them. In this fashion, the rulers have an incentive to be responsive to the needs and demands of the ruled, and the citizens can hold the rulers accountable if they fail to be responsive. Elections are the central mechanism for achieving majority rule in representative democracies. Though representatives are often chosen by plurality rather than outright majorities, in principle all citizens retain the power to decide whether representatives will continue for another term.

In a democracy every citizen has a right to vote and thus a direct voice in choosing elected officials. By creating insecurity of tenure for major officeholders, elections create incentives for the elected to respond to the needs of the electors and also provide recourse for the electors if the elected are not being responsive

Political Parties

For elections to truly hold representatives accountable, a democratic system must offer citizens meaningful choices. The institution that typically fills this need is the political party, defined as an organization that puts forward candidates for public office. To provide an element of choice, at least two competing parties must propose candidates. With competition, voters can choose the party that best represents their preferences. Political parties must accept one another's existence as a necessity for a functioning representative democracy. Accordingly, the party (or parties) in control of the government must allow the opposition party (or parties) to criticize what current government leaders are doing and to propose alternative courses of action for the consideration of voters. That is, the party in control of government must recognize the political freedom of those out of power.

Interest Groups

Beyond holding periodic elections, a representative democracy must provide for continuous communication between the leaders in government and ordinary citizens. This communication is critical to ensuring that citizens' views on public issues are transmitted to those who make major political decisions and thus fosters majority rule. Political parties fulfill this function to some extent; decisive election results can send a clear message to government. But elections occur only once every few years, and citizens need ways to communicate their changing needs between elections. Although citizens have the freedom to express their opinions individually, communication is more effective if diverse individual views are aggregated and transmitted in a coherent way. Citizens in a democracy also have the freedom to organize around common interests and communicate those interests to government.

An institution that has emerged to promote such communication is the interest group. Interest groups aggregate the interests of like-minded individuals and organize to press their common views on government decision makers. Interest groups are likely to contain only a small proportion of the total population, but they enable elected officials to gain some understanding of how a number of people in a common situation—for example, students, businesspeople, or farmers—feel about matters, such as student loan programs, taxes, or farm price supports. Moreover, because communication is a two-way process, interest groups not only press demands on decision makers; they also transmit proposals by political leaders back to their memberships. Just as parties compete to place their candidates in public office, interest groups vie to influence public policy. If the system is operating properly, these groups check and balance one another's efforts, and no one group or small collection of groups dominates the political process.

REPRESENTATIVE DEMOCRACY IN THE UNITED STATES

Although these institutions and principles characterize representative democracies in general, the way democratic government is implemented in different nations varies considerably.

Central Beliefs of Democracy in America

At the core of the American political system is a belief that people are, for the most part, rational and capable of deciding what is good for them personally. Even if the average person is often incorrect, no elite group is assumed to be wise enough or unselfish enough to rule in the interests of all members of society. To ensure that the interests of everyone will be taken into account, the bulk of the population has the right to influence decisions that affect their lives through mechanisms such as elections, and government has the obligation to make this possible by protecting individual rights to liberty and free expression.

These central beliefs underpinning American democracy—that fundamental individual rights are inviolate and that there is a universal prerogative to participate in collective decisions—constitute a general commitment to popular sovereignty. Accordingly, we expect the American political system, in process and substance, to reflect and uphold the three core principles of democracy. Yet no political system produced by human beings completely lives up to its ideals; a gap always occurs between the ideals and the operation of the political institutions designed to embody them. To better understand how the American system lives up to the ideals embedded in the core principles of democracy, it is important to understand not just what a democracy is, but also what it is not.

Fallacies Associated with Democracy in America

In practice, a political system based on popular sovereignty contrasts sharply with a number of popularly held fallacies, or incorrect beliefs, about democracy. One fallacy is that democracy promises the best policy decisions. It does not. Democracies in general, including certainly the democracy in America, make no promises to produce the most effective, efficient, or fair policy decisions. Representative democracy handles disagreements about what we ought to do by allowing everyone to get involved in the conflict. The result is often untidy, confusing decisions with which few are wholly satisfied. The outcomes, in other words, are frequently less than optimal. What we end up with is usually not what we want, but rather what we can live with. Such outcomes do not represent the failure of democracy. The whole point of a democratic system is to broker compromises among competing points of view and arrive at decisions that the majority supports and the minority can tolerate.

A second fallacy is a belief that democracy boils down to majority rule, that the American system is predicated on the majority always getting what it wants. The founders of the American form of democracy placed no particular trust in the majority, and in the United States the majority has never been given the freedom to decide all matters that affect people's lives. If people have fundamental rights, as the founders believed, then the majority must be kept from depriving the minority of those rights. Liberal representative democracy is founded on the notion that although government should respond to the wishes of the majority, the majority is limited. Certain fundamental rights cannot be taken away, even by majority vote. For example, in the United States and Great Britain, majorities of the population are Protestant, but they are not allowed to tell people of Catholic, Jewish, or other faiths how to worship. Likewise in Western democratic nations, the individual's right to private property is respected, and personal goods cannot be taken for public use without compensation. It is precisely such limitations on the scope of government that distinguish democratic societies from totalitarian ones. Majority rule, in other words, does not outrank political freedom or political equality.

A third fallacy is that social conflict is caused by the institutions of representative democracy and the people who occupy them. Representative institutions reflect rather than cause social conflict. Indeed, if the diverse views and conflicting interests that exist in society as a whole did not show up in our representative institutions, then they would not be representative. Political scientist Benjamin Barber

POLITICS IN PRACTICE

COLLEGE STUDENTS: VALUES, VOTING, AND VOLUNTEERING

October 13, 2011, was the designated day for the National Student Solidarity Protest, an event designed to show support for Occupy Wall Street, the more or less spontaneously formed movement to oppose economic and social inequality that quickly drew international support and attention. Word of the planned student protest spread quickly through social media, and Occupy Colleges, a grassroots group set up to connect college students to the broader movement, confirmed that more than 100 (by some counts 150) colleges and universities would join in with a day of demonstrations. The great day of protest dawned, and on most of those campuses . . . not much happened. On some campuses no one showed up at all.

The point here is not that the Occupy movement, or at least college student participation in the movement, is a complete bust. It's just that for all the passion, dedication, and involvement of a few, it's clear that the majority of college students are less interested in politics, are more poorly informed about political issues, and participate in political discourse at lower rates than most other demographic groups—not exactly a formula for ensuring that the core democratic principles are sustained over the long term.

Consider the following: Less than a quarter of college students say they are interested in politics; less than 10 percent regularly talk about politics with their friends; less than a fifth belong to any form of political group; and as a group, they score abysmally low on measures of political participation. Only a third routinely vote in elections. Things did trend up a bit during the presidential election of 2008 as many college students became part of Obama's "Yes We Can" presidential campaign. Slightly more than 50 percent of people 18–29 cast ballots that year. This uptick did not last; by the 2010 midterms, voting among that age group was down to 24 percent. If popular sovereignty depended on college students, government would not have much to respond to; it's hard for majority rule to work if the majority doesn't bother checking in at least once in a while. Political freedom for college students mostly means the freedom not to get involved or even to pay attention.

Yet compared to their peers without college experience, college students actually are well informed and have high rates of participation. Most college students fall into the 18- to 24-year-old age group, and more than 90 percent of people in that age group who are in the labor force rather than in school rarely read a newspaper. A similar majority rarely talk about politics with their friends. More than a third report they almost never vote.

Though college students in general and young people in particular are for the most part disengaged from politics, they are certainly involved in other ways. Voting might be out on the nation's college campuses, but volunteering is definitely in. Two-thirds of students report volunteering time in their community, and a majority view volunteering as a more important way to bring about social change than voting.

So overall, college students are uninterested in politics and barely participate in the political system, but they are involved in their communities and give generously of their time to service-based organizations. What does this mean? Do college students understand and live the ideals of democracy? No.

argues that we must realize that in democracies, "representative institutions do not steal our liberties from us, [but rather] they are the precious medium through which we secure those liberties" (1996, 20). In other words, representative institutions help ensure that the people's often conflicting views are expressed and dealt

That may seem an overly harsh assessment to draw from reading the statistical tea leaves in a handful of opinion polls. Yet what those polls consistently indicate is this: college students view politics as too divisive, too removed from their day-to-day lives, and too inefficient a way to solve problems. In contrast, volunteering with a community service organization—helping out at a food bank, tutoring in a school, and so on—brings with it a concrete feeling of contributing to a communally desired goal. Fair enough. Volunteer organizations do important work and do make important and very real differences in people's lives. College students make a real civic contribution when they volunteer.

Yet volunteering is not a particularly good civics lesson. Here's why: Voluntary service organizations tend to have noncontroversial goals and attract people with similar attitudes toward those goals. What they tend to lack are the very things that characterize democratic politics: adversarial goals, organized opposition, dissenting views, divisive issues—that's democratic politics. That sort of conflict is not why people are typically attracted to volunteering. Who wants to volunteer to do good deeds only to find most of their time engaged in knock-down arguments about what should be done or who should get what?

Despite the many undeniable good deeds and worthy goals achieved by volunteering, it tends to promote a misunderstanding about democratic politics. Achieving noncontroversial, service-based goals prompts those who volunteer toward unrealistic attitudes: "Look what we did! Why can't those bozos in Washington do the same thing?" (Hibbing and Theiss-Morse 2003, 186–187).

Those "bozos in Washington" are dealing with the harsh realities of making decisions in a democracy. That means working without a consensus, dealing with sharp disagreement, and striving for what you can live with, not necessarily what you feel good about. College students are absolutely correct if they see politics as messy and combative; they are also correct to believe their participation in politics will not bring about the changes they really want. The obstacle to those changes, though, is not the political system: it is other people and other groups who oppose those changes and have just as much right to participate as anyone else.

How do you deal with dissenting views? How do you constructively engage with people with whom you disagree? How do you accept that what you want—a policy, a candidate, a campaign—may well lose? These are the tough issues of living in a democracy. Given what the polls say about their attitudes toward politics and government, college students are not striving particularly hard to find answers. Indeed, they do not seem to be particularly interested in asking the questions. Doing this requires being informed and getting involved in the messy end of politics, involvement that makes no promises to deliver the immediate satisfaction that comes with doing good deeds.

SOURCES Center for Information and Research on Civil Learning and Engagement. "Quick Facts: Youth Voting." http://www.civicyouth.org/quick-facts/youth-voting/ (accessed January 12, 2012).

Jarvis, Sharon E., Lisa Montoya, and Emily Mulvoy. 2005. "The Political Participation of College Students, Working Students and Working Youth." The Center for Information & Research on Civic Learning and Engagement. http://www.civicyouth.org/PopUps/WorkingPapers/WP37Jarvis.pdf (accessed May 12, 2006).

The Panetta Institute. 2002. "Volunteerism, Education, and the Shadow of September Eleventh: A Survey of American College Students." http://www.panettainstitute.org/lib/02/hart_05.html (accessed September 16, 2003).

Sanchez, Claudio. 2011. "College Students Join Occupy Wall Street Protests." National Public Radio. http://www.npr.org/2011/10/14/141343966/college-students-join-occupy-wall-street-demonstrations (accessed January 30, 2012).

with. They are designed not to make these conflicts disappear but to provide an arena and a set of ground rules where they can clash.

Exposing these fallacies is not intended to paint a cynical portrait of American democracy but rather to paint a more realistic one. Representative democracy is first and foremost about process, in how decisions are made. The system of representative democracy seeks to embody core democratic principles by instilling them into the institutions and mechanisms that organize the political system and by embedding a set of beliefs about individual liberty in the principles that operate it. For the whole system to be judged democratic, the outcomes, not just the process, must also reflect core democratic principles. Outcomes, though, are secondary; as long as they respect the core principles, outcomes do not have to be wise or effective to be democratic. Decisions made by representative institutions can be irritating, ineffective, silly, or even downright wrong but still be democratic. A messy, less than optimal policy in which all views and rights are taken into account is not a failure of democracy. A failure is a fast, efficient policy where the dissent is ignored or, worse, quashed. (For a view of what could be considered a failure of democracy, see the Politics in Practice feature "College Students: Values, Voting, and Volunteering.")

THE CHALLENGE OF AMERICAN DEMOCRACY

The practice of democratic politics is always going to be messy. Conflict, confusion, and compromise are a central part of the package even in democratic societies where citizens share ethnicity, religious beliefs, and cultural roots. In a large, diverse society such as the United States, the practice of democracy is even more challenging.

Diversity and Difference

The United States is one of the most populous countries on the planet and geographically one of the largest. Its people are highly mobile and come from diverse religious, cultural, demographic, geographic, racial, ethnic, and socioeconomic backgrounds. The astonishing diversity in these characteristics produces a wide range of different political interests and preferences. Blacks and whites may hold broadly different views about the merits of affirmative action. Latinos and blacks may have different ideas about what rights, if any, should be granted to undocumented immigrants. An urban city dweller in New York, Chicago, or Los Angeles likely has little interest in farm subsidies; those same subsidies may be the central topic of conversation in the coffee shop of a rural agricultural community in Nebraska, Kansas, or Iowa. Conservative Christians may view the posting of the Ten Commandments in public buildings and on public monuments with pride and approval; Muslims and agnostics may view such actions with trepidation or even fear. A wealthy individual may view the capital gains tax as unjust; a poor individual may not know what the capital gains tax is and may not care. For a college student at a public university, there may be no more important issue than government support for higher education, at least as it affects tuition; for senior citizens, Social Security may be much more important than subsidizing the studies of teenagers at the local state college.

This vast diversity in the backgrounds and interests of American citizens leads to different ideas of what we should do and who should get what. The challenge for American democracy is to manage all these differences within a democratic framework, to make decisions in a way that ensures the rights of all are upheld in both the process and substance of government decision making. Given that many of these differences seem unbridgeable—for example, differences on abortion, immigration, budget deficits, government bailouts, and the war in Afghanistan—this is an enormously ambitious undertaking for a democratic system.

Dynamics

An additional element of American diversity is change over time. Getting a firm handle on American politics is sometimes difficult because the conflicts processed by democracy are shaped by a constantly changing backdrop. This changing context continually shapes and reshapes questions of what we ought to do.

Consider that the first census of the United States, taken in 1790, indicated that the 13 original colonies accounted for 900,000 square miles of land, forming a relatively narrow corridor along the eastern seaboard. Within this narrow corridor were fewer than 4 million people. Both of these basic characteristics have changed almost beyond recognition. Geographically, the United States grew west, steadily pushing its boundaries to the Pacific and beyond. Today, the 50 states include roughly 3.6 million square miles and a population of about 309 million. Population and geographic growth have a profound effect on politics. States, for example, do not grow at the same rate (see Figure 1.1), and because the number of representatives a state sends to Congress is based on population, population shifts can alter the size of a state's congressional delegation. Presently, power in the Congress is following population trends and shifting south and west. What New Yorkers and Wisconsinites want the government to do is becoming less important than what Californians and Texans want.

It is not just overall growth that presents a challenge. The population is becoming more diverse ethnically and economically. In the past few years, Latinos eclipsed African Americans as the largest minority group. In 1980, the wealthiest 5 percent of Americans received a little less than 15 percent of all the income generated in the country, and the poorest 20 percent of Americans received about 5 percent of the income. Thirty years later, the wealthiest 5 percent of Americans receive more than 20 percent of the income, and the poorest 20 percent receive about 4 percent of the income (U.S. Census Bureau 2008). As America becomes more urban and more racially and ethnically diverse, and as the gap grows between the poorest and wealthiest citizens, political interests and ideas about what we should do change. America is no longer a nation of farmers, so agriculture policy is less important to most people. America is much less white, so the concerns of ethnic minorities occupy a larger space in the political spectrum.

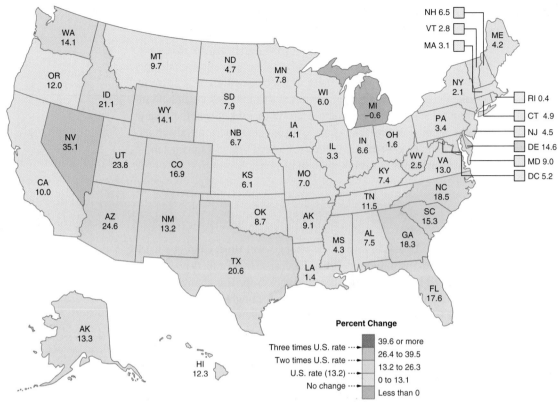

FIGURE 1.1 Population Growth in the United States, 2000–2010

Source: http://www.census.gov/prod/cen2010/briefs/c2010br-01.pdf.

Women are increasingly represented in jobs traditionally held by men in law, business, and politics. This shift in the gender makeup of the workforce can lead to conflict over such issues as salary structures. Women still earn only about 80 percent of what their male counterparts earn in comparable jobs (U.S. Census Bureau 2008). The churn of social, economic, and demographic change is reshaping the political environment.

Ideology and Partisanship

Americans have different ideas about what government should and should not do, and they have different preferences about who should and should not run the government. An **ideology** is a consistent set of values, attitudes, and beliefs about the appropriate role of government in society (Campbell et al. 1960). Ide-

ideology A consistent set of values, attitudes, and beliefs about the appropriate role of government in society.

ology is important to democratic politics because it helps people figure out what they do and do not support even on issues they have little knowledge of or interest in. You might not know anything at all about capital gains taxes, but if you know conservatives are against them and you consider yourself a conservative, then you are likely to also oppose them. These sorts of broad ideological cues are pretty much all the information Americans use to figure out their positions on a wide variety of issues (Bawn 1999). In America the range of ideological beliefs runs across a spectrum from liberals (the left) to conservatives (the right).

America is a diverse society and responding to the variety of perspectives and goals of such a highly diverse population is a challenge for elected officials. Although elected officials cannot satisfy all of these demands, a core principle of democracy is that the rights of all will be upheld in both the process and the outputs of democratic decision making.

Traditionally, conservatives favor the status quo and want any social or political change to respect the laws and traditions of society. Traditionally, liberals believe that individual liberty is the most important political value and that people should be free to express their views and live their lives as they please with minimal limitations from government or from traditional values. Generically, conservatives are more likely to oppose regulating individual economic choices and more likely to support regulating individual moral choices. Liberals do the opposite. However, ideological labels in the United States are, at best, only rough guides to how individuals orient themselves to political issues. Some readers of this text will support gay rights yet consider themselves conservative, and other readers will oppose gay rights yet consider themselves liberal.

Most Americans do not have particularly strong ideological beliefs. Over the last several decades, an average of about 50 percent of Americans identified themselves as moderate or reported that they did not know what these terms meant (Figure 1.2). Of those who did report having ideological beliefs, about 27 percent identified themselves as conservatives, and about 17 percent identified as liberal, but very few Americans placed themselves in the extreme categories (about 2 percent on each extreme).

Many Americans wed their ideological beliefs to their support for a political party. **Partisanship** in American politics is viewed as a psychological attachment to a political party (Campbell et al. 1960). This means that most people view one of the parties as standing for their "brand" of politics. Broadly speaking, Republicans represent the conservative and Democrats the liberal brand of politics. According to one poll, in 2012 roughly a third of Americans considered themselves Republicans, a third called themselves Democrats, and a third aligned with neither of the two major political parties (Rasmussen Reports 2012). Political parties (as we discuss in chapter 7) are the dominant organizing force of American politics: they provide coherence to elections, mobilize voters, and organize the government.

partisanship A psychological attachment to a political party.

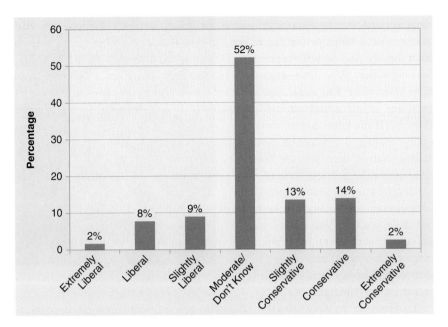

FIGURE 1.2 **Ideological Self-Identification of Americans**

Source: Constructed by the authors from data in American National Election Studies, *The ANES Guide to Public Opinion and Electoral Behavior* (Ann Arbor: University of Michigan, Center for Political Studies), http://electionstudies.org/nesguide/gd-index.htm#3.

Because neither party has the support of a commanding majority and because many citizens either have weak party ties or shuttle their support between the parties, parties are more likely to reflect the differences of Americans rather than bridge them.

False Consensus

Despite the huge variation in everything from ideology to ethnicity, religion, geography, wealth, and partisanship, Americans by and large believe their views are shared by a majority of others (Hibbing and Theiss-Morse 2003, 132n3). This highly unrealistic view of politics is known as **false consensus**, the tendency of people to believe their views are "normal" or "common sense" and therefore shared by most people. False consensus creates a challenge and a danger to democratic decision making. If people believe their views represent the majority position, and the government fails to adopt that position, this creates a perception that the democratic system is somehow not working—something or someone is elevating the preferences of a minority over the preferences of the majority. In the popular mind, that something or someone is often viewed as a special interest. In reality, however, the false consensus rests on an unrealistic and uninformed view of politics and the democratic process. Though huge majorities support democratic principles and the American political system in the abstract, there is more

false consensus The tendency of people to believe their views are normal or represent common sense and therefore are shared by most people.

disagreement than agreement on specific proposals or issues. Many see the disagreements as evidence that something has gone wrong. In reality, the noisy clash of interests is the natural outcome of a democracy as diverse, dynamic, and ideologically mixed as the United States. Democracy in such a place is always going to be marked by conflict as much as consensus, something those who attribute their own views to others will not appreciate.

MEETING THE CHALLENGE?

Does the U.S. political system live up to the challenges of democracy? Does its organization and operation account for diversity and change in a way that upholds core democratic principles in both the process and substance of resolving questions of who gets what? The purpose of this book is not to answer these questions for you, but to give you the tools to make up your own mind. If your answer, in a general sense or on a specific issue, differs from your classmates' answers, do not be surprised. Reasonable people have long disagreed about how the concept of democracy translates into the practice of democracy in the American political system.

The Case for American Democracy

The case for American democracy rests on the assessment that our political techniques and institutions operate, for the most part, according to core democratic principles. The American political system, in this view, is a highly **pluralistic** one, where power is fragmented and distributed widely among diverse groups and interests. Businesspeople, laborers, farmers, African Americans, Latinos, students, the elderly, gays—virtually every conceivable group and interest has access to the political process. Although some may have more political assets—money, numbers, and campaign and propaganda skills—all have at least some political resources. At a minimum, all have the vote.

Although some citizens may be more active in the political process than others—so-called political elites, activists, or influentials—they ultimately represent a wide-ranging set of interests from the entire polity. The political moves and countermoves of this broad variety of political elites produce the energy for the American political system to work. They compete vigorously with one another but abide by the democratic rules of the game. They remain committed to the core principles of a democratic society, and they respect the fundamental rights and freedoms associated with majority rule, political equality, and political freedom—individual liberty, freedom of expression, the right to privacy, and the like. Indeed, these political activists are counted on to defend these principles when other less politically aware and less educated individuals oppose them. In the final analysis, supporters of the pluralistic

pluralistic A term used to describe a society in which power is widely distributed among diverse groups and interests.

view feel that American democracy serves the interests of a wide variety of individuals and groups. Although competing elites may take the initiative in public affairs, they must also take into account the interests of ordinary citizens. The elites require these ordinary citizens to provide support for public policy and to win elections. The entire process takes place within the prescribed democratic procedures, moderates differences among diverse people, and provides for social peace and progress.

Major Criticisms of American Democracy

Although most students of American democracy support the system, it has had its share of critics. Such dissatisfaction has numerous sources and is often based on disappointments with the outcomes of the political process. Despite decades of effort, for example, we remain far from any solution to numerous major social problems, ranging from racial tension to the decline in credibility of public officials. These failures provide a basis for questioning the operation, ideals, and assumptions about the political system.

One of the major criticisms of American democracy is that it is not nearly as pluralistic or inclusive as its supporters claim. Many Americans believe that candidates and officeholders are more interested in manipulating public attitudes than in understanding and acting on them. Republicans and Democrats are charged with standing for little more than the acquisition of power and with robbing voters of meaningful choices rather than providing alternatives. Some critics argue that significant minorities—including African Americans, Latinos, Native Americans, the poor, the young, and women[2]—are poorly served by the American political process. These groups are proportionally underrepresented in major political institutions, such as Congress, the executive branch, and the Supreme Court, and none are as effectively organized as the more dominant affluent groups, which casts an unflattering shadow across the sunny pluralist portrait. Moreover, organized groups do not check and balance one another as pluralist orthodoxy claims. Instead, each concentrates on getting what it wants from government: business interests are served by the Department of Commerce, farmers by the Department of Agriculture, unions by the Department of Labor, and so on. Instead of regulating these groups in the public interest, government is organized to dole out favors to those with political muscle at the expense of the general taxpayer.

Political scientist Morris Fiorina (2006) offers a critique of the process. He sees the intense party-based differences in American politics as evidence that government is not responsive to citizens. He argues that ideological extremists on the left and right have captured control of the parties' nominating process. In order to win party nominations, politicians must take extreme positions to appeal to these ideologues. Although most voters are not strongly ideological and prefer moderate, commonsense policies, party elites serve up two extreme candidates, and vot-

---

[2] Women are not technically a minority. They constitute more than half of both eligible voters and the population as a whole. But they may be considered a social minority in the sense that they have historically been both economically and politically disadvantaged in comparison to men.

ers are forced to choose the one who is the least distasteful. "The result," according to Fiorina, "is a disconnect between the American people and those who purport to represent them" (2006, 51–52).

For such critics, the American system is not pluralistic, but **elitist**, in the sense that the political system is dominated by a set of organized, influential interests that are checked neither by one another nor by the general populace. These political elites are like professional athletes; they are devoted to the game they play, they are highly trained, they know all the rules and inside tricks, and they have access to a wide range of resources devoted solely to helping them win. When the rest of us try to get involved in politics, it's like 11 spectators coming out of the crowd to take on the Dallas Cowboys—even if the spectators manage to get on the field, the scoreboard will still end up reflecting the interest of the elite athletes. Critics of an elitist state of affairs thus offer a different picture of the American political system. The privileged status of elites and their overrepresentation in government enables them to set the public agenda and to determine which issues government considers of legitimate concern and which it does not. The result is a biased system that favors the status quo and provides an advantage to established groups over unorganized ones.

The contrasting overviews of American democracy represented by the positive pluralistic portrait and the negative elitist critique are not absolutes. Leading advocates of both lines of thought recognize elements of the other in the reality of American political life. Pluralists acknowledge that some groups have greater control over the outcomes of political decision making than others; elitists observe that although a handful of organized interests control many major political decisions, they do not control all of them.

Making systematic sense of politics, as you may have guessed, is not easy, especially in a large, dynamic country such as the United States. Although we cannot provide a definitive resolution to these debates, political science provides the tools to help you draw your own conclusions.

MAKING SENSE OF POLITICS: POLITICAL SCIENCE

Political science is the academic discipline dedicated to the study of government, political institutions, processes, and behavior (Isaak 1985). It is the job of political scientists to explain the how and why of the authoritative allocation of values—who gets what and why. Political scientists are interested in these sorts of questions: Who has power? Is it elites, or is sovereignty broadly shared? What determines power and power relationships in society? Is it class, ethnicity, socioeconomic status, or the will of the people? Who votes? Is it rich people or poor people, the young or the old? Why do they vote the way they do? Is it ideology, loyalty to a party, or something else? Why are some people conservatives and others liberal? Why are some people Democrats and others Republicans?

elitist A term used to describe a society in which organized, influential minority interests dominate the political process.

political science The systematic study of government, political institutions, processes, and behavior.

Answers to these and similar questions have direct bearing on the main goals of this book. Understanding who votes and why, for example, can help us better form a judgment of the political system. If certain groups disproportionately participate in politics, this raises questions about the true extent of majority rule and minority rights. If certain laws and rules—for example, voter registration requirements—let some groups gain more power and influence than others, this raises questions about political equality. If other laws—for example, campaign finance laws—limit the ability of groups to get their message out to citizens and to government, this raises questions about political freedom.

The Roots of Political Science

To effectively study politics in general and democratic politics in particular, it is important to know something about the field of political science, which is both a very old and a very new academic discipline. Political science's roots are in philosophy, law, history, and economics; political science claims people such as Plato, Aristotle, Thomas Hobbes, John Locke, James Madison, and John Stuart Mill as its intellectual forebears. All were serious students of politics and are mostly remembered as normative political philosophers. **Normative** theory seeks to prescribe how things should be valued, what should be, and what is good or just, better or worse. As normative political philosophers, these individuals were interested in these sorts of questions: What is the *best* form of government—democracy, autocracy, or oligarchy? What constitutes the legitimate and *just* use of power? What are the *fundamental rights* of man? What are the *best* means to serve the public interest?

Political scientists continue to pursue these questions with vigor, but in modern times, the study of politics is now focused on describing and explaining institutions, processes, attitudes, and behavior as they *are* rather than as they *should* be. This sort of empirical approach to studying politics has a long history. Five hundred years ago, Niccolo Machiavelli became a champion of realist political theory, an approach that seeks to objectively record politics and to understand how it works in practice rather than figure out how it should work in theory. It was not until the last 60 years or so, however, that this sort of approach came to dominate the study of politics and to shape the modern discipline of political science. Rather than asking, "Is democracy the best form of government?" modern political scientists are more likely to ask, "Why do interest groups form?" or "Why does government pay attention to some issues and not others?" These latter sorts of questions are **empirical**, meaning they can be answered by careful observation. Using the scientific method to answer these empirical questions puts the "science" in political science.

The Scientific Method

Science is a method of acquiring knowledge that has three basic goals: description, explanation, and prediction. The heart of the scientific process is the for-

normative Theories or statements that seek to prescribe how things should be valued, what should be, what is good or just, and what is better or worse.

empirical Questions and debates that can be answered by careful observation. Systematic empirical observation is the foundation of science and the scientific method.

science A method of acquiring knowledge through the formulation of hypotheses that can be tested through empirical observation in order to make claims about how the world works and why.

mulation of hypotheses that can be tested through empirical observation. The hypotheses are drawn from explanatory frameworks—called theories or models—about causal relationships, or how one or more factors *cause* a particular outcome. Theory is vital for political scientists who adopt science as the best means to gain useful knowledge about government and politics—not theory in the normative sense (e.g., a theory that claims democracy is the best form of government) but theory in an empirical sense. Rather than a claim about how the world *should* work, an empirical theory proposes testable explanations or hypotheses of how the world *does* work.

For example, consider a political scientist who wants to answer the following question: why do people vote the way they do? There are many potential answers, but one of the best-known explanations is the social-psychological model, or Michigan model, of voting behavior. Briefly, the Michigan model, championed by researchers at the University of Michigan, claims people form psychological attachments to political parties at an early age. This attachment results in a strong tendency to vote on the basis of partisan loyalty even if a voter disagrees with most of the policies a particular party's candidate supports. (For a more in-depth discussion of the Michigan model, see chapter 11.) This theory suggests the following research hypothesis: people will vote on the basis of party loyalty. This hypothesis can be tested empirically through systematic observation of voters' behavior. If it is correct, partisanship should predict whom citizens vote for.

Like other scientists, political scientists do not go looking for evidence to support their hypotheses. They begin by assuming their hypothesis is false and require overwhelming evidence to reject that assumption. Technically, the opposite of the research hypothesis is the **null hypothesis**—there is no relationship between the variables—and it is the null hypothesis that is tested. Thus, a political scientist would analyze data on voting patterns with the general aim of demonstrating that citizens' party loyalties are not associated with how they vote. Only if the data made an exceedingly strong case against this claim would a scientist reject the null hypothesis and accept the research hypothesis. Note that the null hypothesis is *rejected* or *not rejected*, but it can never be proven. And accepting the research hypothesis does not prove that the theory is true. Rather, this test provides empirical evidence consistent with the theory. We continue collecting data and testing and rejecting more hypotheses until the evidence begins to accumulate in support of a theory or leading to new theories. The process is similar to Sherlock Holmes's approach to solving mysteries: "eliminate all other factors, and the one which remains must be the truth" (Doyle 1890, chap. 1). As demonstrated in chapter 11, political scientists have tested the Michigan model extensively and found it to be a fairly robust explanation of why people vote the way they do.

Political scientists are continually constructing and testing such theories or models of political institutions, processes, and behavior. Although political scientists have not found a universal law of politics (at least not yet), we have managed to formulate a number of theories that adequately explain why at least parts of the political world work they way they do. Exploring all of these theories would require a separate book.

null hypothesis A statement positing that there is no relationship between the variables being observed. It is the opposite of the research hypothesis.

Theoretical Frameworks in Political Science

Some textbooks adopt a single theoretical framework to organize all of the chapters. The dominant framework in political science is rational choice theory. Rational choice theory has contributed much to our understanding, but it is not the only theory of politics. To provide a sense of how political science uses theory to make sense of the political world and to help us make sense of politics in America, in this book we often use and contrast different models from three of the most prominent theoretical frameworks. Two of these—rational choice models and behavioral models—have a longer history in political science. The third framework—containing evolutionary and biological models—is a more recent and cutting-edge development that is seeking to integrate political science with large sectors of the life sciences, such as biology, genetics, and neuroscience. These theories do not appear in every chapter of the book. Some topics—civil liberties and civil rights, for example, both important for understanding the full picture of American politics—have not been extensively analyzed using the scientific method, but they can be understood by observing legal and historical evidence. Most of the chapters include discussions of what we have learned from political science research, but covering all three models is not always appropriate. In some cases, the models focus on similar questions and offer competing explanations. In other cases, the models focus on different questions and offer complementary explanations. A brief introduction here will help prepare you to start thinking about politics like a political scientist and give you a sense of how political science is constantly seeking to generate and investigate new explanations of the political world.

RATIONAL CHOICE MODELS OF POLITICS Rational choice models of politics borrow from economic theories that assume people do what they do primarily out of self-interest. The basic idea is that humans are goal-oriented, have preferences, and can rank their preferences from most to least desired based on the amount of **utility**—that is, satisfaction or enjoyment derived from each one. People make choices rationally by doing or choosing what they believe will give them the most satisfaction for the least cost in a given situation (this is said to maximize their utility). For example, when you go to a restaurant, you pick from the menu the meal that achieves your ultimate goal (satisfying your hunger) and maximizes your utility (you may enjoy a hamburger more than broccoli). So how does this help us understand politics?

Well, to begin with, the simple assumptions at the heart of rational choice actually do a surprisingly good job of explaining big chunks of democratic politics. For example, as strange as it seems today, in the middle of the twentieth century, one of the things that Americans found most frustrating about politics was the tendency of the Republican and Democratic parties to sound more alike than different on many major policy issues. This was not just irritating to voters who couldn't perceive a meaningful choice, but a real puzzle for political scientists as well. Why would political parties not offer more meaningful policy choices in a democratic

utility The amount of enjoyment an individual receives from a given situation or outcome.

system? In his classic work *An Economic Theory of Democracy* (1957), Anthony Downs tried to, among other things, figure out exactly that. Starting from the assumption that all people are utility maximizers, Downs reasoned that if the primary goal is to win an election, a party or candidate needs to take policy positions that will appeal to more voters than those espoused by the competition. If most voters prefer moderate policy positions, then in a two-candidate election, both candidates will appeal to this center (Downs 1957, 117–118). As we noted earlier, most Americans do not have strong ideological beliefs, so in general elections both Democrats and Republicans try to appeal to the middle rather than the ends of the ideological spectrum. The result is the often-heard complaint that there isn't a "dime's worth of difference" between major party candidates. Downs's theory, in other words, describes and explains the relatively middle-of-the-road politics that typifies the U.S. system.

Rational choice theory can also help us form judgments about how democracy and politics are practiced. Consider majority rule. If the political system works according to Downs's theory, American democracy is in pretty good shape. The government is going to reflect majority preferences because that's where all the votes are. But what about minority rights? If the major parties ignore minority voices or, worse, appeal to the majority by pushing policies that limit the political freedom of minorities, then the assessment of American democracy is less rosy. The point is, Downs's theory provides an explanation of how politics works, and that theory can be empirically tested. If observation shows the explanation is correct, we know something about how politics in the American system works and can use that knowledge to form judgments about how that performance reflects the basic principles of democracy.

BEHAVIORAL MODELS OF POLITICS In contrast to rational choice, behavioral models of politics draw from psychology and sociology rather than economics. At their root is the assumption that humans behave not according to a self-interested cost–benefit calculation, but as a response to an environmental stimulus. The Michigan model, which suggests that a socialization process leads us to psychologically attach ourselves to a particular party, is a good example of such a theory. According to the Michigan model, this partisan attachment develops in childhood and adolescence (Greenstein 1965). We develop partisan attachments because Mom and Dad called Democrats one thing and Republicans another at the dinner table or because we admired a particular leader at a formative time in our lives and transferred those feelings to his or her party. That socialization process leads us to respond to the stimulus of an election by voting our party affiliation.

Behavioral models have been enormously influential in all of the social sciences and are generically labeled the "standard social science model" because of the widespread assumption that people respond in predictable ways to particular environmental situations (Tooby and Cosmides 1992). How do behavioral models help us understand politics? Consider the implications for majority rule if significant proportions of Americans are socialized to be apathetic about politics. What if at the dinner table Mom and Dad disparage politics as a worthless enterprise and politicians as corrupt and self-serving? What if the social environment teaches that politics is a dirty business that's best avoided altogether? It's hard to see how majority rule can be exercised if most people can't be bothered with politics. Again, the larger point is that the behavioral approach helps us know more about how politics works and puts us in a better position to systematically judge the performance of American democracy on the basis of the core principles.

EVOLUTIONARY AND BIOLOGICAL MODELS A recent development is the study of the political world through evolutionary and biological models. It may seem a little odd for political scientists to be turning to evolution and biology, but the reasons for doing so are straightforward. As one scholar recently put it, "evolutionary biology underlies all behavioral disciplines because *Homo sapiens* is an evolved species whose characteristics are the product of its particular evolutionary history" (Gintis 2007). Humans, in other words, are animals too. It makes sense, therefore, to use theories that have proven themselves capable of explaining much of what goes on in the animal world and apply them to human affairs. Evolutionary frameworks have been used for decades to explain the social structure and behavior of species from bees to chimpanzees.

Economists, anthropologists, psychologists, and yes, political scientists are beginning to understand that these same evolutionary theories provide a powerful set of tools to make sense of everything from consumer behavior to voting behavior. Evolutionary frameworks suggest that at least some of our attitudes toward politics and government; our preferences for particular types of policies, institutional arrangements, and political leaders; and our reasons for engaging in certain types of political behavior are partially inherited and/or shaped by evolutionary forces. Some of this may sound surprising, but social scientists have tested a number of hypotheses along these lines and have found strong evidence to support them.

For example, political scientists have found that at least some of our political attitudes are inherited (Alford, Funk, and Hibbing 2005). Other research using brain imaging techniques found distinct differences in how Democrats and Republicans look at candidates (Tierney 2004). The evolutionary and biological approach is a new method for building models of political attitudes and behavior that helps us think about and understand politics in new and different ways. For one thing, it suggests that liberals and conservatives see, experience, and react to the world from different perspectives, and no amount of informed debate is going to change those perspectives. The rational choice, behavioral, and biological models do not always agree—sometimes they have competing and contradicting explanations of why people vote the way they do, hold the attitudes they have, and so on. Political scientists are busily conducting empirical studies to assess which does the better job of explaining particular elements of politics, and in some cases, there is fierce debate over what model the current evidence supports.

GENERAL APPROACH AND ORGANIZATION OF THE BOOK

With the basic concepts of politics, government, and democracy in hand, as well as a little historical perspective on the American context and some insight into how American democracy is judged and how it is systematically studied, you should be in a good position to tackle the rest of this book. In what follows we present the information needed for you to make your own judgments about politics and democracy in America.

The book is divided into four parts. Part 1 consists of four chapters analyzing the constitutional framework. Chapter 2 looks at the political forces that led to the drafting and ratification of the U.S. Constitution and analyzes the values and assumptions underlying that framework. Chapter 3 focuses on one major element of this framework and a dominant feature of American politics—federalism, a system that divides power between state and national governments. Chapters 4 and 5 examine the liberties and rights guaranteed by the Constitution and how they have (or have not) been extended to various groups.

Part 2 addresses the general subject of connecting citizens to government—that is, how citizens encourage those in power to be responsive to their needs and how citizens hold them accountable for their actions. Chapter 6 focuses on the major institutional mechanism for connecting citizens to government between elections—the interest group. Chapter 7 examines the role that political parties play in organizing politics and translating public preferences into coherent policy agendas. Chapter 8 looks at the mass media's role in shaping opinions and structuring the public agenda. Chapter 9 explores the general nature of Americans' political views, how those views are acquired, and the various outlets for expressing those views in the political process. Chapters 10 and 11 examine elections by reviewing the processes of nominating and electing candidates and analyzing voting behavior, as well as other forms of political participation.

Part 3 focuses on the institutions involved in official decision making in government. These institutions are the Congress (chapter 12), the presidency (chapter 13), the bureaucracy (chapter 14), and the courts (chapter 15). We examine these institutions in terms of the kinds of people who serve in them and how they got there, the institutions' general structure, and the procedures that each utilizes to carry out its activities. In addition, we analyze the relationships and interactions among the officials who serve in these separate institutions.

Part 4 concludes the book. In chapter 16, we examine how the processes and institutions of the American political system combine to make public policy.

The appendices contain important supplemental information and documents. We include a glossary of all terms used in the book, the Constitution of the United States, the Declaration of Independence, and two frequently used *Federalist Papers* (Numbers 10 and 51).

Top Ten Takeaway Points

1. Politics is the authoritative allocation of values; government is the institution that can legitimately use coercion to allocate values for all people in a society.

2. Democracy is a form of government characterized by popular sovereignty, which means that the power to authoritatively allocate values is shared by all citizens. Popular sovereignty is dependent on a political system's commitment to upholding three core democratic principles: majority rule, political freedom, and political equality.

3. For a political system to be considered truly democratic, both the process and outcomes of the system must abide by the three core principles.

4. Democracy has two basic forms: direct democracy and representative democracy. The political system of the United States includes elements of both but is primarily a representative democratic system.

5. Representative democracies have common elements to their political systems, including elections, political parties, and interest groups.

6. The American political system gets mixed reviews on how well it abides by the core principles of democracy. Some see a pluralist system that does a good job of upholding the core principles. Others see an elitist system that routinely violates the core principles.

7. Politics in the United States is complex. The country is large with a diverse population characterized by constant change.

8. Political science is the academic discipline that systematically seeks to describe and explain politics using the scientific method.

9. Systematic explanations of the how and why of politics include rational choice, behavioral, and biological models. Each can be used to provide a deeper understanding of how and why politics works the way it does.

10. The purpose of this book is to provide sufficient information to allow the reader to make informed, independent judgments about the politics and practice of democracy in the American political system.

Key Terms and Cases

absolute majority, 7
autocracy, 5
democracy, 5
direct democracy, 10
economic equality, 9
elitist, 27
empirical, 28
equality of opportunity, 9
equality under the law, 8
false consensus, 24
government, 5

ideology, 22
initiative, 12
liberal democracy, 13
majority rule, 7
minority rights, 7
normative, 28
null hypothesis, 29
oligarchy, 5
partisanship, 23
pluralistic, 25
plurality, 7

political equality, 8
political science, 27
politics, 4
popular sovereignty, 6
referendum, 12
representative democracy, 13
science, 28
simple majority, 7
social equality, 8
sovereignty, 5
utility, 30

KEY QUESTIONS

Why did Federalists want a new constitution to replace the Articles of Confederation?

What is the Madisonian dilemma, and how does the U.S. Constitution try to solve this dilemma?

How does the meaning of the U.S. Constitution change?

© The Signing of the Constitution of the United States in 1787, 1940 (oil on canvas), Christy, Howard Chandler (1873–1952)/
Hall of Representatives, Washington D.C., USA/The Bridgeman Art Library

GIVEN ITS PURPOSE, the U.S. Constitution is a remarkably succinct document. It is a complete instruction manual that has required relatively few revisions to guide the operation of one of the world's major representative democracies for more than two centuries. It sets up the framework of a democratic process; specifies the powers, obligations, and limits of the major institutional actors; and, with the Bill of Rights included, articulates fundamental liberties of individuals that must not be violated by government. In short, the operating guidelines for a nation of more than 300 million are contained in about 4,400 words,[1] a text that can easily be stuffed into a back pocket. As humorist P. J. O'Rourke observed, the owner's manual of a midsize sedan is five times as long and twice as confusing, and it seats only four (1991, 11). No wonder the Constitution is revered as a remarkable achievement and an embodiment of successful democratic ideals.

The Constitution is also surprisingly misunderstood. Americans express abiding faith in and support for the Constitution, yet large numbers have never read it, and few know the politics that produced it. It seems to be viewed almost as the product of divine guidance, a sage bequest of universally agreed-on democratic wisdom brought down from the Revolutionary mount by the founders.

Historical reality contrasts sharply with this idealized portrait, and more than one scholar has suggested that the motives of some of the Constitution's framers were considerably less than pure. A closer look at the personalities who gathered in Philadelphia during the sweltering summer of 1787 to hammer out the Constitution strips away some of the sober semi-divinity that is often used to characterize them. For example, Luther Martin, a fierce advocate of states' rights, was not even sober. He was a heavy drinker who severely damaged the cause of states' rights by giving a rambling, six-hour, apparently alcohol-soaked speech to a room full of uncomfortably hot and irritated delegates (Collier and Collier 1986, 158–161).

---

[1] The total does not include the 17 amendments subsequent to the Bill of Rights.

This is not to suggest that the Constitution was a happenstance product of bumblers. The Constitution's authors included dazzling intellectual and political talents such as James Madison, Alexander Hamilton, Roger Sherman, Gouverneur Morris, and Charles Pinckney. Yet the founders also had serious disagreements among themselves and the full complement of human foibles and flaws that Martin serves to exemplify.

The point is that the Constitution is a supremely political document. It is the product of a lengthy debate over the big question of "what we ought to do" that has governed all similar debates in the polity since its adoption. Embedded in it is the clearest articulation of the goals and purposes of American democracy. Knowing what the Constitution says, why it says it, and how its meaning has changed over time provides a foundation for understanding why American government operates the way it does. To that end, this chapter examines the essential elements of constitutions in general and the circumstances that shaped the content and evolution of the U.S. Constitution in particular.

THE CONCEPT OF A CONSTITUTION

A **constitution** is the basic framework of government that defines the nature and conduct of public authority. A constitution consists of three essential elements:

1. The *functions* of government: the powers and responsibilities that reside in the public rather than in the private sphere
2. The *structure* of government: the institutions and mechanisms that constitute the framework of government
3. The *procedures* of government: the manner in which government carries out the powers and responsibilities entrusted to it

constitution A document or unwritten set of basic rules that provides the basic principles that determine the conduct of political affairs.

Together, these elements provide the basic rules and guidelines for the exercise of political authority. Note that this is a definition of constitutions in general. The functions, structure, and procedures specified by a particular constitution determine whether the government is an autocracy, oligarchy, or democracy.

Thus, a democratic constitution spells out how the core principles of democracy are to be upheld. Consider, for example, the powerful role of public officials and institutions in a representative democracy. They have the authority and power to make binding decisions regulating individual and group behavior. A constitution performs a similarly powerful role in relation to the public officials themselves; it determines what they can and cannot do and the nature of their relationship with other officeholders and the general populace. A state of mutual dependence and influence, therefore, characterizes a representative form of government. The people grant public officials the power to enact laws and decrees, but ordinary citizens ultimately control how that power is exercised. A democratic constitution spells out that popular sovereignty is the basis of political authority and constrains those who exercise that power from limiting the political freedom of others.

A constitution, then, establishes a set of legal relationships between leaders and the led. It is the heart of a nation's political process, and it shapes the process by determining the rules for accessing and exercising political power. The content and form of a constitution are in turn shaped by a political process as groups struggle to write the rules to favor their own interests.

CIRCUMSTANCES THAT LED TO THE CREATION OF THE CONSTITUTION

To understand the U.S. Constitution, we need to appreciate two sets of contemporary circumstances that led to its creation. The first is the historical antecedents—the Declaration of Independence, the Articles of Confederation, and the various state constitutions—that provided a basic philosophy of governance. The second is the economic and social conditions that created dissatisfaction with the forms of governance established by these earlier frameworks.

Historical Antecedents of the Constitution

THE DECLARATION OF INDEPENDENCE The **Declaration of Independence** lays the foundation of American constitutional theory. Penned by Thomas Jefferson with little input from other members of the committee established by the Second Continental Congress,[2] the declaration justifies the struggle for independence with a republican theory of government based on the concept of natural rights. Borrowing from the ideas of John Locke, Jefferson's elegant prose asserts

Declaration of Independence A document written by Thomas Jefferson that lays the foundation of American constitutional theory. In the document, Jefferson justifies the struggle for independence with a republican theory of government based on the concepts of natural rights and popular sovereignty.

Thomas Jefferson wrote the Declaration of Independence, and John Hancock was the first to sign it in July 1776. In the document, Jefferson presents a comprehensive idea of popular sovereignty, one that laid the foundation for the Constitution's major principles.

that "all men are created equal" and that they enjoy "unalienable rights" that include "life, liberty and the pursuit of happiness." These statements reject the arguments of philosophers such as Thomas Hobbes, arguments that suggest that people surrender certain natural rights when they leave the state of nature. The Declaration of Independence provides the basis of republican government, declaring that people create governments to secure these rights, and governments derive their "just Powers from the Consent of the Governed." If a government fails to protect these rights, "it is the Right of the People to alter or to abolish it, and to institute new Government." Together, these ideas can be viewed as a comprehensive conception of popular sovereignty (Becker 1922; Wiecek 1992).

The legal status of the Declaration of Independence is somewhat ambiguous. Although Congress placed it in the U.S. Code under the heading "Organic Laws of the United States of America," the Supreme Court has rarely interpreted it to have binding legal force. Some legal authorities even deny that there is a constitutional right of revolution. Nonetheless, the Declaration of Independence is a basic statement of constitutional principles and lays the foundation for American constitutional order (Wiecek 1992).

THE ARTICLES OF CONFEDERATION The **Articles of Confederation** served as the first constitution of the United States. A committee of the Continental Congress began drafting this constitution in June 1776—even before independence had been declared—though bickering and political divisions meant that the document was not submitted for approval by the states until November 1777.

The Articles of Confederation established a national government consisting of a **unicameral** (one-house) legislature; there was no independent executive or judiciary branch. Under the Articles, the national government's powers were limited primarily to raising an army and navy, entering into treaties and alliances, and sending and receiving diplomatic representatives—matters of war and peace that wartime experience indicated should be vested in the nation. The national government had no authority to regulate interstate and foreign commerce, which the Confederation's framers associated with the Acts of Trade and Navigation passed by the British Parliament that helped spark the Revolution.

The national government also lacked the power to levy taxes, so it had no control over its revenues. Although the national government could requisition funds

Articles of Confederation The first constitution of the United States.

unicameral A legislature with one chamber.

[2] The committee included John Adams, Benjamin Franklin, Roger Sherman, and Robert Livingston.

from the states for expenses, it had no authority to compel payment. Instead, the states themselves had to levy the taxes to pay these requisitions, and they often refused to do so. The authority to provide troops for the national military also resided with the states. Lacking the authority to make the states meet their obligations, and bereft of the power to tax or conscript individuals, the national government lacked the means to fulfill the basic governmental responsibilities entrusted to it. Moreover, there was little chance of changing these arrangements because any alteration of the document required unanimous consent of all the states.

STATE CONSTITUTIONS AS MODELS OF GOVERNMENT While the national government was off to a fragile start, the states were busy asserting their independence not only from Great Britain but also from one another and from any national government that might be formed.

Principal features of the Articles of Confederation—for example, a dominant legislature and weak (or nonexistent) executive and judiciary—reflected institutional arrangements already included in several state constitutions. In most states, for example, the governor was chosen by the legislature; only four states had a popularly elected executive. There were, however, some notable exceptions to this general pattern. New York, for example, had a strong governor system. State judiciaries were also weak and largely subservient to their legislatures, which frequently appointed judicial officials and gave them only limited powers.

Terms of legislators were short—only one year in most of the states. Rhode Islanders were even more wary, allowing their representatives only six months. For the popular legislator, there was an additional limitation in the form of forced rotation. Most state constitutions (and the Articles of Confederation) put term limits on legislators and allowed the recall of unpopular elected officials at any time.

State constitutions and the Articles of Confederation clearly went to some lengths to uphold at least some of the core principles of democracy. Recall provisions and the dominance of legislatures, for example, reinforced majority rule by giving the people frequent opportunities to hold their representatives accountable. Yet whatever their democratic elements, state constitutions and the Articles of Confederation shared a common weakness: they produced weak and ineffective governments. The central concern reflected in these constitutions was a distrust of centralized power. The colonists' experience with British governance had led them to see a strong, centralized government as a threat to the core democratic principle of political freedom. The Revolution, after all, had been fought in no small part because of the colonists' resentment of taxes imposed by a legislature to which they sent no delegates and in which they had no voice. This certainly seemed to violate the democratic principle of political freedom.

Yet state constitutions (and the Articles of Confederation) focused too much on limiting governmental power. Rather than being too powerful, the state and national governments of the early United States were often too weak to effectively do much at all. This weakness carried enormous risks—including the very real potential that the United States would fail as a political system.

Hard-won experience at the state level led to constitutional innovations that later served as examples for the framers of the U.S. Constitution to follow. For example, New York developed a strong governorship free of legislative dominance in order to handle military and civilian affairs. This experience showed the worth of an independent executive and demonstrated that such an executive was not necessarily a threat to political freedom. Encouraged by John Adams, voters in Massachusetts adopted a constitution that included a popularly elected house of representatives and an "aristocratic" senate apportioned on the basis of taxable wealth. It also included a popularly elected governor vested with considerable powers (such as a veto) who was eligible for reelection and an independent judiciary. Both the New York and Massachusetts constitutions would help shape the deliberations at the Constitutional Convention.

Economic Conditions

The United States in the 1780s faced a period of major adjustment following its successful revolt against Great Britain. Within a few years of the end of the Revolutionary War in 1781, America was plunged into a depression. Accounts differ as to how serious it was. Some claim the critical period was brief, and the corner turned by the time the Constitutional Convention met in mid-1787. Others claim it was serious enough to threaten the existence of the new nation. There is general agreement that the economic downturn affected groups differently; small farmers and the few hired laborers of the day experienced little of the effect, but people in commerce and finance were hit hard.

Domestic rivalries worsened the economic problems. Fierce economic protectionism developed as states levied duties to raise revenue and to protect local interests against out-of-state competitors. Lacking the authority to regulate interstate commerce, the national government was powerless to remove the obstacles to free trade within the nation. Adding to the economic woes were the worsening fortunes of the creditors who financed both public and private ventures in the young nation. Debtors often used the political process at the state level to lighten their financial obligations. For example, some states enacted "stay" laws that postponed the due dates of promissory notes. Another type of law allowed a debtor to declare bankruptcy, pay off his obligation at less than face value, and begin his financial life anew with a clean slate. Another advantage for debtors was the issuance of cheap paper money by state legislatures. This practice fueled inflation, meaning that the face value of debt was worth far less than the money originally borrowed.

Even more financially frustrated were those who had lent the nation money to fight the Revolution. They had no way to collect on public securities issued by a government that lacked the financial ability to pay its debts. Similarly affected were veterans of the war, who had volunteered their services on the promise of compensation via proceeds from government bonds. Given the precarious financial situation facing the new nation, there was a risk that the government would default on its debts.

Although the United States had theoretically achieved an independent status in the family of nations, its sovereignty was vulnerable even after the guns had fallen silent. The structure of government lent itself to internal divisions and united the states in little more than name. Economic strife pitted one group against another, and the world's major powers remained active on the North American continent. Spain closed the mouth of the Mississippi to all shipping. The supposedly vanquished British troops refused to withdraw from some northwestern forts until the claims of British creditors were honored. The new nation tottered on the uncertain economic and political legs of its newfound independence. George Washington, the Revolutionary War's great hero, observed that something had to change in order "to avert the humiliating and contemptible figure [they were] about to make on the annals of mankind" (Collier and Collier 1986, 3).

Group Rivalries and the Movement for a Convention

The groups particularly aggrieved in the postwar period were manufacturers, merchants, shipowners, and creditors. The professional classes—lawyers, doctors, newspaper editors, and so on—sympathized with their clients, as did former soldiers who felt cheated out of their rightful claims for services rendered in the cause of nationhood. Combined, they composed a potent group that wanted change. After the Constitution had been drafted, they were to come together to support its adoption under the name of **Federalists**.

Federalist interests were for the most part concentrated in the cities, but some rural Americans also found their interests jeopardized by postwar conditions, including commercial farmers who produced a surplus of crops that they wanted to sell in interstate and foreign markets. Most were large landholders who ran agricultural operations dependent on slave labor; they found common cause with merchants whose futures were also linked to commerce.

Opposing the Federalists were people who did not depend on trade for their livelihoods. At the core of this opposition were small subsistence farmers satisfied with scratching out a living on poor soil remote from river valleys, producing crops for their own families or marketing small surpluses in nearby localities. Also included were small businessmen, artisans, mechanics (the small laboring class of that time), and debtors who welcomed government assistance in their perennial struggle to keep one step ahead of creditors. This coalition of interests, labeled **Anti-Federalists**, resisted ratification of the Constitution.

As a group, the Federalists were wealthier and better educated, and they worked in higher-status occupations. Anti-Federalists tended to be lower-class, obscure individuals of modest means. Although the leadership of the

Federalists The group of people who supported the adoption of the Constitution and favored a stronger national government.

Anti-Federalists The group of people who opposed a stronger national government than what existed under the Articles of Confederation and opposed the ratification of the Constitution.

Patrick Henry, a lawyer from Virginia and a controversial member of the Continental Congress, made the first speech when it convened. Despite being a well-known representative for the Anti-Federalists, who did not support the idea of a strong central government, Henry did not attend the Constitutional Convention.

Anti-Federalists did include a number of prominent Revolutionary-era luminaries—such as Richard Henry Lee, Patrick Henry, and George Clinton—the Anti-Federalists could not match either in numbers or in fame those who lent their skill and prestige to the Federalist cause, such as George Washington, Alexander Hamilton, and James Madison.

Two events in the fall of 1786 enabled the Federalists to act on their desires for a stronger national government. One was a meeting at Annapolis, Maryland, convened to discuss problems of interstate trade and the possibility of adopting a uniform system of commercial regulations. Delegates from only a few states showed up, and most had Federalist sympathies. The Federalist majority, notably Hamilton and Madison, seized the opportunity to issue a report to the Continental Congress suggesting that a commission be assembled the following May to revise the Articles of Confederation.

The second event was an armed revolt in western Massachusetts by farmers who were resisting state efforts to seize their property for failure to pay taxes and debts. **Shays' Rebellion**—named for its leader, Daniel Shays—was put down, but some Americans regarded it as a threat to the very existence of the United States. Among those concerned was George Washington, the most popular American of all. Appalled by the news that a former officer in his army had brought the state of Massachusetts to the brink of civil war, Washington lent his great prestige to the movement for a convention.

THE CONSTITUTIONAL CONVENTION

Pushed by these two events, in February 1787 Congress called on the states to send delegates to a convention in Philadelphia to revise the Articles of Confederation. All except Rhode Island, which was dominated by debtor interests, eventually responded, though some states responded more quickly than others. Although the convention was supposed to open on May 14, 1787, a quorum was not achieved until May 25. The New Hampshire delegation did not arrive until July 1787, some two months after the deliberations began.

Shays' Rebellion An armed revolt by farmers in western Massachusetts who were resisting state efforts to seize their property for failure to pay taxes and debts.

The Founders

The most important feature of the Constitutional Convention was that an overwhelming proportion of the delegates were Federalists. As soon as the convention assembled, it made two important decisions: it named George Washington the presiding officer and bound the delegates to secrecy. Naming Washington as presiding officer gave the convention immediate credibility, and the Federalist majority could exercise a larger degree of influence behind closed doors than in open public debate.

The Anti-Federalists matched and perhaps exceeded their opponents as a proportion of the general populace. Given their numbers, it is somewhat puzzling that more Anti-Federalists did not attend the convention, especially since the state legislatures that selected delegates had strong Anti-Federalist sentiments. There are two possible explanations. One is that some Anti-Federalists did not want to dignify the convention with their presence. The best-known instance was Patrick Henry, whose oft-quoted reason for staying away was that he "smelt a rat." The second possible explanation is that Anti-Federalists thought attendance was unnecessary because the convention's legal mandate was limited to revising the Articles of Confederation. The Anti-Federalists believed they could block anything contrary to their interests because such changes had to be approved by all states. As it turned out, the convention quickly abandoned its assignment of reworking the Articles of Confederation and secretly began drafting a blueprint for a new government.

Anti-Federalists were represented in this enterprise (Luther Martin was one example), but they were outnumbered. And most Anti-Federalists who were in attendance belonged to the social, political, and economic elite; the nation's subsistence farmers, who constituted the rank and file of the Anti-Federalist cause and who were the most numerous economic group in the nation, were hardly represented at all. In fact, all 55 delegates, Federalist or otherwise, were decidedly unrepresentative of American life and interests. Most were lawyers, most were college-educated, and most had political experience. Three-quarters had served in the Continental Congress, eight had signed the Declaration of Independence, and most were dominant figures in the political lives of their states. Although unrepresentative, they were a gathering of political talent of the highest order, a collection with few historical comparisons.

Most delegates took an active role in the proceedings, but a few are remembered as the convention's dominant figures. The most influential was James Madison of Virginia. Madison was hardly a dashing Revolutionary hero, as were some of his contemporaries. Short, frail, and uncomfortable with public speaking, he nevertheless possessed a towering intellect. He spent months preparing for the convention, poring over treatises on government and historical accounts of the ancient Greek city-states, and he arrived at the convention with a well-defined plan for a new government. Called the **Virginia plan**, it was the first major proposal presented to the convention, and it formed the basis of the Constitution. Madison's contributions went far beyond his labors at the convention. He was a key figure both before and after the convention, and his diary constitutes the main

Often called the father of the Constitution because of his huge contribution to its writing and ratification, Madison also collaborated in the writing of the Federalist Papers, which described the justifications for the political institutions and processes the Constitution established. He was elected to the first national Congress, and after serving as secretary of state under Jefferson, he served two terms as the fourth president of the United States.

Virginia plan The first major proposal presented at the 1787 Constitutional Convention; the basis of the Constitution.

historical record of the four-month proceedings. Because of these efforts, Madison is remembered as the father of the Constitution.

Ranking only slightly below Madison in importance were the two delegates from Pennsylvania: James Wilson and Gouverneur Morris. Wilson was a Scotsman in his mid-forties; a lawyer known for his penetrating logical mind, he placed great faith in the common people. Morris, 11 years Wilson's junior, was a swashbuckling figure. Tall, handsome, and known for his biting wit, Morris viewed the common people with aristocratic mistrust. Despite their differences, both advocated a strong federal government with a powerful executive, and through their service on influential committees at the convention, they shaped both the content and the phraseology of the document that ultimately emerged.

Two of the most famous figures present were George Washington and Benjamin Franklin, both of whom made significant contributions to the convention. Washington did not play an active role in shaping the Constitution, but his enormous national prestige and the assumption that he would be the nation's first chief executive provided the convention and the document it produced with a crucial air of legitimacy. Franklin was past his peak of political creativity in 1787, but his justly famed wit served to cool tempers. These two renowned and revered figures played key roles in the fight for ratification simply by lending the Constitution their approval.

Agreement, Disagreement, and Compromise at the Convention

There was a good deal of common ground among the delegates at the convention. Key among these agreements was the consensus on the need for a stronger national government with the power to fulfill the responsibilities entrusted to it. The dilemma was how to achieve this goal. How could a government be powerful enough to protect and serve the common good without tempting tyranny by placing power into too few hands? This conundrum was complicated by the delicate question of relations between state and national governments. The states would have to approve the Constitution, and it was universally recognized that the states had a legitimate interest in defending their sovereignty. So although there was broad agreement on the need for a stronger central government, differences over specifics often divided the convention into shifting and competing groups: large state versus small state, North versus South, and of course, Federalist versus Anti-Federalist.

Thus, the proposed structure of the new government percolated through several proposals. For example, Madison's Virginia plan called for a **bicameral**, or two-house, legislature with a popularly elected lower house and an upper house nominated by state legislatures. Representation in each was to be based on the financial contributions or population of the state. This plan was supported by large states, whose representatives would dominate the national legislature, and op-

bicameral A legislature with two chambers.

posed by small states. A rival proposal was the **New Jersey plan**, which proposed a one-house legislature with equal state representation, similar to that established by the Articles of Confederation. This favored small states, which would wield equal power with their more populous neighbors. The conflict was resolved by the **Connecticut Compromise** or Great Compromise, so called because delegates from Connecticut worked hard for its acceptance. It proposed a two-house legislature, with a House of Representatives apportioned on the basis of population and a Senate representing the states on an equal basis. Similar battles were fought over the composition and selection of the executive branch (these are detailed in chapter 13).

Such political compromises are a notable feature of the document produced by the convention. Some of these compromises seem unsavory, and some left fundamental issues unresolved. For example, Northern and Southern states were split over the question of slavery. The South wanted slaves counted for purposes of representation (even though there was no thought of allowing slaves to vote) but not for purposes of taxation. Northern states favored the reverse. The bargain struck was to count each slave as three-fifths of a person for both representation and taxation. As for the very controversial question of ending the slave trade, the convention simply put it off for the future with a provision that barred Congress from outlawing it until 1808. The unresolved question of slavery perpetuated a problem that neither the bloody Civil War in the nineteenth century nor an extended battle for civil rights in the twentieth has fully resolved.

A number of factors contributed to the willingness of delegates to accommodate their sometimes sharp differences. Many believed that the nation was on the brink of dissolution and that this was the last chance to secure a government that united the states into a single country. Since most of the delegates were Federalists, they agreed on the essential structure of government, even if they differed on the details. This underlying consensus permitted the delegates to find ways to compromise on how to apply these principles. The secrecy of the proceedings also fostered compromise. Free of public scrutiny and pressures, the delegates could change their minds and modify their stands as they groped for answers to the nation's most difficult problems.

The Limited Role of Religion

Of the values and motivations that influenced the delegates to the constitutional convention, religion played a limited role. Although the delegates were Christian (except for a few Deists), a review of notes on the debate at the constitutional convention reveals few references to religion or God (see Benton 1986). The few references that were made do not suggest that the founders attempted to base the Constitution on an explicitly Judeo-Christian belief system. On the contrary, they viewed religion as belonging to the private rather than public sphere. Their

New Jersey plan A proposal presented at the Constitutional Convention that called for a one-house legislature with equal representation for each state.

Connecticut Compromise (Great Compromise) A proposal at the Constitutional Convention that called for a two-house legislature with a House of Representatives apportioned on the basis of population and a Senate representing each state on an equal basis.

primary concern was to protect the individual's religious beliefs from the government, not to base a government on a particular set of religious principles.

It is this latter concern that is expressed in the one direct reference to religion in the original Constitution, in Article VI, Section 3.[3] This clause states that members of the legislative, executive, and judicial branches of both federal and state governments "shall be bound by oath or affirmation, to support this Constitution; but no religious test shall ever be required as a qualification to any office or public trust under the United States." In effect, this provision prevents government at all levels in the United States from requiring its members to be Christian or Protestant or even to believe in God. Such a requirement would in effect establish an official state religion and thereby use the coercive power of government to persecute those with different beliefs. The practice of requiring religious tests as a qualification for civil and military officers was common in England during the reign of Charles II, a practice explicitly referred to in the ratification debates—and roundly condemned. Oliver Ellsworth, a delegate from Connecticut, argued that "the sole purpose and effect of [prohibiting religious tests] is to exclude persecution, and to secure . . . the right of religious liberty" (Ellsworth [1787] 1986, 522).

There is also indirect evidence that the founders wanted government to be neutral with respect to religion. For example, the presidential oath of office allows the president to "swear *or affirm* allegiance to the Constitution" (Article II, Section 1, emphasis added). Article VI offers other government officials the same option to indicate their support for the Constitution by "oath or *affirmation.*" Permitting "affirmation" to substitute for an oath accommodates religious beliefs that forbid swearing and imposes the same level of personal responsibility on someone who is not religious as swearing does for a religious person (Mount 2006b).

The Draft Constitution and the Articles of Confederation Compared

As noted earlier, a constitution establishes the basic principles on which government operates by defining (1) the *functions* and powers of government, (2) the *structure*—that is, the institutions and mechanisms—of government, and (3) the *procedures* through which government carries out its powers and responsibilities. The Articles of Confederation were inadequate on all three dimensions. Table 2.1 compares key provisions of the Articles and the Constitution to show how the Constitution sought to correct the Articles' weaknesses while preserving their protections of individual rights and liberty.

The Articles and the Constitution do have some important features in common. For example, both set up representative forms of government founded on

---

[3] The Constitution concludes, "done in Convention by the Unanimous Consent of the States present the Seventeenth Day of September in the Year of our Lord one thousand seven hundred and Eighty seven." This was a standard way of writing dates at the time rather than an explicit reference to religious principles.

the notion of governance with the consent of the governed, and Congress is the primary representative institution in both systems. Governing with the consent of the governed is an essential part of the definition of democracy, but neither the Articles nor the Constitution established a true representative democracy. Representation in Congress under both systems is based on states rather than on individuals, which gives small states disproportionate power in violation of the democratic principle of political equality. The overarching weakness in the Articles of Confederation was the lack of centralized power adequate to govern a nation. Under the Articles, Congress had the authority to declare war and to raise and equip an army and navy, but it had to rely on state governments to supply the armed forces. The Articles gave Congress the power to apportion taxes among the states, but the states collected the taxes, and there was no power to compel states to pay their portion. The states and the national government both had the power to coin money, making the nation's money supply insecure. And Congress had no authority to regulate interstate commerce. Moreover, the absence of executive and judicial institutions was a key structural deficiency that aggravated the national government's ability to exercise what limited powers had been granted to it.

So it was not a lack of democratic principles per se that the Constitution sought to correct, but the structural deficiencies inherent in the Articles. In contrast to the Articles of Confederation, the Constitution gives Congress sole authority to raise an army and navy, levy and collect taxes, coin money, and regulate interstate commerce. The Constitution also established independent executive and judicial institutions to carry out the powers of government.

The Constitution made some important changes to governmental procedures as well. Representatives to Congress under the Articles were appointed by state legislatures, so representation was indirect. Under the Constitution, members of the House are directly elected, so ordinary citizens have direct control over part of the national government. Government decision making under the Articles required a supermajority—nine of thirteen states, with each state having one vote.[4] Although the Constitution requires a two-thirds majority for certain actions—overriding presidential vetoes, proposing amendments to the Constitution, expelling members of Congress, ratifying treaties in the Senate—most actions require only a simple majority in each chamber.

The proposed expansion of national government powers raised concerns about protecting individual liberty. One of the major objections to the Constitution was the absence of a bill of rights. Because the Articles granted such limited power to the national government, there was little concern that it would threaten

---

[4] Nine was the number of states necessary to achieve a two-thirds majority of the original 13 states. Another potential weakness of the Articles was the problem that would arise if new states were added. For example, 9 of 14 is less than two-thirds, and if the number of states grew to 18, then 9 would be less than a majority. But because amending the Articles required agreement of all states, it might have been difficult to correct this problem.

TABLE 2.1: THE ARTICLES OF CONFEDERATION AND THE CONSTITUTION COMPARED

Provision	Articles of Confederation The United States of America	U.S. Constitution The United States of America
FUNCTIONS		
MAJOR POWERS		
Declare war	Congress	Congress
Army	Congress decides size of force and requisitions troops from each state according to population	Congress authorized to raise and support armies
Navy	Congress authorized to build a navy; states authorized to equip warships to counter piracy	Congress authorized to build a navy; states not allowed to keep ships of war
Treaties	Congress	President, subject to ratification by the two-thirds of Senate
Taxes	Apportioned by Congress, collected by the states; no power to compel states to pay	Laid and collected by Congress
Coin money	Both states and the United States	United States only
Regulation of interstate commerce	No power to regulate interstate commerce	Congress
Staffing government	Congress authorized to appoint ambassadors, maritime judges, and other "civil officers"	President appoints executive branch officials, ambassadors, and federal judges, subject to advice and consent of the Senate
POWERS PROHIBITED		
Bills of attainder	Not prohibited	Prohibited to both states and Congress
Ex post facto laws	Not prohibited	Prohibited to both states and Congress
Religious test to hold office	Not prohibited	Prohibited to both states and Congress
STRUCTURE		
GOVERNMENTAL STRUCTURE		
Form of government	Representative; confederation	Representative; federation
National–state power relationship	States required to abide by acts of Congress, but each state retains sovereignty and all rights and powers not expressly delegated to the United States	U.S. Constitution and federal laws are the supreme law of the land, and take precedence over state constitutions and laws that conflict
LEGISLATURE		
Structure and name	Unicameral, called Congress	Bicameral, called Congress: House of Representatives and Senate
Presiding officer in Congress	President of Congress	Speaker of the House of Representatives; vice president is president of the Senate
Representation in Congress	Between two and seven delegates per state	Two senators per state; representatives apportioned according to state population

Provision	Articles of Confederation The United States of America	U.S. Constitution The United States of America
EXECUTIVE		
Executive power	None specified; Congress authorized to appoint civil officers to manage affairs of the United States	President
Commander in chief	Appointed by Congress	President
JUDICIARY		
National judiciary	Only maritime judiciary	Established one Supreme Court; Congress authorized to create inferior courts
PROCEDURES		
SELECTION OF REPRESENTATIVES		
Members of Congress	Delegates appointed by state legislatures in the manner directed by each legislature	Representatives elected by popular vote; senators appointed by state legislatures
Qualifications for office	None; determined by the state legislatures	U.S. citizen, resident of state, at least 25 years old for House and 30 years old for Senate
Term of legislative office	One year	Two years for representatives, six for senators
Term limits	No more than three out of every six years	None
Recall members of Congress	State may recall its delegates at any time	None
Congressional pay	Paid by states	Paid by the federal government
LEGISLATIVE PROCEDURES		
Voting in Congress	One vote per state	One vote per representative or senator
Vote required to enact legislation	Nine (of 13) states	Simple majority in both House and Senate and signed by the president; some actions require two-thirds majority
When Congress is not in session	Committee of states has the powers of Congress	President can call Congress into session
INTERGOVERNMENTAL		
New states	Admitted upon agreement of nine states, with open invitation to Canada to join	Admitted upon agreement of Congress
Adjudicate disputes between states	Congress	Supreme Court
Extradition of criminals	Accused criminals who flee to another state shall be returned to the state having jurisdiction upon demand of the executive power of that state	Same provision
Full faith and credit	States must grant "full faith and credit" to other states' records, acts, and judicial proceedings	Same provision
AMENDMENT AND RATIFICATION		
Amendment	When agreed to by all states	Proposed by two-thirds of states or two-thirds vote in Congress; ratified by three-fourths of states
Ratification	Consent of all states	Consent of nine states

Source: Adapted and expanded by the authors from Mount (2006a).

individual liberty. States retained the bulk of governmental power, and a number of state constitutions contained bills of rights. But these protections varied across states, and the national government had no authority to protect individual liberties from encroachment by the states. Although most explicit protections of individual rights in the Constitution were added later in the Bill of Rights, the delegates at the convention were concerned about limiting certain abuses of government power. The proposed Constitution included some important prohibitions on governmental power—both state and national—that are absent in the Articles. For instance, the Constitution expressly prohibits passing ex post facto laws or bills of attainder, and as discussed earlier, it prohibits religious tests of those seeking public office.[5]

Thus, the convention proposed a new governmental structure intended to correct the defects of the Articles of Confederation. When the delegates met on September 17, 1787, and 39 of the 55 signed the Constitution, however, their work had not ended. In a very real sense, it had only begun. They now faced the task of persuading their fellow citizens to approve what they had done.

The Ratification Campaign

Ironically, some of the conditions that promoted agreement at the convention made the subsequent ratification process difficult. Anti-Federalists did not see national disintegration as imminent, and they believed that the difficulties attributed to the Articles of Confederation were manageable or temporary. Although they constituted a minority of convention delegates, Anti-Federalists were well represented in state legislatures and the general populace. The secrecy that had promoted cooperation at the convention invited suspicion and resentment among those denied information about the proceedings.

Before the convention dissolved, the delegates made some decisions designed to facilitate the adoption of the proposed Constitution. They ignored the unanimous consent required by the Articles of Confederation and specified that ratification could be secured with the approval of nine states. This provision meant that a single state such as Rhode Island, which had no representatives at the convention, would not be able to block the entire enterprise. Aware of the Anti-Federalist sentiments in state legislatures, the delegates also specified that elected state conventions were to be the ratifying bodies. The Federalists could influence the selection of representatives to these conventions, as well as shape the broader course of deliberations. Ratification was also given a boost by the Continental Congress.

---

[5] Note that the Bill of Rights originally applied only to the national government. As discussed in chapter 4, most of the specific protections in the Bill of Rights have been applied to states through the "due process of law" clause in the Fourteenth Amendment added after the Civil War.

This body, which the new Constitution proposed to put out of business, somewhat surprisingly forwarded the convention's instructions to the states.

Having slanted the rules of ratification to favor adoption, the Federalists set out to transform their opportunity into reality. They labored to get themselves and their sympathizers elected as state convention delegates, and 25 of the Constitution's 39 signatories were so chosen. They developed strategies for convention proceedings. They began a campaign to win public support for the new Constitution.

The Federalists had some notable political advantages, including the endorsements of Washington and Franklin, which were worth thousands of votes in and of themselves. Trading on the important contacts of such luminaries also provided an important communications network for the various state and local campaigns. And the Federalists had a vital asset that their opponents lacked—a positive program to sell. The Anti-Federalists had been neatly maneuvered into the position of favoring some changes in the Articles of Confederation but having no concrete plans to make them. Lacking a viable alternative, Anti-Federalists were forced to adopt a negative, defensive stance in the ratification battle, while the Federalists argued that rejection of the Constitution would lead to a return of the chaos promoted under the Articles.

Still, even with such advantages, ratification was no sure thing. Although the Constitution held obvious appeal to states such as Delaware and New Jersey that were burdened with heavy taxes and debts and squeezed by high interstate duties, other states, such as Rhode Island, offered little hope. And there was genuine and fierce opposition to the Constitution in other states. Four states were crucial because of their size and political strength: Massachusetts, New York, Pennsylvania, and Virginia. If one of these major states failed to ratify, even a legally constituted union of nine or more states would be shaky.

Federalist activities in these key states reveal the efforts they were willing to make to get support for the Constitution. The Pennsylvania state legislature had been in session in the upstairs chamber of the Philadelphia State House even as the convention was finishing its work on the Constitution downstairs. The day after the convention adjourned, the state assembly obtained an unofficial copy of the document. The day after that, the document was printed in the newspapers, and within a week, a rising tide of public opposition threatened to engulf the chances of ratification in the state. The Pennsylvania legislature threatened to swing to the Anti-Federalists in upcoming elections, even before the assembly had summoned a state ratifying convention. Realizing the danger of allowing a legislature dominated by Anti-Federalists to set up the procedures for electing the ratifying convention, the Federalists pushed a motion calling for a ratification convention even though the Continental Congress had yet to officially present the Constitution to the states for approval. Sensing their opportunity, 19 Anti-Federalists bolted from the chamber during a noon recess on September 29, denying the legislature a quorum and hence the legal ability to pass the motion. In response, the sergeant at arms of the Philadelphia legislature assembled a Federalist mob that physically carried two of the recalcitrant representatives back to the chamber, forced them into their seats, and barred the doors! The two captives were enough to muster a quorum, and the Federalists passed the necessary motions to secure a ratifying convention (Morgan 1992, 150–151).

Even in relatively open and free debate, the Federalists often faced tough opposition. In Virginia, James Madison—with the able assistance of future Supreme Court Justice John Marshall—had to take on the formidable opposition of Patrick Henry and future president James Monroe. Although he was not a participant at the state convention, George Washington's influence was clearly felt in Virginia's 89–79 vote for approval. The vote in New York was 30 to 27 in favor of ratification.

With the major states in the fold, the Federalists had their victory, and the other states eventually fell in line to make approval unanimous. The pangs of the formation and adoption struggle were over.

CONSTITUTIONAL PRINCIPLES

What had the Federalists created? What were the underlying objectives of the Constitution, and what democratic ideals and purposes did it embody? Embedded in the document approved by the states is a set of values and goals shared by the delegates to the Constitutional Convention. These values were most clearly articulated by Madison, who—along with Hamilton and John Jay—wrote the best-known explanation and defense of the Constitution. The **Federalist Papers** were originally published as a series of political essays under the pseudonym Publius with the express purpose of persuading New Yorkers to ratify the proposed Constitution. They were subsequently published together as *The Federalist,* and they remain the single best source for understanding the justifications for the political institutions and processes the Constitution established. In a real sense, they constitute the theory that lies behind the practice of American politics.

Madison wrote 30 of the 85 essays, and his contributions make clear that the democratic principle he cherished most was liberty: the individual's right to choose reasonable goals and exercise the means to reach those goals. Madison also recognized that unchecked liberty could cause problems. Freedom to pursue individual goals and the means to achieve them meant there would be an uneven distribution of wealth; some people would be better at acquiring worldly goods than others.

Madison was very much attached to the notion of private property rights, which he saw as the cornerstone of his notion of political freedom. Yet he also reasoned that the unequal distribution of property could cause problems. In *Federal-*

Federalist Papers A series of 85 political essays written by James Madison, Alexander Hamilton, and John Jay with the intent of persuading New Yorkers to ratify the proposed Constitution. They remain the single best source for understanding the justifications for the political institutions and processes the Constitution established.

ist Number 10 (all essays in *The Federalist* are titled by the order of their original publication; see this book's appendix for *Federalist* Number 10), he observed that societies naturally divide into various factions. He defined **faction** as

> a number of citizens, whether amounting to a majority or a minority of the whole, who are united and actuated by some common impulse of passion, or of interests, adverse to the right of other citizens, or to the permanent and aggregate interests of the community.

The causes of factions are numerous and can include religious and political differences. But Madison argued that

> the most common and durable source of factions has been the . . . unequal distribution of property. Those who hold and those who are without property have ever formed distinct interests in society. Those who are creditors and those who are debtors, fall under a like discrimination.

Yet Madison did not divide the world into two simple classes, the rich and the poor. He viewed property as a distinguishing characteristic of a variety of groups, all willing to act in their own self-interest to the detriment of the interests of others.

The existence of factions sets up a difficult problem that is sometimes called the **Madisonian dilemma**: how can self-interested individuals administering strong governmental powers be prevented from using those powers to destroy the freedoms that government is supposed to protect? Madison and his contemporaries were under no illusions about the civic altruism of their fellow citizens. They thought the rich would use political power to exploit the poor, and the poor to plunder the rich; those attached to one religious belief or partisan agenda would similarly use power to force their beliefs on others, with little regard for individual liberties.

To avoid these ugly consequences, Madison saw two options: either remove the cause of factions or control the effects. He rejected the first option as not only impossible but also repellent. The only way to remove the cause of factions was to eliminate individual differences and give everyone the same "common impulse of passion, or of interests." Individual differences were rooted in human nature, and nothing, least of all government, would make them disappear. So Madison turned to the other option—controlling the effect of factions. He believed minority factions posed little difficulty because the majority could always protect its interest by voting them down. The more serious threats were factions that constituted a majority. Madison realized that a majority of his fellow citizens were capable of quashing or persecuting a minority to serve their own interests. As Madison put it, the grand objective of the constitutional undertaking was "to secure the public good and private rights against the danger of such a faction, and at the same time to preserve the spirit and form of popular government."

faction In James Madison's terms, "a number of citizens, whether amounting to a majority or a minority of the whole, who are united and actuated by some common impulse of passion, or of interests, adverse to the right of other citizens, or to the permanent and aggregate interests of the community."

Madisonian dilemma The problem of limiting self-interested individuals who administer stronger governmental powers from using those powers to destroy the freedoms that government is supposed to protect.

To achieve this goal, Madison rejected morals or religion as an effective check on the self-interested appetites of humans. Since "men are not angels," society itself would have to take on the job of blunting and controlling the opinions and wishes of a majority that threatened private rights and the public good. He argued that this restraint could be best accomplished through a **republican form of government**, defined primarily as representative government.[6] The two primary goals of republican government are to create a government that governs with the consent of the governed and to, at the same time, limit a tyrannical majority from using the power of government to infringe on personal liberty. Thus, a republic can be distinguished from a monarchy in that representatives who exercise power are responsible to the people either directly through election or indirectly through appointment by representatives who are elected. Yet it differs from pure or direct democracy in that representatives make decisions on behalf of the people rather than allowing the people to make binding decisions directly by majority rule.

In essence, Madison was making an argument for how the U.S. Constitution would uphold the core values of democracy. Popular sovereignty would be achieved through a representative form of government but with limits on those who hold power. Majority rule was accepted, but Madison placed special emphasis on the rights of the minority. Political freedom and political equality were tied to the notion of individual property rights and the right of like-minded people to pursue their own interests as they saw fit.

The Constitution includes a number of features designed to incorporate and uphold these basic principles, outlined in the following pages.

Written Constitution

The first notable feature of the U.S. Constitution is that it is a written document. Constitutions may be written or unwritten, and although almost all contemporary constitutions are written, at the time of America's founding, a written constitution was quite innovative. Before the American and French Revolutions, a constitution was conceived as something that evolved from a nation's history and practice. The notion that a constitution could be "drafted" was met with contempt in England. English writer Arthur Young ridiculed the American and French idea of a written constitution as "a new term they have adopted; and which they use as if a constitution was a pudding to be made by a receipt" (quoted in Pritchett 1976, 2; Zink 2009, 442).

A written constitution essentially reverses the traditional view. As political scientist C. Herman Pritchett explains, the founders' view was that a

> constitution was a formal written instrument, a "social contract" drafted by a representative assembly and ratified by a special procedure for determin-

republican form of government A form of government in which the government operates with the consent of the governed through some type of representative institution.

---

[6] This discussion describes the founders' view of republican government and does not refer to the platforms and principles of any contemporary political party that may use the name.

ing public assent. . . . The constitution brought the government into existence and was the source of its authority. The government was the creature of the constitution. (1976, 2)

Recall that a constitution defines the fundamental rules and powers under which government operates. It also establishes the "rule of law" so that no one, not even the lawmakers, is above the law. The discussion and debate at the Constitutional Convention focused on creating a stronger central government that would protect individual liberty. James Wilson, one of the most influential delegates, offered a comprehensive theory of the written American Constitution. An analysis of Wilson's writings (Zink 2009) shows that he agreed that the primary purpose of the Constitution was to secure individual liberty based on natural rights. Yet Wilson recognized the inherent tension between the notion of inalienable natural rights and the need to establish a common identity in the new nation. He believed that the written Constitution would minimize this tension "by cultivating within each citizen a refined understanding of the complex interdependence of liberty and law" (Zink 2009, 448).

Governmental powers can be established and limited in ways other than through a written document. Great Britain, for example, is among the few nations that still has an unwritten constitution. Nonetheless, writing down the basic rules and processes of government for everyone to see is one way to establish limits on governmental power: if what government can and cannot do is written down on parchment, then it will be more apparent if government exceeds its legitimate authority. Yet words on parchment alone cannot prevent abuse of power. Traffic lights, for example, are generally effective in regulating the safe flow of traffic through a busy intersection. But just as a traffic light cannot prevent someone from running the light and crashing into crossing traffic, writing down powers and limitations on government cannot prevent self-interested individuals from using those powers to infringe on liberty. Thus, although the founders provided a written constitution to create a stronger government that would also remain limited, they included a number of other features to protect liberty.

Representative Government

One of the most important republican principles incorporated into the American Constitution is representative government. This system operates with the consent of the governed without establishing a direct democracy. A representative system allows deliberation and refinement of public views by passing the views through a body of citizens whose knowledge of the public good is superior to that of the general populace. In addition, representative government permits effective popular rule over a much larger area than direct democracy does, bringing under its control a greater variety of people and interests than direct democracy. Representative democracy also makes it difficult for groups with diverse interests to band together into a majority that could threaten the basic rights of minorities or the general public.

Fragmentation of Power

Another way to protect liberty is to divide power among a number of different institutions and offices so that no single individual has absolute power (as under a monarchy), and no single class or faction is able to control government. The Constitution fragments power in different ways.

SEPARATION OF POWERS A major feature of the Constitution aimed at pitting leaders against one another is the principle of **separation of powers**. The concept is borrowed from the French political philosopher Charles Montesquieu, who argued that liberty is associated with the dispersal of power and tyranny with its concentration. As framed by the Constitution, separation of powers might more accurately be termed as separation of processes. Each of the three branches of government is authorized to carry out a separate portion of the political process: the legislature makes the laws, the executive implements them, and the judiciary interprets them.

These processes are not wholly independent of one another. Although each of the branches is assigned the major responsibility for one of these processes, each to some degree also participates in the principal activities of the others. For example, Congress has the primary responsibility for enacting legislation, but the president is authorized to recommend measures to Congress and to veto laws passed by that body. Similarly, Congress can decline to appropriate money to fund the operation of executive branch departments, and the Senate can affect the president's execution of laws by failing to approve his nominees for major positions in the executive branch. Congress can influence the courts' interpretations of the laws through its power to define their jurisdiction—that is, the kinds of cases they are entitled to hear.

The three branches can thus **check and balance** one another's influence and political power. One branch can assert and protect its own rights by withholding its support for the essential activities of another. But because the three branches are also dependent on one another, the system of shared processes also requires them to cooperate. In this fashion, the separation of processes and checks and balances complement each other to achieve the desired effect in the political system. The first prevents one branch from usurping the responsibilities of another; the second allows each branch to counteract the influence of the others. The result is a

separation of powers The idea that each branch of government is authorized to carry out a separate part of the political process.

check and balance The idea that each branch of the federal government should assert and protect its own rights but must also cooperate with the other branches. Each branch is to serve as a limit on the others' powers, balancing the overall distribution of power.

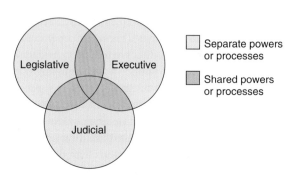

FIGURE 2.1 **Separation and Overlap of Government Powers**

fragmentation of political power. Figure 2.1 illustrates the separation and overlap of processes among the branches of government.

The separation of powers calls for more than just separation of process; it also requires separation of personnel. People who serve in one branch of government are not allowed to concurrently serve in another branch. For example, an individual may not hold a congressional office and a position in the executive branch at the same time. Allowing such a practice would obviously permit power to concentrate.

Another aspect of the separation-of-powers doctrine reflected in the American system is the separation of **constituency**. That is, different groups with different interests choose the personnel of the three branches. As originally envisaged in the Constitution, the president would be selected by the electoral college, an independent group of electors chosen by means specified by each state legislature, none of whom could be a member of Congress. Senators also were chosen by state legislatures, whereas members of the House of Representatives were popularly elected from smaller political districts. Members of the national courts were to be nominated by the president and confirmed by the Senate, so that a single branch of government did not choose them. Once appointed and confirmed, judges serve for a term of good behavior, which amounts to life tenure. Thus, the personnel of the three branches have largely separate and independent bases of political support and power.

FEDERALISM Madison conceived of another check on the majority, which we examine in detail in the next chapter. Federalism is the constitutional division of powers between the national government and the states. In Federalist Number 10, Madison argues that such a division of powers limits the threat of faction: "the influence of factious leaders may kindle a flame within the particular states, but they will be unable to spread a conflagration through the other states."

Madison's system for checking the evils of factionalism was to create a series of dikes to interfere with the free flow of majority will. First, majority interests are filtered by the actions of their elected representatives, who are expected to have more refined views of the public good than the voters themselves. Second, the wishes of the majority are diluted because republicanism allows government to take in a wide variety of interests. And finally, the majority will is directed into many channels by the joint effects of federalism and the separation of powers. Madison wrote in *Federalist* Number 51,

> In the compound republic of America, the power surrendered by the people is first divided between two distinct governments, and then the portion allotted to each subdivided among distinct and separate governments. Hence a double security arises to the rights of the people. The different governments will control each other, at the same time that each will be controlled by itself.

Grasping the importance of this idea is fundamental to understanding the American political system. The system was designed to make it difficult for any faction, even a majority, to wield broad political power. The Constitution essentially divides the various elements of sovereignty, divides them again, and then parcels off the pieces to different institutional actors governed by different processes and character-

constituency The group of people served by an elected official or branch of government.

federalism A political system in which regional governments share power with a central or national government, but each level of government has legal powers that are independent of the other. This division of power between the national and state governments attempts to balance power by giving independent sources of authority to each and allowing one level of government to serve as a check on the other.

ized by different constraints. It is enormously difficult to get a government designed in such a fashion to do anything that a portion of the population opposes. The reason American government is often slow, conflict-riddled, and able to produce only brokered compromises is that it was designed to be exactly that way. The idea is to make it so difficult to bring together all those pieces the Constitution carefully distributes that government is likely to take action only in those rare circumstances when the public will and the public good are so unified as to be indistinguishable.

Mixed Government

There is good reason to believe that the founders provided separate constituencies not only to preserve the independence of the different branches of the national government but also because they wanted them to represent different social and economic interests. The idea of **mixed government** is that it should represent both property and the number of people. The Constitution did not mandate property qualifications for officeholders or voters, but it is significant that originally only the House of Representatives was popularly elected. Direct election of senators was not authorized until adoption of the Seventeenth Amendment in 1913.

mixed government The idea that government should represent both property and the number of people.

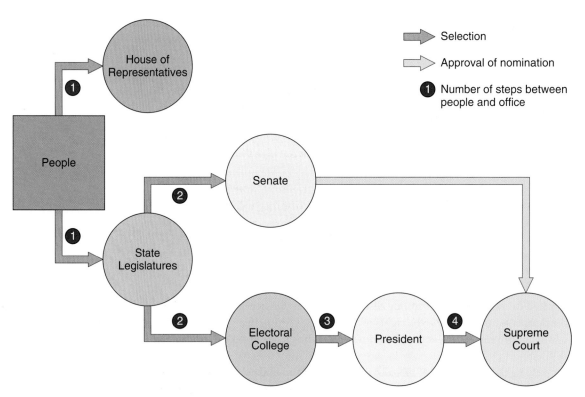

FIGURE 2.2 Relationship between the People and the Selection of Officeholders under the Original Constitution

Other offices were to some extent insulated from popular influence. As Figure 2.2 illustrates, members of the Senate were two steps, the president was three steps, and the Supreme Court was four steps removed from the direct control of the people. Furthermore, the longer terms of senators (six years), the president (four years), and Supreme Court members (life) would make them less subject to public pressures than members of the House of Representatives. Because fewer people were chosen for these three political bodies, they would be more prestigious than the lower house of the national legislature. This greater prestige in turn would attract better-qualified people to these bodies, and because property ownership was considered a reflection of natural ability, the individuals chosen would be those of economic substance from the upper social classes. Thus, in all probability the founders expected the House of Representatives to represent the interests of the common people who owned no private property of consequence. The Senate—with its smaller, more prestigious membership, insulated from popular control by its longer terms of office and (then) indirect method of selection—would constitute the more aristocratic division of the legislature.

CHANGING THE AMERICAN CONSTITUTION

A constitution necessarily reflects the interests and values of the groups responsible for its original formulation. In time, new groups arise that are dissatisfied with the existing distribution of values, and they often seek to rewrite the rules of democratic governance to change this distribution. Recognizing the political motivations of such changes, humorist Will Rogers once observed,

> See where there is a bill up in Congress now to change the Constitution all around. . . . It seems the men who drew up this thing years ago didn't know much and we are just now getting a bunch of real fellows who can take that old parchment and fix it up. . . . Now when they get the Constitution all fixed up they are going to start in on the Ten Commandments, just as soon as they find somebody in Washington who has read them. (1974, 14)

Constitutional change is always political. The press of events and the emergence of different attitudes on the part of leaders and the populace occasionally create a need to alter a nation's fundamental framework. Every democratic system must provide a mechanism to achieve such accommodations or run the risk that frustrated individuals and groups will turn to violence to achieve their goals. The question, therefore, is not whether a democratic constitution will be changed, but how. The U.S. Constitution can be changed through a formal amending process and through a number of other processes as well.

The Anti-Federalists sought to establish the first ten amendments (the Bill of Rights) to the Constitution in order to protect individuals against arbitrary government action and promote political equality. Many of the later amendments are also concerned with equality, but the fight to achieve these rights was long and difficult. In the mid-1800s, Susan B. Anthony and Elizabeth Cady Stanton began what would be a 50-year campaign to secure the right of women to vote, and both died before the Nineteenth Amendment to the Constitution was passed in 1920.

Formal Amendments

One important method of changing the Constitution is the process of formal amendment. This consists of two distinct stages: (1) the proposal of the amendment and (2) the ratification of the amendment. The Constitution provides two options for each stage.

The two methods of proposing amendments are a two-thirds vote in both houses of Congress and a national convention called by Congress at the request of two-thirds of the states (34 of the 50 states). To date, the only method that has ever been used to propose any amendment is the first, a two-thirds vote in Congress.[7]

The authority to propose amendments under this method rests exclusively with Congress; the president has neither the responsibility to sign amendments nor the authority to veto them. But the president is not prohibited from politically supporting or opposing proposed amendments. During his administration, for example, President Clinton actively lobbied members of Congress to defeat a balanced budget amendment and urged them to propose an amendment granting Washington, DC, full representation in Congress.

Since the convention method has never been used, the details of this process are largely unknown. Do two-thirds of the state legislatures have to pass resolutions with exactly the same wording, or are similar resolutions on the same issue sufficient? Is there a time limit on how long it can take for two-thirds of the states to request a convention? If a convention is called, how many delegates will attend the convention, and how will they be apportioned among the states? How will delegates be selected? Will they be popularly elected, appointed by state legislatures, or selected by state governors? Will the convention require a simple majority or a supermajority (two-thirds or three-fourths, respectively) to propose amendments? Is the convention limited to proposing the amendment for which it was called, or can delegates propose additional amendments—or perhaps even become a runaway convention and rewrite the Constitution entirely, as happened in 1787?

Congress has the constitutional authority to resolve these issues, and the answers will inevitably involve political choices, not strictly legal or constitutional

---

[7] The requirement is two-thirds of those present and voting, not two-thirds of the chamber's entire membership. Since amendments typically involve very important issues, however, few members miss these votes.

POLITICS IN PRACTICE

EFFORTS TO CALL A CONSTITUTIONAL CONVENTION

Since the Constitution was ratified in 1789, there have been more than 400 applications from states to call a convention to propose amendments. In the first century following ratification, there were relatively few such petitions. In the last half of the twentieth century, however, applications to call constitutional conventions proliferated, with more than 90 percent of all requests being made during that time period. About half have come since the 1960s.

Applications in the last half-century have been motivated almost exclusively by conservatives outraged by liberal Supreme Court decisions on such issues as busing to achieve integration of public schools, reapportionment of congressional districts, school prayer, and abortion. Most of the time, only a handful of state legislatures pass resolutions requesting a convention, far less than the two-thirds of states necessary to oblige Congress to act. In fact, no issue has yet garnered requests from the required two-thirds of states to start the amending process. Given the difficulties of coordinating political action across a large number of state legislatures, it is perhaps not surprising that all of the amendments proposed to date have been initiated by Congress.

Some issues have come close to mustering requests from the required number of states. One is the movement to call a convention to propose an amendment requiring a balanced federal budget. Indiana was the first state to call for a convention on a balanced budget amendment in 1957. Thirty-one other states submitted similar applications, just three states short of the 34 required. The effort appeared to have stalled and seemed to be moving in reverse when Alabama rescinded its 1976 application in April 1988.

Although it has never been used, this provision giving states the power to initiate the process of amending the constitution is important. Even if an effort falls short, the threat of a constitutional convention may pressure Congress to act, especially if the number of states calling for a convention nears the required two-thirds mark. For example, Congress proposed the amendment to allow for the direct election of senators in response to the pressure of states requesting a convention. Moreover, such calls have been instrumental in raising public consciousness about issues and have increased the pressure on politicians to propose remedies other than constitutional amendments.

SOURCE Weber, Paul J., and Barbara A. Perry. 1989. *Unfounded Fears: Myths and Realities of a Constitutional Convention.* Westport, CT: Greenwood Press, 2–7, 56, 74.

ones. Although the convention method of proposing amendments has never been used, it is important because the Constitution provides states with the means to initiate the formal amending process. Yet Congress retains considerable authority to determine exactly how a convention would be called and how it would operate. (See the Politics in Practice feature "Efforts to Call a Constitutional Convention" for a brief history of this yet-to-be-used method of changing the Constitution.) Thus, proposing amendments is ultimately a political process, and Congress plays a key role regardless of the proposal method used.

Ratification is also a political process, and states determine whether a proposed amendment will be ratified. After an amendment has been proposed, it must be ratified by three-fourths of states (38 of the 50 states) before it can become part of the Constitution. There are two ways for states to ratify amendments: by votes of state legislatures and by conventions held in the states. Congress specifies which ratification method is to be used. Only the Twenty-First Amendment (repeal of prohibition) has been ratified by state conventions so far. In this case, there was concern that political forces favoring prohibition controlled key leadership positions in state legislatures and might be able to thwart popular support for repeal. Congress specified state conventions, apparently in the hope that they would more accurately reflect popular sentiment.

Most successful amendments have been ratified within about two years of being proposed—the median number of months is 25 (see Table 2.2). Although

TABLE 2.2: LENGTH OF TIME BETWEEN CONGRESSIONAL APPROVAL AND ACTUAL RATIFICATION OF THE TWENTY-SEVEN AMENDMENTS TO THE U.S. CONSTITUTION

Amendment		Time required for ratification	Year ratified
I–X	Bill of Rights	26.5 months	1791
XI	Lawsuits against states	11 months	1795
XII	Presidential elections	6.5 months	1804
XIII	Abolition of slavery	10 months	1865
XIV	Civil rights	25 months	1868
XV	Suffrage for all races	11 months	1870
XVI	Income tax	42.5 months	1913
XVII	Senatorial elections	11 months	1913
XVIII	Prohibition	13 months	1919
XIX	Women's suffrage	14 months	1920
XX	Terms of office	11 months	1933
XXI	Repeal of prohibition	9.5 months	1933
XXII	Limit on presidential terms	47 months	1951
XXIII	Washington, DC, vote	9 months	1961
XXIV	Abolition of poll taxes	16 months	1964
XXV	Presidential succession	22 months	1967
XXVI	Eighteen-year-old suffrage	3 months	1971
XXVII	Congressional salaries	2,438 months	1992
Median		**25 months**	

Sources: Congressional Research Service, *The Constitution of the United States: Analysis and Interpretation* (Washington, DC: U.S. Government Printing Office, 1973), 23–44 (92d Cong., 2d sess., S. Doc. 92–82); *Congressional Quarterly Weekly Report* (1992), 1423.

Table adapted from Harold W. Stanley and Richard G. Niemi, *Vital Statistics on American Politics 1999–2000* (Washington, DC: CQ Press, 2000), 303.

three amendments lingered substantially longer, in most cases if there is not sufficient support in the states to ratify within two or three years, the amendment is likely to die. (For a look at some proposals that did not succeed with ratification, see the Politics in Practice feature "Proposed Amendments That Were Not Ratified.") The Constitution does not specify a time limit for states to act on proposed amendments, although beginning with the Eighteenth Amendment (proposed in 1917), Congress instituted a seven-year deadline on ratification.[8] Amendments proposed before 1917 had no time limits; it was generally considered that such proposals were dead if the states did not act within a reasonable time so that a "contemporaneous consensus" would be reflected in the decision.

The absence of a deadline presented an interesting political dilemma in one case. Reacting to a political furor over congressional pay hikes in the 1990s, Michigan and New Jersey dusted off an old proposal and became the 38th and 39th states to approve the Twenty-Seventh Amendment, which requires an election to intervene before a congressional pay raise can take effect. This amendment was originally submitted to the states along with other proposals that became the Bill of Rights, and its May 7, 1992, ratification came 203 years after its proposal!

The Anti-Federalists were primarily responsible for the first 10 amendments, which are mostly concerned with political freedom and political equality. They were concerned with **civil liberties**, protecting individuals against arbitrary government action. Many of the remaining amendments revolve around the central democratic principle of equality. The Thirteenth, Fourteenth, and Fifteenth Amendments relate to race; the Nineteenth, Twenty-Third, Twenty-Fourth, and Twenty-Sixth govern the voting rights of women, residents of the District of Columbia, people who live in jurisdictions where a poll tax is levied, and citizens between the ages of 18 and 21. These amendments were designed to safeguard disadvantaged groups' access to the political process and the social and economic life of the United States. It is important to note that these amendments primarily affect the states, not the national government.

The Seventeenth and Twenty-Second Amendments also relate to political participation, but they deal with the suffrage rights of all voters, not particular groups. The Seventeenth Amendment provides for direct election of senators, thus allowing all voters to choose members of the upper house of the national legislature. The Twenty-Second Amendment limits the length of presidential terms by preventing voters from choosing the same person more than twice. The two amendments are based on somewhat different assumptions about human capacities: the Seventeenth expresses faith in the electorate's ability to choose good senators; the

---

[8] Initially, Congress placed the time limit in the body of the amendment. With the proposal of the Twenty-Third Amendment in 1960, the deadline was placed in the submission resolution. The importance of the change is that resolutions are not bound by the two-thirds rule; a simple majority is enough to pass resolutions because they are not a formal part of the amendment. Thus, when the seven-year limit on the Equal Rights Amendment (proposed in 1971) was about to expire, Congress extended it for three more years on a simple majority vote. In 1978, when Congress proposed an amendment to treat Washington, DC, as if it were a state for purposes of representation, it reverted to the practice of placing the time limit in the body of the amendment.

civil liberties The freedoms and protections against arbitrary governmental actions given to the people in a democratic society.

PROPOSED AMENDMENTS THAT WERE NOT RATIFIED

Only 33 of the thousands of constitutional amendments introduced in Congress since 1789 have been submitted to the states for ratification. Twenty-seven of these were ratified and added to the Constitution. Six have not become amendments. Congress set a time limit of seven years for the required three-fourths of states to ratify most of these proposals, and two proposals failed when their time limits expired. But there are still four proposals with no time-limit provisions that theoretically could be ratified. It is unlikely that any of these will surface again because their central issues have been addressed in statutes passed by Congress or by other amendments.

The four proposed amendments with no time limits deal with apportionment of U.S. representatives, the issue of titles of nobility for citizens, slavery, and child labor. The first of these was among a total of twelve proposals submitted by the First Congress. It dealt with apportionment of House districts, providing one representative for every 30,000 people until there were 100 members in the House, at which time Congress would regulate the proportion until the size reached 200 members. At that point, Congress could increase the size beyond 200 so that each representative would represent no more than 50,000 people. The last recorded action on this amendment was ratification by Connecticut and Georgia in 1939; to date, only 12 states have ratified the amendment. Today, membership in the House is capped at 435 by a statute passed by Congress. Every ten years, after the census, the 435 House seats are reapportioned among the states, with some states losing and others gaining seats depending on whether a state's population has grown or declined. Once the seats are reapportioned, the actual drawing of congressional

districts is the responsibility of state legislatures. With the size of the House fixed at 435, each member currently represents a district containing more than 680,000 people. If the proposed limit of 50,000 constituents per member of Congress were followed, the House would need 6,000 members to represent a population of 300 million.

Another amendment without a time limit concerns U.S. citizens' use of titles of nobility and other honors bestowed by foreign governments and monarchs. The proposed amendment, passed by Congress on May 1, 1810, would have denationalized any U.S. citizen who accepted honors or titles of nobility without prior congressional approval. Twelve states ratified this amendment, one short of the 13 required at the time it was submitted. As more states were admitted to the Union, the number required to validate the amendment increased: Louisiana became the eighteenth state in 1812, increasing to 14 the number of additional states necessary to reach the three-fourths requirement. The issue has subsequently been dealt with by statute. For example, naturalized citizens must renounce titles or orders of nobility according to a law passed in 1906. An 1881 law limited congressional approval of honors to the acceptance of a "decoration or other thing," since the awarding of such honors by other governments cannot be prevented. In 1958, Congress passed a law authorizing retired U.S. government personnel "to accept and wear . . . decorations, orders, medals, emblems, presents and other things" (Private Law 85-704).

Congress proposed another constitutional amendment with no time limit on March 2, 1861. It stated that no constitutional amendments could authorize Congress to interfere with state laws regarding slavery. This amendment was proposed as a gesture of compromise in an effort to avert the attempted secession of southern states. Only three states ratified it. It was rendered moot by the conclusion of the Civil War and ratification of the Thirteenth Amendment abolishing slavery. Two interesting procedural details are associated with this proposal. One is that President James Buchanan signed the amendment, but presidential approval of constitutional amendments is unnecessary. Another is that although Congress specified that state legislatures were to decide about ratification, Illinois used a constitutional convention to ratify the amendment. This irregularity did not generate much controversy, since the number of states ratifying was so far short of the required number.

The last amendment with no time limit was proposed on June 2, 1924. It would have given Congress power to regulate child labor. Although Congress had established the practice of attaching time limits in 1917, it did not attach a time limit to this proposal.

Only 28 states have ratified the proposal. The ratification process provoked controversy that ended up in the Supreme Court when the state of Kansas first rejected the amendment in 1925 but then reconsidered and ratified it twelve years later. In the case of Coleman v. Miller (1939), the Supreme Court held that Congress has the ultimate authority to decide whether there will be a time limit and whether a proposed amendment has been properly ratified by the requisite number of states. The record of state actions on proposed amendments reflects changing attitudes about child labor. Both state and federal statutes now regulate child labor.

As noted, two proposals failed when the time limit set by Congress expired. One of these, known as the Equal Rights Amendment (ERA), was submitted to the states in 1972 with a seven-year time limit. The core provision was a mere twenty-two words: "Equality of rights under the law shall not be denied by the United States or by any State on account of sex." The proposal

had wide initial support, and 22 of the necessary 38 states ratified it in the first year after it was proposed. But momentum stalled as opponents organized. When the time limit expired in 1979, only 13 more states had ratified the amendment, three short of the necessary number. Some states that had ratified the amendment passed resolutions rescinding their earlier action, although given the ruling in Coleman, it is not clear that states may retract ratification. Just as time was about to expire, Congress extended the limit to 1982. But no additional states ratified the proposal in this period. Some supporters of the ERA argue that if three more states were to ratify the amendment, Congress could certify that it has been ratified by the required number of states even though the time limit has expired. Such action seems unlikely and would certainly provoke controversy.

The final proposal that failed to be ratified concerned congressional representation for Washington, DC. Since the citizens of Washington, DC, are not part of any state, they have no voting representatives in Congress. The House allows the citizens of the nation's capital to send a nonvoting delegate, but they have no voice in the Senate. The amendment proposed in 1978 would have treated the District of Columbia as if it were a state for purposes of representation and in voting for president and vice president. This means that the residents would have had two senators, at least one representative, and the same number of electoral votes as states with similar populations. When the time limit expired in 1985, only a handful of states had ratified the amendment. Congress had inserted the time limit in the amendment itself, rather than putting it in a separate transmittal resolution, as was done with the ERA. Any extension of the time, therefore, would require a two-thirds vote.

SOURCE Virginia Commission on Constitutional Government. 1961. *The Constitution of the United States of America*. Richmond: Virginia Commission on Constitutional Government.

Twenty-Second reflects a fear that voters may fall victim to the entreaties of a demagogue.

Four of the amendments—the Eleventh, Twelfth, Twentieth, and Twenty-Fifth—bear no particular imprint of group influence or political philosophy. Rather, these amendments relate to changes brought about by the press of particular historical events, and they primarily deal with the structure and procedures of government. For example, the Twelfth Amendment specifies that members of the electoral college must cast separate ballots for president and vice president; this amendment was a direct result of the election of 1800, in which Thomas Jefferson and Aaron Burr—the presidential and vice presidential candidates of the same party—received the same number of electoral votes. The Twentieth Amendment reduces the time between the election and inauguration of the president and vice president.

Two other amendments altered powers and procedures of the national government. The Sixteenth allows the federal government to levy an income tax, and as already discussed, the Twenty-Seventh limits the authority of members of Congress to give themselves a pay raise by requiring an election to intervene before the raise can go into effect. The remaining two amendments—the Eighteenth and Twenty-First—resulted in no net change, first establishing and then repealing prohibition of alcohol.

Although amendments have produced important changes in the Constitution, only 27 amendments have made it past the hurdles embedded in the process, and of these, 10 came at once, and 2 counteract each other. Thus, in more than two centuries, the Constitution has undergone lasting formal alteration on only 15 occasions. But formal amendments to the Constitution are responsible for only a portion of the vast changes that have occurred in the functions, procedures, and structure of the American political system over this period. These changes have been a result of other processes—specifically, of custom and usage and of interpretation by officials of the three branches of the national government.

Constitutional Change through Custom and Usage

Constitutional change through **custom and usage** occurs when practices and institutions not mentioned in the written document evolve in response to political needs and alter the structure, functions, or procedures of the political system. For example, political parties are not mentioned in the Constitution. Indeed, the founders probably viewed parties as examples of the factions Madison discussed in *Federalist* Number 10. Nonetheless, political parties developed soon after ratification in response to the demands of electoral politics. Although not formal government institutions, parties have fundamentally altered the structure and procedures of government. For example, members of Congress are chosen in partisan elections, and Congress itself is organized along party lines.

Political parties have also changed the way the electoral college operates. The founders created the electoral college in part because they did not trust ordinary citizens to exercise sound judgment in choosing a president. The Constitution mandated

custom and usage The term used to describe constitutional change that occurs when the practices and institutions of government not specifically mentioned in the Constitution change over time through use and evolution.

that "each state shall appoint, in such manner as the Legislature thereof may direct" a number of electors equal to its number of senators and representatives (Article II, Section 1). Each state originally appointed one slate of electors. As political parties developed, they began nominating slates of partisan electors, and the popular vote in a state now determines which party's electors cast that state's electoral votes for president. Thus, although the constitutional provisions governing the electoral college have not been significantly altered by formal amendment,[9] the operation of the electoral college has changed significantly from the original intent of the founders; it has become more democratic through a process of custom and usage.

Executive Interpretation

The Constitution contains three types of powers. **Enumerated powers** are powers explicitly granted to government or to a particular institution. Article I, Section 8, for example, lists the powers of Congress (power to declare war, to raise an army and navy, to coin money, to regulate interstate commerce, and so on), and Article II enumerates specific powers of the chief executive (the power of commander in chief of the army and navy and the power to make treaties with the advice and consent of the Senate, to see that the laws are faithfully executed, to receive ambassadors and other public ministers, and so forth). **Implied powers** are those not formally specified by the Constitution but rather inferred from the powers that are formally specified. Implied powers flow from the "necessary and proper" clause in Article I, Section 8, which empowers the national government to make other laws that are "necessary and proper for carrying into Execution the foregoing Powers and all other Powers vested by this Constitution in the Government of the United States, or in any Department or Officer thereof."

Inherent powers (or prerogative powers) are not derived from either enumerated or implied powers but are those that are essential to the functioning of government or a particular office. Federal courts, for example, issue fines and incarceration for contempt of court on the grounds that courts cannot perform their judicial functions without the ability to control courtroom misbehavior. Similarly, presidents periodically claim certain inherent powers as chief executive or commander in chief. In 2006, President George W. Bush authorized the National Security Agency (NSA) to engage in electronic eavesdropping on American citizens without a warrant, although warrants are required by the Foreign Intelligence Surveillance Act (FISA). President Bush argued that as commander in chief he had the inherent power to protect America from terrorist attacks and that Congress does not have the authority to limit the president's espionage power during wartime. Although the formal powers of the president have changed little since George Washington first exercised

enumerated powers The powers specifically listed in the Constitution as belonging to the national government.

implied powers Those powers belonging to the national government that are suggested in the Constitution's "necessary and proper" clause.

inherent powers (prerogative powers) Powers that are not listed or implied by the Constitution but that rather have been claimed as essential to the national government.

---

[9] The Twelfth Amendment specified that electors were to cast separate votes for president and vice president, but this provision did not change the goal of removing selection of the president from direct popular control.

them, the political powers of the presidency have expanded significantly through executive interpretation. Such interpretation derives mainly from the concept of inherent or prerogative powers; presidents have claimed them as an essential characteristic of the executive office, as illustrated in the previous paragraph. An early example of executive interpretation occurred when George Washington interpreted the power to "receive ambassadors and other public ministers" to mean that the president also had the authority to recognize foreign governments. This interpretation significantly expanded presidential powers beyond those specifically enumerated. Perhaps the best-known example is **executive privilege**, the right of the president to withhold information on matters of national sensitivity or personal privacy. For example, in the early years of the George W. Bush administration, some members of Congress wanted to know who was meeting with Vice President Cheney to help develop national energy policy. President Bush refused to provide this information, arguing that getting candid advice required protecting the confidentiality of those actually tapped to give it. Another example is the president's ability to dismiss high-ranking members of the executive branch. There is nothing in the Constitution about the procedure for removing executive branch officials. Does the president have the power to do this unilaterally as part of his power as chief executive, or is the Senate's approval also required? That issue surfaced as a factor in the impeachment action against President Andrew Johnson shortly after the Civil War and eventually led to a number of court decisions after Presidents Woodrow Wilson and Franklin Roosevelt also removed key executive officials from their positions.

Legislative Interpretation

Each time Congress enacts legislation, it must interpret the Constitution. Some laws passed by Congress are so far-reaching that they fundamentally alter the responsibility and functions of the government. For example, the Social Security Act of 1935 involved the federal government in basic social welfare services, and the Employment Act of 1946 gave the national government responsibility to use its power to promote economic prosperity and full employment. Both laws were highly controversial when first enacted, and opponents argued that they were beyond the constitutional scope of government. Congress's interpretation prevailed. Today, government's responsibility in these areas is generally accepted.

Judicial Interpretation

executive privilege A prerogative power of the president to withhold information on matters of national security or personal privacy.

judicial review The power to review decisions of the lower courts and to determine the constitutionality of laws and actions of public officials.

Judicial review refers to the power of courts to declare the acts and actions of legislatures and executives unconstitutional. It is an extraordinary power that seems to challenge the democratic principle of majority rule. And nowhere does the Constitution explicitly grant courts the authority to nullify the actions of elected officials. In a prime example of constitutional change through judicial interpretation, the Supreme Court itself claimed the power of judicial review in 1803 in the case of *Marbury v. Madison,* which is discussed in detail in chapter 15.

It is hard to overstate the importance of judicial interpretation in the American political process. For example, Supreme Court interpretations of the "equal protection of the laws" clause of the Fourteenth Amendment altered the composition of both the House of Representatives and state legislatures and also revolutionized race relations in this nation. Judicial interpretation has promoted political and social equality in American life.

CHAPTER TWO
Top Ten Takeaway Points

1 A constitution establishes the basic principles on which government operates by defining (1) the *structure*—that is, the institutions and mechanisms—of government, (2) the *functions* and powers of government, and (3) the *procedures* through which government carries its powers and responsibilities. In defining these basic principles, constitutions establish a set of legal relationships between the leaders and the led by determining the rules for accessing and exercising political power.

2 The Declaration of Independence, the Articles of Confederation, and state constitutions provided the philosophical foundations on which the Constitution is based. In these historical antecedents is a commitment to popular sovereignty through representative government, limited powers for the central government, and dominant legislatures.

3 The major deficiency of the Articles of Confederation, the first constitution of the United States, was the central government's lack of sufficient power to govern. Civil unrest and the inability of the national government to respond to economic priorities fueled a movement to create a stronger national government. Those who favored a new constitution giving more power to the national government were called Federalists; those opposed were known as Anti-Federalists.

4 In February 1787, the Continental Congress called on the states to send delegates to a convention in Philadelphia for the purpose of amending the Articles of Confederation. Although there was considerable support in the general populace for the Anti-Federalists' opposition to a strong central government, few Anti-Federalists attended the convention.

⑤ Federalists, who agreed that the national government should be more powerful, dominated the convention. The delegates quickly abandoned the attempt to revise the Articles of Confederation and decided to write a new constitution.

⑥ Although there was disagreement about specifics, there was enough common ground for acceptable compromises to be reached. The most important was the Connecticut Compromise.

⑦ The Constitution produced by the delegates corrected the major deficiencies in the structure, function, and procedures of government under the Articles of Confederation. The stronger central government it created achieved popular sovereignty through representative government, while limiting the power of government to infringe on individual liberty, by fragmenting governmental power.

⑧ Although the Constitution created a stronger national government, power was divided among three coequal branches. The legislative, executive, and judicial branches each had some ability to check abuses of power by the other branches.

⑨ Power was also decentralized through creation of a federal system in which the national government was granted limited powers and states retained sovereignty in other jurisdictions. The Constitution had to be approved by nine states to be ratified. The ratification battle was a bruising political contest. The Federalists just managed to pull out majorities in several key states. Rhode Island was the last state to ratify in May 1790, and the Constitution was officially ratified and took force in May 1791.

⑩ There are several ways to change the Constitution. In addition to changes by formal amendment, the Constitution has been changed by custom and usage and through legislative, executive, and judicial interpretation.

CHAPTER TWO

Key Terms and Cases

Anti-Federalists, 43
Articles of Confederation, 40
bicameral, 46
check and balance, 58
civil liberties, 65
Connecticut Compromise (Great Compromise), 47
constituency, 59
constitution, 38
custom and usage, 68

Declaration of Independence, 39
enumerated powers, 69
executive privilege, 70
faction, 55
federalism, 59
Federalist Papers, 54
Federalists, 43
implied powers, 69
inherent powers (prerogative powers), 69

judicial review, 70
Madisonian dilemma, 55
mixed government, 60
New Jersey plan, 47
republican form of government, 56
separation of powers, 58
Shays's Rebellion, 44
unicameral, 40
Virginia plan, 45

③ FEDERALISM

KEY QUESTIONS

Why does the United States use a federal system to divide power between different levels of government?

What are the advantages and disadvantages of federalism?

How has the "Great Recession" changed state–federal relations?

IMAGINE THAT YOU ARE FLAT BROKE: no job, no money, no food, no prospects, a pile of overdue bills on the table, and creditors banging at the door. Out of the blue, your rich uncle calls and offers you a million dollars. Would you take the money?

At first glance, it's a no brainer: take Uncle Sugar's dough and enjoy the sweet ride back to solvency. Yet what if Uncle Sugar put some strings on his handout? What if you only got to spend the money on what he thought was important, and that didn't include some of your bills? What if he insisted that you had to spend all the money right away, but as part of the deal, you had to commit to giving monthly $10,000 checks to his favorite charity for the next ten years? That means you'd be on the hook for another large bill even after Uncle Sugar's dough was long gone. What if he said you had to be at his beck and call for the next 20 years to run his errands, and from painful experience you knew that running his errands would be time-consuming and annoying beyond belief and would you a fortune in gas? What if Uncle Sugar said that if you took the cash, you could watch only the TV programs he wanted you to watch, and you had to buy the foods he liked (and you hated)? What if he said you had to start rooting for his favorite football team?

You get the idea. At some point, Uncle Sugar's dough isn't worth the hassle, no matter how much of a financial pickle you're in. In 2009, some state governments were publicly wondering whether they were in just this sort of situation. Early that year, the federal government had passed the American Recovery and Reinvestment Act (ARRA), which among other things sent about $200 billion to the states to fund a wide range of programs, from transportation to education.

The states needed that money. The great recession of 2008–2009 had left most state governments with gaping holes in their budgets, forcing them to slash public services. As jobs disappeared and the economic machinery slipped its gears, some states were getting desperate. Things were so bad in California that Mike Genest, director of the state's Department of Finance, spent February 2009 trying to figure out whether the state could legally declare bankruptcy (Goldmacher 2009). No wonder California officials were grateful to get an estimated $50 billion in federal stimulus money. In 2009, most state officials were in favor of the federal stimulus money, but even then some expressed worries about the ARRA's fine print. Governors in nine states openly considered rejecting millions in federal stimulus money to expand unemployment benefits.

The problem was that the federal money was for the short term, but the expansion of the benefits would last much longer. The basic problem was a bigger version of Uncle Sugar's million: people who write large checks usually want something for their money. The federal government made no bones about what it wanted in return for all that cash it sent to the states; it wanted its policy priorities addressed. Such a situation potentially creates a big source of conflict for the American political system. States are not supposed to take orders from the federal government. The Constitution establishes the states as independent, sovereign governments that have authority over a broad swath of domestic policy. Yet can the states retain that independence if they are dependent on federal money and subject to the strings that come with the cash? This choice between financial support and policymaking independence can be tough. Still, at least in some cases, states have been willing to say, "Thanks, but no thanks" to the federal government's money and the strings that come with it. For example, in 2011, governors in Ohio, Wisconsin, and Florida turned down billions in federal support for development of high-speed rail systems. At the time, those states desperately needed the jobs and investment represented by the federal dollars, but the states ultimately decided that the extra costs they would have to pick up over the long term did not justify taking the dough. High-speed rail is a federal policy priority; at least some states wanted to invest their resources in their own policy priorities.

This sort of conflict cuts to the heart of the American political system: who has the power to do what, and who pays for it? This is the fundamental question of American federalism. In a real sense, the debate about the appropriate roles of state and national governments that lay at the heart of the struggle between Federalists and Anti-Federalists has never been fully resolved. Defining those roles is at the center of many important political struggles. States still seek to protect their independence from one another and from federal encroachment, and the federal government still struggles to provide the regulatory uniformity that characterizes a nation-state. We can see signs of this continuing struggle in the Tea Party movement. Many arguments made by Tea Party–backed candidates in the 2010 congressional elections and by several candidates competing for the Republican presidential nomination in 2012 were remarkably similar to Anti-Federalist themes in the ratification debate.

Conservatives and liberals take one side or the other of the issue, depending on what is at stake. Some conservatives often echo Anti-Federalist arguments championing states' rights. Yet on some issues—same-sex marriage and medical marijuana, for example—they are quick to support sweeping legal intervention by the federal government. Some liberals turn to the federal government to provide uniform solutions to important issues such as civil rights but prefer leaving other issues, such as same-sex marriage and medical marijuana, with the states.

An important prerequisite to understanding the complicated nature of American politics is understanding the division of power between different levels of government. This chapter provides a basic grounding in federalism by outlining the concept of federalism and its relation to other ways of distributing governmental power, detailing the federal system adopted in the United States, tracing the evolution of state–federal relationships, and examining the consequences of these arrangements.

THE CONCEPT OF FEDERALISM IN CONTEXT: CONFEDERAL, UNITARY, AND FEDERAL SYSTEMS

All political systems divide and delegate power. What distinguishes one system from another is where sovereignty resides. In chapter 1 we identified three forms of government—autocracy, oligarchy, and democracy—based on whether one, few, or many exercise power. Another way to classify governments is based on *how* sovereignty is divided between a central (national) government and regional (state) governments. This approach identifies three distinct types of political systems: confederal, unitary, and federal.

Confederation

In a **confederation**, regional (state) governments are sovereign, and the central (national) government is created by—and can exercise only the authority granted to it by—unanimous agreement of regional governments. Powers of the weak central government extend exclusively to foreign policy or issues confronting the entire collection of states, and the national government has no direct power over the citizens of the sovereign states. Two other features typically associated with a confederation include the right of a component government to withdraw from the larger union and a requirement that all members of the union consent to any change in the division of powers between the two levels of government. Figure 3.1 illustrates relationships in a confederation.

confederation A political system in which the central government receives no direct grant of power from the people and can exercise only the power granted to it by the regional governments.

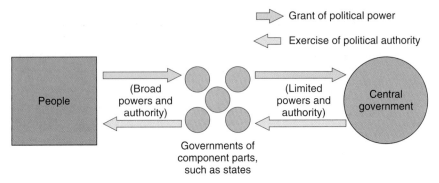

FIGURE 3.1 Confederation

A familiar example of a confederal system is the United States under the Articles of Confederation. The original Congress could not exercise direct control over people or states to enforce its authority. It had to rely on state governments to provide money and troops for the Revolutionary War, and it needed state courts to enforce its laws. A modern-day example of a confederation is the United Nations (UN). In this body, around 193 nation-states—such as the United States, China, Mexico, and Kenya—are the component governments, and the UN itself is the central political unit. Member nation-states remain sovereign, and the UN exercises only those powers granted to it by its members: it depends on voluntary contributions of money and military forces for its operations, it cannot force its provisions on individual members, and nations are free to withdraw from it at any time.

Unitary Government

In a **unitary system**, sovereignty resides wholly in the central government. The central government may (and usually does) create regional governments, but these local units can exercise only the powers delegated and authorized by the central government (Figure 3.2). The central government retains the most exten-

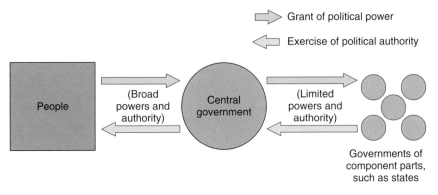

unitary system A political system in which the power is concentrated in the national government, and the regional governments can exercise only those powers granted them by the central government.

FIGURE 3.2 Unitary System

sive and important powers, and it may reduce or take back any powers it grants to the lower political units.

Most countries have unitary governments. An example of a unitary relationship in the United States is the relationship between every state government and its local governments. In this case, the state (central) government is sovereign over its villages, cities, counties, and school districts. These local governments exercise only the powers allowed them by the state government, and they do not have the power to block any changes in state–local relationships, nor can they legally withdraw from the jurisdiction of a state government.

Federalism

Standing somewhere between the confederate and unitary options is **federalism**, a system in which central and regional governments share sovereignty. Each level of government has its own jurisdiction and set of responsibilities. In the American system, for example, neither the national government nor any individual state is dependent on the other for its political power. The same is true of other federal systems. Provinces in Canada, cantons in Sweden, and *Länder* in Germany have power bases independent of their national governments. Figure 3.3 illustrates federal relationships.

The two essential features of a federal system are (1) that each level of government is granted power directly by the constitution and (2) that each level possesses and exercises some powers that are legally independent of the other. A federal

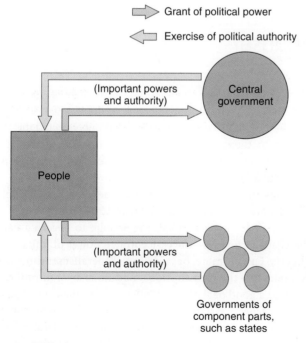

FIGURE 3.3 Federalism

federalism A political system in which regional governments share power with a central or national government, but each level of government has legal powers that are independent of the other. This division of power between the national and state governments attempts to balance power by giving independent sources of authority to each and allowing one level of government to serve as a check on the other.

system has two other important characteristics. First, both levels of government must participate in any decision to change the division of powers between them. For example, in the United States, the states play a role in amending the federal Constitution. Second, the component parts are not free to voluntarily leave the union. This was the major legal issue underlying the American Civil War. The Southern states claimed that they had the right to secede from the Union, and the Northern states disagreed. The question was decided in favor of the North on the battlefield and in the courtroom.

Notice that all three types of government involve a division of power. What keeps the categories distinct is the *how* power is divided: in confederations, the regional governments decide how to divide power; in unitary systems, the central government decides how to divide power; in federal systems, a constitution divides power so that each level has some power independent of the other. Although confederal, unitary, and federal systems are distinct, the distribution of power varies within each of these categories. As weak as the national government was under the Articles of Confederation, it had much more power than the UN has today. France and Great Britain have unitary governments, but counties and towns exercise more power in Great Britain than in France because of the British tradition of local self-government. In federal systems, the relative power of states and the national government varies. For example, in the United States, all states have equal sovereignty, whereas in India and Russia, some states have more autonomy than others; overall, power is more centralized in the Russian Federation than in the United States (Zhuravskaya 2010).

WHY FEDERALISM?

Federalism is the primary institutional feature of the U.S. Constitution. It is also an innovative feature of the Constitution. The founders rejected the forms of government familiar to them—unitary and confederal—and invented federalism. Why did they invent a new type of government? We can see practical political and philosophical motivations.

Federalism was the only option that made sense given the political environment. The experience with the Articles of Confederation had made clear to them that a confederacy was not strong enough to govern a nation, and as colonists, they had learned how the concentrated power of unitary government threatened liberty. Furthermore, because Anti-Federalist sentiments ran high in many states, politically the Constitution stood no chance of ratification unless the states retained a good deal of independence from the central government.

In opting for a federal system, however, the founders were doing more than bowing to the demands of their political environment. A federal system was compatible with a guiding philosophical principle of the Constitution—fragmentation of power. They made a conscious choice to create a political system that trades off some goals for others.

Advantages of Federalism

DISPERSAL OF POWER A primary objective for the founders was to disperse power. Federalism preserves the right of the states to be autonomous governments accountable to their own citizens rather than to the national government. A key reason the founders wanted states to share this responsibility—to be partners of the federal government rather than its subordinates—was the idea that having strong and independent states would prevent the federal government from gaining too much power and threatening the rights of citizens. Americans have always feared concentrations of power, and dividing power between the states and the federal government was an attempt to provide balance. If the states remained sovereign governments, power remained closer to the people and thus would be less likely to be used against their will. Federalism thus institutionalizes and safeguards the division of powers that the founders believed to be so critical to a well-constructed republic.

ACCOMMODATION OF DIVERSE INTERESTS With independent political power granted to states, local interests and political priorities are respected and represented. States have broad latitude to pursue their own policy paths, allowing them to respond to the wishes of their citizens rather than to the dictates of the federal government.

POLICY EXPERIMENTATION Variation in laws and public policy across states is one of the most commonly cited advantages of federalism. As Supreme Court Justice Louis Brandeis observed, state governments are the "laboratories of democracy." Public policy experimentation provides important lessons not only for other states but also for the national government. Expansion of the vote to women is one example of a policy implemented in some states before it became a national policy.

Disadvantages of Federalism

Institutionalizing a division of power, accommodating diverse interests, and allowing state and local experimentation are clear advantages of the American system of federalism. But there are also some disadvantages.

FACTIONS Recall that James Madison defined a faction as any group, either a minority or a majority, that is motivated to act in a way that harms individual rights or is contrary to public interest in general. He was especially concerned about majority factions (*Federalist* Number 10). Smaller political units tend to be politically, socially, and economically more alike than the larger nation of which they are a part. As a result, these political units are more likely to be dominated by factions, and because of their sensitivity to local interests, state governments may be more vulnerable to a tyranny of the majority. The nation's history is replete with examples of dominant factions appropriating the power of state and local governments and denying minority groups equal rights, precisely the sort of behavior Madison feared. One example is the systematic disenfranchisement of African Americans following the Civil War, especially in Southern states. Whites in many of these states used their majority status to enact Jim Crow laws to deny blacks equal political, social, and economic opportunities.

COMPLEXITY AND INEFFICIENCY Though experimentation in public policy has advantages, it leads to a bewildering variation in state laws. In Nebraska, the speed limit is 75 miles per hour. Cross into neighboring Iowa or Kansas at that velocity, and you immediately break the law. In other words, crossing a state line means entering a different political jurisdiction with different legal standards. All this variation makes coordinating intergovernmental action difficult, creates headaches for those who engage in interstate business and must deal with a patchwork of regulatory requirements, and can catch even a conscientiously law-abiding citizen unaware. Your status as a traffic scofflaw depends not only on what you do but also on what state you do it in.

ACCOUNTABILITY The variation can also make it harder for the citizen to hold government accountable. For example, who gets the blame or credit for the policies and programs funded at least in part by the federal government—the federal government, because it put up the cash and insisted on some general rules about how it was spent, or the states, which also kicked in a lot of dollars, implemented and administered most of these programs, and independently created programs of their own? Or both? When popular public services get slashed, who gets the blame: the states that will not raise taxes or the federal government that is cutting grants? Such questions can be frustratingly hard to answer in a federal system.

DIVISION OF POWERS IN THE AMERICAN FEDERAL SYSTEM

Federations differ on the particular methods they use to divide political power. The United States uses a written constitution to divide political power, with specific grants of authority going to the national government and the rest being reserved for the states. As a result, the central operative questions in politics include not just "who gets what?" but also "what level of government gets to decide who gets what?" The answer to the second question often determines the answer to the first. To formulate an answer to this second question, you need to know how the Constitution divides power between state and federal governments.

The Powers of the National Government

Article I, Section 8 of the U.S. Constitution spells out certain powers given to Congress. These include the power to levy and collect taxes, to borrow money, to regulate interstate commerce, to coin money, to declare war, and to raise and support an army and a navy. The specific grants of power given to the national government are called enumerated powers. But the national government's powers are not limited to these. Included in Article I, Section 8 is a vague and sweeping grant giving Congress the power "to make all laws which shall be necessary and proper for carrying into execution the foregoing powers" (often called the "elastic" clause of the Constitution). With this statement, the founders expanded the authority of the national government beyond its enumerated powers by giving it implied powers. Madison strongly favored implied powers. The logic behind these powers is the impossibility of listing in detail every specific power the national government would be authorized to take in every conceivable situation.

Enumerated powers make it clear that the power of the national government is meant to be limited, yet the potential for increasing central government's influence through the doctrine of implied powers is hard to overestimate. The scope of this potential was first tested in the case of **McCulloch v. Maryland** (1819), which involved a dispute over whether the central government had the power to create a national bank. The national bank was originally created as part of a broad economic program formulated by Secretary of the Treasury Alexander Hamilton. President George Washington had some doubts about the constitutionality of this proposal and got conflicting advice from two key members of his cabinet—Hamilton and Thomas Jefferson.

Hamilton acknowledged that establishing a bank was not one of the national government's enumerated powers but argued that the "necessary and proper" clause gave it the implied power to do so because the bank would be a convenient way to keep and administer the revenues Congress raised by taxing and borrowing. Hamilton interpreted *necessary* as "convenient" or "appropriate." Jefferson, in contrast, interpreted *necessary* as "indispensable." A national bank was not indispensable to safeguarding federal funds (they could be deposited in state banks, for instance) and was accordingly beyond the authority of the national government. Washington sided with Hamilton and signed the national bank bill into law. A quarter of a century later, the bank became the center of a constitutional controversy when the state of Maryland taxed a branch of the national bank located within its borders. On instructions from his superiors, the bank's cashier, James McCulloch, refused to pay the tax on the grounds that it constituted state interference with a legitimate activity of the national government. In deciding this case, the Supreme Court affirmed Hamilton's interpretation that *necessary* meant "appropriate," not "indispensable."

This early judicial test opened the door to the expansion of federal government activities through the use of implied powers. Yet enumerated powers have been broadly interpreted and have, if anything, given the federal government greater opportunities for expanding its influence. This is especially true of the power

McCulloch v. Maryland An 1819 court case involving a dispute over whether the central government had the power to create a national bank.

to regulate interstate commerce and the power to tax and spend for the general welfare.

The constitutional issue boils down to the same thing in both instances: how narrow or broad an interpretation to give the applicable phrases. The Supreme Court has interpreted the interstate commerce clause to give the national government the power to license the operation of boats on New York State waters (*Gibbons v. Ogden* 1824), to regulate what farmers can feed chickens (*Wickard v. Filburn* 1942), and to prohibit private acts of racial discrimination (*Heart of Atlanta Motel v. United States* 1964 and *Katzenbach v. McClung* 1964). Passenger vessels are considered interstate commerce even if they are not directly engaged in the buying and selling of goods; what farmers feed chickens affects the interstate market for wheat; and individuals who racially discriminate while serving substantial numbers of interstate travelers or while relying on interstate commerce for their supplies are held to interfere with the rights of minorities to travel and engage in interstate commerce.

The general pattern of court decisions led some students of constitutional law to conclude that, given the interdependent nature of American economic and social activities, the Supreme Court would consider almost no activity beyond the scope of the interstate commerce power. In recent decades, however, the Supreme Court has shown a willingness to limit the use of the commerce clause. For example, in *United States v. Morrison* (2000), the Supreme Court ruled that the federal government did not have the power to provide a civil remedy for sexual assault. The case turned on the Violence against Women Act of 1994, which gave rape victims the right to sue their attackers in federal court. Congress justified its intrusion into what is traditionally an area of law left wholly to the states by using the interstate commerce clause. The argument was that fear of violence prevented women from such activities as traveling alone and going out at night. Because these actions are often associated with work obligations and may involve crossing state lines, Congress could invoke the interstate commerce clause. The Supreme Court disagreed and, for the first time since the 1930s, rejected a congressional argument that a popular activity constituted interstate commerce.

As was the case with the "necessary and proper" clause, the power of the national government to tax and spend for the general welfare provoked a debate between two of the nation's early leaders: Hamilton and Madison. These coauthors of *The Federalist* disagreed about what the national government had the power to tax and spend money on. Madison argued that the national government could tax and spend only for the activities it was specifically authorized to undertake. Hamilton held that the power to tax and spend was independent of the other enumerated powers. In other words, in Hamilton's view, Congress had the power to tax and spend for functions it could not otherwise control.

Again, a series of Supreme Court decisions decided the issue on Hamilton's terms. The implications for the expansion of federal power are considerable; this means Congress can use its taxing power as an indirect method of regulating an activity, such as by taxing gambling. Since the meaning of "the general welfare" has undergone a similarly broad interpretation, the taxing and spending power of Congress has evolved into a powerful tool.

Regulation of interstate commerce and taxation, the two powers the founders thought most crucial to the operation of a national government, have become the major bases for the constitutional expansion of national government. The federal government has significantly expanded its power since its founding.

The Powers, Rights, and Obligations of State Governments

The Constitution focuses more on the national government than on states. Nonetheless, states are granted certain powers and rights under the Constitution, and states are required to fulfill certain obligations to one another.

STATE POWERS In contrast to the federal government, state governments receive no specific grant of powers from the Constitution. In fact, in its original form the Constitution made no mention at all of state prerogatives. The Federalists argued that all powers not granted to the national government would remain with the states. But because the lack of explicit guarantees was a sore point with Anti-Federalists, the Federalists promised that if the Constitution was adopted, it would be amended to include a guarantee of states' rights. This promise was kept with the Tenth Amendment pledge that "the powers not delegated to the United States by the Constitution, nor prohibited by it to the states, are reserved to the states respectively, or to the people."

The constitutional questions raised by the Tenth Amendment center on the scope of national powers. Advocates of states' rights argue that the amendment is an important check on the expansion of the federal government into state prerogatives. For much of the twentieth century, however, judicial interpretation tended to provide legal support for almost any activity the federal government wished to undertake. This interpretation provided an important nationalizing influence on American federalism. A shift in the stance of the Supreme Court during the 1990s reversed the trend. For example, in *United States v. Lopez* (1995), the Supreme Court ruled the Gun-Free School Zones Act of 1990 unconstitutional. The Court reasoned that this federal law banning possession of firearms within a thousand feet of any school had nothing to do with commerce and therefore exceeded the federal government's authority. In other words, the states had jurisdiction, not the federal government.

Although such court decisions show that the Tenth Amendment still provides important protections for state independence, the general source of political authority for the states comes from their own constitutions, which specify each state's powers and limitations. As long as these constitutions do not

In a federal system of shared powers, the responsibilities and authority of differing levels of government often overlap. When issues or problems affect both governments, agencies from different governments have to coordinate and work together. Here a U.S. Border Patrol agent and a Texas State Trooper question suspected illegal aliens. Though illegal immigration is technically an issue of federal law, illegal immigrants also present challenges to state and local governments.

© Eddie Seal/Bloomberg via Getty Images

contravene the U.S. Constitution or conflict with legitimate federal statutes and treaties, states are generally free to establish their own form of government and responsibilities. This means that, unlike their federal counterpart, state legislatures exercise plenary, or comprehensive, power (Tarr 2000, 7). You can think of the constitutional difference between state and federal governments like this: Congress needs authorization from the U.S. Constitution to do anything, whereas states can do anything they want as long as it is not expressly forbidden by the U.S. Constitution or their own state constitution.

State powers include **police power**, or the authority to pass laws for the health, safety, and morals of their citizens. This grant of political authority is in many ways much broader than any given to the national government. States also have **concurrent powers**, or powers that the national and state governments can exercise. For example, both levels of government have the authority to tax and to borrow money. The large jurisdictional overlap of concurrent powers and the vaguely defined divisions between state and federal authority arising from the Tenth Amendment, the "necessary and proper" clause, and the broad interpretation of enumerated powers mean that federal–state relations are often marked by tension. Who has the authority to do what? The ability and authority to answer that question is the key to power in the American political system. Given the wide range of possible interpretations of national and state constitutions, the question is often frustratingly hard to answer.

STATES' RIGHTS The Constitution guarantees the states certain rights in the American federal system. First, the Constitution guarantees the states that the central government will protect them from invasion and insurrection. National defense is a responsibility of the central government, and Article IV, Section 4 declares that the invasion of any state is an invasion of the United States. States are thus freed from the obligation of maintaining standing military forces. If local authorities are unable to maintain law and order, the governor may ask the president to send federal military troops to assist.

Second, the Constitution guarantees the states a republican form of government. The term is not precisely defined by the Constitution but is generally taken to mean a government based on the consent of the governed and representative institutions—in other words, a representative democracy founded on the notion of popular sovereignty. The enforcement of this constitutional guarantee is political rather than legal. The federal courts generally have declined jurisdiction and have deferred to Congress to determine whether a state has a republican government. Senator Charles Sumner (D-MA) once expressed concern that this clause is a "sleeping giant" because it potentially gives Congress authority to intervene (some might say meddle) in local affairs. Politics, rather than legal limitations, constrain this type of congressional intrusion.

A third constitutional guarantee to the states is equal representation in the Senate. This system of representation is inconsistent with the principle of political equality because sparsely populated states have more than their fair share of representation in the Senate, and the most populous states have less than

police power The authority of the states to pass laws for the health, safety, and morals of their citizens.

concurrent powers The powers listed in the Constitution as belonging to both the national and state governments.

their fair share. For example, in 2010, the least populous state, Wyoming, had roughly 0.18 percent of the nation's population, whereas the most populous, California, had 12.0 percent, but each state had two U.S. senators (or 2.0 percent). Thus, Wyoming's representation is about 11 times greater than its share of the population, and California's is only one-sixth of its share. Equal representation in the Senate is a constitutional recognition that states are units of government that have special status not possessed by other units of local government such as counties or cities.

Fourth, under the Constitution all states are equal after admission. Every state has the same degree of sovereignty, with the same rights and powers. The president or Congress has occasionally tried to mandate certain conditions of statehood, but such requirements are unenforceable if they would give the new state more or less power than other states. For example, President William Howard Taft vetoed legislation admitting Arizona as a state because he objected to a provision in the proposed state constitution permitting voters to recall state judges. Once the offending clause was deleted, Taft signed the act, and Arizona became the forty-eighth state in 1912. The new state promptly restored the recall provision (Peltason 1982, 122). Similarly, in 1907, Congress attached a provision to the enabling act passed prior to Oklahoma's admission as a state, prohibiting Oklahoma from moving its state capital from Guthrie for ten years. Two years later, the voters of the state approved a referendum to move the capital to Oklahoma City. When the residents of Guthrie sued in federal court to enforce the provision of the enabling act, the Supreme Court held that the provision could not be enforced because once Oklahoma had become a state, it was on equal footing with all other states and thus had control over the location of the seat of government (*Coyle v. Smith* 1911). There is no seniority when it comes to state power and sovereignty: once a territory achieves the constitutional status of statehood, it is equal to all other states.

Finally, states have the right to decide how or whether the Constitution is to be changed. At least three-fourths (38) of the states must agree to any changes in the Constitution. This requirement is a major protection of states' rights and sovereignty because amendments must be approved by the states acting as governmental units through either state legislatures or state conventions. In other words, the Constitution gives the states, not the people, the power to approve amendments. This means that the 13 least populous states, which represent about 4 percent of the nation's population, can block a change favored by the other 37 states, which represent the other 96 percent of the nation's people.

OBLIGATIONS OF STATES The Constitution imposes certain obligations on the states. Article IV, Section 1 requires states to grant **"full faith and credit"** to one another's public acts and records. This provision ensures that important civil obligations, such as property rights, wills, and marriages (with the possible exception of same-sex marriages), will be valid and honored in all states.

This provision applies only to civil proceedings. Because states have the right to establish their own criminal laws and punishments, a state is precluded from

"full faith and credit" The provision in the Constitution that requires states to honor the civil obligations (wills, birth certificates, and other public documents) generated by other states. Note: states apparently are not required to recognize marriages under "full faith and credit."

enforcing the criminal laws of another state. The constitutional obligation of one state to another in the area of criminal law is limited to **interstate rendition**. If a person accused of a crime flees across state lines, Article IV, Section 2 says that the governor of the state to which the criminal has fled shall deliver the criminal back to the state with jurisdiction over the crime.

THE ADDITION OF NEW STATES New states were added to the original 13 states by congressional action as specified in Article IV, Section 3. New states cannot be formed by combining or dividing existing states without their consent.[1] Once admitted, states have equal sovereignty and powers with all other states.

Federal troops were called in to help desegregate Central High School in Little Rock, Arkansas, in 1957 (as shown here). Desegregation was opposed by many at the local and state levels. When segregation was ruled unconstitutional by the U.S. Supreme Court, however, state laws mandating racially separate schools were invalidated. State laws cannot violate the U.S. Constitution, which is the law of the land.

The typical procedure for adding states to the Union is as follows:

- Congress forms an incorporated territory.
- Residents of the territory petition Congress for admission as a state.
- Congress passes a resolution called an **enabling act**, authorizing the residents of the territory to draft a state constitution and hold a referendum to approve it. The resolution must be approved by the president.
- When the proposed state constitution is approved by the majority vote of both houses of Congress and signed by the president, the territory becomes a state on equal footing with all other states.

Texas is a special case because it began as an independent nation, the Republic of Texas, and then negotiated with Congress for statehood. The congressional resolution admitting Texas as a state contains a provision authorizing Texas to divide itself into five states if the state legislature desires. Although some Texans claim this could be done unilaterally without congressional approval, the Civil War and Supreme Court rulings have established that Texas has the same rights, powers, and limitations as other states, so such action would require consent of Congress as well.

interstate rendition The obligation of states to return people accused of a crime to the state from which they fled.

enabling act A resolution passed by Congress authorizing residents of a territory to draft a state constitution as part of the process of adding new states to the Union.

[1] Five states were formed from other states with the consent of Congress and the legislatures of the affected states: Vermont from New York in 1791, Kentucky from Virginia in 1792, Tennessee from North Carolina in 1796, Maine from Massachusetts in 1820, and West Virginia from Virginia in 1863 (Peltason 1982, 122). The West Virginia case is a little different from the others. The Virginia legislature voted to secede and join the Confederacy. Several counties wanted to remain in the Union, and representatives from those counties formed a new Virginia legislature that approved the formation of West Virginia during the Civil War.

The most recent discussion about adding a new state involves Puerto Rico. Puerto Rico is an unincorporated territory of the United States. Its residents are U.S. citizens, but they pay no federal income tax. Puerto Rico's special commonwealth status gives it greater control over local matters than territories such as Guam, American Samoa, and the Virgin Islands. At 3.73 million, Puerto Rico's population is similar to Oklahoma's 3.75 million, and it is bigger than roughly half the states. Yet citizens of Puerto Rico cannot vote in presidential elections, and they have no voting representatives in Congress. They do have a nonvoting delegate to the House but have no voice at all in the Senate. Puerto Rico has held several plebiscites (nonbinding votes allowing citizens to express an opinion) on statehood, the most recent in 2012. Though pluralities in these votes generally supported statehood, it is unlikely Puerto Rico will become the fifty-first state any time soon.

Washington, DC, poses difficult issues relating to statehood and representation. Since the passage of the Twenty-Third Amendment, U.S. citizens who reside in the nation's capital have voted for president, but they have no voting representation in Congress. Like Puerto Rico and the territories, they have a nonvoting delegate in the House and none in the Senate. Yet about 600,000 people live in the District of Columbia, about 40,000 more than the population of Wyoming. Because the Constitution establishes Washington, DC, as the seat of the national government, it is neither a state nor a part of a state (see the Politics in Practice feature "Federalism and Democracy in the Nation's Capital").

Admitting new states has always been an inherently political process. In the early years of the republic, the politics of gaining admission to the Union revolved around the issue of slavery. The Civil War resolved this issue, but it did nothing to end the intensely political conflicts that surround application for statehood. For example, Utah's struggle for statehood dragged out for nearly half a century because of a political fight over the definition of marriage. From the first request in 1849 to 1896, when statehood was finally achieved, the political obstacles centered largely on suspicion about the Mormon Church's practice of plural marriage. In effect, the federal government required the church to alter its views on marriage as a condition of statehood, thus regulating intimate relationships a century before the question of same-sex marriages arose (Lyman 1986, 1–5).

The admission of the last two states, Hawaii and Alaska, amply demonstrate the politics surrounding statehood. Hawaii's statehood was long delayed, partly because of suspicion of the traditional political, social, and economic systems of a Polynesian culture. Granting Hawaii statehood presented Congress "with an unprecedented dilemma: . . . the question of equality under the nation's Constitution for a noncontiguous area with an essentially nonwhite population" (Bell 1984, 5). Hawaii finally gained statehood in 1959. Alaska was admitted that same year after a political struggle of more than a decade that involved concerns about the indigenous nonwhite population and some partisan bickering.

POLITICS IN PRACTICE

FEDERALISM AND DEMOCRACY IN THE NATION'S CAPITAL

Washington, DC, has 40,000 more residents than Wyoming and three fewer votes in Congress. Wyoming has the smallest population of any state but has two U.S. senators as guaranteed by the Constitution. It has one representative in the House of Representatives, again getting the minimal level of representation guaranteed by the Constitution. In contrast, DC is guaranteed no votes by the Constitution, and that's exactly what it gets: no votes.

DC resides in a sort of democratic limbo, simultaneously serving as the seat of the federal government but having no rights to representation in that government. This condition is a product of DC's odd position in the federal system. Technically, DC is a federal city, whose existence and governance is dictated by Article I, Section 8, Paragraph 17 of the Constitution. This provision grants Congress the power to rule over a geographical area not to exceed 10 miles square that constitutes the capital of the national government.

This makes DC a unique entity in the federal system. It is neither a state nor a local government. It is clearly not a sovereign jurisdiction; the federal government can grant to or retract from local authorities whatever powers it sees fit. At various times during the past two centuries, Congress has done everything from giving DC virtual home rule to putting it under the control of local governments in neighboring states to having important decisions directly made by the federal government. It has allowed residents of DC to elect the district's local officials, has appointed those officials, or has operated under some mix of the two systems. And although DC residents are essentially stuck in a unitary system—the local government draws its power from the national government, not from its citizens—they have no voting rights when it comes to representation in the central government.

This arrangement has struck many as unfair. The simple fact is that residents of Washington, DC, do not enjoy the same rights as residents of the 50 states. Most obviously, they have no right to equal representation. The single delegate the House has granted to Washington, DC—and to other U.S. territories— is a representative who has most of the privileges of membership: speaking on the floor, serving on committees, and introducing legislation. The delegate can vote only onw procedural matters, though, not on actual legislation. In the Senate, residents of DC are not represented at all.

There have been periodic attempts to redress the inequities that consign DC residents to second-class citizenship within the federal system. Most notably, DC became part of the electoral college in 1963 (it has three electoral votes). Prior to that, residents not only had no representative in Congress; they also had no say in presidential elections. Still, if no candidate gets a majority of electoral votes, sending the election of the president to the House of Representatives, DC has no vote.

There have been a number of attempts to get DC similar representation in the legislative side of the federal government. Most recently, in 2009, a bill was introduced to give DC a full-voting member of the House. These sorts of bills, however, are controversial. For one thing, it is not clear they would be constitutional (the Constitution says nothing about representatives from non-states). For another, giving DC voting representatives has controversial partisan implications. One of the key objections to DC gaining full voting rights on par with states is the potential impact such a move would have on the Senate. The addition of two senators conceivably could tip the balance of power in that chamber. Neither party wants to strengthen the other side, and given DC's voting patterns, it's certain the district's senators would tend toward the liberal end of the spectrum and most likely be Democrats. On top of that, states jealously guard their prerogative of equal representation in the Senate and are loath to dilute that power by inviting others into the club.

SOURCES   Council of the District of Columbia. 1997. "History of Self-Government in the District of Columbia." http://www.dcouncil.washington.dc.us (accessed September 23, 2003).

Washington Post Editorial Board. 2009. "The Democrats Dodge on Voting Rights." Washington Post. http://www.washingtonpost.com/wp-dyn/content/article/2009/10/28/AR2009102804142.html (accessed December 4, 2009).

Refereeing Power Conflicts

The Constitution makes some provisions for settling conflicts between state and federal operations. Article VI declares that the U.S. Constitution, laws passed by Congress, and treaties made by the national government shall be the **"supreme law of the land."** State constitutions and laws are subordinate to the supreme law, and if there is a conflict between a state provision and a federal provision, the latter is enforced. The Constitution thus establishes a hierarchy of law; the U.S. Constitution is superior to both national laws and state laws and constitutions, and national laws and treaties are superior to state constitutions and laws. Given the vague and broad constitutional language, this means that the ultimate umpire in the federal system is the Supreme Court, which has the final say on how to interpret the Constitution.

The Supreme Court has historically tended to favor the federal government in apportioning powers, but the states are far from helpless in these conflicts. For example, the federal system ensures that state interests play an important role in the national government. Although Congress is the lawmaking branch of the national government, members of Congress are elected to represent state and local—not necessarily national—interests. Most members of Congress, at least those interested in reelection, have a fundamental interest in ensuring that national legislation either positively benefits their constituents or, at least,

does not harm them. For example, in 2009, the Republican leaders in Charleston County, South Carolina, formally censured their state's senior U.S. senator and fellow Republican, Lindsey Graham. The Charleston County GOP was upset with Graham's willingness to work with Democrats on several issues, especially on climate legislation that Graham saw as a key national and international priority. Charleston County Republicans obviously did not see it as such and sought a censure by the state party organization to go with the rebuke issued by the county party (Associated Press 2009). Graham, in short, faced a conflict between the preferences of local and state interests and his beliefs about what was in the best interests of the nation. These conflicts have no easy solution, but elected officials who consistently choose the latter over the former run the real risk of being replaced by someone willing to reverse the order of priority.

Vincent C. Gray (right) holds a unique elected positions in the American political system; as mayor of Washington, D.C., is he is the chief executive of the nation's only federal city. As a federal city, Washington, D.C., is not sovereign—it can only exercise the powers granted to it by Congress.

© Photo By Douglas Graham/Roll Call

"supreme law of the land" The idea that the U.S. Constitution, laws passed by Congress, and the treaties made by the federal government are supreme, and state constitutions and laws are subordinate to them.

THE EVOLUTION OF FEDERALISM

A historical analysis of governmental development in the United States points to one overriding pattern: the growth of activities at *all levels* of the political system. Though the fortunes of state and federal governments have waxed and waned in their relationship to each other, taken as a whole, local, state, and national governments all provide more services and regulate the actions of their citizens to a greater extent today than at any time in the past. Government expenditures tell this story clearly: At the beginning of the twentieth century, the total expenditure of all levels of government was less than $2 billion; in 2012 the federal expenditures alone were nearly $4 trillion. That's a four followed by twelve zeros, a staggering sum that accounts for outlays at only one level of government.

One of the key reasons for this increase is the larger role of the federal government. Even though government spending at all levels has risen, the proportion of total government expenditures accounted for by the federal government has increased, while the proportion accounted for by states has decreased. At the beginning of the twentieth century, the federal government accounted for about 35 percent of all government expenditures. At the turn of the twenty-first century, the federal government accounted for more than 50 percent of all government expenditures. The figures for states are roughly reversed: states started out the twentieth century accounting for about 60 percent of government spending and started the twenty-first century accounting for 30 percent (Advisory Commission on Intergovernmental Relations 1994; U.S. Census Bureau 2001).

Three historical events drove these long-term trends: World War I and its aftermath (roughly 1914 to 1922); the New Deal response to the Great Depression (roughly 1933 to 1938); and the buildup and aftermath of World War II (roughly 1938 to 1948). State and federal spending as a percentage of the nation's gross domestic product (GDP) is a good indicator of government activity. Figure 3.4 shows increases in federal activity during these crises. War and economic depression meant the growth in the federal government's spending was, to some extent, expansion by default. Military matters have always been the primary concern of the national government, and World Wars I and II required harnessing a large portion of the nation's resources to the military effort. Government activity at the state and federal levels increased in response to the Great Depression in the 1930s. The federal government was in a better position to respond to this crisis than state or local governments because it had power over currency, the banking system, and the regulation of interstate economic activities. It also had a superior tax base, since the Sixteenth Amendment, ratified in 1913, gave Congress the authority to levy an income tax.

For similar reasons, the federal government has taken the lead role in addressing national crises of a much more recent vintage. Fighting two wars in Iraq and Afghanistan, the nation was hit in 2008 and 2009 with the worst economic downturn since the Great Depression. In response to a threatened economic implo-

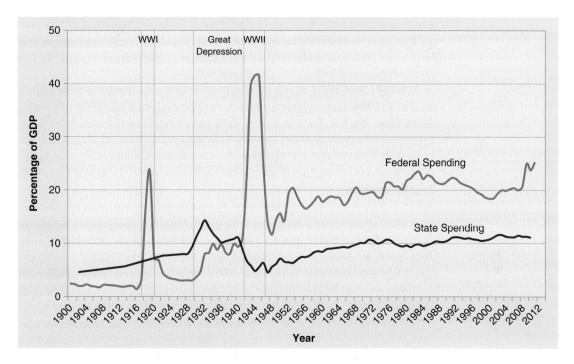

FIGURE 3.4 **Federal and State Expenditures, 1900–2011**

Source: Constructed by the authors from data in the Budget of the United States Government, Table 15.3, "Historical Tables: Total Government Expenditures As Percentages of GDP, 1948–2008," at http://www.gpoaccess.gov/usbudget/fy10/sheets/hist15z3.xls.

sion, the federal government injected billions into propping up banks, bailing out major auto manufacturers, buying a major share in the world's largest insurance company, and becoming the single largest source of revenue for state and local governments. Federal government spending, which had held steady between 18 and 22 percent of GDP for roughly half a century, jumped to 25 percent of GDP in 2009, 2010, and 2011. This figure is expected to fall somewhat between 2012 and 2016, but even then it is projected to remain at or above 22 percent of GDP for the foreseeable future (Office of Management and Budget 2012).

Though the federal government's role has significantly increased over the past century, it would be inaccurate to conclude that the history of federalism is a story of federal expansion at the expense of state and local governments. States and localities remain the primary regulatory powers for such major domestic activities as education and law enforcement. Moreover, aggregate spending patterns conceal complex intergovernmental relationships surrounding changes in spending on particular activities. States and localities are not slowly disappearing into the shadows cast by the federal government's fiscal power. Their capabilities and responsibilities have increased dramatically during the nation's history, and they have not by any means evolved into supplicants of the federal government. At times, states have fiercely fought to maintain independence from the federal government, and states have established a broad set of working relationships with the federal government that account for a great deal of the domestic policy we take for granted. Roads, schools, utilities, and much more are built and maintained as a result of combined federal, state, and local policies.

Although attempting to systematically describe the evolution of federalism is likely to provoke some debate, federalism can be categorized into three reasonably distinct eras. Each is characterized by a different model of federalism: dual federalism, cooperative federalism, and new federalism.

Dual Federalism

Dual federalism views federal and state governments as independent sovereign powers with separate and distinct jurisdictions. The central government has jurisdiction over national concerns: conducting national defense, coining money, and regulating interstate and foreign commerce. The states have responsibility for local concerns: exercising "police powers," including public safety, and managing education, health, and welfare.

In theory, national and state responsibilities are clearly divided. Each level of government is supreme in its own policy arena, and the other level has no constitutional basis to enter that arena uninvited. During the nineteenth century, the Supreme Court adopted dual federalism as the guiding principle to referee conflicts between state and federal governments. Compared to contemporary times, dual federalism was practiced to some extent. The federal government, for example, was less involved in the daily lives of its citizens during the formative years of the republic than it is today.

Still, intense controversies have always marked federalism. As discussed earlier, the ink was barely dry on the Constitution before Hamilton, one of its authors, began to loosely interpret its provisions to expand the federal government's power. In the first few decades after the adoption of the Constitution, Federalist sentiments dominated politics, and the federal government established itself as a central force.

This early expansion of national government fortunes underwent a sharp decline when Andrew Jackson became president in 1829 and set about resurrecting the Anti-Federalist states' rights platform. Jackson appointed Roger B. Taney as chief justice of the Supreme Court. Taney is generally acknowledged as the author of the dual federalism doctrine, and his rulings represented a clear philosophical break from those of his predecessor, John Marshall, who had been much more receptive to Federalist arguments.

Even though the federal government may have been less involved in the daily lives of its citizens, it was often involved in standoffs with state governments. These conflicts sometimes became so intense that even Jackson found himself on the nationalist side. For example, in the 1830s, states' rights advocates favored the doctrine of **nullification**, the act of declaring a national law null and void within a state's borders. In 1832, South Carolina nullified a set of national tariffs and threatened to secede from the Union. Jackson responded by threatening to use federal troops, and South Carolina dropped its secessionist stand.

dual federalism The idea that the national and state governments are sovereign, with separate and distinct jurisdictions.

nullification The act of declaring a national law null and void within a state's borders.

Other states threatened to leave the Union because of disagreements with federal policy. The New England states threatened to secede en masse during the War of 1812 in response to a federally ordered trade embargo. The most notable of these disagreements was, of course, the Civil War, when 11 Southern states broke away and formed the Confederate States of America (CSA). The CSA's defeat in the subsequent American Civil War settled the lingering questions of nullification and secession, and for a time power came back to the federal government. Three amendments—the Thirteenth Amendment outlawing slavery, the Fourteenth Amendment guaranteeing due process and equal protection of the laws, and the Fifteenth Amendment prohibiting denial of the right of citizens to vote on the basis of "race, color, or previous condition of servitude"—served to limit state power in these areas. During Reconstruction, the federal government became the dominant partner in the politics of many Southern states.

Toward the end of the nineteenth century, the country entered a period of explosive economic growth, sometimes referred to as the Gilded Age, fueled by freewheeling capitalism. During this era the doctrine of dual federalism strongly reasserted itself, even in areas traditionally considered the domain of the national government. The dominant industrial capitalists of the day did not support strong central government regulation of business, interstate or otherwise. These sentiments were often reflected by the Supreme Court, which declared unconstitutional federal laws establishing a minimum wage and regulating the use of child labor. Still, the newly industrialized economy provided the impetus for greater federal regulatory powers, and World War I accelerated the movement to give the national government a more prominent role. Although this expansion of federal power blurred the line separating state and federal jurisdictions, dual federalism lingered as the operative model until a severe economic crisis pushed the federal government into a more central role.

Cooperative Federalism

In contrast to dual federalism, **cooperative federalism** recognizes an overlap in state and national responsibilities. Accordingly, state and federal governments have to work together, coordinating their actions to serve and respond to the needs of citizens.

The impetus for the cooperative model of federalism was the Great Depression, although it had been practiced in rudimentary form even before the Constitutional Convention. For example, in 1785, Congress passed a statute, supplemented by the Northwest Ordinance of 1787, giving states large sections of public lands to be developed for educational purposes. The basic form of this legislation—a grant from the central government so that the states could achieve a desired policy end—remains the basic mechanism of cooperative federalism.

Initially, federal grant programs to the states mostly involved land, a resource that the national government had in abundance. Toward the end of the nineteenth century, the form of grants shifted from land to cash, and instead of being once-

cooperative federalism The idea that the distinction between state and national responsibilities is unclear and that the different levels of government share responsibilities in many areas.

Since its beginning in 1965, Head Start has been a federally funded program that has brought education and health care programs to underprivileged children all over the country. Administered jointly by the Administration on Children, Youth and Families; the Administration for Children and Families; and the Department of Health and Human Services, it operates with a paid staff of just under 200,000 and a volunteer staff of nearly 1.5 million workers. In addition to its general outreach to communities, it funds grants to the American Indian and Migrant Programs in order to further help these special needs groups.

grants-in-aid A form of national subsidy to the states designed to help them pay for policies and programs that are the responsibility of states rather than the national government.

only gifts, the grants came in the form of continuing appropriations. This new form of subsidy became known as **grants-in-aid**, and it is the reason cooperative federalism is sometimes called *fiscal federalism,* recognizing that cooperation among the levels of government is often characterized by financial relationships.

Grants-in-aid became more common in the early twentieth century as the federal government tapped the lucrative new revenue source of the income tax and became more willing to involve itself in regulating the economy. Federal grants-in-aid expenditures jumped from $5 million in 1912 to almost $34 million in 1920. Most of these funds went to education, highways, and agricultural extension programs, but Congress laid the basis for modern assistance programs by providing money for maternal and child health care.

During the New Deal, the use of grants-in-aid exploded and became perhaps the central characteristic of American federalism. State and local governments were ill prepared to deal with the massive economic dislocation of the 1930s. Facing a social disaster of unprecedented proportions, the federal government stepped into the breach. Between 1932 and 1935, grants-in-aid expenditures swelled from $200 million to more than $2 billion. Instead of having the federal government administer burgeoning new programs in welfare, health, employment security, and public housing, President Franklin D. Roosevelt chose to funnel the money and much of the program responsibility through state and local governments.

The outbreak of World War II temporarily slowed grants-in-aid programs, as the national government conserved its resources for the military effort. But the war propelled the federal government into an unprecedented centralization of power. Among other things, the federal government regulated wages, prices, and industrial production. Beginning in 1948, grant expenditures began to rise again, and by 1954, they had reached their prewar level of $3 billion. During the administration of President Dwight D. Eisenhower in the 1950s, the amount of grants-in-aid money increased as an explicit attempt to counter the centralization of domestic programs in Washington.

The 1960s and early 1970s witnessed a major surge in grants-in-aid programs similar to the surges of the 1930s. As part of President Lyndon Johnson's Great Society initiative, roughly two dozen grants-in-aid programs were enacted in 1964 and 1965 alone. During the next two presidential administrations, more than one hundred grant programs were created. These programs tended to concentrate on the problems of large metropolitan areas and covered a broad range of policy issues dealing with economic development, education, and race relations. They brought another important feature to the evolution of grants-in-aid: some grants went directly to private groups, bypassing state and local governments.

By the early 1980s, the federal government was funneling huge amounts of money to states and localities, which in turn used the funds to finance an enormous expansion of the programs and policies they provided to citizens. Federalism was now characterized by the politics of grants-in-aid—a struggle between state and national government not over whether the federal government *should* be involved in policy areas that were traditionally the responsibility of the states but over *how* the involvement should be conducted.

The political battles over grants-in-aid reflect changing policy priorities over the past half-century. In the 1940s and 1950s federal assistance for health programs accounted for less than 10 percent of all federal grants to states and communities. Since the mid-1990s, health care programs have been the largest single category, accounting for close to 50 percent of federal grants-in-aid in recent years (see Figure 3.5). Federal grants to state and local governments currently account for 16 percent of all federal expenditures.

Given a choice, state policymakers tend to favor **general revenue sharing**, a type of grant that originated in the early 1970s and that comes with no strings attached. In general revenue sharing, the federal government gives money to states and localities to use as they wish. Federal policymakers, however, tend to favor **categorical grants**, programs that provide funds for a defined area of activ-

general revenue sharing. A type of federal grant that returns money to state and local governments with no requirements as to how it is spent.

categorical grants A type of federal grant that provides money for a specific policy activity and details how the programs are to be carried out.

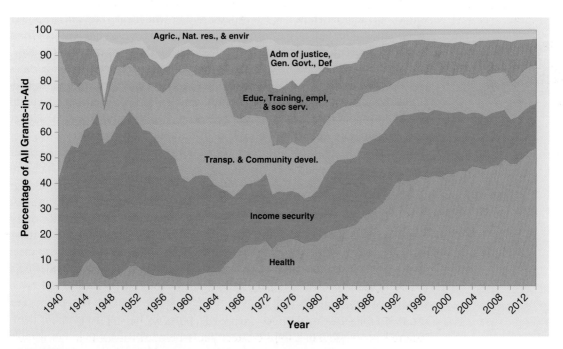

FIGURE 3.5 **Changing Priorities in Grants-in-Aid, 1940–2014**

Source: Constructed by the authors from data in Budget of the United States Government, Table 12.2—"Total Outlays for Grants to State and Local Governments, by Function and Fund Group: 1940–2014," http://www.gpoaccess.gov/usbudget/fy10/sheets/hist12z2.xls.

ity, such as education or public housing, but that also specify how the programs are to be carried out. Categorical grants allow the federal government to use the power of the purse to exercise maximum control over various policy responsibilities of state and local governments. Somewhere between general revenue sharing and categorical grants are **block grants**. Block grants provide funds for a general policy area, but they allow states and localities greater discretion than categorical grants in designing the programs being funded.

As grants-in-aid programs multiplied, they produced major problems of coordination and control for all government levels. No single, centralized mechanism manages grants-in-aid. Instead, they are controlled piecemeal by a dizzying array of departments and bureaus, many of which operate according to their own rules and regulations. The compartmentalization of hundreds of programs sometimes means the federal left hand does not know what the federal right hand is doing. The Department of Transportation, for example, might help develop a highway that displaces low-income urban residents, creating a shortage of low-income housing that ultimately becomes a major concern of officials in the Department of Housing and Urban Development. Legislators, governors, mayors, council members, and other officials charged with tracking overall public needs find it difficult to control the activities of specialized agencies and establish priorities among them.

Though these problems are significant, the two central drawbacks associated with cooperative federalism are its expense and its tendency to concentrate power in the hands of the federal government. State and local government revenues from income, sales, and property taxes nosedived during the recession of 2008–2009, and federal grants-in-aid became the largest single source of revenue for states and localities in 2009 and 2010. Those federal dollars come with strings attached. Grants-in-aid may require matching funds, which means that states must put up part of the money for a project, which the federal government then matches dollar for dollar (or sometimes three or four dollars for a dollar). Some complain that this matching requirement distorts states' authority to set priorities because states have an incentive to shift their tax revenue away from high-priority problems to get the federal subsidy that deals with a lower-priority problem. Other strings attached to federal grants-in-aid are aimed at quality control and at ensuring that the money is spent honestly and efficiently. For example, the American Recovery and Reinvestment Act (ARRA) did not just send billions in federal aid to states and localities. Instead, it required the governments spending the money to meet strict reporting and accountability requirements. This information, compiled on a government website (recovery.gov), allows anyone with Internet access and a web browser to find out how much stimulus money is being spent not just in any state, but in any zip code. Government watchdogs generally have applauded this commitment to transparency, but the reporting requirements have put considerable administrative and accounting burdens on states and localities.

By far, the most controversial string attached to federal grants-in-aid is the so-called **crossover sanction**. Crossover sanctions are conditions placed on the receipt of grant money that have nothing to do with the original purpose of the grant. They are, in effect, the fee exacted for access to the federal treasury, and

block grants A type of federal grant that provides funds for a general policy area but offers state and local governments discretion in designing the specific programs.

crossover sanction Conditions placed on grant money that have nothing to do with the original purpose of the grant.

that fee is state acquiescence to the federal government's policy preferences. For example, the national government effectively set the national minimum drinking age at 21 by threatening to withhold highway funds from states that did not adopt this policy. Constitutionally speaking, setting the legal drinking age is the legislative province of the states. But the Supreme Court ruled that the federal government was allowed to place conditions on offers of financial aid as long as the states had the right to refuse the aid. The other options, such as raising taxes or going without the federal funds, were largely unpalatable to state politicians and the electorate. So the states accepted the conditions and the money. There has been a uniform drinking age of 21 in all states since the mid-1980s.

New Federalism

New federalism was a movement to take power from the federal government and return it to the states. Just as the era of cooperative federalism overlapped the era of dual federalism, no clear date marks the beginning of new federalism. The term *new federalism* was first used by President Richard Nixon to describe an early 1970s plan to reverse the trend of federal government expansion triggered by the Great Society programs of the 1960s. Nixon had mixed success. The main policy associated with Nixon's new federalism was general revenue sharing, which was popular with state and local governments but which hardly promoted their independence from the federal government.

The first president to attempt a systematic reversal of cooperative federalism was Ronald Reagan. In the 1980 presidential election, Reagan campaigned vigorously against the concentration of power in Washington and promised to cut states free from the regulatory thicket that bound them to federal government dictates. President Reagan had some success in this effort. Federal grants-in-aid had increased from less than 1 percent of GDP in the 1940s to about 3.4 percent when Reagan took office in 1981. When he left office in 1989, spending on grants had fallen to 2.3 percent of GDP (see Figure 3.6).

But President Reagan's push to make federalism more state-centered quickly ran into several problems. First, cutting regulations and federal grants (including eliminating general revenue sharing entirely) did not simply cut the federal budget. It also shifted policy power and responsibility to the states, a process termed **devolution**. In essence, Reagan was proposing a radical restructuring of program and funding responsibilities between national and state governments, and this was opposed by Congress, which feared diminished influence over federal policy priorities, and by state officials who feared the loss of federal dollars that were now a critical revenue source. Thus, given the opposition, reducing federal grants (and their attendant regulations) was a hit-and-miss affair. When Reagan's successor, President George H. W. Bush, left office in 1993, federal spending on grants-in-aid had climbed to around 3 percent of GDP, and it remained at that level through the 1990s. Second, many of Reagan's supporters began to realize that there were advantages to federal (as opposed to state) regulation, and they started to oppose the effort to turn regulatory power over to the states. Such reconsideration was

new federalism A movement to take power away from the federal government and return it to the states.

devolution The return of policy power and responsibility to the states from the national government.

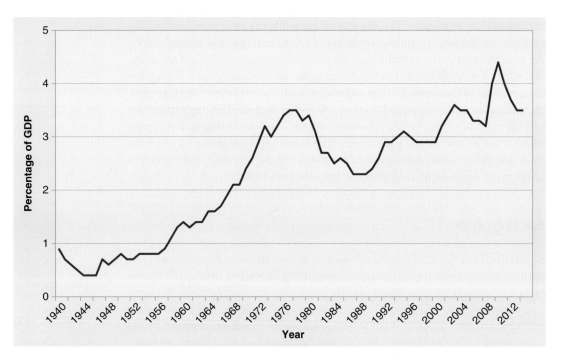

FIGURE 3.6 **Grants-in-Aid as a Percent of GDP, 1940–2114**

Source: Constructed by the authors from Budget of the United States Government, Table 12.1—"Summary Comparison of Total Outlays for Grants to State and Local Governments: 1940–2014," http://www.gpoaccess.gov/usbudget/fy10/sheets/hist12z1.xls.

especially true of business groups. Facing the prospect of 50 systems of regulation in areas such as consumer product safety and the environment, businesses began lobbying Congress for uniform and standardized federal laws.

New federalism picked up steam in the 1990s with the election of Bill Clinton, a former Democratic governor sympathetic to state interests, and a Republican Congress that made taking power away from Washington its campaign battle cry. The most dramatic of the new federalism initiatives of this era was the 1996 welfare reform law that ended the Aid to Families with Dependent Children (AFDC) program and gave states more flexibility to design and run their own welfare programs. The drive by Congress and the president to push more responsibilities toward the states was supported by a series of Supreme Court decisions that put more teeth into the Tenth Amendment. Among other things, the Supreme Court ruled that the federal government could not force local law enforcement agencies to perform criminal background checks (*Printz v. United States* 1997) and that citizens could not use a federal law to sue a state in a state court (*Alden v. Maine* 1999).

New federalism represented a rethinking of which level of government should bear primary responsibility for a particular policy area and which level of government should pay for the programs in that area. Many saw this as potentially constructive; the give-and-take over program and funding responsibility would result in policy responsibilities evolving to their "natural" level of government. For example, because of its broader tax base and national reach, the federal government was seen as better suited to manage redistributive policies (policies that take something from one group and give it to another, such as Social Security and welfare programs). State governments, on the other hand, were seen as better suited to handle developmental policies (roads, education, and the like) (Peterson 1995).

Though a good idea in theory, in practice the new federalism movement never managed to get federal and state governments to agree to such a neat (and perhaps sensible) division of policy responsibilities. States took on big redistributive policy responsibilities. Welfare, for example, is a redistributive policy where responsibility has shifted significantly away from the federal and toward the state level. This raised concerns that states would adopt stingier welfare programs because generous welfare programs might attract disadvantaged people from less generous states. This is good for the states they leave because it reduces states' welfare costs. It is bad for the states they move to because it forces taxpayers in those states to shoulder a disproportionate share of the burden in providing a social safety net. The obvious way to avoid being the sucker in this scenario is for a state to slash its welfare benefits. Doing so then encourages surrounding states to do the same, and the net result is a "race to the bottom" (Peterson and Rom 1990; Rom, Peterson, and Scheve 1998).

By the beginning of President George W. Bush's administration, it was clear that governmental commitment to the philosophical underpinnings of new federalism was suspect, especially at the federal level. The federal government continued to pass **unfunded mandates**—provisions in federal statutes requiring states and localities to take on certain responsibilities without covering any of the associated expenses. For example, the signature domestic policy of Bush's first term was the No Child Left Behind (NCLB) law. This law not only requires state and local governments to pay for large portions of a federally mandated program but also shifts power over education—constitutionally a responsibility of state governments—toward the national government. Bush was a former governor, and he came to office as a strong supporter, at least rhetorically, of the new federalist philosophy. Yet the first years of his presidency were marked by a sagging economy and devastating terrorist attacks in New York City and Washington, DC; early military successes in Afghanistan and Iraq were followed by unexpectedly difficult guerrilla campaigns; and the economy took the biggest downturn since the Great Depression during his last year in office. Recession and war traditionally focus power on the national government because it can better deal with such challenges. Here, this was the case: states and localities followed the lead of the federal government.

State–federal relations during the Clinton and George W. Bush years were sometimes described as **ad hoc federalism**, in which a state-centered or nation-centered view of federalism is adopted on the basis of political ideology (Baybeck

unfunded mandates Federal mandates for which the federal government does not pay any associated costs.

ad hoc federalism The process of adopting a state- or nation-centered view of federalism on the basis of political convenience.

and Lowry 2000; Smith, Buntin, and Greenblatt 2004, 52). Rather than a commitment to a particular vision of what state and federal governments should or should not do, the issue at hand (and who supported it) determined whether federal policymakers employed the states' rights or federal supremacy argument.

The new federalism movement stumbled because of the unusual strength and coherence of a single political party, which for much of the Bush presidency controlled the White House, both houses of Congress, and a majority of governorships and state legislative chambers. Ironically, this was the Republican Party in control, traditionally the party of states' rights and of limited federal government. A centralized and coherent Republican Party structure seemed to help overcome the fragmented nature of the federal system and allow party policy preferences to be achieved in a more national, top-down fashion (Krane and Koenig 2005). **Preemption**, in which Congress expressly gives national laws precedence over state laws, was a hallmark of several important policy areas during the Bush administration (examples include the No Child Left Behind law, which mandated that states follow federal education policies, and the Real ID Act, which set federal requirements for state-issued driver's licenses and identification cards). Certainly by the end of the Bush presidency, state and local governments saw the federal government as having largely abandoned the ideals of new federalism. In 2008, Larry Naake, executive director of the National Association of Counties, summed up the prevailing mood on the local-state relationship with the federal government: "Congress and the administration don't look at us as partners, but as a political organization they can use or [as] people trying to get handouts or money" (Greenblatt 2008, 24).

Federalism and the Great Recession

Ironically, even as federal policymakers philosophically abandoned the push to devolve power from national to state governments, their inability to move forward on key domestic issues created an opening for state policymakers to assert their independence. Partisan gridlock stymied federal action on such high-profile issues as immigration and the environment, and state governments stepped into this policy vacuum and became the leaders and innovators on a broad range of policy issues.

For example, frustrated with federal inaction on illegal immigration, states began enacting their own immigration policies. Arizona passed a law allowing the state to revoke the licenses of businesses knowingly hiring undocumented immigrants. Oklahoma passed laws requiring people to demonstrate proof of citizenship or legal immigration status to receive certain government benefits. Equally fed up with federal foot dragging on environmental policy, states forged their own path. For example, in 2007, six states and two Canadian provinces formed the Western Climate Initiative with the explicit goal of developing policies to reduce greenhouse emissions (Dinan 2008).

preemption Congress expressly giving national laws precedence over state and local laws.

Indeed, state and local governments became so prominent in taking the lead on domestic issues that, in June 2007, a cover article in *Time* magazine posed the question "Who needs Washington?" (Grunwald 2007). In the next two years, it would become abundantly clear that state and local governments needed Washington, and in the worst possible way. The great recession of 2008–2009 scrambled state–federal relations and all but killed the last vestiges of new federalism. With massive budget deficits threatening their new policy innovations and the most basic of public services, state governments came to rely heavily on federal aid. They were saved by the billions in aid flowing from the federal American Recovery and Reinvestment Act discussed in the opening section of this chapter.

State reliance on federal government grant money offers the federal government an opportunity to reshape national–state relationships according to federal preferences. In some cases, the federal government has eagerly seized this opportunity. For example, under President Barack Obama the federal government has pursued sweeping health care, education, and financial reforms, all of which have used federal budgetary and regulatory powers to push the states to follow federal policy priorities. Yet in pursuing these initiatives, the Obama administration has demonstrated a willingness to work with states and to make the federal regulations at least somewhat responsive to state policy priorities and concerns. For example, states can choose not to participate in some elements of the health care reform or choose to do more than the minimal standards set by federal regulation. This has been a more collaborative approach than that pursued under Obama's predecessor.

The recession has clearly shaken up power relationships between the federal and state levels of government, though what this means for the long term is hard to say. At least in the short term, it means more power is concentrating at the federal level. Yet states have pushed back against the recent expansion by the federal government. For example, more than half of the states mounted legal challenges to various aspects of the Patient Protection and Affordable Care Act of 2010 (popularly known as Obamacare) on the grounds it violated state sovereignty. In *National Federation of Independent Business v. Sebelius* (2012), the Supreme Court upheld the key provisions of Obamacare, including, most controversially, its requirement that citizens buy insurance or pay a penalty for failing to do so. Essentially, the Court ruled that this mandate did not violate state sovereignty because it was effectively a tax, and the Constitution clearly gives the federal government the power to levy taxes. The Court expressly rejected the argument that the law was justified under the interstate commerce clause; this is important because it signaled that the Court was not willing to further expand federal government power with another generous interpretation of the clause. Indeed, it is possible to interpret the Court's reasoning in the case as declaring limits on federal government power rather than agreeing to expansion of federal government power. So for the near-term future, economic circumstances have given the federal government the ability to assert its preferences over those of the states, but it is not clear that this dominance will continue for the long term (see the Politics in Practice feature "Federalism and the Golden Rule").

FEDERALISM AND THE GOLDEN RULE

There's an old saying about the Golden Rule: "he who has the gold gets to make the rules." These days there is no doubt about who has the gold. As the only government with the power to print money, that would be the federal government. And the federal government is not shy about using this power to make some policy rules that the states, like it or not, have to follow.

The American Recovery and Reinvestment Act (ARRA) provided the federal government with an opportunity to reshape federal–state relations for the short term, and perhaps for the long term too. It's not just the money that is driving this reengineering of federalism, though the money is considerable. In recent years the federal government became the single largest source of revenue for state and local grants, sending about $450 billion annually to states and localities. It's less the eye-popping numbers, though, than the conditions that go with that aid that may allow the federal government to seize a more centralized policymaking role over the states.

Historically, federal grant programs have been highly diffuse, which has made it extremely hard for the federal government to impose anything like centralized control over policy at the state and local levels. Consider, for example, a city that wants to gain access to federal money to do energy audits and retrofits in residential areas. There are not one, not two, but dozens of programs from which the city can seek grant aid. Each one of those programs is separate, each with its own list of requirements and mandates.

Given this extreme decentralized nature of federal grants, the federal government has difficulty assessing what it's getting for its money, and it's especially hard to figure out whether money is being wasted or even spent fraudulently. And the Obama administration has seemed intent on addressing this issue. A new template for federal grants-in-aid emerged from the ARRA experience. A key element of this is the federal government's insistence on transparency and accountability for every dollar spent. The federal government has set up a massive database to track all ARRA spending and is holding states' and localities' toes to the fire in accurate reporting to that database (there's even a government website dedicated to the public reporting of this data; you can check it out yourself at recovery.gov).

Above and beyond insisting on greater accountability, the federal government is reshaping its grants-in-aid programs to focus more on measurable, long-term outcomes and is judging state and local government performance by those yardsticks. Those who do not meet the policy and program performance standards may face serious consequences as the federal government seeks other institutions to meet its policy goals.

As an example of this, the federal government under President Obama has become much more interested in funneling grants not to states or localities but to "metros"—that is, large urban areas that consist of multiple municipalities and counties that have formed cooperative regional levels of government to coordinate policy in key areas such as transportation. The metros are where most Americans live and where most economic activity in the United States is generated. In driving to get the most bang for its grants-in-aid buck, the federal government has announced a willingness to deal directly with these metros rather than sending grants to individual states or localities.

The federal government's move toward using grants-in-aid to reshape its role in domestic policy and to achieve greater centralized control over its policy goals brings mixed news to state and local governments. On the one hand, the federal government is in some ways asserting greater power and influence in areas traditionally the domain of states and localities. On the other hand, in recent years states and localities have had little choice but to go along. They have needed the money, and their only real option has been the federal government. And if you want to play with someone else's gold, you play by their rules.

SOURCES Dinan, John, and Shama Gamkhar. 2008. "The State of American Federalism 2008–2009: The Presidential Election, the Economic Downturn, and the Consequences for Federalism." *Publius: The Journal of Federalism* 39: 369–407.

Harkness, Peter. 2009. "Tying Federal Funding to Regional Cooperation." *Governing*. http://www.governing.com/column/tying-federal-funding-regional-cooperation (accessed November 24, 2009).

Posner, Paul. 2009. "The Next Federal Grant System." *Governing*. http://www.governing.com/column/next-federal-grant-system (accessed November 24, 2009).

CHAPTER THREE
Top Ten Takeaway Points

1 Federalism is a political system in which regional governments share power with the national government. In the system established by the U.S. Constitution, states are sovereign powers and are partners of, rather than subordinates to, the federal government.

2 Two other primary means of dividing power in a political system exist. In a confederation, the central government is subordinate to the regional governments. In a unitary system, power is concentrated in the central government, and regional governments can exercise only the power granted to them by central authority.

3 Federalism offers some general advantages. It allows experimentation and gives regional governments the ability to tailor policy more closely to local preferences. It has disadvantages, such as creating an often confusing patchwork of laws and regulations across a nation.

4 The Constitution grants the national government enumerated and implied powers. Enumerated powers are specified in the Constitution. Implied powers come from broad constitutional clauses such as the power to "make all laws which shall be necessary and proper" (Article I, Section 8). Enumerated and implied powers have been interpreted broadly and have allowed the constitutional expansion of the national government.

⑤ The Constitution gives no specific powers to state governments. The Tenth Amendment says that the powers not given to the national government or prohibited to the states "are reserved to the states respectively, or to the people." The general source of political authority for the states is their own constitutions, which specify each state's powers and limitations.

⑥ The Constitution spells outs certain rights and obligations of the states. Rights include a republican form of government, equal representation in the Senate, equality with other states, and the right to approve any changes to the U.S. Constitution. Obligations include extending "full faith and credit" to the public acts and records of other states and returning criminals who cross state lines to the state with jurisdiction over the crime.

⑦ All state and federal laws, including state constitutions, are subordinate to the U.S. Constitution, in effect making the Supreme Court the ultimate umpire of the federal system.

⑧ Federal and state governments and the relationship between them have evolved considerably in the two centuries the Constitution has been in force. All levels of government have become larger and have played a more prominent role in the lives of citizens.

⑨ State–federal relations can be roughly categorized into three eras: dual federalism, cooperative federalism, and new federalism.

⑩ The great recession of 2008–2009 prompted a shakeup in state–federal power relationships. Generally speaking, economic hardship has increased the power and prominence of the federal government.

Key Terms and Cases

ad hoc federalism, 101

block grants, 98

categorical grants, 97

concurrent powers, 86

confederation, 77

cooperative federalism, 95

crossover sanction, 98

devolution, 99

dual federalism, 94

enabling act, 88

federalism, 79

"full faith and credit", 87

general revenue sharing, 97

grants-in-aid, 96

interstate rendition, 88

McCulloch v. Maryland, 83

new federalism, 99

nullification, 94

police power, 86

preemption, 102

"supreme law of the land", 91

unfunded mandates, 101

unitary system, 78

4 CIVIL LIBERTIES

KEY QUESTIONS

What are civil liberties?

How can civil liberties be balanced with the need to maintain social order?

What happens when exercising one civil liberty violates another civil liberty?

A DEVOUT KID FROM KANSAS who grows up to be a stud college football player and then gets a scholarship to study religion and the law sounds like an all-American sort of guy, right? Well, what if his name is Abdulla al-Kidd? Does that change anything? Apparently it did for U.S. government officials, who detained al-Kidd at Washington Dulles Airport, strip-searched him, shackled him in irons, and shuffled him through detention facilities in three states in two weeks, mostly in harsh conditions in the company of hardened criminals. Testifying before Congress, Federal Bureau of Investigation director Robert Mueller publically and prominently mentioned al-Kidd's detention as evidence of the FBI's progress in neutralizing terrorist networks.

Only al-Kidd was not a terrorist or a criminal. He was not suspected of doing anything remotely illegal. He was picked up as a potential witness who might help the federal government make a case against someone else. After a couple of weeks, he was let out of custody, but the government placed restrictions on his travel, and he remained under a cloud of unwarranted suspicion. His marriage fell apart. He lost his job. Yet the federal government never charged him with anything and never called him to testify against anyone (Sherman 2011).

Most people do not think of the United States as a place where the government deprives citizens of their liberty, ruins their reputations, limits their economic opportunities, and subjects them to harsh and humiliating confinements without reason or justification. Al-Kidd was one of those people. Like all American citizens, he thought he had certain rights and freedoms that the government could not interfere with, at least until that fateful day in March 2003 when he was arrested. He had exercised his freedom of religion by converting to Islam after college and was following his chosen path of studying Islamic law (he was detained as he was leaving for Saudi Arabia—a U.S. ally—on scholarship to pursue these studies). Yet it was his exercise of such constitutionally protected freedoms that probably brought him to the government's attention. Al-Kidd's detention came just a couple years after the

9/11 terrorist attacks, and the federal government had been given new, sweeping powers to investigate and detain its own citizens. Muslims with Islamic-sounding names traveling to Saudi Arabia apparently aroused some sort of suspicion, even if the Muslim in question was born in Kansas and played football for the University of Idaho. Bottom line: there seemed to be no real justification for what al-Kidd had experienced at the hands of his own government, so he decided to do something about it.

That something was to sue Attorney General John Ashcroft. The reasoning was that Ashcroft had taken laws aimed at preventing witnesses from fleeing before they could testify at trial and had used them to justify detaining people in gulag-like conditions for—well, for not much of anything. On its face, this action seemed to violate a number of constitutional guarantees. Accordingly, al-Kidd's lawyers reasoned, Ashcroft should be held personally responsible for knowingly depriving their client of his rights as an American citizen. The U.S. Supreme Court disagreed. In *Ashcroft v. Al-Kidd* (2011), the justices unanimously ruled that the attorney general had immunity from such lawsuits. There was general agreement that al-Kidd had done nothing to deserve his treatment and that such treatment violated his constitutional rights. Yet the justices also agreed that government officials have immunity from civil suits if they are acting within the scope of their duties.

Abdulla al-Kidd grew up in Kansas and was a star football player in college. His all-American credentials, though, did not prevent federal government officials from locking him up and portraying him as a terrorist suspect even though he was never suspected of doing anything illegal.

This controversy highlights one of the central tensions in democratic societies: the need to balance individual freedom with social order. Few people believe that sweeping up citizens on the basis of little more than their religious beliefs serves the broader interests of society. Yet most people also believe that the government needs enough power to go after bad guys who mean us harm, maybe even when the evidence that the "bad" guy is really bad is not wrapped up in a nice neat package. When al-Kidd was detained, only eighteen months had passed since 9/11. At the time the first priority of law enforcement agencies was to ensure that such an attack was not repeated, and they had been given a clear message—that national security trumped at least some individual civil liberties—and a lot of new legal authority. In that sort of situation, should individual rights be upheld? Or should the government have the power to sweep aside these rights in the name of protecting the common good?

There are no universally approved answers to these questions. The problem of balancing the freedom of the individual with the need for social order is a dilemma that raises big questions about the core democratic principle of political freedom. It is a balancing act that requires squarely facing the Madisonian dilemma discussed in chapter 2: how do you give government enough authority to preserve social order and communal values, but not so much that it places unfair and inappropriate limits on individual freedom of choice? In this chapter, we explore how the United States has struggled with this question by examining civil liberties—the freedom of individual citizens—and the constitutional principles that protect them.

THE CONCEPT OF CIVIL LIBERTIES

Civil liberties are defined as the freedoms enjoyed by individuals in a democratic society. They constitute the choices individuals are free to make with little or no interference from governmental authority. Choosing and practicing religious beliefs, speaking our minds, and seeking to form associations of like-minded people are examples of freedoms that American citizens are granted by the Constitution. Civil liberties thus boil down to the core democratic principle of political freedom: they represent a basic guarantee that individual citizens are free to make their own choices and to select their own goals and the means to achieve them.

Yet civil liberties cannot be absolute. Even in democratic systems, governments impose restrictions on individual liberties in the name of the public interest. For example, Americans are guaranteed the rights of free speech and assembly by the First Amendment. Yet there are restrictions on these rights. You cannot use your right of free speech to incite a riot. If you exercise your right to assemble by organizing a mass demonstration, you may be required by government authorities to obtain permits and to satisfy health, safety, and sanitary regulations. Most people see such restrictions as a reasonable way to balance the freedoms of the individual with the need to maintain social order.

civil liberties The freedoms and protections against arbitrary governmental actions given to the people in a democratic society.

Liberty and Authority

Balancing the liberty of the individual with the government authority necessary to maintain social order is not an easy task. Championing the freedom of the individual over the need for social order (or vice versa) is not just a philosophical choice, but a perspective that can change depending on particular time and circumstance. For example, in the immediate aftermath of the terrorist attacks of September 11, 2001, government authority took precedence over individual liberty as citizens sought assurances of personal safety and national security. Congress passed the Patriot Act, legislation that gave the government sweeping new powers to spy on its own citizens, just 45 days after 9/11. This aggressive response to ensure security and social order was popular, at least initially. Yet it soon became clear that the aggressive efforts to tighten national security ran into, and sometimes over, civil liberties. Under the provisions of the Patriot Act, government agencies can secretly search your house or even your library records. Compare these powers with the individual freedoms guaranteed by the Fourth Amendment, which gives individual citizens the right to be secure in their "persons, houses, papers, and effects" and free from "unreasonable searches and seizures." If the government is conducting a "sneak and peak" search of your records to make sure you are not taking an unhealthy interest in extremist religious groups and is doing it without your knowledge, do you still have all the liberties guaranteed by the Constitution?

As 9/11 began to pass into history, the basic justification for the Patriot Act—that the government needs the power to snoop on citizens to help keep those citizens safe—was increasingly questioned. The original legislation passed overwhelmingly; the only U.S. senator to cast a nay vote in 2001 was Senator Russ Feingold (D-WI), who waged a very lonely battle against giving the federal government the power to infringe on the civil liberties of its citizens. In 2006, 10 Senators—nine Democrats and one independent—voted against reauthorizing the Patriot Act. In 2011, when key provisions of the Patriot Act came up for renewal, 12 senators—including two Republicans—cast nay votes. In other words, despite consistent passage of the law by large majorities, opposition in Congress began to grow, from a single senator to a small cadre of Democrats to a slightly larger and more bipartisan core. This growing concern about the power given by the Patriot Act to the federal government reflected increasingly mixed views about whether the law appropriately balanced individual freedoms with the need for social order. In 2011, public support was split, with roughly 40 percent of people supporting the law as a tool for catching terrorists and about a third seeing it as a threat to civil liberties (Pew Research Center 2011c).

The shifting views on the Patriot Act reflect the difficulty of coming up with definitive answers to questions about how the American political system can best balance individual liberty and the authority of government. How much of our civil liberties are we willing to give up for greater assurances of security? Should the government be able to detain people indefinitely without charges? Conduct secret searches? Target groups for surveillance based on their religious or political beliefs?

These questions are hard to answer because the issue is not whether we pick liberty *or* authority; rather, it is figuring out the best mix of liberty *and* authority. Government must have some authority to set and enforce limits on individual freedom to maintain social order because without social order, civil liberties are meaningless. Individual freedom has to be backed by some central authority, or for practical purposes, that freedom ceases to exist. Without that authority, one individual's freedoms extend only to the willingness of the next individual to respect those freedoms. Inevitably, some will use their freedom to deprive others of their liberties, their property, or even their lives—hence the need for central authority, without which social order is replaced by anarchy. Yet democracy does not require complete social order, because this would mean individual behavior being dictated to a large extent by the state, and this too would threaten individual freedom. The government, for example, could almost certainly make the country more secure from the threat of terrorism by increasing the monitoring of individual activities, restricting the freedom to travel, and outlawing certain political groups or beliefs. Doing so, however, would restrict political freedom. The crux of the issue is how a free and secure society can achieve an acceptable balance between the values of individual freedom and the authority needed to maintain social order.

Resolving the conflicts that arise over these two values is difficult and complex, especially when individual liberties conflict. One group or individual exercising its rights may infringe on the rights and liberties of others. You have probably heard the old cliché that you can exercise your rights only as long as doing so does not interfere with someone else's rights. That's wrong. When an individual exercises a right, it inevitably comes into conflict with someone else's right. A classic case is a newspaper editor who exercises freedom of the press by publishing information about a crime that consequently jeopardizes the right of the accused to a fair trail. Is freedom of the press more important than a fair trial? Or does the right to a fair trial justify limiting freedom of the press? In such cases, the authority of government has to choose, in effect, whose freedoms are more important. How does a democratic society go about choosing which individual freedoms take precedence over others?

RESTRICTIONS ON THE GOVERNMENT

The basic approach to dealing with civil liberties in the United States begins with the assumption that citizens should have as much freedom as possible to make individual choices. The rights and freedoms of individual Americans are embodied in the Constitution's Bill of Rights, which provides a starting point for establishing what individuals are free to do without government interference. These freedoms have undergone a considerable evolution over the past two centuries.

The Bill of Rights

A central concern among those who took the initiative in calling the Constitutional Convention was the protection of individual property rights from state governments. But the convention's participants gave almost no consideration to safeguarding civil liberties from the actions of national authorities. Although one of the main reasons for splitting from Great Britain was the lack of guaranteed individual rights, the notion of formally including such rights in the Constitution was brought up only toward the end of the convention, and even then in a half-hearted way. As originally written, the Constitution contained virtually no mention of guaranteed civil liberties (Collier and Collier 1986, 338).

The absence of a guaranteed set of civil liberties—a Bill of Rights—became one of the central issues raised by opponents to the Constitution during the ratification campaign. Even leaders such as Thomas Jefferson, who favored the adoption of the Constitution, were unhappy that the convention had not included a statement of rights. The absence of a Bill of Rights "nearly sank the Constitution" (Collier and Collier 1986, 342). In response, the Federalists backing adoption of the Constitution agreed to make fashioning a Bill of Rights one of the first orders of business of the new government formed after ratification. Acting under a moral rather than a legal obligation, George Washington, in his inaugural address, asked Congress to give careful attention to the demands to amend the Constitution to include a statement of rights.

James Madison took the lead in coordinating the suggestions of state ratifying conventions and introduced the amendments into the House of Representatives. Congress pared the list down to 12, and 10 of the resulting amendments were ratified relatively quickly. These first 10 amendments constitute the Bill of Rights, which became the legal basis of civil liberties in the United States. Both the Anti-Federalists and the Federalists gained from the process. The former saw their initial support for a Bill of Rights vindicated, and the latter gained additional popular support for the Constitution they authored.

Restrictions on State Violations of Civil Liberties

The Bill of Rights was originally interpreted to apply only to the federal government, not to state governments. In the early years of the republic, restricting the Bill of Rights to the federal government made sense for the simple reason that states were well ahead of the federal government in guaranteeing basic civil liberties. Virginia's Declaration of Rights, for example, guaranteed its citizens' basic freedoms of press and religion and the right to a trial by jury, and it was passed years before the Constitutional Convention. In fact, all the early state constitutions either contained a separate bill of rights or incorporated similar provisions as part of the basic document.

Given that state governments already had basic guarantees of civil liberties in their constitutions, it is not surprising that Congress focused on the national government when developing the Bill of Rights. Nowhere did Congress specifically state that the amendments in the Bill of Rights applied only to the national government, but this was most likely the intention of those who drafted them in the early 1790s.[1] In the case of **Barron v. Baltimore** (1833), the Supreme Court explicitly confirmed that the Bill of Rights applied only to the national government.

The application of the Bill of Rights to state governments, however, gradually became an increasingly important question in guaranteeing civil liberties. This question was especially the case in the South during much of the nineteenth and twentieth centuries, when a number of state governments passed laws systematically denying civil liberties to racial minorities. The Civil War had ended slavery, thus freeing African Americans from involuntary servitude, but state laws prevented many from enjoying the full rights and freedoms of citizenship. Following the Civil War, the Thirteenth, Fourteenth, and Fifteenth Amendments seemed to take a large step toward making the Bill of Rights apply to state governments as well as the federal government. Of particular importance is the Fourteenth Amendment, which reads in part, "No state shall make or enforce any law which shall . . . deprive any person of life, liberty, or property, without due process of law." The Fifth Amendment contains a "due process of law" clause that applies to the national government, and the same clause in the Fourteenth Amendment applies to the states. The same clause appearing in both amendments implies that at least part—and perhaps all—of the Bill of Rights is binding on state governments.

These parallel provisions sparked a running debate over what is known as the **incorporation doctrine**, the notion that the Bill of Rights applies to state governments as well as the federal government through the due process clause of the Fourteenth Amendment. Some argued that the Fourteenth Amendment applied the entire Bill of Rights to state governments. Others disagreed, arguing that the due process clause applied the Bill of Rights more selectively to the states, and the applications and limitations should be worked out on a case-by-case basis. The Supreme Court followed the latter course and slowly began using the Fourteenth Amendment's due process clause to apply the Bill of Rights to the states.

An important early example of this piecemeal approach to the incorporation doctrine came in the 1925 case of *Gitlow v. New York*. Here the Supreme Court ruled that the freedoms of speech and the press are such fundamental rights that the Fourteenth Amendment prevents states from unduly limiting these freedoms. Using similar reasoning in other cases, the Court added the other First Amendment freedoms to the liberties so protected. Over the years, much of the Bill of Rights has, provision by provision, been applied to the states. Table 4.1 lists provisions in the Bill of Rights that have been incorporated. Today most, but not all, of the limitations on government in the Bill of Rights apply to the states as well as to the national government. Some of the rights guaranteed by the Bill of Rights that the U.S. Supreme Court has not yet applied to state governments through the due process clause of the Fourteenth Amendment include the Fifth Amendment right to indictment by grand jury and the Seventh Amendment guarantee of a jury trial in civil suits.

Barron v. Baltimore The 1833 Supreme Court case that explicitly confirmed that the Bill of Rights applied only to the national government.

incorporation doctrine The idea that the specific protections provided in the U.S. Bill of Rights are binding on the states through the "due process" clause of the Fourteenth Amendment.

---

[1] The First Amendment states that "Congress shall make no law," and presumably this phrase is read into the amendments that follow, although this is never clarified.

TABLE 4.1: INCORPORATION OF THE BILL OF RIGHTS TO APPLY TO STATE GOVERNMENTS

Year	Amend.	Issue	Supreme Court Case	Vote
1868	XIV	Fourteenth Amendment ratified		
1897	V	Just compensation in taking of private property by government	*Chicago, Burlington & Quincy RR v. Chicago* 166 U.S. 266	9:0
1925	I	Freedom of speech & press	*Gitlow v. New York* 268 U.S. 652	7:2
1927	I	Freedom of speech	*Fiske v. Kansas* 274 U.S. 380	9:0
1931	I	Freedom of press	*Near v. Minnesota* 283 U.S. 697	5:4
1932	VI	Counsel in capital criminal cases	*Powell v. Alabama* 287 U.S. 45	7:2
1934	I	Free exercise of religion	*Hamilton v. Regents of the U. of California* 293 U.S. 245	9:0
1937	I	Freedom of assembly & petition	*De Jonge v. Oregon* 299 U.S. 253	8:0
1940	I	Free exercise of religion	*Cantwell v. Connecticut* 310 U.S. 296	9:0
1947	I	Separation of church & state	*Everson v. Board of Education* 330 U.S. 1	5:4
1948	VI	Public trial	*In re Oliver* 33 U.S. 257	7:2
1949	IV	Unreasonable searches & seizures	*Wolf v. Colorado* 338 U.S. 25	6:3
1961	IV	Exclusionary rule of evidence from unreasonable searches & seizures	*Mapp v. Ohio* 367 U.S. 643	6:3
1962	VIII	Cruel & unusual punishment	*Robinson v. California* 370 U.S. 660	6:2
1963	VI	Counsel in all criminal cases	*Gideon v. Wainwright* 372 U.S. 335	9:0
1964	V	Self-incrimination	*Malloy v. Hogan* 378 U.S. 1	5:4
			Murphy v. Waterfront Commission 378 U.S. 52	9:0
1965	VI	Right to confront adverse witnesses	*Pointer v. Texas* 380 U.S. 400	7:2
1965	IX	Right to privacy	*Griswold v. Connecticut* 381 U.S. 479	7:2
1967	VI	Impartial jury	*Parker v. Gladden* 385 U.S. 363	8:1
1967	VI	Obtaining & confronting favourable witnesses	*Washington v. Texas* 388 U.S. 14	9:0
1967	VI	Speedy trial	*Klopfer v. North Carolina* 386 U.S. 213	9:0
1968	VI	Jury trial in non-petty criminal cases	*Duncan v. Louisiana* 391 U.S. 145	7:2
1969	V	Double jeopardy	*Benton v. Maryland* 395 U.S. 784	7:2
2010	II	Individual right to keep and bear arms	*McDonald v. Chicago*, 561 U.S. ___	5:4

Sources: Stanley and Niemi (2011, 295); Supreme Court of the United States, "2009 Term Opinions of the Court," http://www.supremecourt.gov/opinions/slipopinions.aspx?Term=09 (accessed July 3, 2010)

The most recent amendment to be incorporated is the Second Amendment's right to keep and bear arms (*McDonald v. Chicago* 2010). In full, the Second Amendment states, "A well regulated Militia, being necessary to the security of a free State, the right of the people to keep and bear Arms, shall not be infringed." There has been considerable disagreement over what this statement actually means. Some argue that it guarantees an individual citizen the right to own and carry firearms with little or no interference from government. Others argue that the amendment refers to citizen militias—citizen-based military organizations formed for the purpose of common defense that were common during the founding era—but provides no unfettered guarantee of individual firearms ownership (Williams 2003). Until recently, the few precedents that existed supported the latter interpretation. This position was most clearly expressed in *U.S. v. Miller* (1939), in which the Supreme Court held that the Second Amendment's "obvious purpose" was to ensure the effectiveness of a well-regulated militia and not to guarantee an individual's right to gun ownership. The Court reaffirmed this interpretation in *Lewis* v. *United States* (1980).

The Supreme Court overturned these precedents in ***District of Columbia v. Heller*** (2008), striking down the Washington, DC, ban on the possession of handguns and for the first time holding that the Second Amendment protects an individual's right to possess a firearm for lawful purposes such as self-defense. Although the scope of this newfound right is not yet clear, Justice Scalia noted that "the right secured by the Second Amendment is not unlimited" and that the ruling should not be interpreted as casting doubt on reasonable restrictions such as prohibitions against possession of firearms by felons and the mentally ill or laws banning firearms in sensitive places such as schools.

Because this case involved Washington, DC, it limited federal, not state, power (remember from chapter 3 that the District of Columbia is a federal city). In ***McDonald v. Chicago*** (2010), the Supreme Court ruled that the Second Amendment right of an individual to "keep and bear arms" applies to the states as well as the federal government. The city of Chicago had a ban on possession of handguns similar to the one voided in Washington, DC. The Court reaffirmed, however, that although an outright ban on handguns is unconstitutional, reasonable restrictions such as those mentioned in *District of Columbia v. Heller* are permissible.

Even if a right has not been incorporated and made binding on states, states may extend that right to their residents. The Nebraska constitution, for example, guaranteed rights of firearms ownership to all citizens of that state long before *McDonald v. Chicago* applied the Second Amendment to all states. The right to keep and bear arms is a good example of how states frequently offer broader rights and liberties than those guaranteed by the U.S. Constitution. The Bill of Rights can be thought of as a minimum set of guarantees; states can and often do go well beyond those minimums.

Because most of the liberties guaranteed by the Bill of Rights have been incorporated, in practical terms they provide a common yardstick to judge the minimal set of civil liberties shared by all citizens. This means that virtually all of the important dilemmas pitting liberty against authority, or liberty against liberty, are resolved by the Supreme Court interpreting and applying the Bill of Rights in specific cases. The next sections discuss controversies and Supreme Court decisions surrounding a particular set of freedoms and rights guaranteed by the Bill of

District of Columbia v. Heller The 2008 case in which the Supreme Court struck down the Washington, DC, ban on the possession of handguns and for the first time held that the Second Amendment protects an individual's right to possess a firearm for lawful purposes such as self-defense.

McDonald v. Chicago A 2010 case in which the Supreme Court ruled that the Second Amendment right of an individual to "keep and bear arms" applies to the states as well as the federal government.

Rights and considered fundamental civil liberties: freedom of religion, freedom of expression, the right to privacy, and the protections offered to people accused of committing crimes.

FREEDOM OF RELIGION

Many Americans assume that freedom from government interference in religious matters is a right that predates the founding of the republic. Tradition tells us that Puritans fled England in the early 1620s to escape the dictates of the official Anglican Church and that the right of individuals to worship as they saw fit was a characteristic of the Massachusetts Bay Colony. In reality, the Puritans wanted only the freedom to impose their own religious views on others. They quickly established the Congregational Church and forced all inhabitants under their jurisdiction to follow its religious precepts. Other colonies followed similar practices, and as late as the Revolutionary War, most of them had what were known as established churches, or a particular set of religious beliefs that were favored by the government.

For the most part, these established churches did not survive the Revolutionary period. Rather than a single established church, some of the founders (notably George Washington) wanted all Christian churches to be state religions of equal standing and to be supported by taxation. This notion was opposed by others who thought it unwise to mix church and state and who sought an official separation of the two (those favoring this position included James Madison, Thomas Jefferson, and George Mason). The latter position was written into state law in 1786 in the Virginia Statute for Religious Freedom, which mandated that state government could force no one to frequent or support any religion or religious practice. This general attitude about church–state relations became dominant in other states. Two sections of the Constitution made this attitude national policy. Article VI prohibits the use of a religious test as a requirement for public office, and the First Amendment mandates that "Congress shall make no law respecting an establishment of religion, or prohibiting the free exercise thereof." In *Cantwell v. Connecticut* (1940), the Supreme

The free exercise of religion is a constitutional right familiar to Americans, but the interpretations of how to uphold that right are often controversial, especially with regard to religion in schools. The Supreme Court has consistently ruled that when a public authority supports an activity with religious content (such as prayer in public schools), it is favoring a belief system, which is prohibited by the First Amendment. On the other hand, it has also ruled that government support of secular activities by parochial schools is legal if it does not promote excessive relations between church and state and does not impede or promote religion. What difficulties do you see in comparing these types of rulings?

© Dennis MacDonald/Alamy

Court incorporated this clause of the First Amendment, ruling that it represented a fundamental liberty and was applicable to state governments through the due process clause of the Fourteenth Amendment.

In making the religious provisions of the First Amendment apply to all governments, the Supreme Court was in effect passing on two separate guarantees. The first is that government cannot establish a religion, which means that public authorities cannot show preference for one set of religious beliefs over others, or for religious beliefs in general over nonreligious beliefs. This is the basic definition of the **establishment clause** of the Constitution. The second is that government cannot prohibit the **free exercise of religion**, which means that individuals are free to choose religious beliefs and practice them as they see fit or not to practice any religion at all. These two guarantees are obviously related—if government uses its power to establish a religion, then it also prevents the free exercise of religious beliefs that have not been so established. They are two different ideas, however, and the Supreme Court has made a point of keeping them distinct.

Prohibition against the Establishment of Religion

Controversies over the establishment clause deal with whether public authorities can sanction religious activities or favor a particular religious group or belief. The Supreme Court has generally said public authorities cannot do this directly, although it has allowed public authorities considerable leeway in indirectly supporting secular activities undertaken by religious organizations. Public education provides an excellent case study of how these issues have evolved over the past century.

An early case involving public education and the establishment clause was *Everson v. Board of Education* (1947). This case originated in New Jersey, where state law authorized local school boards to reimburse parents for costs incurred in transporting their children to parochial schools. The key question was whether the expenditures showed favoritism that constituted an establishment of religion. In its majority opinion, the Court for the first time directly articulated the principle of **separation of church and state**, meaning that neither federal nor state government could pass any law supporting one religion or all religions or any law preferring one religion over another. Although the *Everson* ruling called for a sharp separation between church and state, the Court concluded that the transportation expenditures did not support any religious activity, but rather assisted families and were therefore allowable. In directly articulating the concept of separation of church and state, however, the Court laid the foundation for several other cases that had a much broader and more controversial impact on education.

One of the most significant of these cases was *Engel v. Vitale* (1962), which decided that public schools could not officially sanction prayer. The heart of the case involved a prayer written by New York State officials that was read aloud by teachers and students in public schools: "Almighty God, we acknowledge our dependence upon Thee, and we beg Thy blessings upon us, our parents, our teachers, and our country." In a blunt majority opinion, the Court declared,

establishment clause A clause in the First Amendment of the Constitution that states that government cannot establish a religion.

free exercise of religion The First Amendment guarantee that individuals are free to choose religious beliefs and practice them as they see fit or not to practice any religion at all.

Everson v. Board of Education The 1947 case in which the Court for the first time directly articulated the principle of separation of church and state, concluding that transportation expenditures to parochial schools did not support any religious activity but rather assisted families and were therefore allowable.

separation of church and state The idea that neither national nor state governments may pass laws that support one religion or all religions or give preference to one religion over others.

The constitutional prohibition against laws respecting an establishment of religion must at least mean that in this country it is no part of the business of government to compose official prayers for any group of the American people to recite as part of a religious program carried on by government.

A year later, in *Abington Township v. Schempp* (1963), the Court extended this line of reasoning by prohibiting states from requiring Bible reading or recitation of the Lord's Prayer in public schools.

The Supreme Court has struck down state- or school-sanctioned religious activities in most subsequent cases. In *Stone v. Graham* (1980), a Kentucky statute requiring the Ten Commandments to be posted in every public school classroom was ruled unconstitutional. An Alabama statute authorizing a one-minute period of silence in public schools for "meditation or voluntary prayer" met a similar fate in *Wallace v. Jaffree* (1985). In *Lee v. Weisman* (1992), the court ruled that having clergy offer prayers at public school ceremonies that students were required to attend was similarly a violation of separation of church and state and thus a violation of the establishment clause.

What all these cases have in common is some form of governmental authority (state law, school district, public official) sanctioning or supporting some form of religious expression, belief, or activity. The Court has consistently ruled that when a public authority organizes, requires, or officially approves any activity with religious content, it is favoring a particular belief system. This favoritism, the Supreme Court has ruled, constitutes establishment of religion and is prohibited by the First Amendment's establishment clause. This ban has been extended to prevent everything from drawing school district boundaries to create public schools with a particular religious majority (*Board of Education Kiryas Joel Village v. Grumet* 1994) to student-led prayer at high school football games (*Santa Fe Independent School District v. Doe* 2000). More recently, a federal court (though not the Supreme Court) struck down a requirement enacted by a Pennsylvania school district that intelligent design be taught as an alternative to evolution. A group of parents objected to this requirement, arguing that intelligent design—the notion that life was created by an intelligent force rather than by natural selection—was cover for a religion-based creationist belief system that had no place in a public school science curriculum. In *Kitzmiller et al. v. Dover School District* (2005), U.S. District Court Judge John E. Jones III agreed, ruling that the requirement was an unconstitutional violation of the establishment clause.

All of these decisions are based on the idea that the First Amendment clearly states what government cannot do: it cannot establish a religion. But what *can* the government do? The First Amendment is much less clear on this point. Parochial schools engage in a wide range of educational activities that have no direct religious component. Can government support some of these activities, even though that support would indirectly benefit an organization that promotes a particular religion? That indirect support is permissible clearly was the implication of the *Everson* case, which allowed reimbursement for the costs of traveling to a religious school, even as the ruling affirmed the separation of church and state. The

Supreme Court has generally ruled that as long as an activity related to a religious school has a secular purpose, does not impede or promote religion, and does not promote excessive entanglement between church and state, public authorities can support that activity without violating the establishment clause of the First Amendment.

Even so, attempts to use public money or other resources to support activities at religious schools are controversial. Behind these disputes is a more fundamental difference concerning the role that schools, especially parochial schools, should play in a democratic society. Those who support public expenditures for parochial schools argue that they educate a lot of children and thereby save the public school system a good deal of money. Furthermore, say proponents, it is not fair to tax parents for the public schools while they are paying parochial school tuition; such parents are in effect paying twice to educate their children. Finally, supporters of parochial schools argue that such schools do not raise serious religious problems in American society because they devote most of their activities to educating students in secular rather than sectarian subjects.

Opponents argue that sending children into separate schools on the basis of religion is democratically undesirable. A primary advantage of public schools is their democratizing influence, and this includes bringing children of various religious backgrounds together during their formative years. This diversity is seen as particularly important because religious differences are often associated with differences in ethnicity and socioeconomic background. Opponents, therefore, do not want to see government take any action that would foster parochial schools at the expense of public ones. If parents wish to send their children to church-supported schools rather than to public schools, then that is their prerogative. But they must assume the financial burden of that choice and not expect the rest of society to assist them. Just as those who choose to hire private security firms are not exempt from paying taxes to support local law enforcement, those who choose to send their children to private schools are still required to contribute to public schools. Finally, opponents believe that it is not possible to draw clear distinctions between sectarian and secular matters and that religious points of view have an effect on the way that many nonreligious subjects are taught.

Recent Supreme Court rulings on this issue sided with proponents of programs that result in tax dollars going to religious schools. *Zelman v. Simmons-Harris* (2002) considered the constitutionality of a school voucher program in Cleveland, Ohio. The publicly funded vouchers were given to disadvantaged students, who could use them to pay for tuition at private schools. The overwhelming majority of vouchers (more than 90 percent) were redeemed at religiously affiliated schools. Opponents argued that the vouchers represented little more than a way to subsidize religious institutions. Proponents argued that the program was designed to help underprivileged students by giving them the means to leave failing public schools and did not constitute government favoring religion. The financial boon to religious schools was therefore not a policy goal but simply a byproduct of individual choice neither required nor encouraged by government. In a five-to-four decision, the Court sided with proponents of vouchers. *Arizona Christian School*

Tuition Org v. Winn (2011) tackled a similar issue to that considered in *Zelman*. This case was brought by a group of taxpayers who objected to an Arizona law that provided tax credits to people underwriting scholarships for students attending private, primarily religious schools. Again, the argument was that this amounted to little more than a legal ruse to provide indirect public subsidies for religious schools. In another five-to-four decision, the Supreme Court dismissed the suit on the grounds that the taxpayers had no standing—there was no direct government expenditure, and therefore taxpayers suffered no damages or harm. In these two rulings the Supreme Court seems to be saying that indirect subsidies of religious educational institutions such as vouchers and tax credits can be (and in some cases are) prohibited by state constitutions, but they do not violate the separation of church and state mandated by the First Amendment.

Free Exercise of Religion

Controversies involving the free exercise of religion deal with the extent to which the state can regulate individual religious practices. In the late 1870s, the Supreme Court had to decide whether a federal law banning polygamy in the territories violated the First Amendment rights of Mormons who practiced plural marriages. In *Reynolds v. United States* (1879), the court made a clear distinction between religious beliefs and actions stemming from those beliefs. The justices reasoned that Mormons had every right to believe that God permits men to have as many wives as possible but that Mormons had no right to implement this belief because it violated social duty and order.

As *Reynolds* indicates, the free exercise of religion is a liberty subject to some restrictions by government. But the Court has frequently acted to protect individual religious choices from government restrictions. For example, a series of cases in the 1930s and 1940s dealt with Jehovah's Witnesses who acted on their belief that each member of the group is a minister with a duty to spread the gospel. In distributing religious literature in the public streets, Jehovah's Witnesses ran afoul of state and local laws relating to permits, fees, and taxes. The Court ruled that Jehovah's Witnesses had the right to pass out tracts in residential areas. The Court in effect had to balance the right of Jehovah's Witnesses to propagate their faith with the right of individuals to privacy—in this case, to not be bothered by people seeking to convert them (*Cantwell v. Connecticut* 1940; *Minersville School District v. Gobitis* 1940; *West Virginia State Board of Education v. Barnette* 1943).

Few issues better highlight the delicate balance between the right to free exercise of religion and the broader interests of society than religious exercises in state-supported schools. This issue actually spans both the establishment and free exercise clauses. Since its initial ruling banning mandatory prayer in public schools in 1962, the Supreme Court has consistently ruled that because public schools are government institutions, the Constitution prohibits state and local authorities from commanding schoolchildren to pray aloud or silently or to engage in other activities that could be construed as having a religious purpose. Yet none of these decisions prevent an individual from praying in school. The government has no right—and, as a practical matter, no ability—to interfere with such practices. Nor can public authorities prevent religious groups from using public facilities if such access is available to others (*Lamb's Chapel v. Center Moriches School District* 1993; *Good News Club v. Milford Central School District* 2001).

Although the government cannot limit individuals or groups from practicing their religious beliefs, the Supreme Court has also ruled that public authorities are not obligated to subsidize how individuals choose to exercise those rights. In *Locke v. Davey* (2004), the Supreme Court decided that state governments are allowed to withhold taxpayer-funded scholarships for those who choose to study for the ministry. At issue in this case was the constitutionality of Washington State's so-called Blaine amendment. Blaine amendments (named for the congressman who tried, and failed, to add his amendment to the U.S. Constitution) are included in some state constitutions, and they specifically prohibit state governments from funding religious activities. Joshua Davey was a college student who won a publicly funded scholarship and decided to study for the ministry. The state rescinded the scholarship on the grounds that paying to train someone to lead a congregation constituted support of a religious activity. Davey sued, arguing that withholding a scholarship available to students studying in any other field amounted to religious discrimination. The Supreme Court held that Washington State was under no First Amendment obligation to provide the scholarship.

Davey makes an interesting companion case to the *Zelman v. Simmons-Harris* (2002) and *Arizona Christian School Tuition Organization v. Winn* (2011) rulings. In the latter cases the Supreme Court said state governments could, at least indirectly, support activities undertaken by religious organizations. In *Davey*, the Court ruled that even though state governments *could* support such activities, they were not *obligated* to do so. Withholding financial support from religious education imposes no criminal or civil limitations on the free exercise of religion, and states are free to mandate that tax dollars not be used to support any religious activity.

FREEDOM OF EXPRESSION

In addition to freedom of religion, the First Amendment spells out a number of other liberties that government may not interfere with: freedom of speech and the press, the right of peaceful assembly, and the right to petition the government for redress of grievances. Together, these constitute means by which individuals and groups can express their views and communicate them to one another, as well as to public officials. Like religious freedom, the First Amendment liberties relating to expression did not become a matter of major concern for the Supreme Court until the twentieth century. It was not until the 1950s that social and political changes prompted a series of vital First Amendment issues to be decided by the Supreme Court.

General Approaches

There are several basic approaches to dealing with issues of freedom of expression. One is to treat this freedom as absolute. This **absolutist approach** argues that the founders wanted the words of the First Amendment to be taken literally; in other words, the language "Congress shall make no law" means that government cannot take any action that interferes with the free expression of views, no matter how offensive, hurtful, or even harmful they may be. Absolutists do recognize that society has a right to place limits on the freedom of expression, but they want those limits kept to an absolute minimum.

Other approaches to freedom of expression issues differ from the absolutist position in degree rather than kind. Some justices have adopted the **preferred freedoms doctrine** approach to freedom of expression. According to this doctrine, First Amendment rights are so fundamental to achieving a free society that courts have a greater obligation to protect these freedoms than other rights. Justice Oliver Wendell Holmes first expressed this view in the early 1900s. This doctrine supports an argument that courts should take a more active role in First Amendment controversies rather than defer to the Congress and the president.

Other justices have avoided trying to treat freedom of expression issues with a universal philosophy. For example, Justice Felix Frankfurter was known for a pragmatic **balancing test** approach to free expression. Essentially, this approach called for weighing competing values on a case-by-case basis to determine when restrictions on freedom of expression were warranted in order to protect society or the rights of individuals or groups. The significant difference between the balancing test approach and the absolutist and preferred freedoms approaches is that the former rejects the idea that freedom of expression is an absolute value that ought to take precedence over other legitimate concerns.

absolutist approach The view of the First Amendment that states that the founders wanted it to be interpreted literally so that Congress should make "no laws" about the expression of views.

preferred freedoms doctrine The idea that the rights provided in the First Amendment are fundamental and as such the courts have a greater obligation to protect those rights than others.

balancing test The view of freedom of expression that states the obligation to protect rights must be balanced with the impact on society of the action in question.

Specific Tests

Although the general judicial approaches to freedom of expression reflect important basic attitudes, in practice none have been particularly helpful in dealing with the wide variety of freedom of expression issues the Supreme Court has faced in the past half-century or so. The basic problem is that although most justices advocate the greatest degree of freedom possible in matters of individual expression, it has proven difficult to balance that freedom with society's need for order and authority. The Supreme Court has devised various tests to provide a basic rule about when freedom of expression can legitimately be regulated.

CHAPTER 4 CIVIL LIBERTIES

The **"clear and present danger" test** was articulated by Justice Oliver Wendell Holmes Jr. in *Schenck v. United States* (1919) and follows from his preferred freedoms doctrine. The case involved a socialist convicted of violating the Espionage Act by circulating antiwar leaflets to members of the armed forces. According to Holmes, the central issue was whether the leaflets constituted a "clear and present danger" of bringing about "substantive evils" that Congress had a right to prevent. Schenck's activities were deemed to meet this test; the possibility of soldiers refusing to fight was considered a substantive evil, and his conviction was upheld.

The **bad tendency rule** was articulated just a year after the *Schenck* case in *Pierce v. United States* (1920). This case also involved socialists distributing antiwar pamphlets, though there was no indication that any of this literature reached members of the armed forces or had an immediate effect on the war. The case is notable because it eased the "clear and present danger" test for restricting freedom of speech. Instead of requiring that speech raise the probability of an immediate evil before it could be restricted, the bad tendency rule allowed restrictions if speech simply might tend to bring about an evil at some time in the future.

This ruling raised the question of when to use the "clear and present danger" test and when to use the bad tendency rule, a question the Court sought to answer in *Dennis v. United States* (1951). This case revolved around Communists charged with conspiring to overthrow the government. In deciding whether expression advocating the overthrow of the government was protected by the First Amendment, the Supreme Court indicated that the nature of the evil to be avoided had to be taken into account. If the evil was grave enough—such as the violent overthrow of the government—then it was not necessary to demonstrate that the expression would probably result in the immediate occurrence of the evil. But if the evil was less grave, such as a local disturbance, then those seeking to regulate expression must meet the thresholds established earlier. In this case, the Court seemed to say that if the evil is serious enough, the bad tendency test should be employed; if the evil is less serious, the "clear and present danger" standard is applicable.

The difficulty with all these tests, as well as with those applied to other areas of free expression, is that verbal formulas cannot possibly capture all the complexities of social situations. In other words, judges ultimately exercise considerable discretion in deciding freedom of expression issues. This discretion is sometimes used to defend individual liberty against the authority of the state. For example, in *Texas v. Johnson* (1989), the Supreme Court ruled that burning the American flag was a form of expression that had constitutional protection. Despite widespread support for laws outlawing desecration of the flag, the Court ruled that a "bedrock principle" of the First Amendment is that the government has no authority to prevent the expression of an idea simply because it is offensive. This basic idea was reaffirmed in *Snyder v. Phelps* (2011). Fred Phelps and members of his family are the driving force behind the Westboro Baptist Church (WBC), a fundamentalist congregation militantly opposed to homosexual rights. WBC members believed military casualties in Iraq and Afghanistan were God's punishment for America's tolerance of homosexuality. They demonstrated at military funerals, including that of Lance Corporal Matthew Snyder, holding up signs that read, for example,

"clear and present danger" test An approach to determining whether an action should be protected under the First Amendment that considers "whether the words used are used in such circumstances and are of such a nature as to create a clear and present danger that they will bring about the substantive evils that Congress has a right to prevent."

Schenck v. United States The 1919 case that articulated the "clear and present danger" test.

bad tendency rule An approach to determining whether an action should be protected under the First Amendment that considers whether the action would have a tendency to produce a negative consequence.

Texas v. Johnson The 1989 case in which the Supreme Court ruled that burning the American flag was a form of expression that had constitutional protection.

"Thank God for Dead Soldiers" and "You're Going to Hell." Lance Corporal Snyder's father, Albert Snyder, sued the WBC for millions in damages, claiming emotional and psychological harm. Yet in an eight-to-one decision, the Supreme Court said the First Amendment gave WBC a right to picket and express their views at a military funeral, however repugnant or disturbing those views might be to grieving family and friends. In short, the Court once more reaffirmed that the purpose of the First Amendment is to protect the expression of ideas and views that others find disagreeable.

One of the most famous cases of the Supreme Court upholding the right to free speech, even though that speech was considered offensive to many, came in ***Brandenburg v. Ohio*** (1969). Clarence Brandenburg was a member of the Ku Klux Klan (KKK) who was filmed by a television crew giving speeches that alluded to gaining "revengeance" against blacks and Jews, castigated the government for oppressing whites, and called for a march on Washington, DC. Brandenburg was convicted for inciting people to break the law. The Supreme Court, however, overturned his conviction, ruling in a unanimous decision that Brandenburg's speech, though supportive of lawbreaking in the abstract, contained no incitement to commit an "imminent or specific" crime. This **imminent lawless action test** replaced the old clear and present danger test and protects a broader range of speech.

Although the Court ruled that burning flags is protected speech, in *Virginia v. Black* (2003) it ruled that burning crosses is not. The key issue in this case was a Virginia law that made it a felony to burn a cross for the purpose of intimidating any person or group. The Supreme Court rejected the argument that cross burning with the intent of racial intimidation was constitutionally protected free speech. In this case, the Supreme Court used its discretionary power to limit the freedom of the individual in the name of protecting security and social order.

In *McConnell v. Federal Election Commission* (2003), the Supreme Court upheld Congress's right to limit some forms of political speech immediately before an election. The issue here was not what was said or how, but where and when it was said. The McCain-Feingold Act of 2002 banned special interest groups from running issue ads within 60 days of a federal election. Opponents of the law sued, arguing that the law violated First Amendment rights in a way that was particularly offensive; in effect, the law served to weaken the voices of citizens when they were most likely to be heard—that is, right before an election. The Court disagreed, ruling that the money underlying these ad campaigns raised the possibility of perceived or actual corruption and that the government had a basic interest in preventing both. That interest overrode the right of special interest groups to speak loudly in an election.

Yet in ***Citizens United v. Federal Election Commission*** (2010), the Court overturned its decision in *McConnell v. Federal Election Commission* and struck down a provision of the McCain-Feingold Act that prohibited all corporations and unions from broadcasting "electioneering communications" that mentioned a candidate within 60 days of a general election or 30 days of a primary. This ruling effectively prevented Congress from limiting independent campaign spending, on the grounds that such expenditures reflected political speech protected by

Brandenburg v. Ohio The 1969 case that upheld a KKK member's right to controversial speech, which supported lawbreaking in the abstract, *because* it contained no incitement to commit an "imminent or specific" crime, establishing the imminent lawless action test.

imminent lawless action test As decided in *Brandenburg v. Ohio*, speech is protected if it contains no incitement to commit an "imminent or specific" crime. This test replaced the old "clear and present danger" test and protects a broader range of speech.

Citizens United v. Federal Election Commission A 2010 Supreme Court case holding that a provision of the McCain-Feingold Act prohibiting corporations and unions from broadcasting "electioneering communications" within 60 days of a general election is an unconstitutional limitation on the First Amendment guarantee of free speech. It also held that corporations and labor unions can spend unlimited amounts of money in campaigns.

the First Amendment. The decision was enormously controversial for its potential to increase the political influence of those with deep pockets. The ruling cleared the way for independent-expenditure political action committees dubbed "Super PACs," which can accept unlimited donations and spend as much as they want. These Super PACs were used to funnel massive amounts of money into the 2010 and 2012 elections, much of it spent in the form of negative advertising. Though it will take more election cycles to fully evaluate the impact of *Citizens United*, the experience thus far has done little to diminish the fears of the ruling's critics who worried it would increase the influence of those with fat checkbooks and make already negative electoral environments even more cynical and sharp-tongued (see the Politics in Practice feature "Should Corporations Have Civil Liberties?").

It is probably fair to say that over the years, the Supreme Court has shown more than a little inconsistency in its rulings on freedom of expression (e.g., it is legal to burn a flag but not a cross). The point to keep in mind is what the court is striving for in each of these cases: to balance the right of individual expression with the need to preserve social order. The simple fact is that there is no generally agreed-upon standard that can be universally applied to every specific case.

Unprotected Speech

The Supreme Court has ruled that some forms of expression are always beyond constitutional protection and can be outlawed or strictly regulated by the government. Yet even in these cases, the Court has struggled to strike an appropriate balance of competing values and clear standards that both government and individuals can understand and follow.

OBSCENITY Few civil liberty issues have given the Supreme Court more difficulty than obscenity. Rulings in two key 1957 cases, *Roth v. United States* and *Alberts v. California*, clearly articulated that obscenity was not protected speech but was instead a form of expression that could be outlawed by government. Yet despite allowing government to outlaw obscenity, neither case produced a clear definition of obscenity.

In *Roth*, the test of obscenity was whether an "average person, applying contemporary community standards," would find that the dominant theme of the material in question would appeal to prurient interest. The ruling made clear that isolated passages from a film or a literary work

The rapper Eminem has come under severe criticism for his violent and derogatory lyrics. A wide variety of groups have called for suppressing or censoring his lyrics, but Eminem claims the right to freedom of speech and refers to the provisions of the First Amendment to the Constitution for support. The Supreme Court, while admitting that some obscene speech should be regulated, has not been able to provide guidelines for what specific types of speech can be regulated, making enforcement nearly impossible.

© Bill Pugliano/Stringer/Getty Images

POLITICS IN PRACTICE

SHOULD CORPORATIONS HAVE CIVIL LIBERTIES?

Murray Hill was, by far, the strangest person to attempt a run for Congress in 2010. For a start, Murray Hill wasn't a person, or maybe he was. Well, not "he" exactly. Nor was Murray a she. Murray was more of a, well, an "it." But in the eyes of the law, Murray was a person with First Amendment rights. It's just hard to take Murray seriously as a person. Maybe it will make more sense if you know Murray's full name: Murray Hill Incorporated. That's right—Murray is a business, a corporation.

Specifically, Murray Hill is a liberal-leaning public relations firm that, at least until the run for Congress, was best known for its ad campaigns for such groups as the American Federation of Teachers and the National Resources Defense Council. It became the first corporation in the history of the United States (perhaps in the history of humankind) to run for elective office. The campaign was (mostly) a tongue-in-cheek swipe at the reasoning and logic behind the Supreme Court's ruling in *Citizens United v. Federal Election Commission* (2010).

As discussed in the text, the *Citizens* decision was based on the notion that campaign expenditures are a form of expression and thus protected by the First Amendment. Fair enough—if you use your money to buy TV ads or put up billboards touting your political views, you are certainly exercising your right to express your views. Logically, then, the Supreme Court reasoned that being told you cannot spend money to do that restricts your freedom of expression, and the First Amendment says that's a no-no. The decision was hailed by many, including Senate Minority Leader Mitch McConnell (R-KY), who called it "an important step in the direction of restoring the First Amendment rights of these people."

The "people" McConnell referred to, though, were corporations, not individual people. The key legal issue in *Citizens* was whether groups such as unions and corporations had these sorts of First Amendment rights, not whether individuals had these rights. Legally, corporations have always had at least some of the same rights as individuals. They can make contracts and sue and be sued, for example, and courts have repeatedly affirmed those rights. Yet the notion of full corporate personhood—granting corporations *all* the liberties and privileges of individual citizens—is enormously controversial and became a running issue in the 2012 presidential campaign. That spring, while campaigning

could not be used to judge whether the work was obscene; the dominant theme of the entire work had to be judged. The test caused enormous problems in application. There was huge variation in what people considered obscene under this definition, and this variation existed not simply from community to community but also from state to state and even from court to court.

The frustration caused by the Court's inability to provide a clear and universally applicable definition of obscenity was most famously articulated by Justice Potter Stewart in *Jacobellis v. Ohio* (1964). In a concurring opinion, Stewart wrote, "Perhaps I could never succeed in intelligibly [defining obscenity]. But I know it when I see it." Stewart's statement points out a basic problem with enforcing for the Republican presidential nomination in Iowa, Mitt Romney famously replied to a heckler, "Corporations are people, my friend." Some in the audience vociferously disagreed, arguing that people and corporations should not and could not be equated.

The controversy erupted in the 2012 presidential campaign because this was the first electoral cycle where the *Citizens* decision cleared the way for corporations to exercise their First Amendment rights to shovel enormous, unlimited piles of cash into what amounted to independent political campaigns. The issues at the heart of this controversy had been foreshadowed by the mischievous folks at Murray Hill with their 2010 bid for Congress.

Murray Hill's mocking campaign had at least a semiserious point: if corporations really have the same rights as individuals, then by golly, let's see what a democracy looks like when corporations start exercising those rights to the full. For example, why not go the whole hog and get them elected? In a press release announcing the run for Congress, Murray Hill argued that the campaign was the legal and logical result of the reasoning used by the Supreme Court in *Citizens*: "Until now, corporations only influenced politics with high-paid lobbyists and backroom deals. But today, thanks to an enlightened Supreme Court, corporations now have all the rights the founding fathers meant for us. It was their dream to build the best democracy money can buy." Hill's campaign platform was basically that if corporations are going to influence elections through spending gobs of money and have the same legal rights as individuals, why not just cut out the middleman and put corporations in office?

Hill's candidacy, by the way, foundered on an interesting technicality. The Constitution has no requirement that a member of the House of Representatives has to be a person-person as opposed to a corporate-person. It does set a minimum age requirement of 25, though, and Murray Hill was only seven when it decided to run. Maryland election officials barred Murray Hill from the ballot on the grounds it was too young, not because it was a corporation. If a 25-year-old corporation wants to run for Congress, it may yet get on the ballot. So although there is not (yet) a corporation in Congress, Murray Hill's stunt does raise interesting questions about civil liberties, who has them, and how they will be exercised in the future.

SOURCES Good, Chris. 2010. "Murray Hill, Inc. For Congress." *The Atlantic*. http://www.theatlantic.com/politics/archive/2010/02/murray-hill-inc-for-congress/35282/ (accessed February 16, 2010).

Murray Hill for Congress. n.d. http://murrayhillincforcongress.com/ (accessed February 16, 2012).

Politico. 2010. "Pols Weigh in on Citizens United Decision." http://www.politico.com/news/stories/0110/31798.html (accessed February 16, 2012).

Rucker, Philip. 2011. "Mitt Romney Says 'Corporations Are People' at Iowa State Fair." *The Washington Post*. http://www.washingtonpost.com/politics/mitt-romney-says-corporations-are-people/2011/08/11/gIQABwZ38I_story.html (accessed February 15, 2012).

restrictions on sexually explicit expression: those who engage in such expression often do not know whether they are breaking the law because of the elasticity of the definition of obscenity.

In *Miller v. California* (1973), the Supreme Court set three criteria for judging whether a work was obscene:

1. The average person applying contemporary standards finds that the work as a whole appeals to prurient interests (the *Roth* test).
2. The work "depicts or describes, in a patently offensive way, sexual conduct specifically defined by the applicable state law."
3. The work lacks any "serious literary, artistic, political or scientific value."

These guidelines have subsequently been incorporated into federal and state statutes, but thus far they have not surmounted the problem articulated by Stewart. Frequently, the enforcement of obscenity statutes seems to have been driven by the subjective moral judgments of policymakers and politically active groups rather than by any objective standard of obscenity (K. Smith 1999). The problem is that if government is going to be given the authority to completely outlaw some forms of expression, citizens must know exactly what the forms of expression are. If the state has the authority to arbitrarily or inconsistently declare some forms of expression to be beyond constitutional protection, this clearly threatens individual liberty.

The advent of the Internet and the World Wide Web—where pornographic material is just a mouse click away for anyone with an Internet connection—has given new relevance to the debate over sexually explicit materials and free speech. In *Reno v. ACLU* (1997), the Supreme Court found key provisions of the Communications Decency Act, a law passed by Congress that sought to define and regulate the Internet as a broadcast rather than a print medium, to be unconstitutional. The law argued that even sexually explicit materials constitutionally protected as free speech could not be legally sold to minors. In the name of protecting minors, television networks are not allowed to broadcast X-rated movies over the open air waves. Why, proponents of the law argued, should the Internet be any different? The Supreme Court saw things differently. Who is going to decide what is indecent and therefore illegal to post on the Web? Rather than create another endless definitional debate about what is or is not "indecent," "pornographic," or "obscene," the Court ruled the Internet to be the equivalent of a print medium or public forum. Thus, the Court was obligated to provide that medium the broadest First Amendment protection, and it struck down the Communications Decency Act. Yet the Court has also ruled that government can seek to limit minors' access to sexually explicit materials on the Internet. In *United States v. American Library Association* (2004), the Court ruled that Congress was not unduly restricting free speech rights by requiring libraries to install filtering software on computers as a condition of receiving federal funds.

One form of expression that is universally considered obscene is child pornography. To protect children, both federal and state governments prohibit distributing or possessing sexually explicit images of children. Yet even here there has been controversy. The Child Pornography Prevention Act passed by Congress in 1996 banned sexually explicit material that appears to depict minors but that was produced using youthful-looking adults or computer-imaging technology rather than real children. In *Ashcroft v. Free Speech Coalition* (2002), the Supreme Court held that this attempt to prohibit what is sometimes called "virtual child pornography" was overbroad because it bans materials that would not be considered obscene under the *Miller* standards and materials not produced by exploiting real children. Again, we see the Supreme Court engaged in a delicate balancing act, on the one hand trying to maximize civil liberty and restrict government interference with individual choices, and on the other trying to guarantee the government has enough authority to ensure that the free exercise of those liberties does not threaten social order.

LIBEL AND SLANDER Other forms of unprotected speech have run into the same problem. Making false and defaming statements about someone is **slander** when the statement is spoken and **libel** when it is made in print or other media. The Court has ruled that an individual's right to free speech does not extend to using that right to harm others, so slander and libel do not have constitutional protection. This principle has raised concerns about the First Amendment's guarantee of freedom of the press.

The basic requirements for proving libel are as follows:

1. Publication—the statements must be communicated in such a way that third parties can observe them.
2. Identification—the aggrieved party must be clearly specified.
3. Harm—the aggrieved party must suffer as a result of the libel.

The basic defense in a libel suit is truth. If a communication is defamatory but also completely factual, the aggrieved party generally does not have the basis for a successful libel suit. The problem for the press is that the news media often report on issues that portray public figures in an unfavorable light, and under the pressure of deadlines or because they are not privy to crucial information, they could unwittingly libel someone.

There are different standards for public officials than for people who are not in the spotlight, and public officials have a more difficult time winning libel cases than private citizens. In *New York Times Co. v. Sullivan* (1964), the Supreme Court ruled that in order to win a libel suit, a public official who is defamed in press reports must prove not only that a report was false and defamatory but also that it was issued with "actual malice." In other words, false and harmful reports about public officials are not libelous unless it can be proved that the reports were known to be false when they were published or were published with a "reckless disregard" for the truth. However, public officials have discovered that proving malice is a legal hurdle comparable to defining obscenity. In later rulings, the Supreme Court extended the principle in *Sullivan* to include public figures such as movie stars, athletes, and other celebrities (*Curtis Publishing Company v. Butts* 1967; *Associated Press v. Walker* 1967). As a result, this standard gives the press broad liberties to report on public figures in order to inform the public, but public figures have limited recourse if this freedom is used to issue false and misleading statements about them.

THE RIGHT TO PRIVACY

Nowhere does the Constitution explicitly articulate a **right to privacy**. Yet there is nothing new about privacy as a fundamental civil liberty. The Constitution does include numerous amendments and clauses upholding an individual's right to be

slander To make false or defamatory oral statements about someone.

libel To make false or defaming statements about someone in print or the media.

right to privacy An individual's right to be free of government interference without due cause or due process.

free of government interference without due cause or due process. Combined, these can be seen as a right to be left alone.

Privacy became the focus of controversy in the latter half of the twentieth century, when the Supreme Court expanded the right of privacy beyond its link with the traditional protections actually spelled out in the Constitution and granted it independent status. Over a series of decisions, the right to privacy, in essence, became a part of the Bill of Rights. The lead case in this movement was **Griswold v. Connecticut** (1965). In ruling that Connecticut could not prohibit the use of contraceptives by married couples, the Court enumerated a right of marital privacy, even though it conceded that no such right was specifically provided for in the Constitution. Lacking a specific constitutional guideline, the Court argued that various guarantees in the First, Third, Fourth, Fifth, and Ninth Amendments create "zones of privacy" that the government has no right to invade.

In the years following *Griswold,* the Court signaled a willingness to expand this right to privacy. In *Eisenstadt v. Baird* (1972), the Court ruled that it was unconstitutional to prevent the dissemination of birth control information and devices to unmarried people. "If the right of privacy means anything," wrote Justice William J. Brennan Jr. for the majority, "it is the right of the individual, married or single, to be free from unwarranted governmental intrusion into matters so fundamentally affecting a person as the decision to whether to bear or beget a child."

A controversial expansion of the right to privacy came in two 1973 decisions, **Roe v. Wade** and *Doe v. Bolton,* invalidating laws in Texas and Georgia regulating abortions. The Court reaffirmed the right of privacy enumerated in *Griswold,* balancing the mother's right to privacy against the state's interest in protecting the unborn fetus. Justice Harry Blackmun's decision divided pregnancy into three periods. During the first trimester of pregnancy, the decision about whether to have an abortion belongs to the woman and her attending physician without interference from the state. During the second trimester, when abortion poses a greater threat to a woman's health, states can enact regulations to protect the health of the mother. Only during the final stage of pregnancy is the state's interest in protecting the fetus great enough to warrant severe restrictions on abortion, and even then the state must permit abortions to save the life of the mother.

Since *Roe,* the Court has ruled on a number of restrictions on abortion rights enacted by states and municipalities. It has invalidated those requiring the consent of the father and those that require the abortion be performed only in a hospital. Since the 1980s, however, the Court has signaled a willingness to permit restrictions on abortion rights. In *Webster v. Reproductive Health Services* (1989), the Court upheld a Missouri law that prohibited abortion in a publicly funded facility. In *Planned Parenthood v. Casey* (1992), the Court upheld a Pennsylvania law that mandated counseling and a 24-hour waiting period prior to an abortion and also required that minors obtain parental or judicial permission in order to get an abortion. Although these decisions seemed to chip away at the broad privacy rights articulated in *Roe,* the Court has thus far declined to overturn the substance of that ruling.

Although the Court has extended the right to privacy to cover some personal areas of an individual's life, it has also ruled that other behaviors are beyond this

Griswold v. Connecticut The 1965 case ruling that Connecticut could not prohibit the use of contraceptives by married couples, enumerating a right of privacy. Although the Constitution contains no explicit right of privacy, the Court argued that various guarantees in the First, Third, Fourth, Fifth, and Ninth Amendments create "zones of privacy" that the government has no right to invade.

Roe v. Wade The 1973 case in which the Court reaffirmed the right of privacy enumerated in Griswold, balancing the mother's right to privacy against the state's interest in protecting an unborn fetus.

CHAPTER 4 CIVIL LIBERTIES

protection. For example, it struck down a Georgia law allowing news reporters to be sued for publishing or broadcasting the names of rape victims, ruling that states may not impose sanctions for the publication of truthful information contained in court records that are open to the public (*Cox Broadcasting v. Cohn* 1975). In balancing one liberty against another, the Court has generally favored the right to free expression over the right to privacy. Yet the Court has chosen government authority over individual privacy on certain issues. In *United States v. Miller* (1976), the Court refused to extend the right of privacy to individual bank accounts, ruling that the government has the right to obtain records of checks and other transactions. Similarly, the Court has ruled that state laws prohibiting physician-assisted suicide are constitutional (*Washington v. Glucksberg* 1997).

Advances in surveillance and tracking technology have also raised questions about privacy. In *United States v. Jones* (2012), the Supreme Court ruled that law enforcement's use of GPS tracking devices can constitute a search that falls under the protections of the First Amendment. The case involved District of Columbia police officers who, without a warrant and without consent, attached a tracking device to a suspect's car and used it to record the suspect's movements for nearly a month. The Supreme Court unanimously ruled that this violated Fourth Amendment protections, but the justices were split on the reasons. Some justices argued that attaching the tracking device amounted to trespass on private property without a warrant. Other justices, however, argued that the key violation was not trespass on private property, but a citizen's right to a reasonable expectation of privacy.

Other controversial questions about an individual's right to privacy have focused on state laws outlawing consensual sodomy between members of the same sex. In effect, these cases try to decide the question of whether the government has the right to regulate what consenting adults do in the privacy of their own bedrooms. In *Bowers v. Hardwick* (1986), the Court upheld a Georgia law that made it a crime to engage in homosexual sex. In **Lawrence v. Texas** (2003), however, the Court overturned this decision and ruled that the government had no right to regulate or control consensual personal relationships. In both *Bowers* and *Lawrence,* police officers had entered the homes of gay men and caught them having sex. In the former case, the Court ruled that state bans against homosexual acts had deep cultural roots and that the government had the right to enforce these bans in the name of social order. In *Lawrence,* the Court rejected that reasoning and came down firmly on the side of individual liberty, justifying its shift on the grounds that the government has no legitimate reason to intrude into the personal and private lives of individuals. Harvard law professor Laurence Tribe (2004) suggests that *Lawrence* "may well be remembered as the *Brown v. Board* of gay and lesbian America."

Though the right to privacy has been greatly expanded and refined since the *Griswold* decision, broader social movements and issues continually pressure this right. Wendy Kaminer (1999) observed that such individual liberties as freedom of expression and the right to privacy are quick to be subordinated when they conflict with other values central to a particular ideological point of view. On the left, some feminists want individual freedom of expression limited when it is sexually

Lawrence v. Texas The 2003 case ruling that the government had no right to regulate or control consensual personal relationships. This case overruled *Bowers v. Hardwick,* which had allowed states to make engaging in homosexual sex a crime.

explicit because they believe that sexually explicit material involving women perpetuates second-class status for women and encourages violent crimes against women. On the right, some conservatives back the "imposition of moral absolutes," such as making homosexual acts a crime, even in the most private realm of individual behavior. The initial popularity of the Patriot Act shows that a broad cross-section of Americans were willing to give up at least some of their rights to privacy in exchange for greater assurances of security in the wake of terrorist attacks. Ten years after 9/11, a large minority of Americans remained supportive of the Patriot Act's tradeoff between liberty and security, with 42 percent viewing it as a necessary tool that helps the government fight terrorism (Pew Research Center 2011c). This all shows that balancing an individual's right to privacy and society's broader interests is not easy and is often contentious. Individual choices and behaviors—even if they are conducted in the privacy of the bedroom—may be seen as threats to other people's value systems. The need for social order may require citizens to give government at least some limited authority to intrude on their private lives.

CRIMINAL PROCEDURE

One area in which privacy rights are usually respected is criminal procedure. Generally speaking, democracies go out of their way to protect the citizen from the state because government is a powerful institution, and the individual is seldom of equal strength in criminal cases. The state can marshal its vast resources against a single person, who must struggle to defend himself or herself against charges of having committed a wrong against society. To ensure that government does not abuse this power and unnecessarily intrude on civil liberties, a person's rights to privacy and to freedom from arbitrary governmental action are basic values in democracies in general and in American society in particular. It has long been a central feature of Anglo-American legal systems that an individual cannot be subject to criminal sanctions arbitrarily. As early as the fourteenth century, English courts provided that no one could be imprisoned or put to death except by "due process of law." English settlers in America brought with them a concern for the rights of the accused and a determination to protect those rights in criminal procedures.

This solicitude for the rights of the accused in criminal cases has continued to be a hallmark of the American legal system, and it is explicitly codified in the Constitution and in subsequent court rulings. The government is specifically forbidden from violating the privacy of the individual through unreasonable searches and seizures of home or person. The government is also prohibited from arbitrarily arresting people, and in a trial the burden is on the government to prove its charges against the individual "beyond a reasonable doubt." Such prohibitions and requirements are deliberately designed to make it difficult for the government to succeed in any attempt to deny a citizen property, freedom of movement, or the right to life itself. Such protections favor the accused in order to protect the innocent; to lessen the chances that government will punish an innocent person, the Constitution establishes rules and procedures that make it difficult to punish anyone.

The federal system in the United States has resulted in separate legal systems with separate lists of criminal offenses and trial procedures for the nation as a whole and for each of the 50 states. Most "major crimes"—murder, rape, assault, robbery, burglary, and the like—are violations of state rather than federal law and are thus tried in the state courts. Criminal violations of federal law include certain drug-trafficking activities, transporting a stolen automobile across state lines, and plotting to assassinate federal officials, among others.

The rules governing criminal procedure and the rights of the accused in federal cases spring from several sources. The most important is the Constitution, particularly the Fourth, Fifth, Sixth, and Eighth Amendments:

- The Fourth Amendment protects individuals from unreasonable searches and seizures of personal property.
- The Fifth Amendment contains the historic English guarantee that a person cannot be denied life, liberty, or property without due process of law and also includes specific protections from coerced confessions and from being tried twice for the same offense.
- The Sixth Amendment lays down specific guidelines for a fair trial, requiring a speedy and public trial by a jury of one's peers, the right to confront witnesses, and the right to be represented by counsel.
- The Eighth Amendment prohibits cruel and unusual punishment.

Through various cases, most of these rights have been applied to people being tried in state as well as federal courts.[2] Thus, regardless of which level of government charges an individual with a crime, it must abide by a set of basic safeguards and guarantees in these constitutional clauses.

These rights were the source of significant controversy in the twentieth century. A series of rulings expanded the rights of the accused and imposed increased burdens and responsibilities on the government. In general, the Court has expanded rights through interpretation of the Constitution, has applied the rights to the states through the due process clause of the Fourteenth Amendment, and in later rulings has placed limitations on the expanded rights. The swing of the judicial pendulum demonstrates that achieving the "right" balance between individual liberties and social order is an extraordinarily difficult objective that periodically must be reconsidered in a process that is political.

---

[2] The Fifth Amendment's provision requiring indictment by a grand jury and the Eighth Amendment's prohibition of excessive bail have not been applied to trials in state courts.

Exclusionary Rule

One of the most controversial interpretations of the Fourth Amendment's protections against unreasonable searches and seizures is the **exclusionary rule** first articulated in *Weeks v. United States* in 1914. This ruling said that evidence obtained through an unreasonable search and seizure cannot be used in federal trials. The case of *Mapp v. Ohio* (1961) extended the exclusionary rule to state trials. Excluding evidence of a crime is a controversial way to protect individuals' rights against unreasonable search and seizure. The goal is to deter police from infringing on the rights of innocent people, but it is frustrating to be prevented from using evidence to punish guilty people.

The courts have been unable to find a better way to protect the innocent from overzealous police, but court rulings in the past two decades have backed away from the exclusionary rule. In *Nix v. Williams* (1984), the Supreme Court granted an **inevitable discovery exception**, ruling that illegally acquired evidence can be used in court if it would have been discovered eventually through legal means. In *United States v. Leon* (1984), the Court granted another significant exception to the exclusionary rule, the so-called **good faith exception**. As long as a law officer believes that the warrant authorizing a search is valid, the good faith exception makes evidence obtained in the search admissible even if the warrant is later found to be flawed. This ruling is viewed as a significant weakening of the exclusionary rule because what constitutes good faith is open to broad interpretation.

According to the Fourth Amendment, "probable cause" is required before law enforcement officers or agencies can make any arrest or obtain any search warrant. In other words, before any evidence is collected, and before anyone is taken into custody, there must be some basis for believing criminal activity has occurred. However, there has been considerable debate and controversy over exactly what constitutes probable cause. In *Illinois v. Gates* (1984), the Supreme Court defined probable cause as a "fair probability" that some criminal activity has taken place. Like the good faith exception, such rulings are controversial because what constitutes a "fair probability" is often in the eye of the beholder.

Right to Counsel

One of the rights to the guarantee of a fair trial is the Sixth Amendment right to assistance of counsel in mounting a defense against a criminal charge. As early as 1790, Congress passed a law providing legal counsel for all people charged with capital crimes (those punishable by death), but generally speaking, the ability to exercise this right was limited to people who could afford it. This practice changed in federal cases in 1938, when the Court required provision of counsel to anyone accused of a federal crime (*Johnson v. Zerbst*).

The obligation of state governments to provide an attorney was not firmly established until almost 30 years later. In *Gideon v. Wainwright* (1963), the Supreme Court ruled that the right to counsel is a fundamental part of a fair system

exclusionary rule The rule derived from the Fourth and Fourteenth Amendments that states that evidence obtained from an unreasonable search or seizure cannot be used in federal trials.

Weeks v. United States The 1914 case that said that evidence obtained through an unreasonable search and seizure cannot be used in federal trials.

Mapp v. Ohio The 1961 case that extended the exclusionary rule to state trials.

inevitable discovery exception An exception to the exclusionary rule that states that evidence obtained from an illegal search may be used in court if the evidence eventually would have been discovered through legal means.

good faith exception An exception to the exclusionary rule that allows evidence obtained in a search with a flawed warrant to be admissible as long as the law officer believed the warrant was valid at the time of the search.

Gideon v. Wainwright The 1963 case in which the Supreme Court ruled that state courts are required under the Sixth and Fourteenth Amendments of the Constitution to provide counsel in criminal cases for defendants who cannot afford to hire their own lawyer.

of criminal justice, reasoning that without the assistance of counsel, a trial is stacked in favor of the government. *Gideon* was a landmark case that opened the door to a series of specific questions involving the right to counsel. Most fundamental was what kind of criminal cases initiated the state's obligation to provide a lawyer. In a series of later rulings, notably *Argersinger v. Hamlin* (1972) and *Scott v. Illinois* (1979), the Supreme Court ruled that any charge that carried a potential loss of liberty was serious enough to trigger the state obligation under *Gideon*.

Ernesto Miranda (right) and his attorney John Flynn leaving the U.S. Supreme Court in June 1966 after it overturned the Arizona State court's decision of guilt and a jail sentence of 20 years.

Right against Self-Incrimination

Probably the most famous expansion of the Fifth Amendment right against self-incrimination came in **Miranda v. Arizona** (1966). At issue was a confession to the crimes of kidnapping and rape that Ernesto Miranda made to police officers during a two-hour interrogation. The Court ruled the confession inadmissible on the grounds that once Miranda had been taken into custody or deprived of his freedom of action in any significant way, law enforcement officials were under an obligation to inform him that he had the right to remain silent and that if he gave up this right, anything he said could be used against him in court. This ruling also shifted the Sixth Amendment right to counsel from the trial stage to the police station: *Miranda* required police to inform suspects of their rights to counsel and to have an attorney appointed if they could not afford one.

The basic reasoning behind the *Miranda* ruling was that confessions can be coerced in ways other than beatings. Just being in custody in a strange environment and being questioned by police is a psychologically coercive situation. Furthermore, criminal laws are often complex, and an accused individual may unwittingly admit to criminal acts. Individuals cannot exercise their constitutional right against self-incrimination if they are unaware of it, and they need the help of an attorney to protect their rights.

The *Miranda* decision provoked a storm of protest. Law enforcement officials complained that it would handcuff them in dealing with criminals. The ruling seemed to be placing the rights of criminals above the public interest. Subsequent rulings have placed some limits on the Miranda decision. For example, in *Michigan v. Mosley* (1975), the Court ruled that if a defendant exercises the right to be silent when originally questioned about a crime, but voluntarily

Miranda v. Arizona The 1966 case that established a criminal suspect's right against self-incrimination and right to counsel during police interrogation.

makes statements about a different crime during a subsequent interrogation, later statements are not protected by the original decision to remain silent and can be used as evidence in a trial. In *New York v. Quarles* (1984), the Court ruled that the police are allowed to interrogate a suspect before advising him or her of rights if "public safety" is at risk; this was considered a significant erosion of the rights established by earlier rulings. The Court narrowed the Miranda protections further in 2010. The case of *Berghuis v. Thompkins* (2010) involved a suspect who indicated that he understood the Miranda rights read to him, but he did not explicitly invoke or waive his right to remain silent. After remaining silent through nearly three hours of questioning, the suspect made an incriminating statement that was used as evidence in his trial. The Court held that just remaining silent is not sufficient to invoke the right against self-incrimination; a suspect must make an explicit, unambiguous statement that he or she wishes to remain silent. However, even after lengthy silence, any voluntary statements made imply that the suspect waives the right to remain silent. In *J.D.B. v. North Carolina* (2012), the Court did create a minor expansion of Miranda rights by ruling that police have to take age into account when issuing Miranda rights. The case involved a 13-year-old who was questioned at school by a police officer, during which time he confessed to committing two robberies. The confession was used in court even though the student had not been given a Miranda warning. This was allowed on the grounds that the student was not technically in police custody when he made the confession. The Supreme Court, however, ruled that it is hard for children to assess whether they are in custody or not. Age, the court argued, has to be taken into account when assessing whether someone is in custody and entitled to a Miranda warning.

Although having to let a guilty person go free on a legal technicality is frustrating, *Miranda*'s role in adding to such frustrations is debatable. Ernesto Miranda, for example, was retried and convicted of rape on the basis of evidence other than the coerced confession. (See the Politics in Practice feature "The Strange Fate of Ernesto Miranda.")

Capital Punishment

Capital punishment is one of the most divisive controversies in American jurisprudence. At one time, it appeared that the forfeit of life would be ruled a violation of the Eighth Amendment's protection against "cruel and unusual punishment." In *Furman v. Georgia* (1972), the Supreme Court outlawed the death penalty as it was then implemented by the states. But only Justices William Brennan and Thurgood Marshall stated that the death penalty was inherently unconstitutional. Other justices claimed that the problem was not the penalty itself but rather how it was applied; it seemed to be applied arbitrarily and was disproportionately used on defendants who were socioeconomically disadvantaged.

Furman thus left open the possibility that new death penalty statutes could pass constitutional muster if they avoided imposing the sentence in a capricious

POLITICS IN PRACTICE

THE STRANGE FATE OF ERNESTO MIRANDA

Ernesto Miranda is best remembered for the landmark Supreme Court case that overturned his rape conviction and obligated law enforcement officers to inform suspects of their right against self-incrimination. What is less remembered about Miranda is that his victory did him little good and even may have helped his killer escape justice.

Miranda was a dropout who grew up in and around Phoenix, Arizona. He had amassed a considerable criminal record by March 1963, when he was arrested and accused of kidnapping and raping a woman he had picked up in his car. Taken into custody, Miranda confessed to this crime and to other charges of kidnapping and robbery.

Although he had confessed to the crimes, Miranda pleaded not guilty in court, and his lawyer unsuccessfully sought to suppress the confessions. Miranda was found guilty and sentenced to 25 to 30 years in prison. He appealed the conviction, seeking a new trial in which the confessions would not be allowed into evidence. His appeal gradually wended its way through the court system, and it was one of six cases bundled together by the U.S. Supreme Court in a review of how police obtained confessions. Because his name was listed first, these cases collectively became known as "Miranda."

The Court ruled that in order to exercise their rights, citizens must first be aware of what those rights are and that it was the responsibility of law enforcement personnel to expressly inform people suspected of crimes of their rights against self-incrimination and to legal representation. On this basis, Miranda's confession was excluded from evidence, and his conviction was overturned.

The standard warning that emerged from this ruling has been immortalized in innumerable movies and television shows: "You have the right to remain silent. Anything you say can be held against you in a court of law. You have the right to an attorney to assist you prior to questioning and to be with you during questioning. If you cannot afford an attorney, one will be provided for you."

Miranda's victory was fleeting. He was retried in state court and again convicted, even though the confessions were excluded from his second trial. He went back to prison and served until he was paroled in 1972.

Upon being paroled, Miranda returned to Phoenix and sold autographed copies of Miranda warning cards from the courthouse steps for $2 each. In January 1976, while playing cards in a Phoenix bar, he got involved in a fight over a $3 bet. As he left the bar, he was attacked by two men and fatally stabbed.

The police tracked down one suspect and read him his rights in accordance with the Miranda ruling. The suspect refused to answer questions, and he went free for lack of evidence.

SOURCE Simonich, Milan. 2000. "Miranda's Life Ended with Warning, No Conviction." *Pittsburgh Post-Gazette.* http://www.post-gazette.com/healines/20000110miran-daside2.asp (accessed October 25, 2000).

manner. Between 1972 and 1975, some 30 states passed new statutes that did exactly that.

In the effort to avoid imposing the sentence in an arbitrary and capricious way, each of these states used one of two basic approaches. One was to make the death penalty mandatory for certain offenses, such as the murder of a police officer. The second was to establish separate procedures for determining guilt and passing sentence, thus essentially holding two trials in cases involving capital crimes: one to determine guilt or innocence and the other to determine whether to apply the death penalty.

In 1976, the Supreme Court heard five related cases involving the constitutionality of death penalty laws in Georgia, Texas, Florida, North Carolina, and Louisiana. It upheld the laws of the first three states and invalidated those of the latter two. Although there were a number of differences in these laws, all of those upheld contained a two-part procedure for determining guilt and sentencing. In contrast, the two that were struck down set mandatory death penalties for certain crimes. The most important of these cases was *Gregg v. Georgia* (1976), where the Court ruled that the death penalty does not, by itself, violate the Constitution. As long as the states took steps to ensure that death sentences were not automatically awarded upon conviction, but came after due deliberation by the sentencing authorities, it was not considered cruel and unusual punishment.

Even though the Supreme Court ruled the death penalty constitutional, its application has continued to raise controversy and concern. The case for the death penalty rests on the argument that some crimes are so repugnant and heinous that, in the name of the greater good, society has a right to assess the ultimate penalty and take someone's life. Yet for a system that tries to maximize individual liberty and minimize government authority, the basic problem with the death penalty is the potential for executing the innocent. In such cases, authority completely and obviously squashes individual liberty and breaks the democratic promise of political freedom. Democracies are less likely to employ the death penalty than nondemocratic nations. About 60 percent of democratic nations do not use the death penalty for any crime. In contrast, about 80 percent of nondemocratic nations employ the death penalty. The United States is one of only a couple dozen democracies that employ the death penalty for ordinary crimes such as murder. Among the Western representative democracies, typically thought of as the U.S. peer group—democracies with highly developed economies that originated in western Europe or the British Commonwealth—only the United States still enforces the death penalty (see Figure 4.1).

A second objection to the death penalty is that its application is racially biased—minorities tend to be disproportionately represented on death row, and numerous studies indicate that death penalty sentences are more likely when the victim is white (Death Penalty Information Center 2012). These concerns have driven a long-running battle between opponents and proponents of the death penalty. In 2003, Illinois governor George Ryan, citing a system "fraught with error," commuted the death sentences of 167 death row inmates. Ryan's decision came after investigations showed at least 13 men convicted and sentenced to death were later exonerated and set free. His decision was celebrated by death penalty opponents and harshly criticized by proponents, who argued that the net result of the action was to literally let people get away with murder while trampling the rights of victims.

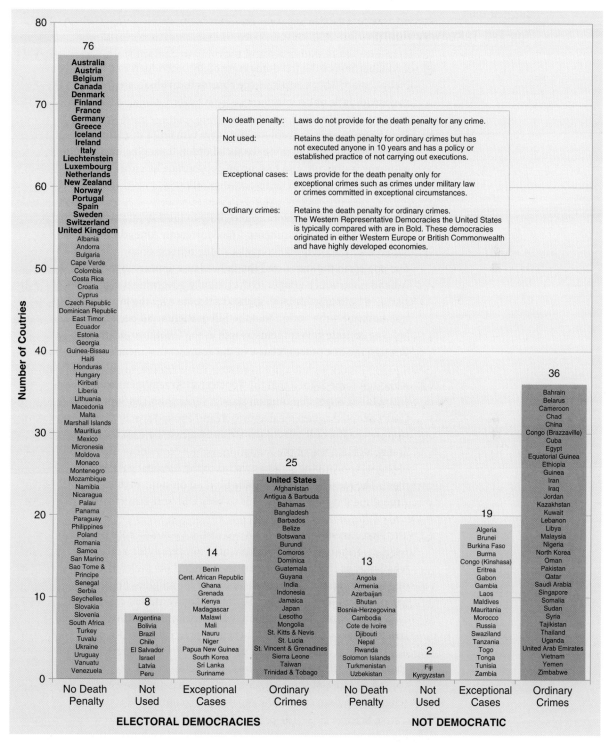

FIGURE 4.1 Democracies and the Death Penalty

Source: Constructed by the authors from Freedom House (2006) and Amnesty International (2006).

Top Ten Takeaway Points

① Civil liberties are the freedoms enjoyed by individuals in a democratic society. They constitute the choices individuals are free to make with little or no interference from governmental authority.

② Civil liberties are not absolute, and there remains a need for constraints on them to preserve social order. Balancing liberty and authority is difficult, and finding an appropriate balance is one of the central dilemmas of democratic societies.

③ The Bill of Rights originally applied only to the federal government, not to state governments. The Fourteenth Amendment added after the Civil War contains a "due process of law" clause that applies to the states, and the same clause appears in the Fifth Amendment, which applies to the national government. The same clause in both amendments sparked a debate over the incorporation doctrine—the notion that the Bill of Rights had been made binding on state governments as well as the federal government through the due process clause of the Fourteenth Amendment.

④ Although some argued that the Fourteenth Amendment made the entire Bill of Rights binding on state governments, the Supreme Court adopted a piecemeal approach and applied specific provisions in the Bill of Rights to the states on a case-by-case basis. Today, all but a few of the limitations on government in the Bill of Rights apply to the states as well as to the national government. The most recent right made binding on states is the Second Amendment right of individuals to keep and bear arms.

⑤ The First Amendment contains two distinct guarantees to protect religious freedom: First, government cannot establish a religion, which means that public authorities cannot show preference for one set of religious beliefs over others, or for religious beliefs in general over nonreligious beliefs. Second, government cannot prohibit the free exercise of religion, which means that individuals are free to choose which religious beliefs to practice or not to practice any religion at all. These two guarantees are related because if government uses its power to establish a religion, then it also prevents the free exercise of some religious beliefs. These guarantees of religious freedom call for the separation of church and state.

⑥ The First Amendment's specific guarantees of freedom of speech and the press, of the right of peaceful assembly, and of the right to petition the government for redress of grievances establish a general right to freedom of expression. Freedom of expression is the means by which individuals and groups can express their views and communicate them to one another as well as to public officials. Freedom of expression is not absolute and can be limited in some circumstances, and some forms of expression such as libel and slander and obscenity are not protected forms of expression.

⑦ Although the Constitution does not explicitly articulate a right to privacy, the Supreme Court has held that various guarantees in the First, Third, Fourth, Fifth, and Ninth Amendments create "zones of privacy" that the government has no right to invade.

⑧ The rules governing criminal procedure and the rights of the accused are found in the Fourth, Fifth, Sixth, Eighth, and Fourteenth Amendments.

⑨ The exclusionary rule prohibits the use of evidence and confessions obtained in violation of constitutional rights in federal or state trials. This practice is controversial, but the courts have been unable to find a better way to protect individuals' rights from unreasonable illegal government action.

⑩ The Eighth Amendment prohibits "cruel and unusual punishment." Few Supreme Court justices have taken the position that capital punishment is inherently unconstitutional. Recent challenges have focused on whether the death penalty is applied in ways that satisfy constitutional rights.

5 CIVIL RIGHTS

KEY QUESTIONS

What are civil rights?

What is the difference between civil rights and civil liberties?

What groups have historically been denied civil rights?

JENNIFER GRATZ was determined to gain admittance into the University of Michigan at Ann Arbor, an institution not far from her home in Southgate, a working-class suburb of Detroit. Founded in 1817, the university's motto—"An uncommon education for the common man"—seemed particularly apt for the blue-collar Gratz. Neither of her parents, a retired police sergeant and a secretary, was a college graduate, and she would have to bootstrap her way into one of the most prestigious public universities in the nation.

She was willing to put in the work to achieve this dream. She finished high school ranked twelfth in her class of 298, with a GPA of 3.76. She did well on the ACT (eighty-third percentile). She was the vice president of the student council, the homecoming queen, and a math tutor, and she participated in athletics. She was so focused on Michigan that she did not even bother applying anywhere else. When she was rejected, she was stunned. Rejections from major universities are not uncommon, and upon receiving them, most students try to make the best of their other options. Not Gratz. She made a federal case of her rejection—literally. She sued, and the case went all the way to the Supreme Court.

Gratz believed that what had kept her out of the University of Michigan was not her record, but her race. Gratz is white, and at the time the University of Michigan's admissions system gave preference to minorities. Applicants were ranked on a point system that, although heavily tilted toward academic achievement, also awarded points for membership in certain groups. These groups included state residents (extra points for applicants from Michigan), legacies (points if your parents or stepparents went to the university), scholarship athletes, and those from socioeconomically disadvantaged backgrounds. Also included were racial minorities. At the heart of the Gratz lawsuit was the claim that this latter category amounted to an unfair and unconstitutional racial preference.

The university disagreed. In a selective school such as Michigan, there are always more applicants than available slots. Everyone agreed that the admissions process should emphasize academic merit. The university, however, argued that other factors, including race and ethnicity, should be taken into account because a diverse campus has a number of social, cultural, and academic benefits. Besides, given the highly competitive nature of Michigan and the existing emphasis on academic merit, it seemed highly unlikely that the small weight given to race had made any real impact on the decision regarding Gratz's admission. Eliminating race as an admissions factor, the university argued, was less likely to let more people like Gratz in than it was to keep minorities out (Younge 2003).

At stake in the Court's decision was not just the University of Michigan's admissions policy, but the broader concept of **affirmative action**, or governmental actions designed to help minorities overcome the effects of past discrimination and compete on an equal basis with the majority. Throughout the history of the United States, the majority has erected social, political, and legal barriers that exclude minorities from participating in the political process because of their race, gender, religion, or other characteristics. This exclusion denies minorities the core democratic principles of political equality and minority rights. The effects of this sort of discrimination can persist even after the barriers are eliminated.

Affirmative action policies serve to help certain groups overcome these lingering disadvantages created by past discrimination. In doing so they are designed to help restore and uphold core democratic principles such as political equality and political freedom. Yet some see affirmative action not as a way to uphold these principles but as a means to destroy them. The core of this argument is that affirmative action seeks to redress discrimination against one group by discriminating against another group. This view was the underlying issue in the Gratz lawsuit and in a companion case that examined the admissions process for Michigan's law school. There was a delicate balancing act here. Most agreed that a diverse student body served a greater social good; the question was whether this could be achieved without discriminating on the basis of race.

In *Gratz v. Bollinger* (2003) the Court walked something of a middle line. It struck down Michigan's undergraduate admissions system but

affirmative action Governmental actions designed to help minorities compete on an equal basis and overcome the effects of discrimination in the past.

upheld the right of public universities to use race as a factor in the admissions process. Universities can continue to use race as an admission criterion, but only if they can demonstrate that doing so promotes the educational benefits that flow from a diverse student body (Biskupic 2003). The Supreme Court decision did nothing to dampen the controversy over affirmative action policies, however.

Gratz went on to become the executive director of the Michigan Civil Rights Initiative, an organization that successfully spearheaded a ballot initiative to amend the Michigan state constitution to ban affirmative action policies by state institutions; it was overwhelmingly passed by state voters in 2006. Among other things, the amendment specifically prohibits higher educational institutions such as the University of Michigan from granting preferential treatment to anyone on the basis of race, sex, or national origin. Other states passed similar initiatives limiting affirmative action or even seeking to ban it outright.

Opposition to affirmative action from some perspectives is understandable. Some studies show that people like Gratz (working-class whites) are indeed disadvantaged by college application processes (Espenshade and Radford 2009). Yet this reflects exclusion by class as much as race. There is also still plenty of evidence that nonwhites suffer systematic discrimination, and not just in college applications. So perhaps there is as strong a case to expand affirmative action as to end it.

Regardless of the ultimate fate of affirmative action, it is a certainty that controversies over whether certain groups in American society are being systematically denied rights and liberties enjoyed by others will continue. How such rights are guaranteed by government, and what government does when those rights are denied, cuts to the heart of the core democratic values of political equality and minority rights. In this chapter, we explore the struggles undertaken by several groups in attempts to achieve equality.

THE CONCEPT OF CIVIL RIGHTS

Civil rights are the rights of all citizens to legal, social, and economic equality. The key word here is *all*. The liberties granted by the First Amendment, for

civil rights The obligations placed on government to protect the freedom of the people.

example, are supposed to apply equally to all citizens. Your race, socioeconomic status, age, or sexual orientation is not supposed to matter. As civil rights, these liberties belong to all in society, not just to those who have a certain skin pigment or sexual preference. Yet these factors have mattered and in some cases still do. Certain liberties and freedoms are denied to some simply because they belong to a particular group. If and how civil liberties are guaranteed to all groups and what government should do when those rights are denied to specific groups cuts to the heart of the core democratic principle of political equality. It is this group aspect and the government's responsibility to act or not to act that distinguishes civil rights from civil liberties.

In chapter 4, we learned that individual citizens have civil liberties, or the freedom to make individual decisions. In order to ensure they enjoy those freedoms, limits are placed on the coercive power of government to prevent government from using its power to arbitrarily deny individuals the right to exercise their civil liberties. Civil rights, in contrast, impose an obligation on government to actively use its coercive powers to ensure that those freedoms are not arbitrarily denied to certain categories of citizens. The metaphor of the "shield and sword" (*Pollock v. Williams* 1944) serves to clarify the distinction between civil liberties and civil rights. Questions of civil liberties—the shield—center on the issue of protecting individual freedom from government interference. Questions of civil rights—the sword—center on the issue of government's obligation to take action to protect individual freedoms from other outside interference. The shield, or civil liberty, is a negative safeguard: "it enables a person whose freedom is endangered to invoke the Constitution" to invalidate government action (Carr 1947, 3). The sword, or civil rights, is a "positive weapon wielded by the federal government, which takes the initiative in protecting helpless individuals by bringing criminal charges against persons who are encroaching upon their rights" (Carr 1947, 5).

Historically, both federal and state governments have tolerated unequal treatment of citizens based on characteristics such as race, gender, and religion. The most notorious example is the treatment of African Americans. In the name of political pragmatism, the founders accepted the institution of slavery and enshrined in the Constitution the value of slaves (referred to as "other persons") as three-fifths of a person for purposes of taxation and representation (Article I, Section 2). Since most blacks were slaves at the time, the Constitution itself violated the civil rights of a large section of the population on the basis of race. Even for free African Americans and even after the abolition of slavery, basic liberties such as the right to vote were systematically denied on the basis of race.

African Americans are not the only group to wage an extended battle over the federal government's duty to prevent their freedoms from being arbitrarily denied. Other racial and ethnic minorities—including Native Americans and Latinos—have suffered like discrimination and have faced similar obstacles. Additionally, it is not just racial and ethnic groups that have been systematically denied rights and liberties. Other groups include women, people with disabilities, and gays and lesbians. Age has also been a battleground for civil rights. During the Vietnam War, young people were angry that their government could send them to fight in a war but would not allow them to vote and have input on the decision to wage the war in the first place. This concern was the driving force behind the Twenty-Sixth Amendment, adopted in 1971, that guarantees all citizens aged 18 or older the right to vote. On the other end of the spectrum, advocates for the elderly have fought mandatory retirement and age discrimination in employment. Other groups with civil rights agendas include everyone from welfare recipients to smokers.

In short, the list of groups that have fought or are fighting extensive civil rights campaigns is long, and to do them all justice would require a book unto itself. Although we cannot examine every struggle to gain equal access to the rights and privileges of citizenship in one chapter of a textbook, we can examine some representative cases to give a sense of how groups denied civil liberties have sought to get government to act not just as a shield, but as a sword.

AFRICAN AMERICANS

Slavery systematically denied civil rights to large numbers of African Americans for almost the entire first century of the republic's history. The end of the Civil War brought with it a constitutional ban on slavery. In the postwar period, the federal government embarked on a program to bring liberated slaves, who were concentrated in the South, into the mainstream of American life. Congress passed legislation granting African Americans the right to sue, to give evidence in court, and to buy, sell, and inherit property. New federal laws also outlawed segregation in transportation, schools, and public accommodations. The Fifteenth Amendment specifically prohibited states from denying any adult male the right to vote on the basis of race, color, or previous condition of servitude.

Benefiting from the newfound political rights guaranteed by the federal government, African Americans made significant gains toward political equality. African Americans were elected to Congress and to numerous state and local offices. However, these advances were made possible by federal occupation forces that remained in Confederate states following the Civil War. This federal presence helped ensure that the new constitutional protections were enforced. Those federal forces and the protection they represented were withdrawn following a political deal struck between Northern Republicans and Southern Democrats in the disputed election of 1876. Southern Democrats acquiesced in the selection of Republican Rutherford B. Hayes over their candidate, Samuel J. Tilden, in return for Hayes's agreement to withdraw troops from the South when he came to office.

Racial Segregation

With the federal government's protection removed, the systematic denial of African Americans' civil and political rights spread throughout the South. Initially, **racial segregation,** or the separation of people based on their race, was based on tradition. Gradually, however, state laws segregated public schools, transportation, and accommodations by race. Other laws politically disenfranchised African Americans through a series of legal techniques such as **poll taxes** (fees required for casting a ballot), **literacy tests** (a requirement that citizens demonstrate their fitness to vote by passing a reading or comprehension test), and the exclusion of African Americans from Democratic Party primaries. In the last two decades of the nineteenth century, lynching was used to deter African Americans from exercising their constitutional rights. By the early years of the twentieth century, segregation of African Americans through intimidation and disenfranchisement was complete in the southern states.

At about the same time, however, the locus of race problems began to shift. The overwhelming proportion of African Americans had been concentrated in the rural South. But millions began migrating to urban areas in the North to escape oppression and improve their lives economically. Northern cities were less than welcoming. African Americans were often shut out of white neighborhoods by residential segregation ordinances and restrictive covenants forbidding the sale of property to nonwhites. These legal means of oppression were sometimes augmented by beatings and bombings. The end result was that African Americans were often concentrated in low-rent, racially exclusive ghettoes. In terms of day-to-day life, northern ghettoes were probably better than southern plantations, but discrimination and segregation remained a central fact of life in the North as well as the South.

African Americans' reaction to being systematically denied their civil rights varied. Some, such as Booker T. Washington, urged accommodation. Others, especially a group of northern intellectuals, argued for a more active pursuit of political equality. Among the best known of this latter group was W. E. B. Du Bois, who in 1909 joined with prominent white intellectuals such as philosopher John Dewey and lawyer Clarence Darrow, among others, to form the National Association for the Advancement of Colored People (NAACP).

The Judicial Strategy to End Segregation

racial segregation The separation of people based on their race.

poll taxes A technique used to keep certain groups from voting by charging a fee to vote.

literacy tests Reading or comprehension tests that citizens are required to pass to demonstrate their fitness to vote.

Because African Americans were often prevented from exercising their right to vote, elected officials in the state legislatures and governors' mansions were unresponsive and even hostile to demands for racial equality. Excluded from the electoral process, African Americans turned to the federal courts for help in securing fundamental constitutional rights.

The NAACP became the major group fighting for civil rights and led the way in court battles to end segregation and disenfranchisement. Soon after its founding, the NAACP began a successful series of test cases on several legal fronts. Its initial victory came in *Guinn v. United States* (1915), in which the Supreme Court invalidated the **grandfather clause** of the Oklahoma constitution, a clause that exempted people whose ancestors were entitled to vote in 1866 from the literacy test. Only whites had the right to vote that year.

In the three decades following *Guinn,* the NAACP scored a number of other notable victories. The most significant was the fight to get equal treatment in public facilities such as schools. The Fourteenth Amendment prohibits states from passing or enforcing any law that would deny "any person within its jurisdiction the equal protection of the laws." Southern states responded by passing laws requiring **separate but equal** accommodations for blacks and whites in public facilities such as public transportation. An 1896 Supreme Court decision, *Plessy v. Ferguson*, ruled that separate public facilities for people of different races satisfied the Fourteenth Amendment's equal protection clause, provided they were "equal."

Initially, the NAACP tried to chip away at the "separate but equal" doctrine on a case-by-case basis. The first big victory came in *Missouri ex rel. Gaines v. Canada* (1938). The University of Missouri had refused to admit a qualified African American student to its law school, but the state offered to pay his expenses at a school in a neighboring state that admitted blacks. The Supreme Court ruled that this policy did not satisfy the state's constitutional responsibilities. "Separate but equal," in other words, meant separate but equal within the state.

After this case, the Supreme Court began to pay closer attention to whether separate facilities were actually equal. In the early 1950s, NAACP lawyers decided to abandon the policy of chipping away at the "separate but equal" doctrine and to advance the argument that separate facilities for different races in and of themselves violated the equal protection of the law clause of the Fourteenth Amendment. The strategy was vindicated in **Brown v. Board of Education** (1954), one of the most important civil rights decisions ever made by the Supreme Court. A unanimous Court overturned the "separate but equal" precedent set by *Plessy.* To give added weight to the ruling, Chief Justice Earl Warren wrote the opinion declaring that separate educational facilities are inherently unequal. Even if all the tangible characteristics of schools—such as classrooms, libraries, curricula, teachers' salaries, and teachers' qualifications—are equal, wrote Warren, the intangible quality of education is not equal in racially segregated schools. Racial segregation of public schools deprives African American children of equal protection of the laws because "to separate them from others of similar age and qualifications solely because of their race generates a feeling of inferiority . . . that may affect their hearts and minds in a way unlikely ever to be undone." The following year, the Court ordered states to dismantle the system of segregated schools "with all deliberate speed" and entrusted the federal district courts to require local school boards to comply. There was resistance to integration of the schools throughout the Deep South, and the federal judges entrusted with enforcing the Constitution were at the center of legal battles for more than a decade to follow (Peltason 1961).

grandfather clause A provision in election laws used in conjunction with literacy tests to prevent African Americans from voting. People whose ancestors were entitled to vote in 1866 (i.e., whites) were exempt from passing the literacy test, but African Americans, whose ancestors were slaves, had to pass the literacy test in order to vote. This clause was ruled unconstitutional in 1915.

separate but equal A practice in southern states to comply with the Fourteenth Amendment's "equal protection" clause by passing laws requiring separate but equal accommodations for blacks and whites in public facilities. The Supreme Court ruled such laws unconstitutional in 1954.

Plessy v. Ferguson An 1896 Supreme Court decision ruling that separate public facilities for people of different races satisfied the Fourteenth Amendment's equal protection clause, provided the facilities were "equal."

Brown v. Board of Education The 1954 case in which a unanimous Court overturned the "separate but equal" precedent set by *Plessy v. Ferguson* and declared that separate educational facilities are inherently unequal.

The Revolution in Race Relations

Although the NAACP scored significant victories in court, the legislative and executive branches of government initially did little to secure the rights of African Americans. Southern senators successfully filibustered an attempt to enact anti-lynching legislation, and even liberal presidents of the first half of the twentieth century showed little commitment to the civil rights of African Americans. Franklin Roosevelt, for example, introduced no major civil rights legislation; he issued an executive order establishing a Committee on Fair Employment Practices in 1941 only after being threatened with a march on Washington to secure job opportunities for minorities.

The first significant steps for racial equality were taken shortly after World War II, when President Harry Truman outlawed segregation of the armed services and of civilian jobs in national government and mandated that the federal government would do business only with firms that did not discriminate in hiring. Truman also proposed a broad civil rights program to Congress and appointed a committee to study race relations. Truman's successor, Dwight Eisenhower, followed up on the process of desegregating the armed forces and pushed to end segregation in the District of Columbia. The Civil Rights Act of 1957 created the U.S. Civil Rights Commission and was the first civil rights law to be passed by the federal government since the Reconstruction period following the Civil War.

By the mid-1950s, then, the judicial, executive, and legislative branches of the federal government finally had begun to take proactive steps to uphold the civil rights of African Americans. At about the same time, the civil rights movement abruptly rejected the status quo in race relations, and a large segment of the African American community refused to accept the inferior position it had been assigned in American society. As part of the civil rights movement, people began engaging in acts of **civil disobedience**, or deliberately disobeying laws viewed as morally repugnant. An event that epitomized this development was the December 1955 arrest of Rosa Parks, an African American seamstress who refused to move to the back of a municipal bus in Montgomery, Alabama. The arrest sparked a bus boycott led by a young minister, Dr. Martin Luther King Jr., and ultimately led to government action to outlaw racial segregation.

What had been a battle waged by a relatively few well-educated, middle-class African Americans became a broad movement that cut across social and economic lines. The legal battles and conciliatory negotiations with government and white leaders that had been used by groups such as the NAACP and the National Urban League came in for sharp criticism. According to Martin Luther King Jr. and others of a new generation of civil rights leaders, what was needed was direct action by the masses, including peaceful boycotts, sit-ins, and protest marches. People were no longer willing to wait for the outcome of lengthy courtroom campaigns to win rights for their children. They wanted those rights for themselves, and they wanted them soon. The reasons for this sudden shift are varied. In World War II many African Americans serving in the armed forces had the novel experience of being treated with respect by white people in France and Great Britain who gave

civil disobedience Deliberately disobeying laws viewed as morally repugnant.

them a social acceptance they had never enjoyed in their own country. Coming back from military service, they naturally resented returning to an inferior position in civilian life and desired to do something about it. Furthermore, many were keenly aware of the irony of a country's fighting a war against the racist philosophy of Nazi Germany while at the same time practicing its own brand of racism at home.

The attitudes of whites, though far from uniform, also began to change. Supreme Court decisions and executive actions indicated that the political system was either responding to or promoting more tolerant racial attitudes in the white mainstream. Capitalizing on these changes, leaders such as King began to push for full integration in all aspects of American life. King favored nonviolent tactics, or what was termed **passive resistance**, a technique of civil disobedience where individuals peacefully submit to arrest for refusing to obey laws they consider immoral. The technique was used successfully by Mahatma Gandhi to obtain India's independence from Britain. A broad coalition of new groups emerged, including the Southern Christian Leadership Conference, the Student Nonviolent Coordinating Committee, and the Congress of Racial Equality. Sympathetic whites lent support, particularly college students who went to the South to assist in registering African American voters and integrating public facilities.

On August 28, 1963, Martin Luther King Jr. delivered his "I Have a Dream" speech to over 200,000 people who marched on Washington, DC, that summer.

By the mid-1960s, some African Americans began to feel that nonviolent direct action also was too slow a method of achieving their goals, and some advocated taking civil disobedience a step further and pursuing change through violence. Leaders of the Black Muslims, a group founded in the 1930s, and the Black Panthers, an organization founded in 1966 in Oakland, California, to protect African Americans from police brutality, openly advocated violent revolution. Race riots in Los Angeles, Detroit, Washington, DC, and other major cities in the mid- to late 1960s seemed to be spontaneous mass reactions to police brutality or to the assassination of Martin Luther King Jr., not organized actions coordinated with a particular group's agenda.

Government's Response to the Race Revolution

Although the social turmoil of race relations in the 1950s and 1960s was not pretty, it did seem to affect the political system. In the summer of 1963, more than 200,000 people marched on Washington, where Martin Luther King Jr. delivered his famous "I Have a Dream" speech, one of the most eloquent declarations of the moral force behind calls for racial equity in the United States (see the Politics in Practice feature "I Have a Dream"). This march pressured the Kennedy administration into supporting the expansion of the 1957 Civil Rights Act. After Kennedy

passive resistance A nonviolent technique of protest that entails resisting government laws or practices that are believed to be unjust.

"I HAVE A DREAM"

Address delivered by Dr. Martin Luther King Jr. at the March on Washington for Jobs and Freedom, August 28, 1963.

I am happy to join with you today in what will go down in history as the greatest demonstration for freedom in the history of our nation.

Five score years ago, a great American, in whose symbolic shadow we stand today, signed the Emancipation Proclamation. This momentous decree came as a great beacon light of hope to millions of Negro slaves who had been seared in the flames of withering injustice. It came as a joyous daybreak to end the long night of their captivity.

But one hundred years later, the Negro still is not free. One hundred years later, the life of the Negro is still sadly crippled by the manacles of segregation and the chains of discrimination. One hundred years later, the Negro lives on a lonely island of poverty in the midst of a vast ocean of material prosperity. One hundred years later, the Negro is still languished in the corners of American society and finds himself an exile in his own land. And so we've come here today to dramatize a shameful condition.

In a sense we've come to our nation's capital to cash a check. When the architects of our republic wrote the magnificent words of the Constitution and the Declaration of Independence, they were signing a promissory note to which every American was to fall heir. This note was a promise that all men, yes, black men as well as white men, would be guaranteed the "unalienable Rights of Life, Liberty, and the pursuit of Happiness." It is obvious today that America has defaulted on this promissory note insofar as her citizens of color are concerned. Instead of honoring this sacred obligation, America has given the Negro people a bad check, a check which has come back marked "insufficient funds."

But we refuse to believe that the bank of justice is bankrupt. We refuse to believe that there are insufficient funds in the great vaults of opportunity of this nation. And so we've come to cash this check, a check that will give us upon demand the riches of freedom and the security of justice.

We have also come to this hallowed spot to remind America of the fierce urgency of now. This is no time to engage in the luxury of cooling off or to take the tranquilizing drug of gradualism. Now is the time to make real the promises of democracy. Now is the time to rise from the dark and desolate valley of segregation to the sunlit path of racial justice. Now is the time to lift our nation from the quicksands of racial injustice to the solid rock of brotherhood. Now is the time to make justice a reality for all of God's children.

It would be fatal for the nation to overlook the urgency of the moment. This sweltering summer of the Negro's legitimate discontent will not pass until there is an invigorating autumn of freedom and equality. Nineteen sixty-three is not an end, but a beginning. And those who hope that the Negro needed to blow off steam and will now be content will have a rude awakening if the nation returns to business as usual. There will be neither rest nor tranquility in America until the Negro is granted his citizenship rights. The whirlwinds of revolt will continue to shake the foundations of our nation until the bright day of justice emerges.

But there is something that I must say to my people, who stand on the warm threshold which leads into the palace of justice: In the process of gaining our rightful place, we must not be guilty of wrongful deeds. Let us not seek to satisfy our thirst for freedom by drinking from the cup of bitterness and hatred. We must forever conduct our struggle on the high plane of dignity and discipline. We must not allow our creative protest to degenerate into physical violence. Again and again, we must rise to the majestic heights of meeting physical force with soul force. The marvelous new militancy which has engulfed the Negro community must not lead us to a distrust of all white people, for many of our white brothers, as evidenced by their presence here today, have come to realize that their destiny is tied up with our destiny. And they have come to realize that their freedom is inextricably bound to our freedom. We cannot walk alone.

And as we walk, we must make the pledge that we shall always march ahead. We cannot turn back. There are those who are asking the devotees of civil rights, "When will you be satisfied?" We can never be satisfied as long as the Negro is the victim of the unspeakable horrors of police brutality.

We can never be satisfied as long as our bodies, heavy with the fatigue of travel, cannot gain lodging in the motels of the highways and the hotels of the cities. We cannot be satisfied as long as the Negro's basic mobility is from a smaller ghetto to a larger one. We can never be satisfied as long as our children are stripped of their selfhood and robbed of their dignity by signs stating "for whites only." We cannot be satisfied as long as a Negro in Mississippi cannot vote and a Negro in New York believes he has nothing for which to vote. No, no, we are not satisfied and we will not be satisfied until "justice rolls down like waters and righteousness like a mighty stream."

I am not unmindful that some of you have come here out of great trials and tribulations. Some of you have come fresh from narrow jail cells. Some of you have come from areas where your quest for freedom left you battered by the storms of persecution and staggered by the winds of police brutality. You have been the veterans of creative suffering. Continue to work with the faith that unearned suffering is redemptive. Go back to Mississippi, go back to Alabama, go back to South Carolina, go back to Georgia, go back to Louisiana, go back to the slums and ghettos of our northern cities, knowing that somehow this situation can and will be changed. Let us not wallow in the valley of despair.

I say to you today, my friends, so even though we face the difficulties of today and tomorrow, I still have a dream. It is a dream deeply rooted in the American dream.

I have a dream that one day this nation will rise up and live out the true meaning of its creed: "We hold these truths to be self-evident, that all men are created equal." I have a dream that one day on the red hills of Georgia, the sons of former slaves and the sons of former slave owners will be able to sit down together at the table of brotherhood.

I have a dream that one day even the state of Mississippi, a state sweltering with the heat of injustice, sweltering with the heat of oppression, will be transformed into an oasis of freedom and justice.

I have a dream that my four little children will one day live in a nation where they will not be judged by the color of their skin but by the content of their character. I have a dream today.

I have a dream that one day down in Alabama, with its vicious racists, with its governor having his lips dripping with the words of "interposition" and "nullification," one day right there in Alabama little black boys and black girls will be able to join hands with little white boys and white girls as sisters and brothers. I have a dream today.

I have a dream that one day "every valley shall be exalted, and every hill and mountain shall be made low; the rough places will be made plain, and the crooked places will be made straight; and the glory of the Lord shall be revealed, and all flesh shall see it together."

This is our hope. This is the faith that I go back to the South with. With this faith we will be able to hew out of the mountain of despair a stone of hope. With this faith we will be able to transform the jangling discords of our nation into a beautiful symphony of brotherhood.

With this faith we will be able to work together, to pray together, to struggle together, to go to jail together, to stand up for freedom together, knowing that we will be free one day. This will be the day, this will be the day when all of God's children will be able to sing with new meaning:

My country, 'tis of thee,
sweet land of liberty, of thee I sing;
land where my fathers died,
land of the pilgrim's pride,
from every mountainside, let freedom ring!

And if America is to be a great nation, this must become true.

And so let freedom ring from the prodigious hilltops of New Hampshire.

Let freedom ring from the mighty mountains of New York.

Let freedom ring from the heightening Alleghenies of Pennsylvania.

Let freedom ring from the snowcapped Rockies of Colorado.

Let freedom ring from the curvaceous slopes of California.

But not only that: Let freedom ring from Stone Mountain of Georgia.

Let freedom ring from Lookout Mountain of Tennessee.

Let freedom ring from every hill and molehill of Mississippi.

From every mountainside, let freedom ring.

And when this happens, when we allow freedom to ring, when we let it ring from every village and every hamlet, from every state and every city, we will be able to speed up that day when all of God's children, black men and white men, Jews and Gentiles, Protestants and Catholics, will be able to join hands and sing in the words of the old Negro spiritual:

Free at last! Free at last!
Thank God
Almighty, we are free at last!

SOURCE The Martin Luther King Papers Project at Stanford University. http://www.stanford.edu/group/King. Copyright © 1963 Martin Luther King Jr., copyright renewed 1991 Coretta Scott King. Reprinted by arrangement with the Estate of Martin Luther King Jr., c/o Writers House as agent for the proprietor, New York, New York.

Civil Rights Act of 1964 The landmark law that outlawed racial segregation in schools and public places and barred discrimination in employment based on sex.

Jim Crow laws Laws designed to prevent African Americans from voting.

Voting Rights Act of 1965 Act authorizing the federal government to ensure that eligible voters were not denied access to the ballot, actively protecting the Fifteenth Amendment's promise of voting rights for African Americans.

was assassinated in November 1963, President Lyndon B. Johnson, acting with the moral authority bestowed by the shadow of the slain president, picked up Kennedy's civil rights bill, strengthened it, and submitted it to Congress. The **Civil Rights Act of 1964** is a landmark law that outlawed racial segregation in schools and public places and barred discrimination in employment based on sex. Title II of the law barred racial segregation in public accommodations; Title VI outlawed racial discrimination in any program that received assistance from the federal government; and Title VII banned discrimination by employers and unions based on race, religion, sex, or national origin. That same year also saw the ratification of the Twenty-Fourth Amendment, which made poll taxes unconstitutional and strengthened the voting rights of African Americans.

A year later, Johnson signed the 1965 Voting Rights Act into law. This act targeted **Jim Crow laws** used mainly by southern states to establish racial segregation in all public facilities (such as schools, public buildings, and transportation) and to disenfranchise African Americans by requiring them to pass literacy tests, pay poll taxes, and be of "good moral character," among other things, as prerequisites to voting. Significantly, the **Voting Rights Act of 1965** authorized the federal government to ensure that eligible voters were not denied access to the ballot. For the first time, the Fifteenth Amendment's promise of voting rights for African Americans was actively being protected by the federal government. In the wake of the Voting Rights Act, millions of African Americans registered to vote, making it harder for elected officials to ignore their concerns and pressuring the political system to provide them with full political equality. And the number of black elected officials has increased. In 1965, only five members of Congress were black. As of 2012, there were 44 black members (all were members of the House; there were no African American senators).

Though still proportionally underrepresented, African Americans currently occupy significant positions in all branches of the government, not just the legislature. In 2008, Barack Obama, son of a Kenyan father and a Kansan mother, was the first African American to be elected president in the United States. Other prominent blacks in the executive branch of government as of 2012 include Attorney General Eric Holder and Surgeon General Regina Benjamin. In the judicial branch Clarence Thomas is an associate justice of the Supreme Court.

Affirmative Action

The values expressed in the Civil Rights Act and the Voting Rights Act are now firmly embedded in the American political system, and it is generally accepted that people should not be denied political equality or denied the rights of citizenship on the basis of their race. Accepting these values, however, has not ended the civil rights movement for African Americans. To help minorities who experienced discrimination (unequal or unfair treatment), implementation of affirmative action programs began in the 1970s. This shift from eliminating the legal obstacles to political equality to pursuing programs that actively seek to counter past or present effects of discrimination created a second, long-running political dispute.

The basic argument for affirmative action policies is that inequality cannot be wiped out by removing **de jure discrimination**, or discrimination by law. The effects of discrimination linger long past their official sanction in law. As President Lyndon Johnson put it,

> You do not wipe away the scars of centuries by saying: Now you are free to go where you want, do as you desire, and choose the leaders you please. . . . We seek not just freedom but opportunity. We seek not just legal equity but human ability, not just equality as a right and a theory, but equality as a fact and equality as a result. (Americans United for Affirmative Action 1999)

In other words, equality before the law was not enough. To combat the lasting effects of discrimination—in hiring, college admissions, and promotions—government needed to take proactive steps to help those groups that had been systematically excluded from the full rights and privileges of citizenship.

The argument against affirmative action is that it replaces one form of discrimination with another. Rather than promote equality, opponents argue, affirmative action actually promotes political inequality because it creates "reverse discrimination,"

de jure discrimination Discrimination that is set forth in law.

which simply means punishing whites on the basis of their race. Critics argue that if any race is discriminated against, political equality suffers. Equality before the law, however imperfect, is enough to deliver on the value of political equality.

The big disagreement in civil rights has boiled down to the conflict embodied in these two points of view. Over the past several decades, the Supreme Court has repeatedly tried to strike a balance that allows policies to promote diversity in the name of the greater social good, without promoting outright quotas or favoritism. A key early case was *Regents of the University of California v. Bakke* (1978). Allan Bakke was denied admission to medical school at the University of California, Davis, which had designated a set-aside quota for minority students. Bakke's academic record was superior to that of all of the students admitted under the quota, and he sued, claiming the school violated his Fourteenth Amendment right to equal protection of the law. The Court agreed, ruling that racial quotas violated federal law. The Court also said that although race could be used as a factor in deciding admissions, it could not be the sole criterion.

In later cases, the Court ruled that racial set-asides were constitutional under some circumstances. For example, in *United Steelworkers of America v. Weber* (1979), the Court upheld an affirmative action plan voluntarily agreed to by Kaiser Aluminum Chemical Corporation and a union representing its employees. The plan guaranteed a certain number of jobs to African Americans until the racial makeup of the company's employees reflected the racial breakdown of the local labor force. The Court said that this plan did not violate federal statute because its purpose was to redress the effects of past discrimination.

Affirmative action programs have always been criticized for providing unfair advantages to minorities and for unduly downgrading merit as the basis of social economic opportunities. This has spawned a backlash, and there have been numerous movements to eliminate race as a basis for preferential treatment. In 1996, a solid majority of California voters approved Proposition 209, which prevented the use of race as a criterion in determining school admissions, employment, government contracts, and the like. This law effectively eliminated the state's affirmative action policy. Washington State voters passed a similar ballot initiative in 1998. The Jennifer Gratz–led Michigan Civil Rights Initiative discussed at the beginning of this chapter did the same thing in that state in 2006. Nebraska followed suit in 2008 with a similar ballot initiative. Supreme Court rulings have also chipped away at affirmative action, and the Court let stand a lower court ruling in *Hopwood v. Texas* (1994) prohibiting the use of race and gender in public college admissions policies in Texas, Louisiana, and Mississippi. In *Ricci v. DeStefano* (2009) the Supreme Court ruled in favor of 19 firefighters—17 white and 2 Hispanic—in a discrimination suit involving the city of New Haven, Connecticut. The plaintiffs were all firefighters who had passed promotion exams, but the city had invalidated these results because no black firefighters had passed the exam. The city's reasoning was that it would risk a lawsuit by advancing a predominantly white group that included no blacks. The plaintiffs argued that this was a clear case of reverse discrimination; they were being denied career advancement on the basis of their race. The Supreme Court agreed, arguing that the city's decision amounted to racial discrimination, not affirmative action.

Thus, the debate over affirmative action—the conflict over whether it represents a commitment to political equality or an obstacle to political equality—continues. Proponents of affirmative action continue to argue that it is needed to ensure civil rights and to promote the social good. Derek Bok and William Bowen (1998), for example, examined the academic performance and the postgraduate activities of students admitted under affirmative action programs. They found that these students performed well in even the most selective schools and that after graduation they went on to have positive roles in the broader community. Bok and Bowen concluded that affirmative action had a positive effect on people who had historically been denied equality of opportunity and a positive impact on society as a whole, and they rejected critics' claims that affirmative action punished the deserving to boost the unqualified.

Such studies are provocative but do little to mollify critics of affirmative action who see policies that promote racial preferences as inherently unfair. Proponents of affirmative action reply that African Americans still are not on an even playing field. Implementation of affirmative action policies began in the 1970s; four decades after the federal government first took such positive steps to address historical discrimination, African Americans still lag behind the white majority on a broad variety of measures, ranging from average income to educational achievement. African Americans' earnings relative to whites has improved only slightly over the last 35 years—from around 75 percent of white workers' earnings in the 1970s and 1980s to about 80 percent in the 2000s (see Figure 5.1). And blacks lag even farther behind whites in getting a college education, though the gap has narrowed somewhat. In the 1970s, the proportion of blacks with a college education was less than half the proportion of whites, increasing to about two-thirds that of whites by the early twenty-first century.

Do these disparities reflect an inequality of opportunity that lingers as a result of discrimination? Do they reflect continued **de facto discrimination** (literally, discrimination "by fact")—patterns of segregation and social opportunity? Or are the issues more complex? There are no easy answers to such questions, and the struggle for the civil rights of African Americans is likely to continue.

African Americans are not the only group to have been systematically denied the full rights and privileges of citizenship on the basis of race and ethnicity. Though no other group has suffered the wholesale indignity of being reduced to property or singled out as counting for only three-fifths of a person in the Constitution, other racial and ethnic minorities have also long struggled for political equality. Two of the most notable of these groups are Latinos, the single largest ethnic minority in the U.S. population, and Native Americans.

de facto discrimination Discrimination that exists in fact, in real life, or in practice.

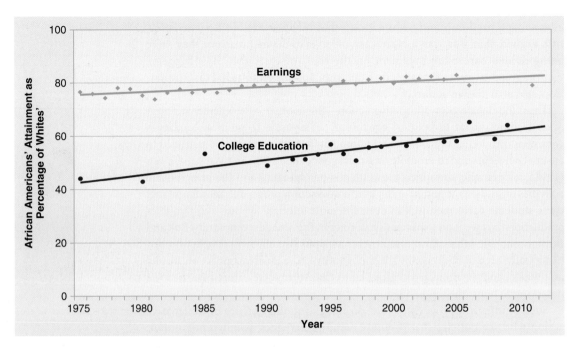

FIGURE 5.1 **African Americans' Earnings and College Education Relative to Whites**

Sources: U.S. Census Bureau, Current Population Survey, Annual Social and Economic Supplements Table P-43: Full-Time, Year-Round All Workers by Median Earnings and Sex: 1960 to 2006. (Workers 15 years old and over with earnings beginning with March 1980, and workers 14 years old and over with earnings as of March of the following year for previous years. Before 1989 earnings are for civilian workers only.)

Bureau of Labor Statistics, "Median Usual Weekly Earnings of Full-Time Wage and Salary Workers by Age, Race, Hispanic or Latino Ethnicity, and Sex, Fourth Quarter 2011 averages," http://www.bls.gov/news.release/wkyeng.t03.htm.

LATINOS

Latinos, or people who came from or whose ancestors came from Spanish-speaking nations or Latin America, are the fastest-growing ethnic minority in the United States. They are also the largest, having passed African Americans as the largest minority group. In 2010, the U.S. Census Bureau estimated that there were 50.5 million Hispanics in the country, or 16 percent of the population, compared to 42 million African Americans or 13.6 percent of the population. Latinos account for roughly half of all population growth in the United States (U.S. Census Bureau 2011). Mexican Americans are the most numerous, and their political power has been increasing in many states, particularly in the Southwest.

The initial experience of Mexican Americans with American society was as a conquered people. The Treaty of Guadalupe Hidalgo, which ended the Mexican-American War in 1848, ceded parts of what are now seven southwestern and western states to the United States. The treaty guaranteed Mexican Americans living in these areas citizenship and certain land grants and rights. But these rights were rapidly abrogated as land was seized by both legal and illegal means by cotton plantation owners, cattle and sheep ranchers, miners, and farmers. Some Mexican Americans struck back with armed raids, and even after the violence subsided, the divisions remained well into the twentieth century.

A half-century after Martin Luther King Jr. gave his famous "I Have a Dream" speech, racial inequities and what the government should or should not do to address those inequities remains a divisive and contentious issue in American politics.

During the Great Depression, the government succeeded in deporting some Mexican Americans, and groups such as the League of United Latin American Citizens (LULAC) had to work hard to gain even a semblance of integration into mainstream American life. About a million Mexican Americans fought in World War II, and Mexican American combat units were often highly decorated. The industrial war effort drew many others into urban centers, where for the first time they obtained high-paying skilled jobs. The GI Bill of Rights enabled Mexican American veterans to go to college and receive other benefits, such as housing and expanded economic opportunities. As a result, Mexican Americans, along with Latinos in general, increasingly refused to accept second-class status and, like African Americans, began to demand social equality. Significant progress has been made, but even after decades of civil rights progress, Latinos still lag behind whites in income and education, and they often face the additional burden of language barriers. Indeed, there are some indications that Latinos have lost ground over the last three decades. Latinos earned about three-fourths the earnings of whites in the mid-1970s. By 2011, Latino earnings had fallen to about two-thirds of white earnings. The gap in getting a college education is even bigger. From 1975 to the 2000s, the proportion of Latinos with a college education remained flat, at only about 40 percent the proportion of whites (see Figure 5.2).

The civil rights struggle of Latinos combines litigation and political activism. Among the groups spearheading these efforts during the past four decades have been the Mexican American Legal Defense and Educational Fund (MALDEF) and the Puerto Rican Legal Defense and Education Fund (PRLDEF). These groups often model their tactics on the litigation pursued by the NAACP, and they have focused their efforts on issues related to education. They have scored notable successes in lawsuits seeking more equitable distribution of resources for schools, implementation of bilingual programs, and equal access to higher education. They have also fought aggressively to protect Latinos' voting rights and to increase their

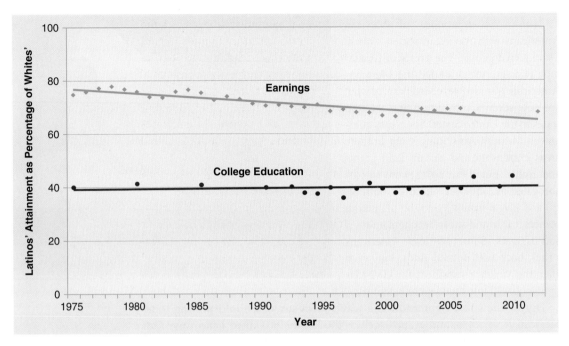

FIGURE 5.2 **Latinos' Earnings and College Education Relative to Whites**

Sources: U.S. Census Bureau, Current Population Survey, Annual Social and Economic Supplements Table P-43: Full-Time, Year-Round All Workers by Median Earnings and Sex: 1960 to 2006. (Workers 15 years old and over with earnings beginning with March 1980, and workers 14 years old and over with earnings as of March of the following year for previous years. Before 1989 earnings are for civilian workers only.)

Bureau of Labor Statistics, "Median Usual Weekly Earnings of Full-Time Wage and Salary Workers by Age, Race, Hispanic or Latino Ethnicity, and Sex, Fourth Quarter 2011 averages," http://www.bls.gov/news.release/wkyeng.t03.htm.

representation in the political process. For example, in *White v. Register* (1973), a test case brought by MALDEF, the Supreme Court overturned multimember electoral districts in Texas, agreeing with arguments that such districts unfairly stacked the deck by making it harder for minority candidates to win a majority.

These sorts of victories, combined with their numbers, have made Latinos an important political force in recent decades, especially in the Southwest. Yet their representation in elected and appointive office still does not reflect their relative proportion of the voting-age population. The number of Latino members in Congress, for example, increased from 4 in 1965 to 32 in 2012 (30 in the House, 2 in the Senate). But this level of representation in Congress is only about one-third as large as the Latino voting-age population. Consequently, issues that resonate in Latino communities, such as bilingual programs and access to educational opportunities, are not always fully represented in the policymaking process. Even when these issues are pushed into the political process, they are often perceived as attempts to limit the rights of Latinos rather than expand them. Immigrant access to public services is perhaps the best-known recent example of this. Much of the growth in the Latino population is being driven by immigration, and Latino immigrants—especially undocumented, or "illegal," Latino immigrants—have faced a backlash. This backlash is ironic because the United States views itself as a nation of immigrants, evidenced by the inscription on the base of the Statue of Liberty welcoming prospective Americans: "Give me your tired, your poor, your huddled masses." Political developments over the past decade or two have sent a clear message that the welcome does not apply to undocumented immigrants (who often end up existing on the margins of the economy and are thus often tired and almost always poor).

Most recently, this message was perhaps most forcefully made by an Arizona law passed in 2010 that made it a state crime (not just a federal crime) to be an undocumented immigrant. The law cracks down on those who hire, transport, or shelter undocumented immigrants and obliges law enforcement officers to check for immigration status and to arrest individuals if there is probable cause to believe they are undocumented. Following Arizona's lead, lawmakers in at least 30 other states introduced similar laws, and five were actually enacted (in Utah, Indiana, South Carolina, Georgia, and Alabama). These laws sparked fierce debate. Opponents saw them as enshrining racial profiling into law and unfairly—and unconstitutionally—targeting the civil rights of Latinos. Supporters argue that states were all but forced to act on illegal immigration because of the federal government's continued inaction on the issue.

Such state-level anti-immigration laws are not new. Proposition 187, for example, was passed by California voters in 1994. This law required California law enforcement, health care, and social welfare agencies to check and verify citizenship status, report undocumented immigrants to federal authorities, and deny undocumented immigrants access to services. LULAC, among others, spearheaded efforts to overturn Proposition 187 in the courts, and it was eventually ruled unconstitutional.

The Arizona law was challenged on similar grounds by a number of groups, including the Mexican American Legal Defense Fund, the NAACP, and the National Coalition of Latino Clergy and Christian Leaders. In *Arizona v. United States* (2012) the Supreme Court upheld the centerpiece of Arizona's law, ruling its "show me your papers" provision constitutional. This, in effect, allows state law enforcement officers to investigate the immigration status of anyone they stop or arrest. However, the Court struck down a number of other provisions contained in the Arizona law—for example, its imposition of criminal penalties for undocumented immigrants who seek work in the state. It is too soon to assess the full impact of the Court's decision on state-level immigration laws, though the ruling does clear the way for states to establish at least some minimal form of anti-immigration laws.

Although measures aimed at illegal immigration have proved popular with voters, they have also prompted political action and organization by Latinos. At least as of yet, there is no broad-scale civil rights movement equivalent to the black civil rights movement of the 1960s, but as a significant and growing portion of the population, Latinos represent a potential powerful political force. Laws such as Proposition 187 and Arizona's illegal immigration law may help trigger that potential into reality. (See the Politics in Practice feature "Undocumented Immigrants, Civil Rights, and Latino Political Power.")

UNDOCUMENTED IMMIGRANTS, CIVIL RIGHTS, AND LATINO POLITICAL POWER

The black civil rights movement of the 1950s and 1960s unified African Americans behind a common cause and created a cohesive and powerful movement for change. But even though Latinos are the largest minority group in the United States, they have never coalesced into a similarly effective political force. Consider, for example, that although Latinos outnumber African Americans in the population, there are more African American members of Congress than Latino members (41–30 in 2012).

There are a number of explanations for this sort of underrepresentation. For one thing, Latino nations are a diverse set of countries with different cultures, outlooks, and their own sets of socioeconomic and ethnic divisions. Unsurprisingly, people with roots in these countries tend to use people with similar homelands as their reference group. In much the way that several generations of European immigrants saw themselves as Italian, German, and Irish rather than "white," Latinos tend to see themselves as Mexicans, Puerto Ricans, and Guatemalans. Without a universal rallying point to unify these disparate groups, it is hard to build a coherent political movement.

The issue that seems most likely to unite and galvanize Latinos is illegal immigration. By some estimates, there are 11 million or more undocumented immigrants in the United States, the greater proportion of them Latino. Many work in low-paying jobs in agricultural, construction, or service industries. Many pay taxes and are productive members of their communities. Yet undocumented immigrants are, by law, denied rights granted to all other groups. Citizenship is the universal requirement to enjoy the core benefits of democracy. For example, without citizenship, one has no right to vote, and making one's views known creates the risk of deportation. In some states, undocumented immigrants may even be denied basic public services.

Many in the Latino community view the nation's approach to illegal immigration as inherently unfair. On the one hand, businesses want cheap labor and all but encourage the hiring of undocumented immigrants, a practice the government does little to discourage. Yet undocumented immigrants live in a shadow world, denied not only the basic rights of citizenship but also the opportunity to earn those rights and become a citizen. Hundreds of thousands of Latinos participated in demonstrations calling for immigration reform in 2006. These demonstrations occurred in most major cities and drew comparisons to seminal movements of the black civil rights movement such as the 1963 March on Washington. It seemed a new Latino civil rights movement was about to emerge, one centered on securing civil rights—or at least the opportunity for civil rights—for undocumented immigrants.

NATIVE AMERICANS

Native Americans, or American Indians, are the original inhabitants of the land that became the United States. As the European settlers moved westward, tribe after tribe was chased off its land, and the remaining tribes were moved onto reservations, mostly in the West. Some scholars and critics have equated the

Almost immediately, however, this movement drew a considerable backlash from those who argued that the comparison to the civil rights movement of the 1960s was misleading. These critics pointed out that African Americans were citizens, legal members of the polity who were being arbitrarily denied rights enjoyed by others simply on the basis of their skin color. Undocumented immigrants, on the other hand, are not citizens and have broken the nation's laws. Though legally recognized immigrants do not have the same rights as citizens (for example, no right to vote), they do have constitutionally protected civil liberties. For example, they have freedom of expression and freedom of religion, have access to public services, and can basically live their lives as they please without government intervention. In other words, for authorized immigrants the issue of civil rights is largely moot.

Some commentators, such as Ian de Silva, view attempts to equate undocumented immigration and the black civil rights movement as "morally bankrupt. . . . If illegal aliens have a moral claim to civil rights, then a band of burglars marching down the street protesting tough burglary laws also deserve moral respect." De Silva is himself a self-described "Third World immigrant who went to a great deal of trouble to come here legally." Others were simply offended by pictures of demonstrators waving the flags of other nations or chanting slogans in Spanish—this struck many as the wrong way to go about demanding the right to become an American.

Whether undocumented immigration will become the catalyst for a Latino civil rights movement is yet to be determined. The mass demonstrations of 2006 did not translate into immigration reform, though in the years that followed, a series of events served to reshape the immigration landscape. High unemployment and a general lack of economic opportunities in the years following the great recession of 2008–2009 dramatically reduced illegal immigration into the United States (by some estimates, the number of undocumented immigrants living in the United States dropped by about a million between 2007 and 2011), and crackdowns at the state and local levels also decreased the incentives for undocumented immigration. The latter has been a political flashpoint for several years. Because the federal government has proven unwilling or unable to comprehensively tackle immigration reform, states and localities have stepped into the breach, and these reforms have a strong anti-immigration focus. (See the "Latinos" section in this chapter for a discussion of the Arizona law.) These laws have, to some extent, fueled political activism among Latinos and civil rights groups who often see these laws as amounting to little more than legalized racial profiling. Thus far, however, opposition to illegal immigration has not coalesced into a movement allowing Latinos to exercise political influence proportionate to their presence in the population.

SOURCES Pew Hispanic Center. "Unauthorized Immigration Population: National and State Trends, 2010." http://www.pewhispanic.org/2011/02/01/unauthorized-immigrant-population-brnational-and-state-trends-2010/ (accessed March 14, 2012).

de Silva, Ian. "Illegal Immigration Is Not a Civil Right." *Human Events Online*. http://www.humaneventsonline.com (accessed June 19, 2006).

Williams, Juan. 2006. "A Hispanic Civil Rights Movement." *Washington Post*, April 10.

treatment of Native Americans by the U.S. government with **genocide**, which is the deliberate destruction of a population.

Historically, native tribes were considered independent nations, and the U.S. government's legal relationship with individuals in the tribes operated through the tribal governments. The Constitution (Article I, Section 8) specifically refers to Indian tribes, granting Congress "the power to regulate commerce with foreign nations, among the several states, and with the Indian tribes."

genocide The killing of an entire race of people.

These relationships were codified in a confusing legal tangle of hundreds of treaties made with different tribal authorities. This government-to-government relationship differentiates the struggle for civil rights for Native Americans from that of other racial and ethnic minorities. The rights of Native Americans derive from their legal status as members or descendants of a tribe that is a separate nation rather than from their race (Strickland 1992).

Government policies toward Native Americans have changed repeatedly. Overall, the nineteenth century saw organized campaigns to rob Native Americans of their traditional ways of life. These campaigns repeatedly demonstrated that Native Americans were being systematically and clearly denied the rights and protections taken for granted by most U.S. citizens, including basic property rights, freedom of movement, and voting rights. Indeed, it was not until near the end of the nineteenth century that Native Americans were formally recognized as persons who were entitled to the rights and protections of the law. This question was addressed in the landmark case of *Standing Bear v. Crook* (1879). Standing Bear was a chief of the Ponca, a tribe that had been relocated by the federal government from its traditional homeland in Nebraska to Oklahoma. The relocation was devastating to the tribe, which suffered from disease and starvation. Among the fatalities was Standing Bear's son, Bear Shield. Honoring a promise to his son, Standing Bear took Bear Shield back to Nebraska to be buried in his ancestral home. On orders from Secretary of the Interior Carl Schurz, Standing Bear was arrested for leaving the reservation in Oklahoma. With the aid of a sympathetic attorney and some government officials, Standing Bear sued for a writ of habeas corpus, a legal action that requires whoever is holding a prisoner to bring him before a court and demonstrate that he is being detained legally.

In May 1879, U.S. District Court Judge Elmer Dundy ruled in Standing Bear's favor, finding that he was being held illegally by federal authorities. More importantly, Dundy set the precedent that "an Indian is a person" and therefore entitled to the rights and protections of the law. This was a critical step in establishing the civil rights of Indians; until Dundy's decision federal authorities had pretty much been able to treat Native Americans in whatever way was politically expedient, regardless of whether it violated their rights.

The decision stopped a long way from fully protecting Native Americans, however. For example, Dundy's ruling never explicitly addressed the question of citizenship and left intact constraints on Native Americans that did not apply to U.S. citizens. For example, even though Standing Bear was set free, the federal government retained the power to arrest Native Americans who left reservations without permission. Native Americans were not formally incorporated as full U.S. citizens with universal voting rights until Congress passed the American Indian Citizenship Act in 1924—54 years after ratification of the Fifteenth Amendment (1870) that formally enfranchised African American men and 4 years after ratification of the Nineteenth Amendment (1920) extending the franchise to women. Although this federal law clearly says that "Indians [are] citizens of the United States," several, mostly western, states perpetuated legal barriers to prevent Native Americans from exercising their right to vote, parallel to the Jim Crow laws used against

African Americans in the South, long after 1924. But "Jim Crow, Indian style" (Svingen 1987; Wolfley 1991) was different in that these laws relied on Native Americans' unique legal status as members of a separate nation under the guardianship of the federal government. Some claimed that Native Americans who lived on reservations were not eligible to vote because they were not "residents" of the state. Others claimed that because state taxes did not apply on the reservation, Native Americans would not have to obey the laws these taxes helped produce. Others refused to give Indians citizenship rights unless they became "civilized" by severing their tribal ties (Berman and Salant 1998; McCool 1985; Wolfley 1991). The Voting Rights Act of 1965 and amendments in 1975 and 1982 helped Native Americans secure their voting rights. Nonetheless, government officials and non-Indian citizens in some states still engage in a number of practices to discriminate against Native Americans and prevent them from voting (Svingen 1987).

Because of this continuing discrimination, like African Americans, Native Americans turned to the courts in their fight for civil rights, and in the past few decades, they have managed to score a number of important victories regarding treaty violations, including rulings granting hunting and fishing rights and awarding substantial financial compensation for past wrongs. Congress has passed laws guaranteeing First Amendment rights and criminal due process protection to Native Americans living in federally supported housing and has also provided welfare, education, and food-stamp programs, community development grants, and federal funds for tribally controlled colleges.

Native Americans' struggle to create a coordinated, broad-scale civil rights movement has been hindered by separate tribal identities, the geographical separation of tribes, and the literally hundreds of separate treaties governing tribal relationships with the federal government. It was not until the 1960s that Native Americans began to take coordinated action. In 1970, the Native American Rights Fund (NARF) was founded to pursue the litigation tactics proven successful by the NAACP and MALDEF. The NARF's legal advocates, who are Native Americans with expertise in Indian law, have successfully used the courts to secure fishing and hunting rights, support tribal land claims, and advance Native American rights in a broad variety of areas.

Other Native American groups have engaged in more radical activities. The best-known incident to focus national attention on the plight of Native Americans was the 71-day occupation of Wounded Knee, South Dakota, in 1973 by 200 members of the American Indian Movement (AIM). The AIM wanted, among other things, a federal investigation into the condition of Native American tribal communities and a review of the 300 treaties between tribes and the federal government. Although this incident did not lead to any major reforms, it served to raise awareness of the grievances of some Native Americans, particularly those who wanted to follow a more traditional form of tribal governance.

Native American groups have had numerous important successes, particularly in reclaiming lands confiscated by the federal government in treaty violations or legitimized by one-sided agreements. However, Native Americans still face a number of challenges. Litigation to protect sacred sites and to gain the right to engage in religious practices involving, for example, ceremonial consumption of peyote has frequently been unsuccessful. A movement to fight negative stereotyping by challenging the practice of using epithets and tribal names as sports teams' names and mascots also has met with mixed success. Some schools have renamed their teams, but others have refused to do so. There have also been vigorous legal challenges over trademark disputes with the National Football League's Washington Redskins and Major League Baseball's Atlanta Braves and Cleveland Indians.

WOMEN

Women differ significantly from the other groups discussed in this chapter—they are not a minority in terms of numbers. Females make up slightly more than 50 percent of the U.S. population, more than 50 percent of college graduates since 1985, and in recent elections, more than 50 percent of voters. But this apparent advantage in numbers has failed to protect women from many of the same types of discrimination suffered by minorities. In the past, women were prevented from voting and owning property and denied political, social, educational, and economic opportunities. Although numerous barriers have fallen, significant obstacles remain.

Historical Background

Though still proportionally underrepresented in all levels of government, females frequently serve in high government office. Hillary Clinton twice won election to the U.S. Senate, made a strong run for the Democratic presidential nomination in 2008, and served as U.S. Secretary of State in President Obama's first administration.

The struggle for women's rights in the United States has been tied to the cause of equality for African Americans. Women made significant contributions to the abolitionist movement that sought to end slavery, but ironically, they discovered that many men who were vehemently opposed to slavery did not extend such passion to the rights of women.

© Scott Olsen/Getty Images

Women were refused the right to participate in the 1833 Philadelphia convention to form the American Anti-Slavery Society, a snub that was repeated at the 1840 World Anti-Slavery Convention in London. Among the women in the American delegation to the latter were Lucretia Mott and Elizabeth Cady Stanton. Outraged at being denied participation on the basis of their gender, Mott and Stanton organized a women's rights convention in 1848 at Seneca Falls, New York. The 300 delegates at this meeting approved a Declaration of Sentiments modeled after the Declaration of Independence: "We hold these truths to be self-evident, that all men and women are created equal; that they are endowed by their Creator with certain inalienable rights; that among these are life, liberty, and the pursuit of happiness" (quoted in McGlen and O'Connor 1983, 389). The convention marked the beginning of the women's rights movement in the United States.

Conventions similar to Seneca Falls met in different cities in the East and Midwest nearly every year until the Civil War. Although Susan B. Anthony and others argued that the struggle for the rights of African Americans and the rights of women were inseparable, the women's rights movement was temporarily suspended during the Civil War. When the movement recommenced shortly after the war, it became clear that although African Americans and women shared a number of mutual interests, they would fight separate battles. Some feminists wanted to add the word "sex" to the statement in the Fifteenth Amendment about "race, color, or previous condition of servitude." Frederick Douglass and other African American leaders opposed linking **suffrage** (the right to vote) for women and African Americans, fearing this would make it easier to defeat the amendment. Some in the women's movement agreed. They argued that if African American men were given voting rights first, it would make gaining the vote for women easier. Ultimately this argument prevailed, and the women's rights movement separated itself from the cause of racial equality.

The women's rights movement was hampered by division. Advocates agreed that female suffrage was necessary but disagreed about broader goals. In 1869, Anthony and Stanton organized the National Woman Suffrage Association, which advocated the broad cause of women's rights and regarded the vote as the means to a general improvement of women's place in society. The same year, Lucy Stone helped form the American Women Suffrage Association to concentrate on suffrage as an end rather than a means and to seek change on a state-by-state basis. The National Woman Suffrage Association was more militant, advocating an amendment to the federal Constitution. The American Woman Suffrage Association tried to appear "respectable" and avoided taking stands on controversial issues involving marriage and religion. Over time, Stone's more conservative organization gained supporters, and the women's rights movement increasingly focused on the suffrage issue. In 1890, the two groups merged into the National American Woman Suffrage Association, which evolved into a single-issue organization pursuing suffrage. In 1890, Wyoming gave women the right to vote, and by 1918, 15 states allowed women to vote (see Figure 5.3).

In time, a new generation of women suffragists threw off the conservative constraints of the National American Woman Suffrage Association. Particularly important was Alice Paul, a militant feminist who formed a small radical group called the Congressional Union in 1913. Its members were generally dissatisfied with the slow and uneven progress in the state-by-state strategy. They sought an amendment to the Constitution and were willing to use unorthodox means to achieve it, including parades, picketing of the White House, mass demonstrations, and hunger strikes. Some were willing to be jailed in order to get the issue onto the public agenda.

suffrage The right to vote.

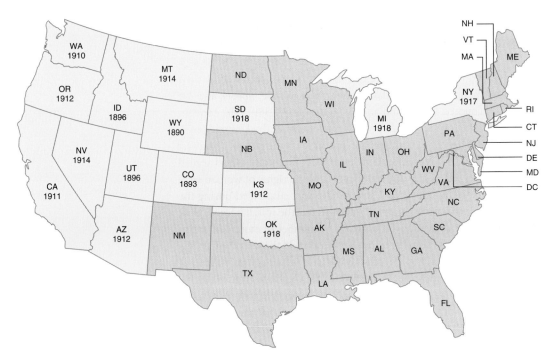

FIGURE 5.3 States (in Yellow) That Allowed Women to Vote before the Nineteenth Amendment

World War I helped promote the arguments of the Congressional Union. Women made many critical contributions to the war effort, and women's rights advocates argued that they had earned the right to vote. Under pressure from the Congressional Union, Congress proposed an amendment giving women the vote in 1919. It was ratified a year later and officially became the Nineteenth Amendment. More than 70 years after the Seneca Falls convention, the Constitution finally guaranteed that citizens' right to vote could not be "denied or abridged" on the basis of sex.

The cause of women's rights won some important victories in the years immediately following passage of the Nineteenth Amendment, including notably a federal law granting women citizenship independent of their husbands. But in general, the broad-based coalition that had grown around the suffrage issue dissolved. Only a few groups continued to actively push for women's rights. Key among them was the National Women's Party (NWP), which had evolved from the Congressional Union. In 1923, the NWP drafted an equal rights amendment (ERA), secured its introduction to Congress, and lobbied vigorously for its passage. The NWP met with little success. The proposal was reintroduced year after year but made little headway.

The movement for women's rights had some modest successes in the broader political arena. The National Federation of Business and Professional Women's

Clubs (BPW), for example, actively campaigned to open up the federal civil service to women, lobbied for equal pay legislation, and came out in favor of the ERA in 1937. But for the most part, women's rights advocates such as the NWP and BPW spent the years between World War I and World War II laboring in vain because they lacked political allies, public support, and a dramatic rallying issue like suffrage.

The Reemergence of Women's Rights

The struggle for women's rights reemerged in American life in the 1960s. This reemergence was not a result of pressure from interest groups outside the political system but rather was prompted by initiatives from within the federal government. When President Kennedy took office in 1961, he appointed Esther Peterson, a longtime labor lobbyist, to head the Women's Bureau in the Department of Labor. Peterson convinced Kennedy to establish the President's Commission on the Status of Women, a body consisting of 13 women and 11 men and headed by Eleanor Roosevelt. In October 1962, the commission issued *American Women,* a factual report on the status of women in employment and education that also contained recommendations for government action. The report was moderate in tone and achieved some concrete results. President Kennedy revised an 1870 law that had banned women from high-level federal employment, and in 1963, Congress passed the Equal Pay Act, which mandated equal pay for equal work performed under equal conditions. Both actions had been recommended by the commission.

Although these represented significant advances, some feminists had serious doubts about the way the reforms were achieved and the slow pace toward ensuring broader equality for women. The Commission on the Status of Women was seen as an easy way for Kennedy to repay his political obligations to the women who had been active in his campaign. Some feminists even suggested that Kennedy's actions were meant to take any remaining political steam out of the drive for an ERA, which the commission opposed in its final report. The 1963 Equal Pay Act was interpreted by some critics as increasing the job security of men by preventing their replacement with lower-paid women.

In the mid-1960s, a series of events converged to stimulate the formation of a new type of interest group to press for women's rights. Betty Friedan's *The Feminine Mystique* (1963) led many women to begin questioning their general situation in society. While commuting to Washington to gather material for a second book, Friedan began talking with women who worked in Congress, the executive branch, and the Citizen's Advisory Council. Many of these women wanted the Equal Employment Opportunity Commission (EEOC) to take sex discrimination in private employment as seriously as it took racial discrimination. A number of them were frustrated with groups such as the National Federation of Business and Professional Women's Clubs and the League of Women Voters, which had refused to launch campaigns against sex discrimination for fear of being labeled "militant" or "feminist."

Within this general atmosphere, a specific issue and a particular event combined to spur the creation of a new feminist interest group. The issue was the EEOC's failure to prevent newspapers from running separate job listings for men and women; the event was the third annual conference of State Commissions on the Status of Women. When the latter met in June 1966, many women wanted the group to pass a strongly worded resolution condemning sex discrimination in employment, but they were informed that the conference was not allowed to pass resolutions or take action. Outraged by the failure of the EEOC to act and disappointed in existing organizations, a group of women formed the National Organization for Women (NOW).

Incorporated in October 1966 with Betty Friedan as its first elected president, NOW passed a strongly worded resolution calling for action to bring women into the mainstream of American society. Instead of shrinking from the feminist label, this group embraced it. The NOW pressured the EEOC for favorable rulings, opposed confirmation of Supreme Court nominee G. Harrold Carswell for his anti-feminist positions, filed suit against the nation's largest corporations for sex discrimination, lobbied for funds for child care centers, and picketed all-male bars.

Women's rights advocates scored a number of important victories in the 1960s and the 1970s:

- The 1964 Civil Rights Act barred discrimination in employment based on sex.
- The Equal Opportunity Act of 1972 extended the coverage of the antidiscrimination provisions of the 1964 Civil Rights Act to educational institutions and state and local governments.
- The Education Amendment Act, also passed in 1972, prohibited sex discrimination in all federally aided education programs.
- A 1974 law extended the jurisdiction of the U.S. Commission on Civil Rights, which was originally set up to study problems of minorities, to include sex discrimination.

The most dramatic congressional victory was the passage of a proposal that had been doggedly building support for a half-century—the Equal Rights Amendment. After the original introduction of the amendment in 1923, it took two decades before first the Republicans and then the Democrats endorsed the measure as part of their party platforms. In the 1950s, the amendment twice passed the Senate but failed to gain approval in the House. By the 1970s, the pressure to pass the ERA had become overwhelming. The amendment was backed by virtually every women's rights group, President Richard Nixon, and a bipartisan group of members of Congress. In March 1972, the ERA finally received the required two-thirds vote in both the House and the Senate and was ready for ratification by three-fourths of the states.

Initially, the ERA had easy sailing at the state level, and 28 state legislatures ratified the amendment in the first year. But in 1973, the Stop ERA campaign began a national drive against the measure. Led by Phyllis Schlafly, an articulate spokeswoman for conservative causes, the campaign drew support from a number of right-leaning organizations, including the John Birch Society, the Christian Crusade, and Young Americans for Freedom. Opponents claimed that the ERA would make women eligible for the draft, deny wives the support of their husbands, and remove children from the custody of their mothers. State legislatures soon felt serious pressure to oppose the ERA, and the ratification movement lost momentum. The deadline for ratification expired in 1979, but women's groups persuaded Congress to extend it until 1982. The extra time did not help, and the ERA movement was halted just three states short of the 38 needed for ratification.

Although the ERA failed, women's rights advanced significantly in the 1980s and 1990s. Among changes made in 1972 to the 1964 Civil Rights Act were the denial of federal funds to any public or private program that discriminated on the basis of sex and the inclusion of Title IX, which required that women's athletics be given equal standing with men's athletics in schools. In 1984, Representative Geraldine A. Ferraro became the first woman to run for the vice presidency on a major-party ticket. The courts became more open to claims of sex discrimination. In 1994, Congress passed the Violence against Women Act. In 1996, the Virginia Military Institute was required to admit women or lose state funding, ending more than 150 years as an all-male state-supported college. In 2002, Representative Nancy Pelosi (D-CA) became minority party whip and then, later that same year, minority party leader. In 2005, she became the first female Speaker of the House. These are the highest offices ever held by a woman in the U.S. Congress. These examples are suggestive of a political system responsive to concerns of sex-based discrimination.

During the same period, women also began to play a greater role in the political, social, and economic life of the nation. Only 2 senators and 11 members of the House of Representatives in the Eighty-Ninth Congress (1965–1966) were women. The 112th Congress (2011–2013) included 92 women, 75 in the House of Representatives and 17 in the Senate. Women also increasingly occupy high-ranking positions in the judicial and executive branch of government. Examples include Madeleine Albright, Condoleezza Rice, and Hillary Rodham Clinton, all of whom served as secretary of state, and Supreme Court justices Sandra Day O'Connor, Ruth Bader Ginsberg, Sonia Sotomayor, and Elena Kagan. Women continue to fall far short of political equality relative to the voting-age population, but the days when a female in a high-ranking public office was a novelty have passed.

Women have also made advances in the economic arena. Women make up roughly half the U.S. labor force, and nearly 70 percent of women work full-time. Women are making significant inroads into traditionally male-dominated career fields, inroads that are reflected in the shifting patterns of education: the percentage of women studying medicine or law is approaching parity with the percentage of men (Institute for Women's Policy Research 1996, 18–25).

Nevertheless, full equality between the sexes remains an elusive goal. Men still dominate national political institutions; women are more likely to live below the poverty line than men; and some career fields remain largely segregated by sex. There also remains a persistent pay gap between males and females, with women earning about 80 percent of what men earn (see Figure 5.4). Much of this gap can be explained by work patterns; women, for example, tend to work fewer hours per year and have less full-time work experience than men. These factors cannot account for the entire gap, however, and some experts suggest that discrimination still plays a role in gender-based wage differences (General Accounting Office 2003). The potential for gender-based wage discrimination was acknowledged by Congress in 2009 when it passed the Lilly Ledbetter Fair Pay Act. Lilly Ledbetter was a longtime employee of the Goodyear Tire and Rubber Company who sued her employer for wage discrimination. After 20 years on the job, Ledbetter was receiving significantly less pay than male colleagues with similar experience. Although no one disagreed that Ledbetter was getting less money than comparable males, there was a big disagreement over whether the disparity reflected gender discrimination or job performance. (Ledbetter's pay, like that of her male colleagues, was determined in large part by performance reviews.) What constituted wage discrimination was never fully defined in this case because in *Ledbetter v. Goodyear Tire and Rubber Co.* (2007) the Supreme Court sidestepped the core issue and ruled against Ledbetter on technical grounds. Under the provisions of civil rights laws at the time, there was a 180-day statute of limitations to file a claim for pay discrimination. In other words, if an employer engaged in wage discrimination, the injured party had six months to sue from the first paycheck issued. Ledbetter's claim fell outside of that six-month window, and the Court said that was enough to nullify her suit. Recognizing that such technicalities ignored very real issues of discrimination that should be addressed, Congress passed the Lilly Ledbetter Fair Pay Act to make it easier for workers to sue employers for wage discrimination. Essentially, the new law says an individual has six months to sue after every unfair paycheck, not just the first one. This nullified the Supreme Court ruling and cleared the way for women to sue whenever they discover their employers engaging in wage discrimination.

Women have made greater progress toward equity with men in getting a college education. Women have been earning a majority of college degrees since the 1980s, and the proportion of the female population with a college education has climbed dramatically in the past four decades. In 1970, about 8 percent of women held college degrees, compared to 14 percent of men. By 2011, about 30 percent of women had a college degree, compared to about 31 percent of men (see Figure 5.4).

To some extent, the broad-based movement promoting women's rights has been a victim of its own success. As one report put it, after three decades of tearing down barriers in employment, education, sports, and other areas of social life, many women are increasingly skeptical of the activism that did so much to achieve these breakthroughs. Indeed, many women now reject the label "feminist" because "they fear being stereotyped as strident, humorless and antimale, or worry that feminists downgrade the importance of motherhood" (C. Clark 1997, 169).

After achieving a series of significant victories, the women's movement has decentralized into often-conflicting camps that pursue contradictory political goals. Victim feminism, power feminism, radical feminism, and liberal feminism take differing stands on abortion, pornography, sexual harassment, and homemaking.

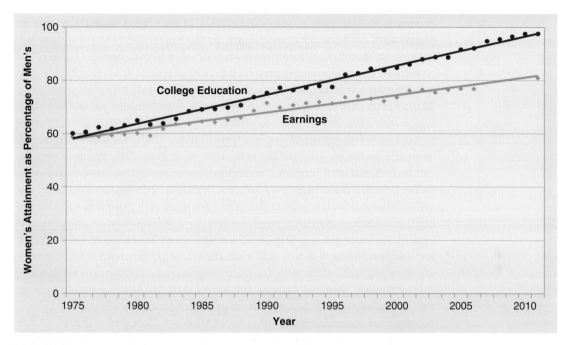

FIGURE 5.4 **Women's Earnings and College Education Relative to Men**

Sources: Bureau of Labor Statistics, "Median Usual Weekly Earnings of Full-Time Wage and Salary Workers by Age, Race, Hispanic or Latino Ethnicity, and Sex, Fourth Quarter 2011 averages," http://www.bls.gov/news.release/wkyeng.t03.htm; http://nces.ed.gov/programs/digest/d10/tables/dt10_008.asp.

Some even suggest that an element of contradiction has crept into parts of the feminist camp. For example, affordable child care—a critical issue for working women—is dependent largely on keeping wages low for child care workers, who are also predominantly female. In other words, the economic interest of the former group of women is working at cross-purposes with the latter (Flanagan 2004). There appears to be little consensus on how, or even whether, the federal government should act to address such issues. Having made enormous advances, the movement for women's rights seems to be undergoing a reassessment, while still falling far short of the goal of full equality.

PEOPLE WITH DISABILITIES

People with mental or physical disabilities have often been the target of particularly virulent forms of discrimination. Their disabilities have been viewed as divine retribution for the sins of families or individuals or as a sign of spiritual uncleanliness. Prior to the twentieth century they were marked for persecution, and many were prevented from fully participating in social, political, and economic life (Humphries and Wright 1992). In the United States, basic care for people with disabilities was seen largely as the responsibility of family and private initiative, and the government made little effort to overcome the barriers that physical or mental disabilities presented to citizens seeking to exercise their rights.

Wounded war veterans were the first group of disabled citizens targeted for assistance from the federal government. The Smith-Sears Veterans' Rehabilitation Act was passed in 1918 to help veterans disabled in World War I. In 1920, it was followed by the Smith-Fess Act, which was the first law to provide broad-based government assistance to disabled citizens. The federal government provided grants to state vocational rehabilitation programs, and states were required to match the funds on a dollar-for-dollar basis. These programs, which were aimed at boosting the economic self-sufficiency of military veterans disabled as a result of their service, had a limited effect. Nonetheless, assistance programs for people with disabilities slowly began to expand. All states had vocational rehabilitation operations by the end of the 1930s, and the Social Security Act of 1935 made the federal government's role in supporting these programs permanent. The reach of government policy began to expand to include medical assistance to those with mental disabilities and broader support for the families of disabled citizens. The range of services and people covered by such programs was expanded even further by the Barden-LaFollette Act of 1943.

World War II created more pressure for the federal government to increase its involvement in assisting citizens with disabilities. In 1947, President Harry Truman helped establish the President's Commission on the Handicapped, which became a vocal advocate for disabled people. In 1954, the Vocational Rehabilitation Act substantially expanded the government's involvement in assisting people with disabilities, providing support for a wide range of physical and mental disorders. Such initiatives were significant, but they were not part of a cohesive civil rights agenda. Rather, they were viewed as extensions of moral obligations.

This view began to change in the late 1950s, when the government began to seriously examine the problems of access for the first time. Access is the ability to get into and make use of public facilities, and it became a focal point for the development of a true civil rights campaign for people with disabilities. Advocacy groups for the disabled point out that they were being segregated from the broader society and denied equal opportunity. A report by the National Commission on Architectural Barriers issued in 1968 estimated that more than 20 million Americans were "built out of normal living by unnecessary barriers: a stairway, a too-narrow door, a too-high telephone" (Percy 1989, 50). Pressure began to build for the federal government to take action to ensure access to public facilities to the greatest extent possible. This pressure resulted

The Americans with Disabilities Act (ADA) extended to people with disabilities formal recognition of their civil rights and protections. It also highlighted issues of access in the private sector, not just in the public sector.

CHAPTER 5 CIVIL RIGHTS

in the Architectural Barriers Act of 1968, a law that mandated designing public buildings to allow access for those with disabilities. This law shifted public policy from a service orientation to a focus on rights.

The new focus on the civil rights of people with disabilities began to bear fruit in the 1970s. First were two important legal victories. *Pennsylvania Association for Retarded Children (PARC) v. Pennsylvania* (1971) contended that the state was arbitrarily denying students with mental disabilities a right to an education because state law assumed that children with mental disabilities were incapable of being educated, and it did not provide due process in excluding mentally disabled students from the public school system. As part of an agreement to settle the suit in 1972, the state acknowledged that it had an obligation to provide a free and appropriate education to students with mental disabilities. In *Mills v. Board of Education of the District of Columbia* (1972), parents of mentally disabled students sued the education authorities in the nation's capital using a similar argument. The court ruled in the plaintiffs' favor and ordered school authorities to provide "a free and suitable publicly supported education regardless of the child's mental, physical, or emotional disability or impairment." Although neither case reached the Supreme Court, both were important civil rights victories for people with disabilities because they established a legal precedent for civil rights action (Percy 1989, 56–57).

The legal victories were followed by important legislation. The 1973 Rehabilitation Act provided some of the same protections to people with disabilities that had earlier been granted to minorities and women, including a prohibition on discrimination on the basis of disability by any program receiving federal funds. The legislation was complex and controversial. It was passed during the tenure of President Richard Nixon but was not implemented by either Nixon or his successor, Gerald Ford. When President Jimmy Carter also sought to delay implementation, his foot-dragging prompted a public outcry. The regulations putting the law into practice were finally signed by Secretary of Health, Education, and Welfare Joseph Califano Jr. in April 1977. Califano said that the law represented "the first federal civil rights law protecting the rights of handicapped persons and reflects a national commitment to end discrimination on the basis of handicap" (Worsnop 1996).

In 1975, Congress approved the Education for All Handicapped Children Act, which required all states to provide a "free appropriate public education" to children with disabilities, thus writing into law the decisions in *PARC* and *Mills*. Like the Rehabilitation Act, this legislation was controversial because of its cost and complexity and its increased federal preemption of what traditionally had been an area under state and local government control. President Ford threatened to veto the bill, but it passed Congress with enough votes to override a veto. The Education for All Handicapped Children Act evolved into the Individuals with Disabilities Education Act in 1992. In essence, this law guaranteed people with disabilities the right to a public education and obligated schools to protect and support that right regardless of the costs they incur in doing so (Biskupic 1999).

The costs associated with the Rehabilitation Act and the Education for All Handicapped Children Act were particularly worrisome to institutions such as schools. They had to invest in physical improvements such as installation of elevators and wheelchair ramps to make their facilities accessible, and they had to make a greater commitment to expensive special education programs. The federal government did make funds available to help cover some of these costs, but it quickly became apparent that part of the financial burden was being passed on to local governments.

The federal government expanded the civil rights protection of disabled individuals in 1988 with the Fair Housing Amendments Act, which was aimed at preventing discrimination in housing. Then, in 1990, Congress passed the **Americans with Disabilities Act (ADA)**, which specifically extended to disabled citizens the civil rights and protections that were the cornerstone of the 1964 Civil Rights Act. Although a landmark victory, the law "was notable more for its sweep than its novelty" (Worsnop 1996, 1, 118). It largely codified existing laws and regulations and extended them to the private sector.

Like the laws it superseded, the ADA was controversial. It required private companies to assume "reasonable" expenditures to meet the legislation's requirements. Businesses complained that the federal government was now able to dictate the width of hallways in a private office building, where a store could display its merchandise, and much more. Although the federal government had the power to make such mandates, it assumed little or none of the cost of actually following through on them (Ferguson 1995).

In enforcing the ADA, the government has tended to concentrate on guaranteeing access to public and civic life and has preferred to negotiate compliance with public and private organizations that have been the target of complaints. For example, the city of Waukesha, Wisconsin, responded to pressure from the federal government to make its city hall accessible. The complaint was initiated by a city alderman who used a wheelchair and had difficulty getting into city facilities, including the room where the council held closed meetings (U.S. Department of Justice 2000). The Supreme Court, however, has signaled a willingness to set limits on the rights of people with disabilities. For example, in *Board of Trustees v. Garrett* (2001), the court ruled that employees of state agencies cannot pursue discrimination claims by using the ADA to sue their employers in federal court. In this case, the Supreme Court ruled against the civil rights of people with disabilities and upheld the sovereign immunity of states, which restricts the rights of individuals to sue states in federal court.

LGBT CITIZENS

Americans with Disabilities Act (ADA)
Specifically extended to citizens with disabilities, the civil rights and protections that were the cornerstone of the 1964 Civil Rights Act. It largely codified existing laws and regulations and extended them to the private sector.

Ethnicity, gender, and disability are far from the only classifications used to arbitrarily deny American citizens full participation in political life. Sexual orientation has also served as a basis for systematic discrimination. Lesbian, gay, bisexual, and transgender (LGBT) citizens have fought to get state and local governments to enact policies preventing systematic discrimination against LGBT individuals and to get the federal government to prohibit denying them employment opportunities for the same reason.

The fight over gay rights has become increasingly partisan in recent years. Many Americans perceive homosexuality as a threat to mainstream family values (Haider-Markel and Meier 1996). The adoption of policies prohibiting discrimination on the basis of sexual orientation has provoked a political backlash, succeeding in some states and localities, failing in others. In *Lawrence v. Texas* (2003) the Supreme Court ruled unconstitutional state laws criminalizing homosexual sex conducted between consenting adults in the privacy of their own bedrooms. This represented a significant step forward for the gay rights movement because, in essence, it said that gay citizens have the same right to privacy as everyone else. Yet in upholding this right, the Court stopped considerably short of granting LGBT individuals full political equality. Nowhere is this more apparent—or more controversial—than in the conflict over same-sex marriage.

The debate over whether same-sex couples should gain the same legal rights available to married heterosexual couples was pushed onto the public agenda as far back as 1993, when the Hawaii Supreme Court ruled that denying same-sex couples a marriage license denied them equal protection rights under the Hawaii constitution. Congress and many states moved quickly not only to squash such laws but also to prevent recognition of same-sex marriages altogether. Congress passed the Defense of Marriage Act, and President Clinton signed the bill into law in 1996. About 30 states have passed similar statutes. These laws stipulate that other states are not obligated to recognize same-sex marriages. Even Hawaii amended its state constitution in 1998 to authorize limiting marriage to couples of the opposite sex.

This did not end the drive for same-sex marriage, however. In 2004, the Massachusetts Supreme Court ruled that denying same-sex couples the right to marry violated the equal protection guarantees of the state's constitution. This ruling pressured the Massachusetts legislature to pass a law legalizing same-sex marriages. Several more states followed suit, and as of 2012 same-sex marriages were legal in nine states—Connecticut, Iowa, Massachusetts, New Hampshire, New York, Vermont Maine, Maryland, and Washington State—as well as Washington, DC. The issue remains highly controversial, and the number of states permitting same-sex marriage is in flux. California, for example, permitted same-sex marriages for about six months in 2008 after the California Supreme Court held that laws limiting marriage to heterosexual couples violated the state constitution. California voters, however, overturned that interpretation in November 2008 when they passed Proposition 8, amending the state constitution to include the ban on same-sex marriage.

In addition to the handful of states that permit same-sex marriage, a number of other states allow civil unions or domestic partnerships between same-sex couples. These unions are not technically or legally a marriage, though they typically confer almost all of the same legal state-level benefits enjoyed by married couples. States with civil union or domestic partnership laws include California, Colorado, Hawaii, Maine, Maryland, Nevada, New Jersey, Oregon, Washington, Rhode Island, Illinois, and Wisconsin (National Conference of State Legislatures 2010a).

Other states do not perform same-sex marriages but do recognize same-sex marriages from other states. Marriages between heterosexual couples are generally recognized by all other states under the "full faith and credit" provision of the U.S. Constitution (see chapter 3). But some legal experts argue that states recognize marriages performed in other states, even if the marriage would not be legal in that particular state, as a matter of public policy and not because they are required to by the "full faith and credit" clause of the U.S. Constitution. For example, 25 states prohibit marriage between first cousins, but those states generally recognize marriages between first cousins performed in states that permit them (National Conference of State Legislatures 2010b). Similar logic suggests that other states would not necessarily be required to recognize a marriage or civil union between a same-sex couple, an opinion underlined in federal law by the Defense of Marriage Act, which bars the federal government from recognizing same-sex marriages performed in states where they are legal. In July 2010, a federal district court in Massachusetts declared that the Defense of Marriage Act is unconstitutional on the grounds that it interferes with states' exclusive right under the Tenth Amendment to define marriage and forces the state to discriminate against its own citizens in order to receive federal funds (*Massachusetts vs. U.S.* 2010), and because it denies same-sex couples equal protection of the law (*Gill et al. vs. U.S.* 2010). The issue is far from settled, and this decision may be reversed by the Supreme Court. And there remains some debate and confusion as to whether states would ultimately be obligated to recognize the same-sex marriage laws of any other state as legal and binding.

Although equality in terms of the legal rights and status of marriage remains an issue of fierce debate and no small amount of confusion, advocates of LGBT rights have scored some notable successes in other areas. In *Romer v. Evans* (1996), for example, the Supreme Court struck down an amendment to Colorado's constitution that invalidated local ordinances seeking to protect gay rights and outlawed similar regulations. This marked the first time the equal protection clause of the Fourteenth Amendment had been extended to LGBT citizens. Numerous companies and municipalities have taken it upon themselves to extend fringe benefits, such as health and life insurance coverage, to unmarried domestic partners—including same-sex partners—of their employees.

The development of LGBT civil rights is still in its early stages compared to similar movements for ethnic minorities and women. Whether the LGBT community can secure the same sorts of successes in gaining civil rights remains unclear.

Top Ten Takeaway Points

1. Civil liberties ensure that government does not use its coercive power to arbitrarily limit individuals' freedom to make the choices they please. Civil rights ensure that government will use its

coercive power to prevent those freedoms from being arbitrarily denied to certain categories of citizens.

❷ Over the course of American history, numerous minorities have been systematically excluded from the political and social mainstream. Unequal treatment of citizens has been based, among other things, on race, ethnicity, gender, physical disabilities, and sexual orientation.

❸ Minorities have engaged in long struggles to get the government to ensure that they enjoy rights equal to those enjoyed by the majority. Each group's struggle has elements unique to that group, though all seek to force the government to uphold the democratic principle of political equality.

❹ Affirmative action involves governmental actions designed to help minorities overcome the effects of past discrimination and compete on an equal basis with the majority. Affirmative action is controversial. Opponents argue that it replaces one form of discrimination with another.

❺ The most notorious example of government tolerance of inequality is the historical treatment of African Americans. The Constitution set the value of slaves as three-fifths of a person. It took the better part of two centuries to get the federal government to guarantee African Americans civil rights, and this remains a contentious political issue today.

❻ Latinos are the fastest-growing and also the largest ethnic minority in the United States. Latinos' struggle for equality has focused on issues related to bilingual education, the protection of voting rights, and increased representation in the political process.

❼ Native Americans are members of tribes that are considered independent nations. The U.S. government's legal relationship with individuals has operated through the tribal governments. This government-to-government relationship differentiates Native Americans' struggle for civil rights from the struggles of other racial and ethnic minorities. Native Americans did not gain full citizenship rights until 1924, but even after they were granted citizenship, some states erected legal barriers to prevent them from participating in the political process.

❽ Women differ from other groups that had to struggle to overcome discrimination in that they are not a minority. After gaining the right to vote, women still had to engage in a protracted political struggle for equality in employment, education, and the political process.

....

⑨ In 1990, Congress passed the Americans with Disabilities Act (ADA), which extended to citizens with disabilities the civil rights and protections that were the cornerstone of the 1964 Civil Rights Act, which prohibited discrimination in employment and education based on race, ethnicity, sex, or religion.

....

⑩ Lesbian, gay, bisexual, and transgender citizens have fought to get state and local governments to enact policies preventing systematic discrimination against them and to get the federal government to prohibit denying them employment opportunities for the same reason. Recent controversy has focused on marriage of same-sex couples.

....

CHAPTER FIVE

Key Terms and Cases

affirmative action, 146
Americans with Disabilities Act, 178
Brown v. Board of Education, 151
civil disobedience, 152
civil rights, 147
Civil Rights Act of 1964, 156
de facto discrimination, 159

de jure discrimination, 157
genocide, 165
grandfather clause, 151
Jim Crow laws, 156
literacy tests, 150
passive resistance, 153
Plessy v. Ferguson, 151

poll taxes, 150
racial segregation, 150
separate but equal, 151
suffrage, 169
Voting Rights Act of 1965, 156

(6) INTEREST GROUPS

KEY QUESTIONS

Why do people form and join interest groups?

What do interest groups do?

Why is it so hard to regulate interest groups?

What influence and power do interest groups have?

IN 2008, Barack Obama campaigned for the presidency on a promise to eliminate the influence of special interests. He broke that promise. We shouldn't be too hard on him, though. He's certainly not the first aspirant to the Oval Office to make—and break—that pledge, and he certainly won't be the last. The fact is that neither the president nor Congress nor the courts will ever eliminate the influence of special interests. Or at least, let's hope so.

That hope may strike many as misplaced. Most Americans think special interests have too much influence, influence that is somehow undermining popular sovereignty because government responds to these special interests rather than to ordinary citizens. Actually, that's not the case at all. In fact, quite the opposite is true. If President Obama or any other federal official actually managed to deliver on the promise of banishing the influence of special interests, *that* would undermine popular sovereignty.

How do we figure that? Well, as *Newsweek* editor Robert J. Samuelson (2008) observes, we as a democracy constitute a collection of special interests. According to Samuelson, "the only way to eliminate lobbying and special interests is to eliminate government." At least, we'd have to get rid of a *democratic* form of government. Give citizens free speech, freedom of association, the right to petition government to redress grievances—in a nutshell, give them the First Amendment—and the inevitable consequence is special interests and lobbying. In short, pretty much the only way to get rid of special interest influence is to get rid of political freedom—in other words, to deliberately violate one of the core principles of democracy.

This might seem like something of a strange argument given the popular image of lobbying and special interests. Generally, special interests are seen as a corrosive, corrupting influence on democracy, conjuring images of fat-cat elites buying votes and favors with campaign contributions. Some of that does happen, and when it does, it tends to get a lot of media attention and reinforce the collective notion of lobbying as seedy and unbecoming. Those running for public office tend to be some of the loudest denouncing this negative influence, rhetorically whipping special interests even as they quietly acknowledge that special interests are an unavoidable part of the democratic system. (See the Politics in Practice feature "Help, There's a Lobbyist in My Campaign!")

What seems to bother people the most about the influence of special interests is the idea that the rich and the powerful are doing their level best to get the government to do what they want it to do. And truth be told, they are. Bankers, lawyers, CEOs, unions—you name a powerful special interest group, and chances are they are lobbying for government to see things their way. Here's the deal, though: they're not the only ones lobbying government. So are hospitals, advocates for the poor, child welfare organizations, and believe it or not, universities, colleges, and people trying to keep your tuition costs down. Shouldn't abused kids, the sick, and college students get to petition government for redress of their grievances?

The answer, of course, is yes, they should. But this is a right shared equally with Wall Street bankers, the National Rifle Association (NRA), labor unions, business groups, farmers, and so on. The pluralist nature of American politics means every group and every interest has an equal right to pester, cajole, plead, and bargain with the government—just as they all have an equal right to make their views known to the public. That's what political freedom is all about.

We must remember that the First Amendment guarantees the "right of the people peaceably to assemble, and to petition the Government for a redress of grievances." This is a straightforward expression of the core democratic principle of political freedom. Political freedom means, in part, having the right to join with others to pursue shared interests. Americans enthusiastically embrace this right. Alexis de Tocqueville, a French aristocrat and political thinker, noted in the early nineteenth century that Americans exercise the right to form associations more often than their counterparts in other nations. Even today, Americans are still joiners.

We must also keep in mind, though, that these freedoms bring no guarantees that everyone's views will be heard or accounted for in the making of public policy. There is certainly no guarantee that the "right" or "just" or "best" view will prevail. There is not even a guarantee that the most popular or best-known view will come out on top.

Why would a government that's supposed to govern with the consent of the governed fail to adopt the most popular view? The answer is that, in general, the American political system is not designed to detect the will of the people and translate it into government action. The government responds less to the will of the people than to the people who are involved in the process; motivated and well-organized groups can be more effectively involved than individuals or less well-organized interests. As political scientist E. E. Schattschneider observed, "What [300] million people can do spontaneously, on their own initiative, is not much more than a locomotive can do without rails" (1960, 139).

The American political system is characterized by a variety of interest groups battling for government action and public support and employing a number of different techniques to achieve their goals. Groups' abilities to achieve their objectives depend not only on having political resources but also on how well they use the resources. Hiring a lobbyist to advocate on your behalf is one way to effectively influence government. Yet there are other options, which include everything from making campaign donations to running public education campaigns. The point is that having a grievance, an opinion, a point of view, or a demand is not enough if you want the government to respond to your concerns. You must get involved in the political process, and doing that means dealing with the fact that a lot of people who hold opinions and points of view that do not necessarily match yours are also involved. It may not matter that justice, logic, common sense, and the facts are on your side. If a group cannot effectively engage in the political system, government is unlikely to respond. Providing understanding of how groups go about achieving their goals and how and why the government responds to these efforts is the purpose of this chapter. The chapter thus examines what interest groups are, who joins them and why, their sources of power and influence, and their place in American politics.

HELP, THERE'S A LOBBYIST IN MY CAMPAIGN!

In 2008, there were 41,386 lobbyists registered with the federal government, and if you believed the rhetoric (which you shouldn't), neither of the major party presidential candidates wanted anything to do with any of them.

Republican John McCain touted his staunch resistance to peddlers of paid persuasion, presenting as evidence his championing of campaign finance reforms and the kudos for those efforts he had received from nonpartisan watchdogs such as Public Citizen.

Democrat Barack Obama did not have the credentials of an anti–special interest crusader like McCain, but he one-upped McCain by keeping a formal distance from lobbyists, and he persuaded his party to do the same. His campaign did not employ registered lobbyists, he declined contributions from registered lobbyists, and he persuaded the Democratic National Committee to do likewise. "We will not take a dime from Washington lobbyists or special interest PACs," said Obama shortly after wrapping up the Democratic nomination.

In fact, both candidates were cozier with lobbyists than they suggested, and they appeared to be playing off a popular but inaccurate stereotype of lobbyists.

McCain, for all his reputation as an anti–special interest crusader, did take hundreds of thousands of dollars in contributions from lobbyists. His campaign also included a number of high-profile staffers with lobbying backgrounds, people such as former U.S. senator Phil Gramm, whose high-powered lobbying clients included such organizations as Swiss banking giant USB. At least 70 McCain fundraisers were active lobbyists.

Stung by criticisms from the Obama campaign, McCain did engage in something of a purge of lobbyists from his campaign in late spring and instituted a set of stricter rules on the involvement of registered lobbyists in his candidacy. The man responsible for formulating those rules for McCain was his campaign manager, Rick Davis. Davis was a former lobbyist.

McCain was hit not just by Democrats; some of his opponents in the Republican presidential primary also

THE CONCEPT OF INTEREST GROUPS

Political scientists have long recognized that the formation and mobilization of interest groups is the natural result of like-minded individuals coming together to pursue a common goal (Truman 1951). Yet there is debate over exactly what an interest group is and how to define it (see Baumgartner and Leech 1998, 22–33). For our purposes, an **interest group** is an organization of people who share a common concern or value and who engage in collective action to make demands on others in society with respect to those interests.

Not every group fits this definition. People who have red hair or who are college students share certain characteristics but have different interests. They make

interest group A group organized around a set of views or preferences and who seek to influence others in order to promote or protect those preferences.

criticized his campaign for being under the influence of lobbyists. One of those complaining the loudest was Mitt Romney. Romney went on to be the 2012 Republican nominee—and employed some of the same lobbyists he had complained had too much influence on McCain in 2008.

In 2008, McCain unsurprisingly became entangled in the public perception of hypocrisy on matters related to lobbyists, but the Obama campaign's claim to the moral high ground on this issue also rang a little hollow. Obama had not erected a foolproof firewall insulating his campaign from lobbyists.

It is true that the Obama campaign did not hire registered lobbyists, but it was quite happy to let them work on the campaign's behalf for free. And although Obama's campaign did not take money from registered lobbyists, it was happy to take money from the (wink, wink) friends and family of registered lobbyists. If there was any hypocrisy, it existed on both sides of this partisan divide.

It was also a problem of the candidates' own making, according to more than one professional observer of politics. Candidates on both sides were playing into a popular—but inaccurate—stereotype of lobbying as a universally corrupting influence on politics. Ross Baker, a political scientist at Rutgers University, argued that the stereotype being played for electoral advantage was simply untrue. Lobbyists are no different from any other group of human beings; some are good, some are bad. Some work for noble causes (aid for abused children); some work for not-so-noble causes (profit-enhancing tax breaks). "It would be as unfair to assume that all lobbyists are like Jack Abramoff as it would be to like all physicians to Jack Kevorkian," said Baker.

The bottom line is that lobbying is not just a constitutionally protected activity; it is a natural product of having political freedom. There is no practical way to inoculate democratic politics from lobbying. If citizens have the right to try to persuade the government to respond to their interests, they can hardly be blamed for acting on that right. Pretending otherwise—as McCain and Obama demonstrated—is less a recipe for clean hands than a red face.

SOURCES ABC News. 2008. "Obama Commends DNC for Cutting Lobbyist Contributions." June 5. http://blogs.abcnews.com/politicalradar/2008/06/obama-commends.html (accessed August 23, 2010).

Baker, Ross. 2007. "In Defense of Lobbying." *USA Today*. http://blogs.-usatoday.com/oped/2007/09/in-defense-of-l.html.

Mooney, Brian. 2008. "Lobbyists Are a Boon As Well As a Bane for McCain, Obama." *Boston Globe*, June 1. http://www.boston.com/news/nation/articles/2008/06/01/lobbyists_are_boon_as_well_as_bane_for_mccain_obama/ (accessed August 23, 2010).

up what sociologists call *categorical groups*. The first basic requirement of an interest group is a shared interest, not simply a common characteristic.

This definition also excludes groups that are not political in nature. Some groups do not make demands on society or seek to influence collective decisions about who gets what. For example, people who share a common interest in classical music may meet to listen to recordings, attend concerts, or sponsor a touring orchestra. But such a group is not an interest group. If that same group demands that a rock music radio station devote an hour a day to Mozart and Beethoven, then the group meets the second basic requirement and can be defined as an interest group because its members work together to make demands on others in society.

The preceding example illustrates that groups can engage in political action without involving government. For example, though labor unions exert extensive influence in and on government, they also make demands on employers and the general public through strikes and picketing. Other groups also seek to satisfy their demands by dealing directly with private individuals and organizations. Students, for example, have sought to bring about major changes in universities through negotiation and confrontation with school officials.

Political action, nonetheless, frequently does involve government. Getting the government involved offers significant advantages because government has coercive power. If, for example, the classical music lovers are unsuccessful in convincing the owners of radio stations to play classical music, they might ask the Federal Communications Commission (FCC), the federal agency that grants licenses to radio stations, to require stations to devote a certain percentage of airtime to serve the public interest in order to keep their broadcast licenses. The harassed radio station owner may decide that it is easier to cooperate with the music lovers than to defend the station's programming decisions before the FCC. Furthermore, the classical music interest group might persuade the city council to subsidize a local orchestra with public funds so that its performances can be broadcast. This politically savvy set of Mozart lovers would thus have taken advantage of the government's ability to require radio stations to conform to certain rules and would have gained tax money taken from people who do not necessarily like classical music.

Interest Group Goals

Political interest groups pursue two general objectives:

1. They seek new positive benefits to *promote* the group's interest.
2. They defend current benefits to *protect* the group's interest.

Engaging in political action to persuade a radio station to play classical music and trying to convince a city council to subsidize a local orchestra are examples of seeking new positive benefits. Groups that are generally satisfied with the present distribution of resources take defensive actions in the political arena to preserve the status quo. Interest groups thus attempt to achieve their objectives by trying to get their group and its goals to be the answer to the question of who gets what.

Interest Group Membership

Political activity in the United States has always been shaped by organized group activity. James Madison was fully cognizant of the role interest groups played in American politics; the groups he called "factions" in *Federalist* Number 10 fit our definition of political interest groups quite well. As Figure 6.1 illustrates, most Americans belong to some form of voluntary organization—about 79 percent in one study. Although many organizations are not political interest groups as we define them in this chapter, on average, 61 percent of the members of these

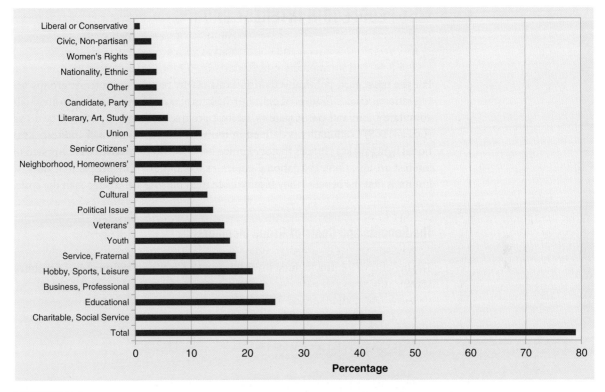

FIGURE 6.1 **Percentage of Americans Affiliated with Voluntary Organizations**

Source: Verba, Schlozman, and Brady (1995, 62–65); figure format adapted from Lowery and Brasher (2004, 33).

organizations reported that their organization took stands on political issues (Verba, Schlozman, and Brady 1995, 62–65).

At the very least, the vast majority of Americans are not far removed from an interest group. For example, many are members of, or have parents or grandparents in, the American Association of Retired Persons (AARP), one of the largest and most powerful interest groups in the nation. The AARP has around 40 million members—roughly one out of every two Americans over the age of 50—with revenues of more than a billion dollars. Among the many issues it addresses are laws to protect pensions, fight age discrimination, and provide health care coverage. Other Americans are members or are related to members of labor or teachers' unions, the American Bar Association, the American Medical Association, or other business or professional groups that lobby some level of government on behalf of their members. Students may be involved in campus or school organizations that make demands on the university for facilities, funding, or recognition. It is likely that some students who read this text are members of the NRA or the Brady Campaign to Prevent Gun Violence, or another group that shares a common interest and makes demands on others with respect to that interest.

WHY PEOPLE JOIN INTEREST GROUPS

For the most part, political scientists explain why people join interest groups using rational choice models of behavior. This explanation assumes that individuals voluntarily join and participate in interest groups because it is **rational** to do so (Olson 1965). Rationality is defined in terms of an individual's self-interest: a rational being makes choices that maximize benefits and minimize costs. Applied to interest groups, then, the rational choice explanation of why people join interest groups is that the benefits they receive from membership are greater than the costs.

The Benefits and Costs of Group Membership

The benefits of joining include the following (P. Clark and Wilson 1961; Salisbury 1969):

- Material benefits
- Solidary benefits
- Purposive benefits

Material benefits are tangible rewards that people gain through membership in an interest group. For example, joining the AARP brings an opportunity for discounts on life insurance. Material benefits may also be nonmonetary, such as safety provisions for coal miners achieved through government regulation that makes mine owners responsible for certain equipment and procedures.

Solidary benefits are "satisfactions gained through friendship and fraternity among individuals involved in a joint enterprise" (King and Walker 1992, 397). Farmers may join a farm organization mainly to socialize with others involved in agricultural work. Recreational shooters may join the NRA because it brings them into contact with others who enjoy marksmanship competitions. The sense of membership and identification, and perhaps even having fun, are important incentives for joining a group. Even though there appears to be nothing tangible here, this still fits comfortably within the rational choice of theoretical framework mentioned in chapter 1. Imagine someone who gains *utility* (satisfaction or enjoyment) from saving money and from the companionship of gun owners. If companionship brings greater satisfaction than saving money, it is rational to pay the membership dues and join the NRA because the benefits outweigh the costs. That is, trading the cost of membership dues for the benefit of interacting with other gun owners brings more satisfaction and enjoyment than keeping the money and forgoing the pleasure of belonging to the group.

Purposive benefits transcend an individual's own material or solidary interests; they are benefits derived from feeling good about contributing to a

rational Making choices that maximize benefits and minimize costs.

material benefits Tangible rewards gained from membership in an interest group.

solidary benefits Satisfaction gained from membership in interest groups such as friendship and a sense of belonging to a group or meeting people with similar interests.

purposive benefits Benefits that interest group members derive from feeling good about contributing to a worthy cause in an effort to improve the lot of society in general, not just the individual concerns of the group's members.

worthy cause. Public-interest groups such as the government watchdog group Common Cause are often largely concerned with purposive benefits. They channel the desire of members to improve the lot of society in general, not just the individual concerns of the group's members. Again, this makes sense from a rational choice perspective—it is perfectly rational to join an interest group if the purposive benefits maximize utility. If someone has an individual preference to serve the greater good over improving his or her own lot in life, it is rational for that person to give up time and money for a group and a cause that will provide no material or solidary benefits to the individual.

Although many people are drawn to issues for personal reasons, interest groups can provide purposive benefits. Wendy Hamilton, whose sister and young nephew were killed by a drunk driver, was president of Mothers Against Drunk Driving (MADD). Here she stands before a display of people killed by drunk drivers in Louisiana. Established in 1980, the special interest nonprofit group has grown to more than 600 affiliates and 2 million members nationwide, and it has successfully sponsored more than 2,300 antidrunk-driving laws. MADD works closely with the National Highway Traffic Safety Administration (NHTSA) to expand programs with the goal of saving lives.

Material, solidary, and purposive benefits are not mutually exclusive. An interest group may provide all three. For example, the United Automobile Workers (UAW) union provides material benefits to its members in the form of higher wages obtained through contract negotiations, sponsors recreational and other activities, and may push for social and economic reforms to benefit groups beyond its membership. Thus, the UAW provides different kinds of incentives to appeal to the different interests or requirements of its members.

The most obvious cost of participating in an interest group is membership dues. But more important than monetary costs are the costs of collective action—the time spent in meetings, in maintaining the organization, and in planning and participating in activities in pursuit of the group's goals. Thus, we typically assume that people form and join interest groups when the benefits (material, solidary, and purposive) outweigh the costs of participating (dues, time, and the effort involved with working with others).

Collective Action, Public Goods, and Free Riders

Although the assumption of rational action is at the heart of mainstream explanations of why people join interest groups, Mancur Olson (1965) points out a fundamental problem: it is not rational to join an interest group if the benefit it produces is a public good. If the benefits of a public good are greater than the costs, then why is it not rational to pony up your share? The answer has to with the nature of public goods. A **public good** is a benefit that cannot be withheld from anyone—even those who do not contribute to the cost of providing the good. For example, an environmental group that pushes for clean air laws is seeking a public good—pleasant outdoor activities, better health, lower medical costs—that will be available to

public good A benefit that is provided to everyone and cannot be withheld from those who did not participate in its provision.

everyone. A rational actor who supports these goals may decline to join the group because he or she will get the benefits of the group's activities without paying any of the costs. In other words, if a group is providing a public good that is available to everyone, it is rational to be a **free rider** and get the benefit without paying anything for it. The term *free rider* is not intended to imply wrongness, as the term "free loader" would. The concept of a free rider simply describes a rational choice to enjoy the benefits of group activity without incurring any of the costs.

The paradox is that securing a public good requires **collective action**—that is, a lot of people have to work together to make demands on others in society to actually produce the public good. It makes sense from a cost–benefit perspective to engage in collective action and produce public goods. Everyone is better off if we have clean air and clean water and if everyone pays their taxes, volunteers for community projects, and generally plays by the rules. And if lots of people work to produce the public good, the cost to each individual is likely to be much less than the benefits gained. If all the Sierra Club members work hard to get clean air laws, you can take as much as you want of the product of all that hard work whether you belong to the Sierra Club or not (breathe in a lungful—it's free!). But even if you are a member of the Sierra Club and are committed to clean air laws, it is not likely that your individual dues are going to make that much difference to the outcome; nor will your presence at a rally or your signature on a petition. The collective action problem presents something of a catch-22: Producing a public good requires organized collective group action, but each individual contribution is such a small part of the total cost that nonparticipation won't be noticed. Because everyone receives the benefits, it's rational to get a free ride and save the costs; but if everyone makes the rational choice, there won't be enough people engaging in the collective action to produce the benefits of the public good.

Some suggest that the notion of purposive benefits helps solve this puzzle. If we observe people making choices that do not seem to maximize benefits, there must be some psychological satisfaction from "doing the right thing" that maximizes utility; either that or people are irrational. Even if we accept the idea that a preference to do the right thing will persuade some to shoulder considerable individual costs simply for the satisfaction of being part of a worthy cause, this idea does not solve the free rider problem because purposive benefits are essentially public goods. In effect, the argument is circular: people join an interest group and engage in collective action to produce a public good because they have a purposive desire to see the public good provided (King and Walker 1992, 397).

Thus, we need to look elsewhere for a solution to this puzzle. Interest groups that can overcome the collective action problem and persuade potential free riders to join are more likely to play a significant role in deciding who gets what. The challenge is to make it more attractive to join than to ride for free.

free rider A person who makes the strictly rational choice to enjoy the benefits of public goods without incurring the costs of providing them, thus presenting a dilemma to the community as a whole.

collective action Action in which a group of people work together for the provision of public goods.

Overcoming the Free Rider Problem

Groups have several ways to overcome the free rider problem. One is to get government to require membership. For example, workers in some states are required to join a union if a majority of workers vote to let the union represent them. This arrangement is called a *union shop* or *closed shop*. But federal law also permits states to legislate an open shop so that workers are not required to join a union. Not surprisingly, labor unions in open-shop states are weaker than those in closed-shop states because of the free rider problem. Why join the union if everyone gets the benefits regardless? The problem is that because the unions are smaller and weaker in open-shop states, they lack the political muscle to achieve their collective goals. Open-shop states with weak unions tend to have lower wages and less job security—the very benefits the free riders may want the most.

Labor unions are not the only group that seeks to use the government to overcome the free rider problem. Some states require lawyers to join the state bar in order to practice law, and many universities require students to pay fees to support student government and other student organizations (see the Politics in Practice feature "Student Activity Fees"). This remedy to the free rider problem, however, is relatively unusual and can be used only if the conditions are right.

Another way to discourage free riding is to use peer pressure to persuade others to do their part in achieving group goals—in other words, the group can threaten to ostracize people who do not join in. Ostracizing people who do not contribute tends to be more effective in small populations in which individuals have frequent face-to-face contact. In small groups, an individual's failure to contribute is more likely to be noticed because each individual contribution is a relatively large part of the collective group effort. In such settings, ostracism can be a powerful behavioral influence. Most people desire a sense of identification with a group, and the possibility of group disapproval, or even exclusion, is an important counter to the temptation to free-ride.

The third and most common approach to entice people to join an organization is to utilize **selective benefits**, or material benefits that are available only to members. These incentives include low-cost life insurance and health plans for union members and technical journals and newsletters for professionals. Selective benefits make perfect sense from a rational choice perspective; they provide a benefit unique to group membership and thus offset the costs of joining. The selective benefits available to AARP members, for example, include everything from hotel and restaurant discounts and discounts on insurance and health care products to complimentary magazine subscriptions (check out the selective benefits of AARP membership at www.aarp.org/benefits-discounts/). These selective benefits alone can easily outweigh the annual membership dues ($16.00 a year in 2012 for AARP). By using selective benefits to encourage membership, groups can overcome the free rider problem and secure a large enough base to engage in collective action to secure public benefits.

selective benefits Benefits provided by interest groups that are available to members only.

POLITICS IN PRACTICE

STUDENT ACTIVITY FEES

Should a Jewish student be compelled to contribute to funding a Nazi group? Should an African American student be forced to help support a Ku Klux Klan organization?

Many colleges and universities require students to pay a general activity fee that is used to fund a variety of student organizations. Some students have objected when the money supports organizations that espouse social or political views they find objectionable or speech they find offensive. Supporters of the general activity fee counter by pointing out that colleges should support the free and open exchange of ideas, even objectionable ideas, because this contributes to the growth of knowledge—a public good.

In 1996, a University of Wisconsin student, Scott Southworth, organized a group of conservative Christian students and sued the university for mandating the payment of student activity fees. These fees subsidized a variety of student organizations, including the Lesbian, Gay, Bisexual Campus Center; the Campus Women's Center; the Madison AIDS Support Network; the International Socialist Organization; Amnesty International; and Students of National Organization for Women. Southworth argued that these groups engaged in political and ideological advocacy for causes he did

not support and that therefore he should not be forced to contribute to them. A federal judge ruled that students may opt out of paying the portion of the fee that funds organizations they find objectionable, and a U.S. appeals court in Chicago upheld the ruling (*Southworth v. Grebe* 1998).

But in March 2000, the Supreme Court reversed these decisions and unanimously voted to uphold the University of Wisconsin's student-fee system (*Board of Regents of the University of Wisconsin v. Southworth* 2000). "The University may determine that its mission is well served if students have the means to engage in dynamic discussions of philosophical, religious, scientific, social, and political subjects in their extracurricular campus life outside the lecture hall. If the University reaches this conclusion, it is entitled to impose a mandatory fee to sustain an open dialogue to these ends," wrote Justice Anthony M. Kennedy in the Court's opinion. As Justice Ruth Bader Ginsburg noted, "people are compelled to pay for all kinds of things being taught that they might not believe in." The Supreme Court's ruling also means that colleges and universities can compel students to not be free riders, at least when it comes to student organizations.

THE ORIGINS AND GROWTH OF INTEREST GROUPS

Interest groups have long played an important role in the American political system. For example, the Chamber of Commerce of the United States, an organization designed to advance the interests of the nation's business community, was formed in 1912. A related group, the National Association of Manufacturers, was established in 1895. The American Farm Bureau Federation dates back to 1919;

today it is one of the largest agricultural interest groups in the nation, with a membership of more than three million. These groups and others like them have been actively making demands on others in society through government action for the better part of a century. But what drives people to form interest groups?

Theoretical Perspectives on the Formation of Interest Groups

Political scientists have suggested several other explanations for why interest groups form.

PLURALIST THEORY The **pluralist explanation** is that interest groups are a natural extension of a democratic system that guarantees freedom of expression and association. An early advocate of this perspective is David Truman, who argued in the 1950s that changes in the political environment encouraged formation of new groups (Truman 1951). New groups are especially likely to emerge when those changes adversely affect interests; people will coalesce around a common cause more readily when they feel threatened. There are numerous examples of this kind of interest group formation. For example, the National Association of Manufacturers—the largest industrial trade association in America—was formed in response to widespread concerns in the business community about the effects of an economic depression. Sometimes the precipitator of such group formation may be government activity, and in some cases, government explicitly encourages it. Theodore Lowi (1969) argues that the Departments of Agriculture, Commerce, and Labor are examples of government delegating the power to formulate and administer public policy to particular clienteles. In other cases, groups form in response to governmental action that is unpopular with a particular interest. The antiabortion group the National Right to Life Committee (NRLC), for example, was founded in 1973 as a direct result of the Supreme Court ruling to legalize abortions in *Roe v. Wade*.

BY-PRODUCT THEORY AND EXCHANGE THEORY A drawback of the pluralist theory is that it does little to explain how latent groups—groups of people who share common interests but are not organized or perhaps even aware of their common circumstances—overcome the free rider problem. Exchange theory and by-product theory were formulated to deal with this puzzle. The central problem is this: if taking the free ride (not joining the group) is the rational choice, how do groups manage to form in the first place?

Viewed from this perspective, the formation of so many interest groups seems less like a natural outgrowth of a pluralistic democracy than the product of mass irrationality. Mancur Olson (1965), the economist who introduced the free rider problem to political scientists, provided a simple answer to this puzzle: **by-product theory**. In a nutshell, by-product theory argues that group leaders overcome the free rider problem either by offering selective benefits—material, social, or recreational benefits available only to members, as described previously—or

pluralist explanation (of interest groups) The idea that interest groups form in reaction to problems created by particular social or economic events.

by-product theory The theory that most people will not engage in collective action with the sole aim of producing public goods. Instead, groups build membership by offering selective benefits available only to group members.

by creating coercive incentives such as mandatory membership in a professional organization. Whereas pluralist theory suggests that groups form because of a spontaneous coalescing of common interests around a common goal, by-product theory argues that special interest groups exist because they have overcome the free rider problem by attracting members using some other means. Any pursuit of a collective goal—NARAL's pursuit of pro-choice laws, the NRA's opposition to an assault weapons ban—is not the main reason the group exists but is in reality a by-product of a successful strategy to recruit members.

Political scientist Robert Salisbury (1969) refined this general argument into an **exchange theory** of interest groups. Exchange theory explains the formation of interest groups as a rational quid pro quo between supplier and consumer. The basic idea is that groups form as a result of a deal—an exchange—between a **group entrepreneur** and an unorganized interest that may be underrepresented or not represented at all. The group entrepreneur invests resources (such as time, money, and organizational skill) to create and build an organization that offers various types of selective benefits (material and solidary) to entice others to join the group. Individuals with a common but unorganized interest join the group in exchange for the benefits of membership. Exchange theory is similar to by-product theory in that it is based on an assumption of rational actors: groups form because they provide a set of benefits available only to members that outweigh the costs of membership. Exchange theory, though, views interest groups as essentially suppliers in a market. Groups form to "sell" a particular benefit package to induce people with certain interests to join (King and Walker 1992; Lowry 1997).

NICHE THEORY One of the most recent explanations for growth in the number of interest groups is niche theory, formulated by political scientists Virginia Gray and David Lowery (1996). Gray and Lowery applied biological concepts such as population ecology (the study of how animals interact with their environment) and carrying capacity (the maximum number of animals a given environment can sustain indefinitely without deterioration of said environment) to interest groups. Just as a biological environment has a certain carrying capacity to support the various species that compete for its resources (such as food and nesting space), a political environment has a certain carrying capacity to support the interest groups that compete for its resources (such as members and financial contributions). An environment—biological or political—is composed of various niches, or spaces that contain an array of resources necessary for survival (Lowery and Brasher 2004).

Niche theory explains the explosive growth of interest groups as the partitioning of policy niches into segments representing narrower and narrower interests. For example, the environmental policy niche was once dominated by general environmentalist groups such as the Sierra Club. The generalist organizations, though, left opportunities for specialized groups to cater to specialized environmental niches (e.g., Ducks Unlimited, a group that focuses on policies re-

exchange theory The theory that interest groups form as a result of a deal—an exchange—between a group entrepreneur and an unorganized interest that may be underrepresented or not represented at all.

group entrepreneur Someone who invests resources (such as time, money, and organizational skill) to create and build an organization that offers various types of benefits (material, solidary, and purposive) to entice others to join the group.

lated to wetlands and waterfowl). Specific groups can fill such specialized niches because new techniques and technologies have, in effect, increased the carrying capacity of America's political environment. For example, changes in communications technology and the growing importance of money in mounting competitive political campaigns have provided opportunities for entrepreneurs to identify and reach particular constituencies, to make their interests widely known, and to make them a potent political force through fundraising activities. Emily's List, the nationwide network of political donors that backs pro-choice female Democratic candidates, is a good example of how such niche organizations have grown. ("Emily," by the way, is an acronym rather than a person. It stands for "Early Money Is Like Yeast"—it raises dough.) Emily's List was started in 1985 by 25 women, many of them already office holders, who operated mostly out of group founder Ellen Malcolm's basement, and within three years Emily's List was raising nearly a million dollars to support pro-choice candidates. Five years after that its membership topped 20,000, and nowadays Emily's List can raise and distribute tens of millions of dollars per election cycle (see www.emilyslist.org/who/history/ and www.opensecrets.org).

Changes in techniques and opportunities for building organizations also have redefined what it means to be a member of an interest group. In the past, associations were more likely to have local chapters established nationwide, to be centered on social divisions such as race or gender, and to involve face-to-face activity with other members of the group. Over the last several decades, special interest groups have become centralized, and membership involvement is more distant. Groups tend to locate their headquarters in the national or state capitals, and the primary role of membership is to send funds to a group of professionals whose full-time job is advocacy of a relatively narrow agenda.

And although the number of interest groups has grown, the average number of members per group has generally declined. With a few exceptions (the AARP being a notable example), groups with national membership bases tend to be much smaller in scale and have a different type of structure and orientation than earlier organizations designed as civic and political associations. At its 1993 peak, for example, the National Organization for Women (NOW) had 280,000 members in 800 local chapters, with no administrative or organizational levels between the local and national groups. By contrast, in 1955 an earlier women's advocacy group, the General Federation of Women's Clubs (GFWC), had 826,000 members in 15,168 local clubs that were divided into organizational networks with hierarchies in each state (Skocpol 1999). The GFWC had a very different orientation than NOW. Unlike the GFWC, NOW is oriented toward advocacy of a tightly defined political agenda and is much less involved in channeling the activism of educated wives and mothers into community-based good deeds. A broad set of social and technological changes—including economic, social, and political opportunities for women—seems to have hurt old-style organizations such as the GFWC, whereas groups like NOW have been created and prosper.

The Growth of Interest Groups

In recent decades, the role of interest groups has expanded considerably. The 1960s through the 1980s saw an explosion of interest group activity in the nation's capital. According to reliable estimates, 70 percent of all interest groups operating in Washington, DC, in the mid-1980s had opened their offices after 1960 (Schlozman and Tierney 1983). Growth of some categories of interest groups has been particularly spectacular. For example, as shown in Table 6.1, the *Encyclopedia of Associations* listed only 117 public affairs associations in 1959. By 1980, the number had grown to 1,068, an increase of more than 800 percent. Other categories of groups also experienced growth over this period, though the rates of increase vary considerably. Since the 1990s, growth in the number of associations has leveled off and even declined in some categories. For example, the health and medical associations category has grown the fastest since the 1990s, but the 52 percent increase is considerably less than the 226 percent increase in the earlier period. Since the 1990s, several categories have declined; public affairs and educational groups, as well as labor unions, have all experienced negative growth in this period. Overall, though, the trend has been one way for nearly half a century. Even with fluctuations in certain categories, the total number of groups listed tripled between 1959 and 2008.

Although groups are active across a broad range of issues, some interests are more prominent than others. Research consistently shows that business interests

TABLE 6.1: UNEVEN PATTERNS OF GROWTH OF INTEREST GROUPS

	Number of associations				Percentage change	
	1959	1980	1990	2008	1959–1980	1990–2008
Labor unions, associations, and federations	226	235	253	239	4.0	−5.5
Business (trade, commerce, tourism)	2,409	3,223	4,086	4,086	33.8	0.0
Environmental and agricultural	331	677	940	1,355	104.5	44.1
Legal, governmental, military, veterans	273	737	1,254	1,720	170.0	37.2
Cultural (religious, nationality, ethnic)	417	1,232	1,744	1,891	195.4	8.4
Recreational (hobby, athletic, social, fan clubs)	539	1,732	3,206	3,251	221.3	1.4
Health and medical	433	1,413	2,227	3,391	226.3	52.3
Educational (engineering, science, arts and humanities)	857	3,415	4,595	3,570	298.5	−22.3
Social welfare	241	994	1,705	2,320	312.4	36.1
Public affairs	117	1,068	2,249	1,966	812.8	−12.6
Total	5,843	14,726	22,259	23,789	152.0	6.9

Sources: Baumgartner and Leech (1998); *Encyclopedia of Associations* (Detroit, MI: Gale).

are the dominant force in both numbers and spending, and labor unions and other citizens' interests are much less prominent. A study of Washington lobbying groups by Frank Baumgartner and Beth Leech (2001), for example, found that business groups were a dominant force among the Washington lobbying community—over 59 percent of registered lobbyists were from business and trade associations, whereas unions accounted for less than 2 percent, and nonprofit citizens' groups accounted for less than 10 percent. An update of this analysis shows that these findings still hold. More than 60 percent of lobbyists in Washington in 2011 represented various business interests (48 percent from financial, construction, communications, and electronics industries and 14 percent from agribusiness, energy, and natural resources); 2 percent represented labor and 12 percent represented educational, nonprofit, civil servant, and religious interests (see Figure 6.2a). We see the same pattern in spending. Of the $3.28 billion spent on lobbying in 2011, 70 percent (almost $2.3 billion) came from business interests, compared to 2 percent (about $66 million) from labor and 8 percent (about $260 million) from education and nonprofits (see Figure 6.2b).

Activity and competition across issues also is highly skewed. Only a small number of issues attract the attention of a large number of groups presenting opposing views, and on many issues there is only one group actively lobbying. Differential success in overcoming the collective action problem may account for some of the

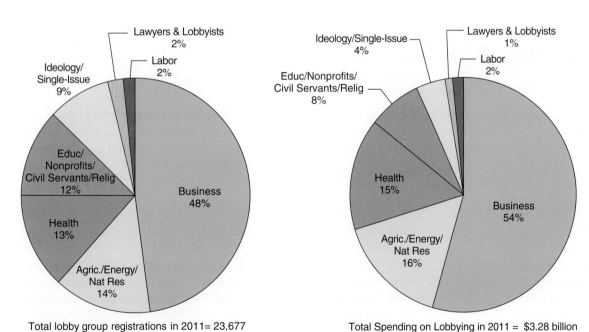

Total lobby group registrations in 2011= 23,677

FIGURE 6.2A Lobby Group Registrations

Total Spending on Lobbying in 2011 = $3.28 billion

FIGURE 6.2B Spending on Lobbying

Source: Constructed by the authors from data from the Center for Responsive Politics, "Influence and Lobbying, Ranked Sectors," at http://www.opensecrets.org/lobby/top.php?indexType=c (accessed October 20, 2012)

differences in activity. Another likely explanation for uneven group activity is that groups successfully stake out their own little niche partitioned from other groups. Baumgartner and Leech (2001, 1204) found that business groups, trade associations, and representatives of state and local governments were active on all types of issues, but on issues "where only one or two groups were active, participation was almost exclusively limited to" these interests. Unions, nonprofits, and citizens' groups were likely to be active on highly visible issues in competition with many other groups, including business.

Thus, group influence tends to be greatest on issues that attract little attention and conflict because there is no one to present an opposing point of view. Those big, controversial issues where we see intense conflict from opposing groups are the issues that Americans see on TV or read about in the papers. As important as these issues are, they are just a tiny fraction of the issues on which groups seek to influence who gets what. The most common type of group influence occurs on small, noncontroversial issues where only one perspective is presented and that are outside the view of the media and most citizens.

Growth in numbers has been accompanied by a shift in the nature of interest groups. One matter of concern is the rapid rise of **single-issue groups**—groups that take positions and are active on only one specific issue (such as abortion, guns, homosexuality, or the environment). There are often single-issue groups on both sides of a question (e.g., the antiabortion National Right to Life Committee and the pro-choice NARAL Pro-Choice America have entirely opposing goals when it comes to abortion), but these groups are similar in that they tend to take extreme, uncompromising positions on a single issue. Critics complain that single-issue groups undermine the democratic process by polarizing the issues and making compromise more difficult. Others respond that these groups just provide a different type of representation. Traditional interest groups represent some economic or occupational interest (such as farmers, businesspeople, or lawyers); these so-called single-interest groups represent ideas about a specific issue (such as protecting the environment, promoting peace, or achieving racial equality). These issues are not necessarily narrow, and such groups are not new to American politics (Tesh 1984). Groups advocating abolition of slavery, the prohibition of alcohol, and women's suffrage were politically active early in our nation's history. The intense conflict over abortion in contemporary politics is not nearly as divisive, or as violent, as the slavery issue was in the 1860s.

Another troubling form of interest group activity is the rise of so-called think tanks that blur the line between research and advocacy. Traditionally, think tanks have been institutions dedicated to the scholarly examination of policy issues of national importance. Although some have a partisan perspective, organizations such as the Brookings Institution and the American Enterprise Institute have long been recognized as sources of creative and independent thinking on policy matters of national importance and not as advocates of a narrow set of interests.

single-issue groups Groups that take positions and are active on only one specific issue (e.g., abortion, guns, LGBT rights, the environment).

The new generation of think tanks is much more ideological and partisan and much more aggressive in trying to influence policy decisions. Some of them depend financially on organizations with a vested interest in the outcome of their research and have been accused of providing scholarly cover to blatantly self-interested agendas (L. Jacobson 1995). These ideological think tanks predominantly espouse libertarian or conservative agendas. Examples are the Citizens for a Sound Economy, which focuses on taxes and regulation, and the Institute for Justice, which has drafted legislative proposals to end affirmative action programs.

INTEREST GROUP RESOURCES AND ACTIVITIES

The ability of interest groups to affect decisions about who gets what depends on a number of factors. To determine whether the role of an interest group has a positive or negative effect, it is necessary to understand where the political power of interest groups comes from and how it is exercised. The sources of interest group power can be divided into two broad categories: political resources and tactics.

Political Resources

Political resources are the tools interest groups have at their disposal to influence the political process. They include membership, money, leadership, and expertise.

MEMBERSHIP The most basic political resource of an interest group is its membership. Several aspects of group membership can provide muscle in the political arena. One is sheer size. Groups that can potentially shift large blocks of voters behind a candidate or a policy proposal often have an advantage over those that cannot. A group such as the AARP, representing millions of senior citizens who are likely to turn out to vote, has a good deal of clout from size alone.

Numbers are not everything. The geographic distribution of the membership is also important. Groups with members spread out over the entire country are likely to have an advantage over groups with members largely confined to a single region. One reason teachers' unions are formidable political players is the wide geographic distribution of their membership. Schools are a recognizable and central component of nearly every community in the nation. Collective action by teachers can bring pressure on the government from all points simply because every congressional representative has a large number of teachers as constituents.

In addition to size and geographic distribution, the status of a group's membership is also a valuable political resource. The American Medical Association and the National Academy of Sciences, for example, do not represent huge blocks of voters, but physicians and scientists have high social status and are respected, so their collective voice is treated with deference.

MONEY Perhaps the most popularly recognized political resource of interest groups is money. A well-financed group no doubt has an easier time in the political arena than one short of cash. But money is a tool, not a guarantee. It is not just how much money a group has but what the group does with the money. Spending money on an unpopular campaign, for example, can diminish a group's political clout rather than enhance it. Such was the case in April 1995, when the NRA mailed a fundraising letter signed by NRA Executive Vice President Wayne LaPierre describing federal agents as fascist thugs who wore "Nazi bucket helmets and black storm trooper uniforms" and who "harass, intimidate, and even murder law-abiding citizens." Former president George H. W. Bush was outraged and called the letter a "vicious slander on good people." Bush turned in his lifetime NRA membership (Spitzer 1998). The letter designed to bolster support for the NRA's position turned out to be a public relations disaster that may have benefited the NRA's opponents.

In order to spend money, groups first have to raise it, and this can be hard work. Interest groups get their money from a variety of sources, including membership dues, fundraising campaigns, special events, endowments, and returns on investments, to mention just a few. All of these sources require a significant investment of interest group resources. Even a stable membership base requires careful tending. For a national organization, staying in contact with members through newsletters, journals, and direct mailings can be expensive. Setting dues that are high enough to defray costs but low enough to retain existing members and attract new ones is a delicate balancing act.

LEADERSHIP AND EXPERTISE The most important sources of political clout are a group's leadership and expertise. With dynamic and forceful leadership, clear objectives, and a well-prepared plan on how to achieve those objectives, a small group operating on a shoestring can be as effective as a much larger and well-financed operation lacking such leadership. When these assets are combined with a large membership and operating budget, the group can be a potent political force. Groups such as the Sierra Club and the NOW enroll less than 1 percent of the adult population as members, but they have committed leaders, chapters operating in all 50 states, and an active membership base (Skocpol 1999). Combined, these assets give them influence in the political arena above and beyond that provided by membership or money alone.

Perhaps the most commonly overlooked source of interest group power is the knowledge and expertise of a group. On matters of health policy, for

One of the most important political resources for a special interest group is competent and dynamic leadership. Grover Norquist, pictured below, is a conservative political activists and founder of Americans for Tax Reform. Before the 2012 election 95 percent of Republican Senators and House members and all but one of the candidates running for the 2012 Republican presidential nomination signed his "Taxpayer Protection Pledge" to oppose all tax increases. Since President Obama's reelection in 2012, where he campaigned vigorously for a combination of budget cuts and tax increases on the wealthy to address the nation's growing debt, a small number of Republicans have backed away from the pledge, but Norquist continues to be a powerful conservative force in the Republican party.

© Photo By Tom Williams/CQ Roll Call

example, the American Medical Association often has clout not only because of its members' status but also because it represents the collective voice of medical experts. Interest groups are not shy about using their expertise as a political tool. A primary objective of interest group lobbying is to provide policymakers with information they can use in decision making. For example, the American Bar Association routinely issues ratings of nominees to the federal judiciary.

Political Tactics

It is one thing to have political resources; it is quite another to exercise political influence or power. Tactics are the ways groups use their political resources to achieve their goals. In order to influence public policy, a political interest group must have access to official decision makers. That is, it must have some means of presenting its point of view to them.

Access is more than just the ability to contact decision makers; it also implies willingness on the part of a decision maker to consider the group's views, whether or not the official ultimately decides to adopt them. To successfully make demands on others in society through government action, a political interest group is largely concerned with deploying its resources to gain access to decision makers. This process is generically referred to as **lobbying**. The term originated from a literal lobby, the entrance hall to the House of Commons, where people who were not part of the government could meet and discuss their concerns with members of Parliament. Today, lobbying is more broadly defined and refers to any activity in which a person or group attempts to influence public policymaking on behalf of themselves or other people or groups (Baumgartner and Leech 1998, 33–34). Lobbying takes on a number of forms, uses a number of tactics, and is aimed at a number of targets.

PROFESSIONAL LOBBYISTS A common approach is to hire a **lobbyist**, an individual whose job it is to contact government officials on behalf of someone else. Some groups—such as trade unions, large trade associations, and corporations with offices in Washington—use their own executives as lobbyists. But many others hire a professional lobbyist to look after their interests in the nation's capital. Professional lobbyists often work for several clients. Some Washington law firms not only carry on standard legal practices but also represent clients on political matters before legislative and executive officials. And although some firms tend to be associated with a particular political party, some large lobbying firms hire highly visible lobbyists from both parties to increase access for whoever their client might be. The Livingston Group, for example, is a high-profile lobbying organization founded by former Republican congressman Bob Livingston. One of his partners is Dennis Hertel, a former six-term Democratic member of Congress (you can get a pretty good idea of what a top-level lobbying firm does by exploring the Livingston Group's website: www.livingstongroupdc.com). Other lobbyist-entrepreneurs specialize in matters that do not require legal expertise and provide services on a

lobbying Activity of a group or person that attempts to influence public policymaking on behalf of the individual or the group.

lobbyists Individuals whose job it is to contact and attempt to influence governmental officials on behalf of others.

fee basis. Often the founders and leaders of groups with purposive goals, such as eliminating handguns, serve as lobbyists for their organizations.

Whatever the arrangement, interest groups look for people who possess the information, skills, and access that make them effective in transmitting group views to decision makers. Former members of Congress are especially sought after as lobbyists because they understand the complexities of legislation, have contacts among former colleagues and staff, and have the right to go onto the floor of the legislative chambers—a privilege that may give them a special type of access to policymakers. However, more lobbyists come from the executive branch than from the legislative branch. There are more former executive branch employees to draw from, and many crucial decisions are made by administrative agencies. It may be more important for an interest group to have a conduit to an agency that implements a law than to the legislature that passes it.

DIRECT AND INDIRECT LOBBYING Interest groups and their lobbyists employ a variety of approaches to communicate their viewpoints to decision makers. Some involve direct contacts with public officials—called **direct lobbying**. Others make use of intermediaries to make the contact, which is **indirect lobbying**.

Lobbyists trying to influence Congress have a number of direct lobbying options. Because the fate of legislative proposals largely depends on the committees that initially consider them, lobbyists routinely appear before these committees to express their groups' viewpoints on pending legislation. Speaking before a congressional committee allows a lobbyist to have direct contact with more than one legislator and makes the group's views a matter of record in the transcripts of committee hearings that are routinely distributed to interested parties. One-on-one contact with individual representatives is usually considered more effective than an appearance before a committee. Members of Congress are frequently absent from committee meetings and may be distracted by other business when they are present. A personal visit ensures attention and is more likely to convey the impression that the lobbyist considers the representative important enough to merit special consultation.

Lobbyists often find it advantageous to work through others who enjoy special relationships with a decision maker they hope to influence. Personal friends or relatives of officials, of course, may provide an entree. One of the most effective ways to reach senators and representatives is through their constituents, especially constituents who can affect their political careers. If a lobbyist can convince, say, a major campaign contributor or a newspaper editor in a legislator's home state to present the group's point in a favorable light, the message is likely to be well received.

Another way to effectively use the indirect approach is to draw on a group's membership. Members of Congress take note of letters, phone calls, and e-mails about issues, and enough contacts—especially from a member's own constituents—can gain a legislator's attention. A flood of mail and calls can alert a decision maker to the importance of an issue. Such tactics are sometimes ineffective, however, because legislators can usually detect a contrived campaign that is pretending to be a grassroots effort (i.e., a spontaneous outpouring of sentiment from voters). Letters that contain the same wording, that were sent on the same day,

direct lobbying Direct contact by lobbyists with government officials in an effort to influence policy.

indirect lobbying The use of intermediaries by lobbyists to speak to government officials, with the intent to influence policy.

and that disproportionately come from a few zip codes indicate that constituents' expressions of concern are not spontaneous. Some political consulting firms specialize in such campaigns, which are called AstroTurf to distinguish them from true grassroots campaigns.

A subtler form of indirect lobbying is to inform voters about a legislator's positions and votes, rather than informing the legislator about voter preferences. Interest groups frequently provide rank-and-file members with "report cards" on legislators. The report lists the percentage of the time a legislator opposed or supported the group's preferences. Table 6.2 shows how several different groups rated some prominent members of Congress. Groups in the first four columns support liberal, labor, and environmental positions, and groups in the last three columns support conservative, business, and low-tax positions. Notice that Democrats tend to have high scores from liberal groups and low scores from the conservative groups, whereas Republicans score high with conservative groups and low with liberal groups. For example, Paul Ryan, the 2012 Republican vice presidential nominee, voted with conservative groups around 90 percent of the time. Ron Paul, who sought the Republican presidential nomination in 2012, gets scores similar to Ryan from anti-tax, business, and conservative groups. But Mr. Paul voted in agreement with the ACLU almost half the time, reflecting his libertarian philosophy of limited government across both economic and social issues. Several Democrats in Congress voted in agreement with business relatively often.

Other possibilities for effective indirect lobbying include having group members talk to their representatives when the politicians are back home campaigning or visiting, having group members who are visiting Washington call on their legislators, and holding a conference in the nation's capital to let lawmakers know firsthand how concerned individuals and groups are about an issue. A less frequently used method is to stage a dramatic demonstration in Washington. This tactic was used by civil rights and antiwar groups in the 1960s, by members of the American Agricultural Movement in the 1970s, and by groups involved on both sides of the abortion debate from the 1980s to the 2000s.

COALITION BUILDING One way to effectively extend a group's influence in the political arena is to join forces with other groups. This process of **coalition building** is a form of indirect lobbying that signals to politicians that a particular issue is of concern to more than just an isolated segment of the public.

One basis for forming a coalition is to focus on common and overlapping interests. Even groups that oppose each other occasionally find common interests. The major automobile manufacturers, for example, banded together with the United Auto Workers to delay the imposition of emission standards. Despite their differing positions on labor–management issues, all feared that they would be economically harmed by the timetable favored by environmental groups.

A second basis for coalition building comes through a process called **logrolling**. This is an exchange of support in which one group essentially tells another, "You support me on my issue, and I'll support you on yours." Logrolling may result in a coalition of uncommon interests—that is, a coalition of groups whose interests do not necessarily overlap but are not directly in opposition. For example,

coalition building A means of expanding an interest group's influence that involves working with other groups.

logrolling The exchange of support on issues between individuals or groups in order to gain mutual advantage.

TABLE 6.2: INTEREST GROUP RATINGS FOR SOME MEMBERS OF CONGRESS

	ADA	ACLU	AFS	LCV	NTU	COC	ACU
Democrats							
Rep. Nancy Pelosi (CA-8), Minority Leader	95	100	100	100	11	40	8
Rep. Steny Hoyer (MD-5), Minority Whip	90	88	100	100	5	14	0
Rep. James Clyburn (SC-6), Assist. Minority Leader	95	80	100	100	2	13	0
Rep. Henry Cuellar (TX-28)	75	69	88	70	14	63	13
Sen. Harry Reid (NV), Majority Leader	75	100	92	100	8	18	0
Sen. Richard Durbin (IL), Majority Whip	95	93	98	100	6	18	0
Sen. Barack Obama (IL)	95	83	100	100	16	39	8
Sen. Hillary Clinton (NY)	95	83	100	71	17	67	8
Sen. Mark Pryor (AR)	65	60	91	14	22	60	29
Republicans							
Rep. John Boehner (OH-8), Speaker of the House	0	18	0	0	76	94	92
Rep. Eric Cantor (VA-7), Minority Whip	0	6	0	0	90	88	100
Rep. Ron Paul (TX-14)	15	43	13	0	95	88	96
Rep. Paul Ryan (WI-1)	0	18	0	20	92	88	96
Sen. Mitch McConnell (KY), Minority Leader	0	7	8	0	97	100	96
Sen. Lamar Alexander (TN)	10	7	10	0	93	100	80
Sen. John Cornyn (TX)	0	7	2	0	99	100	100
Sen. John McCain (AZ)	5	17	0	0	88	100	63
Sen. Susan Collins (ME)	40	47	36	64	72	82	64

Note: Entries are the percentage of the time that the member voted in agreement with the group's position. Scores are from 2010; scores for individuals who are no longer serving in Congress (Obama and Clinton) are from the last year they served.

ADA: Americans for Democratic Action (liberal)
ACLU: American Civil Liberties Union (pro–individual liberties)
AFS: American Federation of State, County, and Municipal Employees (liberal labor)
LCV: League of Conservation Voters (environmental)
NTU: National Taxpayers Union (pro–taxpayer rights)
COC: Chamber of Commerce of the United States (pro-business)
ACU: American Conservative Union (conservative)
Source: Constructed by the authors from data at Barone and McCutcheon (2011) and Barone and Cohen (2009, 2007).

the Chamber of Commerce of the United States typically sides with the American Farm Bureau Federation on agricultural policy issues, and the latter takes the chamber's side on business issues.

SHAPING PUBLIC OPINION Perhaps the most appealing coalition is the public itself. If an interest group can make enough people sympathetic to its desires and persuade them to convey their sentiments to those in public office, it achieves a major strategic objective: other people are lobbying on its behalf. Efforts to shape public attitudes have become an increasingly important tactic.

A group's membership can be used as one vehicle to shape public opinion. For example, in a fight against health care proposals that it considered to be "socialized medicine," the American Medical Association got doctors to distribute literature and talk to patients about the issue. This activity capitalized on patients' tendency to respect their own physicians and to view them as experts. Another tactic is to use well-regarded experts or trusted figures to persuade the public to support a group's cause. For example, NRA members elected Charlton Heston president in 1998. Heston had a long record of Second Amendment activism prior to this election, but Heston is most famous as an actor, especially for his portrayal of Moses in the 1956 movie *The Ten Commandments*. He gave up the NRA presidency in 2003, but Heston's name recognition and the moral authority identified with the characters he played in movies gave the NRA a powerful public champion.

Well-known public figures can bring considerable public attention to interest groups and garner public support for them. Here actor Samuel L. Jackson works the phone banks on behalf of Hope for Haiti, an organization created to raise awareness of, and offer relief services to, the victims of a devastating earthquake in Haiti.

Ultimately, though, probably the most powerful way to shape public opinion and attitude is through the mass media. Appeals can and sometimes do camouflage the partisan self-interest that is their source. For example, letters to the editor may be statements drafted by lobbyists for individual signatures. A similar practice is the provision of "canned" editorials, prepared statements on public issues distributed freely to the press. A harried newspaper editor may welcome such materials; not only might these writings reflect the editor's own views, but they also come free of charge.

Television is another natural outlet for interest groups that seek to shape public attitudes. Public service announcements touting a company's commitment to the environment, for example, may serve as an effective counter to the corporate image being portrayed by environmentalist groups.

CAMPAIGN SUPPORT The most basic support an interest group can provide any public official is help winning office. If the candidate seeks an appointive office, the group's representatives can use their political influence to see to it that those responsible for making the appointment are aware of the nominee's qualifications and the high esteem in which the nominee is held by the organization. Many interest groups become involved in appointments to major executive posts and seats on the federal bench.

Interest groups can also provide important political support for a person running for an elective office. This support can take many forms: giving financial contributions, providing information for political speeches and audiences to hear the speeches, featuring favorable coverage in the organization's newsletter; and helping get voters registered and to the polls. The earlier a group provides political support and the more extensive that support, the more likely the public official is to grant the access that is all-important to the organization (Austin-Smith 1995; Grier, Munger, and Roberts 1994).

There are also dangers when a group irrevocably commits itself to a single party's candidates. The group is unlikely to have much influence if the candidate it supports loses. To minimize this risk, it is not uncommon for groups to contribute money to more than one candidate and to both major political parties. The presumption is that regardless of the outcome, the group will have lent enough support to gain the access it desires.

LOBBYING IN COURT Interest groups also use the judicial process to further their interests. Groups pursue a judicial strategy because court decisions are binding public policies about who gets what. For example, when the Supreme Court ruled that states cannot ban abortion early in a pregnancy (*Roe v. Wade* 1973), it was setting an important national policy. This type of lobbying is governed by different rules and expectations than efforts to influence members of the legislative or executive branches. Lobbyists cannot go to a judge's office and try to persuade the judge to give them a favorable ruling in an important case. Nonetheless, interest groups can influence judicial policymaking in two legal and legitimate ways: filing test cases and filing amicus curiae briefs.

A **test case** is a lawsuit filed to test the constitutionality of some government policy. The lawsuit must be filed by someone who has actually been injured by the policy, and the court's ruling technically applies only to the parties involved in the suit. But because judicial rulings serve as precedents to guide rulings in future cases, some cases represent major policy victories for certain interests. Perhaps the most famous test case is *Brown v. Board of Education* (1954). The Reverend Oliver Brown filed suit on behalf of his seven-year-old daughter, Linda, challenging the constitutionality of the policy of the Topeka, Kansas, school board requiring her to attend an all-black school. The *Brown* case was one of several similar suits posing the same question: do racially segregated schools violate the equal protection clause of the Fourteenth Amendment? But where did citizens of modest means get the huge sums of money required to take this case through the judicial system all the way to the Supreme Court, and how was it that they filed such similar suits all at the same time? An interest group—the National Association for the Advancement of Colored People (NAACP)—provided the resources and the strategy to challenge the segregation policy in the courts. Although the NAACP was not a party in this case (the parties were the plaintiff, Rev. Brown, and the defendant, the Board of Education), the interest group made this suit a test case as part of a political strategy. Since the *Brown* decision, other interest groups have pursued a judicial strategy to promote or protect their interests.

Interest groups can also try to influence judicial decisions by filing an **amicus curiae brief**, which is a legal brief filed by someone or some organization who has an interest in a case but is not an actual party to it. In a lawsuit, the plaintiff and the defendant each file legal briefs making arguments about how the case should be decided. Sometimes other organizations present arguments even though they are not a party in the suit. This procedure is a way for interest groups to present arguments and information as *amicus curiae* (Latin for "friend of the court"). The Supreme Court sometimes quotes from these briefs in their written opinions, indicating that sometimes the arguments in amicus curiae briefs can be persuasive.

test case A lawsuit filed to test the constitutionality of some government policy.

amicus curiae brief A legal brief filed by someone or some organization who holds an interest in a case but is not an actual party.

Understanding what interest groups are, who joins them, and what they do is important. The central concern most citizens have about interest groups, however, is the extent of their influence on political decision making. Are they too powerful? Do they make a positive or negative contribution to the democratic process? In exploring the answers to these questions, keep in mind that interest groups, as Madison recognized, are a natural by-product of a free and open democratic process. Interest group activity, in essence, is the core principle of political freedom being put into practice: in a free and democratic society, people with shared interests must have the freedom and opportunity to band together in order to advance their common preferences. A system of divided powers like that of the United States, with multiple venues in which to seek a response from the government, is especially conducive to group action. At least in theory, this group activity contributes to greater democratic responsiveness. Government has a hard time responding to an individual vote in a presidential or congressional election. It is much easier to get a response with collective input such as an endorsement from the multimillion-member AARP. So interest group activities make a positive contribution to the performance of democracy by helping the government make good on the promise to act on the will of the people.

Some political scientists argue that interest groups act as a more general stimulant to political involvement and activity by giving individuals an opportunity to develop the skills necessary for political participation. This contribution has been called *unintentional mobilization* because it is an unintended by-product of group involvement (Leighley 1996). Also, organized group action on one side of an issue often spawns another interest group taking the opposite position, so interest groups can be seen as promoting pluralism. Interest groups can thus be viewed as making important contributions to a healthy democratic system.

But interest groups are exactly what Madison had in mind in his discussion of factions in *Federalist* Number 10. All the dangers Madison associated with factions potentially apply to politically active interest groups. Many may seek to advance their agendas by suppressing the preferences of others. As a result, interest groups may contribute to low levels of satisfaction with the performance of democracy. It is important to realize that not all interest groups are equal. Some have more resources and more influence. Some interest groups exercise power in very specific policy niches where they do not have to compete with other interests to influence who gets what.

Interest Group Power and Influence

Have interest groups become too powerful? Do a handful of groups exercise undue influence? Is the result a political process that is elitist rather than pluralist?

Researchers have found evidence to support affirmative answers to such questions.

It is clear that well-organized, well-financed groups have enough political muscle to hinder adoption of visible, controversial policies they oppose. Furthermore, the groups themselves may be dominated by a small number of elites who are less concerned with compromise than are other members. Although most interest groups look democratic in the sense that rank-and-file members have some say over policy decisions and the election of officers, in practice an active minority usually runs the organization. Attendance at an annual convention by rank-and-file members who have limited knowledge of the group's operations does not place a meaningful check on the actions of the group's leadership. There is no group of officeholders to counter the ruling clique, so rarely is there any organized opposition to the current leadership. Unlike the broader political arena, the internal operation of interest groups is not governed by a system of checks and balances.

Of particular concern is the organized collection and disbursement into the political arena of huge amounts of money. Corporations and labor unions have long been prohibited from making campaign contributions directly to candidates. To get around this ban, interest groups use **political action committees (PACs)** to raise funds and make political contributions on a group's behalf. Over the last several decades, the number of PACs and the amount of money they pump into the electoral process have exploded. Currently thousands of PACs spend hundreds of millions of dollars every national election cycle. Figures 6.3 and 6.4 document the increasing prominence of single-issue groups mentioned earlier. The number of single-issue PACs has rivaled corporate PACs in recent years; if trends continue, single-issue PACs will be the largest category in a few years (see Figure 6.3). And single-issue PACs spend much more on political campaigns than all other categories of PACs, accounting for nearly one-third PAC spending in election cycles since 2003–2004 (see Figure 6.4).

PACs contribute money directly to candidates' campaigns, but federal law limits the amount. In recent election cycles, new forms of political organization have developed that rival traditional PACs as sources of cash and controversy in political campaigns. The legal status of these organizations can get complicated, and the practical differences between these organizations are sometimes subtle and not well understood by many citizens, who know the organizations only through the television or radio ads they sponsor. Roughly speaking, these newly evolved forms of PACs can be lumped into three categories: Super PACs, 527 groups, and 501(c) groups.

A **Super PAC** is a type of political committee that can raise unlimited sums of money from corporations, unions, associations, and individuals to independently support or oppose political candidates. Unlike traditional PACs, Super PACs may not contribute directly to or coordinate with political candidates' campaigns (Center for Responsive Politics 2012a, 2012b; Levinthal 2012).

Named after sections of the Internal Revenue Code that regulate tax-exempt organizations, 527 and 501(c) groups are like Super PACs in that they can raise and spend unlimited amounts of money but face some restrictions on how that

political action committees (PACs) Organizations specifically created to raise money and make political contributions on behalf of an interest group.

Super PAC A type of political committee that can raise unlimited sums of money from corporations, unions, associations, and wealthy individuals to independently support or oppose political candidates. Unlike traditional PACs, Super PACs may not contribute directly to or coordinate with political candidates' campaigns.

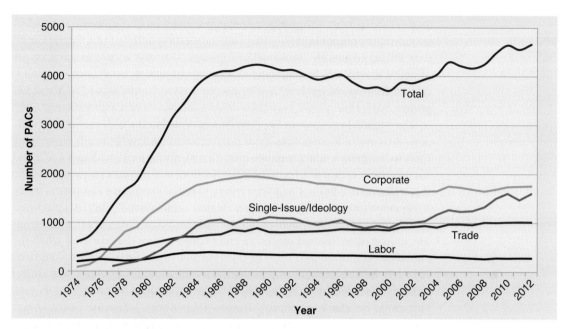

FIGURE 6.3 Number of PACs, 1974–2012

Source: Federal Election Commission, "PAC Count—1974 to Present," http://www.fec.gov/
press/summaries/2011/2011paccount.shtml.

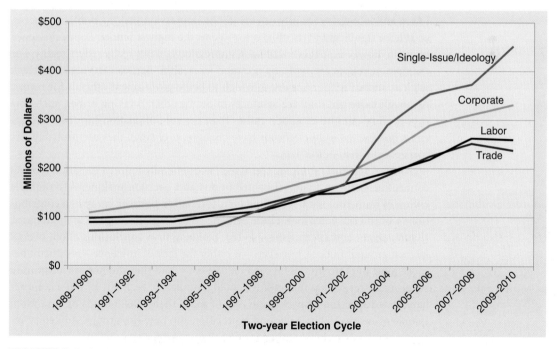

FIGURE 6.4 PAC Spending 1990–2010

Source: Constructed by the authors from Federal Election Commission reports, http://www.fec.
gov/press/bkgnd/cf_summary_info/2010pac_fullsum/4sumhistory2010.xls.

money can be spent. **527 groups** can engage in voter mobilization and issue advocacy, but they cannot expressly advocate the election or defeat of a federal candidate. **501(c) groups** are "social welfare" groups. They may engage in certain types of political activities, including advocating for or against candidates, but political activities cannot become their primary purpose. Unlike Super PACs and 527 groups, 501(c) groups can keep their donors and names of members secret.

The potential influence of 527s was demonstrated in the 2004 presidential election when one of these groups, Swift Boat Veterans for Truth, ran ads disparaging Democratic presidential candidate John Kerry's military record. Super PACs and 501(c) groups appeared first in the 2010 elections and played a prominent role in the 2012 election. Super PACs spent more than the candidates' campaigns in the 2012 campaign for the Republican presidential nomination. Political ads produced by these groups are often highly negative, and they allow deep-pocketed contributors to keep their favored candidate competitive and in the race even when the candidate's organization is short of cash. Former House Speaker Newt Gingrich's 2012 run for the Republican presidential nomination, for example, was almost certainly extended by an independent Super PAC called Winning Our Future. This group benefited enormously from a single donor, billionaire casino owner Sheldon Adelson, who contributed millions to the Super PAC to keep Gingrich competitive even as his own campaign struggled to raise funds (the Gingrich campaign organization ended nearly $5 million in debt).

More than 50 years ago, Will Rogers quipped, "America has the best politicians money can buy" (quoted in Sterling 1979, 63). The activities of PACs, Super PACs, and lobbyists certainly can create the impression that the political process, or at least significant parts of it, is for sale to the highest bidder. Political science research, however, suggests that such impressions do not really reflect reality. For example, lobbyists are typically pictured as stealthy figures carrying little black satchels stuffed with money with which to bribe government officials for favors. Although there certainly are instances of public officials taking bribes, such corrupt dealings are the exception rather than the rule. If relationships between interest groups and public officials have changed over time, they are probably less corrupt now than in the past.

Political scientists studying this issue have generally found a remarkably weak connection between financial contributions and decision making. A systematic review of numerous studies looking for a correlation between campaign contributions and roll call votes found little evidence that votes in Congress are purchased (Baumgartner and Leech 1998, 14–15). Drawing firm conclusions about overall interest group influence, however—or rather the lack of influence—is difficult because most of these studies focused on one issue, and they did not use a common set of measures so that the findings could cumulate (Leech 2010). But a comprehensive study of the lobbying activities of more than 1,000 groups on a random sample of nearly 100 issues found no relationship between groups' monetary resources and receipt of what they wanted (Baumgartner et al. 2009).

Even if there is no direct connection between money and votes, the primary goal of interest groups is to gain access, and some studies find evidence that contri-

527 groups Tax-exempt organizations that can raise and spend unlimited amounts of money to influence elections. They can engage in voter mobilization and issue advocacy, but they cannot expressly advocate the election or defeat of a federal candidate.

501(c) groups Tax-exempt organizations that can raise and spend unlimited amounts of money to promote "social welfare." They may advocate for or against candidates, but political activities cannot become their primary purpose. They can keep their donors and names of members secret.

butions do help groups get a foot in the door (Austin-Smith 1995; Grier, Munger, and Roberts 1994; Wright 1990). But other research shows that groups associated with PACs do not have an advantage over constituents in gaining access to elected representatives. A study of who gets appointments with members of the House of Representatives found that "members give priority to constituent requests over PACs" (Chin, Bond, and Geva 2000, 545).

Another common view of interest groups is that they use their access to pressure elected officials to do their bidding. Indeed, interest groups are often referred to as "pressure groups." But systematic research has found very little evidence of group lobbyists pressuring policymakers into doing something they don't want to do. Instead, we find that interest groups spend most of their time talking to friends and allies (Baumgartner et al. 2009; Hojnacki and Kimball 1998). And what do they talk about? Basically, groups provide policymakers with information and political support to help them pursue goals they already agree with (Ainsworth 1997).

Researchers studying the details of how bills are crafted in committee have found evidence that interest group activity does influence public policymaking. This influence, however, turns out to be much less clear-cut than the quid pro quo, or money-for-favors, process often imagined by the general public (R. Smith 1995). Contributions, direct lobbying, and the various other tactics employed by interest groups can indeed influence what sort of bill comes out of a committee (Hall 1996). But an interest group's chance of getting what it wants depends much more on opposing interest group activity than on the money given to a campaign and the number of direct contacts with an official. A clash of interests and their associated lobbying efforts puts a significant constraint on group influence.

Indeed, a clash of interests can elevate the role of public officials as independent decision makers. Groups opposed to gun control, for example, were able to block or defeat legislation in Congress for many years in part because there was no organized group supporting the legislation. Passage of the Brady Law, requiring a five-day waiting period to purchase a handgun, came about at least to some extent because lobbying by Handgun Control, Inc., countered efforts by the NRA (Spitzer 1995, chapter 4). Political scientist Diana Evans (1996, 301) concludes that "Far from viewing members of Congress as their pawns, a stereotype evidently cherished by much of the public, lobbyists saw committee leaders as powerful decision-makers, especially in cases of conflict." But most issues are not like gun control or abortion, and they do not attract a lot of attention and controversy from opposing interests. Rather, most issues draw the attention of a tiny number of groups that may not disagree; on these issues, well-heeled groups use their access to quietly push through specific policy provisions favorable to their interest (Baumgartner and Leech 2001).

Furthermore, interest group success is affected by whether the group is trying to get some new benefit from government or trying to protect benefits it already has. Because governmental power is fragmented and policymaking requires not one but many decisions, groups defending the status quo have an advantage over groups pushing for new benefits. A proposal to provide new benefits must

survive multiple decision points in Congress, a possible presidential veto, a likely legal challenge, and numerous smaller decisions in the bureaucracy that will implement the policy. In contrast, groups that would be harmed by the change can defeat, or at least delay, the new policy if they prevail at just one of the many decision points in the process. Research by Frank Baumgartner and his associates replicates the long-known power of the status quo—they found no change at all in about two-thirds of the issues they studied over a four-year period. But an important insight of this research is that when policy change does occur, it tends to be large and substantial rather than incremental (Baumgartner et al. 2009).

A discussion of power in a democratic society also needs to recognize that the relationship between interest groups and public officials is a two-way process: private groups not only make demands on officials but also serve as potential bases of support for the officials. In other words, interest groups and their lobbyists act as an effective communications vehicle between the broader electorate and government officials. They provide a way for citizens with similar interests to make sure that the govern-

The NAACP (National Association for the Advancement of Colored People) has served as a communication vehicle between minority groups and government officials for more than 95 years. Because of its long history, the group seeks to protect the advances it has already achieved while still working to eliminate the current adverse effects of racial prejudice and discrimination. Here members prepare for a march to honor the late Rev. Dr. Martin Luther King Jr. on the 40-year anniversary of his "I Have a Dream" speech in Washington, DC.

ment is aware of and responds to their preferences. Interest groups often perform important services for those who are in office, including furnishing factual information, proposed drafts of legislation, and written speeches that can be delivered to constituents.

Regulation of Interest Group Activity

Despite concerns about their political influence, interest groups are only lightly regulated. Lobbying is regarded as a legitimate method of influencing public policy and is considered part of the rights of free speech, assembly, and petition protected by the First and Fourteenth Amendments. Congress has placed two types of restrictions on lobbying: (1) limits on the kinds of activities in which interest groups may engage and (2) requirements that lobbyists and organizations disclose their identity and certain basic facts about their operations. Both types of restrictions have been ineffective.

Federal law prohibits bribery; it is unlawful to offer a member of Congress "anything of value" for the purpose of buying a vote or otherwise trying to influence his or her official actions. Legislators who sell their votes are subject to criminal charges. Although the law prohibiting such activity is fairly clear, in practice it is hard to enforce. It is difficult to prove that a favor was tendered for the purposes forbidden by law. For example, it does not constitute bribery for a lobbyist to promise future political support in an attempt to influence how a member of Congress votes. Informing a politician that group members will be happy if the politician votes a particular way is an act of free speech protected by the First Amendment. There are few things more valuable to officeholders than votes.

In the 1970s, Congress passed legislation requiring lobbyists and interest groups with business before the national legislature to make their financial arrangements a matter of public record. That is, Congress took the approach of illuminating lobbying activities rather than prohibiting them. The **Federal Election Campaign Act (FECA)** in 1971 allowed unions and corporations to form political action committees to raise and contribute campaign funds to candidates. In 1974, Congress amended FECA to create the Federal Election Commission (FEC) to collect and report information on campaign contributions. These amendments limited individual contributions to $1,000 and PAC contributions to $5,000 in each election.[1] The law also tried to place limits on how much a candidate could spend, but the Supreme Court held that mandatory limits on candidate spending violated the First Amendment (*Buckley v. Valeo* 1976). In 1979, campaign finance laws were changed to permit unlimited contributions to political parties for "party-building" activities.

Thus, individual and PAC contributions to candidates were limited; these direct contributions to candidates are known as **hard money**. But candidates—millionaires, for example—could spend as much of their own money as they wanted, and all candidates were free to raise unlimited amounts of hard money as long as it was from individuals and groups that had not already given the maximum. Groups also could spend as much money as they wanted for advertising on political issues as long as the ads were not coordinated with a particular candidate. And contributions to political parties for party building were unlimited; such unregulated contributions are called **soft money**.

These sorts of efforts to reduce the amount of money spent on campaigns were largely ineffective. Soft money contributions soared in the 1980s and 1990s, and the total amount of hard money contributions also went up as candidates used new techniques, such as direct mail solicitations, to raise huge amounts of money from many small contributions. The most effective feature of FECA was the disclosure requirements: contributions had to be reported to the FEC, and campaign spending by interest groups and political parties also had to be reported.

Concern over the potentially corrupting influence of all this money in the political arena led to the most recent attempt at reform—the **Bipartisan Campaign Reform Act (BCRA)** of 2002, better known as the McCain-Feingold Act for its main Senate sponsors, John McCain (R-AZ) and Russell Feingold (D-WI). This law raises limits on hard money contributions during each election cycle to $2,000 from individuals and $5,000 from PACs. The main target of the reform

Federal Election Campaign Act (FECA) A 1971 act that allowed unions and corporations to form political action committees to raise and contribute campaign funds to candidates.

hard money Campaign contributions made directly to candidates and regulated by law.

soft money Campaign contributions given to political parties rather than directly to candidates.

Bipartisan Campaign Reform Act (BCRA) A law that limits hard-money contributions during each election cycle to $2,000 from individuals and $5,000 from PACs.

---

[1] These are contributions to candidates for Congress. Regulations for presidential campaigns are treated differently, which we discuss in chapter 10.

is soft money, which the BCRA bans outright. It also restricts "issue ads" run immediately before an election. Issue ads are political commercials run by interest groups that support or oppose some issue (such as abortion, gun rights, or protecting the environment). Numerous interest groups on both the left and the right strongly opposed this provision.

A strange coalition of interests (including the NRA, the NRLC, the American Civil Liberties Union, the AFL-CIO, the Republican National Committee, and the California Democratic Party) challenged the law in court, arguing that it unconstitutionally infringed on basic First Amendment rights of free speech and association. The Supreme Court rejected these claims and upheld the law's major provisions (*McConnell v. Federal Election Commission* 2003). In a 2007 case, *Federal Election Commission v. Wisconsin Right to Life,* the Supreme Court struck down BCRA's restriction on issue ads as an unconstitutional restriction on free speech. This decision weakened BCRA somewhat, but the main problem for comprehensive campaign finance regulation was less the legal challenges to BCRA than the legal loopholes that interest groups quickly identified and exploited.

One of the unintended consequences of the BCRA was that it encouraged the formation of the 527 groups discussed earlier. Technically, 527s are not supposed to directly advocate the election of any federal official. This restriction creates an essential difference between PACs and 527s; in effect, PACs deal in hard money and are regulated by the FEC, whereas 527s deal in soft money and are hardly regulated at all. As a result, 527s have few limits on how much they can raise or spend.

Two court decisions in 2010 are responsible for Super PACs and 501(c) groups being able to raise and spend unlimited amounts of money to support oppose political candidates. In **Citizens United v. Federal Election Commission** (2010) the Supreme Court ruled that corporations and labor unions have a First Amendment right to spend unlimited amounts of money from their general treasuries to advocate the election or defeat of political candidates. Interpreting the decision in *Citizens United,* the Federal Court of Appeals for the D.C. Circuit ruled that the size and source of contributions to groups that make only independent expenditures could not be limited (*Speechnow.org v. FEC* 2010). Although these groups still cannot coordinate expenditures with candidates or parties, what does and does not constitute "coordination" is a matter of dispute. The Federal Election Commission has defined coordination as "in cooperation, consultation or concert with, or at the request or suggestion of, a candidate, a candidate's authorized committee or their agents, or a political party committee or its agents" (Federal Election Commission 2011). Although some campaign finance experts argue that there can be no communication whatsoever, others say that Super PACs and campaigns cannot share specific details about political ads, but discussion of overall strategy is permitted. As of May 2012, the commissioners had been unable to resolve this dispute (Associated Press 2012). Furthermore, campaign staff members often leave the campaign to run a Super PAC, and many of the same individuals donate the maximum amount permitted to the campaign and much larger, unlimited amounts to Super PACs (Kesler, Vance, and Novak 2012; Maguire 2012).

Citizens United v. Federal Election Commission A 2010 Supreme Court case holding that a provision of the McCain-Feingold Act prohibiting corporations and unions from broadcasting "electioneering communications" within 60 days of a general election is an unconstitutional limitation on the First Amendment guarantee of free speech. It also held that corporations and labor unions can spend unlimited amounts of money in campaigns.

These independent groups have created the political equivalent of bare-knuckle brawling in high-profile elections, and the influx of unlimited money into future elections is likely to intensify the brawl. Yet lobbyists who work for special interest groups have incentives to be more restrained in their attempts to influence policymakers. Despite the lack of effective legal regulation of lobbying, there are certain informal codes of behavior that most lobbyists follow. Aside from matters of individual conscience, lobbyists desire to protect their reputations with their colleagues and, more importantly, with public officials. Lobbyists who provide false or misleading information to public officials quickly lose the very thing they have worked so hard to achieve: access to those officials. A lobbyist who steps over the informally agreed-upon line between legitimate advocacy and false or misleading polemics is quickly cut off from important people who make vital decisions affecting the lobbyist's group. Denial of access is a powerful deterrent to lobbyists who may be tempted to engage in improper activities in order to influence public decisions. No member of Congress wants to give the appearance of being in the pockets of special interests, and in the wake of a lobbying scandal, the safe path is to spend less time with lobbyists—to ignore their phone calls, to decline answering their e-mails, and to avoid face-to-face meetings. This cut-off from access is what lobbyists fear above all else. Lobbyists without access are of no use to their clients.

CHAPTER SIX

Top Ten Takeaway Points

① An interest group is a politically oriented organization of people who share common attitudes on some matter *and* make demands on society with respect to that matter.

② Political interest groups pursue two basic objectives: (1) they seek new benefits to promote the group's interest, and (2) they defend current benefits from outside threats to protect the group's interest.

③ People join interest groups for (1) material benefits, which are tangible benefits such as discounts on goods or services; (2) solidary benefits, which are intangible benefits such as the pleasure of socializing with like-minded people; and (3) purposive benefits, which are benefits that transcend the individual and the group and are aimed at others.

④ Many of the material benefit interests that groups pursue are "public goods." Public goods are provided to everyone and cannot be withheld from people who do not contribute to the cost of providing the good. Interest groups that seek public goods face the problem of free riders. People can receive the benefits of group activity without joining the group or contributing to its operation. Groups seek to avoid free riders through laws that require group membership, selective benefits provided only to group members, and social pressure.

⑤ Interest groups form in reaction to social or economic events because of the activities of organization entrepreneurs and in response to the carrying capacity of the political environment.

⑥ The large increase in the number of interest groups in recent years may be a result of the partitioning of a policy niche into groups representing narrower and narrower interests. The partitioning of policy niches increases the carrying capacity of a political environment so that it can support more interest groups competing for the resources they need to survive (such as members and financial contributions).

⑦ The ability of interest groups to achieve their objectives depends on political resources (membership size, geographical distribution, status, financial capacity, leadership, and expertise) and the success of political tactics (directly lobbying public officials, indirectly lobbying through third parties, mobilizing membership and voter education campaigns, coalition building, shaping public opinion, and involvement in electoral campaigns).

⑧ Many citizens are concerned about the power of interest groups, and there is a widespread perception that well-organized and well-funded interest groups have undue influence over lawmakers. Most academic research finds little evidence of a quid pro quo, or money-for-votes, relationship between interest groups and policymakers. What powerful interest groups want is to gain is access to policymakers and the opportunity to argue their cases.

⑨ It is difficult to regulate interest group activity, and the regulations that do exist are hard to enforce. Constitutional guarantees of freedom of speech, freedom of assembly, and the right to petition government for redress of grievances virtually invite organized interest group activity and provide strong protections for it.

⑩ Rather than preventing or constraining certain actions or behaviors, laws regulating interest groups generally seek to make interest group activity a matter of public record through rules such as financial disclosure requirements. Informal rather than formal regulation tends to restrain flagrantly unethical behavior such as offering bribes to public officials or providing false or misleading information. Such behavior is as likely to result in reducing access to public officials as it is in guaranteeing it.

CHAPTER SIX

Key Terms and Cases

527 groups, 214
501(c) groups, 214
amicus curiae brief, 210
Bipartisan Campaign Reform Act (BCRA), 217
by-product theory, 197
Citizens United v. Federal Election Commission, 218
coalition building, 207
collective action, 194
direct lobbying, 206
exchange theory, 198

Federal Election Campaign Act (FECA), 217
free rider, 194
group entrepreneur, 198
hard money, 217
indirect lobbying, 206
interest group, 188
lobbying, 205
lobbyist, 205
logrolling, 207
material benefits, 192
pluralist explanation, 197

political action committees (PACs), 212
public good, 193
purposive benefits, 192
rational, 192
selective benefits, 195
single-issue groups, 202
soft money, 217
solidary benefits, 192
Super PAC, 212
test case, 210

7 POLITICAL PARTIES

I N SEPTEMBER 1796, six months before the end of his second term as president, George Washington announced that he would not be a candidate in the upcoming election. In what became known as his Farewell Address (Washington 1796), he set forth his hopes and fears for the young republic and expressed his concern that the nation would be destroyed by the "baneful effects of the spirit of party." He acknowledged that parties might help preserve liberty "in Governments of a Monarchical cast," but "in those of the popular character, in Governments purely elective, it is a spirit not to be encouraged." He feared that "the spirit of party" in the new American republic would agitate "the community with ill-founded jealousies and false alarms," spread animosity between groups, and foment "occasionally riot and insurrection."

Washington's plea for the political system to turn away from parties went unheeded. As early as the Second Congress (1791–1793), officeholders had splintered into two factions. The Federalists coalesced around the political ideas and agenda of Alexander Hamilton, and the Democratic-Republicans gathered around the ideas and agenda of Thomas Jefferson and James Madison. Midway into Washington's second term, both factions were sufficiently organized "to coordinate presidential elections, extend their concern over issues, and capture the affiliation of essentially all national politicians" (Aldrich 2011, 83). Between the end of Washington's second term and the start of Jefferson's first, the Federalists and the Democratic-Republicans transformed themselves from loosely identifiable factions into the progenitors of modern political parties.

Historically, public sentiment about political parties in the United States has largely reflected Washington's initial suspicion and distrust. Scholars and professional political observers, however, argue that in organizing the first recognizable parties, Hamilton, Jefferson, and Madison contributed to the long-term health of the democratic process. Political scientists in particular have largely accepted that parties are a central, and probably necessary, democratic institution. Morris Fiorina

(1980) argues that the only way collective responsibility can exist in a democratic political system such as the United States is through political parties. E. E. Schattschneider, one of the best-known political party scholars, put the matter more bluntly: "democracy is unthinkable save in terms of parties" (1942, 1).

THE CONCEPT OF POLITICAL PARTIES

The Challenge of Defining American Political Parties

An immediate problem in studying political parties, especially in the context of American politics, is deciding what exactly is being studied. Students of government have experienced much difficulty defining a political party. Particularly problematic is identifying the features of a political party that distinguish it from related concepts that also help connect citizens to government, such as interest groups.

The definition problem is not new; the writings of some of the founders illustrate the dilemma. In *Federalist* Number 10, Madison used three different terms to describe divisions in society. One is *faction,* a concept explored in chapter 2. Another is *interest,* which Madison calls the most durable source of factions, using as illustrations a manufacturing interest, a mercantile interest, and so on. Madison also refers to the conflict of *parties.* Washington's Farewell Address is similarly vague; his condemnation of the "spirit of party" seems to reflect a general unhappiness with the divisiveness and bickering among citizens rather than a criticism of a particular kind of political organization.

A basic way to distinguish parties from other political groupings is to define a **political party** as an organization that nominates and runs candidates for public office under its own label in pursuit of two goals: (1) to win governmental offices and (2) to enact policies favored by the party. Anthony Downs (1957) viewed parties as teams competing for governmental power. Although political parties frequently coalesce around an ideology or core party principles and propose policies consistent with those principles, the relative weight of the two party goals—winning office and enacting policies—varies across party systems and over time within party systems. For the two major parties in the United States, winning office is paramount. As Downs observed, "parties formulate policies in order to win elections, rather than win elections in order to formulate policies" (1957, 28).

political party An organization that nominates and runs candidates for public office under its own label.

Comparison of Political Parties and Other Political Groupings

Political parties are in some ways similar to interest groups; notably, both are organizations that engage in political action to achieve policy goals. Yet there are important differences. Political parties are not just a special type of interest group.

The most important difference distinguishing parties from interest groups is that they use fundamentally different methods to influence the political process. Political parties nominate and run candidates for office under a party label. Interest groups do not run candidates for office but instead use a variety of lobbying techniques, including supporting the election of candidates sympathetic to the group's particular interest.

A second major difference is that political parties address a broad range of issues, whereas the focus of interest groups is narrower. In order to appeal to a broad electorate, political parties and their candidates must address the full range of large and small issues of concern to voters—foreign affairs, the economy, abortion, gun control, support for classical music, and so on. In contrast, interest groups are more effective if they limit their attention to the few specific concerns of their members. Individuals participate in interest groups because they share a set of attitudes on some specific matter, such as classical music. Group members agree on their love for classical music and will support group activities to promote it. But classical music lovers do not necessarily agree on gun control, and if the group takes a position on such an issue, it risks splintering the group.

A third difference is that interest groups are private organizations, whereas parties are quasi-public. This distinction is important because private organizations can establish whatever membership requirements they wish. As private organizations, interest groups can restrict membership by income, professional qualifications, or even gender or race. Public organizations are legally prohibited from enacting such restrictions. Although political parties are not part of government, the U.S. Supreme Court has held that they are quasi-public organizations because they perform a "state function." Thus, according to the Court, the Texas Democratic Party could not declare itself a private club and limit participation in its primaries to white voters (as it once attempted to do) because such action prevented citizens of other races from effective participation in the political process (*Smith v. Allwright* 1944).

Parties also differ from factions. Historically, factions preceded political parties; they were groups of people who joined together on an ad hoc basis to win some political advantage. In the days of a restricted electorate and relatively few elective offices, factions formed around candidates, and they were able to control elections fairly effectively. As the right to vote expanded to include a greater diversity of social groups, more inclusive and permanent organizations became necessary. Particularly important was the task of making clear to voters which candidate represented which group. The crucial step that turned factions into political parties was running candidates for office under a common label.

Today, the term *faction* refers to an informal group that is part of a larger political entity. The term commonly identifies a segment within a political party based on a personality, a philosophy, or a geographical region. Thus, people speak of the religious right faction of the Republican Party or the southern faction of the Democratic Party. In this sense, *faction* is synonymous with *wing* or *division*.

Membership in American Political Parties

Another difficulty in studying parties is the problem of identifying the membership. In contrast to interest groups and political parties in other countries, most Americans do not formally join a political party and pay dues. The French Socialist Party and the American Farm Bureau Federation can quantify with fairly rigorous accuracy their membership; the Republican and Democratic parties in the United States cannot.

A useful attempt to overcome these difficulties was formulated by political scientist V. O. Key (1964). Key defined political parties in terms of three distinct, though overlapping, elements associated with different activities:

1. Party in the electorate
2. Party in government
3. Party organization

The **party in the electorate** consists of ordinary citizens who identify with the party and who usually support the party's candidates with votes and campaign contributions. Although these partisan supporters are most active at election time, they tend to hold similar views on many political issues in periods between elections.

The **party in government** is the elected and appointed officeholders at the national, state, and local levels who are considered representatives of the party. Because partisans in different branches and levels of government share a party label and have similar views on many issues, they often use their official powers to pursue common policies.

party in the electorate The component of a political party that is made up of the people in the public who identify with a political party.

party in government The component of a political party that is made up of elected and appointed government officeholders who are associated with a political party.

party organization The component of a political party that is composed of the party professionals who hold official positions in the party.

The **party organization** refers to more or less professional party officials and workers, including those who hold a party office (e.g., convention delegates and national, state, and county party chairs and party committee members) and party activists (e.g., professional campaign consultants, financial donors, and unpaid volunteers) who provide a variety of essential resources to the party organization and candidates mostly during elections.

Incentives for Associating with Political Parties

The general incentives for associating with political parties are similar to those previously described for interest groups: material benefits, solidary benefits, and purposive benefits. Political scientists classify people who participate in party activities into two major categories based on their primary motivation: (1) **party professionals**, whose incentives for participating are primarily material and social in nature (J. Wilson 1962), and (2) **policy-motivated activists** (Aldrich 2011, 187–188), whose incentives are primarily purposive and social. These two types of party activists hold different views about compromise, political patronage, and the internal governance of the party.

The material incentives that motivate party professionals to participate in politics include tangible rewards, such as patronage jobs and government contracts. These individuals are also motivated by social incentives. In general, they get satisfaction from the game of politics for its own sake—the quest for victory, the maneuvering for advantage, and the camaraderie of working and socializing with other party members. They like the exercise of political power and the deference paid to them because of the positions they hold and the influence they wield.

The professionals tend to place great emphasis on winning elections, mainly because their jobs and livelihood depend on it. Although they may personally favor a particular program, party professionals evaluate policy primarily in terms of whether it can attract political support. If a policy threatens to cost the party an electoral victory, professionals will work to moderate the party's position or even abandon the policy altogether. Professionals understand the importance of compromise in politics and are tolerant of people who differ on political matters. As for the internal operation of the political party, professionals expect it to be an oligarchy in which the people in top positions make the decisions (Aldrich 2011; J. Wilson 1962).

The prototype of a party organization run by professionals was the old-time political machine. A **political machine** is a party organization headed by a "party boss"; political machines and party bosses once maintained their power and control over government offices with such techniques as control over nominations, patronage, graft and bribery, vote buying, and rigging elections (Plano and Greenberg 2002, 111). The political organization also sponsored picnics, beer parties, and other events for supporters, many of whom were immigrants looking for new friends and social outlets. In return, the boss received votes from the recipients of this largess, political contributions from those on the public payroll (usually a set percentage of their salary known as a "lug"), and kickbacks from those with government contracts.

In contrast, policy-motivated activists are less concerned with using political parties to further their own interests; instead, they want to use parties to help other individuals or groups or society in general. They believe in certain principles and are dedicated to implementing those principles in public policies—for example, banning abortion or protecting the environment. Party activists of this kind are also referred to as "amateurs" (J. Wilson 1962), "purists" (Polsby and Wildavsky 2000, 44; Wildavsky 1965), and "intense policy demanders" (Cohen et al. 2008a). Unlike the "professionals," who must win in order to get the material benefits that motivate them (government jobs and contracts), these activists get satisfaction from doing the right thing as they see it and supporting candidates

party professionals Party activists whose incentives for participating in party activities are primarily material and social in nature.

policy-motivated activists Party activists whose incentives for participating in party activities are primarily purposive and social. They are dedicated to implementing certain principles in public policies, and they are less willing to compromise those principles than are party professionals.

political machine A political organization characterized by a reciprocal relationship between voters and officeholders. Political support is given in exchange for government jobs and services. Headed by a "party boss," political machines and party bosses maintain their power and control over government offices with techniques such as control over nominations, patronage, graft and bribery, vote buying, and election-rigging.

POLITICS IN PRACTICE

WHEN IS A TEA PARTY REALLY A PARTY?

The Tea Party movement became one of the most talked-about forces in politics in recent years. Little wonder—as a genuine grassroots movement channeling all-too-genuine anger at government, the Tea Party caught entrenched interests in both political parties by surprise with its sudden emergence and major impact.

The Tea Party activists first got the political establishment's attention with its vocal opposition to federal health care proposals in 2009 and 2010. They flooded town hall meetings put on by members of Congress and sent them back to Washington with an earful of complaints (not to mention the odd threat of electoral vengeance and a sometimes vehement but baffling call to "keep the government's hands off [their] Medicare"). Just in case Congress didn't get the message, Tea Party participants started to make a difference in electoral politics. In 2010, they helped elect a Republican (Scott Brown) to the Senate seat of a late liberal icon (Ted Kennedy) in what is typically considered a pretty liberal state (Massachusetts). The Tea Party also began to reshape the Republican Party by playing an influential role in some GOP primary elections. In 2010 they helped defeat three-term U.S. senator Bob Bennett (R-UT) and in 2012 did the same for U.S. Senator Richard Lugar (R-IN). Bennett and Lugar were long-standing Republican Party favorites but lost their party's nomination to rivals who were backed by Tea Party organizations. That sort of clout will get Congress's attention pretty fast.

The problem for Congress, or anyone else trying to "get" the Tea Party message, is that it's not entirely clear what the Tea Party message is. Ask Scott Brown. One of his first votes as a newly minted senator was cast in support of a $15 billion jobs bill, and he was promptly excoriated by various wings of the Tea Party movement for not "getting it," even though he'd apparently gotten it on the campaign trail just a few weeks before.

The Tea Party movement is, at least for the time being, clearly a force in politics. It's clear what that force is being applied to: incumbent politicians, especially incumbent Republicans deemed not conservative enough by Tea Party standards. Not clear is what

who agree with their policy goals. All else being equal, policy-motivated activists prefer to be on the winning side, but they would rather support a loser who espouses their principles than a winner who does not. Compared to professionals, policy-motivated activists are less willing to compromise their principles and the policies that follow from them (Cohen et al. 2008a).

In actual party organizations, few individuals perfectly fit either category (see the Politics in Practice feature "When Is a Tea Party Really a Party?"). So-called political professionals, for example, are interested in political programs, and most policy-motivated activists will compromise, especially if the choice is achieving part of their goals or nothing. In addition, the tools and activities of party professionals have changed over the years. Machine politics have waned as a result the Tea Party is a force for. Some observers have expectantly looked for the Tea Party movement to develop into a legitimate third party, but it is not clear how the movement can do this with such a diffuse message, organization, and policy agenda, especially since the movement seems to already have a clear party bias—it certainly seems to be more for Republicans, or at least more against Democrats.

Currently, the Tea Party is demonstrably not a political party, certainly not by the definition we use here. The Tea Party does not run candidates for office under its own label. It has no real centralized organization or authority and instead is more of a loose coalition of grassroots activists who are not happy with the way things are going. In some places this unhappiness reflects libertarian preferences for less government, and the Tea Party movement is pretty much independent of either major political party. In other places the Tea Party is essentially an offshoot or adjunct of the Republican Party. In still others it reflects the real political fringe: conspiracy theorists and survivalists who see various people and groups hatching nefarious plots to overthrow the republic.

The Tea Party does engage in some of the things political parties traditionally are associated with, including mobilizing voters. Yet it has failed, at least thus far, to provide much of the connective glue that serves as a primary contribution of political parties to representative democracy. Political parties, remember, do things like aggregate interests and put forward clearly delineated policy choices for voters. Generally speaking, it is clear that the Tea Party is against some things—bigger government, massive federal debt, and so on. But thus far, it has no cohesive message or proposal on what to do about those problems. Some of the policy proposals that are repeatedly heard from the Tea Party, or at least from some of its more strident elements, include banning the Federal Reserve and outlawing the income tax. These proposals have little traction among policymakers. Some other ideas routinely reported from Tea Party gatherings (e.g., forming citizen militias, preparing for a coming revolution or apocalypse) seem more likely to lessen than increase the movement's mainstream credibility. This in turn could limit its ability to connect its participant's interests in a meaningful way to the government—in other words, its ability to become a political party in fact by running competitive candidates for office.

It is, in sum, hard to describe exactly what the Tea Party is, or even what it is for. It is relatively easy, however, to state what it's against and with certainty what it is not (at least not yet): a political party.

SOURCE Barstow, David. 2010. "Tea Party Lights Fuse for Rebellion on Right." *New York Times.* http://www.nytimes.com/2010/02/16/us/politics/16teaparty.html (accessed February 26, 2010).

of reform movements. Modern party leaders continue to focus on winning elections, but they use public polling, computer technology, modern fundraising techniques, and media campaigns to build and maintain party organizations. And just as parties change, so do individuals: policy-motivated activists evolve into professionals of sorts, though they are a different kind of professional than those old machine politicians (Aldrich 2011).

Nonetheless, the primary political orientation of many people and organizations can be characterized as essentially professional or policy-motivated in nature. Assessments of American political parties often turn on whether they are judged by the standards of a political professional or a policy-motivated activist.

WHY PARTIES? THE HISTORY AND DEVELOPMENT OF AMERICAN POLITICAL PARTIES

The beginning of this chapter indicated that American political parties were founded on a paradox: a conviction that parties would be ultimately harmful and the simultaneous organization of early parties by many of the same men who espoused disdain for parties. Madison and Washington were particularly concerned that internal divisions could imperil national unity at the very time the young republic was dealing with the disruptive forces of regional and economic rivalries. Hamilton, who showed little faith in common people, spurned the idea of political organizations that would enable the public at large to influence decisions he believed were best left to those of superior intellect and training. This paradox raises a question: "Why parties?" Political scientists generally agree that political parties are essential in order for democratic government to work, but they have proposed different explanations for why parties develop.

A Sociological Explanation of Political Parties

V. O. Key's definition and explanation of political parties suggest an answer based on role theory. **Role theory**, borrowed from sociology, is a behavioral model of politics based on the assumption that human beings have a psychological need for predictability in their relations with each other. This need for predictability leads to the creation of roles. A role is a pattern of behavior that society generally expects of particular individuals based on their social status or the position they hold. Expectations associated with particular roles are based on the values and norms of the society. And for the most part, these expectations are met. In your role as a student, for example, you are expected to behave in particular ways; the role of teacher brings with it expectations of a different set of behaviors. But in either case, what an individual does in response to a particular stimulus can be explained in terms of the constraints imposed by the expectations associated with the role he or she occupies. These roles work together and develop into a system of social structures and institutions that perform certain functions and help society run smoothly (Parsons 1961).

V. O. Key suggested that a "party system" was analogous to the "system of relationships between . . . two football teams. Each team has a role to play in the game, a role that changes from time to time. Within each team a subsystem of relationships ties together the roles of each player" (1964, 206). Thus, Key's theory is that political parties perform a number of roles—recruit candidates, engage in activities to mobilize and influence voters, and coordinate the actions of those who get elected to office. As parties perform these roles, they develop into institutions that serve an important social function that makes popular government possible. In particular, Key argued that popular government "compelled deference to popular

role theory A behavioral model of politics based on the assumption that human beings have a psychological need for predictability in their relations with each other.

views, but it also required the development of organization to communicate with and to manage the electorate" (1964, 201).

A Rational Choice Explanation of Political Parties

More recently, political scientists have turned to rational choice models to explain political parties. The answer of John Aldrich's book (2011) to the "Why parties?" question is that ambitious politicians create political parties to overcome collective action problems in order to achieve the goals of election and policymaking.

Aldrich identifies three distinct party systems in American history. The first party system—Federalists and Jeffersonian Democratic-Republicans—was created by Alexander Hamilton, Thomas Jefferson, and James Madison to solve the instability of voting in the early Congresses. Initially, congressional majorities were put together to pass individual bills through a process of vote trades. Such majorities are inherently unstable—that is, new majorities could be put together to overturn previous decisions, resulting in an incoherent set of policies. The first parties developed around the "great principal" of just how powerful the federal government should be. Because the "great principal" resolved the social choice problem of unstable majorities in the early Congresses and continued to be *the* central issue for the new government, it provided the basis for durable voting blocs that would hang together on lesser issues.

The specific proposal that precipitated the formation of America's first party system was the economic program that Hamilton, as the first secretary of the treasury in the Washington administration, submitted to Congress in 1790. The most controversial part of Hamilton's plan was creation of a national bank. This and other political controversies led to the creation of the Federalist and Democratic-Republican parties.[1] The driving force behind the political and policy agendas of the Federalists was Hamilton, and Washington was its popular leader. Madison, who was serving in Congress, and Jefferson, who resigned from the Washington administration in 1793 over the national bank issue, organized the Democratic-Republican opposition.

Party voting patterns appeared in Congress first, and divisions were apparent in the campaign to succeed Washington. Federalist candidate John Adams defeated Democratic-Republican Jefferson in 1796. Partisan battles quickly turned nasty. The Alien and Sedition Laws, passed in 1798, made it a crime to criticize the government or government officials, and the Federalists used these laws to jail or fine about 25 Democratic-Republicans who criticized President Adams. Many of those jailed were newspaper editors. These actions helped trigger a backlash, and

---

[1] The label "Democratic-Republican" is somewhat confusing. The party has also been referred to as the Anti-Federalist Party, the Jeffersonian Republican Party, and the Republican Party. The label used here is traced to a later incarnation of the Democratic Party during the Jackson administration that claimed to resurrect the Republican principles of Jefferson and Madison (Aldrich 2011, 331n10).

"by 1800 elections were publicly and undeniably partisan" (Aldrich 2011, 79)—the Democratic-Republican ticket of Jefferson and Aaron Burr decisively defeated the Federalist team of Adams and Charles Pinckney, and Democratic-Republicans also won control of the Senate and the House.

Thus, within two decades of forming, the United States went through crucial stages of political development that led to the establishment of a more or less permanent party system. Washington was initially viewed as a patriot king who would rule in the interests of the people. But it quickly became apparent that there were major differences of opinion on important issues that could not be settled by a neutral political figure, no matter how fair-minded or popular. Equally apparent was that traditional electoral organizations—factions based on local or state political personalities—did not have sufficient scope to capture control of Congress and the presidency. Permanent, visible, and broad-based organizations were required for such a task. So the world's first democratic parties came into being. When the Federalists grudgingly gave up power after the election of 1800, they established another crucial political first: the peaceful transfer of power from one party to another. Orderly, nonviolent competition has characterized the American party system ever since.

The parties changed over the years. The Federalists slowly disintegrated, disappearing completely around 1816. The demise has been ascribed variously to differences between Hamilton and John Adams, to the party's elitist political philosophy that precluded recruitment of broad-based support, and to the pro-British attitude of many Federalists during the War of 1812. There was a brief period of one-party government following the demise of the Federalists, a so-called "era of good feeling" that culminated in the near-unanimous election of James Monroe to the presidency in 1820. The good feeling was short-lived. The Democratic-Republican Party divided into competing factions, one organized around John Quincy Adams and the other around Andrew Jackson. These factions gradually became independent and evolved into genuine parties in their own right. The followers of Adams became known as the National Republicans, and followers of Jackson and Martin Van Buren became the Democrats. Thus began America's second party system.

The second party system—one of mass parties—was created by Martin Van Buren and Andrew Jackson to solve collective action problems of mobilizing a diverse and expanding electorate. Whereas the first party system had featured parties in government formed to create policy, the second party system featured parties in the electorate formed exclusively to win elections. It worked. Ambition for national office attracted politicians to the parties, and the "spoils" of office—selective benefits—bound them together and helped mobilize voters. In the election of 1824, voter turnout was less than 30 percent. Jackson won a popular vote plurality but failed to win a majority of electoral votes. Four years later, Jackson was back, this time with the help of Van Buren and the new mass-based Democratic Party; voter turnout rose to over 50 percent, and Jackson won the presidency. The National Republicans were eclipsed by the Whigs in the late 1830s. The Whigs were initially organized not on the basis of any coherent set of principles or a single personality, but from a coalition that sprang up to oppose Martin Van

Buren, who succeeded Jackson as the Democratic Party's leading figure in the mid-1830s. With two mass parties in place in 1840, voter turnout climbed to over 78 percent (Aldrich 2011, 104). The Whig candidate, William Henry Harrison, won the presidency in 1840. True two-party competition had returned.

Competition between Whigs and Democrats continued into the mid-1850s, when the Whig party disappeared and was replaced by the Republican Party. The Republican Party ran its first presidential candidate, General John Fremont, in 1856. Since then, the Democratic and Republican parties have dominated American politics in the oldest continuous two-party competition in the world.

The third, candidate-centered party system evolved to serve the needs of ambitious politicians. Although the party names remain the same and competition is still between two major parties, changes in the nature of the Republican and Democratic parties in the 1960s resulted in a different type of party system. In this system, parties do not dominate the candidates, but rather the party machinery has been taken over by policy-motivated activists who use the party to serve their needs as ambitious politicians. Although technological innovations make it possible for candidates to run their own campaigns, party organizations continue to provide resources and services candidates need. It's much less costly for ambitious politicians to take over existing party machinery than to create their own new machinery, and policy-oriented activists assist in this takeover (Aldrich 2011, chapter 6).

Thus, rather than viewing parties as a system of roles that constrain behavior and perform certain functions for society, rational choice theory explains parties as the result of the rational choices that ambitious politicians make to solve collective action problems. But notice that Key's definition of party in terms of the three elements is consistent with Aldrich's rational choice theory.

TWO-PARTY COMPETITION IN AMERICAN POLITICS

Figure 7.1 provides an overview of American party competition since 1789. Except for Federalist dominance under George Washington and Democratic-Republican dominance during the era of good feeling in the 1820s, American politics has been characterized by competition between two major parties. Although various minor parties have run candidates and have occasionally had an important influence, none has seriously threatened to replace a major party.

The General Types of Party Systems

Political scientists distinguish three types of electoral situations based on the number of parties—one party, two parties, or multiple parties—that effectively compete for power. In a **one-party system**, representatives of a single political

one-party system A political system in which representatives of one political party hold all or almost all of the major offices in government.

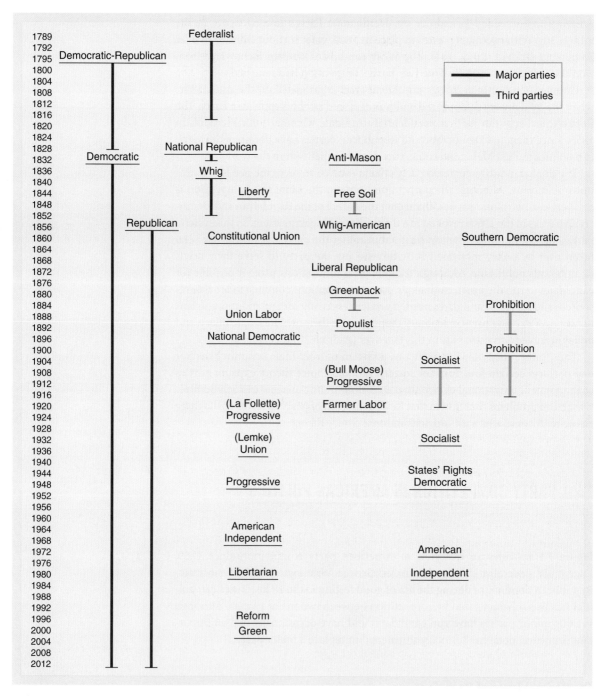

FIGURE 7.1 American Political Parties since 1789

Note: In 1824 and later, the chart indicates the years in which the presidential candidate of a political party received 1.0 percent or more of the popular vote. Minor parties are not included if the minorparty candidate is also the candidate of one of the two major parties (as happened in 1896 when the Populists endorsed William Jennings Bryan, the Democratic candidate). Party candidates sometimes run under different designations in different states (in 1968 George C, Wallace ran for president under at least ten party labels). In such cases the vote totals for the candidate were aggregated under a single party designation. Sometimes candidates run under no party label as H. Ross Perot did in 1992. (In 1996 Perot under the Reform Party label.)

Source: Stanley and Niemi 2011 (Figure 1–3, 10), adapted and updated by the authors.

party hold all or almost all of the major offices in government. This condition may prevail where only one party is legally permitted to run candidates, as in Nazi Germany and fascist Italy in the 1930s. Political systems that use government coercion to prevent opposition parties from competing for power are not democratic. There are instances of political systems in which opposition parties are legally recognized, but one party dominates electoral contests. In Mexico, for example, the Institutional Revolutionary Party (PRI) won election after election against weak opposition for about 70 years until Vicente Fox Quesada of the National Action Party (PAN) won the presidency in 2000. Democrats enjoyed the same sort of electoral dominance in southern states from the end of Reconstruction until the 1970s. Electoral competition in one-party democracies tends to be among factions within the dominant party.

Most contemporary democracies are **multiparty systems**, in which three or more parties effectively compete for political offices, and no single party can win sole control of the government. Multiparty systems are common in parliamentary systems in which the legislature chooses the leaders of the executive branch. These political systems are typically characterized by ruling coalitions. In other words, parties combine to form a government and divide up cabinet seats among all the parties in the governing coalition. Examples of such systems are found in Germany, Japan, and Israel.

Under a **two-party system**, only two political parties have a realistic chance of winning control over a significant number of major political offices. Both parties seek total political power, but neither can eliminate its rival at the ballot box. Each party is capable of capturing enough offices to govern, but the opposition party continues to obtain a sufficiently large enough vote to threaten the tenure of the majority party. The result is that public officials of both stripes must take public wishes and sentiments into account or risk losing to the opposition party in the next election. Such a system works best if the opposition threat is at least occasionally successful, so that the parties alternate in governing. Two-party competition characterizes fewer than 30 percent of the world's democracies. In a widely respected comparative study of political parties, Arend Lijphart (1984) found that only 6 of the 21 nations that have been continuously democratic since the end of World War II have two-party systems: Australia, Austria, Canada, Great Britain, New Zealand, and the United States. The tendency of democracies to have multiparty systems continues to hold today, though it may have weakened somewhat since Lijphart's analysis.

American Party Competition at the National Level

The long-term rivalry between the Republican and Democratic parties clearly meets the requirements of two-party competition. From 1856 to the present, each of these two parties, and only these two, has won control of the major institutions of the national government—the presidency, the House, and the Senate. Figure 7.2 illustrates this close competition with plots of the percentage of presidential

multiparty system A political system in which three or more political parties effectively compete for political office, and no one party can win control of all.

two-party system A political system in which only two political parties have a realistic chance of controlling the major offices of government.

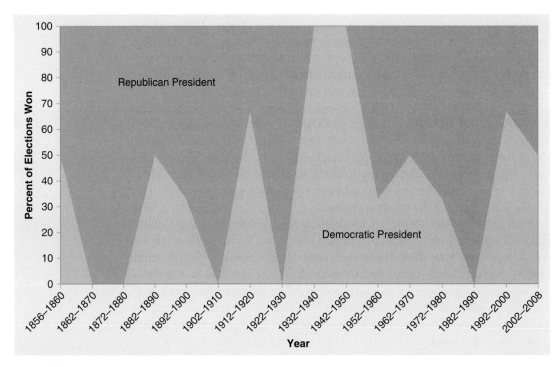

FIGURE 7.2A Competition for presidency

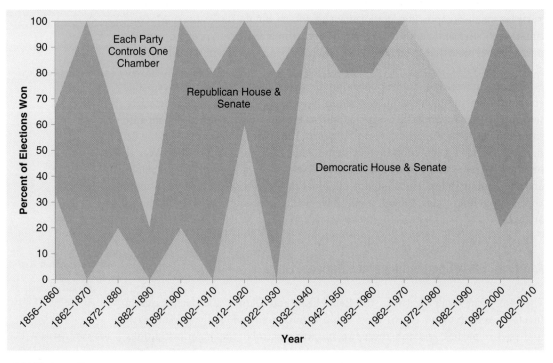

FIGURE 7.2B Competition for Congress

Source: Constructed by the authors.

and congressional elections each party won during each decade of this period.[2] In presidential elections, Republicans were successful in 59 percent of the elections and Democrats in 41 percent. The figure clearly shows the Republican advantage in competition for the presidency. But notice that Democrats show up as competitive players throughout the period.

The competition every two years for control of Congress has been even closer. In congressional elections since 1856, Democrats have won control of both the House and Senate in 34 elections (44.6 percent), and Republicans have won both in 31 elections (39.7 percent); in 13 elections (16.7 percent), Republicans have controlled one chamber, and Democrats have controlled the other. Thus, both Republicans and Democrats have been able to win political power in both the executive and legislative branches of government.

Even in defeat, the major parties still muster substantial political support. Landslide presidential elections, or elections in which the winner gets more than 60 percent of the vote, were rare in the twentieth century. There were only four: Warren Harding in 1920, Franklin Roosevelt in 1936, Lyndon Johnson in 1964, and Richard Nixon in 1972.[3] The popular vote for control of the House has been even closer. The losing party received less than 40 percent of the vote only twice—in 1920, when the Democrats lost, and in 1936, when the Republicans lost.

Although Democrats and Republicans have been able to oust each other from office at fairly frequent intervals, there have been notable periods of one-party dominance. The Republicans largely dominated the executive from 1860 until 1932, with only two Democrats, Grover Cleveland and Woodrow Wilson, winning the presidency during that period (see Figure 7.2A). For the next 20 years, Democrats held the presidency. Similar one-party eras have occurred in Congress. Most notably, the Democrats had majorities in the House of Representatives from 1955 to 1994. On balance, however, the American system at the national level is rightly considered two-party. The roughly equal division of major party victories over 150 years of competition, the close split of popular votes, and the relatively frequent alternation in power place the system squarely in the two-party category.

Reasons for the National Two-Party System

If most democracies are multiparty systems, why does the United States have a two-party system? Scholars have identified several possible causes.

---

[2] We define decades in terms of congressional apportionment periods. The end point of a decade is the year in which the decennial census is taken—that is, years ending in "0"—and the beginning of the next decade is the year ending in "2," the first election after reapportionment. The first period is less than 10 years because the Republican Party did not compete in all the elections before 1860. The most recent decade ended in 2010, and 2012 is the start of the current one that will end in 2020.

[3] A victory is generally defined as a landslide when the winner receives 60 percent or more of the vote. Ronald Reagan came close with 59.2 percent in 1984, and that election is considered a landslide.

© Bonnie Jo Mount/The Washington Post via Getty Images

© Justin Sullivan/Getty Images

The Democratic and Republican parties have won control of major government institutions for over 150 years. At their respective 2012 national conventions, the parties nominated their candidates for president. Democrats nominated President Barack Obama (above) for a second term, and Republicans nominated Mitt Romney (below) to challenge him.

HISTORICAL FACTORS One reason for the formation of a two-party system in the United States is the early division of political loyalties into two broad groups. As discussed in chapter 2, two basic constellations of interests battled over the Constitution: the Federalists and the Anti-Federalists. The Federalists tended to be people who relied on trade for their livelihood (manufacturers, merchants, and the like), whereas the Anti-Federalists tended to be those who did not (subsistence farmers, artisans, and mechanics). Later, the commercial classes supported the Hamiltonian economic program, and agricultural interests opposed it. The first two American political parties formed around these two disparate groups: the Federalists represented business and commercial interests, and the Democratic-Republicans represented agricultural interests.[4] The division was also geographical; commercial interests were concentrated along the coast in the North, and agricultural interests were concentrated in the South and the interior.

Two broad divisions of interests have continued to characterize political parties in the United States. In the Jacksonian era, western frontier forces faced off against eastern moneyed interests. As slavery became a political flashpoint, this East–West schism was replaced by a new sectionalism along North–South lines, reflecting the differing economies of the industrial Northeast and the agricultural South. Lingering memories of the Civil War and the problems of race made North–South differences a major factor in American politics well into the twentieth century. The period from the Civil War until the 1920s was a time of sectional politics, with Republicans in the Northeast, Democrats in the South, and both vying for support in the West and Midwest, regions that held the balance of political power between the two parties.

Beginning in the late 1920s, increasing urbanization and the industrialization of the South and West began to erode this sectionalism. The result was the development of class politics, as the Republicans gathered the support of affluent and upper-middle-class economic groups, and working-class groups, immigrants from central and southern Europe and their children, and African Americans increasingly moved into the Democratic camp. This pattern continues today, but it is complicated by the reemergence of race as a major issue in American politics. As a result of increased African American participation, Democratic officeholders are likely to support generally liberal policy preferences, whereas conservative white southerners and some working-class whites in the North have swung their support to Republicans.

Thus, for much of our history, two parties have been able to aggregate many of the major interests in society into broad coalitions.

ELECTORAL RULES Once political conflicts divide into two camps, the rules of the game—particularly electoral rules—tend to reinforce that initial division. Electoral rules are seldom neutral; they almost always favor some interests over others.

---

[4] Not all individuals followed this pattern. Madison and Jefferson, for example, supported the Constitution but founded the Democratic-Republican Party. Still, most leaders who favored the Constitution became members of the Federalist Party, whereas Anti-Federalists typically became Democratic-Republicans.

In the United States, the rules have undoubtedly given the two major parties important advantages over minor parties.

The system used to elect representatives has a strong effect on whether a democracy will have two parties or multiple parties. Most liberal democracies use a system of multimember constituencies and **proportional representation**, both of which facilitate multiple parties. In such electoral systems, seats are allocated to the parties on the basis of their share of the popular vote. In contrast, the United States uses the **single-member district plurality (SMDP) system**, a winner-take-all system that makes it hard for minor parties to win office. Research by French sociologist Maurice Duverger documented the connection between the electoral system and the number of parties and explained why the single-member district plurality system tends to favor a two-party system (Duverger 1972, 23–32). Political scientists have come to refer to this tendency as **Duverger's Law**.

To illustrate the electoral implications of these two electoral systems, imagine a state entitled to elect ten members to the House of Representatives. In a multimember constituency system, all ten members would be elected statewide, and all ten would represent the same constituency. With proportional representation, the ten seats would be allocated to parties on the basis of their statewide share of the popular vote: a party that got 20 percent of the vote would get two of the seats, a party that got 40 percent would get four seats, and so on. In a single-member district plurality system, in contrast, the state would be carved up into ten separate districts, and voters in each district would choose one representative. The candidate in each district with a plurality of the votes (that is, more than anyone else) wins the seat. This system clearly hinders the development of third parties. Although a minor party may have the support of a substantial minority of voters in the state, it would gain no representation in Congress unless one of its candidates won a plurality in a district. Without at least some success at the ballot box, it is difficult to keep supporters. Political scientists have long noted that democracies using the plurality method are much more likely to have two-party systems, whereas democracies that use proportional systems are much more likely to have multiparty systems (e.g., Lijphart 1984). Josep Colomer, however, argues that Duverger's law has the causal direction upside down. His analysis assumes that political actors make rational choices. Because political parties exist before the election, they choose the electoral system that maximizes their chance of winning. If one party has sufficient support to get a majority, then a plurality electoral system is the rational choice. On the other hand, if support is distributed so that no party can be sure of winning a majority, then proportional representation is the electoral system that makes the most sense. Thus, "it is the number of parties that can explain the choice of electoral systems, rather than the other way round" (Colomer 2005, 1).

The way the chief executive is elected also influences the number of parties. The **parliamentary system** typical of other representative democracies encourages multiple parties. In a parliamentary system, the party that controls the majority of legislative seats chooses the chief executive, who is usually called the prime

proportional representation A method of selecting representatives in which representation is given to political parties based on the proportion of the vote obtained. This method has the effect of encouraging multiple parties.

single-member district plurality (SMDP) system A method of selecting representatives in which a nation or state is divided into separate election districts and voters in each district choose one representative. The candidate in each district with a plurality of the vote wins the seat. This method tends to hinder the development of third parties.

Duverger's Law The tendency for the single-member district plurality system to favor a two-party system, as documented by French sociologist Maurice Duverger.

parliamentary system An electoral system in which the party holding the majority of seats in the legislature selects the chief executive.

minister or premier. The prime minister then forms a government by appointing individuals to run the various government departments or ministries—a secretary of defense, a foreign secretary, a secretary of education, and so on. Since minor parties often win seats in parliament, sometimes no party controls a majority of the seats. When no party has a majority of the seats, the leader of one of the parties will try to form a coalition government by offering cabinet seats to other parties in return for their support. As partners in majority coalitions, minor party representatives can end up in posts of central importance in running the government. In contrast, the United States uses a **presidential system**, in which the chief executive and the legislature are elected independently.

The system used to choose the president in the United States offers a distinct advantage to the two major parties. As we explain more completely in chapter 10, the president is not chosen directly by the popular vote but by the electoral college. The Constitution allocates electoral votes to each state; to win the presidency, a candidate must receive a majority of electoral votes. Each state's electoral votes are allocated on a winner-take-all basis to the candidate who wins a plurality of the votes in the state. Although third party and independent candidates occasionally attract significant popular support nationwide, they often receive no electoral votes because they do not win a plurality of the popular vote in any state. For example, Ross Perot received roughly 19 percent of the popular vote in 1992, but not a single electoral vote. A party that has no chance of winning the nation's highest office is unlikely to be an enduring force in the nation's politics.

Two other types of electoral rules also favor the two-party system. First, state laws regulating access to the ballot are a considerable obstacle to minor parties. Candidates of the two major parties automatically appear on the ballot in every state. Minor parties do not get automatic access to the ballot. In order to appear on the ballot, minor parties must satisfy state laws that typically require them to file a candidacy petition signed by a specific number of registered voters by a certain time prior to the election. This procedure requires considerable organizational and financial resources. If a minor party does qualify for access to the ballot in a state, it may have to repeat this arduous process if it fails to draw a minimum percentage of the vote (usually 5 to 10 percent). Laws regulating who is listed on the ballot are thus a significant handicap for third parties.[5]

Second, public financing of presidential campaigns benefits the major parties. As discussed in chapter 10, presidential nominees of the two major parties can receive full financing of their general election campaigns, whereas those representing minor parties receive partial funding or none at all. And minor party candidates routinely find it difficult to raise funds, since contributors are reluctant to fund candidates who have little chance of winning.

The legal obstacles facing minor parties are typically justified as means for protecting the electoral process from frivolous candidates and parties. Most people

---

[5] A party that fails to qualify to have its candidates listed on the ballot can encourage write-in votes, but it is hard to get voters to support candidates who are not listed on the ballot.

presidential system A political system in which the chief executive and the legislature are elected independently.

do not consider making it difficult for "nuts and crackpots" to get on the ballot to be a serious threat to political freedom. Giving free ballot access to anyone who wants to run for office would increase the costs of administering elections and confuse voters rather than offer real choices. But as we will see, most Americans identify with one of the two major parties, and this view can be seen as self-interested. Supporters of minor party candidates obviously do not consider their proposals frivolous. They claim that Democrats and Republicans, who control the institutions that write the rules, have used that power to limit voters' freedom in order to maintain the status quo and protect themselves.

NATURAL PERPETUATION OF THE TWO-PARTY SYSTEM Another cause of the two-party system is a set of mechanisms that tend to make it self-perpetuating. As we will see in chapter 9, people often develop an attachment to a political party at an early age, and the attachment deepens during their adult lives. In a society where two parties have been dominant for more than a century, it is natural for most citizens to think of themselves as Republican or Democrat. In other words, traditional party patterns embedded in the political socialization process perpetuate the two-party system.

Although minor parties regularly nominate candidates in federal and state elections, only the Republican and Democratic parties have a realistic chance of winning any offices. Ambitious politicians who aspire to political office realize that without one of these labels, their chances of fulfilling their ambitions are small. Not surprisingly, political talent gravitates toward the two major parties rather than to minor parties.

The two-party system also perpetuates itself by channeling political conflict into two major outlets: the organization in power and the one out of power. Support and opposition to the government thus coalesce into two distinct groups. Citizens unhappy with the status quo vote not only against present officeholders but also for candidates of the other major party because that is the only viable alternative to replace the party in power.

Minor Political Parties

Although America is clearly a two-party system, minor or **third parties**[6] have appeared often throughout our history (as Figure 7.1 demonstrates). Despite never capturing a significant number of national offices, third parties have occasionally had a considerable effect on American politics.

As political scientists John Bibby and L. Sandy Maisel point out, two-party politics is not mandated by the Constitution, and public opinion polls consis-

---

third parties Minor political parties that periodically appear but have little success in winning office.

---

[6] Although minor parties are commonly referred to by this term, it would be more precise to label them "third," "fourth," or "fifth" parties depending on their relative electoral strength.

tently find that "voters express a distaste for the major parties" and want an alternative (1998, 3–4). In the 1990s, voters awarded independent presidential candidate Ross Perot significant portions of the popular vote in two consecutive elections, and they elected independent and minor party governors in Maine (Angus King), Connecticut (Lowell Weicker), Alaska (Walter Hickel), and Minnesota (Jesse Ventura). In 2012 there actually was a serious attempt to challenge the two-party system by running a presidential candidate to be nominated by an independent, nonpartisan primary. This effort was backed by some serious money—tens of millions of dollars were spent—and the general idea seems like it should have appealed to an electorate that supposedly craves an end to two-party politics. Americans Elect was founded as a nonprofit organization dedicated to running an online presidential primary, with the winner getting placed on the ballot in all 50 states. The effort fizzled; dozens of candidates were drafted, but none could reach the minimum levels of support the organization required to get onto the online primary ballot. Unable to hold a primary, Americans Elect could not field a candidate, and the effort basically collapsed. This perhaps provides a lesson about the importance of political parties; whatever their faults, they are very good at organizing elections and supporting campaigns for political office.

American political history is littered with minor parties and independent candidacies. Some, such as the anti-Masonic party of the 1830s, contested a single presidential election and disappeared almost immediately. Others, such as the Socialist Party, have fielded candidates in a hopeless electoral cause for a number of years. The Prohibition Party, whose members focused on the evils of alcohol, began running presidential candidates in 1872 and was still contesting the nation's highest office in the mid-1990s. The Communist Party of the 1920s sought a radical overhaul of the entire economic and political structure. The Libertarians, who have had a presidential candidate on the ballot in all 50 states in every election since 1972, seek a drastic reduction of the level of governmental involvement in the economy and in individual lives.

The most notable recent third party movement sprang from Ross Perot's presidential bid in 1992. Perot ran as an independent in that election. The organizational effort associated with this candidacy served as the genesis of a genuine third party—the Reform Party—that backed Perot's run for the presidency in 1996, and it ran 22 congressional candidates in the 1998 elections. Although it failed to elect any members to Congress, former professional wrestler Jesse Ventura was elected governor of Minnesota under its label. The initial promise of the Reform Party as a legitimate contender to the major parties has largely fizzled. Its major issue—out-of-control government spending—evaporated with the appearance of balanced federal budgets, and its "angry middle" constituency disappeared in the economic good times of the mid-1990s (Sifry 1998). Nonetheless, the Reform Party is a good example of the primary characteristic shared by minor parties in American politics: a feeling that certain values or interests are not being properly represented by the two major parties. (See the Politics in Practice feature "Are Political Parties Making America Ungovernable?")

ARE POLITICAL PARTIES MAKING AMERICA UNGOVERNABLE?

Political parties have never been particularly popular, but could they actually represent a threat to democratic governance? Some have actually proposed that the answer to this question is yes, at least during the Obama administration.

The basic argument is this: absent an overwhelming majority both in the electorate and in representative institutions, there has to be some measure of bipartisanship for effective governance. This is in part due to institutional rules—most notably the Senate filibuster, which gives the minority party the power to block legislation favored by the majority. There also is the matter of practical politics; neither party has a monopoly on good ideas, and effectively addressing problems often requires mixing and matching from party proposals rather than picking one or the other. In other words, to get anything done, at least the parties in government (if not the parties in the electorate) have to find some common ground.

The problem is that in the past couple of years the parties in government have had a hard time finding that common ground. When they have managed to get on with each other, the parties in the electorate have not been happy (especially the Tea Party variety). The party organizations, meanwhile, jockey for political advantage in the electoral sweepstakes, and part of that means demonizing the other side. There's a vicious-cycle element to the stridently partisan tones of contemporary politics. Angling for political advantage, one party denounces the policies—and increasingly the people—of the other as beyond the pale. Demonizing the other party, though, makes it harder to work with them after the electoral dust has settled because doing so makes it look like you've sold out your campaign message. When effective governance doesn't happen because the two major political parties cannot get along, then the parties in the electorate get frustrated and angry, the parties in government blame each

GOALS AND TYPES OF MINOR PARTIES Some minor parties have promoted ideologies foreign to the nation's traditional beliefs, most notably parties that have failed to adapt to the political reality of free-enterprise economics introduced into the United States from Europe. Included here are the Socialist Party, which has advocated public ownership of basic industries; the Socialist Labor Party, which seeks to eliminate the capitalist system through essentially peaceful means; and the Communist Party, a group founded in 1919 and notable for its close ties to the now-defunct Soviet Union. Of the three, the Socialist Labor Party has been the longest-lived, running a presidential candidate in every election between 1896 and 1976. The Socialist Party has been the biggest vote-getter, pulling in 6 percent of the popular vote in 1912. The Communist Party's electoral forays have been sporadic and uniformly hopeless. The party's highest vote total was 100,000 in 1932, but this pales in comparison to the 23 million voters who chose the Democratic candidate, Franklin Roosevelt.

The most successful minor parties have, like the Marxist parties, protested economic injustices. But their ideology has been indigenous rather than imported from foreign sources. The Populists, for example, emerged during the 1890s, other, the party organizations stoke those accusations for electoral advantage, and the cycle repeats itself.

In 2010, polls showed that a majority of Republican identifiers (more than 60 percent) believed President Barack Obama to be a socialist, and 40 percent believed he should be impeached. The Republican National Committee was well aware of this; it developed a 2010 campaign strategy explicitly to stoke fears about a socialist takeover of the national government. Having proved successful in 2010—Republicans won control of the House of Representatives that year—accusations about Obama's socialist leanings were repeated during the 2012 campaign. If that's the message winning Republicans campaign on—that the president is leading a shady socialist takeover of government—they leave themselves little room to actually work with the president. To do so would give the appearance of colluding in the socialist takeover that the GOP party organization had warned of.

Still, many professional observers of politics say the fears of partisan gridlock are exaggerated, and the accusations that fly from both sides as just business as usual, albeit on a slightly grander scale. Partisan conflict has always been a blood sport, but this helps absorb and manage the tensions that exist in society. And despite dire warnings from both ends of the political spectrum, the republic is still functioning, and government still works, more or less, as it was designed to. Elected Republicans and Democrats may be at each other's throats in front of the camera and on the campaign trail, but there are enough moderate Democrats and moderate Republicans to create an overlap of common partisan ground in both chambers of the Congress. Maybe that patch of political turf is smaller these days, but it's still there.

Finally, some argue felony disenfranchisement is unfair only if it is permanent. Should individuals who serve their time, get their life together, and become law-abiding citizens have no right to cast a ballot? Should society permanently withhold suffrage for crimes (such as drug use or possession) that harmed no one but the offender? In 14 states, the answer is yes.

SOURCES Barr, Andy. 2010. "Poll: Majority of Republicans Believe Obama Is a Socialist." *Politico.* http://www.politico.com/news/stories/0210/32384.html.

The Economist. 2010. "What's Gone Wrong in Washington?" *The Economist* 394 (8670): 11. http://www.economist.com/node/15545983.

Halloran, Liz. 2010. "Top Republicans: Yeah, We're Calling Obama Socialist." National Public Radio, http://www.npr.org/templates/story/story.php?storyId=124359632.

proposing free and unlimited coinage of silver, a graduated income tax, public ownership of railroads, an expansion of the money supply, and a number of other measures designed to break the financial hold of the industrial East over the producers of raw materials. In 1892, the Populists received 8.5 percent of the popular vote and 22 electoral votes.

The Progressives were probably the most successful third party movement of the twentieth century. The genesis for the Progressive movement came from the liberal wing of the Republican Party, and the group is best known for attacks on abuses of both economic and political power. It proposed government regulation of monopolies and championed the adoption of direct democracy reforms such as the initiative (a way for citizens to propose and enact legislation), the referendum (referring proposed laws to the electorate for the ultimate decision), and the recall (permitting citizens to oust unsatisfactory officeholders between elections). There was then a second Progressive movement that focused on the farmer and echoed the earlier Populist movement. Both Theodore Roosevelt (1912) and Robert La Follette (1924) ran for president under the Progressive label with some success. Roosevelt came in second with 27.4 percent of the popular vote and received 88 electoral votes; La Follette picked up 16.6 percent of the popular vote and got 13 electoral votes.

Racial conflict spawned party competition in the decades following World War II. In 1948, a group of dissident Democrats bolted from their party's national nominating convention over the issue of civil rights. They formed the States' Rights Democratic Party, which was widely known as the Dixiecrat Party, and nominated J. Strom Thurmond of South Carolina and Fielding Wright of Mississippi as candidates for president and vice president. Twenty years later, a third party with similar racial views headed by former Alabama governor George Wallace ran candidates under the label of the American Independent Party. Both of these minor parties carried several southern states in presidential elections. The Dixiecrat ticket received only 2.4 percent of the popular vote nationally, but the party won four southern states with 39 electoral votes in 1948. Wallace's 13.5 percent of the popular vote was concentrated in five southern states giving him 46 electoral votes in 1968.

EFFECTS OF MINOR PARTIES It may appear that third parties have been of little significance in American politics. The most successful minor party foray into presidential politics—Theodore Roosevelt's 1912 run as a Progressive—attracted a little more than a quarter of the popular vote and nowhere near enough electoral votes to be considered a serious threat to the two-party hold over the White House. Third parties have not only failed to capture the main prize in American politics; they have also had little success in attaining other national offices.

The significance of minor parties lies not in the offices they have won, but in their effects on the other two parties. Judged from this perspective, some third party movements precipitated seismic shifts in the American political landscape, up to and including deciding the fate of the presidency. For example, Theodore Roosevelt's Progressive candidacy in 1912 contributed to Republican William Howard Taft's loss in his bid for a second term and helped elect Democrat Woodrow Wilson. The Progressives split Republican loyalties between the traditional party structure and its radical offshoot. George Wallace's strategy in his presidential bid in 1968 was not to win outright; he was a savvy politician who knew that his appeal was largely regional and that his chances of ending up in the White House were slim. His objective was to get enough electoral votes from the South to prevent either the Democrat Hubert Humphrey or the Republican Richard Nixon from winning the majority of electoral votes. This would allow him to be the king-maker who would instruct his electors to vote for the candidate he favored. The idea was to negotiate with Humphrey and Nixon for policy positions in return for the presidency. Nixon got a majority of electoral votes, so Wallace's strategy was never put into action, but it was considered plausible (Bibby and Maisel 1998, 96–97).

Even if they do not decide who ends up in the White House, minor parties have certainly played a major role in deciding who gets the electoral votes of particular states. Rather than take the laborious third party route of gaining ballot access, the 1948 Dixiecrats presented Thurmond and Wright as the official

Democratic nominees in Alabama, Louisiana, Mississippi, and South Carolina. This tactic paid off, and they largely carried these states. In 2000, Green Party candidate Ralph Nader received more than 97,000 votes in Florida, where a margin of a few hundred votes gave Republican George W. Bush the state's 25 electoral votes that made him president. Had Nader not been on the ballot, challenger Al Gore probably would have received enough support from Nader voters to win Florida and the presidency. Several prominent Democrats and even some of those who had voted for Nader in 2000 begged him not to run in 2004 and risk helping to reelect President George W. Bush. Nader ignored these pleas and ran again, but he polled fewer than 500,000 votes and had no apparent effect on the outcome.

The effects of minor parties are felt not only in vote totals. They can help shape the policy orientation of the major parties, which adopt the minor parties' ideas as a way to attract more voters. The Democrats did this in 1896, when William Jennings Bryan adopted the Populists' call for free and unlimited coinage of silver. This position pushed the Democratic Party to the left and separated it from the "sound money" policies of the Republicans. In the aftermath of strong Progressive showings in 1912 and 1924, the Democratic Party absorbed some of the central campaign themes of Roosevelt and La Follette, such as the regulation of large corporations and the promotion of labor interests, which held little attraction for Republicans. The Republicans under Nixon picked up on some of Wallace's American Independent Party's civil rights positions, distinguishing itself on racial issues from the Democratic Party.

This process of absorbing some appealing minor party themes has often led to the demise of the organizations that initially espoused them. The Populists were essentially assimilated by the Democrats; the Progressives eventually trudged home to the Republican Party; and the Dixiecrats returned to the Democratic fold or became Republicans (Dixiecrat Strom Thurmond, for example, switched to the Republican Party).

Thus, rather than serving as viable alternatives to the major parties, minor parties have had a more lasting effect by helping shape the composition of the major parties. Factions within a major party that believe they are losing internal conflicts over key issues may defect to the other major party or begin an independent movement. These movements can have important electoral consequences that prompt a response from the major party. Some third party supporters are not overly distressed if that response signals the demise of their movement: the rationale behind the minor party's formation is no longer valid because the values that were formerly ignored now have major party representation.

Minor parties have played a major role in deciding who gets the electoral votes of certain states. Many believe that Ralph Nader's Green Party campaign in 2000 cost Al Gore the presidential election. Despite being asked not to run in 2004, Nader again put in his bid for the presidency.

Students of political parties see few signs that two-party dominance will end in the near future. Minor parties are likely to have important political roles from time to time. If nothing else, they can signal dissatisfaction with the performance or policy stands of the two major parties. If this signal is strong enough, the major parties will respond.

WHAT POLITICAL PARTIES DO

Defining political parties and knowing why and how they developed are important to understanding their place in American democracy. But what, exactly, do political parties *do,* and how do these activities contribute to the democratic process? Recall that political parties are organizations that run candidates for office under a common label. As they run candidates for office, parties engage in a number of specific activities—they recruit and nominate candidates, develop party positions on issues, disseminate party "propaganda," provide campaign support to their candidates, and sponsor get-out-the-vote drives to encourage potential supporters to vote, among other activities. Note that parties engage in these activities for mostly selfish reasons—to recruit candidates who will appeal to voters, to win office, and to control or influence policy. But as parties pursue their own political self-interest, their activities result in by-products that contribute to the democratic process. Political scientists have identified four major contributions political parties make in democratic governments:

1. Facilitate participation of large numbers of people
2. Promote government responsiveness
3. Promote government accountability
4. Promote stability and the peaceful resolution of conflict

Facilitate Participation

Democratic government relies on the participation of ordinary people. But from a rational choice perspective, participating in democratic politics involves costs, among which the largest are the time and effort required to gather necessary information regarding the issues facing government and to sort out which policies and which candidates serve an individual's interests. Political parties reduce these costs by doing the research and sorting out the issues ahead of time, making it possible for large numbers of people to participate in politics in effective and meaningful ways. In essence, political parties provide a way to overcome collective action problems (Aldrich 2011). Party activities facilitate participation in several ways.

AGGREGATING INTERESTS First, political parties facilitate participation because they aggregate interests and act as intermediaries between citizens and government. Parties seek to put together broad coalitions of different interests for purely selfish reasons—they want people to vote for their candidates. But as parties put these electoral coalitions together, they also aggregate individual preferences into coherent policy agendas that can serve as a plan of action for government (Bibby 1996).

This aggregation of interests provides a more or less organized way to resolve differences about what we ought to do. Like interest groups, political parties channel the views and demands of individuals and groups to public officials. But unlike interest groups that transmit relatively narrow positions, parties aggregate multiple and often conflicting demands into broader, more coherent messages by combining shared and overlapping interests and accommodating differences through compromise. Aggregating diverse interests into a party coalition helps ordinary people participate in politics in a meaningful way.

Political parties facilitate participation by ordinary people. Here local party activists get some help and encouragement from President Obama in his reelection campaign in 2012.

SIMPLIFYING ALTERNATIVES Second, parties facilitate participation by simplifying alternatives for voters. Parties run candidates for public office under their label. To have a realistic chance of winning national and most state elections, a candidate must run under one of the major party labels—either Democrat or Republican.[7] Although party leaders sometimes actively recruit candidates, most candidates for national offices (the presidency and Congress) are self-starters who decide on their own to become candidates. To win a major party nomination, a candidate must survive an often grueling nomination process (discussed in more depth in chapter 10) that chooses a single party standard-bearer from among several candidates vying for the party's nomination. These nominating contests winnow out weaker candidates so that on election day voters choose between, at most, two viable candidates—one Democrat and one Republican—for the various offices.

Although some citizens complain about the limited choice, for many it serves a useful purpose: it reduces the amount of information necessary to decide which

---

[7] Independent and minor party candidates do compete in elections, and they occasionally win seats in Congress, though this is rare. Socialist Bernie Sanders, for example, won Vermont's single House seat running as an independent in 1992, and in 1996, he was elected to the Senate as an independent. Former Maine governor Angus King was elected to the Senate as an independent in 2012. With rare exceptions, only major party nominees have a realistic chance of winning a seat in Congress.

candidate is most likely to serve their interest. It is much easier to keep up with the issues and positions of two candidates than those of ten candidates. Suppose that in the 2008 election for president, rather than choosing either Republican John McCain or Democrat Barack Obama, voters could choose from a long list of candidates. Some voters would no doubt welcome the opportunity to sort out the different qualifications and issue positions of dozens of candidates and find the one closest to their interest. Most Americans, however, are not inclined to invest the time and effort required to dig up information for a lengthy roster of candidates. Without relevant information about the candidates, many citizens would be confused and deterred from voting.[8] Moreover, because most voters identify with one of the two major parties, there is some very useful information printed right on the ballot—namely, each candidate's party affiliation. Simplifying the alternatives reduces information costs and helps many voters—over 129 million in the 2012 presidential election—to participate in the electoral process in a meaningful way.

STIMULATING INTEREST IN POLITICS AND GOVERNMENT Third, the parties' campaign activities facilitate participation by stimulating interest in politics. Parties contest elections and mobilize voters. They fund candidates, engage in media campaigns promoting partisan agendas, and help get their supporters registered and to the polls. That is, political parties have a fundamental interest in promoting political participation among their supporters. Although these activities are self-serving, as parties engage in these campaigns, they raise awareness and interest in politics among mostly disinterested citizens.

Promote Government Responsiveness

Promoting government responsiveness is another important contribution that parties make to democratic governance. To satisfy the core democratic value of popular sovereignty, government must be responsive to the demands of ordinary citizens. Parties help achieve this goal as they organize government and seek to pass a policy agenda (Bibby 1996).

Parties serve as the basis for organizing and operating the national government. Representatives in Congress split into majority party and minority party members. Members of the majority party hold the major leadership positions in

---

[8] Many local elections are nonpartisan in that no label appears on the ballot. Judges in some states and state legislators in Nebraska are also elected this way. The intent is to remove politics from the election process, though removing party labels changes politics rather than eliminates it. Specifically, interest groups and the media become more influential in recruiting and electing candidates. And turnout in these nonpartisan elections tends to be low, at least in part because voters have a more difficult time distinguishing among the candidates.

Congress (for example, the Speaker of the House), and they chair and have a majority of the seats in all standing committees. This organizational control gives the majority party leverage to advance its agenda and suppress the minority party's agenda. The president is also an important policymaker who pursues a partisan agenda. Success in enacting this agenda is greatly influenced by whether Congress is controlled by the president's party (what political scientists refer to as unified government) or by the opposition party (divided government).

Voter choices determine which party wins control of the institutions of government. Because voters base their choices at least in part on party agendas, officeholders are responding to preferences of ordinary citizens when they seek to advance a party agenda. Although government responsiveness may be somewhat clearer under unified government, even divided government may be a reflection of voters' preferences. Morris Fiorina (1996, 72–81) suggests that at least some voters prefer divided government, to check and moderate the extremes of each party's agenda.

Promote Government Accountability

Majority rule requires not only responsiveness but also the means to hold government officials accountable if they are not responsive. Parties act as agents of accountability (Bibby 1996). Particularly important here is the role of the minority party in keeping an eye on the majority. There is, of course, a large degree of self-interest in performing this watchdog function. Uncovering and publicizing questionable actions or broken campaign promises of the party in power may produce electoral benefits for the minority party in future elections. Democrats in Congress certainly tried to elevate the scandal involving Republican super-lobbyist Jack Abramoff into a campaign issue to use against Republicans in the 2006 midterm elections. But this self-interested scrutiny also serves a broader civic function in that the minority party helps to check any abuse of power by the majority, and it aids citizens in holding unresponsive policymakers accountable.

Promote Stability and Peaceful Resolution of Conflict

Finally, some scholars suggest that political parties promote stability and the peaceful resolution of conflict. The process of reconciling and accommodating a broad spectrum of views assists in settling social conflict and developing significant areas of agreement among citizens of various backgrounds and perspectives. The creation of such a consensus contributes to a basic feature of a democratic society: the pursuit and maintenance of political power by peaceful means and, when the populace so desires, the peaceful transfer of that power into other hands. For example, after a difficult campaign in the 2012 election, former Massachusetts governor Mitt Romney expressed disappointment but accepted his loss with grace: "I have just called President Obama to congratulate him on his victory. His supporters and his campaign also deserve congratulations. I wish all of them well, but particularly the president, the first lady and their daughters. This is a time of great challenges for America, and I pray that the president will be successful in guiding our nation. . . . We have given our all to this campaign. I so wish . . . that I had been able to fulfill your hopes to lead the country in a different direction. But the nation chose another leader. And so Ann and I join with you to earnestly pray for him and for this great nation."

This argument is based more on the sociological theory of roles and functions than on rational choice theory. The argument that certain roles in society—in this example, the role of a "good loser" who patriotically places the national interest above his own—reduce conflict and promote stability is controversial. Even if there is a correlation between democratic norms and the stability of a nation, determining the direction of causation is problematic. Some scholars argue that it's likely that a stable democratic nation actually produces "good losers," rather than the good losers producing a stable democratic nation as role theory suggests. It is, after all, a lot less risky to be a gracious loser in a society that does not have a history of putting the political opponents of governmental leaders in jail.

The Responsible Party Model

The extent to which political parties promote these democratic benefits varies across different political systems. Political scientists use the phrase "**responsible party model**" to describe democracies with strong, competitive parties in which one party wins control of the government based on its policy proposals, enacts those proposals once it is in control, and stands or falls in the next election based on its performance in delivering on its promises. The party out of power (sometimes referred to as the loyal opposition) notes every policy failure and every action at odds with popular sentiment; it then uses these failures to formulate new policy agendas and to provide points of contrast and debate in the next electoral cycle. The disciplined political parties of Great Britain are a close approximation of the responsible party model. The parliamentary system unifies control of the executive and legislative branches of government under the prime minister, who is the majority party leader. When the prime minister presents legislation to Parliament, members of the governing party are expected to support it, and members of the loyal opposition are expected to oppose it. A party member who does not vote along party lines is subject to sanctions that might include losing his or her seat.

In theory, this competition over policy encourages government to be responsive to the will of the people. Moreover, competition between disciplined parties helps citizens assign responsibility for government performance. Offering clear policy choices and making it easy to assign credit or blame provides voters with the means to hold an unresponsive government accountable.

Critics, however, have long suspected that the responsible party model is an idealized depiction of the role political parties play rather than a realistic one, particularly in the United States. American political parties are weak and undisciplined. They have no centralized controlling body and few options for enforcing **party discipline**—that is, the means to require party members in public office to promote or carry through on a partisan agenda and to punish those who do

responsible party model A concept that describes democracies with competitive parties in which one party wins control of the government based on its policy proposals, enacts those proposals once it is in control, and stands or falls in the next election based on its performance in delivering on its promises.

party discipline Requiring political party members in public office to promote or carry out the party's agenda and punishing those who do not.

not toe the party line. American political parties sometimes offer similar policy agendas, and officeholders often choose their constituencies or their consciences over their party's policy preferences. Moreover, the American electoral system frequently results in **divided government**—when one party wins the presidency and another party wins a majority of seats in one or both houses of Congress. Divided government makes it hard for voters to assign responsibility and to hold public officials accountable. If a Democratic president signs a law passed by a Republican Congress, who gets the credit or blame? Although there have been periods in American history when parties were stronger, the U.S. party system generally falls far short of the party discipline required by the responsible party model. Nonetheless, party strength in America has varied considerably over time.

THE STRENGTH OF POLITICAL PARTIES

The potential of political parties to fulfill broader democratic functions depends on their viability. A number of political scientists have argued that parties have been declining since the 1950s. If party decline is in fact the case, this raises important questions about the performance and stability of the political system. Specifically, what or who will take over the vital activities traditionally performed by parties? The party decline thesis rests on several pieces of evidence:

- The electorate's attachment to political parties is not as strong as it once was.
- The central role of parties in the electoral process has been eclipsed by the rise of candidate-centered campaigns in which a candidate's electoral chances rest heavily on his or her personal organization rather than on the party's.
- Party voting in Congress occurs less frequently than it once did.
- Party organizations no longer have the power to determine who runs under their party's label.

Other scholars argue that political parties are not likely to fade from a central role in American politics. Parties may be changing, but they still contribute to the democratic process. These researchers present evidence that the party in the electorate and party in government show signs of increasing strength that have persisted into the twenty-first century. Party organizations may no longer unilaterally pick candidates to run under their label, but they have become an important supplier of the resources necessary to run a successful campaign: money, logistical support, and connections to a broad and supportive political network.

In short, whether we see party decline seems to rest heavily on which of the three elements—party in the electorate, party in government, or party organization—we examine, and at what time.

divided government When one party controls the presidency and another controls Congress.

The Strength of Party in the Electorate

The argument that parties are in decline begins with the observation that the electorate is becoming less partisan. Scholars who favor this point of view focus on three indicators:

1. A decline in the percentage of the electorate referring to themselves as strong partisans
2. An increase in the percentage of the electorate calling themselves independents
3. A decline in straight-ticket voting (voting for the same party's candidates for president and Congress)

Several explanations may account for the decline of the party in the electorate. Perhaps the most intuitive explanation is that, as political scientist Martin Wattenberg (1990) argues, political parties are simply less relevant to voters than they once were. Rather than being loyal to a political party, voters are increasingly influenced by issues and candidate image. A candidate's character, views, and appearance increasingly influence voting, whereas the importance of the party label has declined. (Chapter 11 discusses the effect of party on voting behavior in more detail.)

A closer look at the evidence indicates that the trend toward weaker partisanship in the electorate characterized the period from the 1950s to the 1970s but reversed in

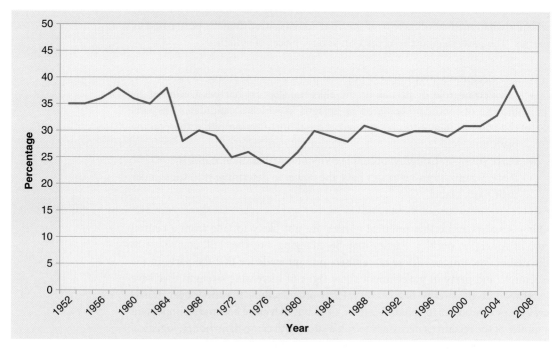

FIGURE 7.3 Strong Partisans in the Electorate, 1952–2008

Source: American National Election Studies, *The ANES Guide to Public Opinion and Electoral Behavior* (Ann Arbor: University of Michigan, Center for Political Studies, 2006).

the 1980s and continued to rise through the 1990s. Political scientists typically measure party identification in the electorate on a scale that identifies strong Democrats, weak Democrats, independents, weak Republicans, and strong Republicans. Figure 7.3 shows the percentage of strong partisans (that is, strong Democrats plus strong Republicans) since 1952. In the 1950s, about 36 percent of the electorate were strong partisans. The percentage fell to around 33 percent in the 1960s and to 25 percent in the 1970s. But "the slide toward weaker partisanship . . . stalled" (Fleisher and Bond 2000b), and the percentage of strong partisans rebounded to about 30 percent in the 1980s and 1990s and continued to climb in the 2000s. The current level of strong partisanship is near the highs in the 1950s.

Another indication that the electorate is becoming less partisan focuses on the rise in the number of independents. Figure 7.4 plots trends in the percentage of Democrats, independents, and Republicans in the electorate. To understand this evidence, we need to consider the definition of *partisans* and *independents*. Studies of partisanship in the electorate reveal that about two-thirds of individuals who initially say they are "independent" admit that they think of themselves "as closer to the Republican or Democratic party" (see Stanley and Niemi 2011, 107). This group is referred to as independent *leaners* because they lean toward preferring one party

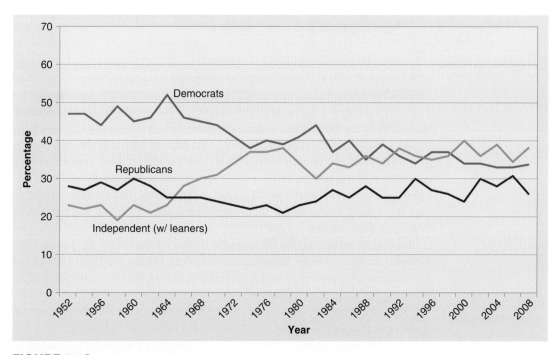

FIGURE 7.4A Party Identification in the Electorate, 1952–2008 (Independent includes leaners)

Source: American National Election Studies, *The ANES Guide to Public Opinion and Electoral Behavior* (Ann Arbor: University of Michigan, Center for Political Studies, 2006).

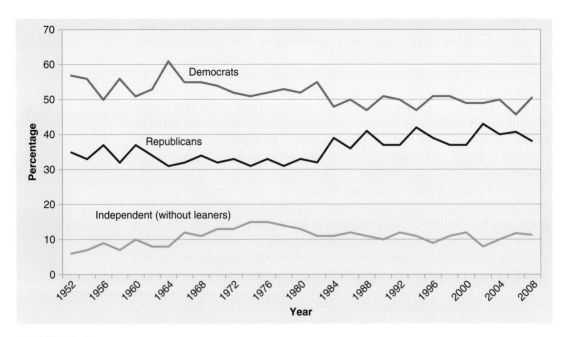

FIGURE 7.4B Party Identification in the Electorate, 1952–2008

Source: American National Election Studies, *The ANES Guide to Public Opinion and Electoral Behavior* (Ann Arbor: University of Michigan, Center for Political Studies, 2006).

or the other. Should we count leaners as independents or as partisans? The choice makes a big difference in whether we find a growing number of independents.

Figure 7.4A shows the trends if the category of independents includes all those who say they are independents (that is, if independent leaners count as independents) and if partisans include only those who express a party preference (strong plus weak partisans in each party). Using this definition, there appears to be a gradual long-term decline in the percentage of Democrats and Republicans and a concurrent increase in the percentage of independents. Indeed, there appear to have been more independents than Republicans since 1966 and more independents than Democrats since 2000.

But it is important not to overstate the decline of party and the rise of independents in the electorate. Independents who lean toward the Democrats or the Republicans exhibit partisan voting patterns. In presidential elections since 1952, for example, independents who lean toward one party or the other have voted for the candidate of the party they favor at about the same rate as (and often higher rate than) weak partisans—an average of 4.8 percent higher for independents leaning Democrat and 1.3 percent higher for independents leaning Republican. This behavior supports the argument that these voters are not true independents, regardless of their initial self-identification as such. Figure 7.4B shows the trends if independents include only those who do not favor one party or the other (pure independents) and if partisans include independent leaners along with strong and weak partisans. In

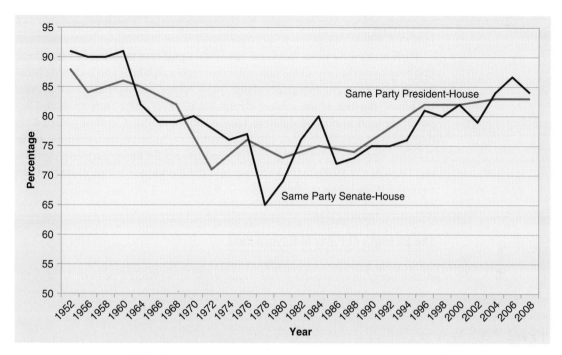

FIGURE 7.5 Straight-Ticket Voting, 1952–2008

Source: American National Election Studies, *The ANES Guide to Public Opinion and Electoral Behavior* (Ann Arbor: University of Michigan, Center for Political Studies, 2006). Information for 2006 provided by Gary Jacobson from Cooperative Congressional Election Study.

this interpretation, about 90 percent of the electorate identify themselves as either Democrats or Republicans, and the percentage of pure independents has increased only slightly. About 7 percent of the electorate identified themselves as independent in the 1950s and 1960s; the number of independents doubled to about 15 percent in the 1970s but then declined and has hovered around 10 percent since the 1980s.

Another indicator of partisanship in the electorate is the percentage of **straight-ticket voters**—that is, voting for the same party's candidates for president and Congress. Figure 7.5 shows that the percentage of straight-ticket voters decreased considerably from the 1950s through the 1970s but then climbed back up from the 1980s to the 2000s.

Although issues and candidate image have increasingly influenced voting decisions over time, the effects of party identification remain strong. And although the influence that party identification had on vote choice declined from 1964 to 1980, it strengthened significantly in the 1984 presidential election. The relationship remained strong in the next five presidential elections—1988, 1992, 1996, 2000, and 2004—"such that party identification is as strongly related to the presidential vote as it has been since" the 1950s (Abramson, Aldrich, and Rohde 2006, 194). When Larry Bartels analyzed the effect of partisanship on voting in both presidential and congressional elections from the 1950s to the 1990s, he concluded that the

straight-ticket voters People who vote for the same party's candidates for both president and Congress.

"conventional wisdom regarding the 'decline of parties' is both exaggerated and outdated" (2000, 35).

Partisan identification, therefore, remains a significant predictor of vote choice and even seems to help shape how voters perceive candidates and issues. As Morris Fiorina observed, arguments about "issue voting" versus "party voting" miss the point: "the 'issues' are in party identification" (1981, 200). Democrats and Republicans tend to express different issue positions, and the level of polarization between partisans (even weak and independent partisans) increased in the 1990s (Fleisher and Bond 2000b). Thus, the trend toward declining partisanship from the 1950s to the 1970s turned around, and the electorate became more partisan from the 1980s to the present.

The Strength of Party in Government

A number of observers have also found evidence of decline of party in government. Two common pieces of evidence to support this perspective are the rise of divided government and a decline in party voting in Congress.

The strength of party in government depends in large part on the strength of partisanship in the electorate. According to political scientists David Brady, Joseph Cooper, and Patricia Hurley (1979), a partisan electorate is a key require-

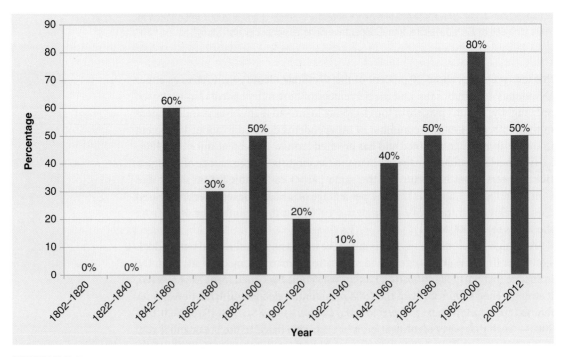

FIGURE 7.6 Elections Producing Divided Government

Source: Constructed by the authors from election results in the public record.

ment for partisan voting in Congress. When voters elect representatives on the basis of partisanship, members of Congress are more likely to be tied to a common party-centered electoral fate. Thus, as the party in the electorate declines, it also erodes the party in government. When the electorate attaches its loyalties to individual candidates rather than to parties, officeholders have more freedom to resist the party line when it conflicts with constituent preferences. Recall that divided government occurs when one party wins the presidency and another party wins a majority of seats in one or both houses of Congress. Figure 7.6 shows the frequency of divided government since the nineteenth century. Although divided government was common in earlier periods of American history, the last two decades of the twentieth century stand out: eight of the ten elections from 1982 to 2000 resulted in divided party control of the presidency and Congress.

Some scholars see divided government as a symptom of weak parties because it hinders the exercise of coordinated government action (G. Jacobson 2001). In order to approach the responsible party model, parties must exercise enough control to get government to at least attempt to follow through on partisan policy agendas. If the major parties split control of the legislature and executive, they may be able to conduct the business of government, but they can hardly claim the sole partisan responsibility for it. Voters have difficulty assigning credit or blame when party control of national governing institutions is split.

Although divided government certainly detracts from the system of government envisioned by the responsible party model, it does not necessarily indicate that parties are weak. Instead, divided government could result from two competitive parties with different strengths—one party strong enough to win the presidency and the other party strong enough to win control of Congress. The evidence presented in Figure 7.2 is consistent with this interpretation. But even if divided government is a sign of party decline, the first six elections of the twenty-first century (2002, 2004, 2006, 2008, 2010, and 2012) produced divided government three times (in 2006, 2010, and 2012), though we cannot be sure what will happen in future elections.

The argument that party in government has declined is bolstered by evidence that party unity within the legislative branch has eroded. Partisanship in the U.S. Congress has never reached the levels common in most parliamentary democracies, although there have been periods when Congress has been characterized by high levels of party voting. A **party vote** is commonly defined as one on which a majority of Democrats vote on one side of an issue and a majority of Republicans on the other. As Figure 7.7 shows, party votes were common from the 1870s to the early 1900s, occurring 80 to 90 percent of the time in some years. The frequency of party votes declined somewhat during the 1920s, rebounded briefly during the New Deal years of the 1930s, and then began a long-term slide, reaching a low point in the late 1960s. In recent decades, however, party in government has become stronger. The proportion of party votes in both the House and Senate increased gradually through the 1970s and then accelerated dramatically in the late 1980s (Fleisher and Bond 2000a). The trend toward increased partisanship in Congress has continued into the twenty-first century.

party vote A vote in which a majority of Democrats vote on one side and a majority of Republicans vote on the other.

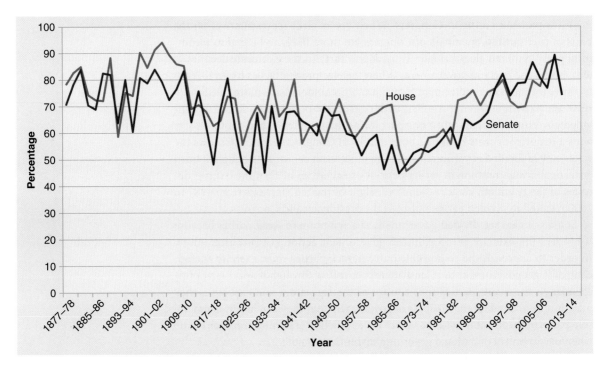

FIGURE 7.7 Party Votes in Congress

Note: A "party vote" is defined as one on which a majority of Democrats vote against a majority of Republicans and vice versa. Entries reflect the percentage of party votes in each Congress, but they are revised to exclude consensus votes (less than 10% voting in the minority) from the denominator. They are interpreted as the percentage of all conflict on the House and Senate floor that is partisan conflict. They are averages of the two years of each Congress.

Source: Constructed by the authors from data at http://voteview.com/downloads.asp.

The recent rise of partisanship in Congress resulted in part from electoral changes. The most dramatic change occurred in the South. Implementation of the 1965 Voting Rights Act brought large numbers of African Americans into the electorate, and white southern Democrats in Congress became more responsive to the interests of their African American constituents. As a result, southern Democrats in the House and Senate became more liberal and began voting more like their northern colleagues (Fleisher 1993; Rohde 1991). At the same time, the most conservative white southern voters began to leave the Democratic Party, contributing to the election of an increasing number of conservative southern Republicans to Congress. Most of the remaining southern Democrats are almost as liberal as northern Democrats. According to David Rohde (1991), when northern and southern Democrats in Congress became more similar ideologically, the Democratic caucus adopted reforms that strengthened the Democratic leadership's ability to promote party discipline.

Another factor contributing to elevated partisanship in the 1980s and 1990s was the election of Ronald Reagan and the Republican takeover of the Senate in the 1980 elections. Republicans interpreted their electoral victory as a mandate to enact a conservative agenda. When House Democrats began to use the rules to prevent votes on the Republican agenda, Republicans turned to conservative activists such as Newt Gingrich. Under Gingrich's leadership, the Republican Party campaigned on the "Contract with America," a coherent policy agenda, in the 1994 elections. Republicans won control of both houses of Congress for the first time in 40 years. As Speaker of the House, Gingrich continued the aggressive use of House rules to enforce party discipline. And these actions in the House may have contributed to the rise in partisanship in the Senate. Recent research suggests that Republican senators who served in the House during the Gingrich years—the so-called Gingrich Senators—are responsible for much of the increased partisanship in the Senate in recent years (Theriault and Rohde 2011).

Republican electoral success in winning House seats was aided by redistricting after the 1990 census. States were encouraged to draw districts so as to increase the number of African Americans elected to Congress. These efforts removed large blocs of reliably Democratic voters from the constituencies of white southern Democratic incumbents. A side effect of drawing districts to elect more African American representatives was the defeat of several moderate white Democrats by conservative Republicans in 1992 and 1994 (Hill 1995). The resulting large turn-over of members created large freshman classes that were more likely to vote the party line than were the members they replaced (Hurley and Kerr 1997).

Thus, electoral changes, rules, and leadership of Congress have all contributed to more partisan voting behavior. Although party discipline in the United States has never attained the levels typical of parliamentary systems, parties remain the primary mechanism for organizing Congress, and party unity remains relatively high even in the face of divided government.

The Strength of Party Organizations

The thesis that parties have declined in strength also rests on some important historical evidence about the decline of party organizations. There is no doubt that modern party organizations have considerably less power than the political machines that once controlled politics in numerous cities and some states. Roughly a hundred years ago, reformers disgusted by powerful and corrupt party machines began pursuing reforms specifically designed to weaken party organizations. One such reform was nonpartisan elections. Numerous cities and one state (Nebraska) adopted nonpartisan elections. The absence of party labels on the ballot made it more difficult for party bosses to mobilize voters in support of their candidates.

Another successful reform was reducing **political patronage**—that is, government jobs and contracts that elected officeholders handed out to those who supported the party. Reformers advocated using a **merit system**—hiring government workers based on their skills and qualifications to do the job rather than on party loyalty. In place of awarding government contracts to party supporters (who often inflated the cost of doing the job and gave kickbacks to the party machine),

political patronage The giving of government jobs to people based on their party affiliation and loyalty.

merit system A system of governing in which jobs are given based on relevant technical expertise and the ability to perform.

reformers proposed a system of competitive bids to award contracts for government work to the lowest bidder qualified to do the job. This loss of control of patronage diminished the role of parties in many voters' political, social, and economic lives. No longer could parties use government jobs and contracts to recruit supporters and maintain their loyalty.

By far the most important of the reforms was the direct primary. The **direct primary**—an election in which rank-and-file voters choose the party's nominees for various offices—transferred the key power for determining who has the right to use the party label in an election from party bosses to voters. Before the direct primary, elected officials would toe the party line or face the threat that party leaders would withhold the party label from them in the next election. Without the party machine's endorsement, candidates had little prospect of getting elected.

Rank-and-file voters are less likely than party leaders to choose candidates on the basis of party loyalty. For example, in recent years, both major parties have been embarrassed by fringe candidates who won party nominations in direct primaries. David Duke, an activist with ties to the Ku Klux Klan, ran as the Republican nominee for governor of Louisiana. And a supporter of political extremist Lyndon LaRouche won the Democratic nomination for lieutenant governor in Illinois. The Republican Party condemned Duke, and the Democratic Party did the same to the LaRouche backer, but neither party could stop the candidate from claiming the party label in the general election. Although these are extreme examples, they illustrate that the direct primary made officeholders much more independent of their parties.

There is evidence, however, that although they differ from the old political machines, modern party organizations are alive and well. A group of political scientists undertook an extensive analysis of party organizations at local, state, and national levels in the 1960s, 1970s, and 1980s (Cotter et al. 1989; Gibson et al. 1989; Huckshorn et al. 1986). In contrast to those who forecast imminent party demise, these researchers saw active organizations busily reinventing themselves as central players in American politics. They found that party organizations at all levels had become more professional. Parties were key sources of funding and logistical support for candidates running under their labels, and they linked party members in differing levels of government and different offices. The research also indicated that parties still remain capable of coherent policy platforms. Furthermore, party organization influences party in the electorate. John Coleman (1996, 821) finds that "strong, competitive party organizations contribute to generalized support for parties" among ordinary citizens.

These scholars do not deny that the reforms adopted around the turn of the twentieth century affected party organization. However, they argue that the reforms did not permanently diminish the relevance of parties but rather obliged them to deal with a new political environment. Parties responded to these changes not by collapsing, but by adapting. For example, the new electoral environment may make candidates more independent in one sense, but they still need campaign funds, a clear message, a way to get the message to the voters, tracking polls, and the host of administrative and logistical services required to run a successful

direct primary The selection of a political party's candidate for the general election by vote of ordinary citizens.

modern campaign. Parties provide all of this and more. By strategically deploying these resources, parties make themselves central players in electoral politics. Indeed, Cotter and his associates conclude that parties operate in "a framework of public regulation and support which protects more than weakens the existing parties" (1989, 168).

Cycles of Party Strength

Thus, we see that party strength rises and falls in cycles over time. At some points, parties have played prominent roles in structuring citizens' vote choice and in making public policy; at other times, their influence has waned. Rather than steadily declining over time, political parties have adapted to changes in the political landscape and have retained a central, albeit altered, place in the political system (Aldrich 2011). As long as political parties continue to attract adherents, they remain viable institutions central to the democratic process, and they have the potential to fulfill their broader functions in the political system.

In chapters 9, 10, and 11 we focus on the role of parties in the electoral process. In subsequent chapters, we analyze the role of the party in the government in making public policy.

CHAPTER SEVEN

Top Ten Takeaway Points

① Although the founders did not incorporate political parties into the Constitution, and although parties have been viewed with suspicion and distrust since their emergence in the early days of the republic, political scientists tend to view them as essential organizations in promoting the long-term health and stability of the democratic process.

② A political party is an organization that nominates and runs candidates for public office under its own label. This characteristic sets parties apart from interest groups, which often try to influence policy but do not run candidates for office under their own labels.

③ Parties can be thought of as consisting of three overlapping elements: (1) the party in the electorate, consisting of ordinary citizens who identify with the party; (2) the party in government, consisting of the elected and appointed officeholders who share a party label; and (3) the party organization, consisting of the party professionals who hold official positions in the party.

④ Political parties' activities produce side-benefits that contribute to the democratic process. Most importantly, political parties link citizens and government by facilitating participation. Parties facilitate participation in three ways: (1) they aggregate individual policy preferences into coherent policy agendas; (2) they structure and simplify alternatives for voters; and (3) their campaign activities stimulate interest in politics and government.

⑤ Political parties contribute to the democratic process in other ways as well: (1) they promote government responsiveness as they organize government and seek to pass a policy agenda; (2) they promote accountability when parties out of power scrutinize activities of the party in power and report mistakes and abuses; and (3) they promote stability and the peaceful resolution of conflict as they reconcile and accommodate a diverse spectrum of views to build broad coalitions.

⑥ Party systems are classified according to the number of parties that effectively compete for power: one-party, multiparty, or two-party. American politics has been characterized by two-party competition throughout most if its history. Democrats and Republicans have dominated political competition in the United States from 1856 to the present in the oldest continuous two-party competition in the world.

⑦ Reasons for the two-party system in the United States include historical factors; electoral rules (including the single-member district plurality system, the electoral college, state laws regulating access to the ballot, and public financing of presidential elections); and a set of mechanisms that tend to make it self-perpetuating.

⑧ Minor or third parties do exist in the United States and have periodically had an important effect on American politics. By siphoning off votes from the major parties, minor parties sometimes influence who wins an election. Minor party issues that attract significant support tend to be absorbed by the major parties.

⑨ Political parties in the United States are not as strong and disciplined as parties in parliamentary democracies, and they fall far short of the responsible party model.

(10) The power and importance of political parties in American politics has varied over time. There was a general decline in the strength of parties in the electorate and in government from the 1950s to the 1970s. Since the 1980s, partisanship in the electorate and in government has been increasing. Party organizations have remained active and vibrant as they have adapted to changes in the political environment.

CHAPTER SEVEN

Key Terms and Cases

direct primary, 262
divided government, 253
Duverger's Law, 240
merit system, 261
multiparty systems, 235
one-party system, 233
parliamentary system, 240
party discipline, 252
party in the electorate, 226

party in government, 226
party organization, 226
party professionals, 227
party vote, 259
policy-motivated activists, 227
political machine, 227
political party, 224
political patronage, 261
presidential system, 241

proportional representation, 240
responsible party model, 252
role theory, 230
single-member district plurality (SMDP) system, 240
straight-ticket voters, 256
third parties, 242
two-party system, 235

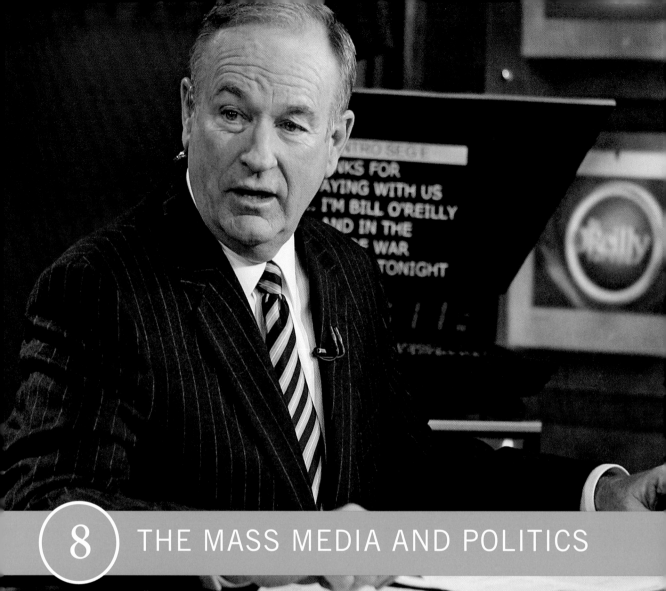

8   THE MASS MEDIA AND POLITICS

KEY QUESTIONS

Does media bias threaten the core principles of democracy?

What are the primary threats to a free press?

Do new media technologies increase civic engagement?

FOX NEWS was called the favorite network of President George W. Bush's administration. Fox News has been called a lot of things by members of President Barack Obama's administration, but favorite is not one of them.

At one point early in Obama's tenure, White House Communications Director Anita Dunn was so ticked off at Fox News that she publically called them biased. "We're going to treat them the way we would treat an opponent," she said, and not "pretend that this is the way that legitimate news organizations behave." Though he didn't mention names, President Obama himself was not shy about airing his displeasure with Fox: "I've got one television station that is entirely devoted to attacking my administration" (Stelter 2009).

Based on the comments of some of its news and talk-show personalities, Obama had some basis for treating Fox as ideologically hostile. Fox news anchor Chris Wallace called the Obama administration a bunch of "crybabies." Former Fox pundit Glenn Beck referred to one White House appointee as a "communist-anarchist radical," branded Obama a racist, and declared that only Fox (and conservative-dominated talk radio) stood between such presumably antidemocratic forces and the safety of the republic. Other Fox shows have (falsely) reported that Obama attended a madrassa (i.e., an Islamic school) and have promoted the "Tea Party" movement in its protests against government (Stelter 2009). None of that seems to reflect the "fair and balanced" motto of Fox News. In its defense, Fox has argued that the White House is conflating its news operation with talk shows and is being overly sensitive to pundits doing what they are paid to do. Fox certainly has not seemed repentant—its ratings trend up during such spats.

Some observers see this sort of thing as just politics as usual. All presidents get sideways with the press at some point. It's certainly no shock to find politicians suggesting that the media are acting recklessly, venally or ideologically, any more than it is to find the media suggesting that those in power are tight-mouthed, underhanded, or thin-skinned. Others, though, see a more fundamental shift in the relationship between politics and the press that is exemplified by the apparent mutual suspicion and hostility between the Obama administration and Fox. It is true that politicians and the press have long had a relationship marked by conflict. But for a century or more the media have taken nonpartisanship as a professional point of pride. Some people—White House communications directors, for example—are now openly wondering whether this era has passed and the press is returning to its more openly partisan origins.

As we'll discuss in this chapter, there is a widely held perception that the media have an ideological or partisan bias (though there's much less agreement on which party or political philosophy the media champions). What does this mean for democracy? If the press is engaging in political bias—or any other type of bias, for that matter—is democracy threatened? Doesn't pushing a particular ideological or partisan point of view represent at least some sort of ethical lapse? Isn't the media supposed to be neutral and unbiased? For at least the last of these questions, there's a short answer: no.

What is crucial to the functioning of a healthy democracy is not neutral media, but free and independent media. A free press means exactly that—that it is free and unregulated. Free does not mean fair, unbiased, or even accurate. It means free of government control; how people use that freedom, with few exceptions, is up to them. The result is not always pretty; at times, it can be downright infuriating. If television networks hire commentators who use their platforms to call the president a racist or refer to government officials as "communist-anarchist radicals," it's reasonable to say they are not promoting neutral or civil debate, but in important ways that doesn't matter. They are engaging in free debate, and that's the essential point: democracy depends on this media freedom in important ways. Limit this freedom, and you limit democracy.

We live in a media-soaked culture, with virtually unlimited access to information. Supplying that information is the **mass media**, a term describing all the means used to transmit information to masses of people. These means include the **print media**, which consist of news-papers, magazines, and books, and the **electronic media**, which consist

mass media All the means used to transmit information to masses of people.

print media Media consisting of news-papers, magazines, and books.

electronic media Consists of television, radio, movies, video and audio recordings, and the Internet.

of television, radio, movies, recordings, and the Internet. Of particular importance to politics is the **news media**: organizations and journalists that cover the news. **News** is defined as accounts of timely and specific events. The print and electronic media partially or wholly devoted to collecting and reporting news in the United States consist of roughly 1,400 daily newspapers; 6,700 weekly newspapers; 1,700 television stations; 15,000 radio stations; hundreds of magazines; and the various publications' and stations' Internet-based counterparts (Newspaper Association of America 2010; Federal Communications Commission 2012). Generically, these are all known as the **press**.

In this chapter, we explore the role of the press in a democratic society. As it turns out, it is the freedom of the media—not its fairness or accuracy—that is most critical to democracy.

news media Organizations and journalists that cover the news.

news Accounts of timely and specific events.

press The print and electronic media that are partially or wholly devoted to collecting and reporting news in the United States.

THE CONCEPT OF A FREE PRESS

A free press is just that—free. Free to say what it wants, investigate what it wants, and report what it wants without government interference or control. Allowing the press to investigate and criticize government, to promote a diverse set of perspectives and viewpoints, and to collect and distribute information with little government censorship or regulation is considered a central characteristic of a democratic society. A free press promotes the core democratic value of political freedom.

The media support political freedom by helping to create what Jürgen Habermas (1991) termed a **public sphere**, a forum where information on matters important to civic life can be freely accessed and exchanged. A free marketplace of perspectives and ideas is critically important because a healthy democracy requires that citizens not only be able to express their opinions and preferences but also be knowledgeable and informed when they make political choices.

For example, in a representative democracy elections are the primary way to connect the preferences of citizens to the actions of government. Elections cannot achieve this goal if citizens have no information about what their government is doing, what issues are important, and what options exist to address those issues. It is difficult, after all, to have preferences about issues, proposals, or candidates if you are unaware that they exist. In any society with a free press, it is easy to find out what the government is doing, identify the important issues of the day, and

public sphere A forum where information on matters important to civic life can be freely accessed and exchanged.

get a broad sense of what actions have been proposed to address those issues. All this information and much more is delivered to doorsteps every morning, and it is available with the flick of a switch or click of a mouse pretty much any hour of the day.

That free flow of information is critical to a functioning democracy not only because it helps inform voters but also because it serves as an important check on government officials. Public officeholders are aware that their proposals and their actions will be recorded and transmitted through the mass media, and they also know there are consequences if that information makes a negative impression on their constituents. Thomas Jefferson (1823) wrote, "The only security of all is in a free press. The force of public opinion cannot be resisted when permitted freely to be expressed."

The media create a public sphere and help uphold the core value of political freedom by serving a number of specific roles in democratic societies. These functions include information dissemination and education, agenda setting, and watchdog and public advocacy.

Information and Education

The news media see their primary role as one of informing and educating the public. They monitor what the government is doing, report its activities to the public, and try to put these activities into context by seeking to explain the meaning and significance of government decisions or actions.

PROCESSING INFORMATION The news media's role in providing information and education is much more complex than simply providing the raw materials for neutral observers to make up their minds on whether they support a particular candidate or oppose a particular policy. People are not neutral consumers of information; they filter what they read, hear, or watch through their own perspectives and biases. People are resistant to messages they do not want to hear and are eager to find support for their own opinions. This makes sense from all of the broad theoretical perspectives we are highlighting in this book. It makes sense from a social-psychological perspective to be more receptive to positive information about the groups you either belong to or view positively and to be equally receptive to negative information about groups you view negatively. Psychological experiments have repeatedly found that people readily accept information that confirms their own views but are much quicker to find fault with information that conflicts with their own views (Vedantam 2006).

It also is perfectly rational to seek out information that supports your preferred point of view. A number of academic studies view the media's information role through the prism of rational choice and conclude not only that it makes sense for utility maximizers to seek information that supports their own preferences, but also that it is rational for the media to serve those preferences. If a large audience shares a particular set of beliefs, it is rational for media outlets to provide information confirming those beliefs. Why? Well, because providing such information serves the rational interests of the media providers—it boosts circulation, viewership, and ultimately advertising revenue and profits (Mullainathan and Schleifer 2005). These findings raise important questions about bias in the media, an issue that is discussed in more detail later in this chapter.

Recent research shows that there is almost certainly a biological basis for how political information is processed. What seems to drive how we process political information is not the reasoning part of our brains, but the emotional part of our brains. One study used brain scans of 10 Republicans and 10 Democrats to study brain activity when people are exposed to information that supports or opposes their partisan viewpoints (in this case, pictures of candidates from the 2004 presidential election). The study found that people tend to react emotionally to the candidates they support; in effect we feel "warm fuzzies" when we see our "favorite." When people are exposed to pictures of the opposing candidate, however, they experience negative emotions that seem to suppress the more rational parts of the brain. In effect, although people accept the candidate they support based on passion and emotion, they pick the "other guy" over, looking for fault (Kaplan, Freedman, and Iacoboni 2007). Biologically, this is what we'd expect to find from the social-psychological framework. People invest themselves psychologically, for whatever reason, in a candidate or a cause. They tend to be relatively immune to rational arguments to dissuade them of that support because their support is based on emotion rather than a conventional cost–benefit calculus. On the other hand, they are quick to pick up on, or independently develop, rationalizations for why the candidates and causes they do not support are wrong.

IMPORTANCE OF THE INFORMATION AND EDUCATION ROLE How people acquire and process political information from the mass media has become an important research topic for social scientists because the information and education function of the media has become increasingly important over the last half-century. During that time, the media have taken on some of the roles traditionally held by political parties. For example, prior to the widespread adoption of primary elections, the job of nominating candidates for office was controlled by relatively small groups of party elites. The rise of the direct primary took the power to nominate candidates from party leaders and placed it in the hands of the voting public.[1] Because voters largely rely on the mass media for information about candidates, this shift in nomination procedures thrust the media into a more prominent role in connecting citizens to government.

The mass media have also taken over some of the traditional party roles for candidates. Historically, candidates relied on party organizations to connect with voters. To reach voters during campaigns, teams of party volunteers banged on doors, organized rallies where candidates gave speeches, and handed out campaign literature. Yet even the most dedicated party machine is an ineffective

---

[1] The direct primary is discussed in more detail in chapter 10.

means of communication compared with the mass media. A television speaks to voters every day, right in their living rooms.

The net effect of these changes is "a new form of campaigning in which the mass media have replaced the political party as the main intermediary between voters and candidates" (Iyengar 1997, 144). Rather than through political parties, most voters now connect with candidates through television screens, newspapers, radios, and the Internet. Candidates are fully aware that the best way to communicate with large numbers of people is through the press, and they engage in sophisticated media marketing campaigns to get their messages out (Patterson 1984).

Although there is little doubt that these mass media appeals can reach a much larger percentage of the electorate than even the most dedicated party effort, their impact on the information and education role of the media is mixed. In terms of quantity, the shift to media-based campaigns undoubtedly led to the availability of more information to citizens and gave candidates more opportunities to get their message to larger numbers of voters. The content of those messages, however, is no less partisan than that of the door-to-door campaigner's. Rather than seeking to educate citizens with civil debate, candidates for office often use their media campaigns to point out the faults of their opponents. There is nothing new about this; as long as there have been elections in the United States, candidates have engaged in mudslinging. The rise of the mass media, especially the electronic media, however, provided the opportunity to do this on a grand scale.

If anything, mass media campaigns have provided a boon for the negative electioneering that has always been part and parcel of democratic politics in America. As one political scientist observed, "more often than not, candidates use their media opportunities to criticize, discredit, or ridicule their opponents rather than to promote their own ideas and programs" (Iyengar 1997, 145). Such has been the case since the nation's founding, but mass literacy and the rise of daily newspapers, not to mention radio, television, and the Internet, make it easier than ever to sling more mud over a wider audience. Many bemoan the attack ads and scathing sound bites, but there is a simple reason for such negativity: it works. Tearing down your opponent can create doubt among voters, making it less likely they will vote in his or her favor. It may make them less likely to vote, period.

DIFFERENT MEDIA, DIFFERENT INFORMATION Given the media's increasingly important role as a central connection between voters and government, the job of informing and educating the public has emerged as a fundamental service to the democratic process. The political freedom of citizens—their freedom to make choices—is tied to the information they have about government officials, actions, and issues. This connection raises the question of how well the media do this all-important job. It turns out that not all media are equal in terms of their ability to convey political information, and not all are equal in their ability to convey political information accurately. Much of this has to do with access.

Though increasingly challenged by the Internet, television remains the dominant mass medium in the United States. Access to television is nearly universal—

virtually every household has a TV—and the potential audience for television news encompasses just about every single citizen. Roughly half of Americans regularly watch TV news, and even more rely on television as a primary source of information about elections and political campaigns. Figure 8.1 reports the results of a survey asking people about their primary news sources for the political campaigns of 2010. When asked for their main campaign news source, about 70 percent of Americans said they relied on television, 27 percent on newspapers, 24 percent on the Internet, 14 percent on radio, and only 1 percent on magazines (note that the figures add up to more than 100 percent because the survey allowed people to give more one than one response; Pew Research Center 2011a).

This survey is interesting not just because it confirms the dominance of television but also because it suggests that Americans are shifting toward the Internet as a primary source of political news; since 2004, reliance on television and newspapers has dipped, and reliance on the Internet as a primary news source has increased. Among younger people (under 30) the Internet is beginning to challenge television as the news media of choice (Pew Research Center 2011a). These trends are clearly reflected in Figure 8.2, which shows where Americans reported getting most of their national and international news between 2001 and 2010. The Internet surpassed newspapers as the primary news outlet in 2008 and, if current trends continue, will rival television within a few years.

These numbers probably underestimate newspaper readership in the sense that traditional newspapers are increasingly setting up sophisticated online editions of their print products; add the online edition to the print edition, and more

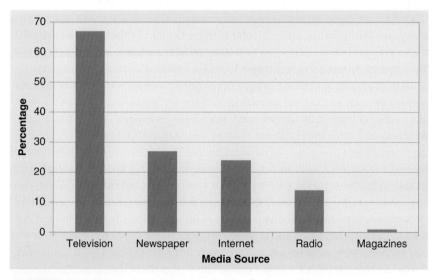

FIGURE 8.1 Campaign News Sources: Percent Media Getting First or Second Mentions

Source: Pew Research Center, "The Internet and Campaign 2010" (2011), http://www.pewin ternet.org/Reports/2011/The-Internet-and-Campaign-2010.aspx.

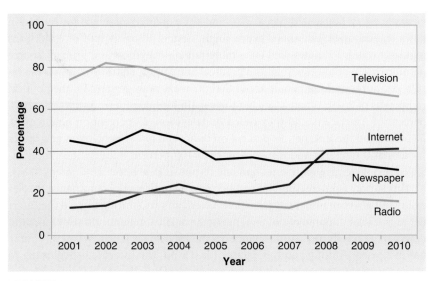

FIGURE 8.2 Primary Source of National and International News

Source: Pew Research Center, "Internet Gains on Television as Public's Main News Source" (2011), http://www.people-press.org/2011/01/04/internet-gains-on-television-as-publics-main-news-source/.

than 40 percent of Americans regularly read a newspaper (Pew Research Center 2006). Still, this confirms rather than contradicts the general conclusion that Americans are increasingly going online to get political news and information.

These shifts in news media consumption are important because different media have different capabilities to convey information. Television is a passive medium; it requires little effort or active involvement on the part of the viewer to get information. You do not even have to be literate to follow a television news broadcast. Yet although television makes it easy to access information, it also has drawbacks. Most importantly, television has tight limits on the amount and depth of information it can convey. One full minute of airtime, for example, constitutes a major story on a national network newscast. Even a longer report, such as those found on shows like *60 Minutes*, cannot contain same amount of information as an in-depth article in a newspaper or news magazine. The print media and their Internet equivalents are less accessible because they require literacy, and the reader must be willing to follow stories as they jump from page to page, but these media can convey not only larger quantities of information but also more detailed information.

Surveys show that people who rely more on newspapers for their information tend to be better informed and more knowledgeable about politics than those who rely more on television. For example, in early 2012 the Pew Research Center conducted a survey designed to assess public knowledge about the candidates running in the Republican presidential primary. Of the four questions asked, 40 percent who relied on newspapers as a main news source got at least three answers correct; that number jumped to 73 percent for those who relied on the websites of major national newspapers such as the *New York Times*. In contrast, only 35 percent of those who relied on television as a major news source got three or more answers correct. The poor scores of the television viewers were about the same as the scores of those who relied on general Internet portals such as Yahoo, Google, or AOL as their main news source (Pew Research Center 2012). This finding is something of a concern because it means some people will be better informed—and thus in a better position to make informed political choices—than others. Young people, immigrants, the less educated, and the poor tend to be more reliant on television as a primary source of political news; these are also groups that tend to be less politically informed and less politically active (Chaffee and Frank 1996).

President Barack Obama gives a televised press conference in the Briefing Room at the White House. Despite spending a good deal of time paying attention to the news, Americans remain politically uninformed, possibly due to their primary news source, television, which is less effective at conveying information than newspapers.

© Brendan Smialowski/The New York Times

It is not just that some media do a better job of informing voters; some media actually produce **misinformation**, or the belief that incorrect information is true. Several studies have found that heavy consumers of political talk radio not only tend to be more misinformed; they also tend to have more confidence in the political viewpoints their misinformation supports. In other words, they are not only more likely to have inaccurate information about politics and government, but they are also more likely to base their political beliefs and actions on that misinformation (Hofstetter et al. 1999).

It is not just conservative radio talk show hosts, though, who have a questionable impact on the quality of civic debate. One study found a "Daily Show effect." *The Daily Show with Jon Stewart* is a faux news program that pokes fun at politics and the media and is very popular among college students (not to mention the authors of this textbook). Increasingly, young people rely on these "soft" sorts of sources for political information rather than "hard" news sources exemplified by major network news and newspapers such as the *New York Times*. Two political scientists, Jody Baumgartner and Jonathan Morris (2006), examined the impact on political attitudes of this shift from hard to soft news sources. Those drawing much of their political information from *The Daily Show* were a pretty informed group, but the show's political humor tended to cause more negative attitudes toward candidates and to generally increase cynicism about politics. Baumgartner and Morris dubbed this impact the "Daily Show effect."

Some argue that these sorts of programs represent a new experiment in political journalism—an emerging hybrid of entertainment and serious news. Shows such as *The Daily Show* may be playing politics for laughs, but their actual impact on the political process is not just funny—it's very real. (See the Politics in Practice feature "A Fake Free Media? The Truth about the Truthy Colbert Bump.")

misinformation The belief that incorrect information is true.

A FAKE FREE MEDIA? THE TRUTH ABOUT THE TRUTHY COLBERT BUMP

The Colbert Report is a Comedy Central program lampooning the sort of conservative, host-centered talk shows that are ratings hits for Fox News. Instead of Bill O'Reilly, Glenn Beck, or Sean Hannity, though, this show revolves around the bumptious, pompous, under-informed, stridently ideological, and largely fake persona of Stephen Colbert.

Colbert, a former regular on Jon Stewart's *The Daily Show*, ramps up the personality of a loud, populist, right-wing bloviator to the nth degree. His stock in trade is a running series of fantastical claims about the world and his (and his show's) impact on it.

Nothing exemplifies this better than the concept of "truthiness." Colbert highlighted "truthy" in a segment called "The Word" in 2005, defining it as what an individual knows to be true not because of facts, evidence, logical argument, or systematic analysis, but in spite of them. Truthy is literally what we want to be true—even if it isn't.

Colbert employed "truthy" as a device to satirize the rationalizations that politicians—particularly those in the Bush administration—used for their policy agendas. Though there is an argument about whether Colbert actually coined the word (according to some sources, it's been kicking around for a while), there is no argument that he popularized it. After Colbert, truthiness became a popular idiom for capturing arguments, perspectives, or worldviews that were presented as real, even though they lacked any rational evidentiary foundation.

At first glance, one of the longest-running examples of truthiness clearly seems to be the claims made on *The Colbert Report*. Among many seemingly truthy claims, Colbert has made a particular point of championing "the Colbert bump." The Colbert bump is the apparently automatic increase in popularity enjoyed by anyone who appears on his show. Beneficiaries of the bump include singers (Toby Keith's album went to number one on the charts after his appearance)

TRUST AND INFORMATION Americans tend to be skeptical about the quality of information they get from the mass media. More than half believe that news organizations often print or broadcast stories that are factually inaccurate. Roughly the same proportion also believes that the press covers up their mistakes rather than admitting to them (Pew Research Center 2007).

Despite this skepticism, Americans seem willing to accept much of what appears in the mainstream media as reasonably accurate, though some news sources are seen as more accurate than others. Americans see most mainstream print and electronic news media—the major television news networks and national daily newspapers, for example—as reasonably credible. Strong majorities also see local television news broadcasts and local newspapers as mostly fact-oriented. In contrast, only 10 percent perceive talk radio shows as fact-oriented, and roughly 70 percent perceive talk radio shows as mostly opinion-based (Pew Research Center 2005).

The credibility of news sources, however, is often as much in the eye of the beholder as in the format or medium itself. The audiences for mainstream news sources are increasingly polarized along partisan lines, and these partisan differences play a large role in determining both media consumption patterns and per-

and writers (Salman Rushdie was knighted after his appearance).

The bump is particularly associated with politicians. The notion that politicians would benefit from appearing on *The Colbert Report* has a particularly truthy ring to it. It's a brave candidate who bears an on-air grilling by Colbert, who tends to ask questions that are less than calculated to endear a politician to his or her constituents (Colbert once asked U.S. Representative Robert Wexler, D-FL, to complete this sentence: "I like prostitutes because . . ."). Funny stuff, watching politicians squirm. House Speaker Nancy Pelosi, though, was apparently not amused and strongly advised Democrats to stay off the program.

A study done by James Fowler, a University of California San Diego political scientist, suggests Pelosi might want to reexamine that advice. Fowler found that the Colbert bump isn't just truthy; it's the truth, or at least it is for Democrats. Using a carefully matched sample of candidates who did and did not appear on the show, Fowler demonstrated that after appearing on the show, Democratic political candidates enjoyed a spike in campaign donations—both in numbers and in amounts. The news was not so good for Republicans, who tended to have something of a Colbert bust—their donations peaked before going on the show.

Fowler's study is interesting not just because it shows that outrageous claims by fake talk show personalities can sometimes be true, but because it shows that a make-believe reality created for television might have a real-world impact. What does it say about democracy if a faux right-wing (or left-wing) pundit with exaggerated, uninformed, and pompous opinions played for laughs helps determine who does or who does not hold elected office?

Well, if nothing else, it shows that the media is indeed free and that a free media is no guarantee that a public will be well informed (though it might laugh a lot). And as for the Colbert bump, maybe there is something to it. Shortly after having his study published, Fowler himself was invited onto *The Colbert Report*. Afterward, he was reportedly more popular among his undergraduates, though we are not sure if this claim is truthy or the truth.

SOURCE Fowler, James. 2008. "The Colbert Bump in Campaign Donations: More Truthful Than Truthy." *PS: Political Science & Politics* 41 (3): 533–539.

ceptions of credibility. For example, 36 percent of Republicans regularly watch Fox News, compared to 11 percent of Democrats. In contrast, 26 percent of Democrats regularly watch CNN, compared to 12 percent of Republicans. Democrats are also more likely than Republicans to get their news from the three networks (ABC, CBS, and NBC; see Figure 8.3a). These partisan divisions become even more lopsided when news talk shows are included. Republicans regularly tune in to conservative talk shows—16 percent regularly watch Bill O'Reilly's *The O'Reilly Factor,* and 14 percent watch *Rush Limbaugh*—compared to only 2 or 3 percent of Democrats who tune into these shows.

Furthermore, partisan audiences tend to view their favored information sources as more credible than others. For example, 35 percent of Democrats believe all or most of the information on CNN, but only 22 percent of Republicans feel the same. There are similar differences in how believable Democrats and Republicans perceive ABC, CBS, and NBC to be. The only news source that Republicans trust more than the Democrats do is Fox News (see Figure 8.3B).

Americans, then, give the media mixed grades for the media's information and education role. On the one hand, Americans consume enormous amounts

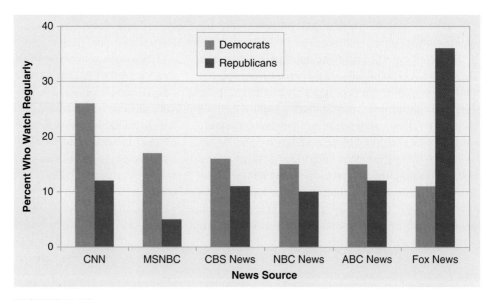

FIGURE 8.3A Partisan Differences in News Sources

Source: Pew Research Center, "Cable Leads the Pack as Campaign News Source," 2012, http://www.people-press.org/files/legacy-pdf/2012%20Communicating%20Release.pdf.

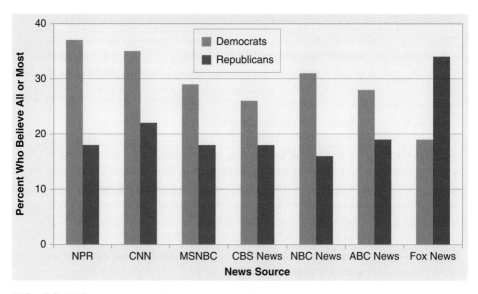

FIGURE 8.3B Partisan Differences in Credibility of News Sources

Source: Pew Research Center, "Key News Audience Now Blend Online and Traditional Sources," 2008, http://www.people-press.org/2008/08/17/media-credibility/.

of information, and they are plugged into the mass media. Daily newspapers, for example, have a total circulation of nearly 49 million (Newspaper Association of America 2010). The average American spends four hours a day watching television (TV Turnoff Network 2004). Millions more tune in to political radio talk shows, and millions read magazines such as *Time* and *Newsweek*. At any given hour of any given day, millions more plug directly into Internet-based news outlets, chat rooms, and politically oriented websites.

Yet the information consumed is viewed as being of mixed quality. Mainstream media outlets are seen as less trustworthy than they were in the past, and the ideology and the partisanship of the viewer determine in no small part what he or she views as a credible information source. Seeing, reading, or hearing is not necessarily believing. These are just the sorts of findings we'd expect given the earlier-discussed theoretical frameworks on how individuals process information. All things being equal, people prefer to have their established beliefs confirmed and therefore seek out news sources that are more likely to do exactly that. News sources that do not provide such confirmation consistently—and this includes virtually all mainstream news media—find their credibility eroding.

Agenda Setting

Media scholar Bernard Cohen famously observed that the press is not very good at telling people what to think but that "it is stunningly successful in telling them what to think about" (1963, 13). This quote sums up the media's powerful role in shaping the public agenda. Simply put, the issues that make the front page of national newspapers and the stories that lead television news broadcasts are the issues that get the most attention from the public and the government. The government cannot pay attention to every single problem at once—it simply does not have the time or the resources. The media's agenda-setting role means it helps the government and the public to focus and prioritize issues and problems.

The media's power to determine the public agenda was confirmed in a study by Maxwell McCombs and Donald Shaw (1972). McCombs and Shaw measured the attention the media were paying to different issues and then asked a group of independent voters what they thought were the most important issues in an ongoing presidential election. What they found was a remarkably strong correlation; in fact, there was virtually no way to statistically distinguish between the prominence of an issue's coverage in the media and how important the issue was ranked by voters.

Yet, although McCombs and Shaw showed that Cohen was essentially correct, other studies have shown that this view of **agenda setting** *underestimates* the impact of the media. Although news reports are unlikely to make us change our fundamental political beliefs, it turns out that the media do play a more complex—and in some ways more influential—role than Bernard Cohen implies.

The media's agenda-setting role goes beyond simply identifying and ordering the list of topics that make up the public agenda. Media outlets also frame these issues for the public. **Framing** means emphasizing certain aspects of a story to make them more important (Iyengar and Kinder 1987). The theory behind framing assumes that our attitudes about any given thing—the president, the deficit,

agenda setting The process of selecting the issues or problems that government will pay attention to.

framing Emphasizing certain aspects of a story to make them more important.

the price of gas, the guy sitting next to us in class—are made up of various characteristics associated with that thing. How much someone approves of the job the president is doing, for example, is a product of such characteristics as the president's ideology and partisanship, the president's personal likability, the state of the economy, and a whole lot more. The media frame an issue by emphasizing particular characteristics. For example, if a media story emphasizes a president's likable personality, that characteristic gets more weight. If a story emphasizes the president's failure to reduce the deficit, that characteristic gets more weight. Framing thus influences how we think about issues or topics by shifting what characteristics relevant to those issues or topics are or are not emphasized (e.g., Chong and Druckman 2007). This clearly goes beyond agenda setting. Framing does not simply influence *what* we think about; it also helps shape *how* we think about issues or topics.

Framing and the broader agenda-setting role of the media ultimately comes down to what Walter Lippmann (1922) called "the pictures in our heads." What issues are emphasized in media coverage and how these issues are framed help us shape our mental picture of those issues.

Watchdog and Public Advocate

Representative democracy is a form of government where the many watch the few. Yet few citizens in modern representative democracies can afford to devote much time to watching government officials. Similarly, not many people have the time or resources to monitor whether the public interest is represented when government decides who gets what, when they get it, and how. If citizens are not watching, who watches to see if government officials are competent and truthful, and who blows the whistle if they are not? Who makes sure that the public interest, not just special interests, is represented in official decision making? The press has traditionally embraced the role of government watchdog, monitoring government officials for signs of corruption or deceit. Increasingly, the press has also taken on the role of public advocate and representative. As *Washington Post* writers Leonard Downie and Robert Kaiser put it, "anyone tempted to abuse power looks over his or her shoulder to see if someone else is watching. Ideally, there should be a reporter in the rearview mirror" (2002, 8).

Journalists not only keep an eye on government, but also see themselves as representatives of the public interest. The public does not send delegates to presidential press conferences, and the public galleries in legislatures are empty much of the time. Reporters, though, are invariably there. One of the roles the press takes upon itself is to use its unique presence and access to stand in for the public, asking questions and probing officials on behalf of the public interest.

There has always been an intense debate both within and outside the journalism community on how the press performs its watchdog function. For example, during the administration of President George W. Bush, critics argued that the press failed to question aggressively enough the justifications for and conduct of the war in Iraq. Yet others argued that far from being too timid with the Bush administration, the press was too aggressive and willing to put a good story above the good of the nation.

A good example of these contradictory judgments is the complicated and strained relationship that existed between the Bush administration and the *New York Times*. Between 2001 and 2003, the *Times* published a number of high-profile stories confirming the Bush administration's main justification for going to war with Iraq—that the regime of Saddam Hussein had weapons of mass destruction (WMD). In 2004, that coverage came under intense criticism. No evidence was ever found of a WMD program, and the intelligence information the government used to support the case to the contrary was found to be at best wrong and at worst deliberate misinformation. This led to criticisms not only of the Bush administration but also of the *Times*; the newspaper was charged with uncritically accepting the administration's case for war rather than critically examining that case as a good press watchdog would do. The *Times* itself admitted to some of these charges after an internal investigation showed that a series of stories were poorly sourced; the credibility of some stories apparently rested on Iraqi defectors eager to support a U.S. invasion whose claims were anonymously confirmed by the Bush administration, which was using these same claims to buttress its case for war. The newspaper's editors said, "We wish we had been more aggressive in re-examining the claims as new evidence emerged—or failed to emerge" ("From the Editors" 2004).

A newspaper that helps the government make the case for war on the basis of questionable sources and information—surely this is a newspaper one would expect the Bush administration to enjoy a good relationship with. In fact, the Bush administration's public relationship with the *New York Times* was as vitriolic as the Obama administration's relationship with Fox News. President Bush and Vice President Dick Cheney delivered blistering criticisms of the newspaper when it printed a story on a secret program to gather data from thousands of financial transactions without first seeking warrants from courts. Bush and Cheney argued that the program was a tool critical to gathering intelligence on and disrupting the activities of potential terrorist threats. The *Times* saw its publication of the story as fulfilling its watchdog function: the government was bypassing the courts and combing the private financial records of thousands of Americans without their permission, an activity that raises legitimate questions about the limits of government power. If the courts were being bypassed, the only check left on government power was the press, and the *Times* argued it was providing just such a check (Lichtblau and Risen 2006; Hulse 2006). Perspectives on the story tended to split along partisan lines. Republicans tended to side with the administration, viewing the story as tantamount to aiding and abetting terrorists. Democrats tended to view the story as the *Times* somewhat belatedly standing up to the administration and taking its watchdog function seriously.

The contentious history of the *Times*–Bush administration relationship demonstrates the complexities of the watchdog function. Was the *Times* too cozy with the government, helping it support controversial policies and cloaking some questionable activities by basing stories on unreliable or "anonymous sources?" Or was it acting as an important check on a government pushing the envelope of its authority? The answer to both questions, of course, is that it depends. It depends not just on the particular story or issue at hand, but also on how the issue or story is viewed. Whether the *Times* was a principled watchdog or a gullible government stooge turns out to be very much in the eye of the beholder.

THREATS TO A FREE PRESS

Democracy presumes the existence of a public sphere where information can be freely accessed and transmitted. Without a public sphere, the core values of political freedom and popular sovereignty are difficult to uphold: unless the people have the means to inform and develop their opinions and points of view, they cannot be truly free, and the will of the people cannot be the highest political authority. The need to maintain a public sphere makes keeping the press free of regulation and censorship a critical issue for democracy.

Yet it is often tempting to place limits on the free access of information. Government officials do not want their misdeeds publicized; entrenched special interests would rather not have the negative side of their agendas broadcast and publicly dissected. Even though the press is seen as a primary defense of political freedom, most Americans seem to favor at least some form of media censorship. For example, during the initial stages of the war in Afghanistan, one survey showed that roughly 60 percent of Americans favored giving the military more power to control how the press reported operations in that theater (Pew Research Center 2001).

Given that majority sentiment may favor some government regulation of the mass media, protecting the public sphere and keeping the media free of government regulation can be difficult. Majority rule is also a core democratic value, and as we learned in chapter 1, democracy requires a balancing act when these values come into conflict. Majority sentiment can threaten a free press in two ways: government control and private control. Either threat is capable of shrinking the public sphere, reducing the effectiveness of the media's democratic roles and, in doing so, limiting political freedom.

Government Control

In the United States, government's authority to control the press is limited. The primary limitation is the First Amendment, which states in part that "Congress shall make no law . . . abridging the freedom of speech, or of the press." The courts have consistently interpreted this provision to mean that the news media have great freedom to report on politics as they choose.

A governmental order to prohibit or censor a news story prior to publication or broadcast is known as **prior restraint**, and the Supreme Court has consistently ruled that, except in extraordinary circumstances, prior constraint violates the First Amendment. The only basis on which the government can prevent publication or broadcast of a news story is if the government can convince a court that the story would harm national security, an exception that is exceedingly rare.

Perhaps the best-known court case dealing with prior restraint is *New York Times* v. *United States* (1971), which dealt with what became known as the Pentagon Papers. The Pentagon Papers referred to a secret government study of U.S. involvement in Southeast Asia that revealed, among other things, that the government had deliberately deceived the public about the impact and success of military operations in Vietnam. In 1971, a copy of the study was leaked to the *New York Times*. A **leak** is a revelation of information that officials want kept secret.

President Richard Nixon sought—and received—a court order preventing the newspaper from publishing its stories about the study. The administration argued that publication of the study would threaten national security by undermining the war effort. But the Supreme Court ruled that this potential threat to national security was not serious enough to justify a prior restraint order, and the story was published.

Congress has occasionally attempted to place some legal restraints on the freedom of the press, but these attempts are notable more for their failures than for their successes. For example, in 1798, Congress passed the Alien and Sedition Acts, which in part made publishing any "false, scandalous, and malicious writing" a crime. This law was mainly used as a legal tool by the Federalist Party to intimidate and silence critical newspaper editors. Opposition to the law was widespread, and after the Federalists were swept from office in the election of 1800, the law was repealed, those convicted of breaking the law were pardoned, and fines were repaid with interest.

However, the federal government has been given considerably more leeway in regulating broadcast media than in regulating print media. The reason is that broadcast media, unlike print media, rely on a public good to transmit information: the airwaves. There are a limited number of broadcast frequencies, and government began regulating their use in 1934 with the passage of the Communications Act.

Prior to this law, something akin to anarchy prevailed on the nation's radio airwaves, with stations broadcasting on the same frequencies and drowning out one

© Bloomberg via Getty Images

Keeping the media free of government regulation can be difficult despite strong limitations like the First Amendment. This image of slain Iraq War soldiers and 359 other photos taken by the Air Force at Dover Air Force Base in Delaware were not released by the Pentagon for publication until an organization (www.thememoryhole.com) requested them under the Freedom of Information Act.

prior restraint The prohibition or censoring of a news story prior to publication or broadcast.

leak The revealing of information that officials want kept secret.

another's transmissions. In the name of the public interest, the Communications Act regulated the nation's airwaves, required broadcast licenses, and established a set of performance standards as prerequisites for obtaining or maintaining a license.

The law also established the Federal Communications Commission (FCC), an independent agency that was empowered to enforce the Communications Act. Today, the FCC is charged with regulating interstate and international communications by radio, television, wire, satellite, and cable. There is no print equivalent of the FCC, and the primary justification for regulating the electronic media is that the industry is heavily based on a limited, public resource: broadcast frequencies.

There has been heated debate over whether the Internet should be treated as a broadcast or print medium. The Communications Decency Act, passed by the 104th Congress, sought to regulate the Internet as a broadcast medium by placing restrictions on indecent content. In *Reno v. ACLU* (1997), the Supreme Court rejected this approach by striking down key provisions of the law. The Court characterized the Internet as a print medium and extended to it the full protections of the First Amendment.

In practice, the regulations imposed on the electronic media are not particularly onerous, though in theory the FCC has the power to revoke licenses and to shut down television and radio stations. Such drastic action is rarely even considered, mainly because such a move would almost certainly provoke a public outcry. Freedom of the press is so embedded as a fundamental value of American society that the government is wary of restricting that freedom even when it has the legal power to do so.

Rupert Murdoch's News Corporation is one of the world's biggest media conglomerates, controlling newspapers, magazines, television stations, book publishers, movie studios, and Internet companies across the globe.

© Brendan Hoffman/Bloomberg via Getty Images

Private Control

Although there are well-established limits on government control of the press, freedom of the press can be limited by private control as well. Left unchecked, market forces also can limit the free flow of information. This restriction occurs in two basic ways.

The first is concentration of ownership. The public sphere presumes a marketplace of ideas, where numerous interests and points of view compete for attention. But what if the mass media are largely in the hands of a few narrow interests? If control of the news media belongs to only a specific few, what prevents them from censoring or distorting information that harms their interests?

The concentration of media ownership into a small number of powerful hands is not just idle speculation. Since the 1980s, there has been a significant change in the patterns of ownership in the mass media industry. Spurred on by new laws that deregulated the telecommunications industry and the widespread adoption of new technologies such as cable television and the Internet, mass media companies began to recognize and pursue multimedia strategies that allowed them to take advantage of shared resources and economies of scale. Currently, just a handful of corporations control a dominant share of the mass media industry in the United States. The "Big Six" of these companies are General Electric, Time Warner, Disney, News Corporation, Viacom, and CBS. Each one of these corporations runs a massive media empire that encompasses every imaginable variation of information media. For example, CBS probably brings to mind the television network and its various divisions—CBS News, CBS Sports, and the like. Yet CBS also owns dozens of radio stations, the publishing giant Simon & Schuster, and a slew of online companies, including ZDnet, Gamespot.com, and CNET. Rupert Murdoch's News Corporation owns not just Fox Broadcasting Company and Fox News but also the *Wall Street Journal,* the *New York Post,* and HarperCollins book publishers. Disney is way beyond Mickey Mouse; besides the studio that made it an icon, it owns ABC, ESPN, a radio network, Movies.com, and its own recording and book publishing operations. Add in a few other companies such as Bertelsmann AG (a German-based media company) and what you have is just a few massive companies owning most mass media outlets not just in the United States, but in the world. You can check out for yourself what companies own what media companies at http://www.cjr.org/resources/in dex.php, a resource provided on the website of the *Columbia Journalism Review.* This concentration of so many media outlets into so few corporate families sets off alarm bells for critics concerned with the impact on the public sphere. For example, would a news organization vigorously pursue a story that reflected negatively on its corporate owner?

The second reason private control may limit the free flow of information is money. Giant media conglomerates such as News Corporation and Time Warner are not in business to promote the public interest or to help realize the core value of political freedom. Like most other businesses, they exist to make money. Profits in the print and electronic media industries are driven largely by advertising, and the larger the audience delivered to advertisers, the more money it is possible to make. Minority and marginalized voices get little attention from corporate media giants—not because big business wants their viewpoints silenced but because there is simply less money in a smaller audience. Some advertisers go beyond simply being interested in media that reach the largest audience: they actually try to influence the information carried by those media. For example, some advertisers have strict policies against buying advertising from media companies whose programming presents their sponsors in a negative light (Herman and McChesney 1997, 7).

The net product of these shifts in the media landscape over the past 20 years is that news itself has become a commodity—a product that is shaped by the forces of supply and demand and packaged to appeal to certain audiences (Hamilton 2004, 7).

Hard news, stories that focus on factual information about important decisions or events, is increasingly deemphasized in favor of **soft news**, stories characterized by opinion, human interest, and even entertainment value. Why? Soft news sells. News has become less focused on the give-and-take of politics or the

hard news Stories that focus on factual information about important decisions or events.

soft news Stories characterized by opinion, human interest, and often entertainment value.

major events of the day and more on whatever will appeal to audience interests. Ratings and circulation, after all, drive advertising revenues.

Among those who are worried about the impact of the profit motive on news gathering are journalists. Most reporters, especially those working for television or radio, believe that the quality of news coverage is being diluted by profit pressures. Opinions among journalists are notable for their contrast with the executives who handle the business side of news organizations. The latter acknowledge that the profit motive is changing what news organizations do and what they report, but they do not see this as a bad thing (Johnson 2004). Political scientists are not so sure. For example, newspapers have been reducing the number of reporters covering state legislatures, even as their importance as key policymaking institutions is increasing. Why cut coverage of an increasingly important part of government? Budgets and marketing. As political scientist Alan Rosenthal puts it, "papers want to find stuff that connects with their audience . . . news that is more entertainment-oriented" (quoted in Boulard 1999). The fact is that covering state government does not pad the bottom line the way covering Hollywood does.

Ultimately, the danger of private control to the public sphere is not that voices will be legally censored or dissent outlawed, or that there will be government regulation of what can be broadcast or printed. The danger is that the information and messages that cannot attract a profit-making audience will simply be ignored.

MEDIA BIAS

Most people do not perceive government censorship or corporate ownership to be the biggest problem with the mass media. Most people believe the biggest problem is media bias. **Media bias** is the tendency to present an unbalanced perspective so that information is conveyed in such a way that consistently favors one set of interests over another.

Virtually everyone believes the media are biased. This perspective was not always the case. Several decades ago, most people regarded the news media as trustworthy and regarded journalists as professionals who did their best to present information in a fair and balanced manner (Erskine 1970). The high regard that Americans once had for the news media has greatly eroded. In the first decade of the twenty-first century, the vast majority of people—as many as 70 percent—believed that stories in the media were often inaccurate, and 60 percent believed that stories were politically biased (Pew Research Center 2009). There is no single or universally accepted answer to why this change has occurred. In general, though, trust in society's institutions has fallen across the board, and the media have shown no immunity to this trend.

Although most people see the media as biased, they see bias in different ways. There are indeed different sorts of media bias, and the evidence on whether bias

media bias The tendency to present an unbalanced perspective so that information is conveyed in a way that consistently favors one set of interests over another.

exists—and if it does, whether it has any negative impact on civic life—varies according to the type of bias being considered.

Political Bias

When most people discuss media bias, they are usually referring to **political bias**, or the tendency to favor a political party or ideological point of view. Political bias has a long history in the American media.

Prior to the advent of electronic media, most print media were openly partisan. For the first hundred years of the republic, newspapers were often little more than propaganda organs for political parties or other organized interests. The Founding Fathers, for example, endured scathing attacks in the press that make the most negative contemporary news stories look mild in comparison.

Consider the career of James Callender, a newspaper editor who made no secret of his political preferences. Writing in the *Richmond Examiner*, Callender called President George Washington a traitor, a liar, and a robber. He referred in print to Washington's successor, John Adams, as a "repulsive pedant," a "gross hypocrite," and a "strange compound of ignorance and ferocity, of deceit and weakness." Callender was put up to some of these character assassinations by none other than Thomas Jefferson, who not only reviewed and approved some of these stories but probably paid their author to write them as well (Daniels 1965, 62–67; McCullough 2001, 537).

The partisan press gradually yielded to the vision of **objective journalism**, which seeks to report facts rather than promote a partisan point of view and seeks balance by reporting both sides of any given story (Alger 1996, 122–123). An early promoter of objective journalism was Albert Ochs, publisher of the *New York Times*, who made it the basis for his paper's news coverage at the turn of the twentieth century. This approach gradually became the standard for the mainstream print press and was adopted by the news organizations of the electronic media.

What objective journalism does not take into account is that people themselves are not objective. As discussed earlier, virtually every theory of how people process information suggests that people will not be neutral consumers of news, regardless of how objective or even-handed those news reports are. Research by political scientists has consistently found that people have a *disconfirmation bias,* or the tendency to dismiss or denigrate information contrary to their own political beliefs, and also an *attitude congruency bias,* or the tendency to uncritically accept information that supports their political beliefs. Alarmingly, researchers have also found that these information-processing biases lead to attitude polarization. This means that people with differing beliefs on a political issue will become further apart on that issue when they consume the same information, regardless of the subjective or objective content of that information (Taber, Cann, and Kucsova 2009).

Few people stop to consider that they might be biased in how they process political information supplied by the media; instead, most are convinced that the

political bias The tendency to favor a political party or ideological point of view.

objective journalism An approach to journalism that places emphasis on reporting facts rather than on analysis or a partisan point of view.

news media are presenting information in a biased way. Yet although most people agree that the press has a distinct partisan and ideological tilt, they disagree on which party or ideology the media actually favor. Conservatives tend to make the most consistent and loudest complaints of media bias, and they see the media as distinctly favoring Democrats and a liberal point of view. This claim is buttressed by research finding that reporters tend to be more liberal and more likely to self-identify as Democrats than the average American. Interestingly, journalists seem to have become a bit more conservative over the past decade or two, though they are still clearly more liberal than the general public. This does not mean the ranks of reporters are dominated by left-wingers. About a third of journalists report they are political centrists, a third say they are a little to the left, and about a quarter lean to the right. Only a small fraction—about 10 percent—characterize their politics as very liberal. When it comes to partisanship, about a third of journalists describe themselves as Democrats and about a fifth as Republicans (Weaver et al. 2006).

Liberals reject the notion of a liberal slant in the media; indeed, they see quite the opposite: a media so cowed and intimidated by conservative critics that it is afraid to give right-leaning issues and candidates the same tough scrutiny it gives to the left. Liberals point not to reporters, but to the owners of the dominant media outlets. As we have already seen, these are mostly giant media corporations headed by conservative-leaning business executives.

The problem with political bias in the media, of course, is that it is critics with a liberal or conservative bias of their own who make the charges. Although both the left and the right are convinced that the media systematically favor their ideological and partisan opponents, academic studies have been unable to substantiate these claims, at least not in any universal sense. Part of the problem is measuring media bias; two people can read the same story and come to very different views about whether it has a particular ideological or partisan slant. It has proven very hard to develop an objective measure that can sort out what subjective views of media bias might actually have merit.

Political scientist Tim Groseclose developed one of the better-known measures of media bias by looking at how many times a media outlet cited think tanks and policy groups in news stories compared to how many times those same groups were cited by members of Congress. The basic idea was to measure the ideological and partisan slant of the press by using the more generally agreed-upon political orientation of lawmakers

The line between news and entertainment has been blurred with an increasing focus on soft news, or stories characterized by human interest or their entertainment value. The relationship between Kirsten Stewart and Robert Pattinson, stars of the *Twilight* movies, receives extensive media attention and gets a wide audience. Hard news, or stories on important decisions or events, is often a tougher sell.

as a reference point. Using this measure, Groseclose's studies find media outlets to have a distinct leftward tilt (e.g., Groseclose and Milyo 2005; Groseclose 2011). Yet this measure is far from perfect and has been criticized for making even conservative-leaning media outlets look liberal. For example, using Groseclose's measure, Fox News, the *Drudge Report,* and the *Washington Times* are all at least slightly left-leaning, even though these media outlets are generally seen as right-leaning.

One of the most systematic investigations of political bias in recent decades was undertaken by David Niven (2002), who examined the tone and type of coverage of specific issues to see whether they changed based on whether they involved Democratic or Republican officeholders. His conclusion was that no such systematic differences existed:

> In a comparison of coverage of two presidents, 200 governors, the mayors of eight cities, and 266 members of Congress, all matched to a member of the opposite party who had the same outcome in office, there is simply no evidence for partisan bias. (Niven 2002, 93)

Other studies produce more mixed impressions. The **propaganda model** suggests that because most mainstream media are corporately owned, the media are biased toward corporate interests. Corporate interests mean profit, not neutrality, so according to this model, the media will supply the news (1) that people want to consume and that advertisers are willing to pay for and (2) that supports social agendas that favor corporate interests—for example, by giving more attention and credibility to pro-capitalist viewpoints than those skeptical of capitalist systems (Herman and Chomsky 2002). In contrast, a study by Riccardo Puglisi (2006) found the *New York Times* to be more oriented toward issues that favor Democratic nominees in presidential campaigns. (Democrats are traditionally viewed as allies of labor, Republicans as allies of the corporate world.)

Despite the overall conclusion that the press has no overall general, systematic partisan or ideological bias, there is a growing sense that individual press outlets are increasingly drifting from the objective journalism model. This drift seems to be driven less by ideological commitment than by the corporate bottom line. For much of the twentieth century, the mass media, be it the print or the electronic media, were oriented toward assembling the biggest audience possible. Practically, that meant appealing to the broad middle of America. When there were only three television networks, for example, none of them could afford to play political or ideological favorites because catering to the political preferences of one segment of the potential audience meant going against the preferences of another. That risked losing those viewers and the ad revenue they represented. The smart play was to not show any obvious partisan favoritism and to structure news presentations that could appeal to the moderate middle. This was a model that lent itself to objective journalism and to making the mass media a vehicle for producing consensus.

propaganda model The idea that mainstream media are biased toward corporate and conservative interests because most mainstream media are corporately owned.

PROPAGANDA AND THE PRESS: PARTISAN REVOLUTIONS IN THE "NO-SPIN" ZONE

Information disseminated through a mass medium that deliberately attempts to influence peoples' emotions, attitudes, and actions with the specific aim of furthering a political or ideological cause is generically known as "propaganda."

During much of the twentieth century, which included two world wars and the half-century-long Cold War, propaganda was an important area of study for academics. As great ideologies competed for the hearts and minds of people within and between countries, scholars systematically began researching what propaganda techniques were commonly used and trying to figure out why they did (or did not) work.

Some of the best-known scholarship in this area was done by the Institute for Propaganda Analysis (IPA), which included some of the best-known communication scholars of the time and political scientists such as Harold Lasswell (he of the "who gets what" definition of politics). These researchers systematically identified a common set of characteristic propaganda devices that have been used ever since to examine different forms of communication for their propaganda content.

These devices include "name calling," or providing negative labels to people or ideas with the aim of getting the audience to reject what the people or ideas represent without examining evidence; "fear" appeals, or attempts to instill in the target audience a belief that something or someone threatens to destroy their ideals and values; and "role-players," or separating people or ideas into good and evil, hero and villain, us and them.

These concepts were used both to analyze the content and effectiveness of ideologies seen as opposing democracy (e.g., fascism, communism) and also to help shape the propaganda efforts of the American government (Lasswell, for example, spent much of World War II analyzing Nazi propaganda and helping to shape an Allied counter-message). They were also used to examine the communication styles of well-known media personalities. Father Charles

That model started to come under pressure about three decades ago. First, we saw the rise of cable television and with it a proliferation of options other than major networks. Then we saw a massive contraction of the print media as people migrated to the Internet, which offered a seemingly endless variety of options for getting news and information. The net result of this proliferation of choices was a destabilization of the mass media model centered on a broad, middle-of-the-road audience, a model that had lent itself to the practice of objective journalism. Although the holdovers from the previous era—major network news, print publications such as the *New York Times,* and National Public Radio—still more or less operate on that model, other outlets such as cable news operations (MSNBC, Fox News), Internet sites (the *Huffington Post,* the *Drudge Report, Daily Kos, Free Republic*), and talk radio (Rush Limbaugh, Michael Savage) are much more likely to frame politics with a distinct ideological or partisan spin (e.g., Baum and Groeling 2008). From a market point of view, this makes sense; in a world with endless options for information, it makes sense to play to the biases

Coughlin, for example, had a radio program in the 1930s that attracted millions of listeners. Though popular, Coughlin's broadcasts were also seen as anti-Semitic and defended (or at least rationalized) some Nazi policies. Under the frameworks developed by the IPA and scholars such as Lasswell, Coughlin's communications were systematically identified as propaganda.

Communication scholars decided to take these same research frameworks and apply them to a well-known contemporary television talk show host: Bill O'Reilly. They focused on Bill O'Reilly partly because of his huge (and international) audience and his use of multiple media (television, radio, and a newspaper column), but also because of Fox News's general claim of "fair and balanced" reporting and O'Reilly's straight-shooting "no-spin zone" persona.

The results of their analysis showed that O'Reilly extensively uses propaganda techniques: name-calling roughly an average of nine times per minute, engaging in classic fear appeals, and routinely dividing the world into "goodies" and "baddies." There was not much evidence of heroes in O'Reilly's communication style—right-leaning media, Christians, and Republicans were most likely to make that grade—but there were plenty of villains. These included foreigners (portrayed as villains 50 percent of the time) and left-leaning media (villains 96 percent of the time).

The same analysis, however, also showed that O'Reilly is not simply a conservative or Republican apologist. President George W. Bush's administration was routinely portrayed as a villain (60 percent of the time), and so was the political right in general (80 percent of the time). O'Reilly may be routinely using the rhetorical techniques of propaganda, but he does not uniformly employ them in the service of a single party or ideology. The larger point of this analysis is not that O'Reilly is consistently propagandizing for Republicans and conservatives—he is not. The take-away story of this analysis is that, whatever else he is, O'Reilly is clearly not objective. The "no-spin zone" largely consists of commentary revolving around some subjective political perspective.

Of course, O'Reilly might challenge this analysis. After all, among the biggest villains on his show are academics (given the role of villain more than 70 percent of the time they are mentioned).

SOURCE Conway, Mike, Maria Elizabeth Grabe, and Kevin Grieves. 2007. "Villains, Victims and the Virtuous in Bill O'Reilly's 'No-Spin Zone': Revisiting World War Propaganda Techniques." *Journalism Studies* 8: 197–223.

of how people process information rather than try to ignore or override those biases. The upshot is that we may be seeing something of a return to the partisan origins of the press. Taken as a whole, the press is still not distinctly liberal or conservative. Individual press outlets, however, are increasingly less shy about adopting a partisan perspective as a means to appeal to a particular audience segment (Starr 2010; see the feature "Propaganda and the Press: Partisan Revolutions in the 'No-Spin' Zone").

Thus, although television news overall may have no systematic partisan tilt, Fox News is viewed as the conservative news channel, and CNN and MSNBC are considered liberal news channels. Networks clinging to the objective model are increasingly seen as untrustworthy by both sides. It is important to note, however, that this bias is at least as much perceived as real; in other words, it is the people who consume and process information that provide the political bias in the press at least as much as the suppliers of that information (Turner 2007).

Racial and Gender Bias

Although it receives considerably less attention, there is actually a better case for racial and gender bias, rather than partisan bias, in the press. For example, academic studies have consistently found that female candidates for elective office are covered differently in the news media than male candidates. Compared to their male counterparts, females tend to get less news coverage. The coverage female candidates do receive tends to disproportionately focus on "women's issues" such as abortion and education, and it places less emphasis on professional experience and accomplishments than it does on personality, appearance, and fashion decisions (Kahn 1992, 1996; Heldman, Carroll, and Olson 2005).

Academic studies have also found a systematic imbalance in the portrayals of African Americans compared to their white counterparts. Press coverage of Hurricane Katrina's 2005 devastation of New Orleans sparked a running debate on the language used in media stories to describe whites versus blacks. The predominantly black victims of Katrina were often described as "refugees." Victims of hurricane disasters that hit proportionately whiter populations were more likely to be described as "evacuees." Widely distributed photos of Katrina victims taking supplies from grocery stories were captioned differently, with whites "finding food" and African Americans "looting" (Sommers et al. 2006). These sorts of differences in media coverage extend to political leaders. Niven's study (2002) also compared the coverage of African American and white mayors. Niven found that, compared to white mayors, African American mayors are less prominently covered in stories reporting good outcomes and are more prominently covered in stories reporting bad outcomes. For example, African American mayors get more coverage than comparable white mayors when a city's murder rate is increasing and less coverage when it is decreasing (Niven 2002, 105).

Communications scholars believe that these imbalances are at least partially the product of the demographic makeup of newsrooms. Conservatives complain that reporters are too liberal, and liberals complain that media owners are too conservative, but both sides ignore what the majority of reporters, anchors, editors, producers, owners, and shareholders have in common: they are overwhelmingly white males.

For example, historically, stories written by male reporters and published in the *New York Times* outnumber the stories written by females by a ratio of roughly 5 to 1 (Mills 1997). The most popular politically oriented talk shows are hosted by white males, and the vast majority of these male hosts are self-described conservatives, libertarians, and Republicans (Numbers USA 2002).

Negativity Bias

Perhaps the most open and obvious bias of the media is a tendency to favor stories that emphasize the negative aspects of politics and government. In presidential campaigns, for example, the large majority of candidates' comments are devoted to making a positive case for their candidacies. The large majority of the media's coverage of presidential campaigns, however, focuses on the negative attacks the candidates make on each other (Morin 2000).

In the media's defense, there are some good reasons for the bias toward negativity. The watchdog function of the press discussed earlier tends to promote an emphasis on reporting incompetence or wrongdoing in government. The press believes that it is the press's responsibility, at least in part, to alert the public to government misconduct, and the logical consequence is that stories emphasizing the negative get more coverage and more prominence.

Moreover, most of what government does is rarely considered news by journalists and editors. Imagine a front-page story headlined, "Government Agency Run Pretty Competently, Does Job Reasonably Well." That describes the humdrum day-to-day reality of government, and it is not considered news. It is the exception to this general rule that gets the attention of the press. There is an old cliché in journalism that says "dog bites man" is not news, but "man bites dog" is. The news media tend to focus on the unusual and the extreme, not on the mundane and the common.

The media's bias toward the negative may prompt people to be negative and cynical about politics. For example, the media tend to emphasize **strategic framing**, which means the story emphasizes which candidate or partisan side is winning or losing. This focus can create a cynical view of the political process, even when the people involved in that process are not being adversarial.

One of the best studies of strategic framing in the past couple of decades was Joseph Capella and Kathleen Hall Jamieson's (1997) systematic study of a high-profile public meeting that occurred in 1995 between President Bill Clinton and House Speaker Newt Gingrich. The New Hampshire meeting was an unusual opportunity for two powerful policymakers to engage in a frank public give-and-take about the major issues facing the nation. Though they disagreed on many points, Clinton and Gingrich were mutually respectful and friendly toward each other. But media reports of this meeting included little emphasis on the issues Clinton and Gingrich discussed or the high degree of civility Clinton and Gingrich showed to each other. Instead, news stories emphasized the strategic elements of the meeting: Who scored political points? Who stumbled? Who won? Capella and Jamieson concluded that the media's relentless focus on the competitive aspects of politics promotes public cynicism about the entire process. There is little doubt that the sort of strategic framing Capella and Jamieson described continues to be a standard approach to media reporting on politics. Media bias thus not only seems to exist, but also has the potential to do long-term harm to the public sphere.

CHANGES IN THE PUBLIC SPHERE

Why has public trust in the media eroded, and why are so many Americans convinced that the media are biased? These are complicated questions that have a

strategic framing Giving prominence in media stories to who is gaining or losing on an issue.

number of answers. As mentioned previously, there has been a general decline in trust in most of society's major institutions during the past three or four decades, and the media are no exception to this overall trend.

Yet the revolution in communications technology has had a particularly notable impact on the media. This revolution occurred at the same time as a number of broad-reaching changes in the political environment. The net result is that compared to the media of the 1990s, not to mention the 1960s, today very different media are shaping a very different public sphere.

As discussed previously, the technological changes include the rise of cable television and the introduction and widespread use of the Internet. Combined, these destabilized a long period during which political news had been dominated by three major television network news organizations, daily newspapers, newsmagazines such as *Time* and *Newsweek,* and radio news organizations such as National Public Radio. Generally, all practiced the objective journalism model.

These technological changes were accompanied by significant developments in the broader social and political environment. For example, the information revolution helped foster the rise of multinational corporations, organizations that defied traditional political boundaries. Japanese companies now make cars in America with components imported from China and Mexico. Multinationals may have tremendous economic clout in a single state or country, but they are not bound to the laws of any single nation; profit, not patriotism or ideology or the canon of journalistic values, is their guiding force. Media companies were not excluded from this trend. Companies such as Time Warner and News Corporation are international conglomerates.

The past 20 years have also seen the rapid expansion of single-issue interest groups (as discussed in chapter 6), which have taken advantage of the new communications opportunities to aggressively promote narrowly focused agendas. Groups such as the National Rifle Association can (and do) raise and spend millions backing candidates who support their policy preferences. Many of those millions are poured into sophisticated media campaigns that focus on narrowly targeted interests. These sorts of developments have had important consequences for the public sphere. Notably, they have resulted in the decline of the media as gatekeepers and the potential for new technology to reshape civic engagement.

The Decline of the Gatekeepers

A **gatekeeper** is someone or some institution that controls access to something. In the mass media, the people who actually make decisions about what to print or what to broadcast (journalists, editors, and producers) and the organizations they work for have traditionally been considered gatekeepers of information. Thirty or 40 years ago, editors and producers at major news organizations could realistically be viewed as society's information gatekeepers—a relatively small group of people decided what political information reached a mass audience. That is no longer the case. Control over information has been pushed downward and made more diverse.

gatekeeper A person or institution that controls access to something.

Individuals now have numerous choices for obtaining very specialized and specific information. Cable television and especially the Internet give individuals enormous control over the sorts of information they gather and consume. In some respects, this development has a positive impact on promoting the public sphere. Citizens now have virtually unlimited access to information, and they are much less reliant on a small number of gatekeepers to decide what information they will or will not get. Because the new technology is often social and highly interactive (think Facebook, chat rooms, and e-mail), some political scientists are optimistic that the technology will make it easier for the average citizen to participate meaningfully in the exchange of ideas and opinions that make up the public sphere (Krueger 2002).

Yet there is also a downside to these developments. The rise of cable television and the Internet has also fueled fierce competition among media organizations, which now have to fight harder to attract and maintain an audience that has an abundance of information options. Some see this cutthroat competition as having profoundly negative effects on the quality of information produced by news organizations. Political scientist David Swanson, for example, argues that the intense competition to find an audience "has led to a loosening of commitments to traditional journalistic values and canons of practice, resulting in news that is more sensationalized . . . and less governed by serious news values" (2000, 411). This argument is backed up in a recent study by Matthew Baum and Tim Groeling (2008), which finds that traditional gatekeepers are increasingly being replaced with nontraditional alternatives, including not just cable news and talk radio, but even amateur bloggers. The standards of what qualifies as news and how that news is presented are very different between traditional and nontraditional gatekeepers. The former is much more likely to stick to the values embedded in the model of objective journalism; the latter is much more likely pick and present stories with a clear partisan or ideological slant.

Historically, the mass media filtered information on the basis of quality as well as its ability to attract an audience. As new media shoulder aside traditional gatekeepers, the quality of information is given much less weight; the focus is squarely on whatever story will attract an audience. News has become a commodity, "a product shaped by the forces of supply and demand" (Hamilton 2004, 8). The result is a public sphere that is at least as dominated by celebrity profiles or the latest diet fad as by important policy issues. Media organizations have discovered that entertaining, rather than educating and informing, gets the bigger audiences and thus the bigger profits.

Information and Civic Engagement

Whatever the negative consequences of changes in communications technology, political scientists are increasingly interested in the potential impact on civic engagement. Social networking sites, Internet chat rooms, e-mail, and the like dramatically lower the cost of exchanging information. Will lowering the barriers and costs of exchanging information expand the public sphere in a positive way? Perhaps not.

In theory, new information technologies hold the potential to draw more citizens into the public sphere. A decade or two ago, scholars were hopeful that computer-based communication options would provide "an inviting opportunity for democratic dialogue" (T. Benson 1996, 61). By creating a virtual commons where people could exchange ideas and opinions in a "spirit of community and civility," the Internet was expected to provide a unique way to expand and improve the public sphere (T. Benson 1996, 61).

But the new communications technology has not lived up to such idealistic hopes. People rarely surf the Web to have their opinions and beliefs challenged; to quite the contrary, they tend to seek out sites and forums that fit their interests and preferences. Interactive forums do not automatically promote civil exchange. One study's conclusions about online media forums are succinctly summed up by a quote taken directly from a forum post: "destroy the scum, and then neuter their families" (Coffey and Woolworth 2003). Hardly the stuff of civil debate.

There are clearly tradeoffs in the rise of new media and how they are employed by a changing democratic society. On one hand, "more citizens have more ready access to more information and opinion than ever before . . . concerning more topics of both public and personal interest" (Swanson 2000, 412). On the other hand, "the Internet is filled with advocacy masked as information, with rumor and innuendo, and with the simply outrageous" (Swanson 2000, 412). The burden of judging information for its reliability and importance to the public sphere has shifted toward the individual citizen and away from gatekeepers who served the old media model using a set of professional standards (Swanson 2000, 412). The new media platforms seem less interested in facts and building civic community than in using outrage to grab audience share, capturing attention "with edgy content that shocks the audience while simultaneously flattering them for their moral and intellectual superiority, as demonstrated by their ability to see through the manipulative smoke, mirrors, and buffoonery offered by the other side" (Sobieraj and Berry 2011).

Some argue that these developments are a good thing, because they expand the political freedom of the individual. If unlimited access to information and access to a virtual press is within the grasp of every citizen, this is a good thing for democracy. Some research supports this positive view of the impact of new information technology on the public sphere. One study, for example, suggests that the Internet significantly enhances voter information about candidates and elections and in doing so plays an increasingly important role in mobilizing voters and encouraging political participation (Tolbert and McNeal 2003).

Others are not so sure. Rather than building democratic community, some see the new media environment as dividing the public sphere. Consider the rising prominence of blogs in politics. There are many political blogs, some of which attract tens of thousands of regular readers and are a part of the daily information consumption patterns of political junkies. Examples include the *Daily Kos* (http://www.dailykos.com), a blog aimed at Democrats and liberals, and Instapundit (http://instapundit.com/), a blog with a libertarian slant. Blogs such as these not only disseminate the views and opinions of their authors but also can have a more direct impact on politics. The *Daily Kos,* for example, has helped raise and distribute to Democratic candidates hundreds of thousands of dollars in campaign contributions. When Markos Moulitsas Zúniga, the man behind the *Daily Kos,* organized a blogger convention in 2006, more than 1,000 political bloggers showed up. This initial gathering grew into its

The freedoms of speech and the press provide a wide open opportunity to express views and exchange information, but this is no guarantee that those views will contribute to a civil or civic debate. Shown here is a billboard paid for by the North Iowa Tea Party that compares President Obama to Nazi leader Adolf Hitler and communist leader Vladimir Lenin. Expressing political views in an uncivil, even inflammatory, fashion has a long history in the United States.

own online community—Netroots Nation—dedicated to pushing its progressive political agenda by teaching people how to use technology to become more effectively involved in public debate. It held its seventh annual convention in 2012 and attracted a long list of liberal luminaries including U.S. Senator Sherrod Brown and economist Paul Krugman. (see the Netroots Nation website at http://netrootsnation.org).

There is little doubt that blogs are here to stay or that their influence will continue to increase. High-profile electoral campaigns attract competing blogs; indeed, sometimes they are covert operations of the campaigns themselves (Kuhn 2004). Although few doubt that blogs are an increasingly influential information source in the political world, there are mixed opinions on whether their overall contribution is positive or negative. Blogs typically make no pretensions to objectivity, and some spew ruthless—and not particularly well-sourced—attacks on perspectives and people from the opposite end of the partisan or ideological spectrum. In some ways, blogs are an unrepentant return to the partisan press of the past. Were he alive today, James Callender would almost certainly have a political blog, most likely a very popular one. Whether the contributions of the contemporary cyberspace Callenders are good or bad undoubtedly very much depends on whether you share their political opinions.

Top Ten Takeaway Points

1 The mass media are the means used to transmit information to masses of people. The mass media include the print media, the electronic media, and the news media. Generically, all are known as the press.

2 The press plays an important role in supporting the key democratic value of political freedom by helping to create a public sphere, a forum where information on issues important to civic life can be freely accessed and exchanged. It performs this role by giving us the information necessary to effectively and responsibly criticize governmental policies and leaders, propose new courses of action, and discuss political issues.

3 Different types of media provide different types of information. Citizens who rely more on newspapers tend to be more knowledgeable about politics than those who rely on other media.

4 The media have several specific roles in a democratic society that help promote the core value of political freedom. These roles include providing information and education, setting agendas, and acting as a watchdog and public advocate.

5 Most theories of how information is processed suggest that people are not neutral consumers of news. Our partisan and ideological viewpoints help determine what information and news sources we consider credible.

6 The media have taken over several of the traditional roles of political parties and are now a primary connection between citizens and government.

7 There are two basic threats to a free press: government control and private control. In the United States, government has always had a limited ability to control the press because of the First Amendment. Private control is more of a concern because profit pressures lead the mass media to ignore opinions and issues that will not attract large audiences.

(8) Most people believe the media are biased, though scholarly evidence supporting these beliefs is inconclusive. There is little evidence of an overall systematic political bias in the media, though specific outlets do seem to be more willing than in the past to employ partisan frames. There is considerable evidence to support the idea of racial and gender bias. Negativity bias is confirmed by most systematic research.

....

(9) A biased press is not necessarily a threat to democracy. Most important is a free press.

....

(10) Changes in communications technology coupled with changes in the broader social, political, and economic environment have changed the mass media in important ways. Technology has increased the size of the public sphere and lowered the costs of participation. Competitive pressures, concentration of ownership, and other trends have diluted the media's gatekeeper function, and some critics argue that the quality of news reporting has been lowered as well.

....

CHAPTER EIGHT
Key Terms and Cases

KEY QUESTIONS

Why is public opinion so important to policymaking in the United States?

Does public opinion really reflect the will of the people?

Where do political opinions come from?

ABRAHAM LINCOLN once said, "What I want to get done is what the people desire to have done, and the question for me is how to find that out exactly" (Crispi 1989, 1–2). Although many people would consider this a worthy and democratic sentiment, others might consider it naïve, foolish, and perhaps even dangerous. It is all of these.

Given what we learned in chapter 1, the democratic appeal of Lincoln's words should be obvious. Lincoln is expressing a straightforward desire to uphold the key democratic principle of majority rule. Majority rule means the government follows the course of action preferred by most people.

Yet Lincoln's desire to have the government do the people's bidding raises two problems. The first is practical: how do you find out what the people want? This problem is far from trivial. In most democracies, and certainly in the United States, citizens are rarely of one mind about anything. The people want government to do different things about everything from budget deficits to military operations in Afghanistan. Ask the people whether they support Policy X to address Problem A, and the answer will almost always be yes. And no. And maybe. It all depends on what particular group of people you talk to.

How is it possible to add up the disagreements and different attitudes into a clear expression of the people's will? Lincoln had no systematic answer to this question. Seventy years after Lincoln's death, Elmo Roper, George Gallup, and Archibald Crossley proposed such a systematic answer. These individuals—a journalism professor, a jewelry salesman, and a market researcher—pioneered scientific public opinion polling (Crispi 1989). Scientific polling provided the first reliable way to assess public opinion on a particular issue or question. As such, public opinion polling is viewed by some as an expression of the will of the people and as a means to measure the preferences of the majority.

The second problem with fulfilling Lincoln's goal to follow the popular will is philosophical: should the government really do what the people want? Even if the answer is yes, how quickly must government respond to the expressed popular will in order to be democratic? Public opinion turns out to be an unreliable basis for making policy because responses to survey questions are often uninformed and do not represent a true attitude (Zaller 1992). And the public often provides fluid and contradictory signals about what government should do. If government responds too quickly, it will find itself out of step with popular sentiment.

Thus, the advent of reliable public opinion polls creates a conundrum: On one hand, citizens rightfully expect government to act on their preferences; this cuts to the heart of the core democratic principle of majority rule. On the other hand, simply translating public opinion into policy can lead to ineffective, irresponsible, and even undemocratic answers to the question of who gets what.

The founders had no knowledge of scientific polling, but they clearly felt that the whims of the masses—what we would call public opinion—should not guide government decision making. Accordingly, the Constitution deliberately avoided establishing a government to quickly translate the will of the people into public policy. Indeed, as discussed in chapters 2 and 3, the Constitution does exactly the opposite. By design, it provides checks on the will of a majority to minimize threats to the rights of the minority and keeps key policymakers at arm's length from popular passions. In doing so, the Constitution seeks to uphold the core democratic principles of political freedom and political equality.

Yet the founders did not renounce the principle of majority rule; they wanted a system that would govern with the consent of the governed. Popular governments existed long before scientific polling. In these early popular governments, the preferences of the citizens were communicated to government leaders through direct political participation rather than through surveys and opinion polls. Political participation has multiple forms, including voting, lobbying, circulating petitions, and sending mail (or e-mail) to public officials. The founders were very clear about protecting citizen rights to participate in this fashion, to petition government and speak their mind about public policy; that's what the First Amendment to the Constitution is all about. Yet clearly there is friction and contradiction between the core democratic principles and the system established by the founders. The founders wanted the government to be responsive to the preferences of citizens (to uphold the principle of majority rule), but not too responsive because they feared the majority might seek to trample the political equality and freedom of a minority.

The founders tried to balance the inherent conflicts between these core principles by creating a system of government that would respond to the public will but act in the public interest. They did this by deliberately insulating much of government from the stormy winds of public opinion but also making clear that the government's authority and legitimacy rested on the will of the people. This is a tough balancing act to pull off without shorting at least one of the core principles.

In this chapter, we examine how well the American political system achieves this difficult balancing act by looking at what public opinion is, how it is measured, where it comes from, and the central role it plays in the American political system. This analysis provides a context for an examination of how political participation translates individual opinions, attitudes, and beliefs into action to influence public policy.

THE CONCEPT OF PUBLIC OPINION

Public opinion is the sum of individual attitudes or beliefs about an issue or question. Although this basic definition is simple, straightforward, and mostly accurate, it oversimplifies what is, in fact, a complex concept. What citizens think or feel about an issue depends on a variety of factors, most of which can change quickly. Measuring and understanding public opinion on any given issue is more than just a problem of arithmetic, or simply adding up who is for or against a proposed policy. To fully appreciate what public opinion is, it is useful to break it down into its basic elements: direction, stability, intensity, and salience.

Direction

The term **direction** refers to whether public opinion is positive or negative (favorable or unfavorable) about a given issue. On some issues, public opinion has no clear direction. Consider abortion, for example. Public policy on abortion is a controversial issue, and the government is frequently pressured to defend or restrict abortion rights. What should the government do in order to follow the will of the people on this issue?

As it turns out, public opinion is of little help in finding a clear answer to this question. As Figure 9.1 shows, positive and negative attitudes about abortion are more or less evenly balanced, with a slight majority favoring some limits but opposing an outright ban. This division leaves government with no clear signal

public opinion The sum of individual attitudes or beliefs about an issue or question.

direction The idea of public opinion being either positive or negative (favorable or unfavorable) on an issue.

Public opinion does not provide the government with clear guidance for making decisions related to abortion. Although attitudes and intensity have remained strong and stable, direction has been evenly balanced between those for and those against for many years, and the topic's salience wanes unless a specific issue becomes prominent.

© PAUL J. RICHARDS/AFP/Getty Images

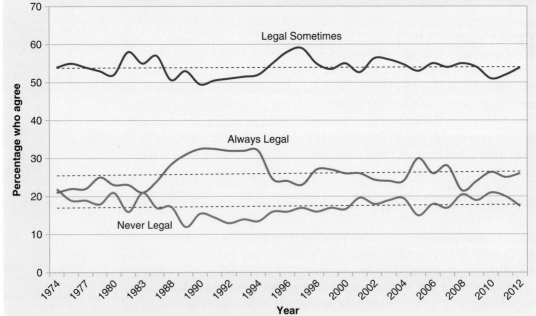

FIGURE 9.1 **Trends in Public Opinion on Abortion**

Source: Constructed by the authors from Gallup polls asking, "Do you think abortions should be legal under any circumstances, legal only under certain circumstances, or illegal in all circumstances?," http://www.gallup.com/poll/1576/Abortion.aspx (accessed June 1, 2012).

from public opinion, with each specific proposal to place limits on abortion the subject of its own controversial debate.

Stability

The element of **stability** is the likelihood of changes in the direction of public opinion. On some issues, public opinion retains a clear direction (or lack of direction) over long periods of time. Strongly pro-choice and pro-life attitudes, for example, have remained relatively stable in the U.S. population for the last quarter-century. During this time, roughly a quarter of Americans believed abortion should be legal in all circumstances, and a slightly smaller proportion believed it should be illegal in all circumstances. The majority of Americans consistently put themselves between these two extremes. Notice that the trend lines of opinions for all three positions in Figure 9.1 are essentially flat. The trends for the extreme positions diverge somewhat in the mid-1990s, but neither position has tended to greatly increase or decrease over more than a quarter-century.

On other issues, however, attitudes and beliefs are more volatile, with the direction of public opinion subject to shifts because of new information or experiences.

stability The likelihood of changes in the direction of public opinion.

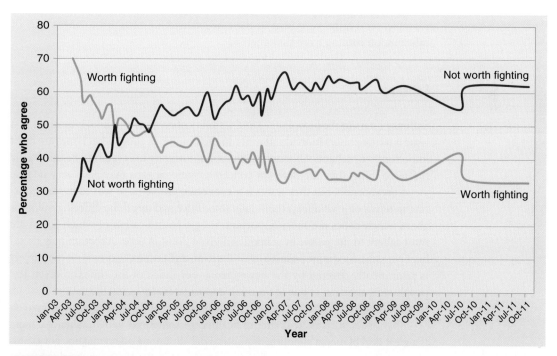

FIGURE 9.2 Public Support for the War in Iraq

Source: Constructed by the authors from data from a poll asking, "All in all, considering the costs to the United States versus the benefits to the United States, do you think the war in Iraq was worth fighting, or not?," http://www.washingtonpost.com/wp-srv/politics/polls/postabc poll_110311.html (accessed October 25, 2012).

Contrast the stability of abortion attitudes with public opinion on the Iraq war. Figure 9.2 shows that support for military action in Iraq varied tremendously from the invasion in 2003 to the end of the war in 2011. Initially, large majorities of Americans—about 70 percent—thought the war was worth the costs. A year later, Americans were about equally divided on whether the war was worth the costs. By the beginning of 2005, a majority—around 55 percent—of the public believed the war was not worth the costs. Since then, a strong majority of Americans have questioned the wisdom of invading Iraq. From 2010 until the end of the war, more than 60 percent of the public thought the war in Iraq had incurred more costs than benefits to the United States. Thus, public opinion completely reversed itself on one of the nation's most important and visible foreign policy decisions of the post–Cold War era.

Intensity

How strongly people hold the attitudes and beliefs is the **intensity** of public opinion. Low intensity tends to make public opinion less stable, given that people are more willing to change their minds if they are not strongly attached to one point of view. Public opinion on issues where large numbers of people have intensely held views tends to be more stable. People with strong pro-choice or pro-life views, for example, tend to be very firm in their beliefs and are resistant to arguments or information coming from the other side.

Salience

Salience refers to the prominence and visibility of an issue and how important that issue is to the public. Individuals differ in their opinions about what issues are most important—or salient. Although salience and intensity may seem to be essentially the same thing, they are different concepts. Some citizens may have very intense views on abortion, but they may view economic problems or war as more important in terms of what affects their daily lives. If we add up all the differing opinions about which issues are most important, we get an indication of which issues are most salient to the public in general at a given point in time. Abortion may be salient periodically if a proposal to limit abortion rights or a court case on the subject is prominently covered by the news media. For much of the time, however, few people view abortion as one of the most important issues facing the nation. Instead, the economy and crime consistently show up as two of the most important issues.

Other issues, such as civil rights or health care, sometimes gain in salience if there is a great deal of media attention or political debate among policymakers. For example, in polls taken during the civil rights movement in the 1960s, civil rights consistently appeared among the most important issues facing the nation, and health care appeared toward the top in 1993–1994 when President Bill Clinton made it a legislative priority. When the nation is at war, war becomes more salient, as was the case with Vietnam from the mid-1960s to the mid-1970s and with the wars in Iraq and Afghanistan. An economic recession can also make certain issues more salient, and

intensity How strongly people hold the beliefs or attitudes that comprise public opinion.

salience The prominence or visibility of an issue or question and how important the issue is to the public.

this was certainly the case as the United States sought to recover from the great recession of 2008–2009. In recent years, most polls indicated that Americans thought the economy, the federal deficit, and health care were the most important issues facing the nation. Iraq and Afghanistan became less salient as the recession and a historical reform of health care policy dominated the public agenda (see Figure 9.3).

To provide the government with a clear signal on what it is expected to do in response to a particular question or issue, the elements of public opinion must come together in a particular way. Public opinion needs to have a clear direction and reflect high levels of intensity, be stable across a reasonable period of time, and concern an issue of high salience. The concurrence of all four elements is rare. On most issues facing the government, one or more elements are missing: public opinion is divided or unstable, attitudes are not strongly held, or the issue is of low interest to most people.

Thus, rather than offering clear guidance, public opinion can often create difficult choices for government leaders. If the public knows little about a complex issue, considers it of little importance, and has no strong feelings one way or the other, public opinion can be a poor basis for deciding questions of who gets what. Public ignorance or indifference creates an obvious problem for a system with a strong preference for the delegate model. If public opinion cannot provide a competent basis for sound decision making, a system premised on following the dictates of public opinion is going to reflect that incompetence.

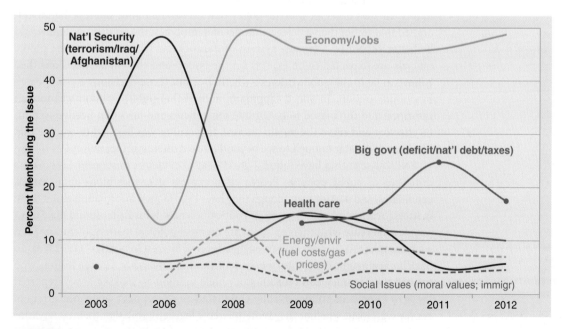

FIGURE 9.3 Public Opinion of Most Salient Issues

Source: Constructed by the authors from polls by Bloomberg, CBS News/*New York Times*, CNN, Fox News, and NBC News/*Wall Street Journal* reported at http://pollingreport.com/prioriti.htm (accessed June 1, 2012). Entries are annual averages of responses to questions asking "the most important issue for the federal government to address today."

THE COMPETENCE OF PUBLIC OPINION

The appropriate role of public opinion in democratic government has been the subject of debate for a long time. Some, like George Gallup, believe that public opinion is a scientifically valid measure of the will of the people. As a direct measure of the will of the people, Gallup viewed public opinion polling as a means to uphold the core principle of majority rule; if scientific opinion polls can accurately gauge the will of the majority, then they should play an important role in guiding political decisions. Gallup seems to endorse a **delegate model of representative democracy**. This view of democracy holds that the job of elected officials is not to act independently, making whatever decisions they feel are in the best interests of the community or society. Rather, their job is to translate the views of the majority, whatever those views may be, into government action. Others strongly disagree with Gallup's perspective, arguing that his view is not only naïve but even dangerous.

Walter Lippmann, a contemporary of Gallup, expressed this contrary view. He argued that public opinion is little more than a collection of individual biases that rest as much on ignorance and prejudice as on knowledge and rational thought. His great fear was that unless citizens were well informed about political issues, public opinion could be easily manipulated by groups promoting narrow interests. Prejudice, ignorance, and the self-interested campaigns of interest groups are hardly the best basis for making policy that serves the public interest. Lippmann argued that rather than a delegate model of democracy, the political system would be better served by a **trustee system of democracy**. In a trustee system, public officials are expected to be experts on the issues, and they make decisions they believe to be in the public interest, whether or not those decisions are supported by public opinion. In effect, Lippmann argued that public opinion was too ill-informed and too biased to be a guide for policies and laws that needed to both be effective and serve the public interest. Governing was best left to an elite that was knowledgeable enough to see beyond its own interests (Lippmann 1949, 195).

Political scientists have found a good deal of evidence to support Lippmann's criticisms of public opinion. People often express strong opinions about issues, candidates, and parties even though they have little factual information about these matters (Sears and Valentino 1997). Political scientist John Zaller found that "most people aren't sure what their opinions are on most political matters, including even such completely personal matters as their level of interest in politics" (1992, 76). To back his argument, Zaller cites the work of another researcher, George Bishop, who studied the accuracy and reliability of public opinion by looking at self-reported levels of interest in politics. Bishop conducted an experiment where one group of people was asked whether they remembered a legislative bill that their congressional representative had voted on in the last 12 years. Only 12 percent could. When this group was asked to describe their level of interest in politics, 45 percent indicated low levels of interest. A second group was asked about their level of interest in politics but was not asked questions about their congressional representative. In

delegate model of representative democracy The idea that the job of elected leaders is to make decisions solely based on the views of the majority of the people.

trustee system of democracy The idea that the job of elected leaders is to make decisions based on their own expertise and judgment, and not just make decisions based on the wishes and preferences of constituents.

this group only 22 percent indicated low levels of interest in politics. Zaller argues that these sorts of findings lead inevitably to the conclusion that

> [people] are heavily influenced by whatever ideas happen to be at the top of their minds. Thus what was most salient to many of the respondents in the Bishop experiment, who had just had an opportunity to observe how little they knew about politics, was that they were apparently not very interested in politics. (1992, 76)

Students of public opinion have long known that responses to public opinion polls are influenced by the wording and the order of the questions. This knowledge can lead to attempts to manipulate public opinion to support a particular issue or candidate. For example, a **push poll** deliberately feeds respondents misleading information or leading questions in an effort to "push" them into favoring a particular candidate or issue. In a push poll, the interviewer might ask the respondent which candidate he or she favors in an upcoming election. If the response is "wrong"—in other words, if the respondent favors the candidate opposed by whoever is backing the push poll—there will be a follow-up question designed to push support away from this candidate. For example, the next question might be "Would you still support this candidate if you knew he favored tax increases?"

The broader question here is that if public opinion is so ill-informed and easily manipulated, can it really serve as a competent guide for making public policy?

ELITE OPINION AND ISSUE PUBLICS

The argument that public opinion is a poor basis for answering questions of who gets what obviously has some merit. Yet it can also be argued that, in at least some ways, public opinion is an informed and reliable basis for guiding government action.

Public opinion can be reasonably judged as informed and reliable in two basic ways, both involving the opinions of smaller, more select groups rather than of the public as a whole. One group that typically has high levels of information backing their opinions is elites, or people with influential positions within society. **Elite opinion** refers to the attitudes of people with large measures of political influence or expertise.

There is convincing evidence that the opinions of elites are more informed than those of the general public (Erikson and Tedin 2002). It is also clear that the opinions of some help shape the opinions of others. For example, I may have little information about an issue, but if an official I admire, or my priest or my boss or a prominent member of my peer group, is against it, I may be willing to follow their lead. Yet despite acknowledgment that elite opinion is more informed and

push poll A type of public opinion poll that intentionally uses leading or biased questions in order to manipulate the responses.

elite opinion The attitudes or beliefs of those people with influential positions within society.

serves as a guide for the opinions of others, using it as the primary basis for political decision making presents a clear conflict with the core principles of political equality and majority rule. The principles, remember, are supposed to reflect the idea of popular sovereignty, or the idea that the power to authoritatively allocate values is shared by all. This idea is hard to square with the notion that the will of the "people" is really the will of a small minority of elites.

The second approach to viewing public opinion as more competent than its critics suggest is to divide opinions by issue, rather than looking at opinions of elites or opinions of the general public. Although most Americans know little about the details of lawmaking and have low levels of information about most issues, many have clear preferences about the issues that are most salient to them. People tend to have higher levels of information on the issues about which they care the most.

Recognizing that people have well-informed opinions only on the issues that are most salient to them suggests that there is not just one general public opinion, but rather opinions held by numerous issue publics. An **issue public** is simply the section of the population with a strong interest in a particular issue. Issue publics tend to be well informed about the policy area in question and are capable of making sophisticated choices, even if the issue is complex. They are much more likely to be knowledgeable about the voting records of elected officials and the positions of candidates on the issues with which they are concerned. Armed with this base level of information, citizens can effectively monitor their representatives and the policy actions of government. They do not have to keep up with every decision and action by all elected officials, all of the time. All they need to do is keep alert to any actions related to the issues that interest them. For example, citizens involved on either side of the gay rights debate do not have to keep up with all the votes and decisions of their representatives. Knowing when representatives vote contrary to their views on same-sex marriage provides an informed basis for political opinion that is sufficient to keep government accountable (Hutchings 2003).

Because issue publics can offer an informed perspective on policy, these opinions should be recognized and respected in a representative democratic system. Although measuring the opinions of numerous issue publics presents challenges, some argue that these challenges also offer an "exciting opportunity for more often engaging American voters in direct debates on policy priorities and direction. Such debates . . . are a sign of a vibrant democracy" (Lake and Sosin 1998, 70).

Despite their problems, public opinion polls can make a positive contribution to democratic governance. Many agree with "the common-sense view that when effective public opinion polls came on stream they positively added to the other modes of citizen expression" (Converse 1996, 649). Even the confusion created by the muddled and mixed messages that opinion polls often provide is not necessarily a bad thing. Instability and mixed direction show political leaders that the policy choices are not as clear, or the stakes as high, as they are often portrayed to be in partisan debate. Low levels of intensity and salience can demonstrate the need to transmit a clear and understandable message to the voters.

In short, even if they lack clarity, polls can still serve a positive democratic purpose by prodding politicians into making a better case for their policy agendas. The backing of public opinion provides a large measure of legitimacy to govern-

issue public A section of the public with a strong interest in a particular issue.

ment action. If polling does nothing else, it forces public officials to fight for and justify that legitimacy rather than simply assume it exists.

INTERPRETING PUBLIC OPINION POLLS

Obviously, public opinion is complex and contradictory, and many groups seek to measure and influence the public mood by putting a particular spin on everything from the president's job performance to whether or not it was worth invading Iraq. The net result is that public opinion often produces more confusion than clarity about the preferences of the majority. This raises questions about whether public opinion can ever be fully and objectively understood.

The short answer is no—assessing public opinion is an interpretive art, and on most issues, there is plenty of room for disagreement about the real state of the public's preferences. It is possible, however, to have an understanding of how public opinion polls work. This knowledge is essential to being an informed and effective participant in contemporary civic life.

Polling expert Brad Edmondson suggests that whenever "a poker-faced person tries to give you the latest news about how Americans feel" (1996, 10), you should ask some questions of your own. Edmondson suggests asking four basic questions to help you determine whether a poll is a reliable indicator of public opinion:

1. Did the poll ask the right people?
2. What is the margin of error?
3. What was the question?
4. Which question came first?

Did the Poll Ask the Right People?

The validity of a poll, or its ability to accurately represent what it claims, is tied to the people who answered the questions. It is not possible to ask all Americans their opinion of a particular candidate or issue. When a poll finds that a certain percentage of Americans are for or against something, that percentage is an estimate. Pollsters make that estimate by selecting a relatively small group of people, called a sample, to represent the entire population.

There are many ways to go about getting a sample, and the poll's accuracy depends on the sample type. Scientific polls are based on the concept of random sampling. Although the mathematics used to calculate a random sample can get complicated, the concept itself is easy to understand: in order to use a small group to figure out the opinions and attitudes of a large group, everyone in the large group must have an equal chance of being in the small group. A **random sample** is thus one in which every person in the target population has an equal chance of

random sample A method of selecting a sample (subset of the population) in which every person in the target population has an equal chance of being selected.

Major public opinion polls all predicted that President Harry Truman would lose his bid to be elected to a full term in 1948. Relying on these polls, the *Chicago Tribune* went to press reporting a Republican victory before election returns were reported in many states. The polls turned out to be wrong because they were based on what was known as a "quota sample." In this infamous photo, President-elect Truman displays the embarrassing result of polls that do not use a random sample.

being a poll respondent. If the target population is, say, Republican women, then the target population includes every woman who is a Republican. A random sample of Republican women would be a small group randomly chosen from the entire target population of Republican women. With random sampling, it is possible to get a reasonably accurate assessment of the opinions and attitudes of hundreds of millions of people—the entire population of the country—using a group that consists of a thousand or less.

Other ways to select a group of poll respondents run the risk of creating a **biased sample**, which is a group that does not accurately represent the target population and thus provides inaccurate estimates of the true opinions and attitudes of the target population. Common examples of polls based on biased samples are radio and television surveys based on viewers who are asked to call or e-mail or vote online in response to a particular question. Such polls reflect the views of only those who were tuned into the television or radio program and felt strongly enough about the question to register their views. Because people who were not tuned in had no chance of expressing their views, such polls are not based on a random sample, and they are unlikely to produce an accurate picture of broader public opinion. Polls based on nonrandom samples are often referred to as **straw polls**, which also include "man on the street" interviews and mail-in surveys placed in magazines.

Even a very large nonrandom sample can produce misleading results. The classic example is a 1936 poll conducted by the editors of *Literary Digest* on the presidential contest between incumbent President Franklin Roosevelt, the Democratic candidate, and Alf Landon, the Republican nominee. The sample for this survey was put

biased sample A group of poll respondents that does not accurately represent the target population and provides inaccurate estimates of the true opinions and attitudes of the target population.

straw polls Unscientific polls based on nonrandom samples.

together using telephone books and automobile registrations, and more than 10 million ballots were sent out by the magazine. The resulting sample was huge— more than two million people responded to the survey. The survey results indicated the winner would be Alf Landon, and the magazine used the poll to predict a Landon victory. Never heard of President Alf Landon? Not surprising—Roosevelt won the election by a landslide, and Landon barely mustered a third of the popular vote.

Why was a poll based on a sample of two million so wrong? However large the sample, it was a biased sample. In the mid-1930s, the country was still in the grip of the Great Depression, and only the relatively prosperous had an automobile or a telephone. The well-off were much more likely to be Republicans. *Literary Digest* had essentially taken a massive straw poll of Republicans about who they were going to vote for. Not surprisingly, Republicans responded that they were going to vote for the Republican candidate. Underrepresented in the sample were Democrats, who tended to be less well-off but much more numerous. Though fewer Democrats were asked their opinion, this did not stop them from voting.

What Is the Margin of Error?

Even a scientifically selected random sample will not perfectly reflect the views of a larger population. A well-selected sample approximates the target population's opinions, but it is almost always a little bit off. Fortunately, another useful feature of random samples is that statisticians can calculate the margin of error. The **margin of error** (sometimes called the *sampling error*) is the amount by which the sample responses are likely to differ from those of the population within very tight boundaries that are known as the confidence level of a survey.

Reputable and reliable surveys always report a margin of error and a confidence level. Although the math behind them may seem complicated, margin of error and confidence levels are easy and intuitive to interpret. A poll with a margin of error of 5 percentage points and a confidence level of 95 percent means that there is a 95 percent chance that the sample responses are within plus or minus 5 percentage points of the target population's real opinions.

The size of the random sample determines how large the margin of error is: the larger the random sample, the smaller the margin of error. A useful guide to determining the approximate error of a random sample is shown in Table 9.1. Note that it is the size of the random sample and not the size of the population that is important. A random sample of 1,000 will have a margin of error of plus or minus 3 percentage points in any large population, regardless of whether the sample is drawn from a population of 2 million, 20 million, or even 200 million.

There are two important points to keep in mind. First, the margin of error means that pinpoint precision about public opinion is unlikely; even a well-constructed poll can show only the likely range of public opinion. For example, a poll showing 47 percent of likely voters supporting candidate A and 44 percent supporting candidate B does not necessarily mean that candidate A is ahead. If the margin of error is 3 percent, this means candidate A's support ranges somewhere between

margin of error The amount that sample responses are likely to differ from those of the population within very tight boundaries that are known as the confidence level.

TABLE 9.1: GUIDE FOR DETERMINING MARGIN OF ERROR

Sampling Size	Margin of Error (%)
250	±6.0
500	±4.5
1,000	±3.0
2,000	±2.0

Source: Michael W. Traugott and Paul J. Lavrakas, *The Voter's Guide to Election Polls*, 2nd ed. (New York: Seven Bridges Press, 2000), 123.

44 percent and 50 percent, and candidate B's support is somewhere between 41 percent and 47 percent. In other words, it is possible that candidate B has more support than candidate A.

The second point deals with the **confidence level**. As discussed earlier, a 95 percent confidence level means that there is a 95 percent chance that the true opinion of the population falls somewhere within the boundaries set by the margin of error. That means there is a 5 percent probability that the true opinion of the population falls outside that range. In other words, there is a 1 in 20 chance that the results of the poll are wrong and that the true opinion of the population is outside the margin of error.

These odds mean the probability of a well-constructed poll being wrong is very low, but the possibility cannot be completely dismissed. To make a reasoned judgment on what a poll says about public preferences, it is important, at a minimum, to know the margin of error. Any poll that does not report a margin of error should be treated with skepticism. Without the margin of error, it is hard to judge whether a poll is an accurate barometer of broader opinion.

What Was the Question?

In order to judge the validity of a poll, it is important to know not only the sample on which it was based and the associated margin of error but also the wording of the questions asked. Pollsters have long known that how a question is worded can help determine how a question is answered. Consider this example taken from a real survey: "Do you want union officials in effect to decide how many municipal employees you, the taxpayer, must support?" (Edmondson 1996, 14). This is a leading question, meaning it is worded so as to prompt a particular answer or opinion—in this case, opposition to municipal unions. Such questions do not produce accurate estimates of true opinions.

The process of designing survey questionnaires is known as **instrumentation**. Reputable pollsters are aware of the potential pitfalls of writing questions that mislead, confuse, or prompt off-topic responses. Technical wording that is hard to understand or questions that provoke strong negative or positive biases can easily threaten the validity of a survey. For example, asking whether people support welfare is likely to elicit a more negative response than asking whether people support programs to help the needy. The word *welfare* tends to prompt a negative image

confidence level The chance, measured in percent, that the results of a survey will fall within the boundaries set by the margin of error.

instrumentation The process of designing survey questionnaires.

of individuals working the system and looking for handouts. The phrase "help the needy" conjures up an image of people in genuine distress through no fault of their own. These sorts of wording issues can determine whether a poll shows support or opposition to a particular issue or candidate.

Instrumentation involves not just the wording of questions but also how they are structured. Many surveys rely on closed-ended questions or multiple-choice questions. The advantage of closed-ended questions is that they ensure a degree of uniformity in responses, which makes data processing and analysis easier. Their disadvantage is that they prevent respondents from answering in their own words. By limiting the response options, a survey may miss important information and unanticipated trends (Manheim and Rich 1991, 115–123). For example, limiting respondents to the major-party presidential candidates in a presidential election poll will fail to gauge support for minor-party candidates.

Which Question Came First?

The order of questions in a survey can also affect answers. Edmondson (1996) looks at two polls taken at virtually the same time that used almost identical questions about tax cuts and the federal deficit. One poll reported that 55 percent of Americans believed tax cuts and deficit reduction could be accomplished simultaneously, whereas the other poll reported that only 46 percent of Americans believed this to be possible. This difference, which is well outside the margin of error of the surveys, has to do with the order in which the questions were asked. One poll first asked whether respondents favored a tax cut and then asked whether they would still favor a tax cut if it meant no deficit reduction, and only then were respondents asked whether a tax cut and deficit reduction could be achieved at the same time. The other poll asked only the latter question—that is, whether they thought tax cuts and deficit reduction could happen simultaneously.

What is probably going on here is that respondents in the first poll expressed support for a tax cut in the first question and then were reluctant to back away from that position when questions about the deficit were introduced, even if they favored deficit reduction. Respondents in the second poll had no question setting up a specific position on tax cuts and so were less boxed in by their own previously expressed preferences when the question of tax cuts and deficits came up. This example shows that the order of questions is critical; without knowing the order in which questions were asked, it is hard to form a solid judgment about the validity of the results.

Getting satisfactory answers to the four questions suggested by Edmondson can help determine whether a poll is providing a real reflection of public opinion or is simply a collection of largely meaningless numbers. Of course, it is often hard to get the information required to answer all these questions. Few news reports include all the technical details of polls, especially on matters such as question order. At a minimum, however, it is critical to get answers to the first two questions (whether a random sample was used and what the margin of error is); without this information, it is wise not to invest any faith in poll numbers. (See the Politics in Practice feature "Peasants under Glass.")

PEASANTS UNDER GLASS

There is more than one way to uncover the views and preferences of the man or woman on the street. Opinion polls based on random sampling are the most reliable, but pollsters are also increasingly using another technique that has been nicknamed "peasants under glass."

This technique is the focus group. Focus groups are, in essence, an in-depth conversation with a small number (typically six to twelve) of people. Unlike most polls, in a focus group, it is practical to ask open-ended questions, let people take the conversation where they want to take it, and give them the freedom to make the responses that they want to make. It is not unusual for a focus group to be asked if there were any questions they felt should have been asked, but were not.

Thus, the big advantage of a focus group is that, unlike most surveys, it sets up a two-way flow of information. A focus group consists of a carefully chosen set of people who respond not just to the questions of an interviewer but to one another's thoughts and comments. Leading a focus group is a moderator, whose job is not to complete a survey questionnaire but to keep the group conversation focused on the issue of interest.

Because focus groups are usually chosen to bring together a group of similar people, participants feel more at ease in expressing their true beliefs and attitudes. This approach can offer useful information to political strategists who are trying to figure out what particular groups like or dislike a particular candidate or issue or how they will respond to particular proposals or arguments.

According to former Republican campaign strategist Lee Atwater, focus groups are useful because they give "you a sense of what makes people tick and a sense of what is going on with people's minds that you simply can't get with survey data." In other words, focus groups do not simply help researchers discover what people think but also why they think that way.

Two advantages of focus groups are their ability to gather a lot of useful information in a relatively short time and their ability to follow up on unanticipated responses or group beliefs. Because of this second advantage, focus groups are increasingly popular for those who want to "test run" arguments or proposals before they are made to the general public. For example, rather that make a major policy proposal in stump speech, a presidential candidate may test the proposal through various focus groups. Based on the response, the proposal can be packaged for the maximum desired effect. Focus groups are ultimately a way to observe the responses of the man and woman on the street under controlled circumstances, almost like a scientist observing reactions under a microscope (hence, "peasants under glass").

Focus groups, however, also have disadvantages. The largest and most obvious is that they are not based on a random sample. This means that what a focus group says is not necessarily reflective of the beliefs and attitudes of the population it was chosen to represent. In fact, different focus groups taken from the same population may give different responses to the same general questions.

A second disadvantage is the need for a skilled moderator. A well constructed survey instrument can be administered by anyone with minimal training and a telephone. However, getting useful information from a focus group requires a moderator skilled in group dynamics who knows when to take the lead and when to step back.

In the end, these disadvantages are outweighed by focus groups' potential to obtain personal and in-depth information about beliefs and attitudes, why people have those beliefs and attitudes, and how those beliefs and attitudes shape responses to candidates and issues.

SOURCE American Statistical Association. 1997. *What Are Focus Groups?* Alexandria, VA: American Statistical Association, Section on Survey Research Methods.

Where do people get their opinions? Are they simply random thoughts plucked from whatever is foremost on people's minds when they are asked a question? If so, the consequences for a delegate model of democratic governance are harsh. Deciding who gets what on what is essentially random impulse can hardly be considered a good basis for effective governance.

The central theoretical models used to explain political attitudes and behavior generally assume opinions are more systematic, but they offer mixed help in explaining where those opinions come from. Rational choice theories are of little help. Rational choice takes preferences—and the opinions, attitudes, and biases behind them—as givens. In other words, rational choice accepts that people have strong beliefs and preferences but makes little attempt to explain *why* they have those beliefs and preferences.

Explanations of the origins of public opinion and political beliefs have largely been carried out using behavioral or social-psychological approaches. From these perspectives, public opinion is a complex product of numerous forces. The social-psychological framework suggests that our attitudes and opinions are products of our environments. They are formed as reactions and adaptations to everything from the political leanings of our immediate family members to the broader values expressed in the political system as a whole. These complex forces can be classified into three broad categories: political culture, ideology, and political socialization.

A more recent explanation of the origins of public opinion suggests that there is an innate component to our beliefs. Following the lead of behavioral geneticists, political scientists have found good evidence that beliefs on a broad variety of issues are partially hereditary. These evolutionary and biological models of public opinion show that the complex environmental forces championed by behavioral models are important, but also that they are incomplete explanations of how we come to our beliefs and opinions. What we believe is significantly shaped by who we are.

Political Culture

A stable political system rests on a set of shared beliefs that include a broad agreement about basic political values and the legitimacy of political institutions and broad acceptance of the process government uses to make policy. These shared beliefs constitute **political culture**.

Political culture helps tie a polity together by providing a basic sense of what the nation is, what it stands for, and what political actions will be considered acceptable. A consensus on fundamentals does not mean people agree on specific outcomes. It means that people share a general sense of how those outcomes should be achieved and what those outcomes should not include. Most Americans, for example, express a strong "tribal loyalty" to the political system. At least in the

political culture A set of shared beliefs that includes broad agreement about basic political values, agreement about the legitimacy of political institutions, and general acceptance of the process government uses to make policy.

abstract, Americans believe in the democratic process and believe that the political system set up by the Constitution is the best way to run things. Support for our system does not mean that everyone likes particular officeholders or that we all approve of how particular parts of the system (Congress, the courts, etc.) are doing their jobs. Americans may dislike—even loathe—officeholders and the policies they produce, but the people generally accept the officeholders as legitimate as long as the latter are perceived as holding their positions and passing laws in accordance with the basic principles of the democratic process.

This broad agreement on how decisions should be made has important implications for public opinion. One of the significant characteristics about the beliefs that make up political culture is that they are stable and enduring: direction, stability, intensity, and saliency are no problem at this level. Although Americans have occasionally quarreled over specifics, in general they have maintained a strong belief in and commitment to democratic institutions and processes as the appropriate means to political order. Anything that smacks of authoritarianism or oligarchy tends to find itself on the wrong side of public opinion. Well-heeled special interest groups, for example, are widely believed to wield too much influence, and Americans tend to have negative attitudes toward them—even though many belong to such organizations.

Political culture, then, acts as a unifying force. It sets the boundaries for what opinions, attitudes, and beliefs are considered legitimate. Positive or negative opinions of presidential performance, for example, are "in bounds" even though these attitudes reflect fundamental disagreements among citizens. The notion of getting rid of the presidency and replacing the system of divided powers with a parliamentary system would likely be considered out of bounds because this attitude does not fit with the political culture's broad commitment as expressed by the Constitution.

Policies and actions that contradict the beliefs central to political culture tend to be rejected quickly, if they are considered at all. Political culture is the more or less stable channel through which the changing currents of public opinion flow.

Ideology

Although political culture can help explain very broad patterns in public opinion, it does little to help us understand where opinions on specific issues come from. Abortion rights and the war in Iraq evoke conflicting responses from people who share the same fundamental beliefs that make up political culture. Young people tend to have different views than older people. What is the source of these differing attitudes?

One answer is ideology. As discussed in chapter 1, **ideology** is a consistent set of values, attitudes, and beliefs about the appropriate role of government in society (Campbell et al. 1960). Ideology is critical to understanding public opinion because it gives people preferences about issues even if they have no individual stake in them. Heterosexuals, for example, may have strong opinions about same-sex marriage. Males may have strong opinions about abortion rights. The opinions produced by ideology have important political consequences: they help drive po-

ideology A consistent set of values, attitudes, and beliefs about the appropriate role of government in society.

Young voters are less conservative than older voters. In the 2012 election, young voters (ages 18–29) supported President Obama by a 25-point margin (60–35), while older voters (age 65 and older) supported Romney by an 18-point margin (56–38).

litical participation by prompting people to vote, join interest groups, and contact public officials (Bawn 1999).

Although political scientists have convincingly demonstrated that ideology plays an important role in determining individual opinions on a wide range of issues, this knowledge redefines rather than answers the question of where public opinion comes from. If opinion comes from ideology, where does ideology come from?

There is no unanimous answer to this question. Some argue that ideology is an outgrowth of national traditions and political culture. Others argue that it is a product of electoral systems, group interests, historical events, religious beliefs, family background, life experience, or some combination of these factors (Gerring 1997). Others argue that ideology is part of our individual psychology; some people are just more conservative or liberal than others, just as some people are more trusting, neurotic, or open to new experiences than others (Jost 2006).

Regardless of where ideology comes from, there is little doubt of its powerful role in shaping individual opinions. On many issues, all you need to form an opinion is your self-identity as a liberal or a conservative. This is because the key characteristic of ideology is a consistent, stable, and interconnected set of beliefs about politics and government. Individuals who view politics ideologically tend to have very coherent and consistent views on political matters, adopting regular and predictable patterns on issue positions, regardless of their levels of information.

Americans tend to lean to the right—that is, toward the conservative end of the ideological spectrum. Although a plurality (40 percent) of Americans viewed themselves as "conservative" in 2011, most Americans remain relatively moderate with relatively small numbers at each extreme—10 percent "very conservative,"

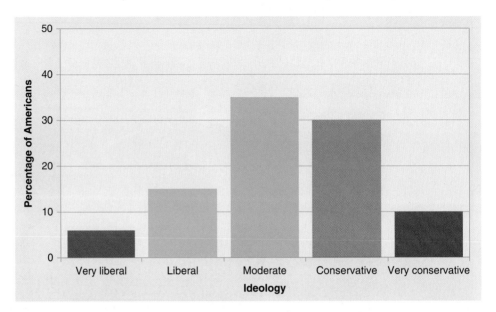

FIGURE 9.4A Political Ideology, 2011

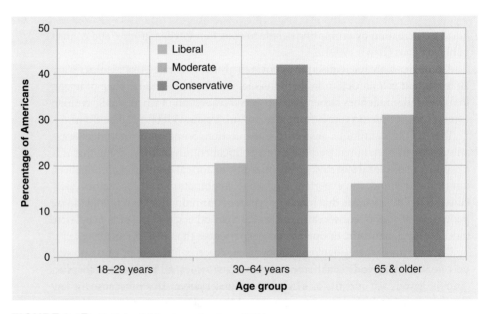

FIGURE 9.4B Political ideology by Age, 2011

Source: Constructed by the authors from Saad (2012).

POLITICS IN PRACTICE

PUBLIC OPINION AND THE CULTURE WAR

We are a nation deeply divided. At least, that's the general impression that many get from examining recent election results. Beginning in the mid-1990s, the winners in national elections were lucky to get 50 percent of the votes cast. President Bill Clinton won in 1996 with 49.2 percent of the vote. George Bush won in 2004 with 50.7 percent of the vote. Barack Obama was the biggest recent popular vote winner, and even he had a bare majority of Americans who voted (roughly 53 percent).

In Congress there is a similar story. Though they controlled the House of Representatives for much of the first decade of the twentieth century, Republicans hardly ever captured 50 percent of the popular vote. Democrats did manage this feat in 2008—mirroring Obama's popular vote share with a minimal absolute majority of about 53 percent. This is what passes for a big win in the popular vote.

Such close election results, with winners lucky to scrape a percentage point or two past a bare majority, initially seem to support the notion of a blue state–red state divide. The blue states (mostly on the coasts and upper Midwest) lean Democratic and liberal. The red states (the South and western middle of the country) lean Republican and conservative. These electoral divisions represent intense divisions in public opinion on a wide range of issues, among them abortion, gay marriage, gun control, and prayer in schools. These issues are at the heart of what some have described as the "culture war," the political battle over how morals and values should be reflected in public policy. Public opinion in the blue states favors abortion rights; public opinion in red states opposes abortion rights. Such intense division in public opinion is reflected in electoral patterns, with candidates vowing to uphold the preferences of their respective constituencies.

As it turns out, this conventional wisdom is more wrong than right. On the vast majority of issues, including hot button culture war topics like "God, gays, and guns," public opinion in blue states and red states are

6 percent "very liberal" (see Figure 9.4a). But young adults (18–29 years old) tend to have a somewhat less conservative ideology than older Americans. Figure 9.4b shows that the number of conservatives increases steadily with age. (See the Politics in Practice feature "Public Opinion and the Culture War").

Political Socialization

Most political scientists see ideology as a product of a broader process called **political socialization**, which is the process of acquiring political values. More precisely, political socialization is the process through which a younger generation learns political values from previous generations. Political socialization thus involves the transmission of values from one generation to another. These values help determine not only our ideology but also our opinions on specific issues. Traditionally, political scientists have organized the major agents of political socialization into five general categories: family, schools, peers, events and experiences, and the media (Erikson and Luttbeg 1973).

more alike than different. That's the conclusion of a study by political scientist Morris Fiorina and colleagues Samuel Abrams and Jeremy Pope. The vast majority of Americans, regardless of where they live or where they stand on the culture war battle lines, identify themselves as ideological centrists. That centrist, moderate political orientation is reflected in public opinion. Most people, for example, favor some gun controls, but are opposed to an outright ban on owning firearms. Most people believe abortion should be legal, but not in all circumstances.

If public opinion on even the most controversial issues is so centrist and moderate, why does America seem so deeply ideologically and politically divided? Is the blue state–red state divide just a mirage? Fiorina argues that it's real enough, even though it does not reflect true public opinion. The moderate middle that represents most people's opinions on most issues translates into a relatively low intensity set of beliefs. Low intensity means that the moderate middle is not particularly inclined to push their political opinions too far; for most people it is simply not worth the effort, because it is not something they feel strongly about.

What this means is that those who do have intense beliefs about particular issues are the people who dominate the debate over those issues. Because they also tend to be organized and heavily involved in the political process, they are also the people and groups that candidates for office tend to pay attention to. In other words, it is the extremes of public opinion that get the attention, even though they represent minority beliefs. People at both extremes of the spectrum on issues such as abortion and gay rights do indeed have deep, fundamental, and perhaps irreconcilable differences.

At least according to Fiorina, however, those people do not represent majority public opinion. They play such a prominent role in defining politics simply because they are more involved in the process. America is not polarized by its beliefs; majorities on even the most controversial issues are usually found in the middle. The moderate middle, however, is relatively silent about its views. The extremes on either end, on the other hand, try to be as loud as possible in expressing and supporting their opinions. It is these extremes of public opinion that are unevenly geographically distributed, not the moderate majority viewpoints that most Americans espouse.

SOURCE Fiorina, Morris, with Samuel J. Abrams and Jeremy C. Pope. 2005. *Culture War? The Myth of a Polarized America.* New York: Pearson Education.

Some of these agents, including family, have an effect early in life. Others, such as coworkers or fellow students, can influence political opinions in a person's adulthood. Some of these agents involve groups where there are face-to-face relationships over long periods of time (family or church, for example). Others involve secondary groups such as labor unions or professional associations, where contact among members is more limited and involves different people across time. The broader point is that political socialization is a lifelong process—the agents of political socialization can shape our opinions about political matters at any age. Understanding the agents of political socialization offers a way to understand where public opinion comes from.

FAMILY The family is the most influential agent in shaping individual political attitudes, and it exercises its major effect during the individual's most impressionable years. For most people, the family enjoys a near monopoly over a person's political attention during the early years of life, and children often learn to orient themselves toward politics and government by imitating their parents. For example, if parents think and speak well of the president, children tend to echo that support.

political socialization The process through which a younger generation learns political values from previous generations.

If parents are cynical about government and politics, believing that politics and politicians are corrupt, their children tend to adopt those beliefs. Additionally, children tend to espouse the political party affiliation of their parents.

Political scientists have long recognized that the family's influence becomes less monopolistic as people are exposed to other agents of political socialization, but political attitudes do tend to persist across generations within families (Jennings and Niemi 1975). How a child is politically socialized by the family generally has a lasting effect on his or her opinions.

Political socialization involves the transmission of values from one generation to another. By reinforcing a commitment to the United States and its political system, pledging allegiance to the flag is a form of political socialization familiar to most children who attend school in America.

SCHOOLS Schools also play a major role in shaping political attitudes. Like family, schools are an important part of a child's life. In fact, one of the reasons for establishing public school systems is to ensure the transmission of the "right" political values to the next generation. Yet there are important differences between schools and family as agents of political socialization.

A major difference is that schools have less influence on fundamental political orientations such as ideology and partisanship. In the United States, there has always "existed a tradition of strong dissent to a public system of education that teaches political doctrines" (Spring 1998, 10). And although any number of groups and individuals may try to use public schools to promote their political agendas, the ability of schools to actually influence specific ideological or partisan political opinions of students seems limited.

Rather than instilling particular attitudes about particular issues, candidates, or parties, schools play a more central role in reinforcing the broader set of beliefs that make up political culture. For example, in school children learn to salute the flag, recite the pledge of allegiance, sing patriotic songs, and honor the nation's heroes. The very notion of public school systems in the United States was based, at least in part, on the desire to promote democratic attributes such as a tolerance of different opinions. This sort of socialization is more likely to promote positive feelings about the nation and its system of government than it is to turn children into fervent Democrats, Republicans, or supporters of abortion rights or gun control.

Schools do play a direct role in opinion formation, but this is because they are places where people from different backgrounds and different ideas come into frequent contact with one another. Postsecondary education in particular exposes young adults to political and cultural diversity. Exposure to diverse ideas is a central characteristic of higher education, and students often change their attitudes and opinions about political issues while in college. This change is at least partially due to college faculties and student populations that tend to be more politically, ethnically, and socially diverse than their counterparts in high schools. Change of opinion in college tends to have less to do with professors brainwashing easily swayed undergraduates than with exposure to different peer groups with different political perspectives. Close physical proximity to people with different attitudes—coupled with the feeling of many students that they have broken with the past—helps promote the formation of new political attitudes and new ways of looking at the political world.

PEERS Peer groups are important agents of political socialization, not just in school but throughout life. The political attitudes of adults can be influenced by peers from formal or informal networks where common interests are shared. These networks include churches, clubs, ethnic groups, neighborhoods, and professional and recreational associations. Peer influence on political attitudes depends on how important political concerns are within the group, the extent of agreement on such matters among group members, and how closely an individual identifies with the group.

Individuals' political attitudes may also be shaped by groups to which they do not belong, at least not in any formal sense. Such groups are called **reference groups** because they provide signals that people use to get their social and psychological bearings. For example, a white liberal may identify with the National Association for the Advancement of Colored People (NAACP), which promotes policies designed to help African Americans, without personally joining the group or receiving any material benefits from the policies the group supports. Reference groups can provide negative as well as positive symbols. A candidate's association with radical groups, such as the Ku Klux Klan or fundamentalist groups that refuse to condemn acts of terrorism, may be enough to turn opinions and votes away.

EVENTS AND EXPERIENCES Our own experiences and the larger political context in which they take place can have a powerful effect on our opinions and attitudes. Someone who has just been mugged, for example, is unlikely to be convinced by statistics that show crime is declining.

Presidential elections are cyclical events that periodically shape public opinion. Following the inauguration of a new president, the new executive typically enjoys a honeymoon period. The conflict of the election is past, and most Americans are willing to give the new president a chance to do the job. Initial job approval ratings of our two most recent presidents were in the mid-60 percent range (see Figure 9.5). After the inauguration, however, public opinion of the president can be driven up or down by other events. The terrorist attacks of September 11, 2001, were a powerful example of how an event can shape public opinion. Prior to the attacks, President George W. Bush had middling job approval ratings from the public, and opinion polls showed little evidence that the public considered a sustained campaign against terrorism a policy priority. Following the attacks, opinions of the president's job performance became overwhelmingly positive as people reflexively drew together and backed the nation's leader in a time of crisis. This effect is known as a "rally 'round the flag" response of public opinion. Rally events occur following dramatic presidential actions in response to international and military crises (Mueller 1973). For example, there was a much smaller rally in

reference groups Groups that influence the political attitudes of non-group members.

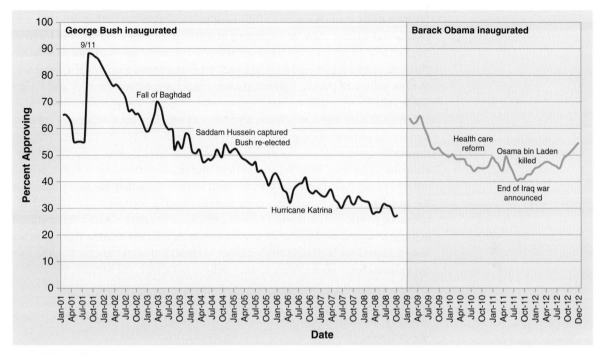

FIGURE 9.5 Presidential Job Approval

Source: Constructed by the authors from Gallup Polls reported at http://pollingreport.com/ obama_job1.htm (accessed October 24, 2012). Entries are monthly averages of responses to the question asking, "Do you approve or disapprove of the way [George W. Bush/ Barack Obama] is handling his job as president?".

President Bush's job approval after the invasion of Iraq in March 2003 and the fall of Baghdad in April.

Other experiences helped drag down President Bush's approval; prolonged, bloody, and inconclusive campaigns in Iraq and Afghanistan, the bungled response to Hurricane Katrina in September 2005, and an economic downturn in 2007 and 2008 all helped shift public opinion on Bush. In the last two years of his administration, public approval of Bush's job performance collapsed, and he received some of lowest job approval ratings of any modern president.

Barack Obama took office with approval ratings typical of newly elected presidents. Controversy over the economic stimulus package and health care reform, as well as the relatively weak economic recovery, led to a steady decline over the first two years of his administration. There was a small rally event in May 2011 following the announcement of the death of Osama bin Laden. The rally, however, was short-lived, and President Obama's approval rating slipped over the next several months. Obama's approval rating then began to increase following the October 2011 announcement that American troops would leave Iraq by the end of the year. His approval rating continued to improve though most of 2012 and exceeded 50 percent by November. President Obama was reelected, continuing a historical pattern that presidents with public approval above 48 percent on election day win reelection, while less popular incumbents usually lose.

THE MASS MEDIA Another way to influence political opinion is through the mass media—television, radio, newspapers, magazines, and the Internet. The Internet has become an increasingly important tool of political and partisan persuasion (Browning 1996; Hill and Hughes 1997), yet television remains the most important source of political information for most Americans (Stanley and Niemi 2011, 162).

Regardless of the media form, a number of scholars have expressed concern that media outlets shape public opinion in a negative way. The concern rests on the media's potential to make people skeptical and cynical about politics and government in general. Scandal, corruption, and incompetence are a staple of media reports on politicians and government. Some believe that the strong focus on the negative makes Americans more distrustful of government and more cynical about politics, even though federal officeholders operate under strict ethical guidelines and almost certainly engage in less unethical behavior than in other historical periods (F. Harris 1995, 61–62). Although studies indicate that the media only reinforce what people already believe to be true, the negative tone about politics, especially in television news programs, tends to promote negative opinions about government institutions, and these opinions persist even when more objective measures of government's job performance are positive (Hibbing and Theiss-Morse 1998).

Political campaigns may take advantage of the negative socialization effects of television by running negative ads. Viewers of these ads become more cynical about the political system and the ability of an average citizen to influence the democratic process (Ansolabehere et al. 1994). This increased cynicism makes people less likely to vote. A political campaign can exploit this socialization effect by aiming its ads at an opponent's supporters. Rather than trying to persuade voters to support a particular candidate or set of issues, the objective is to cut into the opponent's support by making those supporters less likely to vote. Of course, most candidates will not let an opponent run attack ads without replying in kind. The net effect of all the carefully crafted mudslinging in 30-second television ads is to create a very troubling socialization effect: increased cynicism, apathy, and even anger.

The mass media also play another important socialization role by helping to create shared perceptions of social trends. On many issues there is a disconnect between what people experience personally and the perceptions of broader social trends generated by news reports. The latter are often more negative than the former, and they play an important role in shaping opinions. For example, consider that most Americans express satisfaction with their local schools, with most people grading them highly. News reports on public education, however, are almost always negative, stressing the worst of the educational system. As a result, although most people see their own public schools as doing well, they view public schools generally as performing poorly. There is a similar disconnect on many other issues: Americans are generally satisfied with their own families, communities, and workplaces but also believe that these institutions are in trouble nationally; people rate the U.S. health care system poorly, even though they rate their own health care positively (Loveless 1997).

Biological Models of Public Opinion

Biological models of public opinion argue that attitudes and opinions also have a genetic component. In this framework, beliefs and attitudes are seen as products of an interaction between inherited predispositions and the complex environmental factors championed by the behavioral approach.

There is actually good evidence, from research done on twins, to support these claims. As most people know, there are two kinds of twins: (1) identical twins (called monozygotic twins), who share 100 percent of their genetic material, and (2) fraternal twins (called dizygotic twins), who like most siblings share only 50 percent of their genetic material. As siblings, twins are usually raised in the same environment (same family, same schools, same political culture, etc.). Yet like some other siblings, twins are sometimes raised apart because of divorce, adoption, or other events. Twins raised separately obviously have different environments: different family, different schools, and sometimes even different political cultures. Twins thus make an excellent basis for trying to sort out whether genes shape opinions and beliefs. There is a certain amount of variation on genetics and environment, and using statistical techniques, researchers can quite accurately sort out how much of the variation in a given attitude or belief is being driven by genetics or environment.

When researchers examined political opinions and beliefs using data sets based on twins, they found that a surprisingly large component of the variation in these beliefs could be attributed to genetics. One of the original studies to take this approach was done more than 20 years ago by a team of researchers headed by Nick Martin, an Australian behavioral geneticist (1986). They found a strong genetic component to political beliefs such as support for the death penalty. More recently, a team of political scientists focused on this issue using a large twin data set and found that on issues such as school prayer and property taxes, a third or more of the variation in expressed opinions was the result of genetics rather than the environment (Alford, Funk, and Hibbing 2005).

Does this mean there is a gene that determines what your opinion will be on school prayer or abortion? No. What it means is that your genes influence your opinions in combination with the environment. Take for example, religiosity, or the extent to which an individual is religiously devout. Twin research has found a strong genetic component to religiosity; in other words, people do seem to inherit a predisposition to be religiously devout. Yet how that devotion is expressed seems to be almost wholly environmental. Whether you are a devout Methodist, Catholic, Jew, Muslim, or member of any other faith is more a product of the environment you find yourself in than any genetic predisposition. Political attitudes and beliefs are similar. You may inherit a predisposition toward being more politically oriented than someone else, but whether that heightened political intensity leads you to be a fervent Republican or Democrat—or to hold the range of opinions those partisan labels imply—is shaped more by the environment than anything else.

This research, in other words, does not support the notion of genetic determinism, or the idea that your genes automatically determine what you believe and how you behave. What it supports is the idea that there is a biological component to our opinions and behaviors. The origins of our opinions and beliefs, in other words, rest partly in the predispositions we inherit through our genes and partly in the broader political and social environment, but mostly through a combination of the two.

PUBLIC OPINION AND PARTICIPATION

Neither the government nor citizens have to rely on confusing public opinion polls to assess the will of the people. The attitudes and beliefs that make up public opinion can also be expressed through **political participation**, or the translation of a personal preference into a voluntary action designed to influence public policy. In other words, political participation is the process of turning an opinion into a direct contribution to the process of determining who gets what.

Rather than wait for a pollster to ask their opinion, trust that the poll is well constructed and fairly represents their views, and then sit back and hope that government acts on the results, people can express their will directly through involvement in the political system. The causes and consequences of political participation are addressed in chapter 11. What is important for the purposes of this chapter is recognition that public opinion polls are not the only way to connect the attitudes and preferences of citizens to the actions of government.

Political participation involves everything from voting to writing letters or e-mails to government officials to joining an interest group. These activities may seem like a better guide to the will of the people than a public opinion poll. If an attitude or belief provides enough motivation to get someone to go vote or join an interest group, this certainly seems to indicate that an issue is salient and that an attitude is intensely held. The problem with participation is that not all people participate equally. As a result, some groups and their preferences exert a disproportionate influence on the political process. Some Americans do not participate at all; others limit their participation to occasionally casting a ballot; and still others concentrate on specific types of political involvement.

Scholars who study political participation as a means to connect the will of the people to the actions of government have raised persistent concerns that varying rates of participation across racial, ethnic, and socioeconomic lines mean that some preferences will be given more weight than others. This concern is consistent with the elitist perspective of the American political system.

Political scientists have found strong evidence that the voting rates of particular groups can determine election outcomes (R. Jackson 1997) and that disproportionate participation of those higher on the socioeconomic scale results in policies that favor their interests at the expense of those on the lower end of the scale (Bennett and Resnick 1990; Gant and Lyons 1993; Hill and Leighley 1992). But

political participation The translation of personal preference into a voluntary action designed to influence public policy.

not all research findings support this elitist perspective on participation. There is some systematic evidence that government can and does manage to respond to the broader currents of public opinion, and not just to those who participate (Erikson, Wright, and McIver 1993).

Thus, participation may or may not be an accurate indicator of "what the people desire to have done," as Lincoln suggested. It indicates what the people who participate desire to have done, but even in a presidential election, that adds up to little more than half of eligible voters. Moreover, those who do participate tend to be distinct from the broader electorate in a number of important ways: they are older, better educated, and more prosperous; they are less racially and ethnically diverse than the public at large; and they are more likely to be dissatisfied with the status quo, distrustful of government, more partisan, and more confident that their views not only deserve to be respected but should receive a satisfactory response from the government (Verba, Schlozman, and Brady 1995).

We have come full circle, right back to the lament of Lincoln that opened the chapter. Varying rates of participation mean that elections cannot be counted on to reveal what the people—all of the people—really want. Although estimated turnout in the 1860 presidential election was a remarkable 82 percent of eligible voters, Lincoln won the presidency with less than 40 percent of the popular vote. Even with near-universal participation, how could Lincoln respond to the preferences of "all the people" when over 60 percent of them expressed a preference for one of his three opponents? If scientific polling had been available then, Lincoln still would have found it difficult to determine what "the people" wanted done. Public opinion turns out to be more complex than Lincoln imagined.

CHAPTER NINE

Top Ten Takeaway Points

① Public opinion is the sum of attitudes or beliefs about an issue or question and is seen as one expression of the will of the people.

② Public opinion has four elements: direction, stability, intensity, and salience.

③ Most people believe public opinion should play a significant role in guiding government decision making, a belief that reflects a commitment to the core democratic principle of majority rule and to the delegate model of representative democracy.

④ The problem with public opinion is that it is often ill-informed, fragmented, and subject to rapid change. Because of this, the government of the United States is deliberately designed to shield policymakers from the excesses of public opinion.

⑤ Opinions are typically not the product of rational or knowledge-able analysis. They tend to be products of ideology, socialization, and political culture. Recent research also suggests that there is a biological component to opinions, with people inheriting predispositions toward certain political beliefs.

⑥ Understanding the reliability and validity of public opinion polls is an important civic skill. Getting answers to four questions is usually enough to discern the worth and accuracy of a poll: Did the poll ask the right people? What is the margin of error? What was the question? Which question came first?

⑦ There is disagreement about the appropriate role of public opinion. Some believe public opinion is too poorly informed to contribute to competent judgments about complex issues. Others argue that public opinion has a rightful place in the broader democratic debate and is more informed and sophisticated than its critics give it credit for.

⑧ Issue publics, or people with a strong interest in a particular issue, tend to be well informed about that particular policy area and capable of making sophisticated choices.

⑨ Public opinion polls are not the only way the people can make their will known to the government. Political participation sends a direct message by translating personal preference into voluntary action.

⑩ Political participation is an imperfect reflection of the will of the people because different groups participate at different rates. Generally speaking, the well-off, the better-educated, and the middle-aged are more likely to participate than the poor, the poorly educated, and the young.

Key Terms and Cases

biased sample, 312
confidence level, 314
delegate model of representative
  democracy, 308
direction, 303
elite opinion, 309
ideology, 318
instrumentation, 314

intensity, 306
issue public, 310
margin of error, 313
political culture, 317
political participation, 328
political socialization, 322
public opinion, 303
push poll, 309

random sample, 311
reference groups, 324
salience, 306
stability, 305
straw polls, 312
trustee system of democracy, 308

What features must be present to make elections effective?

Why is the process of nominating candidates as important as the process of electing them?

How does the process of nominating and electing the president differ from the nomination and election of members of Congress?

PRESIDENTIAL elections are generally viewed as highly competitive. In the last six presidential elections, the winner managed to get more than 50 percent of the popular vote only three times: Barack Obama in 2008 and 2012 and George W. Bush in 2004. Yet Bush's margin of victory over Democrat John Kerry amounted to less than a percentage point. Obama became the nation's first African American president in 2008, with a more decisive margin of victory (about 6 percentage points) over Republican John McCain. President Obama's bid for reelection against Republican challenger Mitt Romney in 2012 remained close throughout the campaign. On election eve national polls showed the race tied, and both candidates were urging supporters to turn out and vote. The closeness of the national popular vote in presidential contests, however, sends a misleading signal about elections in the United States. The truth is, most elections, most of the time, are not very competitive at all.

If you look at the races state by state, this holds true even for presidential races. In 2012 Romney won most states in the Deep South by margins approaching 60–40. Obama won California (the nation's most populous state) and New York with similarly lopsided victories. Both campaigns focused on Ohio and a half-dozen other states (Colorado, Florida, Iowa, New Hampshire, North Carolina, and Virginia). For most states in the past six presidential elections, there was not much competition at all.

Yet at least the presidential elections are vigorously contested and interesting, even if only in a limited number of geographic pockets. Congressional contests, on the other hand, are typically snoozers. In recent elections, more than 80 percent of House members coasted to victory with more than 60 percent of the vote. Even in 2010, when Republicans picked up 63 seats in the House of Representatives, the largest gain of seats for a party since the 1938 elections, most House incumbents still won by lopsided margins. Senate elections are a tad more interesting. In 2010, almost 30 percent of Senate races (about 11 of 37) were competitive.

In 2012, more than half (18 of 33) of Senate races were competitive—an unusually high number.

Competitive races are important because elections play a critical role in the achievement of popular sovereignty—without vigorous competition that gives voters a choice between at least two viable alternatives, representatives have less incentive to be responsive to the voters, and elections do not provide a realistic chance to hold unresponsive representatives accountable. Elections amount to choosing the decision makers, and these are the most critical choices citizens make in terms of shaping government policy and holding it accountable for its actions. Yet elections in the United States, even in a widely touted "change" election such as 2008, are mostly one-sided affairs. Where is the choice if the outcome is in the bag before a vote is cast?

In this chapter, we explore how candidates are elected to office. To fully understand the crucial role of elections in a democracy, we first need to understand the rules and procedures that structure the electoral process.

THE CONCEPT OF ELECTIONS

election A collective decision-making process in which citizens choose an individual to hold and exercise the powers of public office. Elections are the primary mechanism that representative democracies use to achieve popular sovereignty.

nomination The process through which political parties winnow down a field of candidates to a single one who will be the party's standard-bearer in the general election.

general election The process by which voters choose their representatives from among the parties' nominees.

An **election** is a collective decision-making process in which citizens choose an individual to hold and exercise the powers of public office. Elections are the primary mechanism that representative democracies use to achieve popular sovereignty—that is, to make government responsive and accountable to the will of the people.

Elections to choose the president and members of Congress consist of two steps: nomination and the general election. **Nomination** is the process through which political parties winnow down a field of candidates to a single one who will be the party's standard-bearer in the general election. In the **general election**, voters choose their representatives from among the parties' nominees.[1]

---

[1] Although independent and minor party candidates may also be choices on the general election ballot, in the United States only the major party candidates—Democrats and Republicans—are likely to have a realistic chance of winning office.

METHODS OF NOMINATING CANDIDATES

How candidates are selected has important consequences for the operation of democracy. William Marcy "Boss" Tweed, who headed the powerful Tammany machine in New York during the 1850s and 1860s, once said, "I don't care who does the electing as long as I do the nominating" (Thomsett and Thomsett 1994, 14). A sure way to influence a general election is to determine the choices available to voters. Parties in the United States have used three methods of nominating candidates—legislative caucus, conventions, and direct primaries. The method of nominating candidates has changed over time and differs for president and Congress.

Legislative Caucus

The need for a mechanism to choose who would carry party labels into the electoral arena arose with the development of political parties. Races for local offices, state legislatures, and even the House of Representatives presented no great difficulty. These elections involved a limited number of voters living in a reasonably compact political district. Parties simply held meetings, called caucuses, of their most active supporters to nominate candidates.

Selecting candidates for statewide offices presented more of a challenge. Transportation and communication were primitive, and it was no easy task to assemble party activists from all over a state. Nominating candidates for president and vice president presented the same difficulty on an even larger scale. The initial solution to this problem was to give the **legislative caucus** responsibility for choosing nominees for state and national offices. The party's members in a state legislature assembled to select candidates for statewide office, and party members in the House of Representatives caucused to select candidates for president and vice president. In short, members of the party in government chose candidates for offices representing large constituencies.[2]

Although convenient, allowing members of Congress to select presidential and vice presidential nominees presented several problems: it violated separation of powers; it did not represent elements of the party in states where the party had lost; and party activists who were not members of Congress had no voice in choosing the party's nominee for president.

legislative caucus A method of selecting political party candidates that calls for party members in the state legislature to select candidates for statewide office and party members in the House of Representatives to select a party's candidates for president and vice president.

---

[2] Chapter 7 explains the three elements of a political party: party in electorate, party in government, and party organization.

Convention

The nomination method that emerged to tackle the drawbacks of the caucus approach to nominations was the **national party convention**, a meeting composed of delegates from various states. In 1832, the Democratic Party under Andrew Jackson became the first major party to use the national convention.[3] The convention quickly evolved into the dominant means of choosing candidates at both the state and national levels. Delegates to state conventions were sometimes chosen directly by local party members. But more commonly, delegates were selected by county conventions, whose delegates had in turn been selected by party members in smaller political units. The state convention then chose candidates for statewide office and the delegates to the national presidential convention. This system allowed rank-and-file party members to participate in choosing delegates, but the delegates, not the rank and file, made the key decisions. Candidate selection, in other words, shifted from party in government to the party organization, but it still excluded the party in the electorate.

Disillusionment with the convention began to grow in the early twentieth century as powerful party insiders learned how to manipulate the system to their own advantage. Meetings to choose delegates were often called without notification of all interested people and were packed with ineligible participants. Disputes between rival delegations from the same area were common, and the convention that ultimately decided which was the "real" delegation often did so unfairly or without full knowledge of the facts. Foes of the convention began pushing for an entirely new way to nominate candidates that would shift power from the party organization to the party in the electorate.

Direct Primary

The direct primary allows voters to choose party nominees for public office. In the convention system, voters have an indirect role—they choose the delegates who choose the nominee. A direct primary removes the go-between, allowing voters to select the nominee. Wisconsin passed the first law for a statewide direct primary in 1903. Today, all 50 states use the direct primary for some, if not all, nominations.

Primary laws vary from state to state. Some states, for example, hold **closed primaries** in which only registered party members may vote in a party's primary. That is, only registered Democrats may vote in the Democratic primary and only registered Republicans in the Republican primary; voters who register as independents may vote in the general election, but they cannot participate in party

national party convention A nomination method in which delegates selected from each state attend a national party meeting to choose the party's candidates for president and vice president.

closed primaries Elections to choose a party's nominees for the general election that are open only to party members.

---

[3] A minor party, the anti-Masons, was actually first to employ a national convention in 1831. The anti-Masons had no appreciable representation in Congress and could not use the legislative caucus effectively.

primaries. Other states hold **open primaries** in which independents—and in some cases voters from other parties—participate in a party's primary.[4]

Direct primaries increase the influence of rank-and-file voters at the expense of party leaders. The shift in power away from party leaders, however, is less in closed primaries than in open ones. Proponents of open primaries argue that they are more democratic because they allow all interested citizens to participate in the selection of candidates, and they criticize closed primaries as infringing on citizens' ability to participate in the electoral process. Defenders of closed primaries argue that participation by independents may undermine a party's chances by supporting candidates who are unacceptable to most party members. In open primaries, supporters of the opposing party also have an incentive to cross over and try to get weak candidates nominated so that they will be easier to defeat in the general election.

NOMINATING PRESIDENTIAL CANDIDATES

Both major parties nominate their candidates for president and vice president in national party conventions composed of delegates from the states. To win a party's nomination, a candidate must get the support of a majority of delegates at the convention. The rules that govern the nominating contests that choose the delegates influence the participants' strategies and tactics. Rules are not neutral. Because rules inevitably advantage some interests at the expense of others, they can determine outcomes.

The Allocation of National Convention Delegates

Both parties use similar criteria to decide how many delegates each state party is entitled to send to the convention: state population and support for the party's candidates in the state. Table 10.1 shows the number of delegates each state party sent to the national conventions in 2012. The most important determinant of the size of a state's delegation is population—large states get more delegates than small states get. The two most populous states, California and Texas, for example, had the largest delegations at both party conventions, whereas the delegations of the

---

[4] Another option used in Alaska, California, and Washington is a "blanket primary" in which voters can vote for some offices in one party's primary and other offices in another party's primary. The Supreme Court invalidated this type of primary in *California Democratic Party v. Jones* (2000) because it violates the political parties' right to freedom of association. Alaska and Washington also modified their primary systems. The Court upheld Louisiana's nonpartisan primary, which is discussed later in this chapter.

open primaries Elections to select a party's candidate for the general election that are open to independents and, in some cases, to member of other parties.

TABLE 10.1: SIZE OF STATE DELEGATIONS AT THE 2012 NATIONAL PARTY CONVENTIONS

State	Democratic Convention	Republican Convention	State	Democratic Convention	Republican Convention
California	611	172	Oregon	**84**	**28**
Texas	288	155	Oklahoma	**50**	**43**
New York	384	95	Connecticut	88	28
Florida	300	50*	Iowa	**65**	**28**
Illinois	215	69	Mississippi	45	40
Pennsylvania	250	72	Arkansas	55	36
Ohio	191	66	Kansas	53	40
Michigan	203	30*	Utah	34	40
Georgia	124	76	Nevada	44	28
North Carolina	158	55	New Mexico	50	23
New Jersey	171	50	West Virginia	46	31
Virginia	123	49	Nebraska	44	35
Washington	120	43	Idaho	31	32
Massachusetts	136	41	Hawaii	35	20
Indiana	106	46	Maine	37	24
Arizona	79	29*	New Hampshire	**35**	**12***
Tennessee	91	58	Rhode Island	41	19
Missouri	102	52	Montana	31	26
Maryland	120	37	Delaware	32	17
Wisconsin	111	42	South Dakota	29	28
Minnesota	107	40	Alaska	24	27
Colorado	86	36	North Dakota	27	28
Alabama	69	50	Vermont	27	17
South Carolina	62	25*	Wyoming	22	29
Louisiana	71	46	Other (DC; Terr.)	172	78
Kentucky	73	45			
			Totals	**5,552**	**2,286**

* State penalized 50 percent of its delegates for holding its nomination contest earlier than permitted by party rules. States sorted from largest to smallest.

Source: Constructed by the authors from data at The Green Papers, http://www.thegreenpapers.com/.

least populous states, Wyoming and Vermont, were among the smallest. In addition, both parties give extra delegates to states with a record of supporting their candidates. Democrats use votes cast for the Democratic presidential candidate to award these extra delegates, whereas the Republicans reward states for electing a Republican governor, congressional delegation, and presidential electors. Oklahoma and Oregon, for example, are about equal in population, but strongly

Republican Oklahoma has a larger delegation at the Republican convention, whereas strongly Democratic Oregon has a larger delegation at the Democratic convention.

The Method and Timing of Delegate Selection

State law determines the method state parties use to select delegates, whether the process will be open or closed, and the date when the parties select delegates. The parties select national convention delegates in two basic ways:[5] (1) the **caucus method**, in which national convention delegates are chosen at a state convention; and (2) a **state presidential primary**, in which voters directly elect delegates.

Over time, there has been a trend of increasing use of primaries to choose national convention delegates. Figures 10.1a and 10.1b show the number of presidential primaries and the percentage of national convention delegates chosen in primaries. The first time a presidential candidate used primaries as a major part of a nomination strategy was in 1912. Although relatively few delegates were chosen in primaries over the next 50 years, states began switching to primaries in the 1970s. In the last several elections, more than two-thirds of delegates at party conventions were chosen in primaries. With the rise of the direct primary, power over the nomination process has shifted away from professionals and toward amateurs.

This shift in power has had a profound effect on nomination campaigns. First, the nomination calendar is now critically important. To attract the media attention and the broader support necessary to be considered serious contenders, presidential candidates have to do well in the early competitions for delegates. The first two nominating contests are the Iowa caucuses and the New Hampshire primary. Although only a handful of delegates are at stake, these contests are widely perceived to have enormous influence on the fate of presidential nominees.

A poor showing in these initial contests can severely wound a campaign. The perceived importance of these early contests has led to **frontloading**, in which states leapfrog their primaries and caucuses to earlier dates in the delegate selection process in an effort to gain more influence in the choice of a presidential nominee. Frontloading crams the selection of a disproportionate number of delegates into a few weeks at the beginning of the process.

Figure 10.2a illustrates frontloading of the process over time. The point at which two-thirds of delegates have been chosen is a reasonable benchmark. In most instances, by the time two-thirds of delegates have been chosen, it is unlikely that any of the remaining candidates will be able to win enough delegates

caucus method A method of selecting the delegates to a political party's national convention by permitting the state conventions to select representatives from their states.

state presidential primary A method of selecting delegates to a political party's national convention in which the voters directly elect delegates.

frontloading The tendency of states to move their primaries earlier in the season in order to gain more influence over the presidential selection process.

---

[5] Delegates were once handpicked by party officials, but this method has largely disappeared. Although the Democratic Party continues to set aside a number of delegate slots for party leaders and elected officials (PLEOs)—governors, members of Congress, and party officials—these constitute a small proportion of delegates at the national Democratic convention. These delegates are popularly known as "super delegates." The competition between Barack Obama and Hilary Clinton was so close in 2008 that these super delegates had significant influence on the outcome.

(a) Number of States Using Primaries

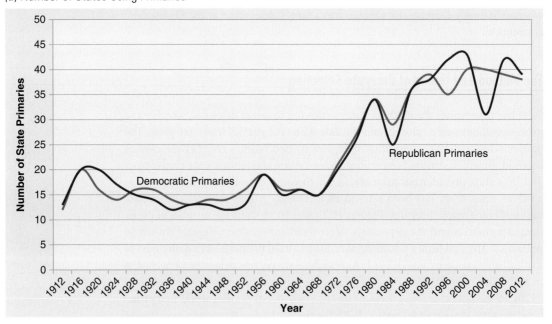

(b) Percent of Convention Delegates Chosen in Primaries

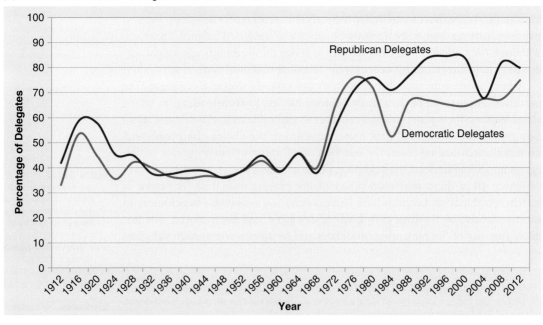

FIGURE 10.1 **Increasing Use of Presidential Primaries to Choose Convention Delegates**

Source: Constructed by the authors from Stanley and Niemi (2011, 55) and Berg-Andersson (2008, 2012).

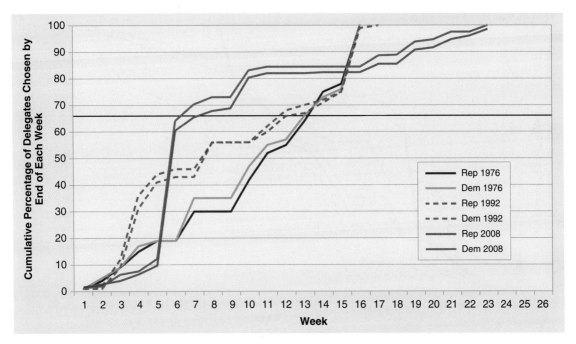

FIGURE 10.2A Increasing Frontloading of Delegate Selection 1976–2008

in the upcoming contests to stop the front-runner. In 1976, delegate selection was spread out over about 16 weeks, and two-thirds of delegates had not been chosen until the thirteenth week. By 1992, the process was becoming more frontloaded, with two-thirds of delegates chosen by the twelfth week. In 2008, two-thirds of delegates to both party conventions were selected in six weeks. Frontloading had become a major concern by 2008, and both parties attempted (without success) to persuade states to spread out the process.

Frontloading has several undesirable consequences. First, to have any chance of success, candidates must lay the groundwork early. A serious candidate must be familiar with the relevant laws and selection methods in all 50 states and understand the political situation in each. This requires political expertise, a well-administered national organization, time, and money—lots and lots of money.

Second, candidates need to raise a lot of money early. Having money does not guarantee that a candidate will win the nomination, but the absence of money guarantees a loss. Frontloading has so shortened the time available to select delegates that candidates who do not have national name recognition, a national organization, and enormous sums of money at the start of the nominating contests have little chance of winning the nomination.

Third, the shortened time "degrades campaign quality." William Mayer and Andrew Busch observe that the almost insurmountable advantage of front-runners "substantially reduces the field of viable candidates" (2004, 3). When so many delegates are chosen in just a few weeks, early primary voters do not have

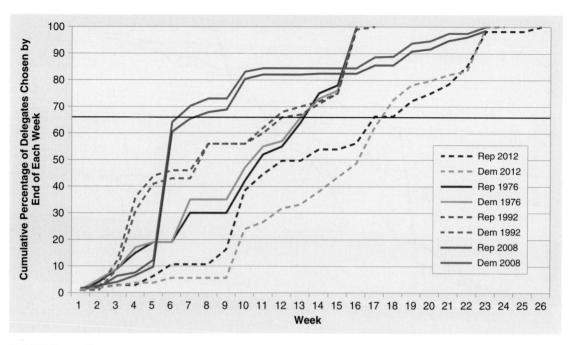

FIGURE 10.2B Delegate Selection in 2012

Source: Information on 1976 and 1992 constructed by the authors from Mayer and Busch (2004); information on 2008 and 2012 constructed by the authors from data at Berg-Andersson (2008, 2012).

adequate time to get to know the field of candidates in order to make a "deliberate choice," and late primary voters are deprived "of any meaningful choice at all."

The Republican Party seemed to rein in the trend toward frontloading in 2012. Primaries and caucuses were spread out over 26 weeks, and two-thirds of delegates were not selected until the seventeenth week (see Figure 10.2b). The national parties, however, have limited control over the nomination calendar. Recall that state legislatures set the date and method of selecting delegates to the party conventions. The primary sanction available to the party is to reduce the delegation size of states that violate the rules. In 2012, for example, the Republican National Committee (RNC) adopted a rule that cut a state's delegation size in half if it held its contest too early. Nonetheless, five states ignored the RNC's calendar and accepted the penalty, suggesting that the attention gained from having an early contest gives a state greater influence than delegate votes at the convention. Thus, frontloading is likely to continue to be a problem in future elections.

The Nomination Campaign

As political scientist John Haskell observed, "everything important in the presidential nomination campaigns revolves around the selection of delegates who

© Photo by Kevork Djansezian/Getty Images

The nomination campaign is a winnowing process to determine which of several candidates can gain enough delegates to win their party's nomination. Of the eight candidates pictured here, Mitt Romney survived to become the Republican Party's nominee to challenge President Obama in 2012.

will get to the national convention" (1996, 33). To gain a party's nomination, a candidate must get the support of an absolute majority of the delegates at the convention—that is, 50 percent plus one of all delegates. The number of delegate votes needed to win is called the **magic number**. In 2012, for example, the Republican National Convention was composed of 2,380 delegates, so the magic number needed to win the nomination was 1,144. The Democratic convention was larger, consisting of 5,552 delegates, and the magic number to win the Democratic nomination was 2,777. Candidates compete for delegates in the caucuses and primaries, hoping to win the magic number of delegates.

The nomination campaign is a winnowing process to determine which one of several candidates will win enough delegates to be a party's presidential nominee. As Table 10.2 illustrates, sitting presidents running for reelection typically have few if any challengers for the nomination. Bill Clinton in 1996, George W. Bush in 2004, and Barack Obama in 2012 had no opposition for their party nominations. In addition, sitting vice presidents seeking their party's nomination are often viewed as the "heir apparent" and draw little opposition, as in the 2000 presidential election when Vice President Al Gore easily won the Democratic nomination. The party not in power, however, will have numerous candidates competing for the nomination. In 1996, about 10 Republicans competed to challenge President Clinton's bid for reelection, and a similar number of Democrats competed for the privilege of running against President George W. Bush in 2004. The 2012 Republican contest was wide open, with about a dozen Republicans actively competing to challenge President Obama's bid for reelection. The 2008 election was unusual

magic number The number of delegates needed at a political party's national convention for a candidate to be nominated as the party's candidate for the presidency; this number equals 50 percent plus one of all delegates at the convention.

TABLE 10.2: CANDIDATES FOR PARTY PRESIDENTIAL NOMINATIONS 1996–2012

Democrats	Republicans
1996	
Pres. Bill Clinton	**Sen. Robert Dole**
Unchallenged	Steve Forbes
	Pat Buchanan
	Sen. Phil Gramm
	Alexander, Lugar, Dornan, Keyes, Specter, Wilson
2000	
VP Al Gore	**Gov. George W. Bush**
Fmr. Sen. Bill Bradley	Sen. John McCain
	Steve Forbes
	Bauer, Keyes, Buchanan, Smith, Alexander, L. Dole, Hatch, Quayle
2004	
Sen. John Kerry	**Pres. George W. Bush**
Sen. John Edwards	*Unchallenged*
Gov. Howard Dean	
Gephardt, Clark, Lieberman, Kucinich, Mosele-Braun, Sharpton	
2008	
Sen. Barack Obama	**Sen. John McCain**
Sen. Hillary Clinton	Fmr. Gov. Mike Huckabee
Fmr. Sen. John Edwards	Fmr. Gov. Mitt Romney
Biden, Richardson, Dodd, Kucinich, Bayh, Gravel, Vilsack	Fmr. Mayor Rudy Giuliani
	Fmr. Sen. Fred Thompson
	Brownback, Paul, Gilmore, Hunter, Tancredo, T. Thompson
2012	
Pres. Barack Obama	**Fmr. Gov. Mitt Romney**
Unchallenged	Fmr. Sen. Rick Santorum
	Fmr. Rep. Newt Gingrich
	Rep. Ron Paul
	Gov. Rick Perry
	Rep. Michelle Bachmann
	Herman Cain
	Donald Trump
	Palin, Huckabee, Huntsman, Christie, Barbour, Pawlenty, Pence, Daniels, Thune, Johnson, DeMint, Jeb Bush

Party nominees listed first in bold. Entries in *italics* are potential candidates who were high in the polls at some point but did not officially enter the race, and candidates who ran for their party nomination but were consistently low in preference polls, did not raise significant campaign funds, and never won a caucus or primary.

Source: Constructed by the authors.

because neither party had a sitting president or vice president running, so there was open competition for both party nominations.

This winnowing process has a number of filter points that weed out weaker candidates. There are four phases of presidential nomination campaigns (Hadley 1976; Kessel 1992):

1. Invisible primary
2. Initial contests
3. Mist clearing
4. Convention

The phases blend together in the real world, but they are distinct enough to provide analytic clarity to aid understanding of how a nomination campaign progresses.

INVISIBLE PRIMARY An unofficial nomination process begins long before the first official contests to select delegates. The period between the election of a president and the first official contests to pick the next one is called the **invisible primary** (Hadley 1976). During this period, potential candidates test the waters and decide whether to enter the race. They begin raising funds, putting together an organization, seeking endorsements, and maneuvering for political advantage. The invisible primary takes place largely behind the scenes—there are no delegates chosen and few if any formal rules. Although party organizations have no official authority at this stage, party insiders have considerable influence. Political scientists Marty Cohen and his associates (Cohen et al. 2008a, 2008b) describe the invisible primary as a "long-running national conversation" among party office holders and other political notables about which candidate can unite the diverse and sometimes competing parts of the party coalition and win the next presidential election.

Speculation about the potential Republican nominee in 2012 started just days after Obama's inauguration. A Gallup poll conducted from February 1 to February 3, 2009, asked Republicans whom they would "most like to see as the party's candidate for president in the 2012 election." The most common response was "don't know" (36 percent). Only two Republicans were mentioned by more than 10 percent, Mitt Romney (14 percent) and Sarah Palin (11 percent). A number of those prominently mentioned as possible candidates decided not to run—for example, Sarah Palin (the Republican vice presidential nominee in 2008), former Arkansas governor Mike Huckabee (the runner-up for the nomination in 2008), former Florida governor Jeb Bush (President George W. Bush's brother), and popular New Jersey governor Chris Christie. Nevertheless, nearly a dozen candidates formally declared that they were seeking their party's presidential nomination, but only a handful emerged as serious contenders. This early—some might say premature—speculation about party nominees is typical. Soon after President Bush was sworn in for his second term in January 2005, speculation about 2008 began.

The invisible primary serves to sort out and begin solidifying the field of serious contenders who will wage the battle for delegates. The chief criteria for assessing

invisible primary The period of time between the election of one president and the first contest to nominate candidates to run in the general election to select the next president.

the strength of the potential candidates are money, standing in the polls, and endorsements.

The first indicator of which candidates are likely to emerge as major contenders is money. Money to finance a campaign is such an important indicator of a candidate's strength during the invisible primary that political observers sometimes refer to this aspect of the contest as the "money primary." Having enough money to run a national campaign is certainly necessary.

Table 10.3 shows how candidates stacked up in the money primary for the 2008 and 2012 presidential nomination contests. In the 2008 election cycle, fundraising success identified the major contenders in both parties, but not the eventual nominees—Obama and McCain finished second and third, respectively, in the money race. In the 2012 election cycle, only the Republican nomination was contested. Mitt Romney led the Republican field with about $33 million raised during the invisible primary and went on to win the nomination. Romney's path to the nomination, however, was not an easy one, and standing in the money race did not identify the strongest contenders. Texas governor Rick Perry, a distant second in fundraising, was briefly considered a strong alternative to Romney who could appeal to different factions of the Republican Party—economic conservatives, the core of Romney's support, and social conservatives and Tea Party Republicans, who did not trust Romney because he had taken moderate positions on issues such as abortion and taxes as governor of Massachusetts. But Perry failed to emerge as a serious contender for the nomination because of gaffes and poor debate performances. The two candidates who posed the strongest challenges to Romney were Newt Gingrich and Rick Santorum, neither of whom had raised a significant amount of money. Does this mean that money is no longer a good indicator of who will be serious candidates? No, money is still crucial. But in the 2012 campaign we saw the emergence of a new source of enormous sums of money—Super PACs. Recall from chapter 6 that Super PACs may raise unlimited sums of money from corporations, unions, and wealthy individuals, but they may not contribute directly to or coordinate with candidates' campaigns. Because Super PACs cannot coordinate with candidates (and most of the spending occurs after the invisible primary), it is not appropriate to add this money to the money raised by the candidates. Spending by Super PACs, however, helps explain why candidates such as Gingrich and Santorum who would have been dismissed as weak in previous elections managed to stay the contest much longer than expected this time (Hartranft 2012). For Democrats there was no contest for the nomination, but lots of activity. Although President Obama faced no significant opposition for renomination, he nonetheless raised nearly $100 million—more than he raised for his nomination battle in 2008 and more than all candidates combined in the hotly contested race for the Republican nomination in 2012. Thus, raising lots of money is important, but it does not guarantee success. To be a serious contender, a candidate must have a message and run a competent campaign that appeals to voters, as the example of Rick Perry's failed campaign in 2012 aptly demonstrates.

A second early indicator of who the major contenders will be is standing in the polls. These polls ask Republican and Democratic voters whom they would like

TABLE 10.3: PRESIDENTIAL NOMINATION CANDIDATES' STANDINGS IN THE "MONEY PRIMARY"

Democratic Candidates	Campaign Funds 3rd Quarter (millions)*	Republican Candidates	Campaign Funds 3rd Quarter (millions)*
		2008	
Hillary Clinton	$90.96	Mitt Romney	$62.83
Barack Obama	**$80.28**	Rudy Giuliani	$47.25
John Edwards	$30.36	**John McCain**	**$32.12**
Bill Richardson	$18.70	Fred Thompson	$12.83
Chris Dodd	$13.60	Ron Paul	$8.27
Joe Biden	$8.22	Sam Brownback	$4.24
Dennis Kucinich	$2.13	Tom Tancredo	$3.54
Thomas Vilsack	$1.03	Mike Huckabee	$2.35
Mike Gravel	$0.38	Duncan Hunter	$1.89
Evan Bayh	$0.00	Tommy Thompson	$1.16
		Jim Gilmore	$.40
		2012	
Barack Obama	**$99.6**	**Mitt Romney**	**$32.83**
		Rick Perry	$17.20
		Ron Paul	$12.81
		Michele Bachmann	$7.55
		Tim Pawlenty	$5.49
		Herman Cain	$5.39
		Jon Huntsman	$4.51
		Newt Gingrich	$2.91
		Rick Santorum	$1.26

*Money raised as of the end of the third quarter of 2007 and 2011. Party nominee in bold.

Source: Federal Election Commission (2007, 2011).

to see win their party's presidential nomination. Preferences expressed in polls taken years before the election reflect mostly name recognition, giving nationally prominent individuals an advantage. But early favorites often decide not to run, and lesser-known candidates engage in activities to get mentioned in the media and emerge as strong contenders.

Figure 10.3 shows how the major candidates for each party's nomination stacked up in polls taken during the invisible primaries in 2008 and 2012. Both parties had open contests in 2008. The early front-runner for the Democratic nomination was Hillary Clinton (see Figure 10.3a). Obama and Edwards had respectable standings in the polls, but Clinton appeared so dominant that many thought she would sew up the nomination early. Giuliani was the early favorite

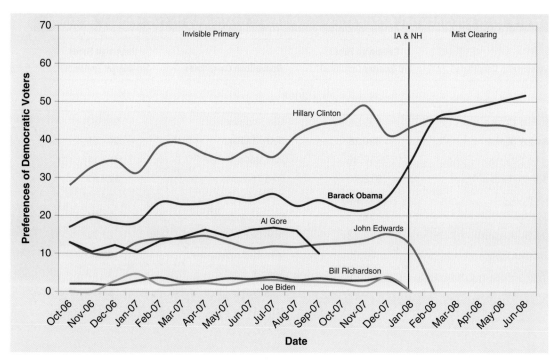

FIGURE 10.3A Democratic Invisible Primary 2008

among Republican voters, but several other candidates—McCain, Romney, and Fred Thompson—appeared to be strong enough that some expected the race to drag on (see Figure 10.3b). These views held throughout the invisible primary. On the eve of the Iowa caucuses, Clinton was still way ahead among Democratic voters. Guliani was still ahead among Republican voters, but Huckabee had risen in the polls, and McCain had slipped; there was a four-way tie among Huckabee, McCain, Romney, and Thompson for second place. As the campaign progressed through the remaining stages of the nomination contest, McCain ended up winning the Republican nomination quickly, whereas competition between Obama and Clinton did not end until the last primary was over.

There was vigorous competition for the 2012 Republican nomination. Mitt Romney led a crowded field in most of the 15 months before the Iowa caucuses and New Hampshire primary in January 2012, but his approval hovered below 25 percent, with the preferences of most Republicans divided among several others. Social conservatives and Tea Party Republicans were concerned that Romney was not reliably conservative on key issues, but there was no obvious alternative. Some commentators described the campaign as a contest between Romney and "Not Romney"—and at least six candidates auditioned for the role of "Not Romney." Figure 10.3c shows when the potential Romney alternatives climbed and then fell in the polls. Donald Trump surged in the polls in April, but his popularity faded quickly, and he never formally entered the race. Michelle Bachman's

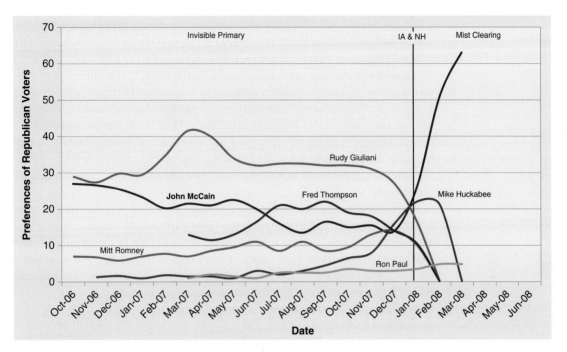

FIGURE 10.3B Republican Invisible Primary 2008

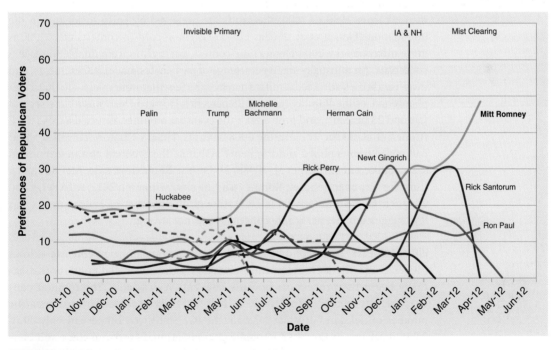

FIGURE 10.3C Republican Invisible Primary 2012

Source: Calculated by the authors from data at http://pollingreport.com/wh08dem.htm; http://pollingreport.com/wh08rep.htm; http://pollingreport.com/wh12rep.htm.

standing started to climb in July after some strong debate performances and her win in the Iowa straw poll, but Rick Perry's announcement of his candidacy in July eclipsed Bachman's rise. After a surge into first place, Perry's popularity peaked in September and started a rapid slide after lackluster debate performances and a series of gaffes. As Perry's standing declined in November, Herman Caine climbed in the polls, only to have his candidacy collapse in November amid accusations of sexual harassment and an extramarital affair. Then it was Newt Gingrich's turn to audition. He climbed into first place in December, but Rick Santorum started to rise in the polls as well. On the eve of the first official contests to begin selecting delegates, it appeared that Gingrich and possibly Santorum could be serious contenders.

The third indicator of who the major contenders will be is endorsements from key members of the party establishment. These party insiders include federal and state elected officials (past presidents, governors, members of Congress, and state legislators), members of the traditional party organization (state and local party officials), and other party notables such as celebrities, interest group leaders, and other party activists. Political scientists have generally dismissed endorsements as having little if any influence on election outcomes, including who wins a party's presidential nomination. Cohen and his associates, however, present persuasive evidence that the accumulation of endorsements in this "endorsement derby" (Cohen et al. 2001) reflects the results of a "long-running national conversation" among party insiders during the invisible primary. In the nine contested nominations from 1980 to 2000, the candidate preferred by party insiders won the nomination (Cohen et al. 2008a, 175–177). The record in contests after 2000 is more mixed. In the 2004 Democratic contest, party elites were unable to reach a consensus. An unusually small percentage of party elites made endorsements, and three candidates attracted similar shares of the few that were made—Richard Gephardt had a slim plurality (around 25 percent), Howard Dean was a close second (around 23 percent), and John Kerry, the eventual nominee, finished a close third (Cohen et al. 2008a, 177). In the 2008 contests, Hillary Clinton "corralled about half of the party's public endorsements"; Obama, the eventual nominee, finished a distant second (Cohen et al. 2008b, 8). On the Republican side, McCain had a slim plurality over Romney. Romney was the clear winner in 2012, with Perry and Gingrich far behind (see Table 10.4), though the number of endorsements was low, suggesting that party elite consensus was not strong.

INITIAL CONTESTS The second phase of the nomination campaign consists of Iowa caucuses and the New Hampshire primary—the first official contests that actually begin the process of choosing convention delegates. These initial contests are important because they are first and only because they are first. The number of delegates at stake is small; the two states combined had only 40 of 2,286 delegates at the 2012 Republican convention. Moreover, Iowa and New Hampshire are not particularly representative of the demographic diversity in America. An Associated Press study ranked states according to how closely they looked like the nation on such demographic factors as race, age, income,

TABLE 10.4: PRESIDENTIAL NOMINATION CANDIDATES' STANDINGS IN THE "ENDORSEMENT DERBY"

Democratic Candidates	Endorsements*	Republican Candidates	Endorsements*
		2008	
Hillary Clinton	46.7%	**John McCain**	**28.7%**
Barack Obama	**29.5%**	Mitt Romney	26.3%
John Edwards	10.4%	Rudy Giuliani	17.0%
Bill Richardson	5.8%	Frank Thompson	15.4%
Chris Dodd	4.9%	Mike Huckabee	5.6%
Joe Biden	2.7%	Duncan Hunter	4.7%
Dennis Kucinich	0.0%	Sam Brownback	2.4%
Thomas Vilsack	0.0%	Ron Paul	0.0%
Mike Gravel	0.0%	Tome Tancredo	0.0%
Evan Bayh	0.0%	Tommy Thompson	0.0%
		Jim Gilmore	0.0%
		2012	
Barack Obama	Unopposed	**Mitt Romney**	**56.0%**
		Rick Perry	11.6%
		Newt Gingrich	10.9%
		Ron Paul	8.6%
		Herman Cain	3.6%
		Jon Huntsman	2.9%
		Michele Bachmann	2.2%
		Tim Pawlenty	2.1%
		Rick Santorum	1.2%
		Gary Johnson	0.7%

*Endorsements weighted by importance of the office. Party nominee in bold.

Source: Calculated by the authors from data from Appleman (2008, 2012).

education, industrial mix, immigration, and urban and rural residential patterns. Iowa ranked forty-first, and only West Virginia and Mississippi were less typical of America than New Hampshire. Which state looked most like America? Illinois (Ohlemacher 2007).

These contests, however, provide the first major opportunity for candidates to generate some favorable national publicity, break out of the pack, and establish momentum for future contests. They also serve to begin culling out weak candidates who fail to meet expectations. (See the Politics in Practice feature "How the Iowa Caucuses Work.")

All candidates enter these contests, and the media devote much time to reporting how the contestants fared, granting favorable free publicity to the perceived

HOW THE IOWA CAUCUSES WORK

The Iowa caucuses traditionally serve as an all-important preliminary heat in the race for a presidential nomination. The winner does not get much in the way of convention delegates, because Iowa sends a miniscule fraction of the delegates needed to clinch a nomination at a national party convention. Instead, what a candidate gets is media attention and momentum.

Yet, while the Iowa caucuses are recognized every four years as the first serious competition among candidates jockeying for their party's presidential nomination, they can be confusing to outsiders. The caucuses are not a primary election, but rather a rolling series of party meetings that start at the local level and culminate in district and state conventions that decide which delegates will go to the national party convention.

Both Republicans and Democrats organize their Iowa caucuses in the same basic four-step fashion:

1. Caucuses in local precincts: These are meetings in each of Iowa's 2,166 precincts, and the main function of these caucuses is to come up with 1,500 delegates to send to county conventions.
2. County conventions: Iowa has 99 counties, and each has its own party convention. The job of the county conventions is to choose 3,000 delegates to send to the congressional district conventions.
3. Congressional district conventions: Iowa currently has five congressional districts. Each had its own convention, which chose district-level candidates to attend the national party convention and the state party convention.
4. State convention: The party's state convention selects at-large delegates to the national party convention.

At each of these stages, presidential hopefuls compete for delegates backing their candidacy, though exactly how these are chosen varies slightly for Democrats and Republicans.

In the all-important first round (the precinct caucuses), Democrats only allow registered Democrats who live in the precinct and are eligible to vote to participate. At the precinct caucuses, attendees join preference groups for candidates. A group must have at least 15 percent of those in attendance. Groups that do not meet the threshold are dissolved, and their members are free to join other groups. Delegates chosen to go to the next level are allocated to candidates proportionally based on the size of their group at each precinct caucus.

Republicans require attendees at the precinct caucuses to be eligible to vote but do not require them to be registered Republicans. Attendees at the Republican precinct caucuses first conduct a secret ballot to see who are the top choices among the candidates, and then delegates to the county convention are chosen by direct election (the winner gets all the delegates) or proportionally on the basis of a straw vote.

Okay, got all that? No? Well, don't worry. Just hope the good folks in Iowa get all the nuances. What they do in the caucuses every four years goes a long way to determining the choice the rest of the electorate gets in the general election.

SOURCE Wayne, Stephen. 2000. *The Road to the White House 2000*. Boston: Bedford/St. Martin's, p. 107.

winner. The perceived winner is not necessarily the candidate who finishes first but rather may be the candidate who does better than the pundits expected. The perceived winner gets headlines across the nation, becomes an instant topic of talk shows, and is granted the image of a winner. This positive attention leads to a rise in the polls and additional campaign contributions.

In the 2008 Democratic contest, for example, Hillary Clinton's unrivaled front-runner status in the invisible primary created high expectations in Iowa. Obama's victory gave him credibility as a serious contender for the nomination and a boost in the polls. Clinton's third-place finish behind Obama and Edwards showed that her nomination was far from inevitable and put more pressure on her to win in New Hampshire. Clinton won the New Hampshire primary the following week, keeping her candidacy alive, but she had to share front-runner status with Obama (who finished second in New Hampshire). Joe Biden and Chris Dodd dropped out of the race after finishing fifth and sixth (Dodd actually finished seventh behind "uncommitted" votes). In the Republican contest in Iowa, the surprise winner was Mike Huckabee, followed by Mitt Romney and Fred Thompson. The win in Iowa showed that Huckabee, who trailed the other major candidates in fundraising, was a viable candidate. McCain finished a distant fourth, making New Hampshire a must-win. McCain's win in New Hampshire stopped his slide. Breaking with the conventional practice, Giuliani did not compete in Iowa and New Hampshire. Instead, he focused on Florida in hopes that a Catholic former New York City mayor would attract more support from all those New Yorkers who had retired there than he would from rural, Protestant voters in Iowa and New Hampshire. The strategy failed, and he dropped out after a poor showing in Florida.

In the 2012 Republican contest, Santorum was the surprise "winner" of the Iowa caucuses—after a recount, Santorum was declared the winner by 34 votes over Romney. A more objective interpretation is that the result was a tie, with Romney and Santorum each getting 25 percent and Ron Paul close with 21 percent. Indeed, because the initial round of precinct caucuses are nonbinding (i.e., no actual delegates are selected), Paul did better than his third-place finish suggests. After subsequent rounds of the caucus process—county conventions, congressional district conventions, and state convention—Ron Paul actually ended up with 21 of Iowa's delegates; Santorum got one, and Romney got none. But "winning" these early contests is not about precise vote counts or even delegate counts—it's all about perceptions. Santorum's perceived victory gave him a big boost in the polls. Romney scored a decisive victory in the New Hampshire primary a week later. Bachman, Perry, and Huntsman dropped out after poor showings in these initial contests.

Concern about the lack of racial and geographic diversity in these early contests led the Democratic National Committee (DNC) to move the Nevada and South Carolina primaries into the first wave of the 2008 contests. The DNC was also trying to get control of the growing problem of frontloading because a number of other states were considering moving their contests earlier. Under the proposed calendar, Iowa would continue to hold the first contest on January 14, 2008, but the Nevada caucuses would be the following Saturday—before the New Hampshire primary. The South Carolina primary then would occur a week after New Hampshire's. But New Hampshire feels so strongly about having the first presidential primary in the nation that state law is written to permit the secretary of state to move the primary earlier if another state holds any kind of nominating contest within seven days of the New Hampshire primary. Thus, New Hampshire officials threatened to hold their primary in 2007 if necessary to preserve their influence over the nominating process. Iowa refused to go along as well. The Iowa caucuses were held January 3, and the New Hampshire primary followed less than a week later on January 8. The national party cannot prevent a state from scheduling its delegate selection contest as early as it wishes, but the DNC voted to take delegates away from any state that did not abide by the new calendar. The threat did not deter Michigan and Florida from moving their primaries to January.

The Republican Party also tried to slow the trend toward frontloading in 2008 and again in 2012. The rule adopted for 2012 provided that Iowa, New Hampshire, South Carolina, and Nevada could hold a contest that would bind delegates to particular candidates as early as February 1, 2012; other states' contests could not occur before March 6. States that held binding contests prior to the prescribed dates would be penalized 50 percent of their delegates. Five states jumped the queue and took the penalty: New Hampshire, South Carolina, and Florida held their contests in January; Arizona and Michigan held theirs in February. Nonetheless, the nomination process in 2012 was less frontloaded than in any contest since 1976 (see Figure 10.2b).

MIST CLEARING The mist-clearing phase begins after the two initial contests, but it does not have a precise duration. Rather, it is an ongoing process analogous to the lifting of an early morning fog, slowly bringing surroundings into focus (Kessel 1992, 9). This phase is characterized by a reduction in uncertainty as weaker candidates are sifted out in the contests that occur in the following weeks. Attention focuses on two or three major contenders. The criteria for assessing success at this stage shifts from perceptions of who exceeded expectations to more objective indicators, such as the number of primaries and caucuses won and the delegate counts.

In 1980, several states began holding their primaries on a single day in early March. Because these states chose a significant portion of delegates to the national convention, this became called **Super Tuesday**. In subsequent presidential elections, more states moved their nominating contests earlier, frontloading the process. This frontloading has tended to shorten the mist-clearing phase. In both 2000 and 2004, for example, party nominations were for all practical purposes settled by Super Tuesday, six weeks after the initial contests. Although no candidate had reached the magic number—that is, a majority of convention delegates—by this point, the front-runners had accumulated such commanding leads in the delegate counts that there was little chance that anyone could win enough delegates in the remaining contests to stop them. The process in 2012 was less frontloaded in part because Super Tuesday was not as "super-sized" as in the past—only 17.1 percent of delegates were chosen on Super Tuesday in 2012 compared to 41.5 percent in 2008. Thus, although Romney won more than half the delegates, this was not enough to make his nomination inevitable.

In 2008, the field of candidates in both parties narrowed quickly after the initial contests to just two or three major competitors. The accumulation of delegates is the most important indicator of success during this stage (see Figures 10.4a, 10.4b, and 10.4c). The pattern of the front-runner locking up the nomination

Super Tuesday The day in early March when several states hold their primaries. These states choose a significant portion of delegates to the national convention.

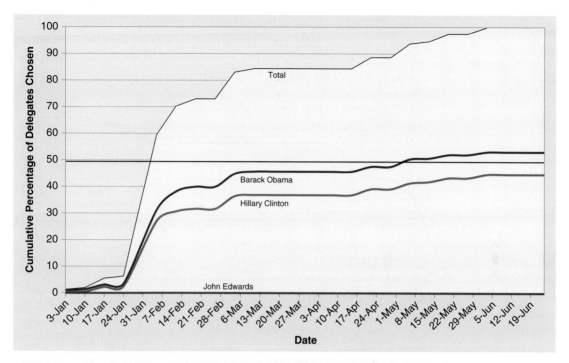

FIGURE 10.4A Mist Clearing: 2008 Democratic Presidential Candidates' Delegate Accumulation

after Super Tuesday continued for Republicans in 2008. Although Romney and Huckabee each won a handful of the subsequent contests, McCain finished first in most of them and quickly pulled ahead in the delegate count (see Figure 10.4b). McCain benefited enormously from a Republican Party rule that allows states to allocate convention delegates on a winner-take-all basis—that is, the candidate who finishes first gets all of that state's delegates. McCain won 10 of the 12 winner-take-all contests, most of which occurred on Super Tuesday. We can see how frontloading combined with winner-take-all allocation quickly swelled his delegate count by looking at the 25 primaries and caucuses after New Hampshire (21 of them on Super Tuesday). McCain won a little more than one-third of the popular vote (37 percent) in these contests, but he received more than two-thirds of the delegates (68 percent). After Super Tuesday, McCain was about two-thirds of the way toward the magic number of delegates required to win, and a week later, he had accumulated nearly 80 percent of the delegates he needed.

Competition between Barack Obama and Hillary Clinton for the Democratic nomination, in contrast, was so close that neither candidate accumulated enough delegates to secure the nomination until the last primary was over. Although the Democratic calendar was just as frontloaded as the Republicans' (see Figure 10.2), different rules explain why the Democratic contest did not end quickly. In particular, Democratic Party rules require proportional allocation of convention delegates (with a minimum 15 percent threshold to be eligible for delegates)—that is, candidates win delegates in direct proportion to their share of the vote in the

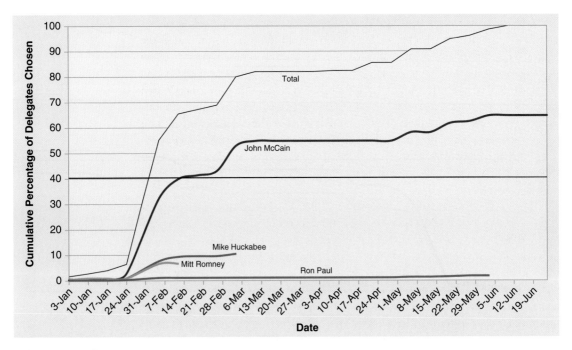

FIGURE 10.4B Mist Clearing: 2008 Republican Presidential Candidates' Delegate Accumulation

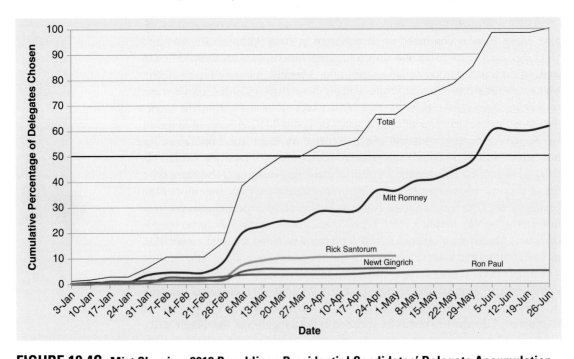

FIGURE 10.4C Mist Clearing: 2012 Republican Presidential Candidates' Delegate Accumulation

Source: Democratic and Republican delegate accumulation for 2008 constructed by the authors from data Berg-Andersson (2008, 2012).

primary. This rule means that candidates who do not come in first still get some delegates (provided they get more than 15 percent of the vote). In some cases, the second-place candidate may end up with as many delegates as the winner because the 15 percent threshold distorts the allocation somewhat. For example, Clinton "won" the 2008 New Hampshire primary with 39 percent of the vote, and Obama came in second with 36 percent, but they each received nine delegates. And although presidential candidates have generally ignored caucus states other than the first one in Iowa, Obama campaigned in these states and won a disproportionate share of those delegates. Thus, Obama was able to accumulate delegates at about the same rate as Clinton and eventually overcame her lead in the polls (see Figure 10.4a).

Romney led throughout the mist-clearing phase in 2012. Although Gingrich and Santorum won several later contests, their victories only slowed but could not stop Romney's march toward the magic number—1,144 delegates—to win the nomination. Gingrich scored the first blow by winning the South Carolina primary on January 21 less than two weeks after New Hampshire. His only other victory was his home state of Georgia on Super Tuesday. Santorum scored three wins—the Colorado and Minnesota precinct caucuses and the Missouri primary— in early February. Winning these contests, however, was largely symbolic because the contests were nonbinding, which means that they did not select any delegates bound to candidates. Such popular-vote victories in the initial contests can influence perceptions and create momentum, but in the mist-clearing phase, attention shifts to delegate counts. It's here that the Gingrich and Santorum campaigns were deficient. To win delegates, a candidate must know the rules and deadlines of each state's delegate selection process. Gingrich and Santorum may have lost delegates because they did not know the rules. Qualifying to be on the ballot in Virginia, for example, requires 10,000 signatures statewide, with at least 400 from each of the state's 11 congressional districts. And candidates had to have these signatures by December 22, 2011—before the first contests. Only Romney and Ron Paul met these requirements. Both Gingrich and Santorum had strong appeal in other southern states, and not competing for delegates in Virginia was costly. Additionally, Santorum won fewer delegates in the Ohio primary than he could have because he had failed to submit a complete slate of delegates by the December 2011 deadline. Although Ron Paul won the popular vote in only one minor contest—the U.S. Virgin Islands caucuses—he got a disproportionate share of delegates in several caucus states where he finished second or third because he knew the rules and vigorously competed for delegates in the subsequent rounds. Thus, although the Republican nomination contest appeared highly competitive, none of the potential "Not Romney" candidates were able stop Romney's steady drive to the nomination.

THE NATIONAL CONVENTION The national convention, composed of the delegates selected in the state primaries and caucuses, is the supreme governing authority of the party. The conventions meet for four days once every four years to nominate candidates for president and vice president and to conduct other party business.

Conventions now serve somewhat different purposes than they once did. As political scientists John Jackson and William Crotty observed, both the media and the public in general have become increasingly disinterested and cynical about national conventions. They argue that conventions have become little more than "marketing devices for the parties, the candidates and the issues and images they want to sell the public in the general election" (1996, 63). The state primaries and caucuses select the presidential nominee, and the convention simply acts as a ratifying body.

Although it is clear that modern conventions are carefully scripted to appeal to a mass television audience, conventions continue to have five major functions:

1. They officially nominate the party's candidates for president and vice president, which ratifies and legitimizes the results of the primaries and caucuses.
2. They approve a platform for the nominees to run on.
3. They provide a mechanism to encourage the losing candidates and disparate party factions to unify in preparation for the general election.
4. They showcase the party and its candidates on national television and create a favorable image with the public.
5. They adopt rules and regulations to govern the party at the convention and in the interim between elections.

The primary function of the national convention continues to be to choose the party's nominees for president and vice president. Whatever may have happened before, the actual nomination occurs at the convention. In recent nomination contests in both parties, the conventions have ratified the winner who secured a majority of the delegates in the primaries and caucuses: the convention has become a body that *legitimizes* the decision about the presidential nominee made before the delegates gather.

The convention typically ratifies the presidential nominee's choice of a vice presidential running mate. A number of considerations go into the choice of a running mate. Generally, there has been an attempt to balance the ticket with someone who differs in important ways from the presidential nominee, to unify the party and appeal to key segments of voters. The most common characteristics to balance are region, ideology, and political experience inside and outside of Washington, DC. In 2012, Republican nominee Mitt Romney selected Wisconsin representative Paul Ryan as his running mate. Ryan appealed to conservative Tea Party Republicans, a key constituency that had never been enthusiastic about Romney. And there was a chance that Ryan might help Romney win the swing state of Wisconsin. In 2008, Barack Obama, a first-term senator from Illinois with no foreign policy experience, picked fellow senator Joe Biden from Delaware. Biden brought a great deal of seniority and experience as chair of the Senate Foreign Relations Committee.

A second important function of the national convention is adopting the platform, which is the central policy document of the party and a statement of its general philosophy. Platforms serve as campaign documents, and they provide a reasonably good indication of what a candidate will do as president. Although they do not deliver on all their promises, presidents attempt to follow through on the broad outlines of the party's basic document.

A third function of the national convention is to promote party unity. Candidates seeking a party nomination generally agree on policy. Unable to differentiate themselves on policy, nomination campaigns sometimes become contentious and personal. The partisan spirit at the convention gives the contestants an opportunity to put aside their personal disagreements and work together to defeat the other party's ticket. Promoting party unity was a major goal of the 2008 Democratic convention. If disagreements prevent the party from unifying, its nominee will be in a weaker position in the general election. Byron Shafer (1988) has found that since 1968, the party with the most harmonious convention has been victorious over a party with a more contentious convention.

A fourth function of conventions is to present a favorable image on national television—what Stephen Wayne calls the "pep rally goal" (2000, 156). As reforms in delegate selection have reduced the chance that conventions will exercise independent choice, this pep rally function has assumed greater, perhaps paramount, importance. According to Wayne, party leaders and the nominee now view the convention "primarily as a launching pad for the general election" (2000, 156). The pep rally goal was paramount at both party conventions since 2000. Traditional party business, such as adopting rules and the platform and even the roll call where delegates cast their votes, has been relegated to the background.

The final function of the convention is to adopt the rules that govern the party. As the supreme governing authority of the party, the convention may affect the party's future operation through its rules. The elimination in 1936 of the Democratic Party rule requiring a two-thirds majority to nominate a candidate reduced the likelihood of a deadlocked convention. Another controversial rule used by Democrats until 1968 was the **unit rule**, in which a majority of a state delegation could require the entire delegation to vote the same way on nominations and other issues, thereby disenfranchising the minority.

Can We Predict Who Will Win Party Nominations?

Except when a popular incumbent president is seeking reelection, numerous candidates seek their party's presidential nomination. Although real competition is typically limited to only two or three "serious" candidates, that competition is vigorous, and the outcome may seem very much in doubt, at least until the contest enters the mist-clearing phase. In short, presidential nomination campaigns seem to be a "vast realm of uncertainty, unpredictability, and chaos. Unknown candidates rise out of nowhere to become front runners; 'can't miss' candidates suddenly see their best-laid plans come undone" (Mayer 1996, 44).

It turns out, though, that political scientists have found indicators that, in elections since 1980, predict quite well the winners of the Republican and

unit rule A rule that permitted a majority of a state's delegation to a political party's national convention to require that the entire state delegation vote the same way (or as a unit).

National Party Conventions are lavishly staged to present a favorable image of their candidates for president and vice president on national television and launch them into the general election campaign. President Barack Obama and Vice President Joe Biden got a significant boost in the polls following the Democratic Party Convention in 2012. This "pep rally" goal has become one of the most important functions of the national party conventions.

Democratic presidential nominations. And contrary to conventional wisdom, winning the initial contests in Iowa and New Hampshire does not predict the eventual winner particularly well. Instead, at least through the 2000 election, a better predictor of the eventual winner was the "winner" of the invisible primary. It may seem a little far-fetched to suggest that we can identify the winner of a contest in which there are no formal rules, no real votes cast, and no delegates selected. Political scientists, however, have identified variables—the leader in money raised, the leader in public opinion polls of party w, and the leader in endorsements of party insiders on the eve of the Iowa caucuses—that are good indicators of the invisible primary winner (Cohen et al. 2008a; Mayer 1996).

There were nine contested nominations from 1980 to 2000 (four Republican and five Democratic). Only one money leader (former governor John Connally in 1980) and one poll leader (former senator Gary Hart in 1988) did not go on to win their party's nomination (89 percent correct predictions); the leader of the "endorsement derby" won his party's nomination in all nine contested nominations. The winners of Iowa and New Hampshire fared much

TABLE 10.5: PREDICTIONS OF PARTY PRESIDENTIAL NOMINEES

Year	Nominee	Invisible Primary "Winners"			Initial Contests Winners	
		Money Leader	Poll Leader	Endorsements Leader	IA Caucuses	NH Primary
Republicans						
1980	Reagan	Connally	**Reagan**	**Reagan**	Bush Sr.	**Reagan**
1984	*Reagan*	*Unchallenged*	*Unchallenged*	*Unchallenged*	*Unchallenged*	*Unchallenged*
1988	Bush Sr.	**Bush Sr.**	**Bush Sr.**	**Bush Sr.**	R. Dole	**Bush Sr.**
1992	*Bush Sr.*	*Unchallenged*	*Unchallenged*	*Unchallenged*	*Unchallenged*	*Unchallenged*
1996	R. Dole	**R. Dole**	**R. Dole**	**R. Dole**	**R. Dole**	Buchanan
2000	G.W. Bush	**G.W. Bush**	**G.W. Bush**	**G.W. Bush**	**G.W. Bush**	McCain
2004	*G.W. Bush*	*Unchallenged*	*Unchallenged*	*Unchallenged*	*Unchallenged*	*Unchallenged*
2008	McCain	Romney	Giuliani	**McCain**	Huckabee	**McCain**
2012	Romney	**Romney**	Gingrich	**Romney**	Santorum	**Romney**
Democrats						
1980	Carter	**Carter**	**Carter**	**Carter**	**Carter**	**Carter**
1984	Mondale	**Mondale**	**Mondale**	**Mondale**	**Mondale**	Hart
1988	Dukakis	**Dukakis**	Hart	**Dukakis**	Gephardt	**Dukakis**
1992	B. Clinton	**B. Clinton**	**B. Clinton**	**B. Clinton**	Harkin	Tsongas
1996	*B. Clinton*	*Unchallenged*	*Unchallenged*	*Unchallenged*	*Unchallenged*	*Unchallenged*
2000	Gore	**Gore**	**Gore**	**Gore**	**Gore**	**Gore**
2004	Kerry	Dean	Dean	Gephardt	**Kerry**	**Kerry**
2008	Obama	H. Clinton	H. Clinton	H. Clinton	**Obama**	H. Clinton
2012	*Obama*	*Unchallenged*	*Unchallenged*	*Unchallenged*	*Unchallenged*	*Unchallenged*
Correct Predictions						
1980–2000		89% (8/9)	89% (8/9)	100% (9/9)	56% (5/9)	56% (5/9)
2004–2012		25% (1/4)	0% (0/4)	50% (2/4)	50% (2/4)	75% (3/4)
1980–2012		69% (9/13)	62% (8/13)	85% (11/13)	54% (7/13)	62% (8/13)

Entries are the candidates who were leaders in each of the indicators in contested nominations since 1980. Correct predictions are in **bold**.
Years in which a sitting president was running for a second term are in *italics* and are listed as *unchallenged*.
Source: Constructed by the authors from data at Mayer (1996, 49–51); Marty Cohen et al. (2008b), Table 10.4; Federal Election Commission (http://www.fec.gov/); and http://pollingreport.com/.

worse, with the states' contests correctly predicting who would win party nominations in only five of the nine contests (56 percent correct predictions; see Table 10.5).

However, these invisible variables did a poor job of predicting the outcomes of the four competitive contests from 2004 to 2012. No poll leader, one money leader

(Romney in 2012), and two endorsement leaders (McCain in 2008 and Romney in 2012) won their party's nomination. The initial contest winners fared only slightly better—two Iowa caucus winners (Kerry in 2008 and Obama in 2012) and three New Hampshire primary winners (McCain and Kerry in 2008 and Romney in 2012) won their party nominations. If we look at all contested nominations from 1980 to 2012, the endorsement leader won his party nomination in 11 of 13 cases (89 percent). The other invisible primary indicators (poll and money leaders prior to the Iowa caucuses) and victory in the initial contests (Iowa and New Hampshire) do a roughly equal job of predicting the eventual major-party presidential nominees.

Why have nominations become less predictable in the three most recent presidential elections? One possible explanation is luck and the small number of cases (or small N, in scientific language). Nine contested nominations from 1980 to 2000 is enough to identify a systematic pattern if one exists (Cohen et al. 2008b, 13), but just barely. Political processes are often influenced strongly by idiosyncratic events, and with a small number of observations, just one or two random events can obscure an underlying process. A limitation of using the results of Iowa and New Hampshire to predict who will win a party nomination is what some call the "your own backyard" effect—that is, candidates from Iowa and New Hampshire and adjacent states tend to have a built-in advantage in these contests. The candidates who won these initial Democratic contests in 1988 and 1992, for example, all had this backyard advantage. Senator Tom Harkin from Iowa and Representative Richard Gephardt from neighboring Missouri won the Iowa caucuses but failed to win the Democratic nomination. New Hampshire is a small state, much of which is in the Boston media market. Former Massachusetts governors Michael Dukakis and Paul Tsongas won the New Hampshire primary; Dukakis went on to win the Democratic nomination, but Tsongas did not. Thus, wins in Iowa and New Hampshire may not tell us much about the strength of candidates in future contests. There are also limits to the invisible primary indicators. For example, Hillary Clinton led in the money primary in 2008 by raising a record $90 million. But Obama, the eventual nominee, was a close second with $80 million, which was nearly double the record-breaking $40 million raised by the money leader Howard Dean in 2004.

The N of 13 for the entire period is still small, and determining whether the lack of predictive power in the four contested nominations since 2000 reflects a fundamental change or just random error is problematic. Marty Cohen et al. (2008b) recognize that four tough nominations after nine comparatively easy ones could very well be due to chance. Yet they also present a good case that some fundamentals have changed as well. They find that

> the communications revolution of the past few years—cable news, blogs, YouTube, and the related increase in visible campaign activity, especially debates—has given candidates more opportunities to make independent

impressions on voters and thereby made it harder for parties to dominate the game. (Cohen et al. 2008b)

Once the parties have chosen their nominees, attention turns to the general election.

ELECTING THE PRESIDENT

The presidency is the single greatest electoral prize in the United States, and it is the only office with a truly national constituency. The presidential election is the focus of more attention, more money, and more effort than any other election. The complex mechanism established to choose the president—the electoral college—is unique to the American political system.

The Electoral College

More Americans cast ballots for president than in any other election, yet the president is not chosen by the national popular vote. The race for the presidency is not a single contest for a national vote, but rather 51 separate elections in the states and the District of Columbia to choose slates of partisan electors. These electors choose the president according to rules and procedures specified in the Constitution.

The **electoral college**, a system "jerry-rigged out of odds and ends of parliamentary junk pressed together by contending interests" (Collier and Collier 1986, 303), reflects disagreement among the founders about how to choose the executive. For example, some wanted direct popular election of the president; others wanted Congress or the state legislatures to have the responsibility. The electoral college was the bargain struck to satisfy these competing preferences (Jackson and Crotty 1996, 104).

The electoral college is not democratic, nor was it intended to be. Some of the founders had a profound distrust of ordinary citizens' abilities to make sound judgments about choosing the president. Convention delegate George Mason, for example, argued that to allow the people to make such a choice made no more sense than "to refer a trial of colors to a blind man" (Benton 1986, 1128). Even Madison, Hamilton, and others who believed that the presidency ought to reflect the will of the people suggested that this popular will should be filtered through intermediaries who would have superior knowledge and judgment. As John Jay explained in *Federalist* Number 64, "the select assemblies [i.e., the electors] . . . will in general be composed of the most

electoral college The institution (whose members are selected by whatever means the state legislature chooses) that is responsible for selecting the president of the United States.

enlightened and respectable citizens." But only a handful of delegates opposed direct election in principle. The primary concern about direct election was more practical than philosophical—delegates worried that voters would not have sufficient information about the candidates to make reasoned judgments because the long distances and slow communications in the new nation would make national campaigns difficult (G. Edwards 2011). The electoral college was seen as a way to solve the communication problem but still give citizens indirect influence.

The 2000 presidential election dramatically highlights the importance of counting electoral votes rather than the national popular vote. The outcome hung in the balance for more than a month after election day while the candidates contested a razor-thin margin in Florida. Democrat Al Gore's victory in the national popular vote over Republican George W. Bush had no bearing on who won the presidency. Neither candidate could win without Florida's 25 electoral votes, so choice of president thus came down to a post-election struggle, largely fought in the courts, to win a single state. Bush won the battle, received Florida's 25 electoral votes, and became president. And the convoluted process of electing presidents became the focus of intense popular interest.

HOW THE ELECTORAL COLLEGE WORKS The electoral college is an awkward electoral device that has attracted its share of critics. The Twelfth and Twenty-Third Amendments, adopted to address some of the criticisms, made only modest changes. The basic legal structure and requirements of the process remain relatively unaltered.

The Constitution calls for each state legislature to choose, by whatever means it desires, a number of electors equal to its total number of senators and House members. Although a state's total representation in Congress determines the number of electoral votes it has, members of Congress and those who hold other national offices are not eligible to serve as electors.

The minimum number of electoral votes a state can have is three—every state has two senators and at least one representative in the House. Seven states—Alaska, Delaware, Montana, North Dakota, South Dakota, Vermont, and Wyoming—have the minimum. Larger states with more representatives have more electoral votes; California is the largest with 55 electoral votes. The total number of electoral votes is 538, the sum of 100 senators, 435 House members, and 3 votes for Washington, DC, as mandated by the Twenty-Third Amendment.

The electors meet in their respective state capitals in December and, as mandated by the Twelfth Amendment, cast separate votes for president and vice president. These votes are transmitted to the nation's capital, to be opened and counted in a joint session of Congress in January. To be elected president or vice president, a candidate must receive an absolute majority of electoral votes—that is, 270 of the 538 votes. The incumbent vice president, who is the presiding officer of the Senate, announces the outcome before the joint session of Congress. One candidate usually receives a majority of the electoral votes, and the vice president officially declares that candidate to be president. This procedure has produced its share of irony. In January 2001, Vice President Al Gore declared his opponent, George W.

THE STRANGE STORY OF THE TWELFTH AMENDMENT AND THE DEATH OF ALEXANDER HAMILTON

The Twelfth Amendment to the Constitution was a direct result of the development of political parties. Originally, each elector cast two votes for president, and the candidate who received the most votes was declared president as long as the vote tally constituted a majority. If no candidate received a majority, the House of Representatives, voting by states (one state delegation, one vote), would choose the president from among the five candidates receiving the highest number of electoral votes. After the choice of president was made, the person with the next highest number of electoral votes would be declared vice president. If two or more contenders received an equal number of electoral votes, the Senate would choose the vice president from among them.

The formation and organization of political parties proceeded at such a rapid pace that, by the election of 1800, the electors no longer served as independent people exercising personal judgment about candidates' capabilities; rather, they acted as the agents of political parties and the general public. In fact, party discipline was so complete that all Republican electors in 1800 cast their two votes for Thomas Jefferson and Aaron Burr. Although it was generally understood that Jefferson was the Democratic Republican candidate for president and that Burr was the candidate for vice president, the Constitution provided no means for the electors to make that distinction on their ballots. The result was a tie between Jefferson and Burr, and as neither won a majority, the matter of deciding a president was thrown to the House of Representatives.

Ironically, the Federalists, despite their crushing defeat in the congressional elections of 1800 at the hands of the Democratic-Republicans, still controlled the lame-duck Congress, which did not expire until March 1801. They were, therefore, in a position to help decide which Republican would serve as president

and which as vice president. Alexander Hamilton had a good deal of influence in the Federalist caucus and played a decisive role. Although friendly with Burr, he did not believe Burr could be trusted with the nation's highest office. In spite of disagreeing with Jefferson on policy matters, Hamilton swung the New York vote behind Jefferson, who became the third president on the House's 36th vote.

One result of this bizarre chain of events was the ratification in 1804 of the Twelfth Amendment, stipulating that electors cast separate ballots for president and vice president. The amendment also provides that, if no presidential candidate receives a majority of the electoral votes, the House of Representatives, balloting by states, will select the president by majority vote from among the three candidates receiving the highest number of electoral votes. If no vice presidential candidate receives a majority of electoral votes, similar procedures are to be used by the Senate in choosing between the two people with the highest number of electoral votes.

A second, albeit indirect, result of this odd presidential election was the death of Alexander Hamilton at the hands of Aaron Burr. Although the two had long been friends, their relationship quickly soured after Hamilton deliberately rejected Burr in the House's presidential balloting of 1800. In 1804, the same year the Twelfth Amendment was ratified, Burr became a New York gubernatorial candidate, and Hamilton once again moved to block Burr's political ambitions. By this time, the relationship between the two men had become so acrimonious that Burr formally challenged Hamilton to a duel to settle their disagreements. In the early morning of July 11, 1804, Burr and Hamilton faced each other with pistols at 20 paces. Hamilton was mortally wounded in the encounter and died a day later, at the age of 47.

Bush, to be president. (See the Politics in Practice feature "The Strange Story of the Twelfth Amendment and the Death of Alexander Hamilton.")

If no presidential candidate receives a majority of electoral votes, the House of Representatives, voting by states, chooses the president from among the top three candidates. Each state has one vote; the state's representatives collectively agree on how to cast that vote. A candidate must receive 26 votes, a majority, to be elected. If no vice presidential candidate receives a majority of electoral votes, the Senate, voting as individuals, elects the vice president from among the two highest candidates. An absolute majority, or 51 senators, is required to elect the vice president.

The original idea behind this convoluted process was to have politically savvy electors, typically chosen by state legislatures, exercise their independent judgment to select the president. If this was the intent, it was quickly dashed. In the first two presidential elections, most state legislatures chose electors, although four states used popular elections to select them. Regardless, there was no division: in 1789 and again in 1793, George Washington got every electoral vote cast. Consensus disappeared with Washington's decision to retire from public office and with the emergence of political parties. More states began having popular elections to choose electors. The founders' original vision of a body of wise men insulated from the winds of public opinion who judiciously picked the nation's highest official faded.

In each state and Washington, DC, the political parties nominate a slate of partisan electors. In November, citizens in each jurisdiction cast votes for president. But the voters are actually deciding which party's slate of electors will win the right to cast the state's electoral votes. Except for an occasional elector who is unfaithful, these electors do not exercise independent judgment. Instead, they are chosen by parties to vote for the party's nominee, and they almost always vote that way.[6]

HOW THE ELECTORAL COLLEGE VIOLATES CORE DEMOCRATIC PRINCIPLES The electoral college violates the core democratic principle of political equality and has the potential to violate majority rule. Although choosing electors by direct popular vote rather than by the state legislatures might appear more democratic in that it gives ordinary people more direct influence, this reform does not prevent the electoral college from violating these core democratic principles.

The basic structure of the electoral college violates political equality because the value of a vote for president depends on where it is cast. For political equality to be achieved in the electoral college, each state's percentage of electoral votes must equal its percentage of the population. Recall that the number of representatives

---

[6] Because the parties choose individuals who have proven their loyalty, unfaithful electors are rare. Between 1820 and 2012, only 18 electors failed to vote for their party's candidates for president and vice president. In 1988, a West Virginia Democratic elector who was supposed to vote for Michael Dukakis for president and Lloyd Bentsen for vice president cast her presidential vote for Bentsen and her vice presidential vote for Dukakis. In 2004, a Democratic elector from Minnesota voted for John Edwards for president. There is speculation that this may have been an error because this elector also voted for Edwards for vice president. About one-half of the states have laws that attempt to bind the electors to vote for the winner, but there is some question about whether such laws are constitutional because the Constitution clearly intends electors to exercise independent judgment.

a state has in the House and Senate determines how many electoral votes it has. Because all states have two senators and at least one representative, no state can have fewer than three electoral votes. As a result, the electoral college gives the smallest states more voting weight and the largest states less weight relative to their populations (Table 10.6). About 12.1 percent of the nation's population resides in

TABLE 10.6: ALLOCATION OF ELECTORAL VOTES, 2012

State	Electoral Votes	Population (millions)	% Under-/Over- Represented*	State	Electoral Votes	Population (millions)	% Under-/Over- Represented*
California	55	37.34	–15.4%	Oregon	7	3.85	4.5%
Texas	38	25.27	–13.6%	Oklahoma	7	3.76	6.9%
New York	29	19.42	–14.2%	Connecticut	7	3.58	12.3%
Florida	29	18.90	–11.8%	Iowa	6	3.05	12.9%
Illinois	20	12.86	–10.7%	Mississippi	6	2.98	15.8%
Pennsylvania	20	12.73	–9.7%	Arkansas	6	2.93	17.8%
Ohio	18	11.57	–10.6%	Kansas	6	2.86	20.4%
Michigan	16	9.91	–7.2%	Utah	6	2.77	24.4%
Georgia	16	9.73	–5.5%	Nevada	6	2.71	27.3%
North Carolina	15	9.57	–9.9%	New Mexico	5	2.07	39.0%
New Jersey	14	8.81	–8.6%	West Virginia	5	1.86	54.5%
Virginia	13	8.04	–7.1%	Nebraska	5	1.83	56.9%
Washington	12	6.75	2.1%	Idaho	4	1.57	46.1%
Massachusetts	11	6.56	–3.6%	Hawaii	4	1.37	68.2%
Indiana	11	6.50	–2.8%	Maine	4	1.33	72.4%
Arizona	11	6.41	–1.4%	New Hampshire	4	1.32	74.0%
Tennessee	11	6.38	–0.8%	Rhode Island	4	1.06	117.8%
Missouri	10	6.01	–4.4%	Montana	3	0.99	73.4%
Maryland	10	5.79	–0.7%	Delaware	3	0.90	91.4%
Wisconsin	10	5.70	0.9%	South Dakota	3	0.82	110.3%
Minnesota	10	5.31	8.1%	Alaska	3	0.72	138.9%
Colorado	9	5.04	2.5%	North Dakota	3	0.68	155.1%
Alabama	9	4.80	7.7%	Vermont	3	0.63	173.5%
South Carolina	9	4.65	11.3%	DC	3	0.60	186.5%
Louisiana	8	4.55	1.0%	Wyoming	3	0.57	203.4%
Kentucky	8	4.35	5.7%				
				Totals	538	309.2	

*Percentage difference between a state's share of the electoral college votes and its share of the U.S. population. Negative numbers indicate states that get less than their fair share of electoral votes; positive numbers indicate states that get more than their fair share of electoral votes. *Source*: Constructed by the authors from 2010 Census data.

California, but California only has 10.2 percent of the electoral college votes (55 of 538). Wyoming, on the other had, has about 0.18 percent of the nation's population, but it has the minimum share of electoral votes (3 of 538), which works out to be 0.56 percent. Proportionally speaking, this means California is underrepresented in the electoral college, and Wyoming is vastly overrepresented.

In addition, votes count more in some states than in others. In most cases, all of a state's electoral votes go to the candidate who wins a plurality of the popular votes. This winner-take-all feature means that the preferences of voters who supported a losing candidate are not represented in the electoral college. In 2012, for example, Barack Obama won about 60 percent of the popular vote in California and got all 55 of its electoral votes, while Mitt Romney won about 57 percent of the popular vote in Texas and got all 34 of its electoral votes. The preferences of nearly five million Romney voters in California and over three million Obama voters in Texas were not represented at all in their state's electoral vote. Moreover, a vote cast in a large state has a much smaller weight in determining who wins electoral votes than votes cast in small states—1 vote out of more than 13 million cast in California has much less weight than 1 out of 250,000 cast in Wyoming.

Election of the president by the House of Representatives when no candidate has a majority in the electoral college also violates the principle of political equality. Because the House votes by state to select the president, the decision is not made according to the "one person, one vote" principle. The House has twice been called on to elect the president, in 1800 and 1824.[7]

Nor does the electoral college ensure that the majority will rule. Five times in the nation's history, the candidate elected president did not get the most popular votes: John Quincy Adams in 1824, Rutherford B. Hayes in 1876, Benjamin Harrison in 1888, John Kennedy[8] in 1960, and George W. Bush in 2000. The electoral college may fail to choose the winner of the national popular vote even if every elector votes for the candidate he or she was chosen to vote for. This can occur because electoral votes are allocated on a winner-take-all basis, regardless of how close or lopsided the vote is in the state. Table 10.7 illustrates an extreme example in which a candidate is on the ballot in only the 11 largest states. If this candidate were to win the popular vote in these states even by a one-vote margin and get no votes in any other states, he or she would be elected president with 270 electoral votes. Although the other candidate would have had a much larger popular vote

---

[7] The Senate was called on to select the vice president in 1837. Martin Van Buren won a majority of electoral votes for president against four other candidates who received some electoral votes. But Democratic electors from Virginia withheld their votes from Van Buren's running mate, Richard M. Johnson, denying him a majority for vice president. The Senate elected Johnson vice president over the runner-up.

[8] Kennedy is typically credited with a small popular vote victory over Nixon. But research by political scientists questions this result. Kennedy's name did not appear on the ballot in Alabama. Instead, only the names of Democratic electors appeared on the ballot, and 6 of the 11 chosen did not support Kennedy. Reports listing Kennedy as the popular vote winner nationwide count all votes for Democratic electors as popular votes for Kennedy, even though some of these popular votes clearly were not for Kennedy. If the popular vote in Alabama is divided in proportion to how the electors voted, Nixon turns out to be the popular vote winner nationwide by a small margin (Gaines 2001).

TABLE 10.7 HOW THE POPULAR VOTE WINNER CAN LOSE IN THE ELECTORAL COLLEGE

State	Electoral votes	Total votes cast in state* (millions)	Minimum votes needed to win state's electoral votes*
California	55	13.04	6.52
Texas	38	7.99	4.00
Florida	29	8.47	4.24
New York	29	7.06	3.53
Illinois	20	5.24	2.62
Pennsylvania	20	5.75	2.88
Ohio	18	5.58	2.79
Georgia	16	3.90	1.95
Michigan	16	4.73	2.37
North Carolina	15	4.51	2.25
New Jersey	14	3.64	1.82
Subtotal for 11 Largest States	**270**	62.92	34.96
Percent of Total	52.4%		**27.1%**
Other 39 States	268	59.14	
Total	538	129.06	

*Popular vote totals are from 2012 presidential election. Votes needed to win state's electoral votes is 50 percent plus 1 of votes cast in the state.
NOTE: votes in the table are based on 2008 returns. We can substitute 2012 returns once we know them.

margin nationally, this popular candidate would receive only 268 electoral votes from the other 39 states.

The mathematical advantage of the small states can also cause the electoral college to fail to choose the popular winner. In the 2000 presidential election, for example, George W. Bush lost the popular vote nationwide, but he won a majority of electoral votes in part because of his success in the smallest states. Bush won 54 electoral votes from 13 of the 19 smallest states, where his popular vote total was about 2.7 million. More than twice as many people—5.7 million—voted for Al Gore in California to give him the same number of electoral votes.

PROPOSALS TO REFORM THE ELECTORAL COLLEGE These defects in the electoral college have led to several reform proposals. In recent years, attention has focused on three basic plans:

1. The proportional plan
2. The district plan
3. The direct popular election plan

The **proportional plan** would divide each state's electoral votes in proportion to the division of the popular vote. For example, a candidate receiving 60 percent of the popular vote in a state would get 60 percent of its electoral votes. Other

proportional plan A plan to revise the electoral college such that the number of electoral college votes given to candidates would be based on the proportion of the popular vote they obtained.

features of the electoral college would remain, such as requiring a majority of electoral votes for a candidate to be elected and having Congress choose the president if no candidate receives a majority.

The **district plan** would return to the method some states used early in the nation's history. The district plan allocates one electoral vote to the presidential candidate who receives a plurality in a House district; the state's remaining two electoral votes go to the candidate who wins a plurality statewide. Thus, a state's electoral votes could be split if the voters in some congressional districts voted for the Democrat and voters in others voted for the Republican.

Either of these reforms could be implemented without amending the Constitution. The Constitution says that state legislatures can choose electors however they wish, so any state legislature could choose to allocate the state's electoral votes in proportion to the statewide percentages or by congressional district. Maine and Nebraska currently use the district plan, and a number of states have considered adopting the proportional plan. In 2008 one of Nebraska's electoral votes went to Obama because he won a plurality in one of Nebraska's three congressional districts.

The **direct popular election plan** would abolish the electoral college and permit voters in the 50 states and the District of Columbia to choose the president directly. A majority of the public has consistently supported direct election for several decades (G. Edwards 2011). Implementing this reform, however, has proved remarkably difficult. Adopting this reform would require a constitutional amendment to abolish the electoral college, and thus far it has proved impossible to muster the two-thirds majorities in both houses of Congress to propose an amendment. Even if Congress were to pass such an amendment, it is unlikely that it would be ratified by three-fourths of state legislatures.

If the goal of reform is to ensure that the winner of the national popular vote is elected president, only direct popular election guarantees it. Table 10.8 shows the elections since 1960 in which one of the reforms would have failed to select the candidate who won the popular vote.

The proportional plan is the reform that would have failed to select the popular vote winner most often. Under the proportional plan, no candidate would have received a majority of electoral votes in six of the 13 elections since 1960. If other features of the electoral college were maintained, these elections would have been decided by the House. The House probably would have chosen the popular vote winners in some of these elections, but there is no guarantee. For example, in 1976 and 1992, minor party candidates would have received enough electoral votes under the proportional plan to deny Carter and Clinton, the popular winners, electoral college majorities. Democrats had a majority in the House in those years, but keep in mind that if the House chooses the president, each state gets one vote, and it takes a majority (26 of 50) to elect the president. Thus, we need to look at the party split in each state delegation to see which party controls at least 26. In 1976 and 1992, 32 state delegations were mostly Democratic, so it's likely that Carter and Clinton would have won in the House. But Republicans controlled the House of Representatives in 1996, and 28 states had more Republicans than Democrats,

district plan A plan to revise the electoral college that would distribute a state's electoral college votes by giving one vote to the candidate who wins a plurality in each House district and two votes to the winner statewide.

direct popular election plan A proposal to abolish the electoral college and elect the president directly by national popular vote.

TABLE 10.8: WINNER OF THE PRESIDENCY UNDER THE VARIOUS ELECTORAL COLLEGE REFORMS

Year	Candidates	Popular Vote	Electoral College Votes	Electoral College Winner	Proportional Plan Votes	Proportional Plan Winner	District Plan Votes	District Plan Winner
1960	Nixon (R)*	49.55	219		266.1	Uncertain/House	278	Nixon
	Kennedy (D)	49.46	303	Kennedy	265.6	27 Dem, 19 R, 4 tie	245	
	Byrd/others	0.99	15		5.3		14	
1968	Nixon (R)	43.2	301	Nixon	231.5	Uncertain/House	289	Nixon
	Humphrey (D)	42.7	191		225.4	27 Dem, 19 Rep, 4 tie	192	
	Wallace (AI)	13.5	46		78.8		57	
	Others	0.6	0		2.3		0	
1976	Carter (D)	50.1	297	Carter	269.7	Uncertain/House	269	Uncertain/House
	Ford (R)	48.0	240		258.0	32 Dem, 11 Rep, 7 tie	269	32 Dem, 11 Rep, 7 tie
	Others	1.9	0		10.2		0	
1992	Clinton (D)	43.0	370	Clinton	231.6	Uncertain/House	324	Clinton
	Bush sr. (R)	37.5	168		203.3	32 Dem, 9 Rep, 9 tie	214	
	Perot	18.9	0		101.8		0	
	Others	0.6	0		1.3		0	
1996	Clinton (D)	49.2	379	Clinton	262.0	Uncertain/House	345	Clinton
	Dole (R)	40.7	159		219.9	19 Dem, 28 Rep, 3 tie	193	
	Perot	8.4	0		48.8		0	
	Others	1.7	0		7.3		0	
2000	Gore (D)	48.4	266		264.0	Uncertain/House	267	
	Bush (R)	47.9	271	Bush	265.0	18 Dem, 28 Rep, 4 tie	271	Bush
	Nader/others	2.7	0		9.0		0	
2012	Obama (D)	51.1	332	Obama	272.2	Obama	262	
	Romney (R)	47.2	206		256.2		273	Romney
	Others	1.7	0		2.1		0	
Times Not Electing Popular Vote Winner		**0**	**2**		**6**		**3**	

*Note: Kennedy is typically credited with a national popular vote victory in 1960. Footnote 8 explains why some political scientists believe that Nixon actually won the popular vote.

Source: Adapted from Wayne 2004, 323–325, and updated by the authors

increasing the chances that the House would have chosen Bob Dole, who finished second in the popular vote. Similarly, in the 2000 election, Republicans controlled 28 state delegations, suggesting that the House probably would have chosen Bush, the runner-up in the popular vote. In the 1960 election, the outcome in the House is uncertain. The district plan would have fared slightly better, though in 1976, Gerald Ford and Jimmy Carter would have tied in electoral votes, throwing the election to the House, and in 2000, Bush would have won a majority of electoral votes under this plan.

Moreover, neither the proportional plan nor the district plan would correct the electoral college's violation of the core democratic principle of political equality. The district plan consistently prevents equal weighting of votes because every state, regardless of population, gets two electoral votes for its two senators and awards two electoral votes to the statewide winner. And since the electoral votes awarded by congressional district go to the plurality winner in the district, the preferences of voters who support the losing candidate in every district are not represented in the electoral vote. The proportional plan does a better job of weighting votes equally, but this plan frequently sends the election to the House. Since voting is by state, small states have disproportionate influence—Wyoming, with about 500,000 people, has the same influence in electing the president as California, with over 36 million people. Thus, neither the proportional plan nor the district plan would reform the electoral college to ensure results consistent with the principles of democracy. Only direct popular election would ensure democratic results.

The electoral college system does have some advantages. By making the presidency a race for states, it preserves the principle of federalism that is the bedrock of the American political system. Although it presents an enormous obstacle to third-party candidates, it also helps promote a stable two-party system. And, however imperfectly, it institutionalizes a check on the tyranny of the majority; demagogues may be able to attract a lot of votes, but they have no guarantee of actually governing unless they win states. As political scientist Judith Best puts it, "the electoral vote system is a model of our federal Constitution . . . that creates one society out of many societies" (1996, 72). Research by George Edwards (2011), however, shows that the electoral college has little to do with preserving federalism—equal representation in the Senate is more important on that score.

The Campaign

Strategy and money are important components of a successful presidential campaign. Strategy is driven not just by the issues, but also by electoral rules. Until recent elections, public financing meant that presidential candidates tended to be on more or less equal financial footing in the general election.

The ultimate goal of presidential candidates is to get 270 electoral votes. Consequently, campaign efforts focus on states with a lot of electoral votes and on **swing states** in which the outcome could go either way. Although the presidential campaign is indeed a race for states, only a small number of large and competitive states receive any attention from the candidates' campaigns. Table 10.9 shows the number of times the presidential candidates campaigned in each state in 2012. The presidential campaigns focused almost exclusively on 12 states: Colorado, Florida, Michigan, Missouri, Nevada, New Hampshire, New Mexico, North Carolina, Ohio, Pennsylvania,

swing states States in which the outcome of a presidential race is unclear, and both candidates have a realistic chance of winning.

TABLE 10.9: PRESIDENTIAL CAMPAIGN STOPS IN THE 2012 PRESIDENTIAL ELECTION

State	Candidates' Campaign Stops	Electoral Votes	Election Margin	State	Candidates' Campaign Stops	Electoral Votes	Election Margin
Ohio	57	18	3.0%	Alabama	0	9	22.2%
Florida	32	29	0.9%	Alaska	0	3	14.0%
Virginia	28	13	3.9%	Arizona	0	11	9.1%
Iowa	25	6	5.8%	Arkansas	0	6	23.7%
Colorado	21	9	5.4%	California	0	55	23.1%
Nevada	13	6	6.7%	Connecticut	0	7	17.3%
Wisconsin	13	10	6.9%	Delaware	0	3	18.6%
New Hampshire	12	4	5.6%	Georgia	0	16	7.8%
201	**95**	**4.8% avg.**		Hawaii	0	4	42.7%
(96% of stops)				Idaho	0	4	31.9%
				Illinois	0	20	16.9%
				Indiana	0	11	10.2%
				Kansas	0	6	21.7%
				Kentucky	0	8	22.7%
Pennsylvania	5	20	5.4%	Louisiana	0	8	17.2%
North Carolina	2	15	2.0%	Maine	0	4	15.3%
Michigan	1	16	9.5%	Maryland	0	10	26.1%
Minnesota	1	10	7.7%	Massachusetts	0	11	23.1%
9	**90**	**6.2% avg.**		Mississippi	0	6	11.5%
(4% of stops)				Missouri	0	10	9.4%
				Montana	0	3	13.7%
				Nebraska	0	5	21.8%
				New Jersey	0	14	17.7%
				New Mexico	0	5	10.2%
				New York	0	29	28.1%
				North Dakota	0	3	19.6%
				Oklahoma	0	7	33.5%
				Oregon	0	7	12.1%
				Rhode Island	0	4	27.5%
				South Carolina	0	9	10.5%
				South Dakota	0	3	18.0%
				Tennessee	0	11	20.4%
				Texas	0	38	15.8%
				Utah	0	6	48.0%
				Vermont	0	3	35.6%
				Washington	0	12	14.9%
				West Virginia	0	5	26.8%
Total stops	**210**			Wyoming	0	3	40.8%
				(0% of stops)		**379**	**21.0% avg.**

Source: Calculated by the authors from data supplied by George Edwards (2011).

Virginia, and Wisconsin. These states had large blocs of electoral votes, were highly competitive, or both. More than 90 percent of the presidential candidates' campaign visits were to these 12 states; the average election margin of the winning candidate in these states was 8.2 percent. In contrast, 32 states with small blocs of electoral votes or in which one of the candidates had a commanding lead received no campaign visits; the average margin of victory in these states was 22 percent.

Not only do the rules help determine where candidates will campaign, but they also determine to a considerable extent how they will campaign. Unlike the long invisible primary associated with the nomination campaign, the general election has tight time limits. After the parties' nominating conventions in 2008, there were only 10 weeks until the general election. This time limit determines the entire strategy of a campaign. As political scientists John Jackson and William Crotty put it, "all the strategic plans, all marshaling and deployment of resources, all the advertising, and every facet of the entire campaign effort works backward from the election date" (1996, 99). The time constraint places enormous pressure on the candidates and their organizations to get their messages out, mobilize their party bases, and attract undecided voters. The option of a front porch campaign in which the candidate stays at home rather than going out to engage the voters has long since receded into history.

Financing the Presidential Election

Running for president is an expensive proposition. Even with the advantage of incumbency and facing no opposition for the 2004 Republican nomination, George W. Bush spent more than $220 million campaigning before the national convention. Facing a crowded field, John Kerry, the eventual Democratic nominee, spent more than $197 million to win the Democratic nomination for president. In 2008, John McCain spent $230 million campaigning for the Republican nomination, and on the Democratic side, Obama spent $454 million, more than twice what Kerry had spent four years earlier (Center for Responsive Politics n.d.).

Although numerous observers express concern about the 2008 corrupting influence of money in politics, efforts to regulate campaign spending must be balanced against constitutional guarantees protecting the rights of free speech and free association. Historically, restrictions on contributions to presidential campaigns have been ineffective. Although Congress enacted several laws in the first half of the twentieth century to prevent corporations and labor unions from contributing money to presidential elections, these laws were circumvented by the channeling of money through intermediaries and political action committees (PACs). Candidates and political parties have also found loopholes in more recent efforts to regulate campaign contributions.

Presidential campaign finance is regulated by the Federal Election Campaign Act (FECA). Its key provisions include the following:

- Public financing of presidential campaigns and overall expenditure limits
- Contribution limits for candidates who accept public financing

- Public disclosure requirements
- Creation of the FEC to enforce the law

In 1976, the Supreme Court ruled that overall spending limits violated individuals' First Amendment free speech rights; that is, the Court ruled that wealthy candidates have the right to spend as much of their own money as they wish on their campaigns. Limits on contributions and expenditures of candidates who accept public funds were ruled constitutionally acceptable (*Buckley v. Valeo* 1976).

Candidates become eligible for public funds as soon as they raise at least $5,000 in contributions of $250 or less in each of 20 states, for a total of $100,000. Once qualified, they receive public funds on a dollar-for-dollar basis for the first $250 received from an individual. Those who accept public financing are bound by a spending limit of about $42 million in the campaign for party nominations and $84 million in the general election. Candidates are not required to accept public financing and the spending limits that come with it. In the 2008 election, for example, Barack Obama declined public financing for both the nomination contest and the general election, so he was not bound by the spending limit.

Campaigns have developed creative methods to avoid the spirit, if not the letter, of campaign finance laws. Campaign contributions can be characterized as either hard money or soft money. The contribution limits established by FECA applied to hard money—that is, money given to expressly support or oppose a candidate. FECA did not regulate soft money, which consists of contributions given to party organizations rather than to individual candidates. Parties use soft money for general party building and for political purposes such as voter registration drives and to run issue ads advocating some cause or issue. Although political activities supported by soft money are not supposed to directly support or oppose a candidate, many observers viewed them as a loophole used to circumvent the contribution limits to indirectly benefit party standard-bearers. In 2002, Congress passed the Bipartisan Campaign Reform Act (BCRA), better known as the McCain-Feingold Act for its main Senate sponsors John McCain (R-AZ) and Russell Feingold (D-WI), to address this problem. The BCRA bans soft money outright, and it restricts "issue ads" run immediately before an election. This law also raised limits on hard money contributions during each election cycle to $2,000 from individuals and $5,000 from PACs. There were plenty of loopholes in this law, however, and the candidates took full advantage of those loopholes in the 2004 and 2008 presidential elections. In 2010, the BCRA became as much loophole as law when the Supreme Court struck down key provisions of the McCain-Feingold law. The Court ruled in *Citizens United v. Federal Election Commission* (2010) that limiting, let alone banning, corporate funding of independent political broadcasts in an election campaign was prohibited by the First Amendment. It will take an election cycle or two to fully assess the impact of this ruling, though many fear that if Congress cannot figure out a way to constitutionally revive key objectives of the McCain-Feingold law, the court has essentially green-lighted unlimited, independent campaign spending by deep-pocketed advocacy groups.

Changes in campaign finance legislation have had important consequences for presidential nominations. Candidates can no longer turn to a few "fat cats" to bankroll their campaigns (unless they themselves are the fat cats). In the absence of a personal fortune, candidates have to raise a lot of small individual contributions. This time-consuming logistical challenge rewards early starters.

Public campaign financing is also available in the general election. Nominees of the parties that received 25 percent or more of the popular vote in the previous presidential election—that is, the Democratic and Republican candidates—are eligible for full public financing; candidates of parties that received between 5 and 25 percent of the vote in the previous election are eligible to receive partial public financing. The major party candidates received equal funding, about $74 million, in 2004. Public financing of the general election "has leveled the playing field between the two major parties in the money available to support their" campaigns (Jackson and Crotty 1996, 186). In 2008, McCain accepted public financing, but Obama declined it, allowing the Democrat to spend a great deal more than the $84 million limit for candidates who accept public financing.

NOMINATING CANDIDATES FOR CONGRESS

Congressional elections differ from presidential elections in a number of ways. There are different rules for winning, smaller constituencies, shifting political jurisdictions, and distinct advantages for incumbents, and there is no public campaign financing. The Constitution leaves the method of selecting congressional candidates to the individual states, so how candidates for the House and Senate gain their party's nomination depends on state law.

Primary Laws

State parties nominate candidates for the Senate and House of Representatives in a direct primary or, at most, a primary and a runoff primary. In most states, the candidate receiving a plurality wins the nomination. Ten states, primarily in the South, require a candidate to win a majority vote to win the nomination, and if no candidate receives a majority, a **runoff primary** is held between the two with the most votes. Southern states adopted the runoff primary because of one-party Democratic dominance following Reconstruction. With no viable Republican party to nominate candidates, winning the Democratic nomination was tantamount to election.

Each state's election law spells out the particulars of how and when the primary is conducted. There are three types of primary elections used to nominate congressional candidates: closed primary, open primary, and nonpartisan primary.

runoff primary A second primary election held between the top two candidates if no candidate received a majority of the votes in the first primary.

A little more than half of the states nominate congressional candidates in closed primaries, and most other states have open primaries. In both cases, voters are limited to casting votes in only one party's primary. Both open and closed primaries produce the same outcome: separate nominees—one Democrat, one Republican, and one candidate from each minor party, if any—to run for each office in the general election.

An exception to this rule occurs in Louisiana, Washington State, and California— the **nonpartisan primary**. In this type of primary, all candidates regardless of party run in the same primary election. A candidate who gets a majority of the primary vote wins the office. If no candidate gains a majority, the top two vote-getters face off in the general election. This means that two Republicans or two Democrats can end up competing against each other in the runoff election. Strictly speaking, this primary is not wholly nonpartisan because candidates list a party affiliation on the primary ballot. It is called nonpartisan because of its structure: it "throws all comers into the pot" and presumably dilutes the importance of partisanship (Kuzenski 1997). Because candidates can list a party preference on the ballot, it might be more accurate to refer to this system as an "all-party election with a run-off."[9]

The Politics of Choosing Congressional Candidates

Generalizing about the politics of congressional nominations is difficult because of the unique and idiosyncratic forces that tend to be present in each nomination contest. Nonetheless, it is possible to identify some general patterns in congressional nominations. The first is the source of the candidates themselves. Senatorial candidates traditionally have been members of the House of Representatives or state governors. Political scientist David Canon (1990) has shown that from 1913, when the Seventeenth Amendment instituted direct election of senators, to 1987, 34 percent of senators were former House members, and 20 percent were former governors. In the 112th Congress (2011–2012), 49 of the 100 senators had served in the U.S. House, and 11 were former governors.

The candidate pool of the House of Representatives is less structured, reflecting the lower prestige of the House relative to the Senate. In general, however, service in the state legislature or in local offices is a stepping stone to Congress. In the 112th Congress, about 214 members had served in their state legislature or held some other elected state office (e.g., lieutenant governor, state treasurer); another 61 had held a local elected office (e.g., mayor, city council, county legislature). Since the 1930s, the proportion of House members with state legislative experience has increased (Canon 1990, 59). Although governors and House members consider the Senate a move up the political ladder, senators and governors generally express little interest in serving in the House.

---

[9] A few states still use conventions as part of the nomination process, although the ability of the party organization to override the party in the electorate is limited in these cases.

nonpartisan primary A type of election used in Louisiana in which candidates from all political parties run in the same primary, and the candidate who receives the majority of the vote obtains the office.

Perhaps the most important generalization about congressional nominations is that incumbents seldom lose. Figure 10.5 shows the number of incumbent representatives and senators defeated in primaries. In elections since the 1950s, an average of between six and seven House incumbents have lost their bid for renomination, about 1.5 percent of those running. As discussed in the next section, Senate races are more competitive than those for the House in the general election, but recent senatorial primaries have been no more competitive than those for the House. Senate incumbents rarely lose in the primary—only eight incumbent senators have been defeated in primaries in the last 30 years.

Unless there are indications that an incumbent is vulnerable, experienced candidates of the other party do not battle vigorously for the honor of going down to defeat in the general election. Previous campaign experience, close relationships with voters, greater knowledge of issues, and superior financial resources give the veteran legislator enormous advantages over his or her opponents. Although surmounting these obstacles in a primary race is not impossible, it is rare enough to constitute the exception that underlines the rule.

Vigorous primary competition does occasionally occur. If the incumbent is perceived to be vulnerable or is not seeking reelection, competitive candidates are likely to jump into the nomination fray. Scandal, a weak showing in the previous election, or a voting record out of tune with the partisan base in the state or district can make an incumbent vulnerable. In 2006, for example, Connecticut

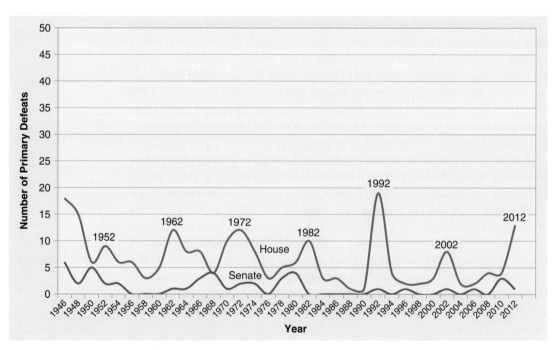

FIGURE 10.5 **Incumbents Defeated in Primaries**
Source: Stanley and Niemi (2011, 43–44) for 1946–2010; the public record for 2012.

CHAPTER 10 ELECTIONS

senator Joe Lieberman's support for the war in Iraq angered the Democratic Party base, and he lost in the primary to an antiwar candidate. Lieberman managed to win reelection as an Independent-Democrat. Senator Arlen Specter of Pennsylvania faced a similar dilemma in 2010. He had been elected five times as a Republican. But Specter's relatively liberal voting record was a recurring irritant to many Republicans, and polls showed that he would likely lose to a conservative candidate in the Republican primary. So he switched parties and ran in the Democratic primary. He lost that one to a more liberal Democrat. Senator Lisa Murkowski of Alaska lost her bid for the Republican nomination to a Tea Party–backed candidate, but she was reelected in the general election as a write-in candidate. In 2012, moderate Republican senator Richard Lugar lost his primary to Tea Party–backed candidate Richard Mourdock. Mourdock's controversial views turned this safe Republican seat into a possible Democratic pickup. Other factors beyond the incumbent's control can create problems for an incumbent too. For example, House incumbents are more likely to suffer primary defeats in election years ending in two—1962, 1972, 1982, 1992, 2002, 2012—because these elections follow the decennial census, which triggers the reapportionment of House seats among states. The resulting redistricting contributes to more defeats because some incumbents must run in altered districts; in some cases, redistricting puts two incumbents in the same district.

ELECTING MEMBERS OF CONGRESS

Unlike presidential aspirants, congressional candidates do not face complex electoral college rules; they do not need a majority of votes to be elected, nor do they have to contend with contingency procedures in the event that they fail to receive a specified proportion of the vote. All they need to do is win a plurality of the popular vote. Senatorial aspirants and House candidates in states with only one representative have an easily defined constituency—the entire population of the state. However, House candidates in states with multiple congressional districts are affected by the way the geographical boundaries of their constituencies are determined.

Apportionment

The Constitution provides for members of the House of Representatives to be apportioned among the states according to population. To keep the allocation of House seats current with changes in state populations, the Constitution requires a national head count—a census—every 10 years. The census has taken place each decade since 1790.

The Constitution does not establish a permanent size for the House of Representatives, leaving the matter to Congress. Following the 1790 census, the membership of the House was set at 105. As both the population and the number of states grew, the size of the House gradually expanded until it reached 435 following the 1910 census. The size of the House was permanently fixed at 435 at that time (Jacobson 2009, 7).[10]

Apportioning seats in a legislature with a fixed size means that after each census, each state gains, loses, or retains seats depending on how its population changed in relation to the national average. The process of adjusting the number of House seats among the states to reflect population shifts is called **reapportionment**. Over the last several decades, population has been shifting away from the Northeast and Midwest to the South and West. From 1942 to 2012, New York and Pennsylvania lost 18 and 15 House seats, respectively, whereas California gained 30 seats and Florida gained 21.

Congressional Districts

For congressional candidates, perhaps a more salient issue is not how many House seats a state gets, but how congressional constituencies are defined within a state. For the first half-century of the nation's existence, each state was free to determine how congressional seats were apportioned internally. Many states elected their representatives at large, which means that all were elected statewide. This arrangement, in which more than one member is elected from the same constituency, is the **multimember district** election system. Another way to choose representatives is the **single-member district** system, in which the state is carved up into the number of districts equal to the number of representatives the state has in the House, and voters in each district choose one representative.

Since 1842, federal law has required representatives to be elected from single-member districts. After each reapportionment, state legislatures must redraw congressional district lines to accommodate changes in the number of seats and to reflect population shifts within the state. The process of redrawing the district lines within a state is called **redistricting**. State legislatures have the responsibility of redistricting.

The partisan stakes are high in redistricting, and they often result in **gerrymandering**, which means the drawing of district boundaries to benefit one interest and hinder another. The term was coined in honor of Elbridge Gerry, a Massachusetts governor who supposedly designed a district in 1812 shaped like a salamander in order to gain a partisan advantage (Figure 10.6). Gerrymanders can benefit several kinds of political interests:

reapportionment The process of adjusting the number of House seats among the states based on population shifts.

multimember district A method of selecting representatives in which more than one person is chosen to represent a single constituency.

single-member district A method of selecting representatives in which the people in a district select a single representative.

redistricting The process of redrawing congressional district lines after reapportionment.

gerrymandering The drawing of district lines in such a way as to help or hinder the electoral prospects of a specific political interest.

[10] When Alaska and Hawaii were admitted into the Union in the 1950s, one seat for each of the new states was temporarily added to the House. After the 1960 census, the membership was again reduced to 435.

CHAPTER 10 ELECTIONS

1. Partisan gerrymanders benefit the majority party.
2. Incumbent gerrymanders benefit current officeholders regardless of party.
3. Racial gerrymanders benefit citizens of a particular race or deny representation to a particular race.

Gerrymandering is accomplished through a process of "packing and cracking." In packing, voters who support the disadvantaged interest are concentrated in as few legislative districts as possible, which means that minority candidates are likely to win those districts by overwhelming margins, but the number of seats they win is smaller than their share of the population. In cracking, such voters are spread out over many districts so that minority candidates are unlikely to win at all because their supporters are spread too thinly to muster a plurality in any district.

As a result of population shifts from rural areas to cities from the 1930s to the 1970s, the distribution of seats in the legislature did not fairly reflect the distribution of the population, and many state legislatures came to be **malapportioned** (badly apportioned). Disparities in the populations of legislative districts became particularly pronounced in states whose constitutions granted towns and counties representation in the state legislature, frequently without regard to their size. In 1960, for example, the most populous district of the California State Senate had 422 times more people than the smallest one. The ratio between the largest and smallest congressional districts in Texas was four to one. Yet neither state legislatures nor successive Congresses were disposed to change the situation. It was asking a lot to expect representatives who came from malapportioned and gerrymandered districts to risk their political careers by changing the system.

Faced with the unwillingness of legislative bodies to remedy the situation, aggrieved parties turned to the courts for assistance. The basis for the court challenge was that the Constitution mandates reapportionment of congressional seats among the states after every census, and the Fourteenth Amendment's guarantee of equal protection of the law requires these new districts to be about equal in population. If legislative districts are not equal in size, then citizens are denied equal protection because every person's vote does not have equal weight—that is, malapportionment violates the core democratic value of political equality.

The federal courts initially refused to deal with unequally sized districts and gerrymandering, on the grounds that legislative apportionment was a political question that they did not have jurisdiction to decide; instead, the remedy of political questions lay with the state legislatures and Congress (*Colgrove v. Green* 1946). Then, in ***Baker v. Carr*** (1962), the Supreme Court overturned the political question doctrine, holding that legislative apportionment was a **justiciable issue** that the courts had jurisdiction to hear and decide.[11]

malapportioned A situation in which the distribution of legislative seats does not accurately reflect the distribution of the population.

Baker v. Carr The 1962 case in which the Supreme Court overturned the political question doctrine, holding that legislative apportionment was a justiciable issue that the courts had jurisdiction to hear and decide.

justiciable issue An issue or topic over which the courts have jurisdiction or the power to make decisions.

---

[11] It may seem strange that legislative apportionment was deemed a political question in 1946 but not in 1962. As discussed in chapter 15, the federal courts are political institutions that make public policy. The apportionment issue was political throughout the debate. In 1962, it was a political question the Court was willing to deal with; in 1946 it was not.

The ruling in *Baker* led to a number of landmark cases addressing the issue of political equality in legislative apportionment. In ***Wesberry v. Sanders*** (1964), the Supreme Court invalidated unequal congressional districts in Georgia. Citing language in the Constitution mandating that representatives be apportioned among the states according to population and that they be chosen by the people of the states, the Court ruled that "as nearly as practicable, one [person's] vote in a congressional election is to be worth as much as another's." The ruling is popularly known as the principle of **one person, one vote**. It means that all legislative districts must contain about equal numbers of people. The same year, in *Reynolds v. Sims* (1964), the Court extended the principle to state legislatures, holding that the equal protection of the laws clause of the Fourteenth Amendment requires state legislative districts to be substantially equal and seats in both houses of a bicameral state legislature to be apportioned on the basis of population.

These rulings, however, did not end gerrymandering. It is possible for a state legislature to distribute residents equally among districts but still benefit the majority party or an incumbent legislator. Perhaps the most controversial redistricting issue of recent years has been racial gerrymandering, in which district boundaries are drawn with the explicit goal of creating a majority block of ethnic minority voters within them. Following the 1990 census, a number of states in the South and Southwest drew up black-majority and Latino-majority districts, which are referred to as **majority-minority districts**. Both the U.S. Department of Justice and various civil rights groups supported such districts as a way to maximize the number of African American and Latino representatives in Congress.[12] Many of the resulting districts did not correspond to local political geography. Some divided towns and communities, and others sprawled across states in a bewildering pattern of spikes and curls that flicked out toward concentrations of minority populations and skirted predominantly white areas. For example, Louisiana's 4th Congressional District, shown in Figure 10.6, was designed to elect an African American to the House. The strange shape resulted from linking widely dispersed communities of African Americans into one district.

In subsequent lawsuits, federal courts began striking down these new districts. In the case of *Shaw v. Reno* (1993), the Supreme Court held that race may not be the sole criterion used in drawing congressional districts.

How best to represent the interests of minorities remains the subject of fierce debate. One side argues that ethnic minorities ought to be represented by members of their own ethnic groups. This view suggests that districts should be drawn to maximize the number of minority representatives elected, to achieve **descriptive representation**, in which the racial makeup of Congress reflects the racial makeup of the nation. In other words, if 12 percent of the population is African American, 12 percent of the representatives in Congress should be African American.

Wesberry v. Sanders The 1964 case in which the Supreme Court invalidated unequal congressional districts, saying that all legislative districts must contain about equal numbers of people. The ruling is popularly known as the principle of one person, one vote.

one person, one vote The idea, arising out of the 1964 Supreme Court decision of *Wesberry v. Sanders*, that legislative districts must contain about the same number of people.

majority-minority districts Districts in which the majority of the population is composed of ethnic or racial minorities

descriptive representation The view of representation that calls for the racial and ethnic makeup of Congress to reflect that of the nation.

---

[12] Racial gerrymanders have not always been used to benefit minorities. During the period between Reconstruction and the 1970s, racial gerrymanders were often used to prevent the election of black representatives.

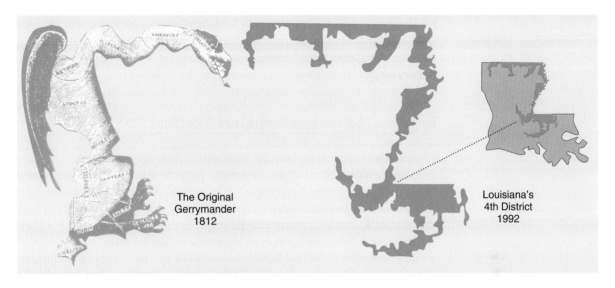

FIGURE 10.6 Gerrymandering, Then and Now

Source: Richard L. Engstrom and Jason Kirksey, "Race and Representational Districting in Louisiana," in *Race and Redistricting in the 1980s,* ed. Bernard Grofman (New York: Agathon Press, 1998).

The other side of the debate contends that a representative does not have to be African American, Latino, Asian, or female to represent those interests. Rather, **substantive representation** of the basic interests of various groups is more important than descriptive representation. Political scientist Carol Swain (1995) argues that increasing the representation of African American interests by creating additional majority-minority districts is ineffective and shortsighted because there are a limited number of places where such districts can be drawn.[13] And there is evidence that packing so many African American voters into majority-minority districts may actually decrease their influence in Congress. Research found that when large numbers of African American voters were removed from the districts of white representatives during redistricting, the voting records of the representatives indicated less support of minority interests (Overby and Cosgrove 1996). After redistricting removed African American voters from their districts, several moderate southern Democrats who had often supported minority interests were defeated in the 1992 and 1994 elections by conservative Republicans who were less supportive (Hill 1995).

Some recent research presents evidence that descriptive representation does benefit minority interests. Electing more African American representatives to partisan legislatures increases African American influence in those bodies and leads to greater policy responsiveness to minority interests. But the relationship depends on the degree of racial polarization. An increase in descriptive

---

[13] In order to draw enough single-member districts to elect a Congress that will descriptively reflect the population, the various groups must be concentrated enough to combine into a district. In some states, African American and Latino populations are sufficiently concentrated to draw such districts. However, drawing a district that is majority female, for example, is not possible—even though women are a majority of the population.

substantive representation The concept of representation that states that officeholders do not have to be minorities to accurately represent minority interests.

representation does not result in policies that are responsive to minority interests if the context is racially polarized, as it is in the South. In less racialized contexts, however, descriptive representation leads to more influence and policies that are responsive to African American interests (Preuhs 2006).

Incumbency Advantage in Congressional Elections

Congressional campaigns resemble presidential campaigns in several ways. Congressional candidates make the same basic political appeals involving personal image, party label, pleas for group support, general positions on issues, and the development of campaign themes. Presidential and congressional candidates have the same basic strategic options and the same basic objectives—to acquire and allocate scarce political resources in an attempt to maximize votes.

There are also important differences between the two types of campaigns. Perhaps the most basic and distinguishing feature of congressional elections is the great **incumbency advantage**. Presidential incumbents do not have a great electoral advantage. Of the eight incumbent presidents who have run for reelection since 1972, only five (62 percent) have been successful. But as Figure 10.7 shows, congressional incumbents are overwhelmingly successful when they run for reelection. Since 1972, for example, an average of 94 percent of House incumbents and 83 percent of Senate incumbents have been reelected. Why are congressional incumbents so successful when they run for reelection? Why are House incumbents more successful than Senate incumbents? The reasons include the nature of congressional districts, resources, and relations with constituents, among others.

DISTRICTS, CHALLENGERS, AND RESOURCES The political makeup of a district sets the general limits of competition. Some districts are overwhelmingly Democratic or Republican, and others are more evenly balanced. Many House candidates run in districts drawn to have a distinct tilt toward one party, whereas candidates for the Senate and the presidency must compete for the votes of a more diverse and competitive statewide or nationwide constituency.

Within the limits set by the nature of the district, several factors determine how competitive a congressional election is likely to be. Most important is the quality of the challenger. Most House incumbents coast to easy, lopsided reelection victories because they run against challengers with no political experience who have little campaign money. Although having large sums of money does not guarantee victory, without adequate funding there is little chance of success. How much money does it take to run a competitive campaign? Political scientist Gary Jacobson estimates that "the minimum price tag for a competitive House campaign under average conditions today is probably [close] to $800,000" (2013, 54). Senate races are typically more expensive, as much as 10 times more expensive in some states. Whereas incumbents are able to raise and spend as much as they need, few challengers can raise enough money to be competitive.

incumbency advantage The tendency for congressional incumbents to be overwhelmingly successful when they run for reelection due to the nature of congressional districts, resources, and relations with constituents, among other reasons.

© Mark Wilson/Getty Images

How to represent the interest of minorities in Congress remains the subject of debate. One side argues that ethnic minorities should be represented by members of their own ethnic group. The other side of the debate argues that a representative does not have to share racial, ethnic, gender, or other characteristics to represent those interests. Democratic Rep. David Wu (right) represents Oregon's first district, which is only about 5 percent Asian.

The few challengers who can raise lots of money pose a serious threat to incumbents. But incumbents spend in response to the magnitude of the threat. Paradoxically, incumbents who spend the most money are the most likely to be defeated. This is because the challengers who are best able to raise campaign money target vulnerable incumbents, who respond by spending huge amounts of money in losing campaigns. In 2010, for example, winning incumbents spent an average of $1,164,689 against uncompetitive challengers who spent about $171,000. But losing incumbents spent an average of $2.5 million against well-funded challengers who spent an average of $1.7 million (Ornstein, Mann, and Malbin 2008, updated at Campaign Finance Institute, http://www.cfinst.org/data/pdf/VitalStats_t3.pdf). As Jacobson observes, "for incumbents, spending a great deal of money on the campaign is a sign of weakness rather than strength" (2013, 54). Humorist Will Rogers showed considerable foresight in 1931 when he quipped, "Politics has got so expensive that it takes lots of money to even get beat with nowadays" (quoted in Sterling 1979, 61).

PERFORMANCE, PERKS, AND PORK-BARREL What a representative does or fails to do over the course of the term can damage or improve his or her chances of reelection.

ELECTING MEMBERS OF CONGRESS 385

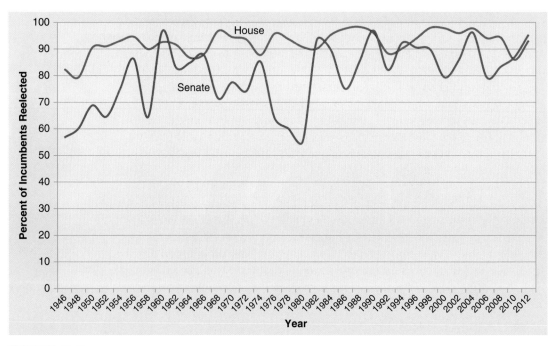

FIGURE 10.7 **Incumbency Advantage in House and Senate Elections**
Source: Stanley and Niemi (2011, 43–44) for 1946–2010; the public record for 2012.

Although they try to avoid it, a few incumbents are tarnished with scandal and suffer at the polls (J. Peters and Welch 1980; Welch and Hibbing 1997).

More typically, incumbents engage in activities intended to please their constituents and discourage vigorous challenges. Members work to bring pork-barrel benefits to their districts, and they use the perquisites of office to appeal to constituents. **Pork-barrel benefits** are government-sponsored projects that bring economic benefits to a member's state or district. This is a pejorative term first used in the mid-nineteenth century to describe projects viewed as a waste of tax dollars that serve no purpose other than to aid the reelection of a single incumbent. Examples include public works projects such as dams, roads, and government buildings; grants to local government or a university; and defense contracts.

Perquisites, or **perks**, are benefits and support services that members need in order to do their jobs. These include an allowance to pay staff members to answer constituents' letters and help with their problems, the franking privilege that allows members to use their signatures instead of buying stamps to send mail to constituents, and a travel allowance so that representatives can make frequent trips home to stay in touch with constituents. (Pork-barrel benefits, perks, and the franking privilege are also discussed in chapter 12.)

Perks are not supposed to be used in a campaign, and there are legal regulations designed to prevent incumbents from using congressional staff or the frank for campaign activities. Nonetheless, critics suspect that pork-barrel projects and the use of perks provide incumbents with considerable electoral benefits. Political sci-

pork-barrel benefits Government-sponsored projects that bring economic benefits to a Congress member's state or district. This is a pejorative term first used in the mid-nineteenth century to describe projects viewed as a waste of tax dollars that serve no purpose other than to aid the reelection of a single incumbent.

perquisites (perks) The benefits and support activities that members of Congress receive in order to help them perform their job.

entist David Mayhew suggests that members of Congress use their offices to make three basic kinds of appeals to constituents. The first is **advertising**, defined as "any effort to disseminate one's name among constituents . . . to create a favorable image" (Mayhew 1974, 49). Advertising activities include sending out newsletters, making frequent visits to constituents, addressing high school commencements, and sending out infant-care booklets. The second is **credit claiming**, an effort to generate the belief that the representative is responsible for government actions that constituents find desirable, such as pork-barrel projects that benefit the district. The third is **position taking**, making public statements on issues that are pleasing to constituents.

These three activities are nonpartisan and are likely to win friends without making enemies. When a member of Congress votes on a controversial piece of legislation, the vote might make as many enemies as friends. But when a member helps a veteran who is having a problem with the Department of Veterans Affairs, it generates goodwill and contributes to the member's reputation as a good representative. Political scientists who have studied the electoral payoff of pork-barrel projects and the use of perquisites, however, have been unable to show that these activities make vulnerable members safe (Bickers and Stein 1996; Cain, Ferejohn, and Fiorina 1987; Feldman and Jondrow 1984).

COMPETITIVE HOUSE RACES The key to electoral competition is having two politically savvy candidates with adequate resources to run vigorous campaigns. If the first law of electoral politics is "you can't beat somebody with nobody," the corollary is "you're not likely to beat somebody with somebody nobody's ever heard of." As we have seen, incumbents are professional politicians who are well known in their districts and can raise the money necessary to mount a vigorous campaign. Incumbency advantage in House elections does not result from the absence of challengers, but rather from the absence of challengers that voters have heard of. The candidates who wage the most vigorous challenges are those who have experiences and attributes that make them known in the district and have enough campaign money to make voters aware of their campaign. Explaining why experienced and well-funded challengers emerge in some districts but not in others, therefore, is crucial to understanding the low level of competition in congressional elections.

Political scientists generally turn to rational choice theory in the study of elections. Gary Jacobson and Samuel Kernell (1981) proposed the "strategic politician theory" to explain variation in the emergence of experienced, well-funded challengers in congressional elections. National political conditions, such as the health of the economy and the president's popularity, influence elections. But national conditions do not directly affect voters' decisions on election day. Instead, the strategic politician theory suggests that voters' decisions are determined mainly by the alternatives available to them. Do voters have a choice between two attractive candidates who run vigorous campaigns appealing for their votes, or do voters have to choose between a candidate they know (the incumbent) and one they have never heard of? The alternatives available to voters are the results of decisions

advertising The activities of members of Congress (such as sending out newsletters or visiting the district) designed to familiarize the constituency with the member.

credit claiming The efforts by members of Congress to get their constituents to believe they are responsible for positive government actions.

position taking Public statements made by members of Congress on issues of importance to the constituency.

made by political elites months before election day. Experienced politicians won't risk promising political careers in hopeless races for Congress, and campaign contributors won't waste money on a lost cause. Thus, these political elites act strategically and run for Congress when the chances of success look favorable. National conditions affect elites' assessment of the odds of success. If the president is popular and the economy is booming, the president's party will field more experienced, well-funded candidates; if national conditions are unfavorable to the president, the opposition party will field more. Because voters "favor attractive candidates who run well-financed campaigns," the party that fields more of these candidates nationally will win more seats held by the other party and lose fewer of its own (Jacobson and Kernell 1981, 2–3). There is strong empirical support for this thesis (Jacobson and Kernell 1981; Jacobson 1989).

But there is also variation across congressional districts—that is, the party advantaged by favorable national conditions does not recruit high-quality candidates in all districts, and the disadvantaged party can still manage to recruit some high-quality candidates in spite of unfavorable national conditions. Bond, Covington, and Fleisher (1985) find that local political conditions and the incumbent's behavior influence how experienced, well-funded challengers assess the odds of success. An incumbent may be vulnerable because the congressional district has been greatly altered by redistricting, because he or she has lost touch with the district, or because his or her party affiliation or voting record does not match the preferences of most constituents. In such cases, a candidate with political experience and access to campaign money is likely to challenge the incumbent.

Some representatives retire or die in each election cycle. Contests for **open seats** in which no incumbent is running are much more competitive. Both parties are likely to field experienced candidates with adequate campaign money. In open-seat House races in 2010, for example, Democratic candidates raised an average of $1.01 million, and Republican candidates raised an average of $1.37 million (Ornstein, Mann, and Malbin 2008, updated at Campaign Finance Institute, 2010a.).

INCUMBENCY IN SENATE ELECTIONS Although incumbency is an advantage in Senate elections, it is a smaller advantage than it is in House races. Unlike House districts, the boundaries of Senate constituencies (an entire state) cannot be manipulated to benefit a particular party or candidate. States also have a ready pool of ambitious, experienced House members, governors, and other statewide officeholders who want to be senators. These experienced politicians make formidable opponents because they have experience representing the same constituents as the incumbent senator and access to a campaign organization and campaign funds.

Other factors also contribute to greater vulnerability for senators. Because states tend to be larger and more diverse than House districts, senators have a harder time developing the close personal bonds with their constituents that are common in the smaller House districts. Senate campaigns receive more media attention, which means that Senate challengers are likely to get more publicity and visibility than House challengers. All these factors make Senate races more competitive than those of the House.

open seats Legislative seats for which there is no incumbent running for reelection.

© Bill Clark/CQ Roll Call

Incumbent Senators seldom lose their party primary. Senator Richard Lugar was a moderate Republican from Indiana. He lost the Republican primary in 2012 to Richard Mourdock, a Tea Party candidate who claimed that Lugar was not conservative enough for Indiana voters. Lugar was shoe-in for reelection if he had survived the Republican primary, but Democratic Rep. Joe Donnelly won the seat because Mourdock's brand of conservativism was too extreme for Indiana voters.

Financing Congressional Elections

Congressional candidates must raise all their funds from private sources. Although candidates for Congress are subject to the contribution limits and the ban on soft money established by the BCRA of 2002, incumbents continue to have a significant advantage over challengers. They can raise more money than challengers because people are generally not motivated to give money to probable losers. Congressional candidates—incumbents and challengers—can also benefit from independent expenditures by Super PACs. Although they cannot coordinate with the candidate's campaign, Super PACs can raise and spend unlimited amounts of money from corporations, labor unions, and wealthy individuals to support or oppose particular candidates.

Raising a considerable amount of money from a wide variety of donors, therefore, is a central task for anyone wishing to make a serious bid for a seat in Congress. Paul Herrnson (1995) observes that there are in effect two campaigns, a campaign for money and then the campaign for votes. Indeed, deciding whether a candidate is a serious contender or a "sacrificial lamb" often begins with an assessment of the campaign's bank balance. Often-quoted advice for those seeking congressional office is to "learn how to beg, and do it in a way that leaves you with some dignity" (Granat 1984).

The amount of money raised and spent on congressional campaigns is nothing short of staggering—about 870 candidates for the House and Senate spent over $1.5 billion in primary and general elections in the 2010 election cycle. Super PACs and other non-connected groups spent an additional $564 million, bringing total spending in the 2010 elections to more than $2 billion. Where does this money come from? Well, almost half of it comes from the business sector (see Figure 10.8). In 2010, business interests contributed about 49.4 percent of the money given to federal candidates. Contributions from organized labor, in contrast, accounted for only about 5.5 percent. (Recall from the discussion of interest groups in chapter 6 that most registered lobbyists in Washington, DC, are from business and trade associations, whereas labor unions account for only a small percentage of them.) Ideological groups provided the second-largest share of campaign money for House and Senate races in 2010—about 14.3 percent of the total.

The relative contributions of the different sectors have changed significantly over the past decade. Ideological groups' share of spending on congressional campaigns, for example, has increased enormously. This sector's contributions increased from only 8.1 percent of the total in 2000 to 14.3 percent in 2010—a relative increase of over 76 percent. In contrast, the share of contributions from business and labor declined over this period. Business contributed 60.1 percent of contributions in 2000, and labor contributed 6.1—relative decreases of 18 percent and 10 percent, respectively, over the decade.

Congressional campaigns are funded by contributions from individuals, PACs, parties, and the candidates themselves. Most of the money—more than half of

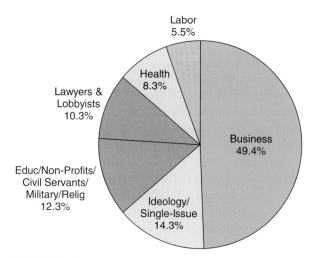

FIGURE 10.8 Congressional Campaign Contributions by Sector, 2009–2010 Election Cycle

Source: Constructed by the authors from data at Center for Responsive Politics (2010)

the contributions to House candidates and more than 60 percent of the contributions to Senate candidates—is donated by individuals (see Figure 10.9). Another important source of campaign money is PACs. In the 2009-2010 election cycle, PACs accounted for about one-third of contributions to House candidates but only 13 percent of those to Senate candidates. House members rely on PAC contributions more than senators because with a two-year term House members must campaign—for money and votes—all the time. But PACs are an important source of funding for both House and Senate candidates, and it is not difficult to understand why. The number of PACs and the amount of money available to them have grown considerably in the past 25 years. The remaining portion of campaign money comes from party committees and the candidates themselves. In recent elections, Super PACs and other outside groups that make independent expenditures have been much more prominent.

A variety of groups utilize PACs to channel their contributions to congressional candidates. Initially, labor was the major user of PACs, and in elections from 2004 to 2008 an average of 98 percent of labor contributions went through PACs (opensecrets.org). In the 2009–2010 election cycle, labor, ideological, and single-issue groups channeled the most—about 70 percent—through PACs (see Table 10.10). Business contributions tend to be from individuals—about two-thirds in 2009–2010. Contributions from lawyers, lobbyists, and the education and non-profit sectors were almost exclusively from individuals. Generally speaking, labor PACs tend to favor Democratic candidates—in the 2010 election, about two-thirds of labor PAC money went to Democrats. Contributions from business are more evenly split between Republicans and Democrats (50 to 44 percent), but there is considerable variation across different types of business. More than 60 percent

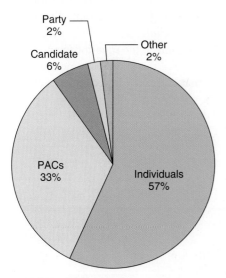

FIGURE 10.9A Source of Campaign Funding for House Candidates, 2009–2010 Election Cycle

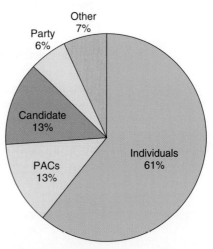

FIGURE 10.9B Source of Campaign Funding for Senate Candidates, 2009–2010 Election Cycle

Source: Constructed by the authors from data at Campaign Finance Institute (2010a); Ornstein, Mann, and Malbin (2008).

TABLE 10.10: PERCENT OF CAMPAIGN CONTRIBUTIONS FROM INDIVIDUALS AND PACS 2009–2010 ELECTION CYCLE

Sector	% from Individuals	% from PACs
Ideology/Single-Issue	19%	72%
Labor	1%	71%
Health	54%	42%
Business total	65%	29%
Lawyers & Lobbyists	89%	10%
Educ., Non-Profits, Civil Servants, Military, Relig.	97%	1%

Note: Percentages may not add up to 100% as money can be given to third party candidates or outside spending groups and PACs.

Source: Constructed by the authors from data at Center for Responsive Politics (n.d.).

of contributions from communications and electronics business (computers, TV/movies/music, telecommunications, and publishing) went to Democrats, and almost 60 percent of contributions from energy and natural resources (oil and gas and mining), agribusiness, and transportation went to Republicans (opensecrets.org). But the clearest bias of PACs is toward incumbents: 82 percent of labor PAC money and 83 percent of business PAC money went to incumbents in the 2010 congressional elections. The only type of PAC that did not show an overwhelming incumbent bias was non-connected PACs—that is, ideological and single-issue groups (Campaign Finance Institute 2010b).

Thus, the rules of the game, campaign strategies, and available resources shape the outcome of both presidential and congressional campaigns. Winners of these contests tend to congratulate themselves for having conducted effective campaigns and praise the voters for having made wise choices. Losers are more likely to blame defeat on circumstances beyond their control: the superior financial resources of the opponent, the formidable obstacle of the opponent's incumbency, their minority party status, or other factors that even their best campaign efforts could not overcome.

Top Ten Takeaway Points

1 Elections to choose representatives in the United States consist of two steps: (1) nomination of candidates by political parties and (2) the general election where voters choose among the nominees selected by the parties.

2 Presidential candidates are nominated in national party conventions, a meeting of delegates from all the states. Delegates to the national party conventions are chosen by rank-and-file party members in caucuses/conventions held in the state or in state presidential primaries. Most convention delegates are selected through primary elections.

3 Presidential nomination contests generally progress through four stages—(1) the invisible primary, (2) the initial contests (Iowa caucuses and New Hampshire primary), (3) mist clearing, and (4) the national party convention.

4 The president is not elected by direct popular vote. Instead, the president is chosen by the electoral college, which consists of electors chosen from the 50 states and the District of Columbia. A state gets one electoral vote for each senator and House member, and the District of Columbia has three electoral votes. The total number of electoral votes is 538 (100 senators, 435 House members, 3 votes for the District of Columbia). To be elected, a candidate must win a majority of electoral votes—that is, at least 270.

5 The electoral college has long been criticized because it violates the democratic principles of political equality and sometimes majority rule. Proposals to reform the electoral college include the proportional plan, the district plan, and direct popular election. Only direct election achieves political equality and guarantees majority rule.

6 Candidates for Congress are nominated by political parties in direct primaries in which rank-and-file voters choose the party nominees who will run in the general election. To be elected to Congress, a candidate must win a plurality of the popular vote in the congressional district or state.

⑦ Representation in the House is reapportioned among the states every ten years following the national census to reflect changes in states' population—that is, states that grow in population gain seats, and states that decline in population lose seats.

⑧ Redistricting is the process of redrawing the boundaries of congressional districts after seats have been reapportioned to the states. State legislatures are responsible for redistricting. The process is a political undertaking that often results in gerrymandered districts with boundaries drawn to benefit a particular interest.

⑨ The distinguishing feature of congressional elections is the incumbency advantage—in elections since 1972, averages of 94 percent of House incumbents and 82 percent of Senate incumbents who have run for reelection have been successful.

⑩ The primary reason incumbents have an advantage is that they typically run against unknown, politically inexperienced challengers who lack adequate funding to run a competitive campaign. Incumbents are generally able to raise more money than are challengers, but spending the most money does not guarantee victory. Incumbents who spend the most money are the ones most likely to lose, given that experienced challengers who can raise lots of money target incumbents who appear vulnerable.

Key Terms and Cases

advertising, 387
Baker v. Carr, 381
caucus method, 339
caucuses,
closed primaries, 336
credit claiming, 387
descriptive representation, 382
direct popular election plan, 370
district plan, 369
election, 334
electoral college, 363
frontloading, 339
general election, 334
gerrymandering, 380

incumbency advantage, 384
invisible primary, 345
justiciable issue, 381
legislative caucus, 335
magic number, 343
majority-minority districts, 382
malapportioned, 381
multimember district, 380
national party convention, 336
nomination, 334
nonpartisan primary, 377
one person, one vote, 382
open primaries, 337
open seats, 388

perquisites (perks), 386
pork-barrel benefits, 386
position taking, 387
proportional plan, 369
reapportionment, 380
redistricting, 380
runoff primary, 376
single-member district, 380
state presidential primary, 339
substantive representation, 383
Super Tuesday, 354
swing states, 372
unit rule, 359
Wesberry v. Sanders, 382

POLITICAL PARTICIPATION AND VOTING BEHAVIOR

KEY QUESTIONS

Why is voter turnout lower in the United States than in other Western democracies?

Why do some people participate in politics whereas others do not?

What best explains why people vote the way they do?

IN MARCH 2012, PAUL CARROLL, an 86-year-old World War II veteran went to cast a ballot in a primary election. Nothing unusual about that—he'd been doing this sort of thing for nearly 40 years in Auora, Ohio, where he lived and had run a local business before retiring. This time was different, though. He was not allowed to vote. From Carroll's perspective, nothing had changed since the last time he cast a ballot—not his residence, his voter registration, or his commitment to participating in the democratic process. What had changed, though, was the law. Ohio is one of a number of states that have recently enacted laws requiring citizens to present a valid photo ID before being allowed to vote. Carroll had a driver's license, but it was expired. He had an official ID issued by the Department of Veterans Affairs, but that was not on the list of acceptable documentation. Rather than being allowed to vote, he was offered a provisional ballot—basically a ballot that counts only upon further verification of a voter's eligibility. The print on that ballot was so small that Carroll could not read it. Besides, by then he was pretty irritated that a law-abiding, upstanding community member with a record of honorable military service was getting such a hassle at the polling place. He did not vote (Scott 2012).

Carroll was not the only one having difficulty casting a ballot. By one estimate, new state laws such as Ohio's photo ID requirement meant roughly five million Americans would find it harder to vote in 2012 than they had in 2010 (Weiser and Norden 2011). For many, this raises red flags. A representative democracy is premised on the notion that elections connect citizens to government. That connection is broken if guys such as Paul Carroll, or pretty much anyone else, find that the law makes it too hard for them to vote. Even if citizens only perceive that this connection is broken—that for whatever reason citizens have no meaningful input into government—then the democratic legitimacy of government is undermined.

The bottom line is that in a democracy citizens need reasonable guarantees that their opportunity to contribute to decisions on "who gets what" is real and significant. If citizens are denied such opportunities, as in Paul Carroll's case, clearly their influence over decisions on who gets what is diminished. If casting a ballot is such a hassle that you simply can't be bothered, then obviously your vote does not count for anything.

In this chapter, we examine not just voting but also political participation in general and its crucial importance to democratic governance. What are the different forms of participation? Why do some people participate and others not? Why is voting the most common form of participation? Are there systematic patterns in who shows up to the polls and the choices they make? What explains how voters choose between candidates? The answers to these questions actually go a lot further in explaining the functioning of the political system and the legitimacy of government than the teething problems of new voting technology. Understanding what the people are doing and why is a prerequisite for judging whether elections—and the other forms of participation—are connecting the will of the people to the government.

THE CONCEPT OF POLITICAL PARTICIPATION

Political participation is the process of turning opinion into an action to influence "who gets what." In a representative democracy, political participation is a primary means of connecting the will of the people to the actions of government. If this connection is successfully made, participation helps uphold the core democratic principles of political freedom and majority rule. A hallmark of a democratic political system is that it counts heads rather than breaking them. If the will of the people is going to provide the fundamental basis for government action, then the people must participate in the political process.

Forms of Political Participation

political participation The translation of personal preference into a voluntary action designed to influence public policy.

Voting in elections is the most obvious way that citizens in representative democracies have to influence government. But political participation is not limited to voting. There are lots of ways to participate in politics. Political scientist Sidney

© T.J. Kirkpatrick/Bloomberg via Getty Images

If the will of the people is going to provide the bases for government action, then people must participate in the political process. One of the main forms of political participation is to campaign for a political candidate. Here a volunteer for Barack Obama's 2012 presidential campaign seeks support for the president's reelection.

Verba and colleagues (Verba and Nie 1987; Verba, Schlozman, and Brady 1995) have indentified four general categories:

- Voting, the most widespread and regularized form of participation
- Campaign activities, such as working for or contributing money to a party or a candidate and trying to persuade others to support a party or candidate
- Citizen-initiated contacts with government officials in which a person acts on a matter of individual concern (e.g., sending an e-mail or speaking to your representative at a public forum)
- Activities in which citizens act cooperatively to deal with social and political problems, including working with like-minded people in interest groups

The Theoretical Basis of Political Participation

Verba argues that participating in these various activities is, more or less, rational: as the costs of participation increase, rates of participation decrease. "Cost" here does not necessarily mean monetary cost (though that might be part of it). Rather, the term *cost* is used more broadly to indicate how easy or difficult it is to participate.

For example, the costs of voting are relatively minor, and this tends to be the most popular form of political participation. Other activities—such as writing letters to public officials, getting involved in civic organizations and interest groups, attending rallies, making monetary contributions, and running for office—require greater levels of time and effort; fewer people engage in these more costly forms of participation. Figure 11.1 shows that Americans' rates of participation in a variety of forms of participation decrease more or less directly with the costs involved. We see that more than 60 percent of citizens voted in recent presidential elections. In contrast, about 30 percent report contacting a government official, only 8 percent report volunteering to work in a political campaign, and only 4 percent report attending a protest. There's little cost associated with voting—basically registering and perhaps standing in line a few minutes at your polling place. Although it doesn't take much effort to fire off an e-mail to a city bureaucrat to complain about the noise a road crew is making, the costs are somewhat higher than voting—you do need to track down the appropriate official to contact, and you need to explain in writing what the problem is, similar to taking an essay exam versus a multiple choice test in the voting booth. Volunteering for a candidate, however, can mean engaging in what amounts to a part-time job for no pay. And attending a protest involves a considerable commitment to an issue—and perhaps some risk to your safety or freedom.

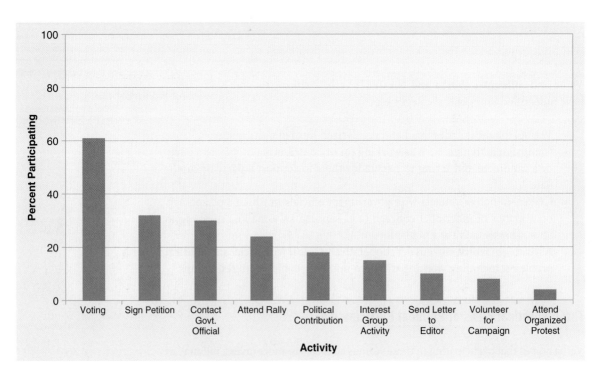

FIGURE 11.1 **Different Forms of Political Participation**

Source: Adapted from Aaron Smith, Kay Lehman Schlozman, Sidney Verba, and Henry Brady, *The Internet and Civic Engagement* (Washington, DC: Pew Internet & American Life Project, 2009), 16.

Is Political Participation in America High or Low?

Are the participation rates reflected in Figure 11.1 high or low? Answering this question requires a benchmark against which to measure the rates. In terms of one obvious benchmark—majority rule—these numbers appear low, with voting in presidential elections being the only activity that attracts more than half of eligible citizens. In a large country such as the United States, though, even a small percentage translates into millions of people incurring costs to participate in politics (Verba, Schlozman, and Brady 1995, 52).

Change over time is another useful benchmark to evaluate participation. There are mixed signs here. It is generally accepted that voting participation has declined over time. (We analyze this issue in more depth a little later in the chapter.) Other forms of participation, on the other hand, seem to have fluctuated or in some cases have even increased. For example, in the late 1960s about 13 percent of Americans reported contributing money to a political campaign, a figure that increased to 23 percent by the late 1980s, but seemed to have dipped to just below 20 percent in 2008. Less than 20 percent of Americans reported attending a political meeting or rally in the late 1960s and 1980s, but 24 percent reported attending similar meetings in 2008 (Verba, Schlozman, and Brady 1995; A. Smith et al. 2009).

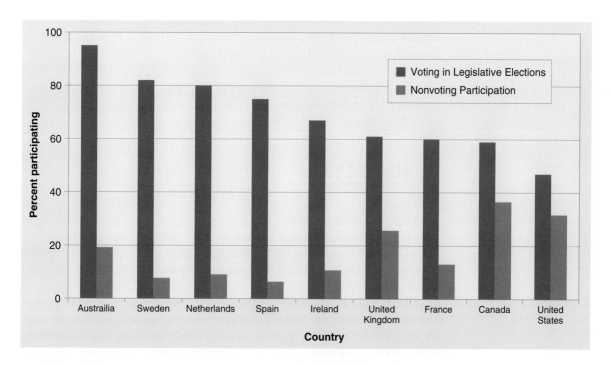

FIGURE 11.2 Political Participation Rates in Selected Representative Democracies

Source: Constructed by the authors with data from the Institute for Democracy and Electoral Assistance, http://www.idea.int/vt/ (voter turnout data); and Wattenberg (2007), Table 1-8, "Nonvoting Political Participation in Established Democracies" (data on other forms of political participation).

A third useful benchmark is comparison of Americans with citizens in other democracies. Figure 11.2 presents such a comparison. This figure shows voter turnout in legislative elections (2005 to 2009) in nine industrialized democracies. The chart clearly shows that voting participation in the United States is generally much lower than in other representative democracies. Lower voter turnout, however, does not necessarily mean that Americans are lazy compared to citizens in other democracies. Although Americans may vote less, participation in activities other than voting (contributing money to political organizations, showing support for a party or candidate, and trying to persuade others) is higher than in most other democracies.

Why do Americans vote less but participate more in these higher-cost forms of political activity than citizens in other democracies? A likely answer is that the costs of various forms of political participation vary considerably from country to country. In the United States there are more barriers to voting than in other countries (for example, generally speaking, it is harder to register to vote in America than in other countries). This means Americans face higher costs to engage in this particular form of political participation. On the other hand, the costs associated with forms of participation such as contacting government officials and participating in community organizations are no higher, and in some cases considerably lower, in the United States than in comparable democracies.

Still, of all the basic forms of political participation, voting has the most visible connection to the core principles of democracy, and it is worth examining in some depth. Participating in elections allows people to participate in decision making about who gets what and allows for direct expression of the will of the people. Exploring who has the right to participate in elections—in other words, the right to vote—provides an excellent starting point for judging the degree of political freedom within a democratic society.

THE RIGHT TO VOTE

The right to vote is known as the **franchise**. Most democracies have a mixed history when it comes to voting rights. In the United States, the franchise was initially very limited, with only white adult male property owners getting the legal right to cast a ballot.

The first major expansion of the franchise was the elimination of property qualifications. In limited form, property qualifications were retained right into the modern era; it was not until *Phoenix v. Kolodziejski* (1970) that the Supreme Court finally eliminated property qualifications by ruling that state laws limiting voting on bond issues to property owners were unconstitutional. Still, for the most part, property qualifications had disappeared by the middle of the nineteenth century, allowing most white male citizens to vote. African Americans, women, Native Americans, and young adults, however, were systematically denied the franchise for far longer.

franchise The constitutional or statutory right to vote.

The battle to enfranchise African Americans began in earnest immediately following the Civil War. The Fifteenth Amendment technically granted African Americans the right to vote, although this right was stripped from many by state laws mandating poll taxes or literacy tests. It was not until the Voting Rights Act of 1965 that the franchise was fully and securely extended to African Americans.

Leaders of the early women's movement had hoped that the initial drive to gain African Americans the franchise would also benefit women. This was not the case, however, and women had to put up with widespread opposition to their political participation. In the late nineteenth and early twentieth centuries, business groups—such as textile manufacturers and brewers and distillers—opposed giving women the right to vote because they feared women would use their newfound political power to harm business interests. The Nineteenth Amendment, ratified in 1920, finally gave women universal voting rights by prohibiting federal and state governments from denying anyone voting rights on the basis of gender. And recall from chapter 5 that Native Americans did not gain universal voting rights until Congress passed the American Indian Citizenship Act in 1924—more than 50 years after the Fifteenth Amendment (1870) formally enfranchised African American men and 4 years after the Nineteenth Amendment (1920) enfranchised women.

Young adults won the right to vote in the 1970s. The Constitution gives states the authority to set voting age requirements, and most states prior to the 1970s had set this age requirement at 21. Many young adults considered this to be unfair. During the Vietnam War, 18- and 19-year-olds were being drafted by the government and sent into combat. If they were old enough to fight and kill for their government, reasoned the generation of the 1960s, they should be old enough to vote. Congress responded to these arguments in 1970 by passing a law that reduced the voting age to 18 in national, state, and local elections. This law was challenged, however, and the Supreme Court ruled that although Congress had the authority to set the voting age in federal elections, it had no such rights for state and local elections (*Oregon v. Mitchell* 1970). It struck some as silly that an 18-year-old could vote for president but be considered too politically immature to vote for city dogcatcher. Congress eventually proposed the Twenty-Sixth Amendment to secure the voting rights of all citizens 18 and older, which was ratified in 1971.

Eliminating property, race, gender, and age requirements extended the franchise to most adult citizens in the United States. Some barriers to voting still remain, although these strike most people as reasonable. Most states, for example, require voters to be U.S. citizens, residents of the jurisdiction where they want to cast a ballot, and registered to vote.

There are other restrictions on groups of people presumed to not have the intelligence or moral character necessary to cast a ballot. These include the mentally ill and convicted felons. In most states, felons are denied the right to vote even after they have served their sentences. This practice, though ruled constitutional by the Supreme Court, is increasingly controversial because such laws tend to disproportionately affect African American men. Overall, a little more than 2 percent of the nation's entire voting-age population has lost the right to vote because of a felony conviction. That number leaps to 13 percent for African American men, and in

POLITICS IN PRACTICE

FELONS AND THE FRANCHISE

Though most adult citizens now have the right to vote, the franchise is still withheld from one large group in U.S. society: convicted felons. About 5.3 million Americans no longer have the right to cast a ballot because of their criminal records. This right is sometimes permanently lost to them—even after serving their time and paying their debt to society.

The voting rights of ex-prisoners are mostly governed by state statute, which means the voting rights of felons vary enormously from state to state. Forty-eight states place at least some restrictions on the voting rights of felons. Most prevent felons from voting while they are in prison or on probation. Twelve states permanently disenfranchise felons; once convicted, they can never vote again.

Some argue there is a rough justice here and that disenfranchising felons is appropriate. If you harm society through criminal activity, you should also lose the right to participate in society's decision-making process.

Others, however, argue that felony disenfranchisement is grossly unfair. It is unfair in the sense that whether you permanently lose your voting rights depends not just on what you did, but where you did it. The exact same crime in Maine and Alabama will have very different implications for individual voting rights—in Maine they are hardly affected at all, in Alabama they are gone for good.

It is also unfair, some argue, because what constitutes a felony varies considerably from state to state. For example, using a false identification card in Maryland is a felony. Two convictions of this crime will result in the state permanently revoking the person's voting rights. The exact same crime in many other states is considered a misdemeanor and will have no impact on voting rights at all.

Some argue that felony disenfranchisement is unfair because it disproportionately affects one group: blacks, especially black males. Overall, about 2.4 percent of Americans have lost their right to vote because of felony convictions. For blacks, it is more than 8 percent; that's nearly two million people. The large majority of these are black males, where crime-related disenfranchisement rates in some states are astonishingly high. In some states, roughly 1 in 3 African American males have been disenfranchised. This raises serious concerns because the criminal justice system is often accused of systemic racism. It raises questions over whether the criminal law is being used as a backdoor to disenfranchise a minority that has historically been denied rights of political participation.

Finally, some argue felony disenfranchisement is unfair only if it is permanent. Should individuals who serve their time, get their life together, and become law-abiding citizens have no right to cast a ballot? Should society permanently withhold suffrage for crimes (such as drug use or possession) that harmed no one but the offender? In 14 states, the answer is yes.

SOURCES Hull, Elizabeth. 2004. "Felons Deserve the Right to Vote." *USA Today Magazine*. January, pp. 50–52.

Sentencing Project. 2009. "Request for a Thematic Hearing on the Discriminatory Effects of Felony Disenfranchisement Laws, Policies and Practices in the Americas", http://www.sentencing project.org/doc/publications/fd_IACHRHearingRequest.pdf some states, almost a third of African American men have permanently lost the right to vote (you can check out how many people are disenfranchised because of felony convictions in your state, as well as see the racial and ethnic disparities in disenfranchisement, through the Sentencing Project's interactive website: http://www.sentencingproject.org/map/map.cfm#map). (See the Politics in Practice feature "Felons and the Franchise.")

Voter Turnout

Ironically, after struggles for two centuries to extend to all citizens the right to vote, fewer and fewer citizens seem interested in exercising that right. As Figure 11.3 shows, roughly 55 to 60 percent of those eligible cast ballots in presidential elections in recent decades. Voter turnout for congressional races in **midterm elections**— that is, the congressional elections held midway between presidential elections—is consistently well below 50 percent.

But is **voter turnout** really declining over time? Answering this question is more complicated than you might think. First, it must be clear what proportion of voters actually vote. Yet there is more than one way to calculate this proportion. A common practice is to calculate turnout rates based on the "voting-age population"—that is, everyone of voting age who lives in one of the 50 states.

midterm elections The congressional and gubernatorial elections that occur in the middle of a presidential term.

voter turnout The percentage of eligible voters who cast votes in an election.

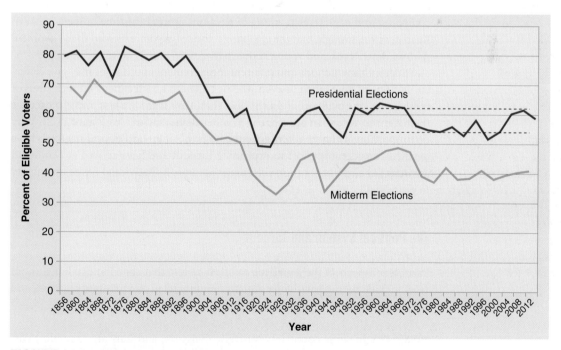

FIGURE 11.3 Voting Turnout, 1856–2012

Source: McDonald, Michael P. 2013. "2012 General Election Turnout Rates." United States Elections Project. http://elections.gmu.edu/Turnout_2012G.html, updated 2/9/13. (accessed March 5, 2013).

But political scientists Michael McDonald and Samuel Popkin (2001) point out that not all residents older than the minimum voting age are eligible to vote—for example, noncitizens cannot vote, and most states do not allow felons to vote. A more accurate estimate is the percentage who vote out of the "voting-eligible population" that excludes from the calculation all those who are disqualified for some reason. Because the voting-age population includes people who cannot vote, it makes turnout look lower than it actually is. McDonald and Popkin argue that if ineligible people are excluded from the calculation, the apparent decline in turnout since 1968 is largely an illusion. Examining the different approaches to measuring turnout by looking at elections from 1980 to 2004 in individual states, Thomas Holbrook and Brianne Heidbreder (2010) find that the voting-age approaches consistently underestimate turnout by two or three percentage points compared to the voting-eligible approach.

Second, regardless of what baseline we use, whether we see a decline in turnout or not depends a lot on where we start and where we stop. If we look at the trend for presidential elections from the 1950s forward, there seems to be not much change in turnout, which has stayed within a band of roughly eight percentage points (between 54 and 62 percent) during the past half-century (see Figure 11.3). Average turnout in presidential elections in the 1950s and early 1960s was a bit more than 60 percent of eligible voters. This dipped steadily to an average of about 55 percent in the 1990s, before once again rising to about 60 percent in more recent presidential contests. Yet if we go back to the nineteenth century, the typical twentieth and twenty-first century turnout rates of 55 to 60 percent look paltry compared to the 80 percent voting in elections around the time of the Civil War. Keep in mind, though, that the eligible electorate was more limited then—women, African Americans, and young people between 18 and 21 were excluded.

Different time periods and different measurement approaches may give different notions of how much or even whether turnout has declined. Yet regardless of these issues, the evidence is pretty clear that Americans are less likely to exercise their right to vote than are citizens in other democracies (see Figure 11.2). Why do proportionally fewer voters go to the polls in America? Political scientists have devoted considerable effort to explaining turnout and have arrived at two broad answers: (1) elements of the political system and (2) individual desire and ability to participate.

The Political System and Turnout

Particular aspects of the American political system that contribute to low turnout rates include voting laws, voter registration practices, the two-party system, and the scheduling and number of elections.

VOTING LAWS In some countries (Australia, Belgium, and Italy are examples) voting is not optional. Citizens are required to vote by law and face fines, loss of voting rights, and social ostracism if they do not. In Italy, for example, the names of nonvoters are publicly posted. In the 1880s, Bavaria came up with an innovative way to encourage voting. In order for an election to be considered valid, two-thirds of eligible citizens had to cast ballots. If turnout fell below the two-thirds threshold, nonvoters were charged with the cost of putting on a new election (Robson 1923, 571–572).

Turnout where there are compulsory voting laws typically exceeds 70 percent and is often higher than 90 percent. Yet although turnout is clearly higher, it is obviously not universal. The punishments associated with compulsory voting laws, as well as the vigor with which they are enforced, undoubtedly vary considerably (Powell 1980, 9). Indeed, compulsory voting laws might more accurately be termed compulsory attendance laws; these laws require voters only to pick up a ballot, not to actually express a preference. In Australia, for example, voters rank-order their preferences on a ballot by putting numbers next to candidates. Many voters, however, cast a "donkey vote," which means they just put a "1" next to the first candidate, a "2" next to the second, and so on until the end of the ballot. In other words, the numbers they list on their ballots have no connection to their preferences. Donkey voting is seen as a form of protest against compulsory voting; it signals that a voter's chief preference was not to be forced to cast a ballot. This raises an important point: compulsory voting reflects the notion of political participation as civic duty, but some question whether legally forcing citizens to vote is democratic. Individual liberty and political freedom in the United States imply not just the right to vote but also the right not to vote.

VOTER REGISTRATION Voter registration requires more effort in the United States than in other democracies. In European countries, it is common for 90 percent or more of those eligible to vote to actually be registered to vote. In the United States, registration rates are considerably lower. The reason for the difference is that in the United States, registering to vote is considered an individual responsibility; it is mostly left to citizens themselves to take the initiative to register. In other democracies, government takes on the responsibility of identifying potential voters and registering them to vote.

Several decades ago, political scientists argued that on the basis of their research, the burden of registration explained a big part of low voter turnout in the United States (Wolfinger 1991). The evidence underlying this argument is that turnout is much higher when it is calculated as the percentage of registered voters rather than the percentage of eligible voters. Persuaded by this logic, in 1993, Congress passed the National Voter Registration Act—the so-called motor voter law—requiring states to provide registration services when citizens go to renew their driver's license or seek other public services. This bill was controversial because, as a group, unregistered citizens tend to be poorer, less educated, and more likely to identify as Democrats. Republicans feared they would be at an electoral disadvantage if turnout increased in this group, though subsequent research suggests Republican fears were unfounded: the law increased registration rates but has had a modest impact, at best, on actual turnout (Knack and White 1998).

Registration laws and procedures vary from state to state. Minnesota and Wisconsin, for example, allow citizens to register on the day of election. Other states require voters to register a month before the election in order to vote in that election. Most states automatically cancel the registration of individuals who have not cast a ballot in a specified period of time (usually two to four years), thus forcing citizens to repeat the registration process if they do not vote on a regular basis.

States also vary in voter verification requirements. Some states card voters at the polls; that is, they require proof that the prospective registered voter is who he or she claims to be before allowing the voter to cast a ballot. Supporters of the most strict identification laws, which require a government-issued photo ID, argue that they help prevent election fraud and thus ensure the integrity of the ballot. Opponents argue that these laws create a burden on voters that is potentially disenfranchising. In 2008 the Supreme Court in *Crawford v. Marion County Election Board* upheld Indiana's voter ID law—one of the toughest in the nation. The court argued that any burdens created by ID requirements were counterbalanced by the law's potential to reduce voter fraud. Critics of the law and the court ruling argue that the net effect will be to make it harder for some people to vote. Some research has found no widespread decline in voter participation that can be attributed to such laws (Ansolabehere 2009). In recent years, however, state governments have passed a large number of laws that make it harder to register or to cast a ballot. These include not just photo ID laws but also requirements mandating proof of citizenship before someone is allowed to register or vote, as well as other restrictions on registering and voting. Maine, for example, recently passed a law ending election day registration. Other states have made it harder to stay registered to vote if you move, have ended early voting opportunities, and have passed new laws disenfranchising those with criminal records. These changes tend to make it harder for the young, the poor, and minorities to register and cast a ballot, and some predict that the cumulative effect of these restrictions could start to noticeably lower turnout among these groups (Weiser and Norden 2011).

THE TWO-PARTY SYSTEM Historically, some scholars argued that two-party systems may not offer voters a meaningful choice, leaving voters with less of an incentive to show up at the polls. This argument is rooted in rational choice theory and was most famously articulated by economist Anthony Downs (1957). He argued that in two-party systems, it is rational for parties to appeal to the average voter, which in the United States means appealing to a middle-of-the-road perspective on politics and policy.

It is perfectly rational for the parties to stake their ground in the middle of the political spectrum because that is where most voters' preferences lie. The problem is that if both parties are chasing the middle-of-the-road voter, they end up with overlapping appeals and make it hard for citizens to differentiate between them. If potential voters cannot see differences between parties or candidates, they will find it troubling to cast a ballot based on individual policy preferences. If this is the case, it is just as rational to go to the beach as to vote. As a Texas politician once said, "the only thing in the middle of the road are yella stripes and dead armadillos" (Hightower 1998).

In recent elections, however, Republicans and Democrats have been less likely to make similar appeals as they seek voters in the center. Indeed, the two major parties have become much more polarized, shifting away from the average voter and closer to the preferences of the more ideologically committed voters that characterize low-turnout primary elections (Masket 2011). Have the parties become less rational? Not really. What candidates have discovered is that it is often no use appealing to the middle-of-the-road voter in a primary election for the simple reason that low-turnout primary elections are not dominated by middle-of-the-road voters. Those who show up to vote in primary elections are more likely to be strong partisans or ideologues. If you want to win a primary election, obviously you have appeal to those more extreme policy preferences. In rational choice terms, it is simply not rational to appeal to the voter on the 50-yard line in a primary election if most of the voters are to be found on the 10-yard or even 1-yard line of your side of the field. The end result is that Republican and Democratic primary winners start running in a general election from essentially their own goal posts, which are a long way from the middle of the political playing field. Even though candidates tend to move to the center in a general election, it is much harder to reach the middle if you start from so far away. When each party represents a clear ideological choice, it is a good thing for strong conservatives or liberals, but moderate voters in the middle may still end up feeling like they have no meaningful choice to represent their preferences and may go to the beach anyway.

ELECTION SCHEDULES AND FREQUENCY Presidential elections are held on Tuesdays, a workday for most Americans. Other democracies encourage voting by holding elections on Saturdays or Sundays. Holding national elections on weekends, or making election day a national holiday, would make it easier for working Americans to show up at the polls (see the Politics in Practice feature "Why Tuesday?"). Some have suggested that it would be fitting to hold national elections on November 11, Veterans Day. The argument here is that this would be an appropriate tribute to the members of the armed forces who have defended democracy and that it would highlight the importance of civic duty and participation (Wattenberg 1998).

Voting requires more effort in the United States than in other democracies. It is harder to register to vote and a slew of new laws place restrictions even on registered voters. Many states now require voters to show proof of identification in order to cast a ballot.

POLITICS IN PRACTICE

WHY TUESDAY?

Why are elections held on Tuesday? Why not Saturday or any other day of the week? In fact, there were good reasons for holding elections on Tuesday, even if those reasons are not as valid as they once were.

Originally, neither the Constitution nor federal law had much to say about when elections should be held. Article II, Section 1 of the Constitution gives Congress the authority to set a uniform election day for the United States. In 1792, the first Congress passed a bill designating the first Wednesday in December as the day on which presidential electors were to assemble and vote in their respective state capitals, and requiring states to appoint their electors at least 34 days prior to that date. Dates for other elections, including elections for Congress, were not mentioned.

In 1845, Congress changed the date for the choice of electors to the "first Tuesday after the first Monday in the month of November of the year in which they are appointed." By this time, most states were choosing presidential electors in popular elections. In 1872, Congress extended this date to the election of members of the House of Representatives. In 1915, after ratification of the Seventeenth Amendment, it was extended to the election of senators.

November was chosen as the month of elections, and Tuesday chosen as election day, for practical reasons reflecting cultural and lifestyle conditions early in the nation's history. The United States was a rural, agrarian nation. Crops were harvested by November, so farmers had free time to travel and vote, and travel was likely to be easier before the onset of winter weather in the northern states. A day's travel was necessary because most rural voters had to travel by foot or horseback to the county seat. Most of the nation strictly observed Sunday as a day of rest, which precluded travel on that day. Saturday was a workday for most people. That basically ruled out weekend elections.

Tuesday was hit upon as a way to allow for a full day of travel between Sunday and election day. Choosing the first Tuesday after the first Monday also prevented election day from falling on the first day of the month, which was frequently reserved for court business at the county seat.

SOURCE U.S. Congress. 1993. *Our American Government.* 102nd Congress, 2nd Session, H. Doc. 102–192, 61–62.

It is not just the timing of elections but also the number that may depress voter turnout in America. Citizens in the United States are called on to vote much more often than in other democracies. The federal system means there are not just federal elections, but numerous elections at the state and local levels too. Citizens in many states elect state agency heads, state and local judges, sheriffs, county officials, mayors, and city councils.

Electing candidates for these offices usually means at least two elections: a primary election and a general election. On top of that, elections are regularly held for special-purpose districts such as school districts, flood control districts, water districts, sewage districts, mosquito control districts, and park districts. In addition, voters are regularly called on to vote for proposed state constitutional amendments, ballot initiatives, and bond issues.

In short, there are a lot of elections, and the United States is far ahead of other democracies in the number of voting opportunities presented to citizens. U.S. voters may be exhausted by a virtually permanent election season. Like the mouse, they may beg, "Don't give me any more cheese; just let me out of the trap."

Individual Desire and Ability to Participate

The mix of reasons listed previously may help explain why voter turnout in the United States is lower compared to other democracies. What it does not explain is why turnout generally declined during the past 40 years, the past couple of election cycles excepted.

This decline is particularly puzzling because it has occurred at the same time as a number of reforms that, at least in theory, should have led to higher turnout. For example, although restrictive registration and voting laws keep voters away from the polls, some states have experimented with simpler registration laws, set up registration booths in shopping malls, and experimented with letting people register online. Yet as registering to vote became easier, voter turnout went down.

The puzzle of voter turnout is tied to the fundamental question of political participation: why do some people participate whereas others do not? There is no single, simple answer to this question. Research has identified a number of the key elements that affect an individual's desire and ability to participate:

- Socioeconomic status, which is simply the social and economic position a person occupies in society
- An individual's psychological engagement with politics
- The broader political and social context with which an individual is connected
- Resources necessary to participate—free time, money, and civic skills
- Group characteristics—age, gender, race

SOCIOECONOMIC STATUS Perhaps the most important determinant of any form of political participation is **socioeconomic status (SES)**. Socioeconomic status is typically measured in terms of education, income, and occupation and serves as a baseline explanation of both the desire and the ability to participate.

Education seems to be especially important. Well-educated people tend to hold high-status positions (business executive, doctor, lawyer, and so on) and earn high incomes. They are likely to be aware of political matters and possess the confidence and intellectual tools to deal with them. They recognize their financial stake in politics (through taxes and fees), and they have professional, intellectual, and social skills that transfer easily to the political arena. In short, SES helps determine whether people have the ability to participate effectively in politics. Generally speaking, higher-SES citizens—those with high income, high education, and high-status occupations—are more likely to show up to the polls than low-SES citizens. But although SES clearly plays an important role in explaining why individuals do

socioeconomic status (SES) The social background and economic position of a person.

or do not vote, overall levels of SES do not necessarily track with voter participation over time. Education and income levels, for example, rose across all levels of society in the four decades between the 1960s and the turn of the century even as the general trend in turnout drifted toward 50 percent in presidential elections. Shortly after the turn of the century, the recession began squeezing incomes, yet voter participation in the presidential elections went up, topping 60 percent for the first time since the 1960s (see Figure 11.2).

Political and social context can influence levels of participation. Living in an area where people put up yard signs, sport bumper stickers, and talk politics can help encourage higher levels of political participation.

PSYCHOLOGICAL ENGAGEMENT People who believe that their opinions are important and that government will respect and respond to their views are said to believe in **political efficacy**. Individuals are more likely to participate if they feel efficacious, regardless of their SES (Milbrath and Goel 1977, 59). Though high-SES people have the skills necessary to participate, it is the psychological engagement with politics that provides the desire to participate.

Psychological engagement, or more accurately the lack of it, may play an important role in explaining voter turnout. **Political alienation** characterizes individuals with deep-seated feelings of isolation and estrangement from the political system (Finifter 1970; Milbrath and Goel 1977; Seeman 1959). Politically alienated citizens tend to have low levels of trust in government and feel the political system does not merit their participation. **Allegiant** individuals, in contrast, express high levels of trust in government.

Although it would seem to make sense that citizens with high levels of political efficacy would participate, and politically alienated citizens would not, the relationship between psychological engagement and voter turnout is not that clearcut. Some argue that alienation and distrust translate into voter apathy, and as alienation and distrust in government have increased, turnout has declined. Others, however, argue that this is a demonstration of "happy politics" (Eulau 1956), or the notion that people who are happy with the political process and who trust government to do the right thing simply see less of a need to participate. Logically, then, people who are unhappy with the government should be more likely to vote; their dissatisfaction with the status quo provides the motivation to go to the polls to try to change things.

Psychological traits beyond efficacy may also play a role in influencing political participation. Recent research has found that an individual's personality can predict his or her level of political involvement. For example, people whose personalities are characterized by openness—they tend to consistently seek out information

political efficacy The belief that one's opinions are important and that government will respect and respond to one's views.

political alienation The feeling of being isolated from or not part of the political process and system.

allegiant Feeling great trust and support for the political system.

and engagement—tend to be more politically engaged (e.g., Mondak et al. 2010). The finding that personality shapes political participation has also raised the possibility that biological factors influence political engagement. Personality traits are known to be heritable, and there is some evidence that individuals' political traits as well as their personality traits are based in the same set of genetic influences (Verhulst, Eaves, and Hatemi 2011).

CONTEXT In addition to SES and psychological attributes, participation is affected by the context in which an individual lives. The broader social network, particularly organizational memberships and the neighborhood, is important in development of civic skills. Political scientists Robert Huckfeldt and John Sprague (1995) conducted an intensive study of political activity in 16 neighborhoods in South Bend, Indiana, during a presidential election. They found that people who live in neighborhoods that reflect and support their party identification are more likely to become politically active—not just voting, but also putting up yard signs, sporting bumper stickers, and making politics a topic of conversation.

Context, though, goes beyond the local level to include the broader impact of the political system and the experiences of the electorate as a whole. The **mobilization** hypothesis posits that "participation is a response to contextual cues and political opportunities" (Leighley 1995, 188). In other words, people are motivated to participate by their political environment. For example, political parties frequently mount "get out the vote" campaigns. These efforts, which may take the form of phone calls, media ads, or direct mail, are aimed at motivating people to actually cast a ballot. Even a simple text message reminding people to vote seems to be enough to significantly increase turnout in a given election (Dale and Strauss 2009). These sorts of mobilization efforts, though, have a mixed impact on participation. On the one hand, they undoubtedly encourage some people to get out and vote. On the other, they mostly tend to encourage certain types of people to get out and vote: the better-off, the better-educated, and the better-informed. This is because the political elites who undertake the mobilization efforts—political parties, special interest groups, and the like—tend to target people who have resources to contribute (money or time), who have a particular partisan or ideological affiliation (these groups want to mobilize supporters, not opponents), or who are key members of social networks (i.e., people who can influence other people). That sort of targeting can certainly mobilize the better-off and better-connected, but it does little to boost the participation of a large mass of voters who do not have those traits (Rosenstone and Hansen 1993).

Rather than mobilization, others argue for the generational effect hypothesis of turnout. This view suggests that the key elements of social context driving voter turnout are the events and experiences that shape a generation's attitudes toward politics. The generation shaped by the Great Depression and World War II was more politically engaged because those events promoted a keen sense of the importance of politics and civic duty. The generations that followed experienced nothing equivalent to mass economic dislocation and a multiyear effort to fight a world war. This resulted in generational effect on turnout (Miller 1992). This

mobilization Efforts aimed at influencing people to vote in an election.

might explain why turnout declined from the 1960s to the 1990s: politics was simply seen as less important and less relevant to baby boomers and generation Xers, and as the electorate came to be more dominated by these generational cohorts and their political context, turnout dropped off (Lyons and Alexander 2000). Currently, key elements of the social context that may shape attitudes toward politics are sustained economic hard times and long and bloody guerilla wars in Iraq and Afghanistan. Could these events highlight the importance of politics and prompt higher levels of political participation in the generation that follows the boomers and the Xers? It's too early to answer this question with confidence, but the generational hypothesis certainly suggests it is possible.

RESOURCES Verba, Schlozman, and Brady (1995) developed a resource-based model that nearly two decades later is still widely accepted as one of the most comprehensive explanations of political participation. Their argument is that individuals need resources in order to participate and that three types of resources are important:

1. Free time after work, household duties, and school
2. Money
3. Civic skills, such as communication and organizational abilities

Individuals who have free time, above-average family income, and the ability to speak and write well or who are comfortable organizing and participating in meetings are more active and effective in politics (Verba, Schlozman, and Brady 1995). Different resources are required for different forms of participation. Contributing money to a campaign, for example, requires surplus income but not much time. Contacting a government official requires time and civic skills. These resources are distributed unequally across the population, which helps explain why some people are more likely to participate than others. But more importantly, the different resources are not equally associated with SES. Money is associated with high SES, by definition. Free time, however, is not; low-SES individuals have as much or more of it than people with high SES.

The connection between civic skills and SES is mixed. Individuals begin acquiring civic skills early in life from family and school. These skills develop throughout adult life in nonpolitical institutions such as the workplace, organizations, and churches and synagogues. High-SES individuals tend to have the civic skills to participate in activities requiring them, such as working in political campaigns or contacting government officials. They probably grew up in families that valued such activity, and as adults, they tend to have jobs and belong to organizations that allow them to practice writing, speaking, and organizing. But school offers opportunities to children from low-SES families to learn civic skills. For example, Verba, Schlozman, and Brady (1995) found that participation in student government contributes to an individual's civic skills. Furthermore, church attendance offers adults opportunities to develop civic skills. Church attendance is not associated with SES; individuals with low income and education have about as much opportunity to make speeches and organize meetings at church as do those with high SES. "In this way," conclude Verba and his associates, "the institutions of civil society operate, as Tocqueville noted, as the school of democracy" (Verba, Schlozman, and Brady 1995, 285).

GROUP CHARACTERISTICS Certain group characteristics—such as race and age—are also associated with participation. The relationship between age and participation is curvilinear: participation is highest among middle-

Voter turnout has important implications for democratic governance. Voting expresses the will of only those people who actually cast their ballots, and government policy favors those who participate.

aged people (say, those aged 45 to 65) and much lower for the very young and very old. Middle-aged people tend to have the greatest stake in the political system, to be aware of how government affects their lives, and to have the resources necessary to participate. Very young citizens participate less in politics because they are less likely to see how politics and government affect them, and they lack other attributes that encourage participation. Young people, for example, may be just starting a career or may still be in school. Participation falls off among older people in part because of infirmities associated with aging. Some research indicates, however, that when differences in education and resources are accounted for, the decline in participation among the elderly is less pronounced. Retired people have the time to devote to politics, and many participate in organizations that provide them with pertinent information about politics and opportunities to develop civic skills.

African Americans and Latinos also participate less than whites. This difference, however, results mostly from factors other than race, particularly education, income, and resources. When SES and resources are controlled for, participation of African Americans and Latinos is not significantly different from that of whites (Verba, Schlozman, and Brady 1995). On the other hand, voter turnout of Asian Americans, another growing ethnic minority, is lower than that of whites even after controlling for SES and other factors (Uhlaner, Cain, and Kiewiet 1989). For other types of participation, there is no significant difference between Asian Americans and whites once the effects of SES and other factors are taken into account (Leighley and Vedlitz 1999).

Voting and Democracy

Scholars have raised concerns that voter turnout—or the lack thereof—has important implications for democratic governance. If some groups participate less than others, are their preferences less likely to be accounted for in the democratic process? This concern is central to the elitist critique of the American system. How can government truly uphold the will of the people and act on majority preferences if a majority of people do not bother to cast a ballot?

Political scientists have approached this issue from a number of perspectives and are divided about the answer. For example, there is solid evidence that government is very responsive to broad currents of public opinion (Erikson, Wright, and McIver 1993). This suggests that people do not actually have to vote to have government respond to their preferences. It is also generally accepted that increasing turnout will not necessarily make a difference in election outcomes. On the other hand, it is also clear that the mobilization of various groups in the electorate is an important determinant of election outcomes (R. Jackson 1997). Disproportionate participation by higher-class citizens logically results in policies that favor their economic interests at the expense of lower-class citizens (Bennett and Resnick 1990; Gant and Lyons 1993; Hill and Leighley 1992). In other words, voting expresses the will of only a portion of the people, and government policy favors those who participate.

MODELS OF VOTING BEHAVIOR

Explaining why people do or do not vote in an election is a complex undertaking. Yet explaining voter turnout is relatively simple compared to the challenge of explaining what happens once a voter enters the voting booth. Why do some people vote Republican and others Democrat? Why do some vote for liberal candidates and others for conservative candidates?

During the past half-century, three theories have dominated the search for an explanation of vote choice: the sociological model, the social-psychological model, and the rational choice model.

The Sociological Model

Researchers at Columbia University developed the sociological model to explain voting behavior in the 1940 presidential election. Initially, the Columbia researchers tried to explain voting choices as consumer preferences. The initial idea was that political candidates could be viewed as "products" offered by political parties and political campaigns as competing marketing efforts aimed at swaying voter preferences.

The consumer preference idea was a bust, mainly because researchers discovered that most voters decided who they were going to vote for well in advance of the advertising campaigns (Niemi and Weisberg 1993, 8). Casting about for an alternate explanation, the Columbia researchers noticed that sociological variables—a fancy term for the characteristics of groups—were strongly correlated with vote choice.

The result was the **sociological model** (sometimes called the Columbia model) of voting behavior. The sociological model uses group-level characteristics such as SES, religion, and place of residence to explain how people vote (Lazarsfeld, Berelson, and Gaudet 1944). At least in the 1940 election, this group-level approach worked well: Catholics, city dwellers, and people with low education, low income, and low-status occupations tended to vote for the Democratic candidate (Franklin Delano Roosevelt). Protestants, rural residents, and people higher up the socioeconomic chain tended to vote for the Republican candidate (Wendell Willkie).

The sociological model still provides a reasonable basis for explaining vote choice. Figure 11.4 shows the voting behavior of various sociological groups in recent elections. For example, people with low income and education still tend to vote Democratic, as do African Americans, Latinos, Catholics, and Jews. Republican candidates still get higher levels of support from whites, Protestants, and people with high income.

Yet as a comprehensive explanation of vote choice, the sociological model quickly fell from favor. Certain group characteristics—such as race, religion, and income—may be associated with differences in vote choice, but they do not always explain why those differences exist. Furthermore, group loyalties shift over

sociological model (Columbia model) A model explaining voter choice by considering factors such as religion, place of residence, and socioeconomic status.

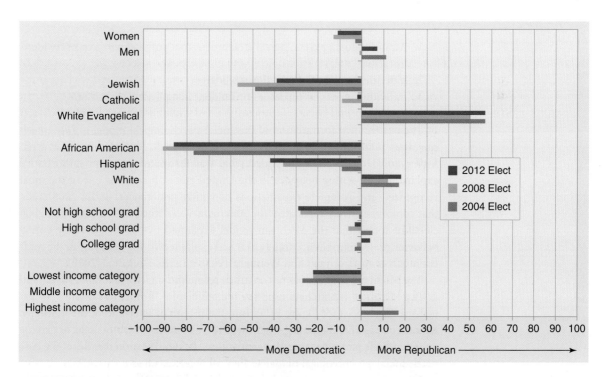

FIGURE 11.4 Voting Behavior of Sociological Groups

Source: Constructed by the authors from "National Exit Polls Table," *New York Times*, http://elections.nytimes.com/2008/results/president/national-exit-polls.html; and "Exit Polls 2012: How the Vote Has Shifted," *Washington Post*, http://www.washington-post.com/wp-srv/special/politics/2012-exit-polls/table.html.

time and are therefore not always reliable predictors of voting patterns. Certainly there have been significant changes in group voting behavior since the Columbia study. Highly educated individuals, for example, are no longer solidly Republican: college graduates favored the Democrat in recent presidential elections. Finally, the conclusions of the sociological model rested on a narrow research base: the sociological model was originally based on a limited sample of voters (taken from a single county in New York State). Other studies based on larger national samples had difficulty replicating the findings.

The Social-Psychological Model

A team of researchers at the Survey Research Center of the University of Michigan began using national scientific polls to address limitations of the sociological model. Beginning with the 1948 election, they interviewed a nationwide sample of citizens to discover how they voted and why. The findings of the Michigan team served as the basis for a new model of vote choice.

The **social-psychological model** (also known as the Michigan model) explains vote choice not as a product of group characteristics but as one of individual attitudes. Specifically, the social-psychological model explains vote choice as primarily a product of three individual orientations:

1. An individual's psychological attachment to a political party, or party identification
2. Individual opinions about the candidates
3. Individual views on the issues prominent in a particular election

The best-known formulation of the social-psychological model is *The American Voter,* published in 1960. Authors Angus Campbell, Philip Converse, Warren Miller, and Donald Stokes provided what was for many years the authoritative explanation for voting behavior in the United States. It remains one of the most recognized and complete explanations of voting preferences, and a 2008 study that comprehensively replicated *The American Voter* study on the 2000 and 2004 elections found that the Michigan model explained twenty-first century voting behavior pretty much as accurately as it had explained voting behavior in the mid-twentieth century (Niemi and Weisberg 1993, 8; Lewis-Beck et al. 2008).

The Michigan model does not so much refute the sociological model as extend it. The Michigan researchers used the metaphor of a "funnel of causality" to explain voter choice (see Figure 11.5). Into the mouth or wide end of the funnel go factors such as SES, religion, gender, and race. These are the factors seen as driving an individual's party identification, and it is party identification that lies at the core of the social-psychological model. Other influences, such as the politics of parents and friends and world events, also affect party identification. Party identification, in turn, shapes an individual's attitudes toward candidates and issues. These attitudes are what lead an individual, finally, to vote a certain way. At the tip or outlet

social-psychological model (Michigan model) A model explaining voter choice that focuses on individual attitudes.

CHAPTER 11 POLITICAL PARTICIPATION AND VOTING BEHAVIOR

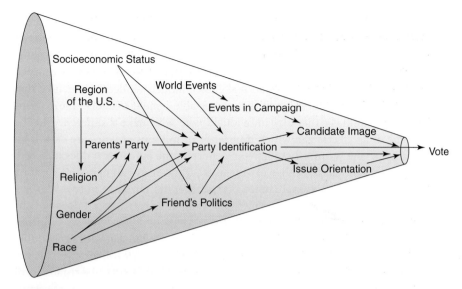

FIGURE 11.5 Funnel of Causality

Source: Luttbeg and Gant (1995), 13.

of the funnel is the individual's actual vote, which is distilled from sociological factors into party identification and from party identification into a certain set of attitudes and opinions about candidates and issues. These final three factors—party identification, perception of candidate image, and issue orientation—play the biggest role in explaining vote choice.

The model thus explains party identification as something largely inherited from parents and the same group-level characteristics dominant in the sociological model. Party identification acts as a "brand" that orients voters toward particular candidates and issues and helps them make choices. The heart of the Michigan model is its focus on party identification and individual attitudes, a focus that continues to dominate explanations of voting behavior.

The Rational Choice Model

The Michigan model's primary competition as a comprehensive explanation of voter behavior is the **rational choice model**. This model argues that voting is the product of a rational cost–benefit calculation. Broadly speaking, rational choice means that individuals will vote if the benefits of doing so outweigh the costs and will cast their ballots for candidates who are closest to sharing their views on the issues.

Unlike the Columbia and Michigan models, rational choice offers fairly precise predictions of voter behavior. For example, as the costs of voting increase (e.g., a long line at the polling place), the rational choice model predicts a lower probability of voting. A second major contribution of the rational choice model is its focus

rational choice model A model of voter choice that suggests that an individual will vote if the benefits of doing so outweigh the costs and will cast his or her ballot for candidates who are closest to sharing the individual's views on the issues.

on issues "which were submerged in the early findings of the Michigan researchers" (Niemi and Weisberg 1993, 9).

Despite the theoretical insight provided by the rational choice model, some scholars consider its theoretical elegance to be a poor match with the reality of voting behavior. Early formal rational choice models tended to conclude that the costs of voting outweighed the conceivable benefit (Tullock 1967, chapter 7). It is unlikely that any individual's vote will make a difference to the outcome of an election in which thousands or millions of votes are cast. If an individual's vote is unlikely to have any effect on the outcome, it does not seem particularly rational to bother to vote at all. This creates an apparent paradox of voting: from the rational choice perspective, the puzzle is not why so few people participate but why so many bother to participate when it does not appear rational to do so.

To solve this paradox, rational choice scholars suggested that voters gain utility not just from the outcome of voting but also from the act of voting. If you believe voting is an important civic duty, voting becomes an important goal regardless of the outcome of the election (Riker and Ordeshook 1968). Critics saw some circular reasoning in this solution: people are rational; therefore, if they vote, voting must be rational; therefore, people who vote must be rational. More refined rational choice approaches argue that voting is a low-cost, low-reward proposition, which means it doesn't take much to sway a citizen to vote (Aldrich 1993). In the vast majority of cases, it takes little effort to show up to the polls, and the payoff in terms of electoral outcomes or satisfaction in doing your civic duty is also pretty low. This means a lot of factors can push a rational individual into voting or not voting: mobilization efforts, the appeal of a particular candidate or ballot issue, and so on.

Rational choice models must also grapple with the information hurdles involved in political participation. To make rational voting decisions on the basis of issues, for example, voters need some minimal level of information about those issues. A good deal of research indicates that most Americans are poorly informed about politics. Because of such practical limitations to the rational choice model, the Michigan model in various modified forms continues to provide the most accepted explanations of voting behavior.

EXPLAINING VOTER CHOICE

According to the Michigan model, the three primary elements that go into a decision to vote for a particular candidate are party identification, candidate image, and issues. Although it is the combination of these elements that is thought to produce a final voting decision, scholars have long recognized that each plays a distinct role in shaping voter behavior.

Party Identification

The Michigan model argues that party identification is the most important determinant of vote choice (Campbell et al. 1960; Lewis-Beck et al. 2008). In contrast to candidate image and issues, party identification is a long-term influence on voting behavior, helping to shape vote choices across many elections.

Early research suggested that an individual's general psychological attachment to a political party begins in childhood and intensifies with age (Campbell et al. 1960, 165). Party identification is also important because voters use it as a form of shorthand or as a "cheat sheet." Voters rarely know everything about the specific issues a candidate supports or opposes. Indeed, they may not know anything at all about some candidates listed on a voting ballot. But most ballots are partisan ballots—they indicate the party affiliation of the candidates. Just knowing a candidate's political party can offer a rough and ready indication of what that candidate supports or opposes. So for a typical voter looking for guidance amid the complexities of personalities, issues, and events, a candidate's party label provides an important reference point. Party labels thus provide a quick and easy, if not 100 percent reliable, way of making judgments about a candidate.

Because of its central importance to explaining vote choice, political scientists have paid close attention to the partisan makeup of the electorate. It is generally recognized that levels of partisanship vary across time. In the 1950s, for example, 75 percent of the electorate identified themselves as Democrats or Republicans. According to the Pew Center, in 2012 less than 60 percent of voters identified with one of the two major parties. (You can check out Pew's data on party identification trends at http://www.people-press.org/2012/06/01/trend-in-party-identification-1939-2012/)

Some scholars see this shift in party identification patterns as heralding the rise of the independent voter, a view supported by an increase in split-ticket voting. Split-ticket voters vote for one party's candidate in one race and for the other party's candidate in another. In the 1950s, straight-ticket voting was common, and party "brand loyalty" was strong across the entire ballot. That pattern changed over the next 20 years as voters became more likely to split their votes between Republican presidents and Democratic congressional candidates, or vice versa (Nie, Verba, and Petrocik 1979). As we learned in chapter 7, however, the decline of partisanship stalled in the 1970s. Most individuals who initially claim to be independent admit to favoring one party, and they vote just like weak partisans. Beginning in the 1990s, the electorate became noticeably more partisan, and straight-ticket voting increased. Party identification is probably more important in determining vote choice today than it was four or five decades ago (Abramson, Aldrich, and Rohde 2006, 194; Lewis-Beck et al. 2008, 127).

The partisan divide in the electorate has been made particularly clear in the red state–blue state divide of the past few presidential electoral cycles. Red states, mostly in the South and the middle of the country, reliably support Republican candidates. Blue states, mostly on the coasts, tend to back the Democratic nominee. Mapping electoral votes onto a map of the United States presents an image of a country starkly divided along geographically defined partisan lines (see Figure 11.6). This image is

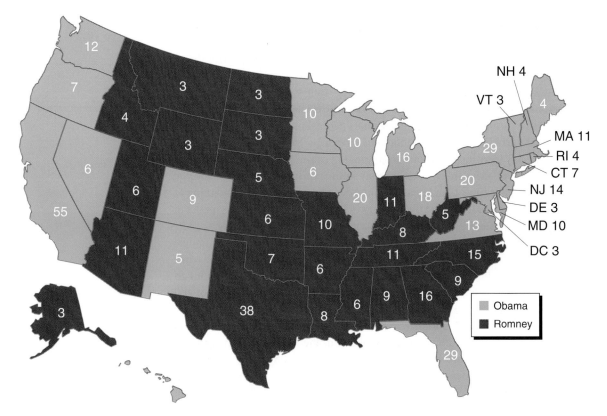

FIGURE 11.6 Red States/Blue States: Electoral Votes in the 2012 Presidential Election

somewhat misleading; there are strong pockets of blue in the red states, and vice versa. Although some states do have electorates with disproportionate partisan loyalties, the red and blue states bleed into each other more than the maps reported in the popular media suggest. There is as much purple—a mixing of red and blue—as anything else. The notion of purple states fits with research suggesting that party loyalties are not as fixed as the red state–blue state divide suggests. Early studies of voting behavior viewed party identification as a fixed and stable political characteristic (Campbell et al. 1960). But the swings over the past 40 or 50 years have convinced some political scientists that party loyalty is more fluid, with party affiliation shifting not just over the course of a lifetime but even within a single electoral season (Allsop and Weisberg 1988).

What explains such shifts in partisan loyalty? Research points to no single explanation but to a combination of factors. Key is the rise of candidate-centered (as opposed to party-centered) election campaigns and the rise of the electronic media. Candidates can make ideological and issue appeals directly to voters through television and radio ads, and this direct connection between candidate and voter may weaken party loyalties (Rapoport 1997). Another explanation is that party loyalty underwent a period of ideological and regional realignment in the 1970s and 1980s (Abramowitz and Saunders 1998). The argument here is that conservative Democrats, especially in the South, slowly shifted to the Republican Party, which traditionally reflects a more conservative ideology. (Southern states, remember, are reliably red states.)

The most recent research suggests that, once established, partisan loyalty is fairly resistant to change, though the intensity of party loyalty can wax and wane depending on a particular set of life experiences or on the context of a particular election. Roughly three in four voters express the same party identification from one presidential election to another. That means a quarter do shift party loyalty, but most of these are weak partisans to begin with (Lewis-Beck et al. 2008, 142). Regardless of what explains shifts in party loyalty, party identification has consistently remained the most reliable predictor of voter choice in presidential elections (Abramson, Aldrich, and Rohde 1999, 174).

Candidate Image

Voter perceptions of the qualities of a candidate are known as **candidate image** (Miller and Levitin 1976). Early studies viewed candidate image as an irrational basis for vote choice because these perceptions are often based on gut-level responses to things such as physical appearance, sense of humor, and family background. These factors were seen as a poor basis for making an informed, issue-based voting decision (Budesheim and DePaola 1994; Goren 1997).

Political scientists, however, also recognized that candidate image could play an incredibly important role in determining vote choice. The candidate viewed as a strong leader or as having high levels of integrity is more likely to gain the confidence of citizens and their votes, regardless of the person's knowledge and experience. The importance of candidate image has increased with the rise of television as the primary source of political information. Television is a passive and visual medium not well suited to in-depth coverage of policy issues and thus tends to elevate the importance of the personal and the symbolic (Carlin 1992; Patterson 1980). Not surprisingly, the personal and the symbolic have thus become a central focus of election campaigns. Television appearances and advertising are often centered on shaping image because they are a way to resonate with viewers' values and emotions and to suitably project a presidential image (Carlin 1992; Kern and Just 1995; Schutz 1995).

In 2008, for example, Democrat Barack Obama was seen an energetic agent for change—an image that helped him connect with an electorate that mostly thought the country was on the wrong track. His relative youth, however, raised questions about his experience; certainly, Republican John McCain's campaign sought to promote an image of Obama as underqualified for chief executive. McCain had experience in spades but turned 72 during the presidential campaign. While Obama sought to project an image of maturity, McCain had to fight an image of being too old and out of touch.

In 2012 the major party presidential nominees had contrasting image problems. Obama was seen as empathetic, likable, and in touch with the concerns of

candidate image Voters' perceptions of a candidate's qualities.

regular folks, but lingering economic doldrums raised questions about his effectiveness as an executive. Supporters of Republican Mitt Romney championed his successful business career as evidence of his strengths as an executive, but they worried about his image as too calculating and too out of touch with the lives and concerns of the average Joe.

In contests for Congress, candidate image is even more important than in presidential contests. People tend to evaluate members of Congress primarily on personal characteristics and qualifications, as well as devotion to district services and local issues. Those who hold office are well aware of this and devote a lot of energy to burnishing their image and "bringing home the bacon" by getting federal dollars for projects and programs in their districts. In voting terms, this adds up to a huge advantage for incumbents (G. Jacobson 2001). Though voters tend to dislike the institution of Congress, they tend to like their own representatives (Hibbing and Theiss-Morse 1995, 45).

Issues

In their analysis of voting behaviors in the 1950s, Angus Campbell and his associates proposed a set of criteria to gauge the importance of issues on voting choices (Campbell et al. 1960). They argued that issues can influence a voting decision only if three conditions are present:

1. The voter must be aware that the issues exist.
2. The issues must be of personal concern to the voter.
3. The voter must perceive that one candidate better represents his or her own thinking on the issues.

When they analyzed voting decisions in the 1952 and 1956 presidential elections, Campbell and his colleagues found these criteria were rarely met: they judged that less than one-third of the electorate voted on the basis of issues. But subsequent research suggests there is more potential for issue-based voting than the highly influential work of Campbell's team suggests. For example, an analysis of the 2000 and 2004 presidential elections using the same Michigan model approach as Campbell and associates found polarization over issues to be an important component of voting behavior (Lewis-Beck 2008).

In contrast to the mid-twentieth century, voters in the early twenty-first century seem to have more fundamental differences on issue preferences, and these differences are reflected in their votes. But it is not just a difference in political eras—the consensual 1950s versus the polarized 2000s—that makes issues important to voting behavior. A key factor is how issues play out in a campaign. If there are clear issue differences between the candidates, and if these issues are a central part of the campaign debate, then voters are more likely to pass the "issue test" suggested by Campbell and his colleagues regardless of what era the election takes place in (Abramson, Aldrich, and Rohde 1999, 132).

Some scholars view this issue test as an overly stringent basis for judging the importance of issues to vote choice. Morris Fiorina (1981) suggests that there are two basic types of issue voting. **Retrospective voting** is based on evaluations of the past performance of the candidate; if voters feel an incumbent has done a good job, they are inclined to support that incumbent at the polls. **Prospective voting** is based on how well a voter believes a candidate will perform once he or she is in office. In practice, voters make both retrospective and prospective judgments, but retrospective assessments seem to be stronger and more influential. In terms of issues, voters seem to use the performance of the incumbent "as a starting point for comparing the major contenders" (Abramson, Aldrich, and Rohde 1999, 57).

VOTING BEHAVIOR AND THE OPERATION OF THE AMERICAN POLITICAL SYSTEM

The political system must balance two necessary but often conflicting qualities: stability and change. Without stability and predictability, the political system would have difficulty making binding decisions about who gets what; without change and openness to new demands, the system risks becoming stagnant and illegitimate.

Elections help the political system achieve this delicate balance because they are driven by both long-term and short-term forces. Long-term forces such as party loyalty or incumbency advantage in congressional campaigns have similar effects across a number of elections; short-term forces such as dramatic events or hot new issues influence outcomes in one or two elections. The former produces stability: most members of Congress, for example, serve multiple terms and provide institutional memory. The latter allows the system to adapt to new events and changing issues; for example, every election brings a significant number of new representatives to Congress, and occasionally this turnover results in the minority party becoming the majority party.

For the most part, long-term forces prevail in elections. An election in which the long-term partisan orientation of the electorate keeps the status quo, at least in terms of which party is in power, is known as a **maintaining election**. When long-term forces give way to short-term forces, what was the minority party prior to the election can become the majority party after the election—such elections are called **deviating elections**. If the subsequent election returns the traditional majority party to power, that election is called a **reinstating election**.

Maintaining, deviating, and reinstating elections are all part of the ebb and flow of democracy and represent long-term stability. Occasionally, however, an election brings about long-term change. The minority party wins an election, but it is not followed by a reinstating election; instead, the new majority stays in power for a number of elections. An election that brings about such a major political

retrospective voting Voting that is based on an individual's evaluation of the past performance of a candidate.

prospective voting Voting that is based on an individual's estimation of how well a candidate will perform duties in the future.

maintaining election An election in which the traditional majority party maintains power based on the long-standing partisan orientation of the voters.

deviating election An election in which the minority party is able to overcome the long-standing partisan orientation of the public based on temporary or short-term forces.

reinstating election An election in which the majority party regains power after a deviating election.

change is known as a **realigning election** or a critical election. Such elections are rare; they require a minority party to become the majority party and maintain that majority over the long term. Typically, realigning elections are a product of two forces: an event or crisis spawns issues that prompt blocs of voters to switch their party loyalties, and new voters are mobilized and disproportionately favor the minority party.

There have been few realigning elections in U.S. history. The last election universally judged to be a realigning election was in 1932. In that year, the majority Republican Party was displaced by the Democratic Party for a long time. This realignment occurred because Republicans were not perceived to be paying enough attention to the needs of immigrant and low-income groups who suffered mightily during the Great Depression. The latter event allowed the Democratic Party to put together a coalition of southerners, ethnic minorities, Catholics, Jews, the poor, urban blue-collar workers, and intellectuals. This coalition (known as the New Deal coalition) sustained the Democratic Party as the majority party in Congress, with relatively few interruptions, until the mid-1990s.

Contemporary Realignment?

Although there have been significant electoral changes over the last 30 years, there is no consensus about whether they add up to a realignment. The New Deal coalition has clearly eroded, and that has benefited Republicans. Some argue that 1980 should be treated as a realigning election. In that year, Republican Ronald Reagan defeated incumbent Democrat Jimmy Carter, and Republicans made significant gains in the House and won the Senate outright. Most reject 1980 as a realigning election: Republicans failed to win control of both houses of Congress that year, and Democrats came back to win the White House with the election of Bill Clinton in 1992.

What 1980 undoubtedly did make clear is that the New Deal coalition was fraying as a reliable basis of Democratic electoral power. In 1980, groups that traditionally had voted Democratic for 50 years shifted their support to the Republican nominee in large numbers. This shift was especially noticeable in the South, where voters began to realign their traditionally conservative ideology with Republican candidates. These changes laid the foundation for a 1990s Republican resurgence. In 1994 Republicans gained control of the House and Senate for the first time since 1953. Six years later, George W. Bush became the first Republican president in nearly 50 years to enjoy same-party control of both houses of Congress.

The Republican majority that emerged in the 1980s and 1990s, however, was never overwhelming. In the 2000 election, Bush actually lost the popular vote. Control of the U.S. Senate was so narrow in the early years of Bush's term that the defection of a single senator—Jim Jeffords of Vermont—from the Republican Party was enough to temporarily let Democrats regain control of the upper chamber. In the 2006 midterm elections, Democrats ousted the GOP as the majority party and took control of both the House and the Senate. Republicans had a disastrous 2008

realigning election An election in which the minority party is able to build a relatively stable coalition to win election, and this coalition endures over a series of elections.

electoral campaign, as Democrats took the White House and majorities in both houses of Congress. Those majorities, however, were under almost immediate assault. In 2010 Republicans, who just two years earlier had been hammered at the ballot box, came back with a vengeance, slicing the Democratic majority in the U.S. Senate, retaking control of the House of Representatives, and scoring a string of smashing electoral victories at the state level. Yet Republican fortunes dipped again in 2012; not only did they fail to gain the White House, they lost seats in both houses of Congress. Though the GOP did retain its majority in the House, even here the news was not all good. Not only did Republicans see their House majority shrink, in 2012 more people actually voted for Democratic House candidates in than Republican House candidates. This volatility from election cycle to election cycle seems to reflect only one consistent lesson: voters are not particularly happy with either major political party.

CHAPTER ELEVEN
Top Ten Takeaway Points

1. Representative democracy rests on the notion that ordinary people have the right to influence decisions about who gets what. Participation in making those binding decisions upholds the core democratic principles of political freedom and majority rule.

2. There are several forms of political participation, including voting, campaign activities, citizen-initiated contacts with government officials, and local community activities. Voting is the most common and widespread form of political participation.

3. Voter turnout in America is lower than in other Western representative democracies, but participation in other forms of political activity is higher.

4. Voter turnout in the United States has generally declined over time, even as the franchise has expanded. Around the time of the Civil War (1860s), turnout was approximately 80 percent. In the 1950s and 1960s, it was more than 60 percent. Turnout in presidential elections during the 1980s and 1990s was below 60 percent. Turnout rose above 60 percent in recent presidential elections, but it is not clear whether this pattern will continue.

5. Various elements of the U.S. election system impose higher barriers to voting than are found in other democracies. Elements of the American political system that might cause low turnout include

voting laws, voter registration practices, the two-party system, and the scheduling and number of elections.

6 An individual's desire and ability to politically participate are affected by socioeconomic status, psychological engagement with politics, political context, resources necessary to participate (free time, money, and civic skills), and group characteristics (age, gender, and race).

7 Political scientists are interested in explaining the choices voters make: for example, why do some people vote for Democrats and others vote for Republicans? Three theories have dominated the search for an explanation of vote choice: the sociological model, the social-psychological model, and the rational choice model. The sociological model uses group-level variables to explain voter behavior. The social-psychological model focuses on individual attitudes. The rational choice model views the decision to vote and the decision of whom to vote for as the product of an individual cost–benefit analysis.

8 Elections turn on both short-term forces (such as the candidates and issues associated with a particular election) and long-term forces (such as stable party loyalties within the electorate).

9 An election that brings about major political change over the long term is called a realigning election.

10 Significant electoral changes over the last 25 years have frayed the Democrats' New Deal coalition and aided Republicans, but there has been no long-term realignment to the GOP.

CHAPTER ELEVEN

Key Terms and Cases

allegiant, 412
candidate image, 423
deviating election, 425
franchise, 402
maintaining election, 425
midterm elections, 405
mobilization, 413

political alienation, 412
political efficacy, 412
political participation, 398
prospective voting, 425
rational choice model, 419
realigning election, 426
reinstating election, 425

retrospective voting, 425
social-psychological model
   (Michigan model), 418
socioeconomic status, 411
sociological model (Columbia
   model), 417
voter turnout, 405

12 CONGRESS

KEY QUESTIONS

What does Congress do?

How is Congress organized?

How does the organization of Congress affect what it does?

© AP Photo/Ron Edmonds

AMERICANS don't like their Congress very much. Public opinion polls typically show that disapproval of Congress is greater than approval. This presents a paradox. Congress, especially the House of Representatives, is the government institution that is supposed to be the closest and most responsive to the will of the people. If most Americans are dissatisfied with the way "the people's branch" is doing its job, doesn't that imply that America's most democratic institution is failing? Maybe. Maybe not.

Americans disapprove of Congress in general, but they approve of their own representatives in the particular (see Figure 12.1). A study by John Hibbing and Elizabeth Theiss-Morse (1995) helps explain this paradox. The authors found that many people believe Congress is less interested in the average citizen than in the rich and powerful. This belief rests on the notion that there is broad agreement on the problems facing the nation, and all the bickering and finger-pointing in Congress impedes quick action to solve these problems. In short, many Americans seem to think that their representative shares their views on the nation's problems, and it's all those other "jerks" in Congress who mess things up.

This finding suggests that Americans lack a basic understanding of how Congress works, which is precisely what Hibbing and Theiss-Morse found. The 535 members of Congress have differing goals and preferences, and they work in an institution governed by rules that could be described as Byzantine. Moreover, our representatives actually contribute to popular misperceptions. Rather than educate constituents about how Congress works and why, they often pander to popular (and misinformed) perceptions. As political scientist Richard Fenno observed, "members run *for* Congress by running *against* Congress" (1978, 168).

As discussed in chapter 9, the voice of the people on most issues is a jarring cacophony of conflict. There is no broad consensus on what government should do to solve the nation's problems, or even on what those problems are. Filtering these conflicting opinions through an institution as large and as complex as the U.S. Congress will not turn discord into harmony. Perhaps all the argument and debate in Congress is just a reflection of the diverse and often conflicting opinions in the public. If so, Congress does exactly what it was designed to do.

Some might be surprised by this conclusion. But Americans often fail to grasp the wide variety of functions Congress serves and how the institution connects its business to the broader political arena. In this chapter, we analyze what Congress is supposed to do, who does it, how it is done, and why. The chapter seeks to provide a foundation for judging whether Congress is fulfilling its democratic responsibilities by connecting the promise and the performance of democracy.

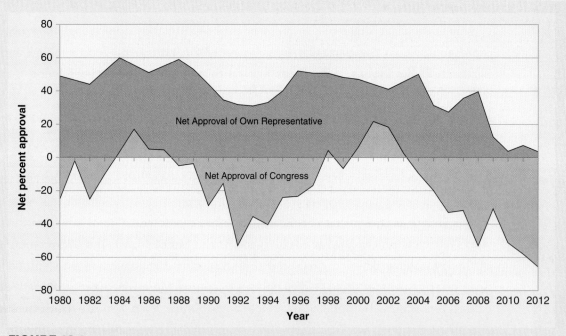

FIGURE 12.1 Americans Don't Like Their Congress But They Do Like Their Congressperson

Source: Approval of Congress: annual averages of all polls available in the year from Gallup Poll, *Washington Post, New York Times, WSJ, USA Today*, ABC, CBS, CNN, NBC, and various other news organizations and polling houses. Own representative: NES (1980, 1982, 1984, 1986, 1988, 1990, 1992, 1994, 1996, 1998, 2000, 2004), http://www.election-studies.org/nesguide/toptable/tab8a_3.htm; *Washington Post*, http://www.washingtonpost.com/wp-srv/politics/polls/postpoll_041607.html; ABC, CBS, FOX, and various other news organizations and polling houses (1989, 1991, 1993, 1995, 2002, 2005–2012).

THE CONCEPT OF THE U.S. CONGRESS

The U.S. Congress is a type of legislature. In general, a **legislature** can be defined as a deliberative council that has the authority to make and repeal laws. In representative democracies, ordinary citizens elect legislators to represent them. There are two general types of legislatures in representative democracies: (1) **parliamentary systems** in which the majority party in the legislature selects its leader to be chief executive, as in the British Parliament and prime minister; and (2) **presidential systems** in which citizens independently elect representatives in the legislature and the chief executive, as in the U.S. Congress and president.

Calling the American national legislature "Congress" follows the precedent of its historical antecedents—the First and Second Continental Congresses and the Congress under the Articles of Confederation. The term "congress" means "a coming together" (Ayto 1990, 131). Traditionally, the term referred to a meeting of representatives of independent organizations (e.g., trade unions, states, and nations) to discuss some problem. Hence, the Continental Congresses were meetings of delegates representing the colonies. The unicameral Congress under the Articles of Confederation represented sovereign states, not the people of those states. As political scientist Charles Stewart observes, this Congress was "an assembly of ambassadors" (2005, 8). Laws passed by Congress under the Articles were not binding on the people directly, but rather were requests to the states to take some action (which the states routinely ignored). The Congress created by the current Constitution does represent the people, and its laws are directly binding on the people. Nevertheless, representation is still tied to states—every state is guaranteed at least one representative in the House and two in the Senate, originally senators were elected by state legislatures, and electors chosen by states elect the president. Moreover, the federal system retains the status of states as self-governing units, though federal laws take precedence over state constitutions and laws if there is a conflict. Continued use of the term for the bicameral Congress created by the current constitution emphasizes the special status of states in this federal system.

Congress is both a representative institution and a policymaking institution. The purpose of Congress, therefore, is twofold: to represent the needs and interests of ordinary people and to translate those needs and wishes into laws that determine who gets what. To assess whether Congress is achieving this dual purpose, it is necessary to understand its responsibilities within the American political system.

RESPONSIBILITIES OF CONGRESS

The national legislature is charged with a dizzying number of tasks. These tasks can be grouped into primary and secondary responsibilities. Primary

legislature A deliberative council that has the authority to make and repeal laws. In representative democracies, ordinary citizens elect legislators to represent them.

parliamentary system An electoral system in which the party holding the majority of seats in the legislature selects the chief executive.

presidential system A political system in which the chief executive and the legislature are elected independently.

responsibilities are performed on a continuous basis and consume the greatest share of members' time. Secondary responsibilities are not necessarily less important; these duties can be essential to achieving Congress's dual purpose. They are called secondary because they come up sporadically and constitute a smaller proportion of the legislator's workload.

Primary Responsibilities

Congress's two primary responsibilities are lawmaking and representing constituents.

LAWMAKING The legislature's foremost responsibility is enacting laws that address the major problems and concerns of American society. **Lawmaking** includes passing the laws and then overseeing government administration of those laws. For example, the Clean Air Act of 1990 "would have a direct impact on the lives of nearly all Americans" because it "was designed to improve the quality of the air we breathe. It would have wide-ranging impacts on health, transportation, and the economy" (R. Cohen 1995, 4). This particular legislation is instructive not only because of its substance but also because it shows Congress at its best and at its worst.

On the positive side, there was clear public support for cleaning up the air, and the legislative process managed to incorporate a diverse set of viewpoints on a divisive set of topics to produce a law that had strong majority support. This is no small achievement. Yet the process of lawmaking was agonizingly slow: the bill was 13 years in the making. Parochial protectionism, special interest meddling, and inter- and intra-party disagreements stalled the process at various points (see R. Cohen 1995). The Clean Air Act was not unique in this sense. Virtually every piece of major legislation has to run a similar gauntlet.

Passing laws to ameliorate social problems is a central function of Congress and an essential step in the policymaking process. The role Congress plays in the policymaking process, however, has changed over the course of the nation's history. The policymaking process (discussed in more detail in chapter 16) involves several steps:

1. *Agenda setting:* government identifies the list of issues and problems to which it will pay attention.
2. *Policy formulation and adoption:* government considers various solutions and formally approves a particular one.
3. *Policy implementation:* government translates the law into action.
4. *Policy evaluation:* government and nongovernment actors assess the successes and problems of public policies (Ripley 1988, 48–55).

lawmaking A legislature's power to enact laws that address major problems and then to oversee government administration of those laws.

The goal of separation of powers in the Constitution was to make legislative and executive powers independent, which suggests that Congress would have primary responsibility for steps 1 and 2 in the policy process, and the president would have primary responsibility for steps 3 and 4. This division of responsibilities has become less clear-cut over time.

Congress continues to be a major agenda-setter, but the legislative branch has come to expect the president to take the lead in initiating policy proposals. Since the 1950s, the president has initiated about one-third of the most important bills considered in Congress (Edwards and Barrett 2000, 122). Congress, of course, does not automatically pass the president's initiatives. Some presidential proposals do not pass, and those that do are often changed substantially as they work their way through the legislative process.

Congress has also delegated substantial lawmaking powers to the executive branch. Congress tends to pass general laws that set broad goals and guidelines for dealing with a problem, while leaving the specifics of implementation to executive branch agencies. Filling in these details is known as rulemaking, a little-known form of lawmaking discussed in chapter 14.

Although Congress has delegated significant legislative power to the executive branch, it has compensated by extending its lawmaking authority to the implementation of policies. The primary way Congress has extended its lawmaking power is through **legislative oversight of administration**, which refers to a variety of tools that Congress uses to control the administrative arm of government. Congressional oversight is often considered another primary function of Congress. Although it is certainly a vitally important activity, just as policymaking has come to mean more than passing laws, we believe oversight of the executive is better viewed as an essential part of lawmaking. Legislative oversight tools (discussed in more detail in chapter 14) include the power to do the following:

- Create or abolish executive branch agencies
- Assign these agencies particular program responsibilities
- Provide or withhold funding for governmental programs
- Confirm or not confirm presidential appointments to the major administrative positions in the executive branch

REPRESENTATION The other primary responsibility of Congress is representation. **Representation** is a complex relationship that involves responding to constituents' needs and demands and informing and educating the public. Political scientists Heinz Eulau and Paul Karps (1977) identify four types of responsiveness that illustrate some of the complexity of representation: policy responsiveness, service responsiveness, allocation responsiveness, and symbolic responsiveness.

The first and most obvious part of representation is **policy responsiveness**—that is, the extent to which the policymaking behavior of the representative is congruent with the preferences of constituents. In the most simplistic terms, representatives are supposed to vote the way their constituents want them to vote. Political science research finds that most citizens know little about how their representatives vote on issues before Congress, and partisanship and ideology are the primary predictors of how members of Congress vote on roll calls.

legislative oversight of administration A variety of tools Congress uses to control administrative agencies, including creating or abolishing agencies, assigning program responsibilities, providing funds, and confirming presidential appointments.

representation The relationship between elected officials and the people who put them in office, involving the extent to which officials are responsive to the people.

policy responsiveness The amount of agreement between the people represented and their elected officials on policy issues.

Does this mean that members of Congress are failing as representatives? Not necessarily. Candidates who win election to Congress tend to reflect the politics and cultures of their constituencies. Consequently, representatives and constituents share many values, including party and policy preferences. Some districts are composed of voters who are mostly Democrats with preferences for liberal policies; these districts tend to elect liberal Democrats. Other districts are mostly Republicans with more conservative preferences, and they send conservative Republicans to Congress. On the most salient issues, representatives tend to follow constituency preferences. Constituents may know little about most policy proposals before Congress, but they are generally aware of high-profile policy issues, and failure to follow constituency preferences on these salient matters invites a negative response at the polls. Thus, there is likely to be substantial policy congruence between most representatives in Congress and their constituents.

A second component of representation is **service responsiveness**, which refers to the variety of tasks that legislators perform for constituents who request assistance in dealing with the federal government. For instance, an elderly constituent might want information about Social Security benefits, or the mayor of a small city may ask for help in applying for a grant for a federal water treatment program. These activities are known as **casework**. In performing casework, members of Congress act as intermediaries between private individuals and the administrative agencies in the executive branch.

A third component of representation is **allocation responsiveness**. Members of Congress are notorious for using their position to see that their state or district gets a share of the benefits of government programs for roads, dams, government buildings, federal grants to local police and fire departments, support for agricultural commodities, and so on. Political scientists refer to such allocations as **distributive benefits**—that is, government expenditures and programs that concentrate benefits in specific geographical areas such as states or congressional districts but for which the costs are spread across the entire population (Evans 2004; Lowi 1969). These are also pejoratively called **pork-barrel benefits**, a term first used in this context in the mid-nineteenth century to describe projects viewed as a waste of tax dollars that serve no purpose other than to aid the reelection of a single incumbent. Although reelection is a primary reason that members of Congress pursue distributive programs, objectively identifying what is wasteful "pork" and what genuinely serves the public interest is a difficult task. By securing these allocations, a representative anticipates and responds to the needs of his or her constituency. A study by political scientist Diana Evans shows that leaders in Congress also use distributive benefits "as a sort of currency to purchase legislators' votes" in order "to build the majority coalitions necessary to pass broad-based, general interest legislation" (2004, 2).

The three types of representation discussed so far involve delivering some tangible benefit—a vote consistent with constituents' preferences, help with

service responsiveness Representation that takes the form of the tasks legislators perform based on the requests and needs of their constituents.

casework Activities of members of Congress to act as intermediaries and help private individuals who are having problems with the administrative agencies in the executive branch.

allocation responsiveness Representation that takes the form of members of Congress ensuring that their district gets a share of federal benefits.

distributive benefits Government expenditures and programs that concentrate benefits in specific geographical areas such as states or congressional districts for which the costs are spread across the entire population.

pork-barrel benefits Government-sponsored projects that bring economic benefits to a Congress member's state or district. This is a pejorative term first used in the mid-nineteenth century to describe projects viewed as a waste of tax dollars that serve no purpose other than to aid the reelection of a single incumbent.

bureaucratic red tape, or government expenditures to assist the district. The fourth type of representation—symbolic responsiveness—draws attention to a psychological component of representation. **Symbolic responsiveness** includes activities that use broad "political symbols in order to generate and maintain trust or support" among constituents (Eulau and Karps 1977, 246). Members of Congress develop close, cordial relations with their constituents. They spend time in the district to show that they are part of the constituency and that they are "at home" there. Richard Fenno, one of the nation's foremost authorities on Congress, refers to these activities as member **home styles**, which are the ways members of Congress present themselves to the various parts of their constituency and explain

their Washington activities (Fenno 1978). Typically, members develop home styles that fit their constituencies. A member who represents a strongly partisan constituency, for example, might adopt a policy-oriented home style, whereas a member from a politically diverse constituency might adopt a home style that emphasizes constituency service.

Fenno found that "constituency" is a complex concept. Members of Congress view their constituencies like "a nest of concentric circles" (1978, 1): the geographical constituency, the reelection constituency, the primary constituency, and the personal constituency. The largest circle is the **geographical constituency**, which consists of everyone and everything within the boundaries of the member's House district. Nested within the geographical constituency is the **reelection constituency**, which is composed of the people in the district whom the member can count on for support. The **primary constituency** is a smaller number of the member's strongest, mostly partisan supporters. An even smaller number of intimate friends, advisors, and confidants are viewed as the **personal constituency**. A member's behavior will vary depending on which constituency he or she is interacting with.

The complexity of representation is especially evident when a member of Congress must choose between the preferences of constituents and the dictates of conscience or the best interests of the entire nation. A pork-barrel project might provide economic benefits and be strongly supported within the district, but what if it is an unnecessary drain on the federal treasury? Should a representative choose what the constituents clearly want or what serves the best long-run interests of the nation as a whole? Such conflicts are more common than most people realize, and they raise a basic question about the exact nature of representation. Edmund Burke, a British political philosopher and member

Members of Congress sometimes have to choose between the preferences of constituents and what they believe to be in the best interests of the country. In 2008 lawmakers approved a controversial $700 billion bailout of the financial industry, a policy many economists agreed was critical to preventing an economic catastrophe. In contrast, many voters, like those pictured here, were intensely opposed to the bailout.

symbolic responsiveness A congressional member's efforts to use political symbols to generate trust and support among the voters.

home style The way a member of Congress behaves, explains his or her legislative actions, and presents himself or herself in the home district.

geographical constituency Everyone and everything within the geographical boundaries of a congressional member's House district.

reelection constituency The people within a Congress member's House district who can be counted on for support.

primary constituency A member of Congress's strongest, mostly partisan supporters.

personal constituency A small number of intimate friends, advisors, and confidants who support a member of Congress.

of Parliament, argued that representatives should be **trustees** who use their own judgment to make the decisions they feel are appropriate for the interests first of the nation and then of their constituents. In contrast, representatives who adopt a **delegate** role simply do what their constituents want, regardless of whether those wants are in the public interest. These contrasting philosophies suggest different decisions: the delegate will vote for the pork-barrel project; the trustee will not (and will face the consequences during the next election). In reality, the philosophical divide is not quite so clear, and representatives often adopt a mix of both delegate and trustee roles; this type of representative is a **politico**.

Representation is a two-way concept. The four components of representation just discussed reflect the view of the relationship as one that flows from constituents to representative. Another aspect of representation focuses on the relationship that flows the other way, from representative to constituent. This aspect is the representative's duty to lead by informing and educating the public.

Scholars have long recognized that a central obligation of representatives is to inform the public about the major issues facing the country and the options for dealing with them (W. Wilson 1885). Thus, when Congress holds hearings on Social Security, pollution, drugs, or the conduct of the war in Iraq, it is helping to educate and inform the American people about the problems on the nation's agenda and the policies that might deal with them. Such activities may be intended to produce an electoral advantage, but they also help inform citizens.

Performing the lawmaking and representative functions has important side effects. By serving the needs of constituents, lawmakers help develop loyalty and allegiance of the public to the political system. The give-and-take of the legislative process accommodates competing demands, which helps ensure that final decisions are acceptable to concerned parties. This accommodation process helps legitimize the political system so that citizens in general are willing to abide by the rules and regulations developed by government.

trustee A representative who uses his or her own judgment to make decisions promoting the best interests of the nation as a whole, with the particular interests of constituents remaining a secondary concern.

delegate A representative who makes legislative decisions based on the interests and views of his or her constituents, regardless of personal preference.

politico A representative whose philosophy of representation is a mix of both delegate and trustee. See also delegate and trustee.

Secondary Responsibilities

Secondary responsibilities may be vital to the overall functioning of the government or the legislative body. They are called secondary not because they are less important, but because they occur only occasionally. These tasks include impeachment, seating and disciplining members, and selecting leaders for the executive branch.

IMPEACHMENT Congress has the power to remove executive and judicial officials of the national government from their positions through the impeachment process. According to the Constitution, officials subject to removal by congressional action include "the president, the vice president, and all civil officers of the United States"

President Bill Clinton was impeached by the House of Representatives in December 1998 on charges of perjury and obstruction of justice, and subsequently tried by the U.S. Senate. Clinton was acquitted in February 1999 when the Senate failed to muster the two-thirds majority required to convict and remove a federal official from office.

(Article II, Section 4). Federal judges are the only other civil officers who are likely to be impeached; because they serve for life, there is no other practical way to remove them for wrongdoing. Other legal procedures exist to remove members of Congress and cabinet secretaries for wrongdoing.

Removal through impeachment is a two-step process. The first step is impeachment by the House. To **impeach** means simply to charge or accuse. The House impeaches an official by passing articles of impeachment by a simple majority. The impeachment resolution serves as a formal charge of wrongdoing, similar to an indictment by a grand jury. If the articles of impeachment are approved, the process continues to the second stage: trial in the Senate. Members of the Senate sit as a jury to hear the evidence and decide whether to acquit the impeached official or remove him or her from office. The House sends "managers" to serve as prosecutors, and the impeached official is represented by defenders. Conviction and removal from office require a two-thirds vote of the Senate. As president of the Senate, the vice president normally presides over an impeachment trial. But if it is the president who has been impeached, the Constitution designates the chief justice of the Supreme Court to preside at the trial in the Senate. Having the vice

impeach To charge or accuse.

president preside over a trial that could elevate him or her to the presidency would be an obvious conflict of interest.[1]

Grounds for impeachment include "treason, bribery, or other high crimes and misdemeanors" (Article II, Section 4). Treason and bribery are straightforward but are rarely the focus of impeachment proceedings. What constitutes "high crimes and misdemeanors" is the subject of some controversy. Kenneth W. Starr, the independent prosecutor whose investigation provided the basis for the impeachment of President Bill Clinton in 1998, once argued that an official could be impeached for poisoning a neighbor's cat (Gettinger 1998). Historically, the bar for impeachment has been set considerably higher, to include wrongdoing that threatens the basic functioning of government in the same way that treason or bribery would. Thus, impeachable offenses may not be limited to illegal acts. If a president were to move to a Middle Eastern country so that he could have several wives, such behavior would surely be impeachable, but it would not be illegal (Black 1974). On the other hand, even serious illegal acts are not necessarily sufficient grounds for removing a president from office. When Vice President Aaron Burr shot and killed Alexander Hamilton, Burr was indicted for murder in two states, but he never faced impeachment.

Impeachment is as much a political process as a legal one. As a member of Congress, Republican Gerald Ford of Michigan said that an impeachable offense is "whatever a majority of the House of Representatives considers it to be at a given moment in history" (Gettinger 1998, 565). Ford was ridiculed at the time, but the impeachment of President Clinton seemed to validate this definition; the House impeached Clinton on a largely partisan vote.

The Senate is likely to prevent the bar from being lowered too far. Senators have broader constituencies than House members, and the Senate has a special status and responsibility under the Constitution that most senators take seriously. The supermajority vote (two-thirds rather than one-half plus one) required to convict and remove an official from office also reduces the chances that a president could be removed for solely partisan purposes.

Impeachment is rare. Only 17 officials have been impeached so far. Two presidents—Bill Clinton and Andrew Johnson—were formally impeached, though neither was removed from office. President Nixon resigned prior to the House vote on the articles of impeachment rather than face an almost-certain Senate trial. Most of the other impeached officials were federal judges; only seven were convicted and removed from office (see the Politics in Practice feature "The Impeachment of Judge Alcee Hastings").

---

[1] Senators take an oath to try the case impartially, but impeachment is a political process. Conflicts of interest are inevitable. In the impeachment trial of President Andrew Johnson in 1868, Senator Benjamin F. Wade (R-OH), president pro tempore of the Senate, took part in the trial and voted for conviction. Since there was no vice president, Wade was in line to become president. President Johnson's son-in-law, Senator David T. Patterson (D-TN), also participated; he voted to acquit. Senator Barbara Boxer (D-CA) participated in the Senate trial of President Clinton. Her daughter is married to Hillary Clinton's brother. In an ordinary judicial trial, individuals with such conflicts would be excluded.

POLITICS IN PRACTICE

THE IMPEACHMENT OF JUDGE ALCEE HASTINGS

The following is an excerpt describing the impeachment process in practice:

In the 1980s, for the first time, the Senate used a shortcut procedure first authorized in 1935 to deal with three impeachment trials of federal judges. The shortcut allowed a special 12-member committee to hear witnesses and gather evidence before the full Senate convened to try the judges. This procedure saved the Senate months of deliberation but resulted in court challenges from the judges, who claimed that their convictions were unconstitutional because the full Senate had not heard the evidence. In 1993, the Supreme Court refused to consider that argument, ruling unanimously in the case of *Nixon v. United States* that the courts could not interfere with the Senate's conduct of impeachment trials because the Constitution gave the Senate "the sole power to try all impeachments."

The Court's ruling was an important affirmation of the Senate's impeachment power, but the unique case of federal judge Alcee Hastings of Florida remained unresolved.

Hastings had been impeached and convicted after having been tried and acquitted of criminal charges. In 1992, he made history by winning election to the House as a Democrat from Florida. Hastings' election raised a new constitutional question: whether conviction by the Senate was sufficient to disqualify a person from holding public office, or whether disqualification required a separate Senate vote.

The Constitution says, "judgment in cases of impeachment shall not extend further than to removal from office, and disqualification to hold and enjoy any office of honor, trust or profit under the United States." In practice, the Senate had treated the punishments as distinct and held separate votes on whether to block an impeached official from holding office again. In three of its seven convictions, the Senate had taken separate votes on disqualification from future office and had twice voted to do so. A disqualification vote was not taken for Hastings, and in January 1993, a federal judge rejected a lawsuit claiming that Hastings' Senate conviction disqualified him from holding office. Hastings took his seat with the rest of the 103rd Congress.

It is not surprising that Hastings was greeted in Washington by skepticism that he would be able to work effectively with members who had voted to impeach him in 1988. But Hastings surprised the skeptics by bearing no apparent grudges about the past and by focusing instead on building legislative influence.

"Succeeding is the best revenge" he said after nine months in office. "My goal was to get beyond people viewing me as an impeached judge. I think I've accomplished that in grand style."

SOURCES Congressional Quarterly, Inc. 1993. *Congress A to Z.* 2nd ed. Washington, DC: Congressional Quarterly, pp. 189–190.

Duncan, Philip D., and Christine C. Lawrence, eds. 1998. *Politics in America 1996: The 105th Congress.* Washington, DC: CQ Press, p. 369.

SEATING AND DISCIPLINING MEMBERS Each chamber also has power over the seating and disciplining of its members. Thus, both the House and the Senate have the authority to judge the fairness of elections. Defeated candidates sometimes challenge the results of close elections on the grounds of voting irregularities. Although both chambers attempt to investigate and resolve such charges impartially, historically partisan interests have prevailed, with the majority party seating its candidate.

The House and the Senate can also **exclude** or refuse to seat individuals who win elections but do not meet the constitutional qualifications of being U.S. citizens, having residence in the state, and being at least 25 years old for House members and 30 years old for senators. Until 1969, each chamber occasionally used exclusion as a disciplinary tool against otherwise-qualified individuals who were disloyal, such as those who supported secession during the Civil War or who were charged with crimes or misconduct. The Supreme Court ended this practice in *Powell v. McCormack* (1969), ruling that a duly elected member could be excluded only for failure to meet constitutional qualifications.

Article I, Section 5 of the Constitution also authorizes both chambers to discipline sitting members for illegal or unethical behavior, though both are loath to exercise this power. Because most members do not relish the task of judging their colleagues, such formal actions are reserved for the most egregious cases. There are several penalties available, depending on the nature and seriousness of the wrongdoing: expulsion, censure or reprimand, and fine.

The most serious punishment, **expulsion**, requires a two-thirds vote and is rarely used. Several members were expelled in the 1860s for supporting the Confederacy in the Civil War, but aside from that, only one senator and one House member have been expelled from Congress. Senator William Blount of Tennessee was expelled in 1876 when it was discovered that he had a plan to provoke the Creek and Cherokee Indians to assist British efforts to conquer the Spanish territory of Florida. The House passed impeachment charges against him, but those charges were dropped because the expulsion had already removed him from office. The House member was Ozzie Myers of New York, who was expelled in 1980 for involvement in a bribery scandal.

The lesser penalties of censure or reprimand and fines require only a simple majority to pass. **Censures and reprimands** are verbal condemnations expressing public disapproval of the member's actions by his or her colleagues. Reprimands sometimes include a fine. In 1997, Speaker Newt Gingrich was reprimanded for violating House ethics rules and fined $300,000 (Katz 1998).

SELECTING LEADERS FOR THE EXECUTIVE BRANCH Congress is also occasionally involved in matters of leadership selection for the executive branch. As discussed in chapter 10, if no candidate for president or vice president receives a majority of the electoral votes, the issue is decided by the House in the case of the president or the Senate in the case of the vice president. Under the Twenty-Fifth Amendment, if the vice presidency becomes vacant, both houses of Congress must approve the president's choice of a new vice president by majority vote. Notice that unlike presidential appointments to judicial and executive branch offices, which must be confirmed only by the Senate, appointment of a new vice president under the Twenty-Fifth Amendment requires approval of both houses of Congress. This procedure has been used twice. The first occasion was when President Richard Nixon nominated Representative Gerald Ford to

exclude The refusal of Congress to seat any candidate who wins election but does not meet the constitutional requirements to hold congressional office.

expulsion The ejection of a member of Congress from office.

censures and reprimands Verbal condemnations of a member of Congress by the House or Senate, intended to punish bad behavior by expressing the public disapproval of the member's colleagues.

become vice president after the resignation of Spiro Agnew in 1973. When Nixon resigned in 1974, Ford became president and nominated Nelson Rockefeller to be vice president.

The Senate also plays an important role in staffing positions in the executive branch and judiciary. The president appoints cabinet secretaries and other high-level executive branch personnel, foreign ambassadors, and federal judges with the "advice and consent" of the Senate. There is little Senate advising before the selection, but the consent provision means that the Senate must confirm the president's appointments to these offices by majority vote. Some nominations have run into trouble and have been defeated or withdrawn. However, the Senate has confirmed more than 96 percent of presidents' nominations, and a study found that nominations enjoy a "presumption of success" (Krutz, Fleisher, and Bond 1998). The Senate typically has been inclined to defer to the president's choice, and senators who are opposed to a particular nominee have had a difficult time overcoming this presumption of success. A more recent study suggests that the "presumption of success" does not hold to the same extent it once did, however. As the parties in Congress have become more polarized in recent decades, opponents increasingly have used Senate rules to block nominations from getting to the floor for an up or down vote (Bond, Fleisher, and Krutz 2009).

OTHER POLICY RESPONSIBILITIES Congress also becomes involved in specialized areas of public policymaking. Both houses join in initiating constitutional amendments. The Senate also has special powers in foreign policy: the Senate must ratify treaties negotiated by the president (by two-thirds vote) and confirm ambassadors to foreign countries appointed by the president (by a simple majority). Finally, Congress exercises legal jurisdiction over the District of Columbia.

MEMBERS OF CONGRESS AND THEIR WORLD

Alexis de Tocqueville, the perceptive French observer of America during the Jacksonian period, referred to the "vulgar demeanor" of the American national legislature. The aristocrats who dominated European legislatures, he argued, were secure in their social positions, less tied to their constituents than to their parties, and more interested in big questions. American legislators derived their social position from service in the assembly, were more tied to their constituents than to their parties, and felt compelled to repeatedly confirm their importance and effectiveness whether there was any basis for such claims or not. Rather than tackle big questions, legislators in America focused on whatever issue was popular, regardless of its substantive merit. "The consequence," Tocqueville wrote, "is that the debates of that great assembly are frequently vague and perplexed and that they seem to drag their slow length along rather than to advance towards a distinct object" (Tocqueville [1835] 1955, 97). Does Tocqueville's analysis accurately portray Congress today? Who, exactly, are the people elected to Congress?

Backgrounds of National Legislators

Tocqueville noted that the national legislature was dominated by lawyers and businessmen, an observation that still holds true today. Although lawyers constitute less than 1 percent of the adult population in the United States, 200 (about 37 percent) members in the 112th Congress (2011–2012) listed law as their occupation. A majority of senators—52 percent—were lawyers, and the proportion of lawyers in the Senate has not fallen below 50 percent since the 1950s. Lawyers are somewhat less prevalent in the House—34 percent of House members in the 112th Congress had a background in law, and lawyers have not constituted a majority of House members since the Ninety-Fifth Congress (1977–1978) (Manning 2010; Ornstein, Mann, and Malbin 2008, 35, 38).

Why so many lawyers? For one thing, the tools of the lawyer's trade are verbal and argumentative facility, negotiation skills, and the ability to analyze statutes and administrative regulations—precisely the talents needed by those who legislate, control the administration, inform the public, and represent constituents. Lawyers are also professionals, which bestows social standing in the community, and their job is to help people with various kinds of problems. For these reasons, lawyers are often regarded as natural legislators.

Businesspeople now rival lawyers as the largest occupational group in Congress—209 (about 39 percent) members in the 112th Congress listed their occupation as business. People in business have some of the same attributes that provide lawyers with their advantages as legislators—they too tend to have relatively high social status in their communities, and they benefit from the high regard Americans have for entrepreneurs.

No other occupation rivals business, public service, or law in the national legislature. The next most common occupation listed for the 112th Congress was education—about 15 percent of members. About 92 percent of the 535 members serving in the 112th Congress listed their occupations as law, business, or education. The remainder consists of an eclectic mix of doctors, ministers, journalists, farmers, scientists, engineers, professional entertainers (a comedian, a screenwriter, and a documentary filmmaker), two professional football players, and three political scientists—Daniel Lipinski (D-IL), Dave Loesack (D-IA), and David Price (D-NC).

The similarities of the modern Congress to that of Tocqueville's time extend beyond the career background of its members. The legislature Tocqueville observed was dominated exclusively by white males. This exclusivity has diminished, but not the dominance. In 2010 the U.S. population was about 51 percent female, 13 percent

POLITICS IN PRACTICE

JEANNETTE RANKIN: FIRST CONGRESSWOMAN

This excerpt describes the life and career of Jeannette Rankin (1880–1973), the first woman to serve in Congress:

A suffragist and pacifist, [Rankin] ran for the House at a time when only a handful of states allowed women to vote and as the nation was about to enter World War I.

Born into a family that believed in education for women and political activism, Rankin graduated from the University of Montana and went on to study social work at the New York School of Philanthropy. She returned west and lobbied for the enfranchisement of women in the states of Washington, California, and Montana.

Rankin ran as a Republican for one of Montana's House seats in 1916 on a platform favoring Prohibition, women's rights, and federal suffrage. (The Nineteenth Amendment giving women the right to vote was not ratified until 1920.) When elected, Rankin said: "I knew the women would stand behind me. I am deeply conscious of the responsibility. I will not only represent the women of Montana, but also the women of the country..."

In the House Rankin worked to further the cause of women. She introduced legislation to grant women citizenship independent of their husbands and sponsored a bill providing for federally supported maternal and infant health instruction. She helped set up a House committee on women's suffrage and tried to ensure that employment generated by the legislation would include women.

In 1917 the House voted on the entry of the United States into World War I. With forty-nine other representatives Rankin voted no, saying, "I want to stand by my country but I cannot vote for war." Her vote brought national notoriety for her.

After her first term in the House, Rankin ran unsuccessfully for the Senate. Out of office, she continued to work for women's rights, and in 1940 she was reelected to the House. Once again she was faced with a vote on U.S. involvement in a war. Rankin was the only member to vote against entry into World War II. Few people shared the view of Kansas newspaper editor William Allen White, who said of her pacifist stand: "It was a brave thing! And its bravery somehow discounted its folly." After the vote, she was forced to lock herself in a phone booth to escape from the curious and angry crowds.

In 1968, when she was in her late eighties, Jeannette Rankin led a Jeannette Rankin Brigade to the Capitol to protest the war in Vietnam. She died at the age of ninety-two.

SOURCE Congressional Quarterly, Inc. 1993. *Congress A to Z: A Ready Reference Encyclopedia.* 2nd ed. Washington, DC: Congressional Quarterly, pp. 318–319.

African American, 16 percent Latino, 4.8 percent Asian American, and 0.9 percent Native American. In the House of Representatives in the 112th Congress, 17 percent of members were women, 7.8 percent were African American, 5 percent were Latino, 1.7 percent were Asian American, and one member (0.19 percent) was Native American. The Senate was even less representative of the nation—including only 17 women, two Latinos, two Asian Americans, one Native American, and no African Americans. (See the Politics in Practice feature "Jeannette Rankin: First Congresswoman.")

© Bettmann/CORBIS

Jeannette Rankin.

Although the numbers of women and ethnic minorities in Congress are low in comparison to their proportion in the electorate, they are high in comparison to the historical representation of women and minorities in Congress. These changes suggest that the future composition of Congress may be increasingly different.

Moreover, descriptive representation, in which the legislature reflects the gender and ethnic makeup of society, is only one of several types of representation. As discussed in chapter 10, substantive representation may be more important. It is possible for white male professionals to understand and respond to the interests of blue-collar workers, women, ethnic minorities, and the poor and to represent their substantive interests in the legislature.

Tenure and Career Patterns

Although the profile of the typical member of Congress has not changed much in the last 200 years, the profile of the typical congressional career has changed dramatically. The most obvious change is that serving in Congress is now a career. In the nineteenth century, a decade was an unusually long time for anyone to be a House member, and serving in the House as a lifetime member was virtually unknown. By the latter half of the twentieth century, the average member of the House of Representatives had been serving for about 10 years, and some members have served much longer (Hibbing 1991).

Tenure has increased for several reasons. Members of Congress are now more likely to run for reelection than they were in the past. In congressional elections since 1946, more than 90 percent of House members have run for reelection, and they are very successful when they run—an average of about 92 percent win reelection (see chapter 10, Figure 10.7). The reelection rate in the Senate is slightly lower—79 percent. Careerism in Congress is not just the result of the electoral advantages of incumbency. Government plays a much bigger role in social and economic life than it did before the twentieth century. Serving in Congress has evolved from a part-time job in a part-time body with limited responsibilities to a full-time job in a full-time body with enormous responsibilities (Hibbing 1991, 3).

The rise of congressional careerists may have fueled cynicism toward government. A common view is that the incumbency advantage allows career politicians to ignore the needs of ordinary people and serve the interests of powerful special interests in Washington. The popularity of term limits indicates that many voters are uncomfortable with public service becoming a career unto itself.

Political scientist John Hibbing (1991) conducted a comprehensive analysis of congressional careers. Consistent with the conventional wisdom, Hibbing found that the longer a representative serves in Congress, the less attention he or she pays to constituency matters. The number of trips to the district decreases, and district offices get fewer staffers. Yet he also found that the more senior members of Congress are more effective legislators; as representatives gain experience, they tend to become more active and successful legislators. First-term representatives might spend more time in the district with their constituents, but they are less likely to play a significant role in shaping legislation. Hibbing concluded that term limits are a bad idea and "would likely result in a devastating loss of legislative acumen, expertise, and activity" (1991, 180).

A study by Jeffery Mondak (1995) supports this conclusion. Mondak developed indicators of House members' competence and integrity. He found that members serving seven terms or more scored higher than members who retired or were defeated before the seventh term (Figure 12.2). Evidence from Mondak's study suggests that electoral defeats and retirements tend to filter out individuals less able to do the job well. In short, making experience and expertise a basis for disqualification from office is likely to deprive Congress of its most able legislators.

Although the length of service in Congress increased considerably from 1789 through the 1950s (Polsby 1968), this trend toward longer service has stabilized. As Figure 12.3 shows, the average length of service in both the House and the Senate has not changed much in the last five decades: the average tenure in Congress has been around 10 years and has exceeded 12 years only once in the House (1991–1992) and four times in the Senate (1995–1996, 2005–2006, 2007–2008, and 2009–2010). Tenure in the House has actually declined since the high in

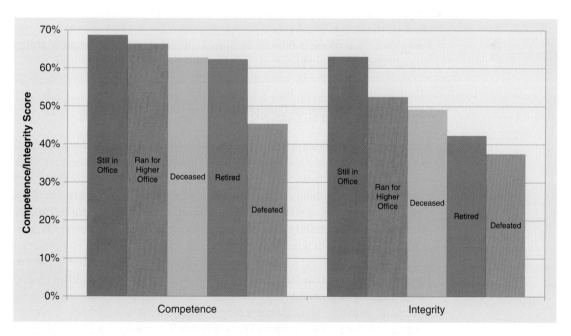

FIGURE 12.2 Competence and Integrity of House Members

Source: Adapted by the authors from Mondak (1995, 1057).

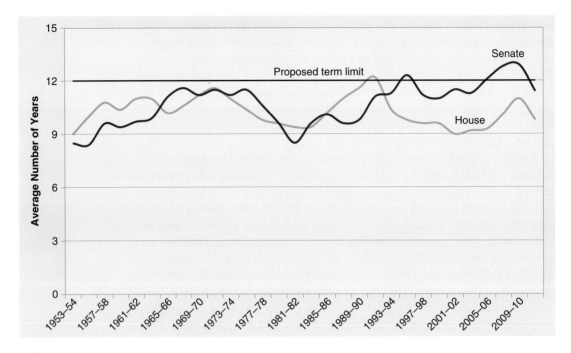

FIGURE 12.3 Average Length of Service in Congress

Source: Constructed by the authors from Ornstein, Mann, and Malbin (2008, 32–34; data for 1953–2008) and Manning (2010, 2011; data for 2009–2012).

1991–1992. Thus, there continues to be substantial turnover in Congress, which casts out deadwood and brings in fresh blood.

Daily Life of a Member of Congress

Busy is the word to describe the typical workday of a member of Congress. One of the most accessible—and amusing—descriptions of a typical member's work routine was penned by the satirist P. J. O'Rourke (1991, 49–65). O'Rourke trailed a congressman for 11 hours of one day. The day began with an 8:00 a.m. breakfast meeting, followed by an 8:30 A.M. breakfast meeting, followed by two committee meetings and a courtesy visit with a volunteer firefighting group from the congressman's district. There was no lunch break. In the afternoon, the congressman huddled with his staff for several hours to come up with coherent and defensible positions on an omnibus farm bill, the reauthorization of a commodities trading commission, a food safety act, a pesticide-control proposal, rural-development legislation, regular and supplemental appropriations bills, a number of foreign treaties, a proposed sale of fighter planes to South Korea, a housing bill, a proposal to close military bases, and a series of bills dealing with U.S. exports. There were 25 issues in all, representing roughly 10 percent of the items on the congressional calendar that week. The congressman had to balance the wishes of his constituents, the preferences of his party, the pressure of congressional leaders, the demands of the president, entreaties from lobbyists, and his own personal viewpoint for each issue. The congressman's position was likely to conflict with at least one of these on each of the 250 items on the calendar that week.

After two hours of trying to map defensible positions, the congressman was expected at a 4:00 P.M. meeting of party colleagues who were elected the same year he was (his "class"). From 5:30 to 9:00 P.M., he was expected at the National Fire and Emergency Services dinner, and from 6:00 to 8:00 P.M., he was supposed to accompany the governor of his state to another official function. O'Rourke did not stay to see how he managed to be in two places at one time: "I was completely exhausted by 7 and went home, leaving the congressman, 20 years my senior, looking as animated and energetic as a full school bus" (1991, 63). The congressman's staff assured O'Rourke that this had been a light day for their boss.

This description shows just one part of the job of serving in Congress. In reality, members of Congress live in two worlds. One is Washington, DC, the world of legislating and overseeing the executive agencies of the national government. This is the world that O'Rourke was describing. The other is the district, the world of listening to constituents in order to learn their wants and needs and to inform them of the issues before Congress.

A reelection-minded member of Congress needs to maintain close ties with his or her district. For those who live near the capital or at least on the eastern side of the country, this is a minor burden, and extended weekends in the district can be the norm.[2] Those who live farther away face a formidable commuting schedule. Even they typically go back to their districts at least two or three weekends a month; few travel home less than once a month. Once in the district, a member often has to hit the road, visiting various communities; attending high school graduations, civic meetings, and functions; and holding town hall meetings with constituents. Living in these two worlds is not easy. It frequently means extended separation from family, balancing time and resources between Washington and home, and the necessity of presenting a parochial face to constituents on home matters and a statesmanlike demeanor on questions of national import.

Congressional Pay and Perquisites

Compensation for members of Congress has been controversial since the beginning of the republic. On one side are legislators who have a heavy workload, grave responsibilities, and limited opportunities for earnings beyond their public paychecks. On the other side are voters skeptical about claims of financial distress from officials receiving what seems to be a generous salary.

The first Congress set legislative salaries at $6 a day. Even then, this was hardly a princely sum, and in 1816, Congress voted to raise its salary to $1,500 a year.

---

[2] Congress customarily transacts official business, roll calls, and the like on Tuesday, Wednesday, and Thursday.

The public response was swift and brutal; in the next election, 60 percent of House members were voted out of office. Congress quickly repealed the law, and legislators went back to the $6 a day stipend, which they raised shortly thereafter to $8. Congress learned early that voting itself a pay raise was electoral arsenic. Almost 40 years passed before it upped its compensation again. Annual salaries increased to $3,000 in 1855, to $5,000 a decade later, and then to $7,000 in 1873. Congressional salaries consistently lagged behind inflation; every attempt at adjustment prompted a backlash. The 1873 increase was so controversial that it was repealed a year later, but it still cost 96 members their seats in the next election (F. Harris 1995, 18).

The modern story of congressional compensation is little different. After Congress voted itself a modest increase in 1983 and again in 1984, public opposition began to grow against a third salary hike proposed in 1987. The raise passed, but in 1989 there was a huge public outcry against a further salary increase. In 1992 (203 years after the amendment was proposed), the requisite number of states finally ratified the Twenty-Seventh Amendment requiring an election to intervene before members could receive a pay raise (discussed in more detail in chapter 2).

Members attempted to insulate their salary from political controversy by making annual cost-of-living adjustments (COLAs) for themselves, federal judges, and other federal workers. Such increases take effect automatically, without a vote, which might attract less public attention and outrage. The 1989 law instituting these adjustments provided members with a cost-of-living increase equal to one-half of one percentage point below the inflation index. Since 1991, members have accepted annual adjustments 12 times and voted to forgo the increase 6 times (Brudnick 2008). In the 112th Congress (2011–2012), the salary for members of Congress was $174,000. Many people believe that this annual salary is more than adequate, since the median family income is roughly a third that of a member of Congress.

Former senator Fred Harris (1995) of Oklahoma presents the other side of the story. Congressional salaries are often lower than salaries earned in comparable positions. Corporate CEOs, for example, typically earn much more than members of Congress, even though legislators arguably have much greater responsibilities and just as little job security. National legislators typically also have to bear the expense of maintaining two residences—one in the capital and one in the district. Keeping legislative compensation down, Harris argues, means that only the wealthy can afford to run for Congress.

In addition to a paycheck, however, members of Congress receive a number of **perquisites** (colloquially called **perks**), or fringe benefits that go with the job. Such benefits include subsidized medical care, inexpensive insurance, a generous pension plan, free parking, and access to their own gym, cafeterias, and barber shop for nominal fees. Other perks help members do their jobs. Members of the House get a **members' representational allowance (MRA)** or more than $1 million per year to pay for office functions, official travel, and staff. Members use this money for office supplies and equipment for the Washington office, for setting up e-mail and web pages,[3] for leasing and equipping one or more offices in their districts so that constituents can contact them locally, and for frequent trips back home to the district.

perquisites (perks) The benefits and support activities that members of Congress receive in order to help them perform their job.

members' representational allowance (MRA) An allowance of about $1 million per year that members of Congress receive to pay for official duties of representation and lawmaking (e.g., office functions, official travel, and staff). It cannot be used for personal or campaign expenses.

[3] Members' web pages can be found at http://thomas.loc.gov/.

The most expensive perk—and one of the most important—is salaries for aides to work in the Washington and district offices. Members can hire up to 18 full-time staff to assist in various tasks, including the following:

- An *administrative assistant* or chief of staff responsible for overall management of the office
- Several *legislative assistants,* each responsible for keeping the member briefed on specific policy areas
- A *legislative director* who supervises the legislative assistants
- An *appointment secretary* to screen and maintain the member's appointments
- A *press secretary* to handle press relations
- Several *legislative correspondents* to answer constituent mail
- One or more *caseworkers* to help constituents with their problems

District offices typically have only one or two staffers; caseworkers are often placed in the district office.

Another important perk is the **franking privilege**. The frank allows members of Congress to send mail that involves official business, such as answers to constituent mail, under their signatures in lieu of postage. Since members get hundreds of letters each week, it would be unreasonable to expect them to pay for postage out of their salaries. Members also use the frank to send periodic newsletters to constituents.

These perks are paid for with tax money appropriated by Congress, and their purpose is to help representatives do their jobs by staying in touch with and responding to their constituents. Perks are not supposed to be used for political purposes, and Congress has adopted a number of rules intended to prevent members from using them in an election campaign (Committee on Standards of Official Conduct n.d.). For example, it is illegal for a representative either to assign staff members to work in the campaign or to send out campaign material using the frank. Mass mailings cannot be sent under the frank within 60 days of an election in which the member is a candidate. In practice, however, the line between representing and campaigning is blurry. Sometimes key staff members take a leave of absence to work in the campaign, and some do campaign work after hours on their own time. The perquisites of the office provide members with an undeniable political advantage; achieving widespread contact with the electorate is an expense that challengers must pay for with campaign money.

BICAMERALISM IN THE AMERICAN CONGRESS

franking privilege The ability of members of Congress to send mail to their constituents free of charge by substituting a facsimile of their signature in place of a stamp.

bicameral A legislature with two chambers.

A distinctive feature of Congress is that it has two separate and independent chambers. The founders designed a **bicameral** legislature for several reasons, including the historical legacy from the British (the British Parliament is also bicameral) and the more immediate example of the colonial legislatures. Many of the latter were also bicameral, with the upper chamber appointed by the king or his representatives and the lower chamber composed of representatives elected by the colonists.

These traditions were not determinative. The national legislature under the Articles of Confederation, for example, was a **unicameral** institution. The two-house legislature is mainly a product of the conflicts discussed in chapters 2 and 3: the political struggle between large and small states and the legal battle over whether national legislators ought to represent sovereign states or individuals. Bicameralism was a compromise that settled both arguments. Bicameralism was also another way to fragment power, which the founders believed would protect basic rights by making bargaining and compromise necessary.

The bicameral legislature serves two major purposes: (1) to represent different interests and (2) to foster deliberative, careful lawmaking. The founders created the Senate to protect the interests of sovereign states and to safeguard property interests. The founders expected the prestigious nature of a Senate seat to attract an aristocratic elite that would be insulated from popular control by indirect election and a long term in office.[4] In contrast, directly elected House members with two-year terms would reflect the interests of the many, the people who had little in the way of worldly goods. Linked to the protection of states' rights and property interest was the belief that the Senate would serve as a check on hasty legislation passed in the House.

The founders also had separate special functions in mind for the Senate and the House. The Senate was to confirm presidential nominees for major positions in the national government and play a major role in foreign policy through its "advice and consent" power on treaties negotiated by the executive with other countries. The House was entrusted with the special and traditional prerogative of lower chambers: originating bills to raise revenue. Although constitutional changes and political reforms over the course of more than 200 years have altered Congress, the House and the Senate remain separate and distinct legislative institutions. Table 12.1 summarizes some important differences.

Leadership in the U.S. Senate

The U.S. Senate has two types of leaders, those designated by the Constitution and those who occupy party leadership positions. The first group exercises largely ceremonial powers and includes the vice president of the United States and the Senate president pro tempore. The second group includes the majority leader, minority leader, and party whips. There are differences in the amounts and types of power that these two types of leaders exercise in the Senate.

---

unicameral A legislature with one chamber.

[4] Election of senators by state legislatures ended in 1913 with ratification of the Seventeenth Amendment.

TABLE 12.1: SELECT HOUSE–SENATE DIFFERENCES

	House	Senate
Institutional features		
Membership	Larger (435)	Smaller (100)
Term of office	Shorter (2 years)	Longer (6 years)
Minimum age for service	Younger (25 years)	Older (30 years)
Electoral arena	Smaller (district)	Larger (state)
Constituency	Narrower (less diverse)	Broader (more diverse)
Formal leadership	Speaker of the House	Vice president (president of the Senate)
Exclusive powers	Raise revenue	Advice and consent; ratify treaties
Committee consideration of bills	Difficult to circumvent committees	Easier to circumvent committee
Scheduling for floor consideration	Speaker; limited consultation with minority	Majority Leader; broad consultation with Minority Leader
"Holds"	No practice of "holds"	Individual Senators can place "holds" on bringing measures to the floor
Rules governing floor consideration	Rules Committee adopts *Special rules* (approved by majority)	*Complex unanimous consent agreements* (requires unanimous consent)
Time for debate	Debate time restricted	Unlimited; Senators can filibuster
Ending debate	Majority vote	Super-majority (60 votes) to invoke cloture
Quorum calls	Usually permitted only in connection with record votes	In order almost any time; used for delay
Amendments to bills	Number & type limited by *special rule*	Generally unlimited
Germaneness	Germaneness of amendments required	Germaneness of amendments *not* required
Decision rule for passing legislation	Majority rule	Super-majority; rules protect minority rights
Informal		
Most powerful leader	Speaker	Majority leader
Level of comity	Lower	Somewhat higher
Reliance on staff	Lower	Higher
Policy focus	Policy specialists	Policy generalists
Degree of partisanship	Higher	Somewhat lower
Member accessibility	Higher	Lower

Source: Adapted by the authors from Moen and Copeland (1999) and Schneider (2008).

Article I, Section 3 of the Constitution designates the vice president as the **president of the Senate**. The vice president is entitled to preside over the chamber, exercising such parliamentary duties as recognizing speakers and ruling on points of procedure. The vice president can cast a ballot only to break a tie. Vice presidents do not have the opportunity to exercise this power very often—only 244 tie-breaking votes have occurred since 1789, an average of about one per year. Vice President Richard Cheney (2001–2008) voted to break eight ties; Vice President Al Gore (1993–2000) voted to break only four ties during his two terms (U.S. Senate n.d.). Except in the rare instances when a tie-breaking vote is necessary, the vice president is not a powerful or important figure in the Senate. And the vice president typically does not preside over the Senate because senators tend to regard the vice president as an outsider, especially if the opposition party controls the Senate.

The Constitution also provides for a **president pro tempore** chosen by the members to preside over the Senate in the absence of the vice president. The party controlling the Senate picks its most senior member to occupy the post. This office is ceremonial and has no special influence. Because presiding over the Senate is generally of little importance, junior members of the majority party take turns exercising the responsibility.

The single most powerful person in the Senate is the **majority leader**, who is elected by members of the majority party. Majority leaders are typically people with considerable experience in the Senate, although long tenure is not always a requirement. For example, Lyndon Johnson (D-TX) gained the post after only one term in office; Johnson held the position from 1955 to 1961 and is generally considered one of the most powerful and effective majority leaders. Several others also won the post in their second term, including Democrats George Mitchell of Maine and Mike Mansfield of Montana and Republicans Bill Frist of Tennessee and Trent Lott of Mississippi.

The majority leader has several tools with which to wield power in the Senate. Most important of these is control over the Senate's agenda. The majority leader knows which senators are for and against a bill and plays a key role in negotiating the rules and procedures under which bills will be debated and voted on. During consideration of legislation on the floor, the majority leader serves as floor leader to deal with the complex system of legislative procedures. The majority leader also influences other important matters, such as committee appointments, the location of government installations, and the distribution of prime office space.

The job of **minority leader** parallels that of majority leader: elected by party colleagues, the minority leader usually has extensive Senate experience, and he or she is the floor leader who watches out for the minority's interest during consideration of bills on the floor and serves as the focal point of communication among senators of the minority party. The minority leader often works closely with the majority leader in legislative scheduling and influences the committee appointments of minority members. The minority leader's power, however, is less than that of the majority leader. The minority leader cannot bestow the same level of rewards and, as the head of the minority party, has a numerical disadvantage in

president of the Senate The person who presides over the Senate and is responsible for many of the parliamentary duties such as recognizing speakers. The vice president of the United States holds this position.

president pro tempore The person chosen by the members to preside over the Senate in the absence of the vice president.

majority leader The person, chosen by the members of the majority party in the House and Senate, who controls the legislative agenda. In the Senate, the majority leader is the most powerful person in the chamber.

minority leader The leader of the minority party in the House or Senate. Works with majority leader to schedule legislation and leads opposition party.

SENATE

President of the Senate Joe Biden (Vice President of the United States)

President Pro Tempore Patrick Leahy (D-VT)

Majority Leader Harry Reid (D-NV)	Minority Leader Mitch McConnell (R-KY)
Asst. Majority Leader (Whip) Richard Durbin (D-IL)	Asst. Minority Leader (Whip) John Cornyn (R-TX)

HOUSE

Speaker John Boehner (R-OH)

Majority Leader Eric Cantor (R-VA)	Minority Leader Nancy Pelosi (D-CA)
Majority Whip Kevin McCarthy (R-CA)	Minority Leader Steny Hoyer (D-MD)
	Asst. Minority Leader James Clayburn (D-SC)

Source: Constructed by the authors.

trying to influence what the chamber does (though, as we will see, the minority can use Senate rules to block action).

Both majority and minority leaders have assistants commonly referred to as **whips** (though both parties have started using the title "assistant majority leader"). The term is a legacy from the British Parliament, which in turn borrowed it from the sport of foxhunting. A whip, or "whipper-in," was responsible for keeping the hounds from leaving the pack during the chase of the fox. By analogy, a legislative whip's job is to keep the rank-and-file members from stepping out of the party line. He or she sees to it that they are present to vote on key legislative measures and that they know the party leader's desire. The whip's ability to fulfill this responsibility is limited. Unlike their counterparts in the British Parliament, party leaders in the U.S. Congress have few rewards and punishments with which to maintain party unity. In the Senate, each party's whip serves mainly as a communication link between the floor leader (a term applied to either the majority or the minority leader) and rank-and-file party members. Table 12.2 lists the leaders of the 113th Congress (2013–2014).

Leadership in the U.S. House of Representatives

The Constitution (Article I, Section 2) provides for a **Speaker of the House of Representatives**. Unlike the constitutionally designated leader of the Senate (the vice president), the Speaker of the House wields considerable power in Congress. The Speaker is the House's most powerful figure. Theoretically elected as an officer of the entire chamber, the Speaker is actually selected by the majority party, making him or her both a House officer and a party official. The Speaker presides over the House, has the power to recognize members who wish to speak, rules on procedural questions, and refers bills to committee. Unlike the vice president, the Speaker may vote but usually does not exercise this prerogative except to break a tie.

whips Assistants to the majority and minority party leaders in Congress who encourage rank-and-file members to support the party's positions. Whips make sure that rank-and-file members are present to vote on key legislative measures and that they know the party leader's desire.

Speaker of the House of Representatives The person who presides over the House. The Speaker is responsible for many of the parliamentary duties, such as recognizing speakers, and is the most powerful person in the chamber.

Nancy Pelosi (D-CA) became the first female Speaker of the House of Representatives following the Democratic victory in 2008. Her tenure was short lived, however, because Republicans won back the majority in the 2010 elections. Here Pelosi turns the gavel over to Rep. John Boehner (R-OH), who served has House Minority Leader before Republicans won control of the chamber.

The Speaker can generally use the same rewards as the Senate majority leader to influence colleagues: assistance in obtaining a favorable committee assignment, appointment to select committees, help with bills, and assistance in a tough political campaign. Like the Senate majority leader, the Speaker is the center of the chamber's internal communication network and serves as a central link with the White House and the Senate.

The position of Speaker became more powerful following the 1994 Republican takeover of Congress. The Republican-controlled House took several steps to curb the power of committees and committee chairs. One of the outcomes of these reforms was to effectively centralize power in the hands of Republican Speaker Newt Gingrich. Gingrich resigned after a disappointing electoral performance in the 1998 midterm elections, but his successor, Republican Dennis Hastert of Illinois, continued to consolidate power in the hands of party leaders. When Democrats regained majority control of the House in the 2006 elections, Democratic Party leader Nancy Pelosi (D-CA) was elected Speaker, becoming the first woman to hold the office. Pelosi continued the pattern of strong Speakers and imposed strong party discipline on her caucus on a number of important issues. In March 2010, she showed her skill as a leader when she rescued President Obama's stalled health care reform by persuading reluctant House Democrats to support the more moderate Senate version of the bill. The close victory—the bill passed 219 to 212 with no Republican support—was so impressive that she has been called "the most powerful Speaker in 100 years" and "the most powerful woman in American history" (quoted in Sawyer 2010). Pelosi's power was short-lived. She was relegated to the status of minority leader when Republicans regained the majority in the 2010 elections. John Boehner (R-OH) became Speaker and continued the pattern of strong leadership.

Next in line behind the Speaker in the House leadership hierarchy is the majority leader. Chosen by the majority party caucus (Republicans call their caucus a "conference"), the majority leader often has strong ties with the Speaker, and the influence he or she wields depends largely on what the Speaker wants it to be. Generally, the majority leader assists the Speaker in scheduling legislation, distributes and collects information of concern to majority party members, and tries to persuade the rank and file to go along with the wishes of party leadership.

The nominee of the minority party caucus, who loses the election for Speaker, becomes the House minority leader. This role is essentially the same as it is in the Senate: to work with the majority leader in scheduling legislation and to lead the opposition party. Party whips have the same general function in the House as in the Senate.

The Committee System

Congress is a collegial rather than hierarchical institution. Power is widely dispersed, and leaders do not have the authority to command rank-and-file members to do their bidding. The committee system institutionalizes the diffusion of power by giving small groups of legislators disproportionate influence.

Standing committees are permanent panels with jurisdiction over particular issues and categories of legislation. The importance of standing committees in Congress is hard to overstate. Woodrow Wilson (1885) referred to them as "little legislatures." In both chambers, standing committees are the primary focus of legislative business, and they wield much power within their areas of jurisdiction. They are powerful for at least two reasons. First, committee members are more knowledgeable than nonmembers about legislation in their issue areas. In Congress, knowledge and expertise are important sources of power. Committee members are more knowledgeable than nonmembers because they have worked on the legislation in committee for a long time, they have attended committee hearings, and they have been kept informed of new developments by committee staff. Second, committee members are more interested in the legislation than the rank and file. Members of Congress with less expertise and less interest than committee members in the issue under discussion often defer to the recommendations of the committee reporting the bill.

The House standing committee system has undergone significant reform. When Republicans gained majority control of the House in 1995, they eliminated a number of committees and subcommittees, changed jurisdictions, imposed term limits on committee and subcommittee chairs, eliminated proxy voting, and

standing committees Permanent committees in Congress that are responsible for legislation in a specific policy area.

cut committee staffs. A primary motivation of these reforms was to shake up the power structure in the House.

STRUCTURE AND ORGANIZATION Standing committees have jurisdiction over particular policy areas. Committee jurisdictions are defined in Senate and House rules and roughly correspond to the major organizational divisions of the executive branch. Senate and House committees are organized along parallel, though not identical, lines. There are 21 standing committees in the House and 19 in the Senate (see Table 12.3).

TABLE 12.3: COMMITTEES OF THE 113TH CONGRESS (2013-2014)

House Committees	Seats	Rep.	Dem.	Majority Seat Advantage	Party Ratio	Over/under seat share	Dominant Member Goal	Transfer Rank
Exclusive Committees								
Ways & Means	39	23	16	7	1.44	0.28	prestige	1
Appropriations	53	29	24	5	1.21	0.05	prestige	2
Energy & Commerce	54	30	24	6	1.25	0.09	policy	3
Rules	13	9	4	5	2.25	1.09	prestige	5
Non-Exclusive Committees								
Judiciary	40	23	17	6	1.35	0.19	policy	4
Transportation & Infrastructure	59	33	26	7	1.27	0.11	constituency	6
Armed Services	62	34	28	6	1.21	0.05	constituency	7
Financial Services	62	33	29	4	1.14	−0.02	policy	8
Homeland Security	33	18	15	3	1.20	0.04	policy	9
Oversight & Government Reform	40	23	17	6	1.35	0.19	policy	10
Foreign Affairs	46	25	21	4	1.19	0.03	policy	11
Natural Resources	47	26	21	5	1.24	0.08	constituency	13
Science, Space & Technology	39	22	17	5	1.29	0.13	constituency	14
Education & Workforce	42	24	18	6	1.33	0.17	policy	15
Veterans' Affairs	25	14	11	3	1.27	0.11	constituency	16
Budget	39	22	17	5	1.29	0.13	policy	17
House Administration	9	6	3	3	2.00	0.84	unrequested	18
Agriculture	47	25	22	3	1.14	−0.02	constituency	19
Small Business	25	14	11	3	1.27	0.11	constituency	20
Exempt Committees								
Intelligence (Permanent Select)	21	12	9	3	1.33	0.17	unrequested	12
Ethicsa	10	5	5	0	1.00	−0.16	unrequested	21
House Party Division	435	234	201	33	1.16			

(Continued)

TABLE 12.3: (CONTINUED)

Senate Committees	Seats	Dem.	Rep.	Majority Seat Advantage	Party Ratio	Over/under seat share	Dominant Member Goal	Transfer Rank
Super-A Committees								
Finance	24	13	11	2	1.18	−0.04	prestige/policy/ constituency	1
Appropriations	30	16	14	2	1.14	−0.08	prestige/constituency	2
Armed Services	26	14	12	2	1.17	−0.05	prestige/policy/ constituency	6
Foreign Relations	18	10	8	2	1.25	0.03	prestige/policy	13
A Committees								
Commerce, Science, & Transportation	24	13	11	2	1.18	−0.04	constituency	4
Judiciary	18	10	8	2	1.25	0.03	policy	5
Intelligence (Select)	15	8	7	1	1.14	−0.08	unrequested	9
Agriculture, Nutrition, & Forestry	20	11	9	2	1.22	0.00	constituency	10
Homeland Security & Govt'l Affairs	16	9	7	2	1.29	0.07	policy	11
Health, Education, Labor, & Pensions	22	12	10	2	1.20	−0.02	policy	14
Small Business & Entrepreneurship	18	10	8	2	1.25	0.03	policy/constituency	15
Environment & Public Works	19	11	8	3	1.38	0.16	constituency	16
Energy & Natural Resources	22	12	10	2	1.20	−0.02	constituency	17
Banking, Housing, & Urban Affairs	22	12	10	2	1.20	−0.02	policy/constituency	18
B Committees								
Veterans Affairs	14	8	6	2	1.33	0.11	unrequested	3
Budget	22	12	10	2	1.20	−0.02	policy	7
Rules & Administration	18	10	8	2	1.25	0.03	unrequested	8
C Committees								
Indian Affairs	14	8	6	2	1.33	0.11	constituency	12
Ethics (Select)a	6	3	3	0	1.00	−0.22	unrequested	19
Senate Party Division	100	55	45	10	1.22			

aHouse and Senate Rules require an equal number of Democrats and Republicans on their Ethics committees.

Sources: rules establishing committee categories are from Schneider (2005, 2006b); dominant goals of committee members adapted from Deering & Smith, (1997); desirability rank from Edwards & Stewart (2006).

Committee size varies considerably. The size of standing committees is determined at the beginning of a Congress. The seats on each standing committee are divided between the majority and minority party using the **party ratio**—that is, the ratio of majority to minority party members in the chamber—as a general guideline. Party ratios on Senate committees generally reflect party strength in the chamber fairly closely. In the 113th Congress, Senate Democrats outnum-

party ratio The proportion of the seats that each political party controls in the House and the Senate.

bered Republicans 55 to 45, resulting in a party ratio of 1.22. The ratio of Democrats to Republicans on most Senate committees matched this ratio closely.[5] Party ratios on House committees are more likely to favor the majority, especially on committees crucial to achieving the party's policy priorities. The party ratio in the 113th House, for example, was (234 Republicans on to 201 Democrats), but Republicans took a disproportionate share of the seats two of the four exclusive committees. The party ratio on the Ways and Means Committee— the committee with jurisdiction over tax policy, Social Security, and Medicare was 1.44. Republicans also took a disproportionate number of seats on the Rules Committee, the committee that formulates special rules (explained below) that determine which bills come to the floor for debate and which amendments will be offered. (see Table 12.3). Taking extra seats on certain key committees is something the majority party does. Democrats followed this practice when they had a majority from 2007 to 2010. Remember that party discipline in the U.S. Congress is low compared to that in parliamentary democracies (see chapter 7). Thus, regardless of which party is in the majority, it needs extra seats on key committees to have a working majority to pass party policies. The minority, of course, complains that underrepresentation on committees reduces their ability to influence legislation at this key stage of the process and "thereby deprives the electorate of the representation it sought in electing those Members" (Tong 2009, 5). This inequitable treatment of the minority may have contributed to the high levels of party conflict in recent Congresses and made it more difficult to find common ground.

Standing committees have subcommittees with jurisdiction over smaller segments of policy. Subcommittees help Congress cope with a large workload, and they permit members to develop more specialized policy expertise.

GETTING ASSIGNED TO A COMMITTEE Party committees determine which members will fill the party's seats on the various congressional committees—that is, Republicans assign Republicans, and Democrats assign Democrats. Members request particular committee assignments, and party committees match up those requests with vacancies on the committees. As a general rule, members who want to continue serving on a committee are allowed to do so.[6] This practice fills most of the seats on the committees. Some continuing members, however, request to transfer to a more desirable committee, and new members need committee assignments. Demand always exceeds the supply of seats for some committees. In deciding who will get a contested seat, reelection is a major consideration. Seniority is also a consideration, especially in the Senate, where seniority is almost always the primary consideration when there is competition for a particular assignment. On some committees, there is a "state seat" tradition where the delegation from the

---

[5] The ethics committees are exceptions; they have an equal number of Republicans and Democrats.
[6] The major reasons that a member would not be allowed to keep a committee assignment are term limits on certain committees—the House Budget Committee, for example—and a change in party control that gives the losing party fewer seats on all committees.

state of the departing member may request that the vacancy be filled by someone else from the state.

COMMITTEE CHAIRS Traditionally, committee chairs were chosen on the basis of seniority. The relevant consideration was not seniority in Congress, but seniority on the committee among majority party members: that is, the usual practice was to appoint the committee member of the majority party with the longest continuous service on the committee. Automatic selection based on seniority insulated committee chairs from pressure from their party caucus and party leaders. In the Senate, committee seniority continues to serve as the primary basis for selecting committee chairs.

The House reforms adopted by Republicans in 1995 sought to place limits on such political power. Republicans ceased using seniority as the primary qualification for chairing a committee, as Speaker Gingrich skipped over the senior Republican on several key committees and handpicked trusted lieutenants as chairs. Democrats also ceased using seniority as the sole criteria for selecting committee chairs. And changes to House rules limited committee chairs to three terms, which further weakened the seniority system.

Although these reforms weakened the role of seniority in selecting committee chairs in the House, they did not eliminate it. The competition to chair committees involves mostly senior members, so committee chairs are still relatively senior majority party members. But criteria such as competence, party loyalty, and a record of raising campaign money to help fellow majority party members have also become important considerations. The Senate continues to rely primarily on seniority, though both parties have adopted rules that the chair "need not be the Member with the longest committee service" (J. Schneider 2006a, 7, 10).

COMMITTEE RANKINGS There are some committees on which almost any member would like to serve; others on which almost no one wants to serve; and many that are desired by some but not others, depending on members' particular political and policy interests. There are two ways to rank the desirability of any given committee: (1) how the committee ranks based on what members say in House or Senate rules and in interviews; and (2) the preferences revealed by members' behavior as they transfer on and off committees. Both methods produce similar, but not identical, rankings.

The formal rules of the House and Senate create different categories of committees, and these categories show how members view the relative importance of committees. (Table 12.3 groups committees according to categories established in the rules.) Members of Congress generally have two major committee assignments, but the rules create different categories that restrict or expand on the two-committee baseline.

House rules divide committees into three categories: exclusive, nonexclusive, and exempt. Most House committees are in the nonexclusive category, and the rules permit members to serve on two of these major committees. The four

exclusive committees—Appropriations, Energy and Commerce, Rules, and Ways and Means—are the most desirable committees in the House, and members assigned to one of them typically receive no other major committee assignment. Restricting exclusive committee members from serving on other major committees is formal recognition of the power and prestige of these committees. The exempt committees—Standards of Official Conduct and Select Intelligence—are exempt from the two-committee limitation, allowing members to serve on these undesirable committees in addition to their two major committee assignments (J. Schneider 2005). Senate rules designate committees as "A," "B," or "C" level. Members may serve on two A committees, one B committee, and one or more C committees. Most Senate committees are in the A category, but four committees—Appropriations, Finance, Armed Services, and Foreign Relations—are called "Super A" committees or the "Big Four." Senators generally serve on only one of the Big Four, though there are exceptions (J. Schneider 2006b).

Interviews with members of Congress also reveal differences in the importance and prestige of committees. Richard Fenno (1973) found that members seek committee assignments to pursue three goals: prestige, policy, and reelection. Committees can thus be classified as "prestige," "policy," or "constituency" committees according to which of the three goals is predominant. Some committees fulfill none of these goals, thereby forming an "unrequested committee" category (Deering and Smith 1997).

Interviews with members indicate that there are a small number of **prestige committees**, which are highly prized and which allow their members to wield tremendous power in Congress (Fenno 1973). In both chambers, the prestige committees include those dealing with major taxing and spending issues: Ways and Means (House), Finance (Senate), and Appropriations (House and Senate). Other prestige committees differ between the House and the Senate according to the particular rules and responsibilities of the chamber. In the House, the Rules Committee, which has special powers to control floor procedures, is a prestige committee, and recently the Energy and Commerce Committee, with its broad jurisdiction, has also assumed this status. In the Senate, Foreign Relations and Armed Services are prestige committees (Deering and Smith 1997, 64, 80). Notice that the "prestige committees" identified in interviews with members are also those codified in the House and the Senate rules as either exclusive or Super A committees.

Most of the remaining standing committees are major policy and constituency committees. These committees have jurisdiction over important policy areas, but members' policy and reelection interests determine which committees are desirable for them to sit on. A representative from a New York City district dominated by financial institutions, for example, might want a seat on the Financial Services Committee, whereas a legislator from a district with a farm-based economy might need a seat on the Agriculture Committee to deal with legislation affecting agribusiness. Classifying Senate committees based on member goals is less clear than in the House (Deering and Smith 1997). Since the Senate is smaller than the House, senators tend to have more committee assignments. Almost every senator can put together a mix of assignments to cover all of his or her prestige, policy,

exclusive committees Four House committees—Appropriations, Energy and Commerce, Rules, and Ways and Means—whose members typically receive no other committee assignments.

prestige committees Congressional committees that are highly prized and allow their members to wield tremendous power in Congress.

and constituency goals, and on several committees no single goal is dominant. The prestige committees in the Senate are not particularly exclusive—there are 98 seats on these four committees, so very few senators are denied a prestigious assignment.

Few members want to serve on the low-ranked "unrequested" committees (Deering and Smith 1997, 77). For example, in both chambers, members do not seek assignment to the Ethics Committee (called Standards of Official Conduct in the House). A party leader in the House expressed members' distaste for sitting in judgment of their colleagues, saying that "anyone who wants a seat on Standards doesn't deserve a seat on Standards" (quoted in Deering and Smith 1997, 77). Other unrequested committees traditionally include the Veterans' Affairs Committee in the Senate and the Select Committee on Intelligence in both chambers.

Members' behavior as they transfer on and off committees also indicates which committees are most desirable: if a member gives up an assignment on the Agriculture Committee to move to the Ways and Means Committee, then it is reasonable to conclude that Ways and Means is more desirable to that member than Agriculture. The most desirable committees, then, are those that members transfer to but do not leave, and members leave the least desirable committees but will not give up an assignment to join them (Groseclose and Stewart 1998; Stewart and Groseclose 1999).

A study (K. Edwards and Stewart 2006) used this technique to rank House and Senate committees from the 104th Congress (1995–1996) to the 110th Congress (2007–2008) (see Table 12.3). The findings are consistent with the other rankings in important ways. The prestigious committees rank at the top; the unrequested ("exempt" and "C") committees rank near the bottom. This method also allows us to see which policy and constituency committees are most desirable. There are some discrepancies, however. The most glaring are the high rank of the Senate Veterans' Affairs Committee (3) and the low rank of the House Budget Committee (17). In interviews, members continue to say that Veterans' Affairs is not a desirable committee assignment, but they are reluctant to transfer off and possibly offend a popular constituency group. The ranking of the House Budget Committee is artificially depressed because the rules require members to transfer off after six years. The intelligence committees dealing with the nation's security traditionally were in the "unrequested" category, but members' transfer behavior ranks these committees as 12 in the House and 9 in the Senate, suggesting members of Congress view service on these committees as relatively important.

HOUSE AND SENATE DIFFERENCES Although committees are a central organizational feature in both chambers, committees are more important and powerful in the House than in the Senate for several reasons. First, the larger membership of the House means that House members have fewer committee assignments (an average of about two) than senators (an average of over three); this scarcity makes committee assignments more highly valued in the House. The surest way to influence legislation in the House is to serve on a committee. Because there are only 100 senators, these lawmakers have opportunities to develop power and influence independent of their committees. The relatively small membership means that senators can build personal relationships with more of their colleagues. In addition, the longer term and the representation of a statewide constituency make the Senate more prestigious than the House, and as a result, senators get more media attention and can develop bases of power outside the Senate, often even on a national scale.

Second, Senate rules allow individual senators opportunities to offer **nongermane amendments** that are not related to the bill under consideration, in some cases bypassing committee action. These amendments are commonly known as **riders** because they are attached to popular bills in an effort to get them a free ride through the legislative process. Riders are generally prohibited in the House.

Third, constituency differences create incentives for House members to become policy specialists and for senators to become policy generalists. Except for states that have only one House member, House constituencies are smaller and less diverse than Senate constituencies. With only a few interests dominating many House districts, a House member benefits from working on one or two committees with jurisdiction over policies important to a single district. Senators representing an entire state with a wide range of interests can benefit from serving on several committees.

RUNNING THE LEGISLATIVE OBSTACLE COURSE

American government textbooks typically include a diagram of how a bill becomes law. The generic diagram reproduced as Figure 12.4 follows a bill through the various obstacles it must overcome before becoming law: from introduction to committee referral, from committee consideration to floor action, from floor action to conference committee, from conference committee back to floor action, and from there to the White House—and back again if vetoed.

Political scientists consider such descriptions to be unrealistic portrayals of how Congress works. Barbara Sinclair (2012) shows that legislation is increasingly governed by what she terms "unorthodox lawmaking." Unorthodox lawmaking involves the use of special procedures and practices that have created "a number of different paths the legislation may follow" (Sinclair 2012, 10). She argues that these "modifications and innovations can be seen as responses to problems and opportunities the members—as individuals or collectively—confronted" (Sinclair 2012, 134).

Although the legislative process is no longer an orderly progression from one point to the next as depicted in the generic diagram, the fundamental nature of lawmaking remains an obstacle course characterized by multiple, sequential decision points. In order to pass, a bill must gain the approval of a group of legislators at each point. Only at the final stage of the process does the majority have an

nongermane amendments Amendments to a piece of legislation that are not related to the subject of the bill to which they are added.

riders A nongermane amendment that is added to a popular bill in hopes that the desirability of the proposed legislation will help the amendment pass.

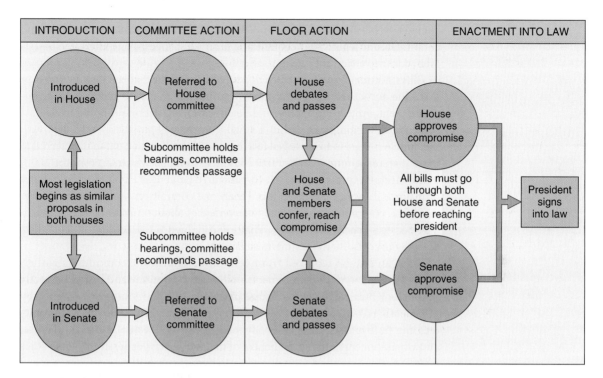

| INTRODUCTION | COMMITTEE ACTION | FLOOR ACTION | ENACTMENT INTO LAW |

FIGURE 12.4 Generic Diagram of How a Bill Becomes Law
Source: Constructed by the authors.

opportunity to express its will, and even there a small minority determines which alternatives the majority will choose from. As a result, the legislative process is not really a process of majority rule. Rather, it is better described as a process of *minorities' consent* because, at each stage, a different minority of members has the power to stall or prevent the bill from going to the next decision point. The most important thing to remember about how a bill becomes law is that there are multiple points of access to the proposed legislation and thus plenty of opportunities for minority interests to slow the bill's progress or kill it outright.

Bill Introduction and Committee Referral

Proposed legislation has numerous sources. Members introduce bills on behalf of the president, interest groups, or constituents. Only members of Congress can introduce bills into their respective chambers. In the House, members accomplish this by placing a proposal into a wooden box called the hopper. Senators can introduce bills from the floor or submit them to Senate clerks.

After it is introduced, a bill is referred to the committee with jurisdiction over the particular issue or area it covers. Committee consideration can be long and complex: a bill is passed down to subcommittee and reported back to the full committee, and legislators negotiate and propose changes, while interested parties lobby for the version they favor.

Bills traditionally were referred to a single committee that had jurisdiction over that issue. As new issues became more prominent in the 1970s and 1980s (e.g., environmental protection, energy, and health care), legislation proposed to address these issues no longer fit within a single committee's jurisdiction. To deal with this problem, the House changed its rules in 1975 to permit a bill to be referred to more than one committee, a practice known as *multiple referral.* From the 100th to the 110th Congresses (1987–2010), about 20 percent of all bills and 34 percent of major bills were referred to more than one committee. Multiple referrals are much less common in the Senate (an average of about 4 percent since 1987), in part because Senate rules allow senators to influence the content of legislation outside the committee structure (Sinclair 2012, 144).

Bills can also be removed from committee against the committee's wishes. In the House, members can remove a bill from committee and bring it directly to the floor by means of a **discharge petition**. This petition must be signed by 218 members—a majority of the House membership. In some cases, committees can be bypassed altogether. Bypassing committees is rare in the House, and when it occurs, it is at the behest of majority party leadership. Senate rules make it easier for an individual senator to bypass committees—any senator can offer legislation as an amendment to another bill that is already on the floor; in most cases, the amendment does not have to be germane (Sinclair 2012, 18–19, 54–56).

Committee Consideration and Action

The most important determinant of the fate of legislation in Congress is what the standing committee does (or more often, does not do). The most common thing that happens to bills introduced in Congress is nothing—most bills are assigned to committees where they are ignored and die at the end of the Congress.

Each committee takes action on a relatively small percentage of bills assigned to it. On these few bills, the committee does additional research. The committee staff studies the bill and provides information to the members. The committee will hold public hearings where interested parties (interest groups, members of the executive agency that administers the program, policy experts, and sometimes celebrities) provide information about the proposal. Committee hearings are typically highly scripted. The committee chair has substantial leeway to decide not only which bills get hearings, but also who the witnesses will be and what positions they will take. In addition to collecting information about the policy, hearings can also be used to test the breadth of political support—and sometimes to build support—for the legislation. Hearings that feature celebrities tend to attract media attention, which gives committee members an opportunity to get some free publicity.

discharge petition A procedure of the House of Representatives that permits a majority of the members of the House (218) to bring a bill out of committee for consideration on the floor.

After the hearings, the committee meets for the markup, where members literally mark up the bill, making changes deemed necessary. After the markup, the committee votes to report the bill to the floor for debate and a vote.

There is no doubt that standing committee action (or inaction) is the most important determinant of whether a bill passes or fails. And members of Congress certainly work hard to get a good committee assignment—that is, one that will help them achieve their goals. Given all this concern with committees, you might think that once members get the desired assignment, they work diligently on all the bills under the committee's jurisdiction. Richard Hall's (1996) study of participation on committees, however, found that participation was far from universal. The number of members participating varied from bill to bill, and it was a largely a different subset of participants on each bill. He quips that his findings "reveal that the standing committees of Congress are not really standing committees; in most cases most of the committee members are standing somewhere else" (Hall 1996, 46).

From Committee to the Floor

Bills reported out of committee have a high probability of passage on the floor. Getting legislation reported from the committees to the floor for consideration and a vote, however, is more complex than it once was. It is not unusual, for example, for a bill to undergo "postcommittee adjustments"—that is, substantial alterations between the time it is reported by a committee and when it is scheduled for consideration on the chamber floor. Party leaders with the cooperation of the committee chair may lead efforts to forge changes to a bill, usually in an attempt to improve the chances of its passage on the floor (Sinclair 2012, 21–24, 57–58).

Furthermore, constraints are often placed on a bill before it gets to the floor for consideration. In the House, the Rules Committee determines what these constraints will be; in the Senate, they are set by the unanimous consent agreement (UCA). These procedural matters are critical in determining whether a bill will pass and in what form.

The House Rules Committee is powerful because it decides what bills come up for a vote, when they come up, and which amendments members will get to vote on. Once a House standing committee has completed its consideration of a proposed bill, it prepares a written report describing what the bill does, what amendments the committee has made, and why the bill should be passed. But before the committee's bill can go to the floor for debate and a vote, it must first go to the Rules Committee, which formulates a **special rule** that establishes the conditions under which the bill will be considered. The Rules Committee thus performs the role of a legislative traffic cop, regulating the flow of legislation from standing committees to the floor. There is no Senate committee that performs this role.

The rule formulated by the Rules Committee sets the date the bill will be brought up on the floor for debate and specifies the conditions of the debate. These conditions normally set time limits; specify which amendments, if any, can be offered; and set other rules that can significantly control the form of proposed legislation and its

special rule A rule formulated by the House Rules committee specifying the conditions under which a given bill will be considered on the House floor.

TABLE 12.4: EXAMPLES OF HOUSE SPECIAL RULES FOR FLOOR CONSIDERATION OF BILLS

Rule for H.R. 2112-Agriculture, Rural Development, Food & Drug Administration and Related Agencies Appropriations Act, 2012

Adopted by record vote of 235-180 on Tuesday, June 14, 2011.

1. Open rule.

2. Provides for one hour of general debate equally divided and controlled by the chair and ranking minority member of the Committee on Appropriations.

3. Waives all points of order against consideration of the bill.

4. Waives points of order against provisions in the bill for failure to comply with clause 2 of rule XXI except for [listed] sections

5. Under the Rules of the House the bill shall be read for amendment by paragraph.

6. Provides that the bill shall be considered for amendment under the five-minute rule.

7. Authorizes the Chair to accord priority in recognition to Members who have pre-printed their amendments in the Congressional Record.

8. Provides one motion to recommit with or without instructions.

Rule for H.R. 2842-Bureau of Reclamation Small Conduit Hydropower Development & Rural Jobs Act of 2011

Adopted by voice vote, after agreeing to the previous question by record vote of 232-177, on Tuesday, March 6, 2012.

1. Modified open rule.

2. Provides one hour of general debate equally divided and controlled by the chair and ranking minority member of the Committee on Natural Resources.

3. Waives all points of order against consideration of the bill.

4. Makes in order the amendment in the nature of a substitute recommended by the Committee on Natural Resources as original text for purpose of amendment, and provides that each section shall be considered as read.

5. Waives all points of order against the amendment in the nature of a substitute.

6. Makes in order only those amendments that are submitted for printing in the Congressional Record dated at least one day before the day of consideration of the amendment and pro forma amendments for the purpose of debate. Each amendment submitted for printing in the Congressional Record may be offered only by the member who submitted it for printing or the Member's designee and shall be considered as read if printed.

7. Provides one motion to recommit with or without instructions.

8. Provides that the chair of the Committee on Financial Services may file a supplemental report to accompany H.R. 3606.

Rule for H.R. 2117-Protecting Academic Freedom in Higher Education Act

Adopted by record vote of 244-171 on Tuesday, February 28, 2012.

1. Structured rule.

2. Provides one hour of general debate equally divided and controlled by the chair and ranking minority member of the Committee on Education and the Workforce.

3. Waives all points of order against consideration of the bill.

4. Provides that the amendment in the nature of a substitute recommended by the Committee on Education and the Workforce now printed in the bill shall be considered as original text for the purpose of amendment and shall be considered as read.

5. Waives all points of order against the committee amendment in the nature of a substitute.

(continued)

6. Makes in order only those amendments printed in the Rules Committee report accompanying the resolution. Each such amendment may be offered only in the order printed in the report, may be offered only by a Member designated in the report, shall be considered as read, shall be debatable for the time specified in the report equally divided and controlled by the proponent and an opponent, shall not be subject to amendment, and shall not be subject to a demand for division of the question.

7. Waives all points of order against the amendments printed in the report.

8. Provides one motion to recommit with or without instructions.

Summary of Amendments to be Made in Order:

Sponsor	#	Description	Debate Time
1. Grijalva (AZ)	#8	Would retain the requirement that states . . . have a process to hear and take . . . action on student complaints . . .	(10 min.)
2. Foxx (NC)	#3	Would repeal a section of the credit hour regulation impacting clock hour programs.	(10 min.)
3. Polis (CO)	#6	Would link state authorization regulations to student outcomes.	(10 min.)
4. Bishop (NY)	#2	Would strike the prohibition on the Secretary of Educ. from . . . promulgating or enforcing any . . . rule defining the term "credit hour."	(10 min.)
5. Polis (CO)	#7	Would require the Secretary to present a plan to prevent waste, fraud and abuse to ensure effective use of taxpayer dollars.	(10 min.)

Rule for H.R. 2560-Cut, Cap, and Balance Act of 2011

Adopted by record vote of 236-177, after agreeing to the previous question by record vote of 235-175, on Tuesday, July 19, 2011.

1. **Closed rule.**

2. Provides four hours of debate equally divided and controlled by the chair and ranking minority member of the Committee on the Budget.

3. Waives all points of order against consideration of the bill.

4. Provides that the bill shall be considered as read.

5. Waives all points of order against provisions in the bill.

6. Provides one motion to recommit.

Source: House Rules Committee, http://www.rules.house.gov/Default.aspx (accessed July 14, 2012).

chances of passage. By controlling the order in which bills are considered, the Rules Committee kills some while allowing others to be decided by majority vote. Some bills are considered under an **open rule** that permits any germane amendment (or sometimes a "modified open rule" requiring that amendments be preprinted in the *Congressional Record*); others come to the floor with a **closed rule** that prohibits all amendments. Frequently, bills come to the floor under a **structured rule** that permits only certain amendments, permits amendments to only parts of the bill, and sometimes specifies the order that amendments will be voted on (see Table 12.4).

The Speaker appoints the majority party's members to the Rules Committee, so the Rules Committee is a tool the majority party leadership uses to help meet policy objectives, keep debate under control, and prevent the minority party from

open rule A rule formulated by the House Rules committee that permits any germane amendment to be considered on the floor.

closed rule The rule that prohibits amending a bill when it is on the floor of Congress for consideration.

structured rule A rule that permits only certain amendments to a bill.

scoring political points by offering amendments that would place majority party members in awkward positions. The majority must approve the rule before the House can consider the legislation. Losing a vote on a rule amounts to losing control of the chamber and is very embarrassing to the majority party leadership. Although rare, it does occasionally happen.

If the rule passes, the House dissolves into the **Committee of the Whole**, literally a committee consisting of every member of the House. Its origins lie with a centuries-old British practice of getting the Speaker, who was a representative of the king, out of his chair so that the House of Commons could act independently of his scrutiny. The advantage of keeping this parliamentary fiction alive is that the Committee of the Whole has less burdensome rules governing debate and requires a smaller quorum than the House itself. While in Committee of the Whole, members debate the bill and consider amendments under constraints of the rule.

Once this process is completed, the Committee of the Whole reports the bill to the House, and the House votes on the bill. The House must approve amendments adopted in the Committee of the Whole, so opponents have a second chance to try to defeat them. Typically, the House votes on all amendments from the Committee of the Whole as a package, and passage is assured. But if the vote on an amendment in the Committee of the Whole was close, the losers in the first round may attempt to change the outcome on the House floor. Such efforts are rarely successful—"after all, the membership of the two bodies is identical" (Sinclair 2012, 44).

Thus, the simple-sounding act of voting on a bill is surrounded by complexities that can make it anything but straightforward. The floor vote is the place where the majority has the opportunity to express its will, but the expression of majority will is limited by the rules governing consideration of the bill and may require multiple tries.

Power is more diffuse in the Senate than in the House. Senate rules and traditions disperse power to all senators. Perhaps the most important protection of individual prerogatives is the Senate rule permitting unlimited debate. The power of unlimited debate gives each senator the power to filibuster objectionable legislation and nominations favored by the majority. A **filibuster** is an effort by one or a few senators to delay action on a bill or nomination by making long speeches and using parliamentary tactics. The goal is to pressure the majority to give up and pull the bill from the floor or at least make changes to remove objectionable provisions.

Senators can signal their intention to filibuster by placing a "hold" on a bill. As defined by a senator, a **hold** is "a notice by a senator to his or her party leader of an intention to object to bringing a bill or nomination to the floor for consideration" (quoted in Oleszek 2008, 1). Holds are an informal tradition of the Senate, and the identity of the senator who placed the hold is secret. Certain provisions of the Honest Leadership and Open Government Act passed in 2007 attempted to end the practice of secret holds, but the practice persists because party leaders continued to honor them. In essence, a hold is a threat to filibuster, and merely the threat is often sufficient to deter the Senate majority leader from scheduling a vote on a bill or nomination.

A filibuster can be stopped if the Senate votes to invoke **cloture**—that is, end debate on a bill. Under Senate rules, it takes 60 votes to invoke cloture.

Committee of the Whole A parliamentary action whereby the House of Representatives dissolves into a committee consisting of every member of the House. This procedure is used to facilitate consideration of legislation because it has less burdensome rules governing debate and requires a smaller quorum than the House itself.

filibuster The effort by a senator to delay the chamber's business by making long speeches.

hold The formal request by a member of the Senate to be notified before a specific bill or presidential nomination comes to the floor.

cloture A procedure of the Senate to end a filibuster; invoking cloture requires votes of 60 senators.

This rule means that a minority of 41 senators can kill a bill by preventing a final vote.

Historically, filibusters were rare, but they have become much more common in recent decades. Once used by individual senators to block legislation they intensely opposed, filibusters have become part of a partisan strategy that the minority party uses to influence legislation (Binder and Smith 1997, 148; Koger 2010). From the 1950s to the 1970s, filibustering was rare, but since the 1970s, filibuster activity (as indicated by the number of cloture votes) has increased precipitously (see Figure 12.5).

Most bills are not filibustered. The Senate conducts much of its legislative business under **unanimous consent agreements** negotiated by party leaders. These agreements define the procedures and conditions under which bills will be considered on the Senate floor. Unanimous consent agreements in the Senate perform a function similar to special rules from the Rules Committee in the House; they set limits on debate, specify which amendments will be in order, and set a schedule for the vote. But there is a big difference. Adoption of a special rule in the House requires a simple majority, and the majority party leadership rarely loses a vote on a rule. Unanimous consent in the Senate means just what it says: any one senator can stop the agreement (see Table 12.5). An objection to a unanimous consent agreement is likely a threat to filibuster, which means that it might take 60 votes, rather than a simple majority, to pass the bill on the Senate floor.

unanimous consent agreement (UCA)
An agreement between majority and minority party leaders on the procedures and conditions under which a bill will be considered in the Senate.

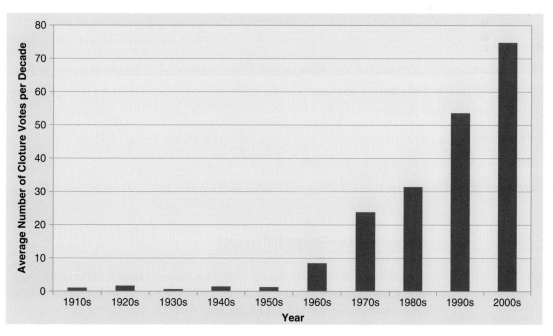

FIGURE 12.5 Increasing Filibuster Activity
Source: U.S. Senate web page, http://www.senate.gov/pagelayout/reference/cloture_motions/clotureCounts.htm.

Following is an excerpt from the Congressional Record of June 29, 2006 where Senate Majority Leader Bill Frist (R-TN) and Minority Leader Harry Reid (D-NV) formalize a unanimous consent agreement on bills dealing with stem cell research.

Mr. FRIST. Mr. President, I ask unanimous consent that at a time determined by the majority leader, after consultation with the Democratic leader, the Senate proceed en bloc to the following bills under the following agreement:

H.R. 810, Stem Cell Research Enhancement Act, discharged from the HELP [Health, Education, Labor, and Pensions] Committee; S. 2754, Alternative Pluripotent Stem Cell Therapies Enhancement Act, discharged from the HELP Committee; S. 3504, Fetus Farming Prohibition Act of 2006.

I further ask consent that there be a total of 12 hours of debate equally divided between the two leaders or their designees; provided further that no amendments be in order to any of the measures; further, that following the use or yielding back of time the bills be read a third time and the Senate proceed to three consecutive votes in the following order with no intervening action or debate: S. 3504, S. 2754, H.R. 810.

Finally, I ask unanimous consent that any bill that does not receive 60 votes in the affirmative, the vote on passage be vitiated and the bill be returned to its previous status on the calendar or in the HELP Committee; and further, other than as provided in this agreement, it not be in order for the Senate to consider any bill or amendment relating to stem cell research during the remainder of the 109th Congress.

Mr. REID. Mr. President, reserving the right to object, it is my understanding that if any one of these three bills or all of them receive 60 votes, they would be passed.

Mr. FRIST. That is correct. Each of these bills will have a 60-vote threshold.

Mr. REID. Mr. President, let me say, first of all, that I extend my appreciation to the distinguished majority leader. This has been difficult. I know that. I would rather that we would just be going forward with H.R. 810, but we will take what we have. . . .

Again, I tell the leader how much I appreciate this and I speak for every Democrat and I speak for people throughout the country. I know this has not been easy.

The PRESIDING OFFICER. Is there objection?

Mr. REID. No objection.

The PRESIDING OFFICER. Without objection, it is so ordered.

Source: *Congressional Record*, U.S. Senate (June 29, 2006, pp. S7169–S7170).

Resolving House–Senate Differences

conference committee A temporary congressional committee made up of members of the House and Senate that meets to reconcile the differences in legislation that has passed both chambers.

Even if a bill clears the many obstacles to passage in one chamber, both chambers must pass an identical proposal in order for it to become law. In some cases, differences can be worked out by informal contacts between the two chambers, or one chamber might agree to accept the version passed by the other. Controversial measures, however, usually require a conference committee to reconcile differences between the House and Senate versions. A **conference committee** is a temporary committee composed of House and Senate members that meets to reconcile differences in a bill that has passed both chambers. Members of a conference committee are called *conferees,* and they are typically selected from among the members of the standing committees that reported the bill. Conference committees traditionally consisted of a handful of the leading members of the committees that originally dealt with the bill. Modern conference committees have increased the membership and have made the job more complicated. For example, 130 representatives from seven House committees and nine senators from two Senate committees were appointed to the conference committee to hammer out the differences in the 1990 Clean Air Act (Sinclair 2012, 3). Members of the conference committee have broad discretion, providing another opportunity to influence legislation. With large membership, complex legislation, and wide disparities between the House and Senate versions of a bill, this final opportunity to negotiate can be complex.

To get legislation out of conference committee, a majority of each chamber's representatives must approve a common bill. This version of the bill is then sent to the respective houses for approval, and neither house can change the version approved by the committee. Each chamber has the choice of approving the bill, sending it back to the committee, or voting it down, which kills the bill.

Conference committees play such an important role that they are sometimes called the "third house of Congress." Because conference committees are composed of the members of the House and Senate standing committees that first handled the bill, Kenneth A. Shepsle and Barry R. Weingast (1987) observe that standing committees have a second chance to enforce the deals made to get the bills passed. Shepsle and Weingast develop a theory suggesting that this "ex post veto" explains why standing committees are so powerful.

Once a bill has been approved, it is sent to the president for signature or veto. Congress can override a presidential veto by a two-thirds vote in both chambers, but as discussed in the next chapter, vetoes are seldom overridden—only about 10 percent of them on average.

Congress's responsibilities, its members, and its operation combine into a process that is more complex and nuanced than many realize. As Sinclair points out, "if the textbook legislative process can be likened to climbing a ladder, the contemporary process is more like climbing a big old tree with many branches" (2012, 48). Some of the branches lead to passage, some lead to alteration, some entrap and entangle a proposal and halt its movement, and some give way altogether.

WHY CONGRESS DOES WHAT IT DOES

This discussion thus far has described the responsibilities and operation of Congress. Political scientists are mainly interested in explaining why members of Congress behave as they do.

Early behavioral studies of Congress relied on sociological theory to explain behavior. Two classic examples are Donald Matthews's (1960) study of the U.S. Senate and Richard Fenno's (1966) study of the House Appropriations Committee. Based on interviews with members, both studies found several norms at work in Congress.

- *Apprenticeship Norm:* Before becoming active participants on major issues, new members are expected to serve an "apprenticeship" during which they watch more senior members and learn how the system (i.e., the committee or the Senate) operates.
- *Hard Work and Specialization Norms:* Members should be "workhorses" who work hard, specialize, and develop expertise on the dull details of particular fields of policy and should avoid being "show horses" who continuously seek publicity.
- *Reciprocity Norm:* Members are expected to help out a colleague if they can, and they expect the colleague to reciprocate and return the favor. These favors might be trading votes or inserting projects in an appropriations bill to help another member's constituency.

The "mavericks" who fail to observe these norms lose the respect of their colleagues and are ineffective legislators. Thus, the sociological explanation of members' behavior and of the operation of Congress as an institution is that these norms come together to form roles that serve particular functions that in turn enable the system to operate smoothly (Fenno 1966; Matthews 1960).

Although these early studies provided important systematic information about Congress, political scientists for the most part have found that rational choice theory offers more convincing explanations. Rational choice models assume that members of Congress are motivated by certain goals—reelection, power, good public policy—and they make choices intended to help them achieve these goals. Thus, members trade votes to get their pet projects adopted not because the "norms" of Congress prescribe this behavior, but because these are rational choices for achievement of their goals (Hall 1996). Three general models of rational choice theory explain congressional behavior: the distributive model, the informational model, and the partisan model. All are based on the rational actor assumption, but they have different policy implications.

The Distributive Model

David Mayhew (1974) was the first political scientist to develop a model of Congress based explicitly on the rational actor model. He begins with the simplifying assumption that all members of Congress are "single-minded seekers of reelection" and asks what types of activity this goal implies (Mayhew 1974, 5). He argues that members of Congress engage in three types of activity to improve the odds of reelection: advertising, position taking, and credit claiming. Advertising includes sending newsletters to those who live in the district and making frequent trips home to create a favorable image among constituents. Position taking means making judgmental statements that will please constituents. What is "pleasing" will vary from district to district. A statement on the Iraq war in a district strongly supportive of President George W. Bush, for example, would have called for a decisive "I support the president on this"; a district in which opinion was divided would have called for waffling: "We must help the Iraqis assume responsibility for defending their new democracy and bring our troops home as soon as possible within parameters consistent with national security." Advertising and position taking are mostly symbolic representation and do not require any actual policymaking.

Credit claiming means taking credit for delivering government benefits. To have an electoral payoff, the claim must be credible. Unlike advertising and position taking, credit claiming involves policymaking. Distributive or "pork barrel" projects are the most obvious way for members to make a credible claim that they are responsible for getting a policy benefit for their constituents. Committees are crucial in the distributive model. Members of Congress seek membership on committees with jurisdiction over policies and programs that are most important to their respective districts, and then they use their committee positions to bring home policy benefits that aid their reelections. Thus, the committee system is an institutional arrangement in which members agree to give up power over policies they care little about in return for power over the policies they care most about (Weingast and Marshall 1988, 145). This reciprocity and vote trading is viewed not as a product of norms, but as a rational strategy to enforce a huge institutional "logroll"—that is, it ensures that one lawmaker won't renege on the deal to scratch another lawmaker's back after the first lawmaker scratches his or hers.

The Informational Model

Rational decision making requires information about the costs and benefits of alternative policies. But members of Congress cannot be experts on every policy, so how do they get the information necessary to make rational choices? Keith Krehbiel (1991) suggests that rational legislators create committees with specialized knowledge to supply the information they need. In this view, committees are agents of the chamber floor. Because committees control what information is provided, specialized committees that are ideologically representative of the whole will provide the most useful information. Committee specialization and reciprocity, therefore, are not the result of norms or the need to enforce logrolls on distributive benefits, but the result of a need for accurate information to cast rational votes on the floor.

The Partisan Model

Gary Cox and Mathew McCubbins (1993) view the majority party as a "legislative cartel" that uses its power to stack committees and control the policy agenda to increase the chances of its members' reelections. Another version of partisan theory is what David Rohde (1991) calls **conditional party government**. He argues that a successful party government depends, or is conditional, on the cohesiveness of policy preferences among members of the majority party caucus. If members of the majority party represent constituencies with diverse policy preferences, the caucus will be reluctant to give party leaders the power to enforce party discipline because forcing everyone in the caucus to toe the party line would threaten the reelection of some members. Yet electoral conditions may change so that nearly all members of the majority party represent constituencies with similar policy preferences. For example, when the 1965 Voting Rights Act brought blacks with liberal policy preferences into southern electorates, conservative white Democrats could no longer afford to ignore those interests, and they started voting more like their liberal northern colleagues. When this "condition" of shared policy preferences among rank-and-file party members is met, the majority party caucus gives more power to party leaders and expects them to use that power to enact the party's legislative agenda. The underlying power relationship is bottom-up rather than top-down: leaders take strong action on behalf of party members who have homogeneous policy preferences because they all represent similar electoral coalitions. A consequence of conditional party government is **party polarization**, given that policy positions (or ideology) within a party become more homogeneous, and policy positions of the two parties tend to move farther apart in order to meet the policy preferences of their constituencies. There is evidence that parties in Congress are becoming more polarized (see chapter 7).

conditional party government When members of the majority party caucus in Congress achieve consensus on policy issues, they adopt reforms that obligate congressional committee chairs and party leaders to try to enact the party's legislative agenda on which there is a consensus.

party polarization Situation in which policy positions (or ideology) within political parties become more homogeneous, and policy positions across the parties move farther apart.

The common feature of all three of these models is that the structure of Congress as an institution is explained by rational calculations. To grasp how and why Congress has such a broad social and political effect, it is important to understand not just what Congress does, but who drives the decisions of the legislature. How Congress executes its role in the political system and how it shapes the broader social fabric are determined largely by the 535 men and women who are members of one of the world's most exclusive clubs.

Top Ten Takeaway Points

❶ Congress's primary responsibilities include lawmaking (passing laws and overseeing government agencies) and representation (responding to constituents' needs and informing the public about the major issues facing the country).

❷ Secondary functions of Congress include impeaching and trying executive and judicial officials, seating and disciplining members, helping select leaders in the executive branch, and fulfilling specialized policy responsibilities such as ratifying treaties and confirming ambassadors to foreign countries.

③ Although there are more minorities and women in Congress today than in earlier decades, membership still does not reflect the diversity of today's American citizens.

④ During the last half of the twentieth century, serving in Congress became a career for many members. In the nineteenth century, a decade was an unusually long time for anyone to be a House member.

⑤ Members of Congress have heavy workloads, and there are enormous demands on their time and attention. Constituents, party leaders, the president, and interest groups often want different or contradictory things, and the member's own preferences may be different from those of these various groups.

⑥ The U.S. Congress has two chambers with two major purposes: (1) to represent different interests and (2) to foster deliberative, careful lawmaking. Both the House and the Senate are organized along party lines, although the specifics of each organization differ considerably.

⑦ Party leaders do not have the authority to command rank-and-file members to do their bidding, but they have a great deal of influence on the operation of Congress. The most powerful person in the Senate is the majority leader, chosen by members of the majority party, whose opposite in the minority party is the minority leader. The Speaker of the House of Representatives is the leader of and most powerful individual in the lower chamber. The Speaker is selected by the majority party and combines the powers shared in the Senate by the vice president and the Senate's majority leader.

⑧ Committees are the core organizational feature of Congress. Standing committees are the most important, being permanent panels with jurisdiction over particular issues and categories of legislation. Committees do research on proposed legislation, revise proposals to accommodate various interests, report the legislation out for consideration on the floor, and conduct oversight of the bureaucracy.

⑨ Some committees are more important and prestigious than others. The prestige committees in the House are Ways and Means, Ap-

propriations, Rules, and Energy and Commerce; prestige committees in the Senate are Finance, Appropriations, Armed Services,
and Foreign Relations.

⑩ The details of lawmaking are often highly complex, and traditional
descriptions of how a bill becomes law oversimplify the legislative
obstacle course. In both chambers, the rules and parliamentary
maneuvering tend to favor those who want to prevent a bill from
becoming law.

Key Terms and Cases

allocation responsiveness, 436

bicameral, 451

casework, 436

censures and reprimands, 442

closed rule, 469

cloture, 470

Committee of the Whole, 470

conditional party
    government, 476

conference committee, 472

delegate, 438

discharge petition, 466

distributive benefits, 436

exclude, 442

exclusive committees, 466

expulsion, 442

filibuster, 470

franking privilege, 451

geographical constituency, 437

hold, 470

home styles, 437

impeach, 439

lawmaking, 434

legislative oversight of
    administration, 435

legislature, 433

majority leader, 454

members' representational
    allowance, 450

minority leader, 454

nongermane amendments, 464

open rule, 469

parliamentary systems, 433

party polarization, 476

party ratio, 459

perquisites (perks), 450

personal constituency, 437

policy responsiveness, 435

politico, 438

pork-barrel benefits, 436

president pro tempore, 454

president of the Senate, 454

presidential systems, 433

prestige committees, 462

primary constituency, 437

reelection constituency, 437

representation, 435

riders, 464

service responsiveness, 436

Speaker of the House of
    Representatives, 455

special rule, 467

standing committees, 457

structured rule, 469

symbolic responsiveness, 437

trustees, 438

unanimous consent
    agreements, 471

unicameral, 452

whips, 455

KEY QUESTIONS

Why has the power of the president grown?

What is the difference between the president and the presidency?

Does the president have enough power to do what people expect the president to do?

PRESIDENTS ARE VERY DIFFERENT—and not just in party, ideology, and policy ambitions. They are different in terms of style. Style makes a big difference.

Take, for example, the styles of President John F. Kennedy and President George W. Bush. Bush and Kennedy faced two of the greatest threats to national security during the past half-century. For Kennedy it was the 1962 Cuban missile crisis, a tense standoff between the United States and the Soviet Union that brought the world to the brink of a nuclear war. For Bush it was 9/11, the devastating terrorist attacks that led to the war on terror.

Kennedy had to deal with Soviet missile sites on Cuba, an island only 90 miles off the coast of Florida. In the event of hostilities, those close-range missile capabilities potentially gave the Soviets a huge tactical and strategic advantage. The United States would have no time to defend or react to a missile strike that was launched from its own backyard.

Some advised immediate military action against the missile bases; others thought such action would mean World War III. Kennedy wanted his Soviet counterpart (Nikita Khrushchev) to remove the missiles of his own accord. Kennedy tried to come up with a response that made clear America's strength and will, while leaving the Soviets an "out"—a way to back down without losing face. Kennedy put together a large and contentious group of experts known as the "Ex Comm" that served to centralize and analyze all available information and to formulate the various scenarios that could produce this result. Out of this came Kennedy's solution: a naval blockade that eventually led to a "peaceful, face-saving resolution to the confrontation" (Crotty 2003, 455).

Bush had to deal with an actual attack on American soil, but there was no obvious nation-state to negotiate with or to hit back. (Most of the terrorists were Saudi citizens, but the government of Saudi Arabia was a U.S. ally.) Bush's approach was not to assemble an equivalent of the Ex Comm to cover the pros and cons of various responses. With little input from anyone, he formulated the "Bush doctrine," which argues for preemptive military action when national security is threatened. He wanted to send a clear message: not only would America hit back, but it also wouldn't wait to be hit first. He made the decision to go to war (Woodward 2002, 15).

Bush assembled a comparatively small war cabinet. Its job was not to employ a broad range of experts to sift through information and provide options or to decide whether to go to war; instead, its job was to hammer out the details of prosecuting wars in Afghanistan and Iraq and dealing with their political implications (Crotty 2003, 460).

Which was the right approach? Kennedy's approach emphasized gathering as much information as possible, seeking contrasting opinions, and involving himself in decision making at all levels. Bush's approach was to make a decision and then turn things over to a small group of people (the "war cabinet") to figure out how to best put that decision into action.

Some see Kennedy's style as a model for how to deal with a crisis: cool and patient under pressure. Others see it as dithering rather than leadership. Some see Bush's style as the better option: decisive and forceful. Others view it as impulsive, reckless, and irresponsible. The point here is not to declare that the Kennedy or the Bush approach is better but to show that the two men had different styles of reacting to a crisis. Such differences have enormous consequences. Differences in style can literally mean the difference between war and peace.

The reason that style can have such momentous consequences is that the office of president of the United States is made up of two fundamental components: (1) the president as an individual and (2) the presidency as an institution. Kennedy and Bush occupied the same office—they sat as the head of the same institution—but were very different individuals. To understand the presidency and its implications for how the nation reacts to particular crises or challenges, it is important to grasp the dual nature of the office.

To that end, this chapter examines the evolution of the institution of the presidency, the influence of the president as an individual, and the implications of the office's institutional structure for the performance of the chief executive.

The president of the United States of America holds the most powerful office on the planet. He (or she) commands the most awesome military machine in history, exerts unequaled influence over national and international policy, and sits as supreme executive in the American political system.

In general, an **executive** is a person or group that has administrative and supervisory responsibilities in an organization. The word derives from "execute," which originally meant "to carry out" or "follow through to the end"[1] (Ayto 1990, 212). The title "president" traditionally referred to the individual who presides over an organization or legislative body to ensure orderly debate. We can find examples of the use of the title in early American governments—for example, John Hancock was "president of the Continental Congress of the United States of America," and Samuel Huntington was "president of the United States in Congress Assembled" under the Articles of Confederation. Although Hancock and Huntington were the first Americans to hold the title "president of the United States of America," neither had any *executive* authority. Rather, the title was used in the traditional sense of presiding over a legislative body, just as the vice president's constitutional responsibility to serve as president of the Senate is a legislative rather than executive power. The declaration of the Constitution of 1789 that "the executive Power shall be vested in a President of the United States of America" (Article II, Section 1) is generally credited as the first time the title was used for the chief executive of a republic who exercised executive powers.[2] Thus, the concept of the president as the chief executive of a nation is an innovation of the Constitution.

The president's powers and unique role within the political system have long created an uncomfortable paradox for the American political system—one that is closely related to the Madisonian dilemma discussed in chapter 2: how do you create a presidency powerful enough to ensure things get done but not powerful enough to run the risk of tyranny? Setting up a chief executive and defining the office's powers and responsibilities were among the most difficult challenges of the Constitutional Convention. The problem was that "the delegates had exceedingly ambivalent feelings about what sort of an executive the new government should have" (Collier and Collier 1986, 284).

---

[1] *OED Online*, s.v. "executive," adj. and n., http://www.oed.com/ (accessed October 25, 2012).

[2] *OED Online*, s.v. "president," n., http://www.oed.com (accessed October 25, 2012); *Encyclopædia Britannica*, s.v. "president," http://www.britannica.com/EBchecked/topic/475206/president (Accessed March 3, 2013); *Online Etymology Dictionary*, s.v. "president," http://dictionary.reference.com/browse/president (accessed July 16, 2012).

executive A person or group that has administrative and supervisory responsibilities in an organization or government.

A clear flaw of the Articles of Confederation was the absence of an executive branch. Convention delegates wanted an executive strong enough to provide clear national leadership and to serve as a real check on the legislative branch. Yet they also feared putting too much power into the hands of a single individual, which could lead to tyranny.

The delegates first agreed on what they did not want in an executive. They did not want a king (Alexander Hamilton was virtually alone in seriously considering resurrecting the British model). Rather than look to Great Britain, the delegates looked to the states. Most states had weak executives dominated by state legislatures. In such a **weak-executive model**, the job of the chief executive is simply to implement the decisions of the legislature. A president in a weak-executive system would have limited terms, would have no veto power, and would be allowed to exercise only the authority explicitly granted by Congress.

But a few states, notably New York and Massachusetts, had strong, independent governors. The **strong-executive model** meant an executive independent of the legislature, with important powers vested in the executive office. The strong-executive model suggested a president as a strong political actor independent of Congress, with veto power, the authority to appoint judges and diplomats, and primary responsibility for foreign affairs.

The Constitutional Convention ended up creating a presidency somewhere between the strong- and weak-executive models. The president was to be chosen by the electoral college rather than appointed by the legislature. The president would not serve at the pleasure of Congress but could be removed for treason, bribery, or high crimes and misdemeanors following impeachment by the House and conviction in the Senate. The Constitution gave the president specific grants of power, including command of the armed forces, the veto, the ability to issue executive pardons, and a very broad, undefined set of rights and responsibilities: "the executive power shall be vested in a President of the United States of America" (Article II, Section 1).

The delegates thus created a strong president but also placed clear limits on the president's power. The president cannot make law by decree; only Congress can pass laws. The president can veto legislation, but Congress can override the veto by a two-thirds vote of both chambers. The president can make appointments to the executive and judicial branches but only with Senate approval. The result is a powerful office, but one that is checked by other branches of government.

Several amendments have altered the basic structure of the executive office formulated at the Constitutional Convention: the Twelfth Amendment on the choosing of the president and vice president; the Twentieth, clarifying the beginning of the presidential term; the Twenty-Second, limiting a president to two terms; and the Twenty-Fifth, specifying the line of succession to the presidency. Despite these changes, the constitutional framework of the presidency has remained mostly intact for more than two centuries.

weak-executive model A model of the presidency in which the executive would have a limited term, would have no veto power, and would be allowed to exercise only the authority explicitly granted by Congress.

strong-executive model A model of the presidency in which the powers of the executive office are significant and independent from Congress.

THE DEVELOPMENT OF THE PRESIDENCY

The presidency today is much more powerful than the office held by George Washington. Most of the changes in the presidency have come not from formal legal alterations but from informal custom and precedent. The power of the presidency, in short, derives in no small part from the legacy of the individuals who have occupied the office. Four basic factors explain the expansion of presidential power:

1. The energy associated with individual executives
2. Vague constitutional provisions that assertive presidents have used to broadly interpret their powers
3. Changing public expectations of the office
4. Congressional delegation of power and authority through law

A Single Executive

In *Federalist* Number 70, Alexander Hamilton used the term *energy* to describe a desirable characteristic of good government, especially in the executive branch. He saw decisiveness and dispatch as important qualities for a good executive. More than anything else, these traits have expanded presidential power.

A good example is the president's ability to make key decisions about committing American troops to military action. Although Congress has the constitutional authority to declare war, presidents have interpreted their power as commander in chief as giving them the right to place military units in combat situations without prior authorization from Congress. The last time Congress formally declared war was to authorize U.S. entrance into World War II in 1941. The major military conflicts the United States has been involved in since then—the Korean War, Vietnam War, and Iraq War—technically were not wars because Congress never made a formal declaration of hostilities. For example, Congress passed a joint resolution in 2002 authorizing the president to use U.S. armed forces

Although the Constitution gives Congress the power to declare war, it makes the president commander in chief of the armed forces. As commander in chief, the president has the ability to make important decisions about committing troops to military action.

© Mark Reis/Colorado Springs Gazette/MCT via Getty Images

BREAKING TREATIES

The Constitution and historical precedent give the president primary responsibility for making treaties with foreign nations. Apparently, presidents can take the lead in breaking treaties for the same reasons.

During his first two years as president, George W. Bush certainly was better known for breaking treaties rather than making them. Against the wishes of Russia, he withdrew the United States from the 1972 Antiballistic Missile Treaty and championed in its place a high-tech (and very expensive) anti-missile system designed to intercept nuclear missiles in flight.

Against the wishes of much of the world, he withdrew the United States from the Kyoto Protocol, a multinational pact aimed at reducing global warming. He also withdrew from treaties or efforts to forge treaties on reducing the global arms trade, banning germ warfare, imposing tariffs on steel imports, and establishing an international war crimes court.

Bush argued that these treaties did not serve the best interests of the country and that his actions simply reflected a president taking a hardheaded and practical view of U.S. interests. Others viewed the moves as evidence of a go-it-alone foreign policy that brought uncertainty into international affairs and left other nations wary of dealing with the United States. These concerns took on particular resonance following the terrorist attacks on the United States in September 2001.

President Bush took on the task of combating terrorism on a global scale—something that made dealing with other nations an absolute necessity. This was a task made harder by Bush's unilateral approach to foreign policy.

The multinational coalition backing the second U.S.-led invasion of Iraq was notably smaller than the coalition that fought in the first Gulf War of 1991. Fighting a lengthy, unpopular, and bloody counterinsurgency campaign in a place like Iraq can never be easy, but allies willing to make significant monetary and troop commitments can ease the burden. Bush found such allies to be in short supply.

Was this simply Bush's foreign policy chickens coming home to roost? Critics of the Bush administration certainly thought so. The basic argument was this: Enlisting international support for any foreign policy initiative is difficult, especially on such controversial decisions as military action. A history of backing out of treaties and ignoring the interests of potential allies, however, is unlikely to make such efforts any easier.

SOURCES Kasindorf, Martin. 2004. "Kerry: Bush's Iraq Choices Undermined American Leadership." *USA Today*. http://www.usatoday.com/news/politicselections/nation/president/2004-05-27-kerryiraq_x.htm.

Nichols, Bill. 2001. "Critics Decry USA Today." *USA Today*. http://www.usatoday.com/news/washington/july01/2001-07-27-bush-treaties-usat.htm.

against Iraq, but this was not a formal declaration of war. Lee Hamilton, former chair of the House International Relations Committee, says, "In the exercise of its . . . war-making power, Congress has basically ceded to the president over a period of years the decision in going to war" (quoted in Lehigh 2002, A27).

In addition to military action, the president retains a dominant role in foreign affairs. The power to negotiate treaties (which require Senate approval) and executive agreements (which do not), to initiate or break off diplomatic relations, and to choose representatives abroad make the president's voice the crucial one in foreign affairs. (See the Politics in Practice feature "Breaking Treaties.")

Historian Arthur Schlesinger Jr. (1973) argues that such expansions of power have led to the creation of an "imperial presidency" that appropriates powers reserved to other branches by the Constitution. Presidents who have acted decisively and assertively have thus significantly expanded the power of the office.

Broad Constitutional Provisions

A key opportunity for aggressive executives to expand their powers is provided by the vague and indefinite opening sentence of Article II: "The executive power shall be vested in a President of the United States of America." This grant of authority allows bold and innovative ventures. Supplementing this provision are other clauses ripe for broad interpretation. For example, the president has responsibility for ensuring "that the laws be faithfully executed" (Article II, Section 3)—a clause that presidents have repeatedly used as legal justification for their actions.

Some presidents resisted the lure to expand their office. James Buchanan and William Howard Taft took a **restrictive view of presidential power**, arguing that the president could exercise only the powers specifically granted by the Constitution. In contrast, Theodore Roosevelt formulated the **stewardship doctrine**, arguing that the president is the steward of the people and should do anything required by the needs of the nation unless it is specifically prohibited by the Constitution. Abraham Lincoln subscribed to the **prerogative view of presidential power**, arguing that the oath of office required him both to preserve the Constitution and to take otherwise unconstitutional measures to ensure that the Constitution itself was well preserved. President George W. Bush took a similar position with respect to the war on terror.

Although earlier presidents could debate the extent of their powers, contemporary presidents do not have this luxury. People expect the president to deliver on a broad set of promises, so the president cannot choose to take the narrow role of caretaker. As political scientist Richard Neustadt put it, the modern president "may retain liberty, in Woodrow Wilson's phrase, 'to be as big a man as he can.' But nowadays he cannot be as small as he might like" (1960, 6).

Public Acceptance of Positive Government

Before the Great Depression began in 1929, government was viewed as having limited responsibility for regulating economic activity. The economic collapse during the Great Depression and the social dislocation it caused changed this

restrictive view of presidential power A view of presidential power that argues that the president can exercise only those powers listed in the Constitution.

stewardship doctrine A view of presidential power that states that the president is a steward of the people and should do anything the nation needs that is not prohibited by the Constitution.

prerogative view of presidential power A view of presidential power, promoted by Abraham Lincoln, that argues that the president is required to preserve the Constitution and take actions to do so that otherwise might be unconstitutional.

attitude. Many Americans welcomed President Franklin Roosevelt's New Deal and its aggressive government intervention into the social and economic patterns of the nation.

Since the 1930s, Americans have increasingly demanded that the government "do something" to ensure prosperity. Economic problems such as unemployment and inflation are now routinely seen as government's responsibility. Government is even expected to mitigate the pain and suffering caused by natural disasters such as hurricanes, tornadoes, floods, and earthquakes. Bold and effective responses to such crises have enhanced the influence of the presidency by creating a sense that the executive can move swiftly and decisively to solve or at least ameliorate such problems. Failure to respond effectively to such crises can diminish the president's leadership. For example, President Bush was on vacation in Crawford, Texas, when Hurricane Katrina struck the Gulf Coast in 2005. Perceptions that he was slow to recognize the magnitude of the crisis and that government's response was ineffective damaged Bush's image as a strong leader. Former White House press secretary Ari Fleischer said that it "turned out to be one of the most damaging events of his presidency" (Fletcher 2006).

This crisis and the increased governmental activity in response to it changed expectations about the proper role of government. Americans have come to accept the concept of **positive government**, a government that plays a major role in meeting or preventing most major crises or problems faced by society. The president is not solely responsible for the rise of positive government; Congress passed the laws and programs expanding governmental activity, and the courts turned away legal challenges to the expanded role. But the energy associated with a single executive makes the president the focal point of these expectations. Expectations of the president go beyond responding to a crisis. The president is routinely expected to manage the domestic economy to produce jobs and opportunity and to conduct foreign policy that promotes peace and democratic values while protecting the nation's economic and strategic interests. As Neustadt observed, Americans have transformed "into routine practice . . . the actions we once treated as exceptional" (1960, 6). The result has been a steady escalation of what the president is normally expected to achieve.

Congressional Delegation of Power

positive government The idea that government should play a major role in preventing or dealing with the crises that face the nation.

In many cases, Congress has specifically delegated additional power and resources to the executive branch. For example, Congress passed several laws in the twentieth century giving presidents an increased role in making budgetary decisions. Some scholars suggest that the legislative branch was too fragmented to be decisive on key policy matters, so Congress followed the public and turned to the president to provide policy leadership. Note, however, that Congress has never abdicated its final authority to amend, change, or block presidential initiatives.

Contemporary Expectations of the President

As a result of these factors, the public has come to expect all chief executives to be presidents of action. The president is held responsible for the economy and for addressing a wide array of social problems. He or she is expected to head the executive branch, conduct foreign policy, nominate federal judges, reflect and shape public opinion, and provide direction and leadership for Congress. The president is also expected to act as the chief partisan for a political party while remaining representative of all Americans.

Although the founders settled on a single executive, the realities of managing broad expectations mean that the modern presidency has become a larger and more bureaucratic organization than in years past. The office of president now stands squarely at the center of the American political system. It has evolved into the center of policymaking, and it has experienced considerable bureaucratic expansion. About 1,700 individuals now make up the institution of the presidency. A broad variety of policy specialists and political advisors enhance the president's ability to meet the high expectations placed on the office. There are experts on everything from national security to agriculture and mass communications.

Yet although presidential power has grown, there is a question about whether it has kept pace with rising expectations. The basic constitutional framework establishes a government of shared powers. If presidents have any hope of meeting the high expectations placed on the office, they must convince political actors in other branches and levels of government to take action. The American system of government makes the president dependent on the actions of others who have power independent of the presidency, and this poses enormous difficulties when it comes to meeting the public's rising expectations. In the seminal behavioral analysis of the presidency, Richard Neustadt (1960, i) defined the problem in terms of personal influence: "what a President . . . can do, as one man among many, to carry his own choices through that maze of personalities and institutions called the government of the United States." Neustadt argued persuasively that to be successful, the president must rely on the powers of persuasion, bargaining, and compromise.

THE PRESIDENT AND THE PRESIDENCY

Most Americans tend to personalize the office of the president in terms of the current occupant, but this perspective ignores the complex organization that lies behind the individual. To fully understand the modern presidency, it is important to grasp how both the individual and the organization contribute to presidential performance.

Political science theory is less developed when it comes to explaining the presidency versus other political institutions. Developing and testing scientific models of the presidency is challenging for a number of reasons: there is a "small n" problem[3]—only 44 cases (presidents) in all to observe—with new cases added only every four or eight years; much of the president's behavior that we need to observe in order to test theories is hidden from public scrutiny; and although some useful information is in presidential papers, it can be decades before scholars can get access to it. Consequently, much of the scholarly analysis of the presidency has been descriptive or biographical. Nonetheless, political scientists have taken some modest steps toward a more scientific analysis of the presidency.

Neustadt's thesis that "presidential power is the power to persuade" can be viewed as relying loosely on a rational actor perspective. The president has policy goals but insufficient power to achieve those goals without the cooperation of other political actors—members of Congress, bureaucrats, and others—all of whom possess independent power to pursue their own goals. "The essence of the President's persuasive task," Neustadt argues, "is to convince [these powerful politicians] that what the White House wants of them is what they ought to do for their own sake and on their authority" (1960, 34). In essence, the president must change the cost–benefit calculations of these other political actors. Neustadt focused on the president's professional reputation as a skilled leader and his popularity with the public as key resources for influencing that cost–benefit calculation.

The President as an Individual

Some presidential scholars have turned to psychology for theoretical guidance, assuming that the way the president handles the powers and duties of office depends on individual personality and character. Family background and life experiences help determine self-confidence, psychological needs, values, and worldview. They also shape the political philosophy and the personal vision of presidential conduct.

Scholars such as Erwin Hargrove (1974) and James David Barber (1992) distinguish between active presidents and passive presidents. "Active presidents" invest a good deal of personal energy into the office, and their personal needs and skills translate well into political leadership. "Passive presidents" devote less time and effort to being president and have neither the inclination nor the ability to effectively exercise political power. Barber (1992) also distinguishes between "positive presidents," who gain personal satisfaction from serving as president, and "negative presidents," who serve because of compulsion or a sense of duty but derive little pleasure from the post.

James Barber (1992) uses these dimensions to identify four types of presidents:

1. Active-positive presidents want results, and they push for change in institutions, policies, and procedures.

---

[3] "Small n" means that there is a small number of cases to observe.

2. Active-negative presidents are preoccupied with acquiring and maintaining power for its own sake.
3. Passive-positive presidents want to be popular, loved, and admired.
4. Passive-negative presidents are characterized by a deep sense of civic virtue and rectitude.

This psychological approach to understanding the presidency has not proven particularly successful. There is little doubt that the background and personality of individual presidents affect their performance, but determining exactly how the former cause the latter is extraordinarily difficult. Part of the problem is context: what a president can accomplish is significantly affected by the type and magnitude of the problems the government faces at the time of his presidency and by the needs, interests, and preferences of the other actors who share power with the president. Rather than character traits causing job performance, the demands of the job may reveal a president's character. Even placing a president into one of the personality categories is imprecise and subjective; there is disagreement, for example, about whether George W. Bush was an active-positive or active-negative.

The Presidency as an Organization

Over the course of history, presidents have used a variety of advisors and organizations to help manage their duties. One presidential advisor, the vice president, is explicitly provided for in the Constitution, although each president determines what role the vice president will play, if any. The cabinet and the Executive Office of the President (EOP) are authorized and funded by Congress. Other people play key advisory roles because of close personal ties to the president. John Kennedy relied on his brother Robert for advice, and George W. Bush frequently turned to his father, former president George H. W. Bush, for advice. Several presidents have turned to the first lady for political and policy advice.

Irrespective of who is president, the presidency is a complex organization made up of many individuals. The major components of the presidency as an organization include the vice president, the cabinet, and the EOP. The various individuals who serve in the executive branch often compete and struggle for access to the president, and some are more influential than others.

VICE PRESIDENT Although the Constitution establishes the office of vice president and sets the same qualifications for the office as for the presidency, it lists no formal executive powers or responsibilities.[4] Historically, vice presidents have not

---

[4] Article I, Section 3, gives the vice president some legislative responsibility as president of the Senate with the right to cast a vote to break a tie. But no formal executive power is granted unless the president dies, leaves office, or is disabled, in which case the vice president assumes the duties of the president.

been central policymakers, and ambitious politicians have shunned the office. John Nance Garner, who gave up the position of Speaker of the House to become Franklin Roosevelt's vice president in 1933, most famously summed up the disdain for the office by saying, "The vice presidency isn't worth a pitcher of warm piss" (Rees 1997, 254).

Some vice presidents have essentially been presidents-in-waiting, for when something arose to prevent the president from fulfilling the obligations of the office. The person with the "best job in the country," Will Rogers once quipped, "is the Vice President. All he has to do is get up every morning and say, 'How's the President?'" (quoted in Byrne 1988, 229). It has become common to describe the vice president as "just one heartbeat away from being president." Since 1960, two vice presidents have ascended to the presidency before the end of the president's term— Lyndon Johnson became president after the death of John F. Kennedy in 1963 and Gerald Ford after the resignation of Richard M. Nixon in 1974. The post has also been a stepping stone to the presidency. Richard Nixon and George H. W. Bush, for example, both were vice presidents who then ran for and were elected president.

Vice presidents are not always condemned to ceremonial roles in the political backwaters. Vice President Spiro Agnew, for example, made harsh public attacks on critics of the Nixon administration. Vice presidents Nelson Rockefeller, Walter Mondale, George H. W. Bush, and Al Gore put their own stamps on the agendas and policies of the Ford, Carter, Reagan, and Clinton administrations (Berke 1999). Vice President Dick Cheney was so powerful that some wags claimed that George W. Bush was just a heartbeat away from being president. Despite the exaggeration in this political humor, close observers do consider Cheney to be "history's most powerful vice president" (J. Goldstein 2008, 384). Vice President Joe Biden has carried on the growing power of the vice president. An experienced Washington observer argues, "The previous two vice presidents, Cheney and his predecessor, Al Gore, significantly changed that power dynamic. But on Biden's watch the 'OVP'—Office of the Vice President— has become something even more: almost a conjoined twin to the presidency" (Hirsh 2012).

CABINET The cabinet consists of the heads of the executive agencies and other officials designated by the president to serve as a council of advisors. The cabinet is more a product of law and historical accident than of constitutional design (Hart 1995). At the Constitutional Convention, Gouverneur Morris offered a detailed and elaborate plan for a Council of State to advise the president. But all that survived in the final draft was a general implication in Article II, Section 2 that a cabinet would exist: the president "may require the opinion, in writing, of the principal officer in each of the executive departments, upon any subject relating to the duties of their respective offices."

The first Congress created the Departments of War, Treasury, and State and the office of attorney general, but it established no formal advisory council. In 1789, George Washington attempted to use the Senate as an advisory council regarding a treaty with Native Americans, but senators refused to discuss the matter in his presence. Angered, Washington left the chamber and turned to the heads of the executive departments for advice. This was the first cabinet.

Every president since has had a cabinet, though its role has varied from one administration to the next. In general, the cabinet's role has declined over time. Reasons for this atrophy are varied. Cabinet secretaries sometimes become advocates for the bureaucratic agencies they head rather than remaining loyal to the president. The White House staff has grown so much that presidents have other sources of expert advice. Many White House staff members were originally part of the president's campaign team and were chosen for their demonstrated loyalty to the president and the president's agenda. By contrast, cabinet members are not necessarily close to the president, did not necessarily play major roles in the campaign, and were frequently appointed either out of electoral debt to some organized group or because the individual's expertise and experience lent credibility to the administration.

The decline of the cabinet as an advisory structure also reflects the evolution of the presidency as a distinct and separate entity within the executive branch. In the past 50 years, the boundary between the White House staff, who are loyal to the current president, and the career civil servants in the permanent departments and agencies of the federal government has become much sharper.

Despite this decline, cabinet members retain important and influential positions in the political system. The head of an executive agency such as the Department of Justice or the Department of Defense has enormous responsibilities and a strong position from which to influence both the policy governing the agency and the way that policy is implemented. Cabinet members can also serve the interests of the president above and beyond providing advice and using their positions to pursue the administration's agenda. Because they hold high-profile positions and are in close proximity to the president, their appointments are useful in strengthening ties to certain constituencies. President George W. Bush, for example, chose Colin Powell as secretary of state for his first term. Powell, an African American, was widely admired for his service as chairman of the Joint Chiefs of Staff. By nominating him, Bush made a symbolic gesture to African Americans, a group that openly questioned the legitimacy of his presidency because of suspicions about voting irregularities. Bush also chose John Ashcroft, a former U.S. senator, as his attorney general. Ashcroft, a favorite of evangelical Christians, helped cement Bush's ties to one of his most important constituencies, even though many other groups viewed Ashcroft's appointment with dismay. President Barack Obama appointed Senator Hillary Clinton, his primary rival for the nomination, to be secre-

© Bettmann/CORBIS

The cabinet consists of the heads of the executive agencies and other officials designated by the president to serve as a council of advisors. Cabinet members can serve the interests of the president above and beyond providing advice and use their positions to pursue the administration's agenda. Because they hold high-profile positions and are in close proximity to the president, their appointments are useful in strengthening ties to certain constituencies. Abraham Lincoln selected a strong cabinet that included all of this major rivals for the Republican presidential nomination: William H. Seward as secretary of state (center), Salmon P. Chase as secretary of the treasury (second from left), and Edward Bates as attorney general (far right). Here Lincoln reads them the Emancipation Proclamation on July 22, 1862.

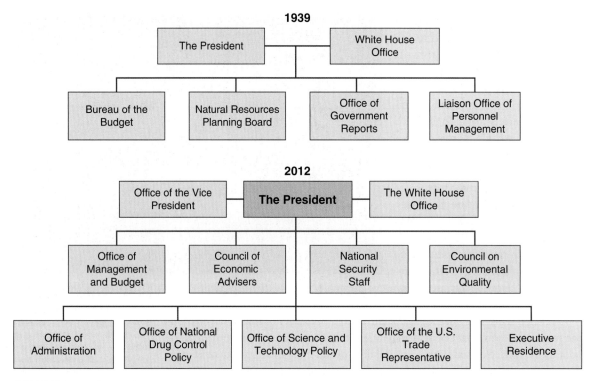

FIGURE 13.1 **Executive Office of the President at Its Inception and Today**
Source: G. Edwards and Wayne (2003); The White House (n.d.).

Executive Office of the President (EOP)
The organizational structure in the executive branch that houses the president's most influential advisors and agencies. The most important include the White House Office, the Office of Management and Budget (OMB), the National Security Council, and the Council of Economic Advisers.

White House Office A section of the Executive Office of the President that houses many of the most influential advisors to the president, including the chief of staff; the White House legal counsel; presidential speechwriters; the president's press secretary; assistants for domestic, foreign, and economic policy; and liaisons with Congress, the public, and state and local governments.

tary of state. The Democratic Party establishment had viewed Senator Clinton as the heir apparent, and Bill Clinton had used his influence as a past president and party leader to support her bid. By appointing her to this crucial and visible cabinet position, Obama helped soothe lingering disappointment with important Democratic Party constituencies. Obama also reappointed Robert Gates, President Bush's secretary of defense. Gates gave the young president credibility with the military, and his appointment signaled the president's desire to work with Republicans in a bipartisan way to solve some of the nation's most thorny problems.

EXECUTIVE OFFICE OF THE PRESIDENT The president's closest and most influential advisors are in the **Executive Office of the President (EOP)**. Congress established the EOP in 1939 after the Brownlow Committee (a blue ribbon committee appointed by President Franklin D. Roosevelt) recommended organizational changes to make the executive branch more efficient. This office has grown in size and complexity over time. The EOP is not part of the cabinet, though cabinet secretaries are members of some of its units. Figure 13.1 shows the organization of the first EOP, in comparison to its modern incarnation.

Among the various units in the EOP, the **White House Office** houses the president's most influential advisors. White House staffers include the chief of staff; the White House legal counsel; presidential speechwriters; the president's press secretary; assistants for domestic, foreign, and economic policy; and liaisons with Congress, the public, and state and local governments. This office also includes the president's personal staff, the vice president, and the first lady's staff.

Over the years, Congress has placed several other agencies under the EOP umbrella. The most important include the **Office of Management and Budget (OMB)**, the **National Security Council**, and the **Council of Economic Advisers**. As the EOP has expanded into a series of agencies with focused responsibilities, staffers have become increasingly specialized. After his first term in office, Franklin Roosevelt had fewer than 100 presidential assistants, most of them generalists with such titles as assistant to the president or counsel to the president. In contrast, under George W. Bush, the OMB alone had more than 500 employees, most of them with specialties in areas such as national security, human resources, or natural resources. With the growth and specialization of the White House Office, the presidency has taken on the trappings of a large bureaucratic organization. Political scientists Lyn Ragsdale and John Theis (1997) argue that the presidency has become "institutionalized" and that it has grown into a large, complex, permanent organization that all presidents must learn to manage once they take office.

FIRST LADY The role of the president's spouse has evolved over time. Originally, the first lady had mostly social duties, acting as a hostess and the like. But over the years, first ladies have become much more prominent as political and policy advisors, reflecting the changing role of women in society.[5]

Eleanor Roosevelt was one of the best-known politically active presidential spouses. She traveled widely to assess social and economic conditions, had her own newspaper column, and was a key member of Franklin Roosevelt's "kitchen cabinet," a group of individuals who were not members of the official cabinet and who fed the president's voracious appetite for information. Taking such a high-profile, nontraditional role was controversial, a problem other politically powerful first ladies encountered as well. President Jimmy Carter's reliance on his wife

© Bettmann/CORBIS

Over the years first ladies have become much more prominent as political and policy advisors, reflecting the changing role of women in society. Eleanor Roosevelt had a very strong effect on this changing role. She traveled widely to assess social and economic conditions, had her own newspaper column, and was a key member of Franklin Roosevelt's "kitchen cabinet," a group of individuals who were not members of the official cabinet and who fed the president's voracious appetite for information. Here she tours conditions in a coal mine in Ohio in 1935 with mine officials and members of the United Mine Workers' union.

Office of Management and Budget (OMB) An agency of the Executive Office of the President that is responsible for assisting the president in creating the budget.

National Security Council A group of presidential advisors made up of the vice president, the attorney general, and cabinet officers chosen by the president to advise the president on national security issues; it is part of the Executive Office of the President.

Council of Economic Advisers An agency of the Executive Office of the President that is responsible for advising the president on the U.S. economy.

---

[5] So far, there have been no first gentlemen, and only two presidents were unmarried during their terms. Thomas Jefferson's wife died before he became president, and in his administration, hostess duties were performed by either his daughters or Dolley Madison, wife of Secretary of State James Madison. So far in the nation's history, James Buchanan has been the only bachelor president. During his administration, the official hostess was his niece, Harriet Lane.

Rosalynn's advice led some to view her as "the second most powerful person in the United States" (Gutin 1994, 521). Bill Clinton appointed his wife, Hillary, to head a task force on health care reform and elevated the position of first lady to a more formal policy role than previous administrations had. Because they had influence and power without having been elected or formally appointed, both Rosalynn Carter and Hillary Clinton were controversial figures during their husbands' presidential terms.[6] President George W. Bush credited First Lady Laura Bush as the most important guiding force in his life, but her role as political and policy advisor was more behind the scenes and less controversial. Michelle Obama also has adopted an uncontroversial role as first lady. Initially, she focused on supporting military families, helping working women balance career and family, and visiting schools to encourage national service. More recently, she adopted a long-term goal of reducing childhood obesity. Obama has engaged in a limited number of political activities, including publicly supporting the president's economic stimulus bill and hosting a White House reception for women's rights advocates to celebrate passage of the Lilly Ledbetter Fair Pay Act of 2009.

Organization of the Presidency and Presidential Effectiveness

As the White House staff has grown, it has become more difficult to control and coordinate. More than three decades ago, political scientist Thomas Cronin observed, "The president needs help merely to manage his help. The swelling and continuous expansion of the presidency have reached such proportions that the president's ability to manage has been weakened rather than strengthened. Bigger has not been better" (1975, 118). Despite this warning, mismanagement of the White House staff has been blamed for a number of crises, ranging from an unsuccessful invasion of Cuba during the Kennedy administration to provision of funds to Nicaraguan rebels in contravention of a congressional mandate in the Reagan administration to a scandal involving the firing of White House travel office staff in the Clinton administration.

Presidents have tried various administrative arrangements to organize the White House staff so that it supports the president's agenda effectively without creating political quagmires. Most presidents use a **hierarchical model**, which sets up hierarchical lines of authority and delegates control through a chief of staff. Other presidents have tried a **spokes-of-the-wheel model**, where the president is in the middle, acting as the hub, and various presidential advisors representing the spokes of the wheel report directly to him. Figure 13.2 illustrates these models.

The hierarchical structure, with clear lines of authority going through a chief of staff, fit well with President Dwight Eisenhower's military experience. It was an efficient system that insulated Eisenhower from small details and allowed him to set

hierarchical model A method of organizing the presidency that calls for clear lines of authority and that delegates responsibility from the president and through the chief of staff.

spokes-of-the-wheel model A method of organizing the presidency that calls for the president to be the center of activity, with numerous advisors reporting directly to the president.

---

[6] Hillary Clinton has a political career in her own right. She was elected to the Senate from New York in 2000, becoming the first First Lady to win elective office. After losing her bid for the Democratic nomination for president in 2008, she was appointed secretary of state by President Obama.

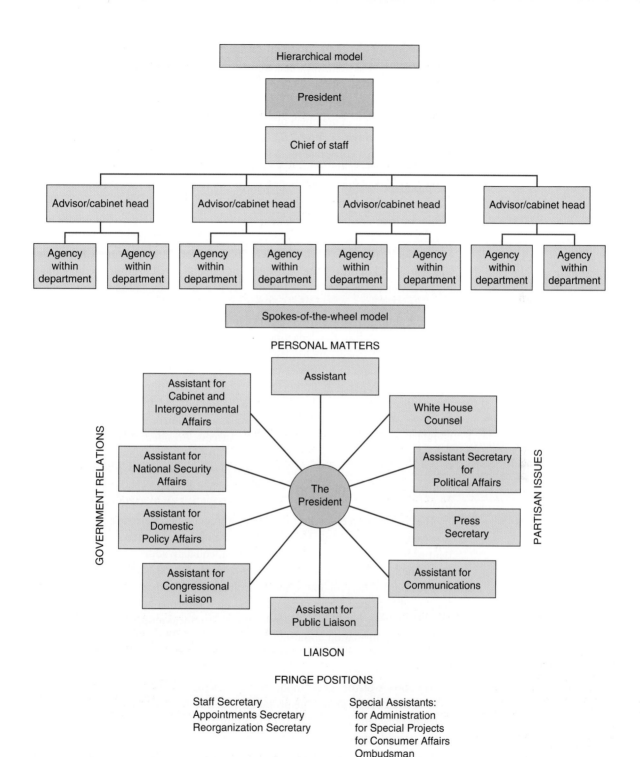

FIGURE 13.2 **Two Models of Organizing the White House Staff**

Sources: Hierarchical model adapted from George and George (1998, 209); spokes-of-the-wheel model adapted from Campbell (1986, 85).

general policy goals and build political support for them. President Richard Nixon also used a hierarchical model, with access to the president controlled by the chief of staff. Although the Nixon White House was efficient from a managerial standpoint, it insulated the president from the perspective and political insights of cabinet members and members of Congress.

President George W. Bush, the first president with an MBA, organized the White House on a corporate model (Crotty 2003; J. Goldstein 2008, 384). In this version of the hierarchical model, sometimes referred to as a "CEO presidency," the president "would be the chairman of the board of the world's biggest conglomerate" (Sanger 2001). President Bush delegated major authority and responsibility to Vice President Dick Cheney, who acted as chief operating officer, and to members of the cabinet, who served as CEOs of their parts of the government conglomerate (Berke 2001; J. Goldstein 2008; Sanger 2001). A strong CEO model that works well in the private sector does not adapt as well in government. Unlike business executives who have clear authority to formulate and implement policy for their corporations, members of the executive branch of government do not have this authority. As we observed in chapter 12, Congress has the power to enact policy, decide on how the departments of government are organized, and oversee how those departments are implementing policy.

President Franklin Roosevelt used the spokes-of-the-wheel model effectively. He ran the staff operation himself and purposely blurred lines of authority to create competition among his staff, to maximize the amount and diversity of information. However, other presidents who tried a similar arrangement, such as John Kennedy, Gerald Ford, and Jimmy Carter, had less success. President Bill Clinton initially tried a spokes-of-the-wheel structure with blurred lines of authority and easy staff access to the president. The system created problems of slow decision making and ineffective communication, and Clinton switched to a more hierarchical arrangement two years into his first administration (G. Edwards and Wayne 2003).

The choice between models represents a tradeoff between the president's need for control over the White House and the need for information to help the president provide broad political leadership to adequately address the nation's problems. The hierarchical model maximizes control with clear lines of authority and responsibility. The problem is that it isolates the president; the president deals mostly with a small group of people who filter information from various sources and report to the president. Under the hierarchical model, the president may not receive information about the full range of opportunities and options available. The president does not keep tabs on lower-echelon assistants, who may take actions the president does not support.

The spokes-of-the-wheel model maximizes the amount and diversity of information available by giving the president access to more advisors. The problem is that the president can end up with too much information to process effectively and may be dragged into micromanaging minor details that could and should be handled by others. If the danger of the hierarchical system is that the president becomes isolated, the danger of the spokes-of-the-wheel system is that the president will be overwhelmed.

THE PRESIDENT'S PRIMARY CONSTITUTIONAL RESPONSIBILITIES

Article II, Sections 1 and 2 of the Constitution define the president's primary responsibilities. These include chief executive, commander in chief of the military, and chief diplomat.

Chief Executive

The executive power referenced in the opening sentence of Article II entails a number of activities. Organizing the presidency and being an effective manager, as discussed previously, are important executive duties. The president can also grant pardons and reprieves. The core of executive power involves implementation of the nation's laws.

Article II, Section 3 does not say that the president implements the laws but rather that the president "shall *take care* that the laws be faithfully executed" (emphasis added). In effect, the president is the chief bureaucrat because executing the laws is mainly the job of the federal bureaucracy. The president has the responsibility of making sure the federal bureaucracy is fulfilling its responsibilities as designated by law.

Administering this vast and varied operation is an enormous challenge. Many of the people who implement the laws are not directly subordinate to the president; the president cannot fire or cut the salaries of individuals in the civil service. Others who serve at the president's discretion, such as cabinet secretaries, often develop political power bases independent of the president.

As chief executive, the president has the power to appoint individuals to fill the most important positions in the executive branch. But here too there are constraints, the most important of which is that appointments require confirmation by the Senate. Although the Senate eventually confirms over 90 percent of presidential nominations to executive branch agencies (cabinet, EOP, and major regulatory agencies), the length of time required for the Senate to act on these nominations has increased for recent presidents. Figure 13.3 shows the average number of months it took the Senate to process executive branch nominations for the last nine presidents. During the Johnson, Nixon, Ford, and Carter presidencies, the Senate generally acted on executive branch nominations in about a month. For subsequent administrations, the time required to act on nominations increased exponentially, doubling to about two months for Reagan, the senior Bush, and Clinton in his first term and then doubling again to nearly four months from Clinton's second term to Obama.

Delaying confirmation of major executive branch officials an extra month or two also delays the president's ability "to take care that the laws be faithfully executed." But not only does it take longer for the Senate to act on executive branch appointments; failure rates have increased as well (see Figure 13.4).

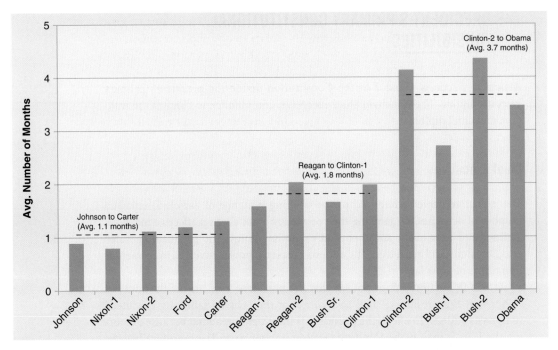

FIGURE 13.3 Increasing Length of the Confirmation Process for Executive Branch Nominations
Source: Bond, Fleisher, and Krutz (2009); Obama nominations updated by the authors.

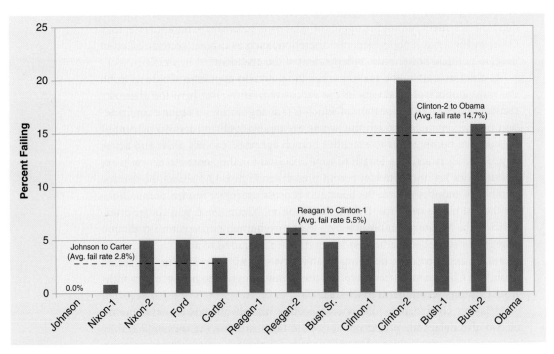

FIGURE 13.4 Increasing Failure Rates of Executive Branch Appointments
Source: Bond, Fleisher, and Krutz (2009); Obama nominations updated by the authors.

Before Clinton, failure rates for executive branch appointments were about 6 percent or less. During Clinton's second term, the failure rate on appointments to the cabinet, EOP, and regulatory agencies jumped to about 20 percent. The failure rate dropped to 8.3 percent during Bush's first term, but climbed up to nearly 16 percent during his second term. The nearly 15 percent failure rate of Obama's executive branch appointments is similar to Bush's. Thus, recent presidents have to wait longer to put top administrative personnel in place, and they are less likely to get their first choice.

Furthermore, the president does not have the authority to determine the particular organization and structure of the executive branch. Instead, Congress determines the number of executive departments and frequently creates executive branch agencies that are insulated from the president. For example, the president appoints individuals to the Federal Reserve Board ("the Fed") and the Federal Election Commission (FEC), but members serve for fixed terms that overlap with the president's term, and these appointees cannot be removed except for wrongdoing.

Commander in Chief

Article II, Section 2 of the Constitution clearly states that "the President shall be commander-in-chief of the Army and Navy of the United States, and of the militia of the several states." Although this is a broad grant of power to the president, the extent of the power is the subject of some dispute. One view is that the president's power is limited to acting as civilian head of the military, with authority for the general policy direction and command of the armed forces. The other view is that this provision empowers the president to take direct operational command. George Washington's response to the Whiskey Rebellion that erupted in western Pennsylvania in 1794 set a precedent that seems to support this latter view. President Washington rode at the head of an army of state militias to suppress the insurrection. President Lincoln also asserted this view during the Civil War, and a number of other presidents, including Franklin Roosevelt, Harry Truman, Ronald Reagan, George H. W. Bush, Bill Clinton, George W. Bush, and Barrack Obama, have acted as if they had direct operational command (G. Edwards and Wayne 2003, 487).

The president has more autonomy in the exercise of the power as commander in chief than in the exercise of other executive powers. Congress has sole authority to declare war, and Congress passes laws establishing funding and regulating the military. But the president has the power—even the duty—to commit military forces to protect U.S. interests without a formal declaration of war.

Attempts to limit the president's authority to commit troops without congressional approval have been largely unsuccessful. One important attempt to limit the power of the commander in chief is the War Powers Act of 1973. This law requires the president to consult "in every possible instance" with Congress before sending troops into action and to report such actions to Congress within 48 hours. Troops must be withdrawn after 60 days unless Congress declares war or passes a resolution authorizing the use of armed force. This law has generally failed to keep presents from committing troops. Presidents view the law as an unconstitutional intrusion on their prerogatives. Presidents Reagan, Bush senior, Clinton, and Obama all ordered military actions that could be considered violations of the War Powers Act. Yet in most instances, they and other presidents observed notification provisions without officially acknowledging them as legitimate: their notification of Congress was "consistent with" rather than "in pursuance of" the War Powers Act. And once the president has taken military action, Congress has been hesitant to withhold support for American troops placed in harm's way.

Taking unilateral action by ordering military operations on foreign soil poses some risks for the president. The risk is small if the conflict can be quickly brought to a successful conclusion, but having American troops in unsuccessful or extended combat operations without the approval of Congress is likely to be politically costly. This was one of the reasons, for example, that President George H. W. Bush sought congressional backing of the Gulf War in 1991 as soon as it became apparent that liberating Kuwait from Iraqi invasion and occupation would require a massive military commitment. Although the second President Bush received congressional approval to use military force against Saddam Hussein in Iraq, extended combat operations and questions regarding whether the invasion was justified eroded support for the war. (See Figure 9.2 in chapter 9.)

Chief Diplomat

The president's central role in foreign policy is a product of tradition and of the unique constitutional authority to "make treaties" subject to ratification by two-thirds of the Senate and to appoint ambassadors subject to confirmation by a majority in the Senate (Article II, Section 2). These constitutional provisions place the president at the center of foreign policy formulation, and presidents have interpreted these powers very broadly. George Washington, for example, assumed that the power to receive ambassadors also conferred the power to formally recognize other nations. Presidents have also used their powers as commander in chief to assert a primary role in foreign policy.

The president is the government official who negotiates treaties. Although the Constitution calls for the president to obtain the advice and consent of the Senate, Washington's attempt to seek advice from the Senate was unsuccessful, as noted earlier, and the Senate's role has been confined almost exclusively to deciding whether to consent. Presidents sometimes discuss controversial provisions of treaties with key senators in an effort to avoid difficulties with ratification, which requires a two-thirds vote. Sometimes, the Senate approves a treaty with reservations or amendments, necessitating further negotiations.

Since 1789, more than 90 percent of the hundreds of treaties submitted to the Senate have been approved—70 percent without any change. Of the treaties that failed, only about 20 were defeated on a floor vote; about 150 others were withdrawn by the president, mostly because they ran into resistance in the Senate. The most famous example of a treaty voted down on the Senate floor is the Treaty of

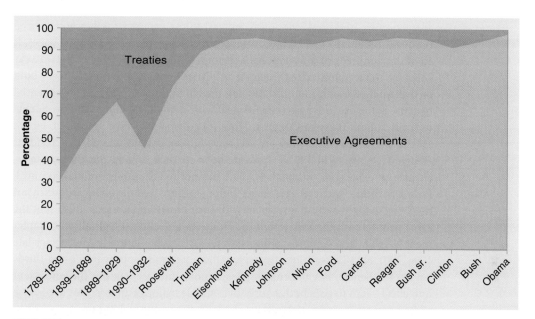

FIGURE 13.5 Proportion of Treaties and Executive Agreements

Source: Constructed by the authors from Stanely and Neimi (2011, 322); Krutz and Peake (2011); Treaties Transmitted = No. of treaties transmitted to the Senate in time period (CIS and Thomas); EAs Concluded = No. of executive agreements listed in Table II-2 in CRS print (p. 39), based off of signed date, updated 2000–2006 using http://www.state.gov/s/l/treaty/c3428. htm and 2007–2010 using Case Act reporting.

Versailles, which ended World War I and established the League of Nations. It failed in large part because President Woodrow Wilson was unwilling to consult with key senators and to agree to compromises. In order to win approval of the Panama Canal Treaty in 1978, President Jimmy Carter agreed to a reservation added by the Senate stating that the United States had the right to use military force to keep the canal open if necessary (G. Edwards and Wayne 2003, 179).

The 90 percent approval rate, however, does not mean that presidents have an easy time winning approval of treaties they have negotiated. Although the Senate rarely turns down a treaty outright, treaties often languish for years in Senate committees that take no action to move them through the process. Presidents have responded to this difficulty by entering into **executive agreements** with other nations. These are treaties in all but name. An executive agreement takes the legal form of a contract between two nations, which does not require two-thirds approval from the Senate. As Figure 13.5 shows, presidents since Franklin Roosevelt (1933–1944) have negotiated many more executive agreements than treaties.

Although executive agreements account for more than 90 percent of all U.S. international agreements, this does not mean that presidents are using this device to usurp the Senate's power under the Constitution. Glen Krutz and Jeffrey Peake present persuasive evidence that the use of executive agreements "is a rational

executive agreements Agreements between the United States and other nations, negotiated by the president, that have the same weight as a treaty but do not require senatorial approval.

adaptation by [the president and Congress] to the complex foreign policy environment" (2009, 187). Most executive agreements involve minor, routine issues. If all of the hundreds of international agreements negotiated during each two-year Congress were submitted to the Senate as treaties for ratification, the Senate would be overwhelmed with minor issues and unable to deal with more consequential matters. Some executive agreements deal with weightier matters, and presidents typically submit these to Congress. The North American Free Trade Agreement (NAFTA), for example, was an executive agreement negotiated by President George H. W. Bush in 1992 to provide open markets among the United States, Canada, and Mexico. Although NAFTA did not require congressional approval, President Bush—and later President Clinton—recognized the political costs of not involving Congress in an agreement with such broad implications. Bush sent the agreement to both the Senate and the House in order to get legislation to implement NAFTA, and Congress approved the NAFTA legislation in 1993 (Ragsdale 1996, 290). NAFTA was not a treaty, so it did not require approval by a two-thirds vote in the Senate. But the enabling legislation—the law that put the agreement into effect—had to pass both houses by a simple majority. In this way, the House of Representatives sometimes plays a role in the treaty-making process—not in ratifying treaties, but in passing the legislation necessary to implement them.

The president's constitutional responsibilities as chief executive, commander in chief, and chief diplomat are relatively well known. The remainder of this chapter focuses on three other major presidential roles: leader of the political party, leader of public opinion, and leader of Congress. In each role, the president needs to persuade others to follow when they may not be inclined to do so.

THE PRESIDENT AS PARTY LEADER

The founders did not anticipate that the president would be the leader of a political party. Indeed, as we learned in chapter 7, the nation's first president warned of the "baneful effects of the spirit of party." Yet Washington's warning went unheeded. By the election of the third president—Thomas Jefferson—in 1800, political parties were already an important feature of American politics. The role of party leader has become a permanent part of the president's job. James Davis argues that of the president's many duties, "none is more important to his longer-term success than that of party leader" (1994, 1). He observes that with the exception of Washington, who became president before the development of parties, America's strongest presidents—Jefferson, Jackson, Lincoln, Wilson, and Roosevelt—have also been strong party leaders.

The role of party leader encompasses the three basic elements of political parties discussed in chapter 7: party organization, party in the electorate, and party in government. America's relatively weak party system significantly constrains the president's ability to lead in each of these areas, and the amount of effort devoted to partisanship and party building varies from one president to the next.

Limitations on the President as Party Leader

Several features of American politics limit the president's ability to act as party leader. First is the traditional mistrust of parties, dating back to the founding of the nation. This suspicion promotes an inclination to be "president of all the people" and a fear that being too partisan is politically risky.

Constitutional fragmentation of powers also limits the president's ability to act as party leader. Federalism has led to national party organizations that are essentially confederations of 50 separate and autonomous state organizations. National party chairs and committees have little authority over state parties, and the president has little hope of centralizing control over such broad and often factious coalitions.

The separation of the national government into executive, legislative, and judicial branches further limits the president's party leadership. Although the president is the nominal head of the party, fellow partisans in other branches have not chosen the president as the leader and have limited influence over the president's policy positions. The reverse is also true: the president has little control over who wears the party's label in Congress and the policies the legislators support. House members and senators have to satisfy local constituencies, not the president, to get elected and reelected. The result is that although the president may be the most visible and influential player in defining the party's position on an issue, he or she will have competition from fellow party members who are officeholders in other branches and the states.

Finally, reforms of the 1880s and early 1900s, especially the decline of patronage and the rise of direct primaries, eroded party discipline and the role of party leaders. Rank-and-file voters, not party leaders, choose the party's standard-bearers in direct primaries. This reform bred independence within parties, and elected officials feel free to take positions contrary to the wishes of party leaders if it serves their reelection needs. Civil service reforms robbed the party of the patronage jobs and contracts distributed to party supporters in return for their electoral help. Thus, party leaders have neither the carrot (jobs for supporters) nor the stick (control of nominations) to secure party loyalty. As the head of the party, the president has not been immune from the weakened position the reforms assigned to party leaders. Even with such limitations, however, presidents must attend to party affairs if they are to be successful.

The President and Party Organization

As an organization, the national party is most active during presidential election years. Between elections, the national party's business is managed by a national party chair and a national committee made up of state party leaders. Although the president is recognized as the titular head of this organization, the president is not an officer of the party and has no formal authority.

Each president decides how much to emphasize the role of party leader. As an academic political scientist before he became president, Woodrow Wilson had a clear vision of the president's role as a strong party leader. He believed that political parties should be the vehicle of presidential leadership, and he envisioned presidents developing a direct relationship with citizens by rallying public opinion in support of administration proposals. As acknowledged party leader, the president would use the loyal support of fellow partisans to enact the administration's program. Franklin Roosevelt was also a strong party leader; he strategically stitched together a New Deal coalition of Democrats from the South and ethnic minorities from the North to transform the Democratic Party into a majority. Recent presidents, such as Ronald Reagan, Bill Clinton, and George W. Bush, made serious efforts to expand and build their national party bases. Barack Obama started party-building efforts immediately after he won the Democratic nomination in 2008, leading some journalists to conclude that he was "more focused on building the Democratic Party than any other candidate in recent history" (D. Goldstein and Klein 2008).

Presidents can shape party organization even before they are elected to office. The candidate who controls a majority of delegates at the party's national convention usually controls most aspects of the convention, including choosing major officers, formulating the party platform, and selecting a running mate. This power offers an opportunity to put together a unified party base behind a set of clear proposals. It also has dangers. If significant numbers of the president's party disagree with the plans, they may fight the platform or force the convention to showcase candidates who opposed the winner. At the 1992 Republican convention, for example, President George H. W. Bush was forced to give more prominence and deference than he desired to supporters of rival Pat Buchanan. The result was public emphasizing of differences between factions in the Republican Party, which was not the preferred outcome of a party leader heading into a tough general election campaign.

The presidential candidate also names the national party chair, typically someone instrumental in securing the candidate's nomination. This power allows the president to influence the party organization between electoral cycles. Historically, the party chair was given a cabinet position, typically as postmaster general, a key source of patronage jobs. (This ended in 1970 when the Post Office Department became an independent government agency.) With the decline of patronage, party chairs are no longer given cabinet positions; the last to have one, Robert Hannegan, resigned his post in 1947.

The President and Electoral Activities

The president occupies a unique place within the electoral process. Many people would prefer the president to be above partisan bickering in the electoral arena, but the president can hardly avoid electoral activities. The presidency is, after all, an elective office, and as the de facto leader of a political party, a president also has some incentive to become involved in congressional campaigns.

PRESIDENTIAL ELECTIONS One of the central difficulties the president faces as party leader is the presidential electoral process. Typically, presidential campaigns are candidate-centered, focusing on election of the candidate rather than the overall success of the party. The candidate's campaign organization is separate from the party, and its loyalty lies more with the candidate than with the party organization.

This separation between candidate and party is increased by the rules governing the selection of presidential candidates. The need to wage primary battles to gain the majority of national convention delegates all but forces presidential candidates to engage in public disagreements with other candidates in the party. Party reforms (discussed in chapter 10) have limited party leaders' control over nominations, and the party organization usually tries to remain neutral in the nomination battles. Winning a presidential nomination has much less to do with the leadership of the formal party organization than with the amount and type of media exposure a candidate receives, the campaign's finances, and the candidate's momentum (Bartels 1993). Since party officials have little influence in the selection of a nominee, they feel less of a bond to the party's presidential candidate.

CONGRESSIONAL ELECTIONS The president can choose to assist the electoral efforts of congressional candidates or to have little to do with them. Presidents sometimes choose a limited role in congressional campaigns out of fear of needlessly antagonizing opposition party members in Congress. Especially during divided government—a president of one party and a congressional majority of the other—the president is dependent on opposition votes to secure the administration's legislative priorities.

The rise of party-line voting in Congress since the 1980s (discussed in chapter 12) has made it more difficult for the president to attract support from opposition party members (Fleisher and Bond 2000b). Although greater partisanship may amplify the benefits of unified government (i.e., a Congress controlled by the president's party), the president's ability to affect who ends up in Congress is limited. The large number of elections for the House of Representatives limits significant presidential involvement to a fraction of them. Even popular presidents find it difficult to transfer their popularity to others, especially when they themselves are not on the ballot.

As discussed in chapter 10, incumbents in Congress usually are in strong positions for reelection. In most congressional races, there is little point in expending effort on a candidate who has a high probability of winning regardless of the president's involvement. Moreover, campaign involvement depends not only on the president's desire and ability to help but also on the congressional candidate's perception of whether such support would be useful.

Bill Clinton's and George Bush's experiences with midterm elections vividly demonstrate the limited effect presidents have on congressional elections. Clinton campaigned vigorously for congressional Democrats in 1994, and Democrats lost control of both houses of Congress. In 1998, Clinton's involvement was much more limited, yet Democrats scored a number of important victories and sliced into the Republican majority in the House of Representatives. Bush engaged in a vigorous campaign to help elect more Republicans to the House and Senate in the 2002 midterm elections. These activities increased the narrow Republican majorities in Congress, but only through a handful of races. In the 2006 midterms, Bush's influence was limited by voter dissatisfaction with the war in Iraq. In 2008, Bush's popularity was so low that GOP congressional candidates viewed him as a campaign liability. In the 2010 midterm elections, Republicans regained control of the House, picking up 63 seats, the largest gain for a party since the 1938 elections. The Republican sweep was due in large part to the unpopularity of President Obama's policies, especially the new health care reform (G. Jacobson 2013, 223–226).

THE PRESIDENT AS PUBLIC OPINION LEADER

Americans have varying attitudes about their government and their elected leaders. They also have different views about specific political and social problems and what should be done about them. The president is a central focus for all these views and attitudes. The chief executive is the symbol and personification of the state and is expected to inspire feelings of loyalty and patriotism, especially in times of crisis. Political opponents closed ranks behind Franklin Roosevelt after the Japanese bombing of Pearl Harbor in December 1941 and behind George W. Bush after the terrorist attacks of September 11, 2001.

As a symbol of the state, the presidency involves some of the ceremony and pomp that are associated with monarchy. Presidential inaugurations are similar to royal coronations, complete with a solemn oath taken in the midst of notables and the multitudes. Other ceremonial aspects of the office include the presidential seal, the music ("Hail to the Chief") that is played at official events, social duties such as entertaining foreign heads of state when they visit Washington, DC, and the lighting of the giant Christmas tree on the White House lawn. Such activities emphasize the chief executive's embodiment of the nation, its government, and its ideals.

Unlike monarchs in democracies such as Great Britain, the president not only reigns but also rules. Part of the president's job is to develop and implement policies that are binding on the entire populace. To achieve policy goals, the president needs to lead public opinion on important issues. At the same time, the president needs to be responsive to public opinion and to respect the limits that public attitudes place on presidential actions. It is a delicate balance.

One of the most important tools available to the president to shape public opinion is the high profile of the office. The public spotlight illuminates almost everything about the president, from stands on issues to reading habits and favorite foods. This public attention provides a bully pulpit, "a unique and imposing podium available only to the President as the one public official . . . elected by the nation as a whole and invested with all the trappings of his great office" (Mervin 1995, 19). Presidents seek to use this bully pulpit well and to establish close ties with a variety of publics in order to convert personal popularity into political effectiveness.

Such has not always been the case. The founders envisioned a president removed from public passions rather than one who shapes and leads them. Insulation from public opinion was a central motivation in developing the electoral college. At least through the end of the nineteenth century, most presidents were somewhat detached from the public.

Going Public

Before becoming president, Woodrow Wilson (1885) argued that the president could remove the shackles imposed by the separation of powers and gain the leverage to act decisively by constructing broad public support for proposals. Modern scholars support Wilson's thesis even as presidents have come to act on it as a matter of routine. As we discussed at the beginning of this chapter, Richard Neustadt (1960) argues that presidential power ultimately rests on the ability to persuade other political actors to do what the president wants. It is much easier to do that when the president has overwhelming public support.

According to Samuel Kernell (1997), contemporary presidents use public support not only as leverage with other political actors but also to evade those other actors. Kernell dubbed the strategy of taking a case directly to American citizens **"going public."** Presidents who go public make increased use of political rhetoric and create political spectacles in an effort to shape public beliefs. Going public is close to the leadership strategy envisioned by Wilson. Presidents make direct contact with the public to build public pressure to act on administration proposals by means of three approaches: personal trips, managing communications with the media, and speeches.

PERSONAL TRIPS One of the earliest methods presidents used to communicate with the American public was a "grand tour." George Washington took a two-month trip through the South in 1791. This trip allowed him to assess the disposition of the people, and it reassured him that the new Federalist government was popular in the South. Modern presidents have continued this tradition. If nothing else, breaking from the confines of Washington, DC, to enjoy the adulation of crowds is reassuring to the president.

Modern presidents often find it helpful to extend their travels abroad. Economic summits, consultations with foreign heads of state, and visits to historical sites and memorials provide a chance to appear presidential and to capture the attention of a variety of publics. Contemporary presidents travel more than their predecessors. Harry Truman, for example, made only 7 foreign appearances; Bill Clinton made 62 in his first two years in office (Ragsdale 1996, 170).

going public A political strategy in which the president appeals to the public in an effort to persuade Congress to support his or her political goals.

Although presidential trips offer opportunities to connect with various publics, they also have risks. Ironically, it was Woodrow Wilson who suffered one of the biggest failures of using personal trips to go public. When his case in favor of the Versailles peace treaty and the League of Nations met resistance in the Senate, he opted for the grand tour strategy to drum up support among the American people. But although he received some support in the West, he ran into a wall of indifference in the Midwest. His tour ended when he fell ill, and his efforts failed to move recalcitrant senators. President George W. Bush's "60 Stops in 60 Days" tour to promote his proposal to reform Social Security also failed to stem the tide of growing public opposition to the private account plan (Villalobos 2006).

There are costs even in a successful presidential trip. Grand tours divert time and attention from other aspects of a demanding job. In recent years, vice presidents and first ladies increasingly have been pressed into service and have journeyed at home and abroad as presidential surrogates. Leading cabinet members are also frequently dispatched to explain administration policies to interest the public and to gauge reaction.

THE PRESS The press is the most important link between a president and the public. As discussed in chapter 8, the press was originally very partisan. The *Gazette of the United States* was the Federalists' party organ, whereas the *National Gazette* spoke for the Democratic-Republicans. During Andrew Jackson's presidency, federal officeholders were expected to subscribe to the party paper. The paper itself was given government contracts to print official notices. Today, the press is independent of political parties but still provides much of the raw material for public opinion.

Presidents recognize the importance of the press. Theodore Roosevelt initiated the practice of granting personal interviews and provided working quarters for reporters in the White House. Woodrow Wilson established the practice of inviting all Washington correspondents to regular press conferences. Contemporary presidents have sophisticated press operations staffed with experts whose primary duty is to interact with and pass information along to the news media.

Over the years, press conferences have evolved into important tools to influence public opinion and gauge the public mind. Presidents have used press conferences in different ways. Some, such as Warren Harding, Calvin Coolidge, and Herbert Hoover, required questions to be submitted in advance, a practice prompted by Harding's difficulty responding to a question about a treaty. Most presidents take spontaneous questions. The frequency of press conferences, though, varies from administration to administration. George H. W. Bush and Bill Clinton made themselves much more available to the press than Ronald Reagan and George W. Bush.

Some of this variation is almost certainly due to the extent that presidents feel at ease with formal press conferences. President Lyndon Johnson preferred to deal with small groups of reporters and experimented with informal, hastily called conferences in a variety of settings. Bill Clinton, on the other hand, was articulate and well versed in the complex details of policy, and he performed well in front of a crowd of rowdy reporters.

Presidents do not limit themselves to press conferences and interviews with the Washington press corps. John Kennedy invited newspaper editors and owners from around the nation to White House conferences where he discussed major public issues. Richard Nixon, who had a strained relationship with the White House press corps, experimented with a number of approaches, ranging from briefings before selected members of news organizations to furnishing editorial writers with transcripts of his speeches and comments. Bill Clinton was an acknowledged master of unscripted media appearances such as talk shows and televised "town meetings."

Much of the interaction between the White House and the press does not directly involve the president. Like other aspects of the modern presidency, the relationship between the media and the president has become highly formalized. Because presidents are concerned about the information the media present, the White House Press Office filters much of the contact between the president and the press. The president's press secretary directs the press to the stories the administration wants covered and presents information that shows the administration in the most favorable light possible. The daily White House press briefing is a key platform for achieving these goals, and so are informal off-the-record communications by administration members. Some scholars claim that the result is "negotiating the news" (Cook 1998).

PRESIDENTIAL SPEECHES When presidents communicate directly with the public, they often do so by means of presidential addresses. Although presidents have always used speeches to educate and persuade the public about issues of importance, the advent of radio and television turned modern presidents into more visible public figures than their nineteenth-century predecessors. Contemporary presidents still address small

Modern presidents use television and radio to communicate directly with the nation. President George W. Bush launched an invasion of Iraq in March 2003 to prevent Iraq from using so-called weapons of mass destruction. The United States and its allies quickly defeated the Iraqi military and the capital, Baghdad, fell on April 9, 2003. President Bush made a highly publicized speech from the deck of the USS *Abraham Lincoln* on May 1, 2003, declaring that "major combat operations in Iraq have ended." This speech became known as his "Mission Accomplished" speech because of the banner with that slogan displayed in the background. However, the announcement turned out to be premature as a growing insurgency and civil war drug on until 2011.

© STEPHEN JAFFE/AFP/Getty Images

audiences on particular issues or topics, but they can use television and radio to communicate with the entire nation.

There are two general types of presidential speeches. A presidential speech on a topic of national importance delivered directly to a national audience over radio or television during the prime evening listening and viewing hours is considered a major address. The president's inaugural address and the annual State of the Union address are major addresses that every president makes. In addition, presidents use major addresses to announce decisions to go to war, to inform the nation of a major international or economic crisis, and to outline their vision of the nation's future (Ragsdale 1996, 146–147).

A minor address is a speech on a substantive policy or political issue delivered to a specific audience, either in person or by use of a broadcast medium. A common example is a commencement address in which the president outlines a new policy proposal. Presidents also make speeches announcing policies at meetings of various business, labor, veterans, police, senior citizen, and professional groups (Ragsdale 1996, 150).

Minor addresses are more common than major addresses. Presidents average about 5 major addresses and 12 minor addresses per year. Though major speeches are less frequent, they can help influence key elites. For example, national public addresses such as the State of the Union speech can positively shape editorials about the president. As "professional persuaders," newspaper editorialists can be important supporters of a president's proposals (Schaefer 1997).

THE LIMITED BENEFITS OF GOING PUBLIC Kernell (1997) provides clear evidence that modern presidents go public more often than their predecessors. The evidence that going public succeeds in raising the president's standing with the public, however, is limited to a small number of case studies.

Presidential scholar George Edwards (2003) conducted a systematic study of the effect of televised speeches by the four most recent presidents prior to Barack Obama—Ronald Reagan, George H. W. Bush, Bill Clinton, and George W. Bush. Edwards compared presidential approval ratings in public opinion polls conducted immediately before and after major televised speeches. He found that the president's speeches seldom moved public opinion. Because of the margin of error in public opinion polls (discussed in chapter 9), public approval must change about 6 percentage points for the difference to be considered statistically significant. Figure 13.6 shows the limited effects of going public. As George Edwards observed, "significant changes [more than 6 points] rarely follow televised presidential addresses. Typically, changes in the president's ratings hardly move at all. Most changes are well within the margin of error—and many of them show a *loss* of approval" (2003, 29). Most of the significant increases followed a major military action; the largest improvement followed the terrorist attacks on September 11, 2001. These changes are more likely the result of the public rallying around the president during an international crisis than the result of a skilled use of the bully pulpit. About one-third of the significant changes are losses in presidential approval following the speech. This evidence indicates that the effects of going public are limited.

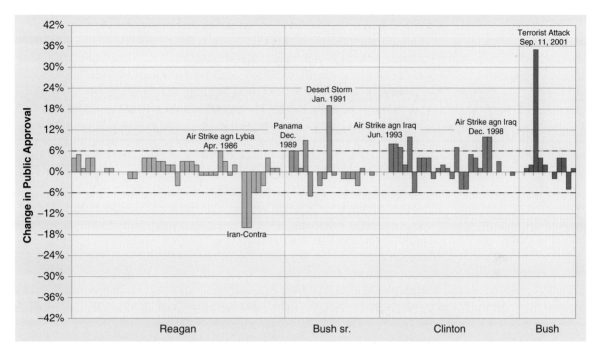

FIGURE 13.6 The Limited Effects of Going Public: Change in Presidential Approval after Televised Speeches

Source: Constructed by the authors from G. Edwards (2003), 30–32.

Presidential Approval Ratings

Regardless of the approach used, in order for going public to succeed, presidents must try hard to influence the perceptions and attitudes of the American people. Public opinion polls on presidential job approval have been taken for more than 50 years. The results of these polls are commonly called the "president's popularity," and politicians and political scientists pay close attention to them. Figure 13.7 shows public approval ratings from Dwight Eisenhower to George W. Bush. With few exceptions, presidents tend to enjoy their highest approval ratings during their first year or two in office. This honeymoon period dissipates as people become dissatisfied with specific decisions, and those who withheld their fire in the bipartisan spirit of support for a newly elected president feel freer to openly disagree with the administration. The tendency for public approval to decline creates pressure to make use of political capital quickly in order to advance a political agenda while the president has broad public support (Light 1983).

The annual averages in Figure 13.7 show overall trends in presidential popularity but also rapid swings. The public's evaluation of the president's job performance is driven by a number of considerations, but the effects of the president's

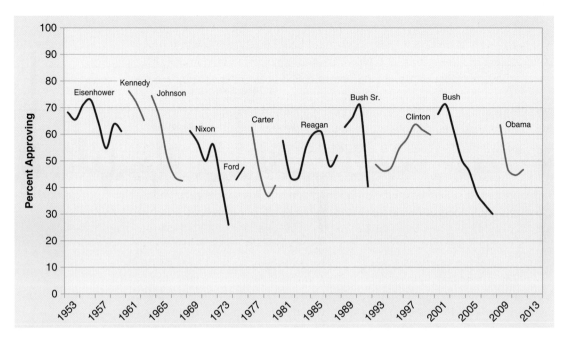

FIGURE 13.7 **Presidential Job Approval**
Source: Constructed by the authors from Gallup polls.

activities are limited compared to the influence of other events over which the president has less control.

The economy, international crises, and scandal are three of the most important determinants of a president's approval rating. The annual averages in Figure 13.7 hide short-term changes, some of which are huge. For example, in February 1991, George H. W. Bush's approval ratings soared to 89 percent following victory during the first Gulf War. Ten years later, his son, President George W. Bush, had similarly astronomically high numbers following the terrorist attacks of September 11, 2001. In both cases, the levels of popularity reflected the "rally around the flag" effect often present when the nation faces an external threat or crisis. Approval ratings for both Bush presidents declined with mounting concerns about the economy and, for George W. Bush, increasing discontent with the protracted war in Iraq.

Scandals can also cause presidential job approval ratings to plummet rapidly. As the details of political sabotage and the White House's obstruction of justice known as the Watergate scandal dribbled out, the 67 percent approval rating of President Nixon following the announcement of a Vietnam peace settlement eroded, bottoming out at 24 percent just before he resigned from office in August 1974. President Reagan's approval rating dropped from 63 percent to 47 percent in a three-month span in 1986 when it became clear that some members of his administration were involved in an illegal scheme to sell arms to Iran and use the profits to fund a Nicaraguan guerrilla movement (Newport 1998).

The scandal surrounding President Bill Clinton's affair with a White House intern is a notable exception to the general rule about scandal dragging down approval ratings. As the scandal developed, Clinton's approval ratings actually went up, ultimately reaching 73 percent in December 1998 as the House of Representatives was voting to impeach him for lying to cover up the affair. The public seemed to make a distinction between Clinton's personal failings (of which they resoundingly disapproved) and the job he was doing as president (which they endorsed).

Going public may occasionally aid in getting specific policies passed, although it provides no guarantees. For example, when Bill Clinton took office in 1993, he sought to deliver on his campaign promise to reform health care. The president, vice president, first lady, and other administration officials took trips and made numerous speeches to drum up support for the plan. But despite an early positive response, public support eroded when details of the complex proposal came to light. Opponents were also emboldened by Clinton's relatively low approval ratings early in his term, which averaged only 52 percent his first year in office (Ragsdale 1996, 193). The opposition went public itself, and despite Clinton's communication skills, his plan did not win congressional approval. President Obama suffered a similar fate in 2010. His most significant legislative accomplishment was comprehensive health care reform (the Patient Protection and Affordable Care Act). Although passage of this law fulfilled a key campaign promise, an intense and unified Republican opposition managed to reverse the support Obama had received from independents two years earlier—independents split 51–43 for Obama (and presumably health care reform) in 2008 but voted for Republicans in 2010 by a margin of 56–37. Democratic losses occurred disproportionately among moderate Democrats (G. Jacobson 2013, 230).

These examples are telling reminders that although presidents are the most prominent actors in the American political system, they are not the only ones trying to influence public opinion. The competition can be tough. Although all presidents use the bully pulpit, and some are effective communicators, their ability to influence public opinion varies from time to time and from issue to issue.

THE PRESIDENT AND CONGRESS

Although Congress has the primary responsibility for making laws, the president plays a key role in influencing legislation. The Constitution gives the president significant formal powers to influence the legislative process, including the responsibility for sending messages and recommendations to Congress and the power of veto bills passed by Congress. In addition to the president's formal powers under the Constitution, other practices have evolved over time that have further increased presidential involvement in the making of laws. Initially started by presidents who wanted to exercise strong legislative leadership, these practices are now considered part of the political duties of office. The practicalities of politics mean that the president has little choice but to actively try to influence decisions made in the legislative branch. And although it is not explicitly spelled out in the Constitution, a number of presidents have claimed that the Constitution gives the chief executive unilateral power to act under certain circumstances—that is, sometimes the president deals with Congress by going around it. This section examines how formal legal power and evolved practices combine to determine presidential influence in Congress.

Messages and Recommendations

Although the assembled senators and members of the House are the immediate target of the State of the Union speech, the president often seeks to reach a larger audience. The message is addressed to all Americans, who can watch the proceedings on television, and the speech is broadcast worldwide. In this speech, the president identifies the problems that the administration views as most pressing and suggests policies to address them. In his 2012 State of Union speech, President Obama stressed that the central mission of our country, and his central focus as president, was rebuilding the economy.

Article II, Section 3 of the Constitution mandates that the president "shall from time to time give to the Congress information on the state of the union, and recommend to their consideration such measures as he shall judge necessary and expedient." Since George Washington's administration, chief executives have followed the practice of annually presenting a message to Congress at the beginning of each regular session. Washington and John Adams gave their messages in person. Thomas Jefferson, a notoriously poor public speaker, sent his message in writing. Subse-

© Photo by Mark Wilson/Getty Images

quent presidents followed Jefferson's practice until Woodrow Wilson surprised Congress and the nation by delivering a message in person shortly after he was inaugurated in 1913. Since then, all presidents, regardless of their oratorical skills, have appeared before Congress to deliver the annual State of the Union message.

Although the assembled senators and members of the House are the immediate target of the State of the Union speech, the president has other audiences in mind. In a sense, the message is addressed to all Americans, who can watch the proceedings on television, and the message is broadcast worldwide as a matter of interest to U.S. allies and adversaries alike. In the speech, the president identifies the problems that the administration views as most pressing and suggests policies to address them. Modern presidents do not limit their recommendations to the State of the Union message. Woodrow Wilson initiated the practice of following the State of the Union address with written recommendations about specific policy topics.

Contemporary presidents go beyond making recommendations to actually developing specific bills. Even though Congress may (and usually does) make changes in administration proposals, the submission of a bill by the president is designed to get Congress to focus on what the White House thinks should be done about a problem. By the middle of the twentieth century, presidents had become so adept at setting the legislative agenda that some scholars openly questioned whether Congress was too unwieldy to be capable of setting its own legislative priorities and needed an outside force such as the president to do it for them (Neustadt 1960). Later in the century, it became clear that Congress is able to independently set its own priorities. For example, the Democratic majority crafted a domestic legislative program without the assistance of President George H. W. Bush, and the Republican majority that won control of Congress after the 1994 elections set and pursued its own agenda without the assistance of President Bill Clinton. Political scientists George Edwards and Andrew Barrett (2000) found that presidents almost always get their legislative items on the congressional agenda—it is rare that a major presidential proposal does not at least get a hearing. Still, presidential proposals constitute only about a third of the Congress's agenda; Congress initiates the other two-thirds.

Nonetheless, the public, the media, and even Congress expect the president to formulate, propose, and actively advance a legislative agenda to address the nation's problems. In fact, Congress has passed laws requiring the president to present proposals to the legislature. For example, the Budget and Accounting Act of 1921 made the executive responsible for formulating and proposing a budget for the federal government.

The Veto

Of the formal powers granted to the president by the Constitution, the veto is probably the most important tool for influencing legislation. The president has three options when presented with a bill passed by Congress:

1. Sign the bill into law.
2. Veto the bill by formally withholding a signature and returning the bill and an explanatory message to Congress; the bill is therefore nullified unless both chambers subsequently pass it by a two-thirds vote.
3. Take no action, in which case the bill becomes law in ten days without the president's signature unless Congress has adjourned; if Congress has indeed adjourned, the bill dies after ten days if the president does not sign it, and the president is said to have used the **pocket veto** to nullify the bill.

The founders originally conceived of the veto as a defensive weapon the president could use to protect the executive from encroachment by a powerful legislature. Scholars such as Neustadt (1960) suggest that the use of the veto is a sign of weakness or failure in the executive because it shows that the president has failed to persuade Congress to adopt administration proposals. But the veto has evolved into a powerful tool to shape public policy. Because of the constitutionally mandated requirement of a supermajority to override, a veto represents a formidable obstacle to legislation. It gives even unpopular presidents without majority party support in Congress an effective way to influence the legislative process. Even as the Watergate scandal politically crippled Richard Nixon in 1973, Congress managed to override only one of his nine presidential vetoes. Veto overrides are rare—across all presidents, only about 7 percent of vetoes are overridden.

The mere threat of a veto is a valuable tool to shape legislation (Cameron 2000). By making clear what features of a particular bill the administration finds objectionable and what must be done to make them acceptable, the president can shape the content of laws sent to the White House. The tactic does not always work, especially if Congress is controlled by the opposition party. The Democratic majority in 1992, for example, sent President George H. W. Bush several bills he had threatened to veto. In effect, they dared him to follow through on his threats, and when he did, Democrats used his opposition to the bills as fodder for political campaigns. Much of the time, though, the threat of a veto provides a lot of leverage in Congress. President Bill Clinton, for example, got budget bill concessions from the Republican majority in 1998 by threatening to veto the appropriations required to keep the government solvent and operating. Having suffered a political disaster when they forced a government shutdown three years earlier, the Republicans were willing to compromise with the president.

Presidential Success in Congress

In terms of the relationship between the executive and legislative branches, presidents succeed when Congress acts in accordance with their recommendations and fail when Congress takes a course of action opposed by the administration. One frequently used measure of presidential success is how often the president's position wins on the House or Senate floor.

pocket veto The veto resulting from a president taking no action, before Congress adjourns, on legislation that has passed Congress.

Like other measures of presidential success, this one is imperfect. It measures success only on matters that come to a floor vote, and some issues never make it that far. President Clinton's health care reform proposals, for example, never made it to a floor vote. But most significant issues do show up in House or Senate roll call votes, and these allow a reasonable basis on which to judge success or failure. Figure 13.8 shows the percentage of times the president got his way on House and Senate roll calls from 1953 to 2011.

This figure shows two important patterns. First, no president has enjoyed complete success or complete failure; all have won some, and all have lost some. This pattern is in stark contrast to parliamentary democracies, where losing an important vote in the legislature is a major embarrassment for the prime minister and may even lead to his or her resignation. Second, presidential success varies. It varies across presidential administrations as well as across chambers and over time within them.

The founders deliberately created a rivalry between the executive and the legislature by assigning important constitutional powers to each. By granting institutional rivals independent bases of political power, the Constitution also ensured that each would be capable of protecting and advancing its interests. The information displayed in Figure 13.8 essentially confirms that these expectations have been met. Members of the first Congress resisted Alexander Hamilton's attempts

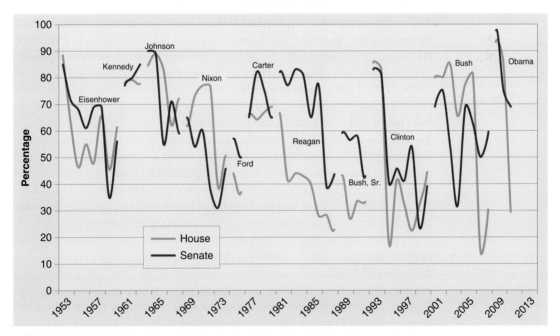

FIGURE 13.8 Presidential Success in the House and Senate
Sources: J. Cohen, Bond, and Fleisher (2013); updated through 2012 by the authors from presidential roll calls indentified by Congressional Quarterly, Inc.

to advance his economic program, and senators and House members have resisted executive efforts to dominate legislative affairs ever since. But it is not only institutional differences that explain the variation in success rates. Other conditions that influence presidential success with Congress are electoral constituencies and cycles, party and ideology, presidential popularity, and the president's bargaining skill.

ELECTORAL CONSTITUENCIES AND CYCLES The president and Congress have very different constituencies. Elected to represent a nationwide constituency, the president tends to see issues from a national perspective. Moreover, the president's diplomatic duties and role as commander in chief require an international perspective. Members of Congress, in contrast, tend to have a more parochial view. They are necessarily concerned with how their particular states or districts are affected. Different constituencies and electoral needs lead to different views of what is in the public interest. The inevitable result is conflict between the executive and legislative branches. The president wins some; Congress wins others.

The executive and legislative branches also operate under separate electoral cycles. The timing of elections has a critical effect on relations between the president and Congress. In a presidential election year, the nation chooses the president, all 435 members of the House, and one-third of the Senate. If the president wins by a large margin, sympathetic House and Senate members may ride presidential coattails into office. Two-thirds of the senators, however, are holdovers from previous elections whose electoral victories probably owe nothing to the president. And two years into the president's term, there is another election in which all 435 House seats and another third of Senate seats are up for election. Not being on the ballot, the president has less influence on these congressional races than on the races that took place two years earlier. The result is that most legislators are insulated from presidential influence.

PARTY AND IDEOLOGY Political scientists have long noted that party and ideology are the strongest determinants of how members of Congress vote. The primary reason is shared preferences—Republicans tend to agree on a wide range of political and policy values, and policies favored by Republicans differ from those preferred by most Democrats. Because presidents are visible party leaders, party consistently exerts a crucial influence on presidential–congressional relations. Simply speaking, members of the president's party are likely to support administration positions because they agree with them, and members of the opposition party are less likely to agree. As a result, conflict between the president and Congress is more pronounced when the two branches are controlled by different political parties, a situation that has been common since World War II. Over the period since 1953, majority presidents have won an average of about 75 percent of roll calls, compared to around 47 percent for minority presidents.

Ideology is also an important influence on roll call voting. As discussed in chapters 1 and 9, an ideology is a consistent set of values, attitudes, and beliefs about the appropriate role of government in society (Campbell et al. 1960). Conservatives have different philosophies about the proper role of government than do liberals.

Party and ideology are related, but they are not the same thing. Although Democrats tend to be liberal, and Republicans tend to be conservative, both parties have had factions of ideological misfits—conservative Democrats and liberal Republicans—who share ideological ground with the rival party. These members have been frequently cross-pressured: their party pulls them in one direction and their ideological beliefs in another. Cross-pressured members of the president's party, therefore, may be less supportive of administration proposals, but cross-pressured members of the opposition party have often been an important source of support (Bond and Fleisher 1990). Minority presidents sometimes have won votes in Congress by forging ideological coalitions with members of the opposition party. President Ronald Reagan, for example, never enjoyed a Republican-controlled House of Representatives, and thus his legislative agenda was always dependent on opposition party votes. Reagan managed to achieve several key victories by securing support from conservative Democrats.

Even members of the president's own party who face no inconsistencies between party and ideology engage in political struggles with the administration on occasion. Members of Congress are representatives of distinct constituencies, and they have their own points of view about the desirability of particular policies. If these come into conflict with the president's preferences, the White House cannot assume that party loyalty will win out. The president's fellow party members may find it politically advantageous to oppose administration positions if they are unpopular with the members' constituents.

PARTY POLARIZATION In the 1980s, the number of cross-pressured members in Congress began to decline, and they had all but disappeared by the 2000s (Fleisher and Bond 2004). Without conservative Democrats and liberal Republicans who often bucked their own party leaders and voted with the opposition, congressional parties polarized. **Party polarization** means that policy positions (or ideology) within a party become more homogeneous, and policy positions across the parties diverge. Thus, with the departure of cross-pressured members from Congress, each party became more ideologically homogeneous—Republicans are conservative; Democrats are liberal—and the parties pulled farther apart because the average Republican had moved to the right, whereas the average Democrat had moved left.

Party polarization has had a profound influence on presidential success in Congress. As the parties polarize, they become more internally cohesive. When parties are cohesive, the president tends to have fewer defections of members of his party, but he is also less likely to attract support from members of the opposition. As a result, party polarization changes the effects of party control. But the effects are not the same in the House and Senate, in large part because they have different rules.

House rules enable a cohesive majority to win. Thus, as members of Congress increasingly vote along party lines, majority party presidents win more, and minority party presidents win less (see Figure 13.9a). In general, a 10 percent

party polarization Situation in which policy positions (or ideology) within political parties become more homogeneous, and policy positions across the parties move farther apart.

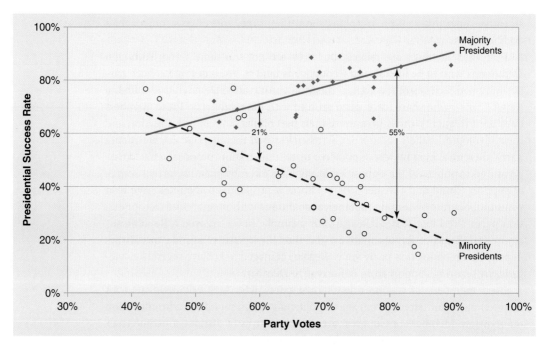

FIGURE 13.9A The Effects of Party Polarization on Presidential Success in the House

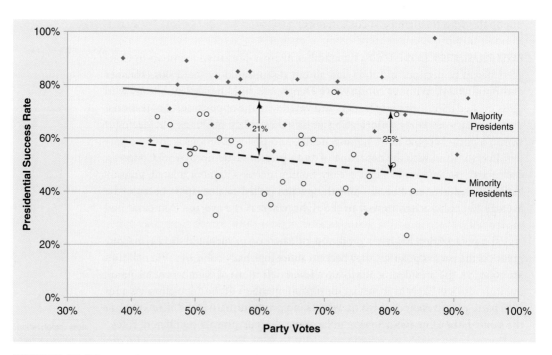

FIGURE 13.9B The Effects of Party Polarization on Presidential Success in the Senate

Source: J. Cohen, Bond, and Fleisher (2013), updated by the authors.

CHAPTER 13 THE PRESIDENCY

increase in party-line votes leads to about 6.5 percent more wins for majority presidents and about 10 percent fewer wins for minority presidents. Because party polarization has opposite effects for majority and minority presidents, the majority party boost—that is, the difference in success rates of majority and minority presidents—grows as party voting increases. The majority party boost is about 21 percent more wins if party-line voting is low (around 60 percent) and about 55 percent if party voting is high (around 80 percent).

The Senate is a different story. Unlike the House, where rules empower the majority, Senate rules and practices protect the minority. As the parties polarized, the minority party began to use these tools, especially the filibuster and the requirement of 60 votes to invoke cloture, in efforts to block action on legislation and nominations it opposed. Filibusters became much more common, and cloture was the only way to stop them. Thus, 60 votes became the de facto threshold to pass any controversial legislation in the Senate (Binder and Smith 1997; Koger 2010).

Party polarization with a de facto 60 vote requirement has made passing controversial legislation in the Senate more difficult regardless of which party has a majority. As party voting increases, success rates of both majority and minority presidents decline (see Figure 13.9b). In general, a 10 percent increase in party votes decreases the success rate about 1.9 percent for majority presidents and about 2.9 percent for minority presidents. Although majority party presidents win more votes on average than minority presidents do, party polarization has little affect on the gap—the majority party boost in the Senate is about 21–25 percent regardless of the level of party voting.

Polarized parties reduce success rates of majority party presidents because a cohesive minority party is more likely to exploit supermajoritarian rules to obstruct the president's initiatives, and there are few if any cross-pressured opposition senators who might be inclined to support the president. Party polarization is likely to reduce the success of minority party presidents as well because a cohesive majority has fewer cross-pressured members who might be inclined to support the president, and the leader of a cohesive majority party is more likely to schedule floor votes that the president opposes.

Thus, party polarization has made party an even stronger determinant of presidential success in Congress. For example, Bill Clinton won more than 80 percent of House and Senate votes in 1993–1994 when Democrats were in the majority. After the Republicans gained control of Congress in the 1994 midterm elections, his success rate plummeted. Facing Republican majorities for the remainder of his time in office, he saw his average success rate fall to 32 percent in the House and 40 percent in the Senate. President Obama suffered a similar fate after Republicans won control of the House in the 2010 midterm elections. Dealing with a Democratic majority in the House during his first two years in office, Obama won nearly 90 percent of the votes on which he expressed a position. With Republicans in control of the House, his success rate took a nosedive to 29 percent (see Figure 13.8).

PRESIDENTIAL POPULARITY Members of Congress are elected representatives and are supposed to be responsive to popular preferences. Consequently, they may be more likely to support administration proposals when the president has high public support. The belief that presidential popularity affects support in Congress is widely accepted by Washington insiders, and there is little doubt that popularity gives the president leverage on some occasions. Public approval helps set the public agenda and determine what issues Congress will consider. However, public approval does not guarantee support.

Academic research has produced mixed results about the ability of presidential popularity to translate directly into desired legislative outcomes. Jon Bond and Richard Fleisher (1990), for example, found that popular presidents were not much more likely to win in the legislative arena than were their less popular counterparts. President George H. W. Bush's record in 1991 is a good example of the limits of presidential popularity. Despite Bush's astronomic approval ratings, Congress did not rally around his policy agenda. He won only 43 percent of the House roll call becomes a target for electoral retribution by the voters who support or oppose the president in question. However, the electoral connection between the president and members of Congress has lessened somewhat with the weakening of presidents' electoral coattails in recent decades (G. Jacobson 1990, 80–81). Moreover, although some voters may use presidential popularity as a voting guide, few have sufficient knowledge to make the connection between their evaluation of the president and the voting behavior of their representative.

Presidential popularity is fluid, so using it as a guide in forecasting roll call votes in Congress is risky. The president's popularity on election day may be very different than it was on the day of a roll call vote on a particular issue. Since election day popularity cannot be predicted with great accuracy, its utility in guiding an elected representative's roll call vote is limited. For these reasons, presidential popularity has only a marginal influence on legislators' decisions to support or oppose the president on roll call votes (Bond and Fleisher 1990; G. Edwards 1989).

PRESIDENTIAL BARGAINING SKILL The president also has a certain amount of patronage to bring to the table in give-and-take with recalcitrant legislators. Although executive positions have increasingly come under civil service regulations that require competitive examinations as the basis for hiring, the president still influences government contracts, grants, defense installations, and the like. Presidents have made sure that military bases have been retained in congressional districts and that legislators were given advance notice of government contracts and grants important to their districts so that they could be publicly announced by congressional offices.

Presidents have also engaged in systematic lobbying efforts on behalf of legislative programs, essentially setting up special interest operations in the White House. Begun in earnest during the Eisenhower era, systematic lobbying varies somewhat from administration to administration. Such efforts usually include legislative liaisons from various executive departments, a central liaison unit in the White House Office, and the vice president. Some of these individuals concentrate on the House, others on the Senate, and they specialize in particular topics and issues. The executive branch lobbyists use the same general techniques as do lobbyists for interest groups, including direct contacts with representatives and indirect contact through congressional staff members, campaign contributors, defense contractors, newspaper editors, state and local party leaders, and others important to a legislator's constituency. They also join forces with private interest groups to work on legislation of mutual interest.

Political pundits, politicians, and some students of the presidency routinely assume that such efforts play a large role in determining presidential success in Congress. It is believed that strong legislative leadership is achieved by the skillful use of the tools at the president's disposal to persuade members of Congress to enact administration proposals. But most of the evidence to support this belief is based on studies of specific bills. More systematic analyses of presidential support from members of Congress, such as those relying on roll call votes on many bills, give less support for this hypothesis (Bond and Fleisher 1990; G. Edwards 1989). Variation in presidential success rests more on party and ideology than on popularity, bargaining skill, and informal powers of persuasion. Success is also due to the political context of the time, which the president has limited ability to shape.

Yet recent research shows that focusing only on roll call votes may underestimate the president's ability to influence legislative outcomes. Matthew Beckmann (2010, 108) argues that trying to influence the roll call vote can be viewed as the endgame in the legislative process. But presidents can't win the endgame unless they are successful in the "early game" (i.e., getting their proposal through the legislative obstacle course to a floor vote). Beckmann's analysis corroborates past research; presidents who "inherit a legislature filled with likeminded lawmakers typically find success on floor votes; those facing a Congress filled with opposition legislators do not" (2010, 108). Yet his analysis shows that presidential lobbying increases the odds of successfully negotiating the initial legislative obstacle course *and* of winning the floor vote that follows. And the president's "political capital"—a combination of public approval and economic growth—"amplifies or diminishes his effectiveness" (Beckmann 2010, 116).

Unilateral Powers

The conventional way presidents influence policy is to persuade Congress to enact the bills they want and to veto the ones they don't (Neustadt 1960). But they have another option—exercise unilateral powers. **Unilateral powers** are presidential directives that carry the weight of law even though they have not been formally endorsed by Congress. Examples include executive orders, signing statements, executive agreements, and national security directives (Howell 2005, 417). These actions not only represent an end run around Congress; they also stand on its head Neustadt's argument that persuasion is the core of presidential power. When they exercise these unilateral powers, "presidents simply set public policy and dare others to counter. As long as Congress lacks the votes (usually two thirds of both chambers) to overturn him [or unless the courts find the action unconstitutional], the president can be confident that his policy will stand" (Howell 2005, 421).

unilateral powers Presidential directives that carry the weight of law even though they have not been formally endorsed by Congress.

POLITICS IN PRACTICE

EXECUTIVE ORDER 10834—THE FLAG OF THE UNITED STATES

What follows is President Dwight Eisenhower's executive order defining the design of the American flag following admission of Hawaii as the 50th state.

Executive Order 10834—The flag of the United States

WHEREAS the State of Hawaii has this day been admitted into the Union; and

WHEREAS section 2 of title 4 of the United States Code provides as follows: "On the admission of a new State into the Union one star shall be added to the union of the flag; and such addition shall take effect on the fourth day of July then next succeeding such admission."; and

WHEREAS the Federal Property and Administrative Services Act of 1949 (63 Stat. 377), as amended, authorizes the President to prescribe policies and directives governing the procurement and utilization of property by executive agencies; and

WHEREAS the interests of the Government require that orderly and reasonable provision be made for various matters pertaining to the flag and that appropriate regulations governing the procurement and utilization of national flags and union jacks by executive agencies be prescribed:

NOW, THEREFORE, by virtue of the authority vested in me as President of the United States and as Commander in Chief of the armed forces of the United States, and the Federal Property and Administrative Services Act of 1949, as amended, it is hereby ordered as follows:

Part I—Design of the Flag

Section 1. The flag of the United States shall have thirteen horizontal stripes, alternate red and white, and a union consisting of white stars on a field of blue.

Sec. 2. The positions of the stars in the union of the flag and in the union jack shall be as indicated on the attachment to this order, which is hereby made a part of this order.

Sec. 3. The dimensions of the constituent parts of the flag shall conform to the proportions set forth in the attachment referred to in section 2 of this order.

Unilateral powers are not specifically spelled out in the Constitution, but presidents argue that Article II of the Constitution, which grants the broad "executive power," provides a legal basis for such actions. Unilateral powers also have historical precedent: presidents of both parties have exercised unilateral powers to some extent since the beginning of the republic. Presidents since Ronald Reagan, however, have resorted to these devices with far greater frequency, in the process attracting widespread criticism from Congress and in the legal community. The controversy has escalated as recent presidents, especially President George W. Bush, increasingly used unilateral powers to achieve their policy goals.

executive orders Directives of the president that have the same weight as law and are not voted on by Congress.

EXECUTIVE ORDERS An **executive order** is a legally binding presidential order directing federal agencies and officials on how to implement laws or policies enacted by Congress. Many executive orders deal with routine administrative matters or symbolic

Part II—Regulations Governing Executive Agencies

Sec. 21. The following sizes of flags are authorized for executive agencies:

| Size | Dimensions of flag | |
	Hoist (width)	Fly (length)
	Feet	Feet
(1)	20.00	38.00
(2)	10.00	19.00
(3)	8.95	17.00
(4)	7.00	11.00
(5)	5.00	9.50
(6)	4.33	5.50
(7)	3.50	6.65
(8)	3.00	4.00
(9)	3.00	5.70
(10)	2.37	4.50
(11)	1.32	2.50

Sec. 22. Flags manufactured or purchased for the use of executive agencies:

(a) Shall conform to the provisions of Part I of this order. . . .

Sec. 23. The exterior dimensions of each union jack manufactured or purchased for executive agencies shall equal the respective exterior dimensions of the union of a flag of a size authorized by or pursuant to this order. The size of the union jack flown with the national flag shall be the same as the size of the union of that national flag.

Part III—General Provisions

Sec. 31. The flag prescribed by Executive Order No. 10798 of January 3, 1959, shall be the official flag of the United States until July 4, 1960, and on that date the flag prescribed by Part I of this order shall become the official flag of the United States. . . .

Sec. 32. As used in this order, the term "executive agencies" means the executive departments and independent establishments in the executive branch of the Government, including wholly-owned Government corporations.

Sec. 33. Executive Order No. 10798 of January 3, 1959, is hereby revoked.

SOURCE The National Archives, The Federal Register. http://www.archives.gov/federal-register/codification/executive-order/10834.html. Accessed August 14, 2008.

proclamations. (See the Politics in Practice feature "Executive Order 10834—The Flag of the United States"). Others implement substantive public policies without input from Congress. Examples include President Lincoln's Emancipation Proclamation in 1862 and the creation of the White House Office of Faith-Based and Community Initiatives in President George W. Bush's first term.

Executive orders can be highly controversial when they go beyond, or even contradict, congressional intent. In response, Congress can amend the law to specify its interpretation and implementation, but the president can veto such an amendment. Practically, what this means is that it can take a two-thirds vote of Congress to overturn an executive order. Executive orders can also be challenged in court, but the courts have overturned very few. A notable example is *Youngstown Sheet & Tube Co. v. Sawyer* (1952), in which the Supreme Court declared President Truman's executive order seizing the steel mills to avert a labor strike unconstitutional.

Though every president has issued executive orders, they were relatively rare until the early twentieth century, when Theodore Roosevelt issued nearly 600 per term (1901–1909). That number climbed steadily to an average of more than 1,100 per term during the Franklin Roosevelt administration (see Figure 13.9). The numbers declined to an average of around 250 per term for presidents after FDR, but the tendency to use executive orders to alter congressional intent has increased in recent administrations (Howell 2005).

SIGNING STATEMENTS When a president signs a bill into law, he can issue a written announcement of how he intends to interpret and apply the law. Such pronouncements are called **signing statements**; specifically, they

> (1) provide the president's interpretation of the language of the law, (2) announce constitutional limits on the implementation of some of its provisions, or (3) indicate directions to executive branch officials as to how to administer the new law in an acceptable manner. (Cooper 2005, 516–517)

signing statements Pronouncements of how the president intends to interpret and apply a law when he signs a bill into law.

Signing statements are controversial because although the bill is signed into law, the president claims that certain parts of it are unconstitutional and will not be

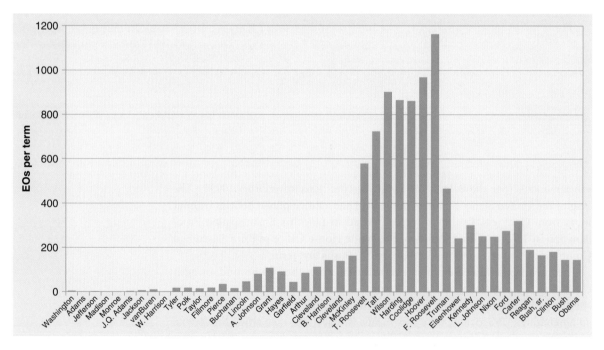

FIGURE 13.10 Executive Orders from George Washington to Barack Obama
Source: Constructed by the authors from data at G. Peters (1999–2012a).

implemented. Some critics argue that this amounts to a line-item veto, but the Constitution provides only two options—veto the bill and send it back to Congress or "faithfully execute" the law.

Signing statements were used as long ago as in the administration of James Monroe (1817–1825), but their use as a means to modify laws to conform to presidential policy goals was not common until Ronald Reagan became president in 1981 (see Table 13.1). The extent to which signing statements are being used to advance the president's policy goals can be gauged by the percentage of such statements that contain constitutional or legal objections to provisions of the bill being signed into law (Halstead 2007). Several presidents before Reagan issued a relatively large number of signing statements. Although only a small percentage raised constitutional objections, signing statements by Presidents Ford and Carter set the precedent for more aggressive use of this tool to protect perceived threats to the president's constitutional prerogatives (Conley 2011). Beginning with Reagan, there was a noticeable increase in the percentage of signing statements raising constitutional objections—about one-third of President Reagan's and nearly one-half of President George H. W. Bush's signing statements contained legal objections to portions of the law. Although President Clinton issued more statements, less than one-fifth included objections. President George W. Bush, in contrast,

TABLE 13.1: PRESIDENTIAL SIGNING STATEMENTS

	Total Signing Statements	Percent with Constitutional Objections
Hoover	16	0.0%
Roosevelt	39	0.0%
Truman	106	0.9%
Eisenhower	142	1.4%
Kennedy	36	0.0%
Johnson	175	2.9%
Nixon	117	3.4%
Ford	137	3.6%
Carter	227	5.7%
Reagan	250	34.4%
Bush, sr.	228	46.9%
Clinton	381	18.4%
Bush	162	72.8%
Obama*	23	47.8%

Source: constructed by the authors from Halstead 2007; Peters 1999-2012b; and Stanley and Neimi 2011, 251-252.

*Signing statements through the end of first term.

issued fewer signing statements than his recent predecessors, but almost three-fourths of these modified congressional intent by raising legal objections. Bush's signing statements were especially controversial because of the unusually expansive interpretation of presidential power. During the 2008 presidential campaign, Barack Obama called Bush's signing statements an "abuse" and promised that he would not use them to get around the intent of Congress (Savage 2009). Shortly after taking office, Obama issued a memorandum negating some of Bush's signing statements (Gerstein 2009). Nonetheless, Obama issued more than 20 signing statements in his first term, almost half of which (48 percent) contained constitutional objections.

NATIONAL SECURITY DIRECTIVES Presidents have more leeway to take unilateral action in the realm of foreign and national security policy than in the domestic arena, in large part because the president controls what information, if any, is available to Congress and the press (Howell 2005, 423–425). The growing tendency to use executive agreements rather than treaties and the president's power as commander in chief to unilaterally launch military action without a formal declaration of war—or sometimes without any prior authorization from Congress—are discussed earlier in this chapter.

Another device presidents use to make national security policy without approval of Congress is the national security directive. A **national security directive**—called National Security Presidential Directives (NSPDs) in the Bush administration—is a type of executive order with the force of law authorizing federal agencies or officials to take some action to protect national security. President Bush relied heavily on national security directives in the conduct of the war on terror. For example, on May 4, 2007, he signed the National Security and Homeland Security Presidential Directive, which was designed to ensure that government will continue to function during a "catastrophic emergency." It authorizes the president to coordinate "a cooperative effort among the executive, legislative, and judicial branches of the Federal Government" to take the place of the nation's regular government during the crisis. Both conservatives and liberals have criticized this directive because the Constitution establishes three equal branches of government with no single branch having the power to coordinate the others and because it does not specify who has the power to decide the emergency is over and restore normal government function. Because such directives concern national security, the information (and sometimes even the title) is often classified. One study estimates that the "titles of only about half" of President Bush's 54 National Security Presidential Directives have been made public, and "there is descriptive material or actual text in the public domain for only about a third" (Aftergood 2008). In some cases, even members of Congress cannot get access to the information. For example, the Bush White House denied a request from Representative Peter DeFazio (D-OR), a member of the House Homeland Security Committee, to examine classified portions of the National Security and Homeland Security Presidential Directive, citing "national security concerns."

national security directive A type of executive order with the force of law authorizing federal agencies or officials to take some action to protect national security.

Top Ten Takeaway Points

1 The office of president of the United States is made up of the president, an individual person, and the presidency, which is a complex institution.

2 The power of the president has grown because of (1) the energy associated with a single executive, (2) vague constitutional provisions that assertive presidents interpreted broadly to enhance presidential power, (3) rising public expectations, and (4) delegation of power and resources to the executive branch by Congress.

3 Presidential scholars suggest that an individual's background and psychological needs allow presidential character to be arrayed along two dimensions: the active–passive dimension is based on how much energy the president devotes to the exercise of power; the positive–negative dimension is based on the extent to which the president gains personal satisfaction from the exercise of power. This psychological perspective, however, has proved to be of limited use in explaining or predicting how presidents handle the job.

4 The major components of the presidency as an institution include the vice president, the cabinet, and the Executive Office of the President (EOP). The president's closest advisors are in the EOP. Historically, the vice president has not been particularly powerful, but recent vice presidents have held significant policymaking and advisory roles.

5 Article II of the Constitution defines the president's primary constitutional responsibilities: chief executive, commander in chief of the military, and chief diplomat.

6 In addition to the formal responsibilities of office, the president is also the party's most visible and prominent leader. Although the founders did not anticipate this role, the strongest presidents have also been strong party leaders, and a president's ability to build and direct a strong party base is often important to the success of an administration's political agenda.

7 The president plays a critical role as a public opinion leader. The high profile of the presidential office and the constant public spotlight that goes with it provide the president with a unique and powerful opportunity to connect with the public. Recent presidents have increasingly adopted a strategy of going public—using speeches to take a case directly to American citizens in an effort to shape public beliefs and influence Congress. The benefits of going public, however, are limited; rarely does a presidential speech produce a significant change in the president's ratings. The economy, international crises, and scandal are three of the most important determinants of a president's approval rating.

⑧ Although Congress has primary responsibility for making laws, the president plays an important role in influencing legislation. All presidents have mixed success in getting their preferences approved by Congress. Differences in constituency, electoral cycles, partisanship, and ideology often give the president and Congress different legislative goals.

⑨ The strongest determinant of presidential success in Congress is whether Congress is controlled by the president's party. Increased partisanship in Congress since the 1990s has enhanced the benefits of majority control, especially in the House. The effects of public approval and bargaining skills on presidential success are limited.

⑩ Presidents interpret their constitutional powers to include some unilateral powers—executive orders, signing statements, executive agreements, and national security directives—that have the weight of law without congressional endorsement. Recent presidents have increasingly used these devices to achieve policies that Congress has not authorized or to alter laws passed by Congress that the president considers unconstitutional.

Key Terms and Cases

14) THE BUREAUCRACY

KEY QUESTIONS

Does a democracy need bureaucracy?

Where does bureaucracy get its power to make public policy?

How do democratic institutions control the power of bureaucracy?

DEAN KLECKNER, retired farmer and former president of the American Farm Bureau Federation, has an alarming message for Iowa voters. "The American farmer is under attack by government run amok," he says. "Over-regulation is killing the American farmer." And what sort of regulations might be threatening the livelihoods of Iowa farmers and the state's agriculture-based economy? Well, here's a doozy: the Environmental Protection Agency (EPA) wants to regulate dust on farms. The federal bureaucracy's dust regulation proposal is about as popular with Iowa farmers as you might expect. Regulate dust on farms? "You can't plow a field without dust," one farmer said. "You can't drive down a gravel road without dust. My dog makes dust."

The fight against the EPA's proposal to regulate dust on farms became a minor cause célèbre during the campaign for the 2012 Republican presidential nomination. Candidate Herman Cain brought up the issue in debates and made it a centerpiece of ads aired in Iowa (the preceding quotes are taken directly from one such ad, which you can view at http://nation.foxnews.com/herman-cain/2011/11/09/herman-cain-ad-epa-wants-regulate-dust). It wasn't just Cain and Iowa farmers taking up the fight against EPA attempts to regulate dust on farms. Representative Rick Crawford (R-AR) slammed the EPA for its bureaucratic meddling, saying from the floor of the House of Representatives, "The regulatory regime must come to realize that our food is grown in the dirt," and in planting, growing, and harvesting crops, farmers work in that dirt and are going to "stir up a little dust." The proposal to regulate dust on farms had a lot of hot-under-the-collar opponents and, as far as we can tell, no supporters. That lack of support is not surprising—not because the proposed regulation is ridiculous (it is), but because the proposed regulation never existed.

It is true that the EPA regulates particulate pollution. This is mostly about what comes out of smokestacks, but to be fair, dust can be included too if we are talking about situations such as construction sites kicking up clouds of the stuff over school playgrounds or high concentrations of cotton dust being inhaled by workers in a textile factory. But regulating dust kicked up by farm dogs? In 2011, EPA Administrator Linda Jackson testified before the U.S. House Committee on Agriculture in a direct attempt to dispel the farm dust regulation story and a series of other myths circulating about EPA proposals. She said that although the EPA is legally obligated to review pollution regulations, it had no plans to expand regulations to govern incidental dust on farms. She also said that the EPA was not planning to regulate cow emissions (another feature of Cain's ads), nor was it planning to write regulations that would treat spilled milk as an environmental threat equivalent to an oil spill.

This all seems a bit surreal. Think about it: a high-level federal executive assuring Congress that the U.S. government is not going to force farmers to make their cows stop farting or kicking up dust—or declare an environmental disaster if a truck carrying the product of their non-farting, dust-free cows turns over on its way to market. It sounds like something out of a Monty Python skit.

There is a larger point here, though, that is anything but funny: people mistrust bureaucracy and are quick to believe the worst. No matter how ridiculous the story, we are willing to believe it if it portrays a government agency doing something stupid, venal, or corrupt. The bottom line is that people hate bureaucracy, so much so that many reasonable people seem quite willing to accept, repeat, and invent patently fictitious horror stories to justify that belief.

It's not surprising that citizens have such a visceral dislike of government bureaucracy; its portrayal in the mass media and popular culture is "typically scathing in nature" (Goodsell 1994, 8). Bureaucracy is blamed for everything from hampering the war on terror to bungling mail delivery. Reviled by politicians and citizens alike, bureaucracy is held to be synonymous with inefficiency, waste, incompetence, and malfeasance. To be sure, some of this criticism is justified. Without doubt there is inefficiency, waste, and incompetence to be found in the bureaucracy. But it is also true that bureaucracy, for the most part, does a good job under very difficult circumstances. What is equally true, though understood by few and accepted by fewer, is that modern liberal democracies simply cannot function without bureaucracy. That's right. Democracy *needs* bureaucracy.

THE CONCEPT OF BUREAUCRACY

Bureaucracy can be defined as a system of public agencies that translate the intent of democratic institutions into action. These agencies, programs, and services are largely, though not exclusively, housed in the executive branches of government, and they do everything from fight wars (the Department of Defense) to repair potholes (municipal or county highway departments) to administer health care programs for senior citizens.

What this means is that bureaucracy, for better or worse, is largely responsible for the performance of pretty much the entire political system. The products of executives, legislatures, and courts—executive orders, laws, and rulings—represent what the government intends to do, not what it actually does.

Understanding the job of bureaucracy is important because democratic governments in the United States promise a great deal—law and order, equal opportunity public education, clean air, libraries, a safe food supply, basic health care; the list is long and growing. All these promises become the responsibilities of the public bureaucracy. Bureaucracy has to take the promise of a law and translate it into reality in order to have successfully done its job. Given this duty, bureaucracy is the part of government that is most involved in the daily lives of citizens. Political scientist Ken Meier (1993, 2) once described a day in the life of a typical American, starting with a breakfast of bacon and eggs (certified fit for consumption by the U.S. Department of Agriculture) and then continuing with a drive to work (the roads, the car, and the fuel all regulated or maintained by public agencies), a walk up a flight of stairs to the office (the stairs inspected by the Occupational Safety and Health Administration), and a climb into bed to sleep at the end of the day (on a mattress with a tag that may not be removed under penalty of law).

The bureaucracy is so involved in our daily lives that most people seem to notice only its absence. For example, the overwhelming majority of letters and packages mailed by the United States Postal Service (USPS) are delivered on time with no problems. Yet it is the small exception—the letter that goes astray—that gets people's attention. Maybe bureaucracy gets its poor reputation from its competence rather than its incompetence. This is not the typical perspective on bureaucracy, but as we shall see, it is one that provides a more realistic understanding of the relationship between the promise and the performance of democracy.

The job of bureaucracy is to make good on the promises of democratic governments. Whatever government decides to do—be it as mundane as building a road or as momentous as going to war—bureaucracy is the actual "doer." For instance, after approving a law to clean up inland waterways, legislators do not fan out to rivers and lakes to take water samples and begin cracking down on polluters. The responsibility for determining what actions the government is obligated to undertake as a result of the law, and for then actually taking those actions, is passed on to a bureaucracy. This procedure sounds reasonable enough in the abstract. In practice, though, it means that bureaucracies deal with translating broad and

bureaucracy The term used to refer to the agencies of the federal government. It also refers to an organizational framework and has negative connotations.

vague intentions into specific actions. Congress passes laws to protect children from accidental harm and consumers from dangerous products. People like that. They are not so thrilled with childproof caps on medicine bottles, one of the specific actions mandated by the Consumer Safety Product Commission to put that general law into action. Those childproof caps do, in fact, save kids' lives by preventing accidental ingestion of medicines. For most people, though, they are simply a constant reminder of how government bureaucracy can make even the small things in life—like trying to get an aspirin out of its bottle—more of a headache.

First and foremost, then, bureaucracy is the management mechanism for government. Public agencies implement, manage, and monitor programs and policies authorized by law, executive order, and regulation. Public agencies take words on paper and translate them into action by issuing contracts, formulating programs, and engaging in any number of other activities, all designed to apply broad laws to specific circumstances.

Bureaucracy is not simply an implementer of policy, however, but rather is a policymaker in its own right. It is not simply the main means to deliver on the promises of democracy; it also helps make those promises. Bureaucracy makes policy in two broad ways. First, bureaucracies and bureaucrats are forced to make informal and formal choices about how to translate into action the broad desires of legislatures, executives, or courts and to apply those desires in specific instances. In the process of making these choices, bureaucrats can be viewed as making policy. For example, speed limits are set by law (usually by state legislatures). Yet in a practical sense, it is really the traffic cop who determines how fast a motorist can go before falling afoul of the law. The legislators, after all, are not on the highway; the police officer is. The ability of lower-level bureaucrats to informally set policy in this fashion is known as the power of the street-level bureaucrat (Lipsky 1980).

The second way in which bureaucracy makes policy is through active participation in the political process. Federal bureaucracies do not wait passively for Congress and the president to formulate policies in Congress and the White House. They help shape those decisions in a number of ways: by conducting evaluations of and analyzing problems, by providing expertise on potential responses to those problems, and by outright lobbying.

Thus, the bureaucracy can be considered a fourth branch of government. The characteristics and organization of that fourth branch of government significantly shape the nation's political system and how it delivers on the promise of democracy.

THE CHARACTERISTICS OF BUREAUCRACY

Agencies in the federal bureaucracy are enormously diverse, and at first glance, organizations as diverse as, say, the Coast Guard and the Federal Deposit Insurance Corporation (FDIC) appear to have little in common. Yet virtually every public agency shares two common characteristics: (1) a broad mission to implement the decisions of government and (2) a common form of organizational structure. Organizational structure is crucial to understanding bureaucracy and how it goes about implementing government decisions. Indeed, to scholars who study the subject, this is what bureaucracy is—not a public agency or a program, but a specific type of organization.

The Weberian Model of Bureaucracy

The best-known description of the bureaucratic model of organization is attributed to Max Weber (Gerth and Mills 1946). Weber's model proposed five distinguishing characteristics of a bureaucracy:

1. *Division of labor.* In a bureaucracy, work is divided according to task specialization. For example, most large bureaucracies employ specialists in personnel, accounting, and data entry. In the public sector, specialists include virologists at the Centers for Disease Control and policy analysts at the Congressional Research Service.
2. *Hierarchy.* In a bureaucracy, there is a clear vertical chain of command, and authority flows downward from superiors to subordinate employees.
3. *Formal rules.* Bureaucracies operate according to standardized operating procedures.
4. *Maintenance of files and records.* Bureaucracies record their actions and keep the records.
5. *Professionalization.* Bureaucrats are appointed on the basis of their qualifications, and government bureaucracies develop a career civil service.

Microsoft, General Motors, and IBM all have this same set of characteristics. What separates public and private bureaucracies is not how they are organized but what they are organized to do. The purpose of most private bureaucracies is to make a profit. The purpose of a public bureaucracy is to implement laws and regulations— that is, to translate the expressed intentions of government into action. Given this purpose, there are several advantages to organizing public agencies along bureaucratic lines. For example, a formal framework of rules and procedures helps ensure stability, predictability, and impartiality in the way an agency carries out its mission.

The neutrality of bureaucracy is responsible, in part, for its unflattering reputation. Most Americans have endured the classic bureaucratic experience of waiting in line, filling out forms, and dealing with red tape. (The term "red tape," by the way, originates from the red ribbons used to bind official documents in the nineteenth century; the ribbon is long gone, but "red tape" remains as a term describing excessive bureaucratic formality.) This is not the sort of process that makes an organization popular. Yet the rules and regulations associated with bureaucracy are designed to ensure equality. It does not matter if you are rich or poor, Democrat or Republican, black or white; when you go to get a driver's license, you have to meet the same qualification standards as everyone else. There is no cutting in line, and there are no exceptions to the testing requirement on the basis of social or political standing. Consider that a public bureaucracy's red tape is a sign of the core democratic principle of political equality in action. As discussed in earlier chapters, the core values enjoy almost universal support in the abstract; in practice, though, they can be downright irritating.

The Merit System

Another characteristic of bureaucracy that relates to the core principles of democracy is professionalization, which means that the people who staff public agencies are there on the basis of merit: they are hired and promoted on the basis of their qualifications and their job performance rather than on their political connections. Public agencies have not always been run on the basis of the merit system. In the **spoils system**, government jobs at all levels are rewards for people's loyalty to a politician or a party. Under such a system, a change of administration (as when a politician or party loses at the polls) results in an immediate large-scale turnover in the bureaucracy.

The spoils system dominated the public bureaucracy for much of the nineteenth and early twentieth centuries. Under the spoils system, getting a government job depended on whom rather than what you knew, and your job security extended only to the next election. The spoils system promoted corruption and incompetence, thoroughly politicizing the bureaucracy (Rosenbloom 1998, 211). It could (and did) lead to many breaches of the core principles of democracy. Bureaucracies operating under the spoils system were involved in everything from playing political favorites (which contradicts the principle of political equality) to rigging elections (which contradicts the principle of majority rule). Although the spoils system has been largely abandoned, a residue of it still exists. The president, for example, appoints the head of many executive agencies. In many cases, though, these appointments must be approved by the Senate, and the appointee must have some qualifications as a prerequisite for gaining that approval.

In contrast to the spoils system, the **merit system** bases government employment on competence rather than partisan fealty. A merit system staffs a bureaucracy by defining the skills and knowledge required to do a particular job and provides a way—typically a written examination—for prospective employees to demonstrate their ability to perform those tasks. A merit system is intended to create a career civil service of competent professionals to run public agencies. Of course, bureaucrats still have their own policy and political preferences, and a merit system does not entirely eliminate politics from the bureaucracy. Compared to a spoils system, however, a merit system greatly reduces the potential for incompetence, corruption, and naked partisanship.

The merit system was formally introduced into the federal bureaucracy by the Pendleton Act of 1883. This law was a direct product of the assassination of

spoils system A system of governing in which political positions and benefits are given to the friends of the winner.

merit system A system of governing in which jobs are given based on relevant technical expertise and the ability to perform.

President James Garfield in 1881 by a disappointed (and mentally unstable) office seeker. This assassination sent shock waves through the political system, turned public opinion against the spoils system, and pushed Congress into considering radical reform of the bureaucracy (Brinkley 1993, 516–517). The Pendleton Act established the principle that government employment and promotion should be based on merit demonstrated through competitive examinations. This principle signaled the end of the spoils system and remains the primary means of staffing the bureaucracy today.

Neutral Competence

Generally speaking, the merit-based civil service system prizes technical competence in government employees above virtually anything else. Most importantly, the bureaucratic form of organization offers a way to install neutral competence into public agencies. **Neutral competence** means that public agencies make decisions based on expertise rather than political or personal considerations.

At least since Woodrow Wilson's administration, reformers have sought to separate the political and administrative functions of government. The general idea is that political functions are performed by elected officials. The president and Congress decide basic issues such as whether the government will wage war, agree to an international trade treaty, or provide or subsidize basic health care and, if so, under what conditions. These are all political decisions: they represent the outcomes of conflicts over what society ought to do. This conflict is processed by the political institutions of a representative democracy into a decision about what action, if any, government should take.

Implementing those decisions is an administrative function and therefore the job of the administrative arm of government—in other words, of the bureaucracy. According to the principle of neutral competence, the bureaucracy does not decide policy or take sides in the political arena. It simply uses its expertise to ensure that policy decisions are implemented in the fashion intended by the institutions of representative democracy. If those institutions make decisions that uphold the core principles of democracy, the bureaucracy ensures that government upholds those values in deed as well as words.

In theory, the bureaucratic form of organization can help separate politics and administration. In practice, though, the record is mixed. As noted previously, the bureaucracy is actively involved in influencing the formation of policies, but as discussed later in this chapter, insulating the bureaucracy from politics is difficult, and some question whether it should even be attempted.

The Bureaucrats

Like the agencies they serve, the roughly 2.8 million federal employees are also an astonishingly diverse group. Because of the merit system, the bureaucracy is

neutral competence The idea that agencies should make decisions based on expertise rather than political considerations.

largely staffed by people hired for their technical expertise rather than for their political or partisan loyalty. Government bureaucrats include doctors, nurses, lawyers, electricians, computer programmers, carpenters, clerical workers, and virtually every other occupational group imaginable. The term *bureaucrat* rarely conjures up the image of a creative arts therapist or a microbiologist, but the federal government employs hundreds of the former and thousands of the latter.

Generally speaking, all this expertise is put to productive use. The stereotype of the ineffective and incompetent bureaucracy is largely inaccurate. Public administration scholars generally conclude that government bureaucracies do a much better job than they get credit for (Goodsell 1994; Sclar 2000). For example, the American Customer Satisfaction Index (ACSI) was originally designed to assess customer satisfaction with various businesses but has been expanded to include a wide variety of federal agencies. Consumer satisfaction varies enormously from agency to agency, with many agencies rivaling or even exceeding the satisfaction scores of private sector counterparts. Other agencies tend to have very low satisfaction scores, but these scores may be as much a result of effective government bureaucracy as anything else. One of the lowest-ranked bureaucracies is the Treasury Department, the department that houses the Internal Revenue Service (IRS). The IRS is pretty good at getting money from people—that's its job—but it can hardly be expected to leave pleased "customers" in its wake (U.S. Government Customer Satisfaction Initiative 2000; Fornell 2010).

Not only do government employees by and large do a good job; they do it relatively inexpensively. Most federal employees are covered by what is known as the general schedule (GS) pay scale (see Table 14.1). There are 15 GS grades, which range in annual pay from a first-year GS-1 at $17,803 to a senior GS-15 with years of experience at $129,517. To put the pay of federal bureaucrats into perspective, a recent college graduate would most likely be hired as a GS-5, GS-6, or GS-7 depending on the area of expertise and qualifications. That means if you went to work for the federal government after graduation, your starting annual salary would most likely fall between $27,000 and $33,000. And if you do go to work for the federal government, it would not be wise to plan on big pay raises—or on any pay raises at all. The GS pay scale was frozen in 2010 and as of 2012 had remained unchanged for three consecutive years.

The one stereotype of the bureaucracy that does hold true is a relative lack of diversity. The typical federal bureaucrat is a white male in his mid-forties who has worked for the government for 17 years. Roughly 67 percent of federal employees are white, and minorities tend to be concentrated in the middle and lower ranks of the bureaucracy. Females are also underrepresented—roughly 56 percent of federal employees are male. As a group, federal employees are also highly educated, with about 44 percent holding college degrees.

---

* current and archived ASCI scores for federal government agencies can be found at http://www.theacsi.org/index.php?option=com_content&view=article&id=27&Itemid=132

TABLE 14.1: GENERAL SCHEDULE (GS) PAY SCALE, EFFECTIVE JANUARY 2012

Grade	Step 1	Step 2	Step 3	Step 4	Step 5	Step 6	Step 7	Step 8	Step 9	Step 10	WITHIN GRADE AMOUNTS
1	$ 17,803	$ 18,398	$ 18,990	$ 19,579	$ 20,171	$ 20,519	$ 21,104	$ 21,694	$ 21,717	$ 22,269	VARIES
2	20,017	20,493	21,155	21,717	21,961	22,607	23,253	23,899	24,545	25,191	VARIES
3	21,840	22,568	23,296	24,024	24,752	25,480	26,208	26,936	27,664	28,392	728
4	24,518	25,335	26,152	26,969	27,786	28,603	29,420	30,237	31,054	31,871	817
5	27,431	28,345	29,259	30,173	31,087	32,001	32,915	33,829	34,743	35,657	914
6	30,577	31,596	32,615	33,634	34,653	35,672	36,691	37,710	38,729	39,748	1019
7	33,979	35,112	36,245	37,378	38,511	39,644	40,777	41,910	43,043	44,176	1133
8	37,631	38,885	40,139	41,393	42,647	43,901	45,155	46,409	47,663	48,917	1254
9	41,563	42,948	44,333	45,718	47,103	48,488	49,873	51,258	52,643	54,028	1385
10	45,771	47,297	48,823	50,349	51,875	53,401	54,927	56,453	57,979	59,505	1526
11	50,287	51,963	53,639	55,315	56,991	58,667	60,343	62,019	63,695	65,371	1676
12	60,274	62,283	64,292	66,301	68,310	70,319	72,328	74,337	76,346	78,355	2009
13	71,674	74,063	76,452	78,841	81,230	83,619	86,008	88,397	90,786	93,175	2389
14	84,697	87,520	90,343	93,166	95,989	98,812	101,635	104,458	107,281	110,104	2823
15	99,628	102,949	106,270	109,591	112,912	116,233	119,554	122,875	126,196	129,517	3321

Source: U.S. Office of Personnel Management, http://www.opm.gov/oca/12tables/indexgs.asp.

Federal government public agencies are organized into a rough hierarchy. If we confine the discussion to the executive branch (Congress and the courts have their own bureaucracies), there are five basic categories of public agency within this hierarchy. At the top are the Executive Office of the President and the cabinet departments. Below them come independent agencies, government corporations, and miscellaneous bureaus (see Figure 14.1).

The Executive Office of the President

At the top of the executive branch hierarchy is the **Executive Office of the President (EOP)**. This is the bureaucracy charged with collectively managing all of the executive branch bureaucracies for the president. The EOP is divided into several agencies with specific tasks. The White House Office consists of the key members of the president's staff who help with the day-to-day administrative responsibilities of the presidency. Also housed in the EOP are agencies specializing in particular policy areas, such as the Council of Economic Advisers and the National Security Council, as well as agencies with broader responsibilities. An example of the latter is the Office of Management and Budget (OMB), which provides a central location for all other agencies to submit program and budget requests and thus plays an important centralizing role in the federal bureaucracy.

Cabinet Departments

Just below the EOP in the bureaucratic hierarchy are the 15 **cabinet departments**, each headed by a cabinet secretary appointed by the president. Congress created each of these departments and has the power to determine their organization and internal operation. The first cabinet departments were State, War (which evolved into Defense), and Treasury, all created in 1789. The most recent is the Department of Homeland Security (DHS), created in 2002 in one of the most sweeping reorganizations of the federal bureaucracy in 50 years.

Cabinet departments are administrative agencies charged with carrying out government operations in general policy areas. These departments are the main institutions of the federal bureaucracy and are responsible for implementing most federal programs and policies. They have the highest profile of all the federal bureaucracies, and the people who run them are often known to the general public.

Cabinet departments are not monolithic and centralized bureaucracies. Many of them are more accurately described as holding companies. They serve as administrative umbrellas covering diverse programs and serving diverse clients. Each department is subdivided into smaller units. The Department of Justice (DOJ) is the

Executive Office of the President (EOP) The organizational structure in the executive branch that houses the president's most influential advisors and agencies. The most important include the White House Office, the Office of Management and Budget (OMB), the National Security Council, and the Council of Economic Advisers.

cabinet departments The 15 largest and most influential agencies of the federal bureaucracy.

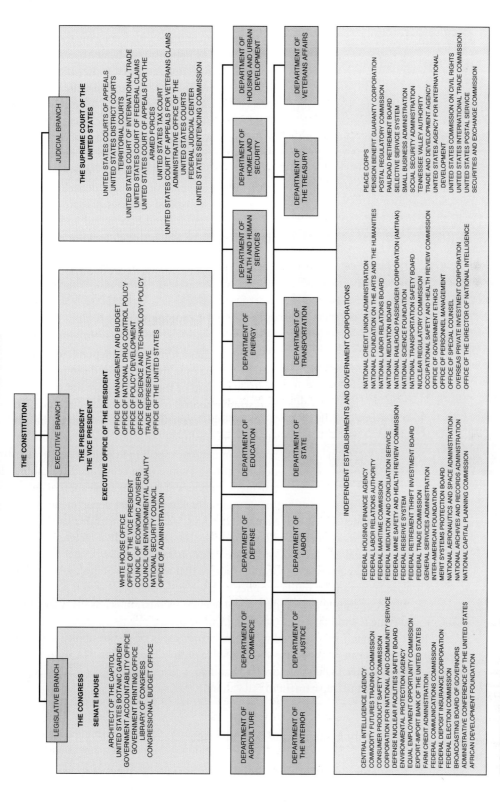

FIGURE 14.1 Organization of the U.S. Government

Source: U.S. Government Manual, http://www.gpo.gov/fdsys/pkg/GOVMAN-2011-10-05/pdf/GOVMAN-2011-10-05-Government-of-the-United-States-4.pdf.

© TATAN SYUFLANA/Reuters/Landov

Secretary of State Hillary Clinton arrives in Jakarta at the beginning of a goodwill visit to Indonesia. The Department of State is a cabinet-level agency, the head of which is appointed by the president and is given major responsibility for executing the nation's foreign policy.

largest law firm in the world, employing thousands of attorneys working in bureaus dedicated to antitrust efforts, civil rights protection, criminal prosecution, and other areas of the law. The DOJ also includes the FBI, the Drug Enforcement Agency, and the U.S. Marshals Service. In addition to lawyers and law enforcement agencies, the DOJ also includes the Federal Bureau of Prisons, which runs the federal prison system. All of these individual agencies may have considerable independence even though they are part of a single department. In fact, many of the individual agencies predate their departmental organizations and have proud and independent histories, some of which stretch back for centuries. The U.S. Coast Guard, for example, operated for more than 200 years before becoming a part of the DHS.

Independent Agencies

The central characteristic of **independent agencies** is their independence from cabinet departments: unlike the Coast Guard or the FBI, they are not under the administrative control of a cabinet secretary. Independent agencies were created to operate outside the cabinet department umbrella for a number of reasons: for example, some did not seem to fit well within any existing department, and some were kept outside of cabinet departments in hopes of fostering fresh approaches to vexing policy problems. Putting agencies outside of cabinet departments also helps clarify policy intent. For example, if NASA were placed within a cabinet department, the most likely candidate would be the Department of Defense. But having the National Aeronautics and Space Administration (NASA) under the control of the military bureaucracy would indicate that the United States intends to use its space program for military rather than scientific and commercial purposes. With NASA operating as an independent agency, its mission is less likely to be seen as serving the military interests of the United States.

Although they generally have narrower areas of responsibility, independent agencies can rival the size and influence of the departments. NASA, for example, has roughly 18,000 employees. That is four times the roughly 4,500 people who work for the Department of Education.

independent agencies Federal agencies that are not part of the cabinet-level executive departments.

regulatory agencies and commissions Agencies that are independent of cabinet departments and are created by Congress to monitor and regulate specific areas of economic activity.

Regulatory Agencies and Commissions

Regulatory agencies and commissions are specific types of independent agencies. They are part of the executive branch of government but are independent of cabinet departments. Examples include the Securities and Exchange Commission (SEC), which regulates stock and bond markets, and the Environmental Protection Agency (EPA), which regulates pollution. What separates regulatory agencies from other independent agencies is the focus of their responsibilities: Congress creates regulatory agencies to monitor and regulate specific areas of economic activity. The main reason for keeping regulatory agencies outside of cabinet departments is to provide them with a degree of insulation from political pressures. The idea is that policy areas such as industrial pollution should be regulated by a neutral referee who serves public rather than partisan interests.

The degree of insulation from political pressure varies. Some regulatory agencies, such as the EPA, are headed by a political appointee—someone who serves at the pleasure of the president. Others, such as the SEC, are headed by presidential appointees—in other words, they have to be nominated by the president and approved by Congress. Once appointed, however, commissioners serve a fixed term and cannot be removed if they make decisions the president disagrees with. Similarly, the Consumer Product Safety Commission is a regulatory agency headed by commissioners serving seven-year terms that overlap with presidential administrations; this overlap makes it more difficult for presidents to use their appointment powers to advance a particular set of interests or to promote a particular political agenda.

Regulatory agencies, or at least government regulations, have been a particular target of anti-bureaucracy criticism, with many arguing that when government regulates with too strong a hand, it ends up limiting individual liberty and acting as a drag on the economy. Conservatives in particular have championed **deregulation**, which means the simplification, loosening, or elimination of government rules (see this chapter's later section for a full discussion of rules and rulemaking). The basic idea is that government rules and regulations are a poor substitute for the natural discipline of free markets. Regulations restrict innovation, nimble decision making, and entrepreneurial activity; remove the regulations, and these activities are promoted, and everyone benefits. At least, that's the theory. In practice, most people are in favor of deregulation only until something goes really wrong; then everyone wants to know why government was asleep at the switch.

For example, the Financial Modernization Act (FMA) was held up as a model of the positives of deregulation when it was passed in 1999. The FMA was designed to deregulate large sections of the financial industry by, among other things, eliminating rules that prevented insurance companies and securities companies from merging with each other. A decade later, the FMA was harshly criticized for promoting the creation of the massive financial institutions whose risky bets plunged the globe into the great recession in 2008 and which had been deemed as "too big to fail" but ended up being bailed out by the taxpayer. That experience led Congress to have second thoughts about deregulating Wall Street and letting the market do its thing.

Congress reversed course from the FMA in 2010, passing the Dodd-Frank Wall Street Reform and Consumer Protection Act, which imposed a new raft of regulations on the financial industry (this law is known as "Dodd-Frank" after Senator Christopher Dodd (D-CT) and Representative Barney Frank (D-MA)

deregulation The reduction or elimination of government rules and regulations that interfere with the efficient operation of market forces.

POURING TOO MUCH OIL ON DEREGULATED WATERS: SECOND THOUGHTS ON GOVERNMENT BUREAUCRACY

Louisiana Governor Bobby Jindal is not what you'd call a big fan of government bureaucracy. He is, or at least was, a big advocate of deregulation and pushed a consistent theme that the government that governs best is the government that governs least.

He made this clear enough in his 2009 response to President Obama's State of the Union speech. "The strength of America is not found in our government," said Jindal, "it is found in the compassionate hearts and the enterprising spirit of our citizens."

Plenty of that entrepreneurial spirit was found in the oil and gas industry that created technological marvels to drill for oil in the deep waters off the Louisiana shore. Overseeing these entrepreneurial efforts was the Minerals Management Service (MMS), which has been described as a "poster child" for the deregulatory agenda favored by politicians like Jindal.

Certainly, as the chief regulator of offshore oil rigs, MMS over the past decade or so has been sensitive to oil industry concerns about the onerous burden of safety and environmental regulations. MMS handed out environmental regulatory waivers and signed off on emergency containment plans that did not seem to include much in the way of actual planning. For example, the BP response plan for an oil spill in the Gulf of Mexico included references to a deceased wild life expert—and a range of wildlife that does not live in the Gulf—but failed to mention the tides that could (and did) carry oil to Florida and even along the Atlantic Coast.

Clearly there was plenty of blame to go around with the BP oil spill. The "drill, baby, drill" spirit, lax oversight from an agency clearly reflecting political preferences for a light regulatory hand, and a company that apparently believed that because a disaster had not happened it could not happen. And it was not just conservative Republicans riding the deregulatory band wagon. The MMS was handing out regulatory waivers

who introduced the legislation into the Senate and the House, respectively). This law also had its critics; some thought it was an overreaction that acted as a drag on economic activity. Others thought it was watered down and did not go far enough. Such criticism is not surprising. Finding the balance between regulations tight enough to protect the public good but not so tight that they strangle economic development and the freedom of individuals and businesses is extremely hard. When things are going well, many may oppose regulations on the grounds that they prevent things from getting even better. Removing or loosening regulation can entail great risk, though. The benefits of regulation are sometimes seen only in hindsight, after the downsides of deregulation have been made disastrously clear. (See the Politics in Practice feature "Pouring Too Much Oil on Deregulated Waters: Second Thoughts on Government Bureaucracy.")

on President's Obama's watch. Just as instructive as what led up to the disaster, however, is what happened after.

Jindal's approach to the federal government and government bureaucracies dramatically shifted course. Rather than less federal government and less regulation, he wanted more. Jindal was far from the only politician whose deregulatory leanings underwent a sudden transformation when faced with a catastrophe that, at least in part, could be traced directly to lax regulation. Bob Marshall, columnist for the *New Orleans Times-Picayune*, described the oil spill disaster as the "fervor for deregulation" chickens coming home to roost, and described Jindal's anxious insistence that the federal government do more in the wake of the blow out as hypocrisy of the highest order.

The rediscovery of the benefits of a strong federal government with vigilant regulatory agencies by Jindal and other deregulatory advocates, "goes beyond preaching caution after the horse is out of the barn," said Marshall. It was people like Jindal who, "helped open the barn door, hung a feed bucket around the horse's neck and then gave it a good slap on the rump to speed it on its way."

One of the few clear things to emerge from the muck spewed into the Gulf by the oil well blowout was that a lot of people prefer a government agency to do less rather than more . . . until something goes really, really wrong. This was pretty much the same scenario following the near collapse of the financial industry in 2008–2009. No one really likes dealing with the annoying and irritating red tape of a tough regulatory agency. What people seem to like even less is dealing with the catastrophic aftermath of a lax regulatory agency.

SOURCES Dionne, E.J., Jr. 2010. "So, Jindal, How's That Deregulation Workin' for Ya?" *Dayton Daily News*. http://www.daytondaily news.com/opinion/columnists/e-j-dionne-jr-so-jindal-hows-that-deregulation-workin-for-ya—734395.htm. Accessed June 7, 2010.

Marshall, Bob. 2010. "Oil Disaster Brought to You by Deregulation." Nola.com. May 23. http://www.nola.com/news/gulf-oil-spill/index.ssf/2010/05/oil_disaster_brought_to_you_by.html. (June 7, 2010).

Prichard, Justin, Tamara Luch, and Holbrook Mohor. 2010. "BP Spill Response Plans Severely Flawed." Associated Press. June 9. http://news.yahoo.com/s/ap/20100609/ap_on_bi_ge/us_gulf_oil_spill_sketchy_plans (June 9, 2010).

Zelizer, Julian. 2010. "The Legacy of 'Drill, Baby, Drill.'" CNN.com. June 1. http://ac360.blogs.cnn.com/2010/06/01/the-legacy-of-drill-baby-drill (August 30, 2010).

Government Corporations

Another set of organizations in the extended family of the federal bureaucracy consists of **government corporations**. These operate in a vague area somewhere between the public and private sectors. The general idea behind government corporations is to shift responsibility for a government task to a nonpartisan arena in hopes of keeping it insulated from politics to the greatest extent possible. Probably the best-known government corporation is the USPS. Other examples include the FDIC, which insures bank deposits, and Amtrak, the nation's passenger rail service. In essence, government corporations are federally established businesses. They have narrow tasks and are run by bipartisan or nonpartisan boards. Most are designed to be self-supporting, although some receive at least some assistance from the federal government.

government corporations Federally established businesses that are narrow in focus and are in part self-supporting.

Other Bureaus

Besides the EOP, cabinet departments, independent agencies, and government corporations, there is a miscellaneous set of executive branch organizations that does not fit into any of these categories. This set includes **advisory committees**, which can be either permanent or temporary and which serve a number of purposes, ranging from providing agencies with technical expertise to providing a means for communicating citizen input to agency operations. In any given year, there are roughly 1,000 advisory committees salted throughout the federal bureaucracy. There are also numerous boards, committees, and commissions that are temporary additions to the bureaucracy. These tend to be small, have well-defined tasks, and have few program responsibilities.

The Politics of Organization

Though we can classify public agencies and sort them into a rough pecking order, there really is no such thing as "the" federal bureaucracy. Rather than a single federal bureaucracy, there is actually a sprawling mass of individual agencies. The 2.8 million civilian employees of the federal government serve in 15 departments, 50 or so independent regulatory agencies, and numerous boards, commissions, and advisory committees. As we have seen, many of these bureaucracies are subdivided into smaller administrative units that have considerable independence. Rather than being a Big Brother, the bureaucracies are more like a vast extended family, replete with third cousins twice removed and siblings who are not talking to each other.

After reading about the confusing stew of departments, agencies, committees, bureaus, and commissions and their seemingly incoherent relationships with one another, you might be wondering whether the organization of the federal bureaucracy makes any sense. The short answer to that is simple: no. At least in terms of being organized to promote effective and efficient administration, the organization of the federal government is not particularly rational or logical.

Consider that, as of mid-2012, not one or two, but at least seven, federal agencies regulated the banking industry. These include two divisions of a cabinet department (the Office of the Comptroller of the Currency and the Financial Crimes Enforcement Network, both part of the Treasury Department), one independent agency (the National Credit Union Administration), one government corporation (the FDIC), one independent government commission (the Federal Trade Commission), one formal interagency body (the Federal Financial Institutions Examination Council), and the central banking system of the United States (the Federal Reserve System, which is headed by a presidentially appointed board of governors and includes 12 regional federal banks). The goals and responsibilities of these agencies overlap, yet there is little in the way of centralized or coordinated control over what they do, and one agency may be all but unaware of the activities of another.

advisory committees Temporary or permanent organizations created to provide information and technical expertise to the bureaucracy.

Especially given the harsh lessons of the financial meltdown of 2008 and the recession it spawned, it is reasonable to ask why the federal government would regulate such a critical part of the financial industry with such an uncoordinated mix of hit-and-miss regulatory agencies. Actually, this mix of agencies is *more* coordinated and centralized than it was just a few years ago. The passage of Dodd-Frank in 2010 eliminated one agency by forcing the merger of the Office of Thrift Supervision with the Comptroller of the Currency and, at least in theory, imposed a more ordered regulatory regime on the financial industry. Dodd-Frank arguably created more bureaucracy rather than less, though. For example, it created the Consumer Financial Protection Bureau (CFPB), a brand new independent unit within the Federal Reserve. The idea behind the CFPB was to take uncoordinated regulatory powers that were spread out over several agencies and concentrate them in a single place. Given the alphabet soup of regulatory agencies governing the financial sector, that seems to make sense, but note the paradox: The idea was to streamline and centralize bureaucratic regulation. And how was this accomplished? More bureaucracy!

Why does the federal bureaucracy contain such redundancy, overlap, and unclear lines of authority? Why, for heaven's sake, are there seven federal agencies regulating financial institutions rather than one? Actually, there is a relatively simple

Heads of federal agencies have high-profile jobs with important policy responsibilities, which means that federal agency heads get lots of scrutiny from Congress. Here Richard Cordray, director of the Consumer Financial Protection Bureau, testifies before the Senate Banking, Housing and Urban Affairs Committee.

© Photo By Chris Maddaloni/CQ Roll Call

answer to all these questions, one directly related to the purpose of bureaucracies: bureaucracies are there to make good on the promises of democratic government, and the constituents of democratic governments often want their government to promise to do things that are not efficient, logical, or even particularly effective.

The reason for seven banking regulatory agencies is that the various sectors of the banking industry do not want to be regulated by a single agency. Credit unions and banks, for example, each wanted their own regulatory agency, each of which has a set of accompanying congressional committees. In other words, the bureaucracy regulating the financial industry is convoluted because it serves a set of political goals. Different sectors of the industry have lobbied government to give them different agencies that regulate different aspects of the business. A good example of this is now defunct—the Office of Thrift Supervision (OTS), which regulated some of the biggest institutions implicated in the massive financial meltdowns of 2008–2009. The OTS had a reputation as a lax regulator, and this is exactly why big companies such as AIG supported the OTS and wanted to be regulated by them (AIG is a massive insurance company that required a massive taxpayer bailout to stay in business [National Public Radio 2009]). In hindsight the OTS regulatory regime was a bad idea; it might have been better to have a tougher regulatory agency watching outfits such as AIG. Had it been in existence, an agency such as the CFPB might have been more effective and more efficient. Yet that misses the point. The job of the bureaucracy is not to be effective or efficient, but to deliver on the promises of democratic governments. Whatever its considerable faults, the OTS was doing exactly that—in the 1990s and early 2000s, less federal regulation was what Congress was demanding, and with the OTS that is just what it got.

This basic rule of democratic governance—bureaucracy responds to the demands of elected government, no matter how silly or dangerous the demands— does not apply just to the financial industry. The pattern is repeated again and again. And it cannot be blamed on the catch-all villain of "special interests." All citizens, in some fashion, have vested interests in government agencies. You, or at least many of your peers, for example, probably want the Department of Education to keep guaranteeing student loans and offering student grants. This demand creates pressure on government—mainly from parents with college-age children—to make promises about higher education and financial aid. The result? A program run by a public agency with rules, regulations, red tape, and the rest of the bureaucratic machinery. (Those of you who have applied for a student loan will be intimately familiar with these details.)

THE POWER OF BUREAUCRACY

Although bureaucracy exists to implement the promises made by the elected branches of government, and the characteristics and organization of the federal bureaucracy reflect the politics of the democratic system, the federal bureaucracy does not simply passively respond to the executives and legislators. Bureaucracy is an independent policymaker. By our definition of politics (the authoritative allocation of values, or the process of deciding who gets what and when and how they get it), the bureaucracy is very much a political branch of government. Every day, bureaucracies make policy decisions about who gets what. Indeed, bureaucracy is a unique form of policymaking institution that combines all branches of government. Bureaucracies are executive branches of government, yet they also exercise legislative and judicial powers. How do they get this power, and how do they exercise it?

Rulemaking

Laws are often vague and provide bureaucracies with only minimal guidelines about the specific actions they must take. Vague laws give bureaucrats considerable discretion in deciding what these actions will be. Recognizing that these choices should not be made arbitrarily, Congress formally requires bureaucracies to follow a decision-making process that is very similar to the legislative process. This process is called rulemaking.

A **rule** is a statement by a federal agency that interprets a law and prescribes the specific action an agency will take to implement that law. **Rulemaking** is the process of deciding exactly what the laws passed by Congress mean. This process has been described as "the single most important function performed by agencies of government" (Kerwin 1994, xi). Once an agency approves a rule, the rule applies to everyone within the agency's jurisdiction and has the force of law. For all practical purposes, rules *are* law. Those annoying childproof caps, for example, are required by Consumer Product Safety Commission (CPSC) rules, and drug manufacturers are legally bound to follow them.

Rulemaking represents the formal process of making choices about what actions the government should undertake, and it amounts to a huge shadow lawmaking process most citizens know little to nothing about. Although it may be unsettling to acknowledge that unelected bureaucrats play a central role in shaping the law, in practical terms it is unavoidable. Passing a law is a difficult process and often requires much compromise. Congress often has more important priorities than thrashing out the minutiae of exactly how a program or policy is to be implemented. As a result, Congress passes laws that are vague about what they specifically obligate the government to do. For example, the Occupational Safety and Health Act was passed "to assure so far as possible every working man and woman in the nation safe and healthy work conditions." That law expresses a noble goal with which few would disagree. Yet how do we put this noble goal into action? What exactly should the government do to ensure that its citizens have a safe working environment? The answers to those questions come not from Congress but from the Occupational Safety and Health Administration (OSHA).

rule A statement of the bureaucracy that interprets the law or prescribes a specific action. These rules have the force of law.

rulemaking The process in which the bureaucracy decides what the laws passed by Congress mean and how they should be carried out.

© Peter Mumford/Alamy

Bureaucracies have the difficult task of creating rules that will implement the (often vague) laws passed by Congress. These rules affect many aspects of our day-to-day lives. For instance, the Child Safety Protection Law was passed by Congress and required the Consumer Product Safety Commission (CPSC) to develop mandatory bicycle helmet standards. The CPSC spent four years gathering comments on their proposed standards before finally issuing them. The standards, however, did not touch on whether children must wear helmets—this was left up to individual states to decide and has resulted in a wide variety of regulations from state to state.

Bureaucracy's responsibility for fleshing out the messy details needed to implement vague laws helps explain how bureaucracy gets its negative image. Passing a law promoting safety in the workplace attracted considerable support in the abstract. In practice, OSHA was left to deal with a myriad of specifics, such as the minimum allowable thickness of ladder rungs and how much cotton dust a textile worker should be exposed to. Issuing a lengthy list of standards for manufacturing ladders seems more like petty bureaucratic meddling than work toward the grand cause of worker safety. Rulemaking is the "dirty work" of politics: detail-oriented, laborious, and necessary. Yet without these specifics, laws are just words on paper, not actions in the real world.

Few federal agencies have the authority to unilaterally issue rules. Rulemaking is governed by the Federal Administrative Procedures Act and other laws passed by Congress. At a minimum, agencies must give public notice of rules, allow interested parties an opportunity to comment on these rules, and publish the finished product in the *Federal Register*. Though the process is unknown to most citizens, most organized interest groups are well aware of the importance of rulemaking and actively participate in the process where their interests are involved. Bureaucracies take public input very seriously, and the rulemaking process is generally acknowledged to be open and to allow for conflicting interests to state their cases. (See the Politics in Practice feature "Rules and Your Bottom Line.")

Adjudication

In making rules, bureaucracies act like legislatures; in judging them, they act like courts. **Adjudication** is a process designed to establish whether a rule has been violated. For example, the National Highway Traffic Safety Administration (NHTSA) uses adjudication to judge whether a particular type or model of automobile violates safety regulations and should be removed from the roads. If the NHTSA believes an automobile violates safety rules, it holds a hearing in which the manufacturer can present contesting evidence and arguments. If the agency deems a recall to be necessary, the manufacturer has an opportunity to negotiate the scope and wording of the recall.

So although the primary mission of bureaucracy is to implement and manage policy, the responsibilities of rulemaking and adjudication make the bureaucracy much

adjudication The process of determining whether a law or rule established by the bureaucracy has been broken.

POLITICS IN PRACTICE

RULES AND YOUR BOTTOM LINE

Ever heard of the federal need analysis methodology? No? Well, it is a complicated formula designed to estimate a family's discretionary income while accounting for things such as asset protection allowances, state and local taxes, and a whole lot of other eye-glazing things that only a bureaucrat could love.

Even if you have never heard of the federal need analysis methodology, there is a decent chance it affects your bottom line. Why? It is used to calculate how much a family can be expected to contribute to college expenses. In short, it determines your eligibility for federally funded forms of financial aid. Virtually all of the billions the federal government spends on financial aid every year is tied to this formula.

Periodically, the Department of Education (DOE) adjusts this formula. These adjustments are not laws, but rules. They provide an excellent example of how rulemaking gives bureaucracy considerable policymaking powers and plays an important role in the lives of citizens—in this case, college students.

The DOE's authority to make these rules is based in the Higher Education Act (HEA), which instructs the department to periodically alter the formula to account for things such as inflation and differences in state and local taxes. Those adjustments, which can mean hundreds or even thousands of dollars in lost or gained financial aid to an individual student, are made not by elected representatives but by bureaucrats. In delegating this authority to the DOE, Congress in effect gave the agency the power not only to make good on the promises of government but to play a significant role in determining exactly what those promises are.

In short, by altering its rules the DOE can, in effect, help determine the level of federal government support for higher education. For example, consider an arcane adjustment to the formula that reduces the allowable income deductions for state and local taxes. Sounds pretty boring until you consider the net impact; it means families are expected to contribute more to college expenses, even though their income has not changed at all. (This exact sort of rule change has happened in the past.) The result of such a rule change is to cut federal government support for higher education by hundreds of millions of dollars and shift those costs to students and their families.

Is it fair that such a significant policy change occurs without any action by Congress? Maybe not, but it is, more or less, the law. At least, it is a rule.

SOURCE Winter, Greg. "Change in Aid Formula Shifts More Costs to Students," *New York Times*, 13 June, 2003. Copyright © by The New York Times Co. Reprinted by permission.

like legislatures and courts—it is a policymaking institution charged with missions as varied, complex, and controversial as those of the other institutions of government.

Bureaucratic Lobbying

Bureaucratic policymaking is not only passive and reactive. Bureaucracies are also active in the initiation of new policies, and they actively participate in the broader political process. As the primary managers of policy, bureaucrats are in ideal positions to identify the problems and limitations of existing laws and programs, and they frequently recommend changes to the president and to the congressional committees with which they interact.

Bureaucracies' power to influence policy formation by legislatures and executives has two sources. First and foremost is their expertise. Knowledge is power, and bureaucracies are vast storehouses of information. The president and the Congress often rely on bureaucracy to collect and present the information needed to fashion policy, and by choosing what information to provide and how to present that information, bureaucrats can affect policy decisions.

The second source of power is close alliances with important clientele groups and the congressional committees that hold jurisdiction over the programs of interest to those clientele groups. The Department of Veterans Affairs, for example, has a powerful ally in the nation's veterans. Few legislators relish the prospect of taking a position that can be perceived as anti-veteran, and this provides a potent source of influence. Politicians and bureaucracy typically use this influence to advance common interests rather than wield it against each other. Some scholars argue that many important policy decisions are made in **iron triangles**, which are stable relationships among a clientele group, the bureaucracy managing the programs that affect that group's interests, and the congressional committees with jurisdiction over those programs. Each actor in this triangle has a shared set of interests, and they are able to work in harness to pursue common goals. Figure 14.2

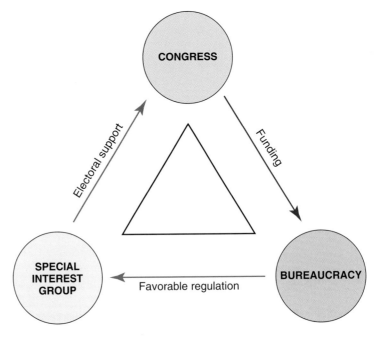

iron triangles A term used to refer to the interdependent relationship among the bureaucracy, interest groups, and congressional committees.

FIGURE 14.2 an iron triangle

shows how the basic relationships in an iron triangle works. Congress provides a bureaucracy with generous funding and political power, the bureaucracy serves its clientele with favorable regulatory or program decisions, and the clientele serves as a special interest group that supports the electoral ambitions of lawmakers. Each corner of the triangle supports the goals and desires of another in a mutually reinforcing relationship. Though they were once seen as "governments within government" that were impervious to democratic control, political scientists have largely concluded that iron triangles are less autonomous and powerful than originally thought (Baumgartner and Jones 1993).

Political scientists have discovered that bureaucracies are more likely to operate in policy subsystems than in iron triangles. **Policy subsystems** are the "interaction of actors from different institutions interested in a policy area" (Sabatier 1988). In other words, they are networks of all the groups that share a particular policy interest. Unlike iron triangles, these networks may include executives, courts, a wide range of interest groups and legislative committees, and just about anyone or anything else that can get itself organized enough to participate in the process. These networks are not nearly as stable as iron triangles, and two actors who work together on one issue may oppose each other on another. Thus, the Sierra Club may champion an effort by the EPA to enforce the preservation of wildlife yet oppose the agency when it seeks to relax rules on power plant emissions.

CONTROLLING THE BUREAUCRACY

The discussion thus far shows that bureaucracy exists to make good on promises made by democratic governments, and to do this, federal agencies have been granted broad powers and structured in a way that makes organizational sense for individual agencies and political sense for the overall bureaucracy. All of these characteristics combine to create a larger concern about the bureaucracy: control. Bureaucrats are appointed, not elected, yet we know that through the process of rulemaking, they for all practical purposes make law. If program or regulatory responsibilities are shared by two or four or six bureaucracies, whom do we hold responsible if something goes wrong?

One of the most consistent concerns about the bureaucracy is the need to ensure that it serves the purpose for which it was intended. We want bureaucracy to serve democracy, not to serve its own interests. This is the classic dilemma at the heart of studying bureaucracy: how do you make one of the most powerful institutions of government abide by the principles of democracy when that institution is not democratic? And make no mistake about it: bureaucracies are *not* democratic. Glance back at the characteristics of the classic bureaucracy given earlier in this chapter. Bureaucracies are hierarchical and authoritarian; their personnel are not hired or fired by elections; their decisions are not put to a ballot. Every

policy subsystem Networks of groups with an interest in a specific policy issue or area.

industrialized democracy has had to come to some sort of arrangement with the increasingly important role of the administrative arm of government. The trick here is to make the bureaucracy accountable to the principles of democracy, rather than vice versa.

Theories of Bureaucratic Behavior

Theories of bureaucratic behavior highlight just how tough it can be to make the bureaucracy accountable to democratic principles. In seeking to explain the choices made by individual bureaucrats and the behavior of entire bureaucracies, political scientists have drawn heavily from the rational choice tradition. Assuming that bureaucrats are rational utility maximizers raises some disturbing implications for the political role of bureaucracies and highlights the need for effective control mechanisms.

Consider the highly influential theory of the budget-maximizing bureaucrat, formulated by William Niskanen (1971). Niskanen was seeking to answer this question: if bureaucrats are rational utility maximizers, what exactly are they seeking to maximize? He reasoned that a bureaucrat's personal utility, or satisfaction, is tied to the budget of the agency he or she works for. Agencies with bigger budgets mean bigger and more important programs, and that means more power, prestige, and opportunities for advancement. Niskanen's theory created a picture of bureaucracies as entities equivalent to corporations run by rational entrepreneurs. Just as rational business executives seek to make decisions that will maximize profit, so will bureaucrats seek to make decisions that maximize budgets. Niskanen's theory of the budget-maximizing bureaucrat thus suggests that bureaucrats will try to "sell" legislatures on the programs and public services they provide not because they serve the public interest, but because funding them serves the rational interests of bureaucrats. The result will be a bloated and expensive public sector, which is good for bureaucrats, but not so good for the taxpayer.

Gordon Tullock (1965) presented an alternative rational choice model of bureaucratic behavior. Tullock argued that bureaucrats maximize utility through career advancement, which is not necessarily achieved by increasing budgets. In Tullock's model, rational bureaucrats maximize utility by highlighting their successes and trying to hide their failures—because doing so increases chances of advancement. The implication here is not necessarily agencies with bloated bottom lines, but agencies that are dysfunctional and incompetent. If bureaucrats have an incentive to suppress information about poor performance and highlight information about successes, then legislatures will have an unrealistic picture of what agencies are doing and what they are capable of. Lacking accurate information about the real capabilities and performance of bureaucracy, Tullock argued, makes it hard for legislatures to figure out when bureaucracies are serving the public interest and when they are serving their own interests.

Rational choice theories of bureaucratic behavior thus highlight the need for effective control of bureaucracy because without effective controls bureaucrats will serve their own interests rather than the public interest. Other theories of bureaucratic behavior, however, especially those in the social-psychological tradition, give a different picture of what motivates bureaucratic decision making. The most famous of these is Herbert Simon's theory of **bounded rationality**, formulated more than half a century ago in his book *Administrative Behavior* (1947). Simon argues that actual humans bear little resemblance to the utility maximizers of classical rational choice models. Maximizing involves considering all possible options and weighing the costs and benefits of all of them to discover which one delivers maximum utility. But identifying alternatives involves costs (time and money), so it's unlikely that a decision maker could identify all of them. And even if one could identify all the alternatives, the information would be so vast and complex that no human being could possibly analyze and evaluate it. Thus, rather than maximize, Simon argues that people satisfice. **Satisficing** means considering possible alternatives until finding one that, in the person's view, is good enough to solve the problem at hand and then choosing it, even though it might not be the "best" possible solution. Because information is costly and people's ability to process it is limited, once a satisfactory solution is found, there is little incentive to continue searching.

Simon's model creates a very different picture of bureaucrats. It does not deny that bureaucrats try to act rationally but argues that their ability to do so is constrained. Bounded rationality takes into account the psychological boundaries to our ability to be utility maximizers; we are not capable of true maximization because we have imperfect information. Instead, we use shortcuts and make decisions based on our values and habits rather than on a rational cost–benefit calculation. The implications of bounded rationality for our understanding of bureaucracy are profound. Consider budgets. Under Niskanen's model, a bureaucrat seeks to make his or her budget as large as possible. Under Simon's model, a bureaucrat is faced with the problem of coming up with a justifiable budget. To overcome that challenge, he or she starts with what worked in the past—last year's budget—and makes incremental adjustments up or down, based on perceived needs and political feasibility. Rather than portraying bureaucrats as people coldly calculating how to build independent empires to serve their own interests, Simon's model portrays them as individuals muddling through the problems they are given as best they can.

Viewed through the lens of bounded rationality, bureaucrats and bureaucracies seem less of a potential threat to the public interest and more as individuals and agencies trying to do a tough job with all the psychological baggage that comes with being human—limited attention spans, imperfect information, and a tendency to rely on personal values as much as on rational cost–benefit analysis when making choices. The result is some good decisions and some bad decisions. Control of the bureaucracy is still an issue from this perspective because public agencies still wield political power; they are delegated significant responsibilities and must be held accountable to democracy.

bounded rationality Herbert Simon's theory that humans are not utility maximizers as suggested in classical rational choice models. Humans satisfice (see satisficing) rather than maximize.

satisficing Considering possible alternatives until finding one that is good enough to solve the problem at hand even though it might not be the "best" possible solution.

Controlling the bureaucracy and making it accountable requires two basic things. First, elected representatives and individual citizens must be able to effectively monitor the bureaucracy. Again, the organization of bureaucracy helps us here; bureaucracies operate by formal rules (which help make clear what they should and should not be doing), and they keep written records. Second, elected officials need a basic set of tools to influence bureaucracy.

Monitoring Bureaucracy

The preferred method of making bureaucracy accountable to democracy is through a process called overhead democracy (Redford 1969; W. Wilson 1887). **Overhead democracy** is the idea that citizens can exercise indirect control over bureaucracy: voters will hold elected officials accountable for their actions through their votes, and elected officials will hold bureaucracies accountable for their actions. Candidates who favor majority viewpoints will win office. To win reelection, these candidates must make some effort to keep the promises they made on the campaign trail. Thus, they have a built-in incentive to keep a close eye on the bureaucracies that will actually deliver on those promises. If the bureaucracy abuses its position and starts violating the core principles of democracy—if it plays favorites or denies people services to which they are entitled—an officeholder is expected to take action. If he or she does not, the officeholder will be voted out in favor of someone who will bring the bureaucracy to heel.

The practice of overhead democracy is more complicated in practice than in theory (Meier 1993). It requires politicians to vigorously exercise their oversight responsibilities, systematically monitoring the bureaucracy to ensure that it is acting in accordance with democratically expressed wishes in much the same way that police officers patrol city streets to spot and deter crime. This process is called **police patrol oversight** (McCubbins and Schwartz 1984). The problem here is that for the individual politician, police patrol oversight rarely pays off. In the vast majority of cases, the agencies are doing pretty much what they are supposed and expected to do. Thus, a legislator's time is better spent crafting new laws, engaging in constituency service, or doing any of the other activities related to election.

Rather than engage in constant monitoring, Congress and its committees tend to rely on **fire alarm oversight**, which kicks into action once an alarm is raised (McCubbins and Schwartz 1984). There are many ways to raise an alarm about bureaucratic wrongdoing. Whistle-blowers (agency employees who bring attention to agency misdeeds), direct contact from constituents, and investigations by Congress's information-gathering agencies such as the General Accounting Office (GAO) all routinely raise alarms. Special interest groups are particularly effective at sounding alarms because they put a good deal of effort into monitoring the agencies that affect their interests. A high-profile failure or disaster can also trigger fire alarm oversight. For example, few people had heard of the Marine Minerals Service (MMS) prior to the massive BP oil spill in the Gulf of Mexico in

overhead democracy The idea that the bureaucracy is controlled through the oversight of elected officials, who are chosen by the people, thus giving the populace control over the bureaucracy.

police patrol oversight The active oversight of the bureaucracy by elected officials to make sure that the bureaucracy is acting according to the wishes of the people.

fire alarm oversight Oversight that becomes active only when there is evidence of bureaucratic wrongdoing.

2010. The job of the MMS, an agency located in the Department of the Interior, is to manage the oil, gas, and other mineral resources in the nation's outer continental shelf. In order to drill for oil in the deep water of the outer continental shelf, companies need to get proper certification from the MMS, a process that includes vetting for safety and environmental impact. It was not until after the disastrous well blowout that spewed millions of gallons of crude oil into the Gulf, causing widespread environmental and economic damage in coastal states, that the president and Congress began questioning the MMS's cozy relationship with oil companies. After it came to light that there had been a number of questionable safety and environmental lapses prior to the blowout, the agency was castigated for lax oversight. The same complaint, though, might have been leveled at elected officials: this was a classic fire alarm scenario, with vigorous oversight of MMS beginning after a catastrophe, not before. Obviously, the big problem with fire alarm oversight is that it is reactive rather than proactive. Relying on fire alarm oversight means Congress begins to tackle bureaucratic problems only after those problems have occurred.

Sometimes, the fire alarms Congress relies on to warn it of problems in the bureaucracy are kept silent. Failure to sound an alarm happens when the relationship between an interest group and a bureaucracy becomes a little too cozy. **Agency capture** describes a bureaucracy run for the benefit of those it is supposed to regulate; it occurs when the regulators appointed to an agency share the same professional and economic values as those they regulate. Some critics compare this to hiring foxes to guard the hen house. Even if regulators do not originally have ties to a regulated industry, over time they can come to identify with industry interests because interaction is so one-sided: representatives of a regulated industry have frequent contacts with the agency and may develop cordial relationships with regulators there, whereas representatives of the broader public interest have only infrequent contacts with the agency. Agency capture upsets any notions of overhead democracy and raises questions about the bureaucracy's ability to uphold the core principles.

Although agency capture is recognized as a possibility by academics and fits well with popular beliefs on the influential role of special interests, systematic research has found relatively little hard evidence that it is a widespread problem. Though there certainly are examples of agencies coddling the regulated (think of the regulatory agencies literally designed around the interests of the finance industry and MMS's close relationship with oil companies), it is actually much more common to find bureaucracies that are vigorously regulating the industries they are supposed to regulate (Meier 1995, 21). The real problem is not that interest groups capture agencies and run them for their own benefit but that interest groups sometimes have little incentive to raise an alarm that would trigger oversight. Why report or publicize negligent or inappropriate agency actions if you benefit from them? This is like making a bundle on insurance if the building burns down. What's the incentive to sound the alarm if you profit from the fire? AIG had little incentive to report OTS for lax oversight, just as

agency capture A term used to describe when an agency seems to operate for the benefit of those whom it is supposed to regulate.

BP had little incentive to complain that MMS was not rigorous enough in its permit process.

Even with its limitations, fire alarm oversight does demonstrate that there are forces providing incentives to monitor the bureaucracy and hold it accountable. Because it implements programs and policies, the bureaucracy is a natural focus for competing interests. Some argue that when they serve a range of clients and interest groups, bureaucracies help to responsibly represent and further those interests. As one scholar put it, "bureaucracies are not just passive actors who respond limply to external demand by politicians and groups. Rather, they integrate and transmit competing values from multiple overlapping constituencies" (Wood 1992).

This role is enhanced by laws that provide individual citizens with considerable monitoring powers and force bureaucratic decision making to be open and transparent. The Freedom of Information Act of 1967, for example, requires bureaucracies to respond to all reasonable public requests for documents. Other statutes called **sunshine laws** require that bureaucratic decisions be made in public meetings. These laws give individual citizens and interest groups the tools to keep tabs on what the bureaucracy does.

Influencing Bureaucracy

All branches of the federal government have at their disposal powerful tools to influence bureaucratic behavior. These tools range from the formal power to create and destroy public agencies to less formal techniques of persuasion that may be handled in an office visit or a telephone call. At least in terms of formal power, each branch of government has a different set of options for getting bureaucracies to follow their wishes.

THE CONGRESS AND THE BUREAUCRACY Congress has the ultimate tool to control bureaucracy: legislation. Federal bureaucracies do not simply interpret the law; they are products of it. Congress has the constitutional authority to create or destroy federal agencies and to determine what programs and polices they administer.

Congress also controls bureaucracy through its power of the purse. Article I, Section 9 of the Constitution states that "no money shall be drawn from the treasury, but in consequence of appropriations made by law." This provision means that every federal agency's budget must be approved by Congress, and it is not unusual for Congress to use the appropriation process to place constraints or demands on the bureaucracy. The power of the purse is, in essence, a living embodiment of the golden rule: who has the gold gets to make the rules.

A final way in which Congress controls the bureaucracy is through legislative vetoes. A **legislative veto** is a provision in a law that allows Congress to reject a proposed action by a public agency. Typically this process involves requiring an agency to inform Congress of proposed actions, and then Congress has the right to reject these proposals. Some legislative veto provisions require both houses of

sunshine laws Laws intended to keep the bureaucracy accountable to the people by requiring that agency meetings be open to the public.

legislative veto Measure that gives Congress the ability to reject an action or decision of the bureaucracy.

Congress to accept or reject rules, although some laws permit just one house, or even an individual committee, to accept or reject rules. The intent here is to give Congress some control over how laws are implemented.

Although the legislative veto is an effective check on the bureaucracy, it has its drawbacks. For one thing, it is not clear whether legislative vetoes are constitutional. The Constitution requires laws to be passed by a majority vote in both houses of Congress and presented to the president for signature or veto. It then becomes the president's responsibility to see "that the laws be faithfully executed." If Congress wants to modify a law, technically it must go through the full process of making a law. The Supreme Court ruled legislative vetoes unconstitutional because they cut the president out of the lawmaking process (*Immigration and Naturalization Service v. Chadha* 1983). Despite this ruling, Congress continues to use legislative vetoes.

Another problem with the legislative veto is that it limits Congress's policy-making role. The legislative veto reduces Congress to a reactive body: it defines a broad goal through legislation and leaves the specifics to executive agencies. Though Congress can block the specifics it finds objectionable, in this process the legislature is reduced to telling the bureaucracy what it cannot do, rather than telling it what to do. The result is to delegate to the bureaucracy a powerful proactive role in determining public policy.

THE PRESIDENT AND THE BUREAUCRACY The president also has several powerful tools to control the bureaucracies. As chief executive, the president is technically the chief bureaucrat. The president is the overall boss of all executive agencies, and like most bosses, the president can exercise a good deal of influence over subordinates.

The most basic tool the president has for controlling bureaucracy is the **appointment power**, which allows the president to choose a wide range of subordinates. Although the elimination of the spoils system dramatically reduced the president's ability to preferentially staff the bureaucracy, the chief executive retains the power to appoint many of the nation's top bureaucrats. These include the secretaries of all cabinet departments, various deputies and undersecretaries, and a wide variety of top-ranking positions in non-cabinet agencies—roughly 3,000 officials in all.

The main advantage of appointment power is that it allows the president to put political allies and loyalists in key administrative positions. The power of appointment presumably puts the bureaucracy under closer control of the president. There are, however, two drawbacks to this system. One, these appointees often lack experience and tend to have short tenures. As many as a third of presidential appointees spend less than 18 months on the job. High turnover makes it hard for the president to provide consistent direction to a bureaucracy. Second, the appointees sometimes "go native," which means they end up becoming advocates of their agency's interests rather than the president's agenda.

The president does not have to rely solely on appointment power to control the bureaucracy. The president also has budgeting power, which, although different

appointment power A power of the president that enables him or her to control the bureaucracy by selecting the people who will head its agencies.

from the budgeting powers of Congress, can be just as effective. Only Congress has the power to approve a budget, but the president has the responsibility of proposing the budget. A president can thus reward or punish agencies by proposing increases or cuts in the annual budget proposal. Congress can change these proposals, but even then, the president can veto an appropriations bill to block agency funding (though such an action would be considered drastic). Even if the money is appropriated over a veto, the president has some limited powers of **impoundment**, or the ability to delay approved expenditures. A president who does not want to spend money appropriated by Congress can also seek to cancel the funding by sending a "rescission message" to Congress. If both houses approve the rescission, the funds are canceled. A president does not have complete control over agency budgets but has more than enough to make any agency wary of getting into a budgetary battle with the president.

The president also has the power to issue **executive orders**, directives that have the force of law even though they are not passed by Congress. These are the equivalent of presidential legislation and are often controversial. For example, Congress was wary of President George W. Bush's faith-based initiative, which proposed to funnel federal grant money into social and community outreach organizations associated with religious groups. The proposal was controversial because it raised constitutional questions about separation of church and state. With the issue stalled in Congress, Bush issued an executive order creating the White House Office of Faith-Based and Community Initiatives. In effect, President Bush on his own authority created a government bureaucracy to run a program that Congress was not willing to formally approve. This bureaucracy outlasted Bush: it was renamed the White House Office of Faith-Based and Neighborhood Partnerships by the Obama administration and given a slightly different focus, but it did not close down.

THE JUDICIARY AND THE BUREAUCRACY The courts have a few simple tools to control the bureaucracy. As the interpreters of law, judges can declare agency regulations, rules, or actions illegal if they fail to meet the constitutional litmus test. In assessing challenges to agency rules or actions, courts pose two broad questions. The first is whether the action is consistent with **legislative intent**. In other words, the court seeks to determine whether the agency's actions are authorized by the relevant law passed by Congress. The second question is whether the action violates **standards of due process**. Even if legislative intent is being followed, courts will seek to ensure that an agency is not depriving anyone of due process guarantees given by the Constitution or the law. For example, federal courts have probably done more than any other branch of the government in restricting local, state, and federal bureaucracies from discriminating in hiring, promotion, and provision of services (Meier 1993, 163–164). In checking for due process, the courts help ensure that bureaucracy abides by core democratic principles such as political equality.

It is important to note, though, that the interest of the courts is typically not whether a bureaucratic action is efficient, effective, or fair or even whether it makes sense. Their concern is almost wholly with whether an action is legal.

impoundment The limited ability of the president to not spend money appropriated by Congress.

executive orders Directives of the president that have the same weight as law and are not voted on by Congress.

legislative intent The intention of Congress when it passes laws.

standards of due process The procedural guarantees provided to ensure fair treatment and constitutional rights.

REFORMING BUREAUCRACY

Because of their central role in the American political process, it is not surprising that bureaucracies are frequent targets of reform efforts. Pledges to change bureaucracy and make it run "more like a business" have been a perennial feature of American politics for more than a century.

Running Government Like a Business

Past efforts to reform the bureaucracy include the Hoover Commission, formed under the administration of Harry Truman and charged with identifying how to improve the efficiency and effectiveness of the bureaucracy. The Grace Commission was formed under the administration of Ronald Reagan and was charged with rooting out government inefficiency and wasteful programs. The National Performance Review was a program of President Bill Clinton's administration that was a sustained effort to "reinvent government." The notion behind reinventing government was to make government agencies more customer-oriented and more entrepreneurial (Osborne and Gaebler 1990). The administration of George W. Bush had no specific plan or program to make government more like a business, but he was the first MBA-holding businessman to become chief executive, and he staffed his administration with the elite of corporate America and ran a CEO-like White House. This was as likely a group as any to make government run more like a business. The Obama administration had no formal business-based bureaucratic reform program and was roundly criticized by various Republicans for not attempting to run government more like a business. A key element of Republican Mitt Romney's 2012 presidential campaign was his experience as a business executive, experience that he argued made him better suited to run government than Obama, who had very little experience in the private sector.

The primary problem with this focus on trying to run government like a business is that government is not a business. All of the formal reform efforts mentioned in the previous paragraph ended up having very little impact on how government is run. Business experience or credentials do not seem to make someone a better (or worse) elected executive than someone without those qualifications. Though there is a common belief that what works in the private sector will work just as well in the public sector, this belief is mostly wrong. Businesses are oriented toward efficiency and productivity, and their ultimate goal is to make money. Government agencies are oriented toward implementing the decisions of democratic governments. This basic mission is often an inherently inefficient proposition (remember all the agencies regulating the financial industry discussed earlier).

© AP Photo/Department of Homeland Security, Charles Reed

Contracting out is the process of hiring a private organization to deliver a public service or program rather than having a government bureaucracy do the job. The Corrections Corporation of America is a private company that local, state, and federal governments have hired to manage more than 60 prisons across the United States.

contracting out Hiring a private organization to deliver a public program or service.

principal–agent model A model explaining the relationship between Congress and the bureaucracy, which states that the relationship is similar to that between an employer who seeks to have work done (the principal) and an employee who does the work (the agent).

Businesses Running Government

Although efforts to make government run more like a business have, at best, had minimal success, there has been much more progress in having businesses run the government. In the past few decades, several Western democracies have sought ways to reduce the size and cost of the public sector while improving the efficiency and effectiveness of public programs. These efforts have resulted in the widespread practice of **contracting out**, or hiring a private organization rather than creating a government bureaucracy to deliver a public service.

The idea is to use the competitive leverage of the marketplace to make public policy more cost-effective. For example, the traditional approach to implementing a policy providing health-care services to the poor meant creating a program and housing it in a bureaucracy. This approach also meant hiring people and providing facilities and other resources at the public expense. Contracting out involves paying a private health care company to provide the service and eliminates the trouble and expense of hiring more government employees or constructing new buildings.

Though contracting out sounds appealing in the abstract, in practice, it has raised a number of concerns. For example, contracting out creates an accountability problem. Political scientists who have studied traditional bureaucratic arrangements have mostly concluded that the bureaucratic tail does not wag the democratic dog (Wood and Waterman 1994). The relationship between Congress, the president, and the bureaucracy can be described by a **principal–agent model**. This model, derived from rational choice theory, is based on the idea of a relationship between a boss who wants some work done (the principal) and an employee who actually does the work (the agent). A number of studies have concluded that this model is pretty much how traditional bureaucracy works. In short, bureaucracy is responsive, not just to Congress and the president, but also to the courts, to media attention, and even to broader currents of public opinion (Wood and Waterman 1994).

Yet whereas traditional bureaucratic arrangements are responsive to democratic controls, it is not clear that the same is true for companies under government contract. Given a program or responsibility by an executive or a legislature, a public agency has three basic responses: work (make every effort to accomplish the policy), shirk (devote its efforts to something else), or sabotage (work to undermine the policy). In trying to ensure that agencies work rather than shirk or sabotage, their principals (Congress and the president) are faced with an information problem. They often do not know the true abilities of a particular set of bureaucrats, and once they give them a job, it is difficult to assess how much effort the bureaucrats expend trying to do that job. These are known as the principal's problems of **adverse selection** (not knowing the abilities of an agent) and **moral hazard** (not knowing the effort of an agent). Adverse selection and moral hazard can make it difficult for a principal to judge whether an agency is working, shirking, or sabotaging a particular policy (Brehm and Gates 1997).

These problems multiply when a principal has multiple agents or an agent from whom it is hard to get information. Both of these scenarios are common in contracting out. Because contracts to deliver a public service are often given to more than one vendor, there is more opportunity for shirking. The result is not a single bureaucracy—required by law to keep records and maintain an open decision-making process—but a network of private organizations, all doing things slightly differently. Some have called this a "shadow bureaucracy," a layer of private companies that depend on government contracts. At the federal level, this shadow bureaucracy has roughly four times the number of workers than the entire public bureaucracy (Light 1999).

It is virtually impossible for government to control this shadow bureaucracy as tightly as it controls the public bureaucracy, and it is much harder to hold it accountable for its actions. Unlike public bureaucracies, for example, private companies often have private decision-making processes and are not required to keep the same sorts of paper trails as public bureaucracies. The logistics needed to keep up with all the contracting out is daunting. In 2011 the federal government's top 100 contractors entered into roughly 660,000 contract actions worth nearly $300 billion. Those contract actions exclude routine stuff such as shipping orders placed with FedEx and UPS, and keep in mind that these numbers are just for the 100 contractors that do the most business with the federal government. The total value of all contracts in 2011 was somewhere between $500 and $600 billion, and the number of contract actions ran into the millions (Federal Procurement Data System 2008). Keeping up with numbers like these in any sort of systematic way would require, well, a bureaucracy.

In addition to the accountability concerns, private sector organizations may not be any more effective or efficient than public bureaucracies. They also may increase rather than decrease the politics surrounding public programs. Big companies, for example, often seek to exert political pressure to reduce competitive bidding, which makes it harder to extract any cost savings. Using private companies also means dealing with profit motive incentives that may conflict with the public interest. Everyone has heard stories of the government paying inflated prices for all kinds of things, from screws to coffee makers. What usually gets left out of these stories is that it was a private company gouging the government by inflating prices and seeking to hide them, and a public bureaucracy exposed the fraud.

adverse selection Principal's lack of information about the abilities of an agent.

moral hazard Principal's lack of information about the effort of an agent.

CHAPTER FOURTEEN

Top Ten Takeaway Points

① Bureaucracy can be thought of as public agencies and the public programs and services they run. The main job of bureaucracy is to translate the intent of democratic institutions into action.

② Scholars of administration and organization use the term *bureaucracy* to describe a specific type of organization whose main characteristics are division of labor, hierarchy, formal rules, maintenance of files and records, and professionalization. Most large and complex organizations have these characteristics, not just public agencies.

③ Federal bureaucracies are organized in a loose hierarchy, but there is no centralized and coordinated control over all public agencies and programs. The responsibilities of federal agencies often overlap, and the agencies often have to report to multiple congressional committees. The structure of the federal bureaucracy is driven more by politics than by the need for organizational efficiency.

④ Because it has to interpret laws and make choices about how to translate them into action, bureaucracy has considerable policy-making powers. Among the most important of these is the power to make rules.

⑤ Rules are statements by a federal agency that interpret a law and prescribe the actions the agency will take to implement that law. Once finalized, rules have the power of law.

⑥ Rational choice models of bureaucracy suggest that control and accountability are critical issues for democratic political systems. Without effective accountability and control mechanisms, rational bureaucrats will serve their own interests at the expense of the public interest. Other theories of bureaucratic behavior suggest that rather than coldly calculating personal maximizing opportunities, bureaucrats search for "good enough" solutions for the problems they face. They rely on experience, habit, and values to make these decisions.

⑦ The size, responsibilities, and power of the federal bureaucracy also create a number of concerns about how to make it accountable to democratic authority. The preferred method of monitoring accountability is overhead democracy, the notion that voters will hold elected officials accountable for their actions and that public officials in turn will hold bureaucracies accountable for their actions.

⑧ Congress, the president, and the courts have a number of powerful tools to control bureaucracy and make it accountable. These include appointment of agency heads, legislative oversight, control of budgets, and judicial review.

⑨ Reform of the bureaucracy is a perennial part of the public agenda. Reform is difficult because many of the assumptions underlying these reform efforts are questionable. Government is not a business, and trying to run public programs like a business creates practical and political obstacles.

⑩ Bureaucracies are not run by democratic principles, but they play an important role in enforcing these principles for the political system. This is especially the case with political equality.

15 THE FEDERAL JUDICIARY

KEY QUESTIONS

Is judicial decision making unavoidably political decision making?

What is judicial review?

What are the democratic constraints on unelected judges' exercise of judicial power?

THOMAS PENFIELD JACKSON does not like Microsoft's business practices and is not shy about letting reporters know it. Bill Gates, he said, "was inherently without credibility" (Bazelon 2002). Antonin Scalia likes Dick Cheney; they have taken hunting trips together.

Nothing unusual here, you say? Bill Gates has platoons of critics as well as legions of admirers. Former vice president Cheney is unpopular with lots of people, but everybody has friends.

What is unusual is not the opinions people have about Gates or Cheney but who holds those opinions. Jackson was the U.S. district court judge who presided over a famous antitrust lawsuit brought against Microsoft. Scalia is a U.S. Supreme Court justice. Scalia and Cheney went duck hunting just three weeks after the Supreme Court agreed to hear a case involving Cheney's refusal to make public whether he met with energy industry officials (including the late Kenneth Lay, the disgraced Enron chief) while formulating the Bush administration's energy policy.

Most people would like to think that judges are wise and neutral, applying the law impartially without prejudice or bias. Yet if someone you believed to be a self-serving prevaricator insisted he was innocent of some wrongdoing, could you objectively assess his claim? How would you feel about making a decision that could potentially expose a close friend to public ridicule and perhaps irreparably harm her career? Might the friendship sway your decision, at least a little?

It is hard to ignore your beliefs and values in answering such questions. This is not simply a matter of bias or prejudice but part and parcel of being a human being. And that's the point: not that Jackson and Scalia were biased but that they are human.

They have likes and dislikes, with strong points of view on certain issues. Can we honestly expect them to ignore their own feelings and beliefs simply because they wear a black robe to work?

Most Americans would like the answer to be yes. Judges are expected to make decisions based on the rule of law, not on partisan fealty, ideological prejudice, personal loyalty, or fear of political retribution. This is why judicial independence is a prized value in the American political system. Federal judges are appointed for life, and that job security is designed to make it easier for people such as Jackson and Scalia to uphold the law, even when it means going against political or personal expectations.

Yet Americans also want judges to be accountable for unpopular decisions. At some level, we recognize that judges are subject to the same range of opinions and biases that we all are, but we do not want judges caving into political or personal pressure. We want them to stand firm for the core democratic principles embedded in law, even when it is the unpopular thing to do. On the other hand, we do not want them using their independence to play favorites from the bench. How do we reconcile independence with accountability?

This question is critical because the judiciary is a political branch of government. It is the job of a judge, after all, to judge—in other words, to decide who gets what. Judges' decisions have affected tax rates, where a child can attend school, and whether a woman has a right to an abortion. A judicial decision ultimately decided the 2000 presidential election. These are all fundamentally political issues with plenty of room for disagreement about what is or is not constitutional or about what does or does not violate the core values of democracy.

Given the central role of courts as interpreters of the law, and recognizing that judges are political decision makers who are far from infallible, understanding the role of the judicial branch in the American political system is essential to assessing how well that system is delivering on the promise of democracy. When they interpret the Constitution, the courts are effectively put in the position of deciding how to uphold that promise. This chapter provides a basic introduction to the federal courts. It covers the nature of judicial power in the political system, the organization and structure of federal courts, who staffs the federal bench, how judges are selected, the power judges hold, and how all this fits into and affects the promise of democracy.

THE CONCEPT OF THE FEDERAL JUDICIARY

The purpose of the federal judiciary in the United States is to serve as the ultimate umpire in the democratic political process. The term *judicial* is related to the concept of *just,* meaning "legal right" or fair[1] (Ayto 1990, 309, 310). Hence, a **judiciary** is a system of courts and judges concerned with administration of justice. The administration of justice involves resolving legal disputes, and to achieve justice, judges' decisions are supposed to be fair and impartial.

As we learned in chapter 1, politics is a process to resolve conflict about who gets what, when, and how, and a democracy is a government that makes decisions consistent with the core democratic principles of political freedom, political equality, and majority rule. But how does a democracy resolve conflicts between core values? In the United States, it is the job of the judiciary to help resolve these conflicts, and the job is not easy. Judges are expected to simultaneously uphold the legitimate will of the majority as expressed in law and uphold political freedom and equality by protecting the liberties of minorities from infringement by tyrannical majorities.

How can judges make impartial decisions when the disputes they must resolve are fundamentally political? The short answer is that judicial power is political power. The framers of the Constitution included provisions designed to insulate judges from political influences. Judges often claim that their decisions are not political and that they don't make the law; they merely *find* the law. Chief Justice John Marshall explained in 1824,

> Courts are the mere instruments of the law. . . . When they are said to exercise a discretion, it is . . . exercised in discerning the course prescribed by law; and, when that is discerned, it is the duty of the court to follow it. Judicial power is never exercised for the purpose of giving effect to the will of the judge, always for the purpose of giving effect . . . to the will of the law. (*Osborn v. Bank of the United States* 1824)

Political scientists refer to this claim as the "myth of judicial objectivity." It is a useful myth; it helps maintain the legitimacy of the courts and protects judicial independence. But it is a myth nonetheless. As we shall see, politics influences every aspect of the judicial process.

---

[1] *OED Online,* n.v. "judicial," adj. and n., http://www.oed.com/ (accessed October 25, 2012).

judiciary A system of courts and judges concerned with administration of justice.

THE JURISDICTION OF FEDERAL COURTS

The term **judicial power** refers to the authority of courts to interpret and apply the law in particular cases. Judicial power is fundamentally political power. The limits and conditions under which courts exercise this power—that is, the types of cases and controversies they can hear—constitute **jurisdiction**. The jurisdiction of federal courts is defined by the Constitution, by laws passed by Congress, and by the courts themselves.

Jurisdiction Defined in the Constitution

The general jurisdiction of the federal courts is succinctly set forth in Article III, Section 2 of the Constitution. Two words used there, *cases* and *controversies,* have been taken to mean that litigation heard by the federal courts must involve an actual dispute in which real people suffer real harm. In other words, courts do not decide hypothetical cases about the interpretation of a statute or its constitutionality. Federal judges cannot render advisory opinions about how or whether a particular law should be enforced. The judiciary is a powerful but passive political actor, exercising its powers only when someone who has actually been harmed by the provisions of a law or a government act brings a constitutional issue before it by means of a lawsuit.

A case brought by a legitimate plaintiff can be heard by a federal court if it satisfies one of two general requirements. The first concerns the subject matter of the suit: it must be litigation involving the U.S. Constitution, a federal law, a treaty, or admiralty and maritime matters. Federal courts have jurisdiction to hear cases brought by private citizens challenging the constitutionality of state or federal laws. Criminal defendants who claim that they were denied individual rights protected by the Constitution can also have their cases heard in federal court.

The second requirement concerns the parties involved in the suit: the Constitution gives certain parties special status to file claims in federal courts. If the United States is suing or being sued, the federal courts can hear the case. The federal courts have jurisdiction over cases affecting ambassadors and other agents of foreign governments and over disputes between foreign governments or foreign citizens and a state or one of its citizens. Interstate conflicts also fall within the federal court's jurisdiction. These conflicts include litigation between the states, between citizens of different states, between citizens of the same state who claim lands under grants of different states, and between a state and a citizen of another state.

Of these cases, suits between citizens of different states are quite numerous and consume a great deal of federal courts' time. In order to keep minor disputes out of federal courts, Congress has passed statutes requiring these cases to involve at least $75,000 before the federal courts have jurisdiction.

judicial power The authority of courts to interpret and apply the law in particular cases.

jurisdiction The types of cases a given court is permitted to hear.

Original and Appellate Jurisdiction

There are two general types of courts, each of which has jurisdiction over fundamentally different types of cases. **Courts of original jurisdiction** are the trial courts that hear cases the first time and make determinations of fact, law, and whether the plaintiff or the defendant wins. The federal district courts are courts of original jurisdiction in the federal court system; these district courts try cases involving alleged violations of federal criminal laws and certain civil lawsuits under federal court jurisdiction. **Courts of appellate jurisdiction** review the decisions of lower courts that are appealed. The U.S. circuit courts of appeal have jurisdiction to hear appeals of decisions made by federal district courts and certain government agencies.

Courts typically have either original or appellate jurisdiction. The U.S. Supreme Court is unique in that it has both. Article III, Section 2 of the Constitution gives the Supreme Court original jurisdiction in cases involving ambassadors, consuls, and other public ministers and in cases in which a state is a party. The Supreme Court's appellate jurisdiction is defined by Congress.

The Power of Congress to Define Jurisdiction of Federal Courts

With few exceptions, Congress sets the jurisdictional boundaries of all federal courts. Congress can take the following actions:

- Forbid courts to handle a certain type of case.
- Allow state and federal courts to exercise concurrent jurisdiction (that is, allow both state and federal courts to hear a particular type of case).
- Assign exclusive jurisdiction; for example, cases involving violation of federal criminal law must be heard in a federal court.

In addition to its power to allocate cases between federal and state courts, Congress also decides at which level in the federal judiciary a matter will be heard. Congress can establish lower courts, determine what cases they can hear, and regulate what matters initially tried in lower courts the Supreme Court can review.

Jurisdiction Determined by Judicial Interpretation

The courts themselves also can define their own power and jurisdiction. The most important power of federal courts in the American political system is the power of **judicial review**, or the authority to review lower-court decisions and to declare laws and actions of public officials unconstitutional. The Supreme Court asserted this power in the case of ***Marbury v. Madison*** (1803), discussed later in this chapter. Although the power of judicial review gives courts considerable influence in

courts of original jurisdiction Trial courts that hear cases for the first time and determine issues of fact and law.

courts of appellate jurisdiction Courts that review the decisions of lower courts.

judicial review The power to review decisions of the lower courts and to determine the constitutionality of laws and actions of public officials.

Marbury v. Madison The 1803 case in which the Court asserted the power of judicial review.

shaping public policy, where and how that power is exercised is constrained by both the Constitution and Congress.

THE STRUCTURE AND ORGANIZATION OF FEDERAL COURTS

The Constitution leaves much of the structure and organization of federal courts to Congress. It calls for "one Supreme Court, and . . . such inferior courts as the Congress may . . . establish" (Article III, Section 1). Congress has created two additional levels of federal courts: district courts and courts of appeals. Congress has also established several specialized courts, such as the Court of Federal Claims and the U.S. Court of International Trade.

Statutes passed by Congress determine the number of judges serving on each court, including the Supreme Court. The Supreme Court has had nine justices since 1869, but the number has varied from as few as five in 1789 to as many as ten in 1863. The number of lower-court judges is determined mainly by caseloads, so that areas with more cases filed have more judges.

The **Judicial Conference**, a committee of district and appellate court judges chaired by the chief justice of the Supreme Court, reviews the needs of the federal judiciary and makes recommendations to Congress. Congress periodically responds to these requests and passes legislation creating new judgeships. This most recently happened in 2003, when Congress created 15 new district court judgeships.

Although the need for more judges to handle an increasing caseload is the primary motivation for expanding the number of judgeships, political considerations inevitably come into play. One study shows that even after the need for new judges has been established, Congress is unlikely to create new judgeships if different parties control Congress and the presidency or if it is late in the president's term (Bond 1980). The reasons are purely political—the majority party in Congress does not want to give a president of the opposing party the opportunity to appoint fellow party members to new judgeships. If a presidential election is coming up, the opposing party in Congress delays expanding the number of judges in the hope that its candidate will win.

The District Courts

Judicial Conference A committee of district and appellate judges that reviews the needs of the federal judiciary and makes recommendations to Congress.

The U.S. district courts are trial courts of original jurisdiction. Although they hear certain classes of cases that are removed from state courts to federal jurisdiction and also enforce some of the actions of federal administrative agencies, these cases are not considered to have been appealed (Abraham 1993, 157–158).

District courts like this one in Albuquerque, New Mexico, deal with antitrust suits, people accused of breaking federal criminal laws, bankruptcy proceedings, and disputes between citizens of different states involving automobile accidents, breaches of contract, and labor cases—among many other matters. This array of cases is heard by more than 650 judges located in the 94 district courts. Every state has at least one district, and each district court has at least one judge. District judges are officials of the federal government and enforce federal laws and the U.S. Constitution, but they are oriented to states and localities.

The district courts are the workhorses of the federal judicial system. Approximately 90 percent of federal cases begin and end in the district courts. In these courts, spirited legal battles occur involving opposing attorneys, witnesses, and possibly a jury. (Parties in federal court often waive the right to a jury trial and have the judge make the decision.) A single judge presides over the courtroom.

District courts deal with a wide variety of matters. This is where the federal government brings antitrust suits and prosecutes people accused of breaking federal criminal laws. For example, Zacarias Moussaoui, suspected of being the "twentieth hijacker" in the September 11, 2001, terrorist attacks, was tried in a federal district court. Bankruptcy proceedings make up a large portion of district court dockets, and the courts also hear disputes between citizens of different states involving automobile accidents, breaches of contract, and labor cases—among many other matters.

This dizzying array of cases is heard by nearly 700 judges located in 94 district courts. Every state has at least one district, and 24 states have two, three, or four districts. No district crosses state lines. Each district court has at least one judge; the Southern District of New York has the most judges—28. The number of judges serving in a district is determined largely by caseload: districts with heavy caseloads need more judges to process the cases in a reasonable amount of time.

Although district judges are officials of the federal government and enforce federal laws and the U.S. Constitution, they are oriented to states and localities (see Figure 15.1). Congress sets the number and boundaries of judicial districts, and the decision to draw districts that do not cross state lines has political implications. By political tradition, district court judges are selected from the states in which they serve, and they live there after appointment. Thus, federal district judges have strong political and social ties to the states in which they serve (Richardson and

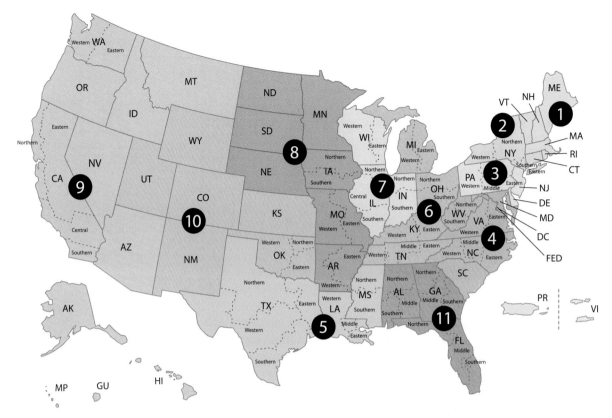

FIGURE 15.1 Federal District Courts and Courts of Appeals

Source: http://www.uscourts.gov/uscourts/images/CircuitMap.pdf.

Vines 1970, 93–98). District court judges occasionally are assigned to hear cases in other districts in order to limit the influence of local political culture on the judge's decision. For example, it was a visiting North Dakota district court judge who issued the 1957 injunction prohibiting Arkansas state officials from interfering with racial integration of Little Rock schools. For the most part, however, district court judges preside over disputes arising in their own local areas.

The Courts of Appeals

The U.S. courts of appeals have only appellate jurisdiction, and they serve as the major appellate tribunals in the federal court system. They review decisions in civil and criminal cases initially heard in federal district courts and the orders and decisions of federal administrative units, particularly the independent regulatory agencies. Of the approximately 10 percent of cases decided by the district courts that are appealed, about 90 percent end in the federal courts of appeals. Thus, only a tiny proportion—about 1 percent—of federal cases go to the U.S. Supreme Court for final disposition.

There are nearly 200 appellate court judges serving on 13 courts of appeals, called circuits, located in various parts of the United States.[2] The size of the courts ranges from 6 to 28 judges depending on the caseload in the circuit. As shown in Figure 15.1, 11 of the appellate courts are arranged regionally, grouping three or more states into a circuit. A court of appeals hears appeals from the district courts located within its circuit. The Twelfth Circuit is the U.S. Court of Appeals for the District of Columbia, which covers the nation's capital. It is one of the most important courts of appeal because it deals with challenges to the rules and regulations issued by most federal government agencies. The Thirteenth Circuit is the Federal Circuit, which is also located in Washington, DC. Unlike all other circuits, however, its jurisdiction is not based on geography. This court has national jurisdiction to hear appeals from specialized federal courts (such as patent cases). Since appellate courts hear appeals from federal courts in several states, appellate court judges tend to be less closely tied to particular states and localities than their counterparts in district courts.

The courts of appeals are **collegial courts** in which a group of judges decides the case based on a review of the record of the lower-court trial. There is no jury at the appellate court level, and the appeals court does not make determinations of fact. Instead, the appellate court decides by majority vote whether the trial court made any legal or procedural errors that would justify a reversal or modification of the lower court's decision.

To expedite the considerable caseload, cases are usually decided by a panel of three judges, allowing several cases to be heard at the same time by different three-judge panels. The chief judge, who is the most senior judge under the age of 65, appoints the panels. Appointments are made randomly to even out workloads and to ensure that the same judges do not always sit together on the same panel. These procedures are intended to prevent a chief judge from stacking a panel with judges who will decide a case in a particular way. The U.S. Court of Appeals for the Eleventh Circuit uses a computerized random assignment process to set the composition of every panel a year in advance (Tarr 2003, 42).

On application of the parties involved in a suit or of the judges themselves, a case can be heard **en banc**—that is, by all of the judges in the circuit. This occurs in fewer than 5 percent of cases; it is restricted to questions of exceptional importance or cases in which the circuit court feels that a full tribunal is necessary to secure uniformity in its decisions or compliance with a controversial decision.

The U.S. Supreme Court

The U.S. Supreme Court sits at the top of the legal hierarchy, and it has both original and appellate jurisdiction (see Figure 15. 2). In practice, it has almost complete

collegial courts Courts in which groups of judges decide cases based on a review of the record of the lower-court trial.

en banc A procedure in which all the members of a U.S. court of appeals hear and decide a case.

---

[2] The courts of appeals were originally staffed by Supreme Court justices who would travel to various regions of the country to hear cases. This practice was called "making the circuit," and it is where the name came from.

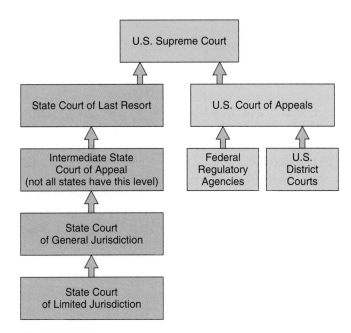

FIGURE 15.2 Structure of the U.S. Judicial System

Source: Adapted by the authors from "Comparing Federal and State Courts", http://www.uscourts.gov/EducationalResources/FederalCourtBasics/CourtStructure/ComparingFederalAndStateCourts.aspx

discretion over the cases it hears, accepting mainly those that have broad implications for the law or government action. The Supreme Court's appellate jurisdiction is regulated by Congress, which has established two major sources of cases for the nation's highest tribunal: (1) appeals from the U.S. courts of appeals and (2) appeals from the highest courts of the individual states. Cases from the U.S. courts of appeals represent the final attempt to gain satisfaction by parties unhappy with decisions made in lower federal courts. Cases from state courts involve controversies that jump from state court systems to the federal court system.

The Supreme Court is the only federal court that can hear appeals from a state court and then only if there is an important constitutional issue involved. Because of its federal structure (see chapter 3), the United States has dual judicial systems: the federal courts deal with federal law, and the state courts with state law. Federal and state courts hold concurrent jurisdiction over some matters, so there is some overlap between the two systems, but state courts are not subordinate to federal courts. State courts enforce state laws using their own legal structure, procedures, and personnel, and they independently exercise the power of judicial review in both original and appellate jurisdictions. If a case involves state matters, it starts in state court and stays in the state court system until it is finally resolved. Each state judicial system has a court of last resort (a state supreme court or its equivalent) that represents the highest level to which a case involving a question of state law may be carried.

The only way a state court case can go beyond the state's court of last resort is if the case raises a federal question. Appeals of such cases go from the state court of last resort directly to the U.S. Supreme Court. For example, a criminal case that raises the issue of whether a state law restricting obscene materials violates an individual's First Amendment right of free speech raises an important federal question. Such a case could be appealed to the Supreme Court to rule on the constitutionality of the state law.

The justification for permitting appeals from the state supreme courts to the U.S. Supreme Court is that when state courts interpret their own constitutions, they are also interpreting the U.S. Constitution. A state constitution can provide its citizens greater protection of the basic rights guaranteed by the U.S. Constitution, but it cannot restrict those rights. Making the U.S. Supreme Court the final arbiter of all questions involving the U.S. Constitution helps ensure that its guarantees are uniformly interpreted and applied. In essence, this link makes the U.S. Supreme Court the ultimate umpire of the federal system.

The Supreme Court exercises discretion over its caseload by choosing relatively few cases for review each year. Of the approximately 9,000 cases appealed to the Supreme Court in a typical year, the Court will decide about 100 on the merits, meaning the Court will actually discuss the cases and vote on decisions. Only about 70 cases will get a full written opinion. Thus, more than 99 percent of cases are disposed of with no written decision explaining the Court's reasoning in reaching that decision.[3] Generally, the Court picks cases that raise important constitutional issues or questions of substantial political importance, or on which different appellate circuits have issued conflicting rulings. The Court formally exercises its discretionary powers over what cases to hear by issuing a **writ of certiorari**,[4] which is granted according to the **rule of four**—that is, four of the nine justices must vote to review a case.

Like the courts of appeals, the Supreme Court is a collegial body, but it does not divide itself into separate panels to hear different cases. Justices have taken the position that the Constitution refers to one Supreme Court, not several, and that all judges should therefore participate in each case. The Court hears cases during a 36-week session from October to June. When the Court is in session, it hears oral arguments from attorneys representing opposing sides of the cases chosen for full hearings. Each side gets 30 minutes to make its case. This time limit is strictly enforced, but the justices frequently interrupt the presentations with questions. The Court occasionally allots more time for unusually complex and important cases. For example, the Court scheduled a total six hours of oral arguments spread over three days on the case challenging the constitutionality of the health care reform law (*National Federation of Independent Business v. Sebelius* 2012).

writ of certiorari An order from a higher court to a lower court ordering the lower court to turn over transcripts and documents of a case for review. The U.S. Supreme Court formally exercises its discretionary powers over what cases to hear by issuing a writ of certiorari, which is granted according to the rule of four.

rule of four Rule according to which four Supreme Court justices must agree to hear a case.

---

[3] When the Court does not accept a case for review, the decision of the last court to rule stands.

[4] A small number of cases get to the Supreme Court through other procedures, including through writ of appeal or by "extraordinary writ," such as habeas corpus. Although some of these cases can be appealed to the Supreme Court as a matter of right, in practice the Court has discretion about whether to hear these cases as well.

Hearing oral presentations is a relatively minor part of the Supreme Court's business; the overwhelming proportion of the Court's work takes place behind the scenes. The justices spend most of their time reading and studying cases and discussing them with their colleagues and their law clerks, who are recent graduates of the nation's top law schools.

The Court decides the cases it has heard in **conference**. Only the nine justices are permitted to attend the conference; clerks and secretaries are not allowed in the room. The justices begin the conference by shaking hands and taking their assigned seats around the conference table. The chief justice presides over the meeting and sets the agenda. Part of the conference is devoted to consideration of petitions for review; under the rule of four, four justices must vote to accept a case for full oral argument.

The next order of business is to discuss and vote on the cases previously argued before the Court. Traditionally, the chief justice speaks first, framing the issues presented by the case. The associate justice with the longest service on the court speaks next, and so on, with the most junior justice speaking last. The justices generally indicate how they will vote during their presentations in conference, although these votes are tentative and sometimes change during the opinion-writing stage.

After the most junior justice has spoken, the justices vote. The outcome of a case is decided by a majority vote, meaning that five of nine justices must support a position for it to become an official Court ruling. The most important decision following this vote is who gets to write the opinion announcing the Court's decision and the reasons behind it. If the chief justice votes with the majority, he or she decides who will write the opinion. If the case is a major one, the chief justice may assume the responsibility, as Chief Justice Roberts did in *National Federation of Independent Business v. Sebelius* (2012), upholding the constitutionality of most of the health care reform law. But opinions are usually assigned to spread the workload among the nine justices. If the chief justice is not on the prevailing side, the most senior associate justice on the prevailing side makes the assignment.

The assignment of writing an opinion is often a delicate political decision. A controversial opinion may be assigned to the justice whose views are closest to those of the minority, the idea being that he or she may be able to win the minority justices over to the majority's side. This tactic can be helpful in a controversial case when the justices want maximum public acceptance, when a premium is placed on a unanimous or nearly unanimous decision by the Court.

The assignment of an opinion does not end the collegial process. Negotiation may continue as the opinion is drafted and redrafted so that a maximum number of justices will join it. The author may even adopt the suggestions and reasoning of other justices in order to attract their votes. But it is often not possible to settle differences. Most cases heard by the Supreme Court are controversial, and the justices typically hold strong views, so a unanimous decision expressed in a single opinion is often not possible.

Until the 1930s, more than 80 percent of Supreme Court decisions were unanimous. Consensus on the Court declined sharply from 1930 to the 1950s, leveling off at an average of about one-in-three unanimous decisions until the 1990s. Since

conference The meeting of Supreme Court justices where they decide which cases they will hear.

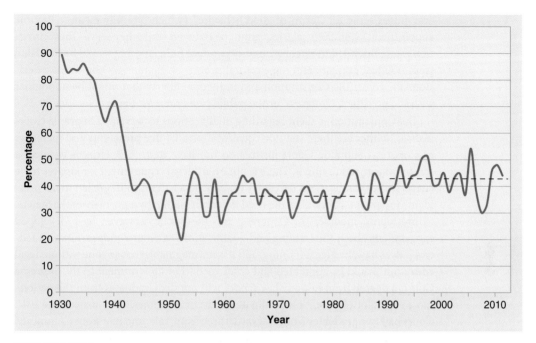

FIGURE 15.3 **Unanimous Supreme Court Decisions**

Source: Constructed by the authors from data at Epstein et al. (2007); data from 2007–2011 from http://www.scotusblog.com/statistics/.

the 1990s, an average of around 43 percent of decisions have been unanimous (see Figure 15.3).

There are four types of opinions. Most decisions are **majority opinions** in which five or more justices agree on both which side wins and the reason for the decision. **Concurring opinions** are sometimes written by justices who agree with the result reached by the majority opinion but not with the reasoning behind it. If a majority of justices cannot agree on both the outcome and the reasons, the case may be decided by a **plurality opinion** in which a majority support the outcome, but the lack of majority agreement on the reason may leave the meaning of the ruling unclear. **Dissenting opinions** are issued by justices in the minority; they disagree not only with the reasoning behind the Court's decision but also with the result. Dissenters do not always write dissenting opinions.

THE SELECTION AND BACKGROUND OF FEDERAL JUDGES

Article III, Section 1 of the Constitution provides for all federal judges to be nominated by the president and confirmed by the Senate. Once confirmed, fed-

majority opinion A decision of the Supreme Court in which five or more of the justices are in agreement on the ruling on which party to the dispute should win a case and the reason that party should win.

concurring opinion An opinion written by a Supreme Court justice who agrees with the ruling of the Court but not the reason behind it.

plurality opinion A decision of the Supreme Court in which a majority of the Court agrees on a decision, but there is no majority agreement on the reason for the decision.

dissenting opinions An opinion written by a Supreme Court justice who is in the minority that presents the logic and thinking of the justices who opposed the majority opinion.

eral judges serve for "terms of good behavior" (which typically means a lifetime appointment), and their salaries cannot be reduced while they serve. These provisions were intended to establish an independent judiciary that would be insulated from political pressure and the electoral process so that judges could make decisions to protect the Constitution and individual liberty that might be unpopular with the president, Congress, or the public (see *Federalist* Papers Number 80).

The Constitution is silent regarding qualifications to serve as a Supreme Court justice. Neither are there statutory qualifications. Unlike presidents and members of Congress, Supreme Court justices do not have to be U.S. citizens or meet a minimum age requirement. There is not even a legal requirement for justices to be lawyers. The qualifications necessary to serve on a federal court are left to the president's judgment, checked by the need for confirmation by a majority of the Senate.

Presidents, members of Congress, and the public, however, have developed expectations about the training and qualifications of federal judges. First, all federal judges have had legal training, and it is unimaginable that anyone without legal education would be appointed and confirmed.[5] For appointment to the Supreme Court, a degree from just any law school will not do. Graduates from the nation's most prestigious law schools dominate the list of Supreme Court justices: the 2012 Court had five graduates from Harvard, three from Yale, and one from Columbia.[6]

A second quality that federal judges have in common is a career in public service. Almost all Supreme Court justices engaged in public service or politics prior to their appointment. Through such activity, they developed ties to presidents and senators who later influenced their appointments. District court judges, for example, have been referred to as "lawyers who know a United States senator." As might be expected, one of the most prevalent kinds of previous public service is that connected with the courts themselves. Many federal judges have served as state judges or district attorneys, and judges serving in higher federal courts often served on lower federal courts.

Finally, although there are no legal age requirements, it is unlikely that individuals who are very young or very old would be considered. Viable candidates for appointment to the federal judiciary, especially the Supreme Court, are those who have distinguished themselves in the legal profession, politics, and public service—and successful careers take time. But at the same time, because presidents want to make appointments that will affect the Court for a long time, they are unlikely to select individuals of advanced age whose service may be cut short by illness or retirement.

---

[5] Early in the nation's history, individuals did not have to attend law school to be admitted to the bar and practice law. Instead, they would "read" the law under the tutorship of a member of the bar for several years. Only 59 of the 110 Supreme Court justices attended law school, and it was not until 1957 that all the justices had law degrees.

[6] The elite education starts before law school. Most of the current Supreme Court justices got their undergraduate degrees at the same elite schools: Princeton (three), Stanford (two), Harvard (one), and Cornell (one). Justice Clarence Thomas attended a Catholic school, Holy Cross, before going to Yale for his law degree; Justice Antonin Scalia attended Georgetown before going to Harvard for his law degree.

A consequence of these expectations is that judicial appointees tend to be disproportionately white, male, and wealthy. As Figure 15.4 shows, President Jimmy Carter (1977–1980) was the first president to appoint significant numbers of women, African Americans, and Latinos to the federal courts (i.e., district courts and courts of appeal). Presidents who followed also increased diversity on the federal bench, but in varying degrees. Bill Clinton made one of the more concerted presidential efforts to increase diversity on the federal bench; during his two terms, Clinton appointed a larger percentage of women, African Americans, and Latinos than any of his predecessors. George W. Bush appointed somewhat fewer women and less than half as many African Americans as Clinton. But Bush appointed a larger percentage of Latinos than any previous president, and only Carter and Clinton appointed more African Americans. Nearly one-half of President Obama's judicial appointments have been women, and more than one-fourth have been African American; the proportion of Latino judges appointed is similar to the proportion under Bush and Clinton. Very few Asian Americans have been appointed to the federal bench. Presidents from Johnson to Bush appointed an average of less than 1 percent. In contrast, more than 10 percent of President Obama's judicial appointments have been Asian American. He nominated nine Asian Americans during his first year in office. Among them was Goodwin Liu, the son of Taiwanese immigrants, who earned his law degree from Yale and became associate dean and professor of law at UC Berkeley School of

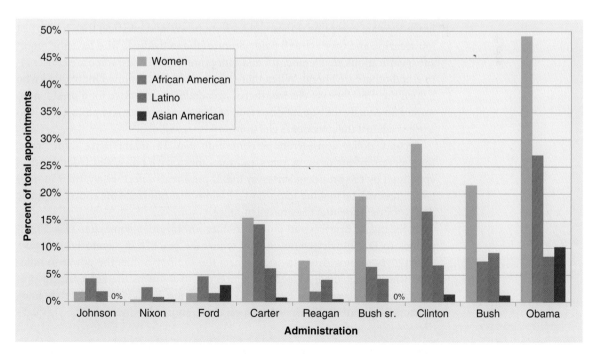

FIGURE 15.4 **Appointments of Women and Minorities to the Federal Courts**

Source: Figure constructed by the authors from Stanley and Niemi (2011), 274–276.

Law. Obama nominated Liu to serve on the Ninth Circuit Court of Appeals. There was speculation that this appointment was meant to groom him for the Supreme Court (Santiago 2010). If so, the strategy failed. A Republican filibuster blocked a confirmation vote, and Liu withdrew in May 2011.

Thus, the pool of prospective Supreme Court justices is limited to the small proportion of the population with legal training from (mostly) the elite universities, in the prime of distinguished careers in law and politics, and with the appropriate character and integrity. When appointments are made from among this relatively elite pool, political considerations inevitably influence presidents' choices. These political considerations include party affiliation and philosophy and balancing the representativeness of the Court.

Party Affiliation and Philosophy

The most important consideration in making appointments to the Supreme Court and the lower federal courts is the nominee's political party and philosophy. With few exceptions, presidents appoint individuals of their own political party who share their political philosophy. Of the 112 justices who have served on the Supreme Court, 90 percent have been of the same party as the president who appointed them. At least two considerations explain the importance of party in making appointments to the federal judiciary. First, old-fashioned patronage considerations lead presidents to appoint members of their own party. Federal judgeships are exceptional jobs: judges have power and prestige; they have great job security; and they are well paid.[7] Some of the individuals who have the requisite qualifications are Democrats, and others are Republicans; some are conservative, and others are liberal. When there are many highly qualified individuals who helped the president get elected, there is generally no incentive for a president to reward an equally well-qualified person of the opposite party and philosophy who worked against the president's election.

Second, policy considerations come into play. Presidents have term limits: they serve for four or eight years and then must leave office. But federal judges appointed by the president serve for life. If presidents select wisely, their judicial appointees will be making important decisions that influence the course of public policy for decades after they have left office.

In the case of district court judges, another consideration comes into play. Nominations to U.S. district courts usually follow the practice of **senatorial courtesy**, which gives senators from the state where the vacancy occurs the power to influence who is appointed. Indeed, the practice actually turns the appointment process around in these cases. Because no district court boundary crosses state lines, senators from states with vacancies expect to recommend individuals who are quali-

senatorial courtesy The practice that allows senators from states with federal district court vacancies to recommend individuals for the president to nominate. If the president fails to follow the home state senators' recommendations, a slighted senator may block the nomination from coming to the floor for a confirmation vote.

---

[7] The chief justice of the Supreme Court earns $223,500, and associate justices earn $213,900; appellate court and district court judges earn $184,500 and $174,000, respectively (as of January 2008). These salaries are lower than those of lawyers at the nation's top law firms, which is where most federal judges would work if they were not judges. Many take significant cuts in pay to become federal judges.

CHAPTER 15 **THE FEDERAL JUDICIARY**

fied and available for the job. The president retains veto power, ruling out nominees who are politically offensive or who fail to meet minimum qualifications. But if the president fails to follow home state senators' recommendations, a slighted senator may object to the nomination and prevent it from coming to the floor for a confirmation vote. Traditionally, senatorial courtesy worked within a party, and opposite party senators could not block a nomination. The partisan nature of senatorial courtesy tended to reinforce same-party appointments. Only in unusual circumstances would a senator recommend that the president appoint someone of the opposite party.

The procedure changed during the Clinton administration. The Senate Judiciary Committee would not hold confirmation hearings on judicial nominees who did not have approval of both home state senators, regardless of party. This change allowed Republican senators to block many of President Clinton's judicial nominees. The procedure changed again after President G. W. Bush took office in 2001. The Judiciary Committee went back to the practice of requiring approval of only one home state senator (Edsall 2001; Masters 2001). This change made it more difficult for Democrats to block Bush's judicial nominees.

Senatorial courtesy is less of a consideration for appointments to appellate courts that hear cases from several states. There is, however, a tendency for each state in the circuit to get a certain number of judges, and the senators from those states do exercise some influence (Masters 2001). Senatorial courtesy does not come into play for appointments to the Supreme Court because the Court hears cases from the entire nation.

Cross-party appointments occur occasionally to further a political purpose. One such case occurred in 1985, when Republican senator Phil Gramm of Texas exercised senatorial courtesy to get President Ronald Reagan to appoint Texas Democratic representative Sam B. Hall to a federal judgeship. Gramm engineered this cross-party appointment in the hope that a Republican would win the special election in Hall's district, which was populated with conservative Democrats. Although the Democrats held on to the seat, political motivations accounted for this cross-party exercise of senatorial courtesy.

When presidents cross party lines for Supreme Court appointments, they typically choose individuals who share their political ideology. Republican president William Howard Taft, for example, appointed two southern Democrats, Horace Lurton and Joseph R. Lamar, to the Court in 1910 and 1911, respectively. Both men were Taft's personal friends and shared his conservative ideology. Taft also hoped that the appointment of Lurton, a Confederate Army veteran, would encourage southern political leaders who held key leadership positions in Congress to help him get his legislative program passed (Abraham 1993, 67).

Balancing the Representativeness of the Court

Other political criteria are less important than party and come into play only sporadically. Concerns about balancing the representativeness of the Supreme Court occasionally influence appointments. The Supreme Court is not intended to be a representative institution. In fact, the Court is often in the position of declaring

MILESTONES OF JUDICIAL SERVICE

The following is an excerpt listing some important firsts in judicial appointments.

Oldest Judges

- The oldest serving federal judge was Joseph W. Woodrough, who was serving as a senior judge of the U.S. Court of Appeals for the Eighth Circuit when he died at the age of 104 on October 2, 1977.
- The oldest serving active judge was Giles S. Rich, who served on the U.S. Court of Appeals for the Federal Circuit until his death at the age of 95 in June 1999.
- The oldest serving Supreme Court justice was Oliver Wendell Holmes, who was 90 years, 10 months when he retired on January 12, 1932.

Youngest Judges

- The youngest federal judge was Thomas Jefferson Boynton, who was 25 when Abraham Lincoln issued him a recess appointment to the U.S. District Court for the Southern District of Florida on October 19, 1863.
- The youngest judge appointed to a U.S. court of appeals was William Howard Taft, who was 34 when he was commissioned a judge of the Sixth Circuit Court of Appeals on March 17, 1892.
- The youngest justice on the Supreme Court was Joseph Story, who was 32 when he received his commission on November 18, 1811.

Longest Serving Judges

- Joseph W. Woodrough served a record 61 years as a federal judge. He served on the U.S. District Court for the District of Nebraska from 1916 to 1933 and on the U.S. Court of Appeals for the Eighth Circuit from 1933 until 1977. He took senior status in 1961.
- Henry Potter was the longest serving judge on a single court and the longest serving active judge. He served on the U.S. District Courts for North Carolina from 1802 to 1857. He previously served on the U.S. Circuit Court for the Fifth Circuit from May of 1801 until April of 1802.
- The longest serving judge on a U.S. court of appeals was Albert B. Maris, who served on the U.S. Court of Appeals for the Third Circuit from June of 1938 until his death in February 1989. Maris, who took senior status in 1958, also served on the U.S. District Court for the Eastern District of Pennsylvania from 1936 to 1938.
- William O. Douglas was the longest serving Supreme Court justice. He sat on the Court from 1939 to 1975.

First Women Judges

- Florence Allen was the first woman to serve on a U.S. court of appeals. She was appointed to the U.S. Circuit Court of Appeals for the Sixth Circuit in 1934.
- Burnita Shelton Matthews became the first woman to serve on a U.S. district court when Harry Truman issued her a recess appointment to

the district court for the District of Columbia in October 1949. The Senate confirmed her nomination in April 1950.

- Sandra Day O'Connor was the first woman to serve as a Justice of the Supreme Court of the United States. She was appointed in 1981.
- Elena Kagan was the fourth woman to serve on the Supreme Court, but her appointment was the first time that two consecutive vacancies were filled with a woman—Sonia Sotomayor was appointed in 2009; Kagan was appointed to fill the next vacancy in 2010.

First African American Judges

- William Henry Hastie became the first African American to serve as a judge when he was appointed to the U.S. Court of Appeals for the Third Circuit in 1950. Hastie had served a fixed term as judge of the U.S. District Court for the Virgin Islands from 1937 to 1939.
- The first African American to serve on U.S. district court as a judge. .. was James B. Parsons, who was appointed to the U.S. District Court for the Northern District of Illinois in 1961.
- Thurgood Marshall was the first African American justice on the Supreme Court of the United States. He was appointed in 1967. Marshall previously served as a judge on the U.S. Court of Appeals for the Second Circuit.

First Latino Judge

- Reynaldo G. Garza became the first Latino federal judge when he was appointed to the U.S. District Court for the Southern District of Texas in 1961. Garza also became the first Latino judge on a U.S. Court of Appeals when he was appointed to the Fifth Circuit court of appeals in 1979.
- Sonia Sotomayor was the first Latina to serve as a Justice of the Supreme Court of the United States. She was appointed in 2009.

First Asian American Judge

- Herbert Choy became the first Asian American to serve as a judge on a U.S. court of appeals when he was appointed to the U.S. Court of Appeals for the Ninth Circuit in 1971.
- Dick Wong became the first Asian American to serve on a U.S. district court when he was appointed to the district court for the District of Hawaii in 1975.

First Native American Judge

- Billy Michael Burrage became the first Native American federal judge when he was appointed to the U.S. District Courts for the Northern, Eastern & Western Districts of Oklahoma in 1994.

First Federal Judge to Be Elected President

- William Howard Taft in 1908 became the first and only former federal judge to be elected president. Taft served as judge of the U.S. Circuit Court of Appeals for the Sixth Circuit from 1892 to 1900. Taft also became the only former president to serve on a federal court when he became chief justice of the United States in 1921.

First Federal Judge Elevated to the U.S. Supreme Court

- Robert Trimble served as judge of the U.S. District Court in Kentucky from 1817 to 1826 when he became the first federal judge to be nominated and confirmed as a justice of the Supreme Court. He served only two years before he died at the age of 51. A total of 31 Supreme Court justices have previously served as a federal judge. With the appointment of Harry Blackmun in 1971, the Supreme Court for the first time had a majority of justices with experience on the lower federal courts.

SOURCE Federal Judicial Center, History of the Federal Judiciary, http://www.fjc.gov/history/home.nsf/page/judges_milestones. html unconstitutional a law favored by the majority of Americans because it violates a fundamental individual right protected by the Constitution. Nevertheless, there is often a strong feeling that the Supreme Court should have representatives of different regions, religions, races, and genders. (See the Politics in Practice feature "Milestones of Judicial Service.")

GEOGRAPHY Early in the nation's history, geographical considerations were often important in making appointments to the Supreme Court. Early presidents felt that having justices from the different regions of the country would help establish the legitimacy of the Court. As the nation expanded, presidents sometimes felt a political need to appoint justices from new states, as when Republican president Abraham Lincoln appointed Californian Steven J. Field, who was a Democrat, in 1863. Until 1891, Supreme Court justices literally had to ride the circuit to serve on the courts of appeals, which reinforced geographical considerations (O'Brien 1996, 70).

In the twentieth century, geography became less important in Supreme Court appointments. The last time geography was a consideration in a Supreme Court appointment occurred in 1969 when President Nixon announced his intention to appoint a "southern strict-constructionist" to the Court. The term *strict-constructionist* was understood to mean a conservative who would resist and perhaps even reverse some of the Warren Court's liberal rulings. The focus on a southerner was meant to attract conservative white Democratic voters in the South to help build a new Republican majority. After the Senate rejected Nixon's first two nominations, both from the South, he appointed Harry Blackmun of Minnesota. Although Nixon did eventually get Lewis Powell of Virginia confirmed, his political goal of attracting conservative southern Democrats to the Republican Party was stalled by the Watergate Scandal, which forced him to resign and contributed to the election of Democrat Jimmy Carter in 1976.

RELIGION Nearly 90 percent of Supreme Court justices have been Protestant. For a long time, there was a historical pattern of having a "Roman Catholic seat" and a "Jewish seat" on the Court (Abraham 1993, 65). Chief Justice Roger B. Taney was the first Catholic appointed, in 1835, and in 1916, Louis D. Brandeis became the first Jewish justice. Breaking the religion barrier was controversial. Brandeis, for example, was condemned as unfit to be a Supreme Court justice in a public statement signed by former presidents of the American Bar Association, and anti-Semitism was barely concealed in the movement to deny his appointment. He is now recognized as one of the great Supreme Court justices.

Religion has become much less of a factor in the contemporary era, and there is no longer much of a demonstrable effort to ensure religious balance on the Court. There had been no Catholic on the Court for several years when President Dwight Eisenhower appointed William Brennan, a Democrat and a Catholic, in 1956. Brennan was a highly respected attorney, but the appointment of an eastern Catholic was seen as a potential help to Eisenhower in the upcoming election (Abraham 1993, 70). Six of the current justices are Catholic: Samuel Alito, Anthony Kennedy, John Roberts, Antonin Scalia, Sonia Sotomayor, and Clarence Thomas. The tradition of the Jewish seat was broken in 1970, when President Richard Nixon filled the vacancy created by the resignation of Abe Fortas with a Protestant, and he later named two other Protestants to the Court. As do all presidents, Nixon claimed that religion was irrelevant and that he was looking for the best-qualified person. There were no Jews on the Court again until 1993, when President Clinton appointed Ruth Bader Ginsburg. His second appointee, Stephen Breyer, was also Jewish. There was no public discussion or controversy about religion in either case. President Obama's appointment of Elena Kagan to the Court in 2010 did generate some discussion about religion. Kagan identifies as a Conservative Jew. Although there was no objection to her religion per se, she replaced the sole remaining Protestant on the Court, retiring Justice John Paul Stevens. Thus, the Supreme Court, long dominated by Protestants, is now two-thirds Catholic and one-third Jewish.

RACE AND ETHNICITY Only two African Americans have served on the Supreme Court. The color barrier on the Court was broken in 1967, when President Lyndon Johnson appointed Thurgood Marshall, saying, "I believe it is the right thing to do, the right time to do it, the right man, and the right place." There is some indication that there is now an African American seat on the Court. When Justice Marshall retired in 1991, President George H. W. Bush appointed Clarence Thomas, who had the right credentials: he is conservative, he is Republican, and he has a law degree from Yale—and he is African American.

Another color barrier fell in 2009 when President Obama appointed the first Latina, Sonia Sotomayor, to the Supreme Court. The politics of this appointment are clear. Latinos are the fastest-growing ethnic group in the United States, and their political power is increasing. Latino votes contributed to Obama's victory in several key states. Now that these race and ethnicity barriers have been broken, we may someday see an Asian American or Native American justice appointed.

GENDER Four women have been appointed to the Supreme Court. The gender barrier was broken in 1981, when President Ronald Reagan appointed Sandra Day O'Connor. Although she was eminently qualified for the job, having graduated near the top of her class at Stanford—where she and Chief Justice Rehnquist had been classmates—the political motivation for this appointment was paramount. During the 1980 presidential campaign, women's groups criticized Reagan for his opposition to the proposed Equal Rights Amendment. In an attempt to reduce the growing gender gap, Reagan made a campaign promise: "One of the first Supreme Court vacancies in my administration will be filled by the most qualified woman I can find." Less than six months into his first year, Reagan fulfilled this campaign promise: O'Connor became a Supreme Court justice in 1981 and served 25 years, voluntarily resigning her position in 2006. President Clinton's first appointment to the Court was also a woman, Justice Ruth Bader Ginsburg. In 2005, President George W. Bush nominated White House counsel Harriet Miers to serve on the Supreme Court. Miers's nomination was torpedoed by broad criticism, however, even from members of the president's own party,

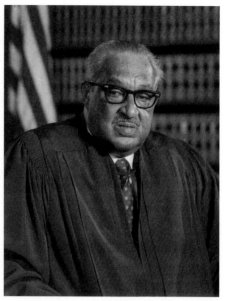

© The Library of Congress

The Supreme Court is not intended to be a representative institution. In fact, the Court is often in the position of declaring unconstitutional a law favored by the majority of Americans because it violates a fundamental individual right protected by the Constitution. Nevertheless, there is often a strong feeling that the Supreme Court should have representatives of different regions, religions, races, and genders. In 1967 the color barrier on the Court was broken by the appointment of Thurgood Marshall (seen here) by President Lyndon Johnson. When Justice Marshall retired, he was replaced by Clarence Thomas, who is also African American.

Sonia Sotomayor is the first Latina to serve on the U.S. Supreme Court. She was appointed by President Obama in 2009.

© Christy Bowe/Corbis

aimed at Miers's qualifications and commitment to conservative principles. She withdrew her nomination barely three weeks after President Bush announced it, and the vacancy created by O'Connors's retirement was eventually filled by Samuel Alito. Sonia Sotomayor, appointed by President Obama in 2009, became the third woman to serve on the Court. Elena Kagan became the fourth woman to serve on the Court in 2010, and this was the first time that two consecutive appointments were women.

Judicial Experience and Merit

It is rare for a president to ignore political considerations and make an appointment based exclusively on judicial experience and merit. Of course, no president wants to appoint an unqualified person to the Supreme Court, so in a sense merit is always the first consideration. In the rare instances when a president has nominated someone with questionable credentials, the Senate typically has blocked the appointment. With few exceptions, Supreme Court justices have been competent and intelligent. (See the Politics in Practice feature "The Politics of Getting to the Supreme Court.")

The connection between judicial experience and merit is tenuous at best. Presidents, senators, and the American Bar Association frequently view service on a lower federal or state court as a prerequisite for "promotion" to the nation's highest court. However, the Supreme Court is unique, and it performs a very different role than trial courts or even courts of appeals. Lower courts deal with the details of the cases at hand: facts and evidence, guilt and innocence. The Supreme Court addresses disputes over the most fundamental issues of politics and society: the meaning of broad clauses in the Constitution and the basic rights of individuals

THE POLITICS OF GETTING TO THE SUPREME COURT

Douglas Ginsburg did not get the job because he smoked dope in college. Levi Lincoln turned down the job because of his failing eyesight. Robert Bork lost the job because he was too ideological. Harriet Miers didn't get the gig because she was not ideological enough.

The job in question was Supreme Court justice, which by most benchmarks is a pretty good gig. The pay is around $208,000—a lot by most people's standards, but less than top legal talent gets in the most prestigious law firms. Still, you can't argue with the job security—once you have the job, you have it for life.

Getting to the Supreme Court, though, is not easy. You usually need top law school credentials, a distinguished career as a jurist, a president who likes your record and judicial philosophy, some appeal to an important political constituency, and an accommodating U.S. Senate that will confirm the nomination. Oh yes, and first you usually need another justice to either die or retire so the job is available. You also need to survive the politics that comes with a nomination to the Supreme Court, and those politics can be pretty brutal.

Between George Washington taking the oath of office and George W. Bush's first day as chief executive, presidents have nominated about 158 people to be Supreme Court justices. In the majority of cases, those nominated have accepted the opportunity to gain one of the most influential positions in the American political system. Some, like Levi Lincoln (who was nominated by James Madison), had their reasons for declining the president's offer.

A few have accepted the official nomination, only to withdraw under pressure. This included Ginsburg, who was nominated by President Ronald Reagan and created a public controversy by admitting that he'd smoked marijuana as a college student. Ginsburg withdrew after it became clear that the public was not comfortable with the notion of a Supreme Court justice using drugs recreationally, even if it had been decades before as a college student.

Ginsburg was actually Reagan's second choice. His first choice was Robert Bork, who was even more controversial because he had a long record of provocative legal arguments, virtually all of them promoting a very conservative interpretation of the Constitution. This record alarmed a wide range of special interests who mobilized a public campaign against him, and he failed to gain confirmation in a Senate vote.

The debate over whether Bork was fit to serve as a Supreme Court justice was so caustic that his supporters coined the verb "bork" to describe the action of blocking a court nominee or subjecting a public figure to unfair media criticism. Reagan is far from being the only president to have problems getting a Supreme Court nominee confirmed. Most recently, in 2005, President George W. Bush unsuccessfully nominated White House Counsel Harriet Miers. Miers withdrew her nomination before a Senate vote after being attacked from both sides of the ideological spectrum. Conservatives did not like her overly moderate political orientation, and liberals and conservatives questioned her qualifications.

Eleven presidents have had at least one Supreme Court nominee defeated in an actual Senate confirmation vote, and Bork's may not even be the most famous (or infamous). A serious contender would have to be Richard Nixon's 1970 nomination of G. Harold Carswell. Carswell was controversial because he had a segregationist past and was considered by many to be a mediocre candidate. Carswell's case was not helped by supporters like U.S. Senator Roman Hruska (R-NE), who said even if Carswell was mediocre, there were lots of mediocre people in the country and "they are entitled to a little representation, aren't they?" Not exactly a convincing argument for appointing someone to one of the most important positions in government.

All this goes to show that the Supreme Court has one of toughest job interviews in politics.

SOURCES King, Florence. 1997. "Misanthrope's Corner." *National Review*. http://www.nationalreview.com/22dec97/gimlet122297. html (Accessed September 15, 2004).

"Defeated Nominees to the U.S. Supreme Court." *WordIQ.com*. http://www.wordiq.com/definition/Defeated_nominees_to_ the_U.S._Supreme_Court (Accessed September 30, 2008).

and society. Experience as a trial judge is not necessarily relevant to resolving disputes over such fundamental questions. Justice Felix Frankfurter boldly asserted, "One is entitled to say without qualification that the correlation between prior judicial experience and fitness for the Supreme Court is zero" (1957, 781). Rather, the job of Supreme Court justice requires a "combination of philosopher, historian, and prophet" (Abraham 1993, 59).

Several great justices had no prior experience as judges, including Joseph Story (appointed 1812), Charles Evans Hughes (appointed 1910), Louis Brandeis (appointed 1916), Harlan Stone (appointed 1925), and Felix Frankfurter (appointed 1939). Among the "great" justices, only Oliver Wendell Holmes Jr. (appointed 1902) and Benjamin Cardozo (appointed 1932) had extensive prior judicial experience, but as Frankfurter argued, their greatness "derived not from their judicial experience but from the fact they were . . . thinkers, and more particularly, legal philosophers" (Frankfurter 1957, 781).

There has been only one clear case in which merit considerations were strong enough to push aside all political concerns: President Herbert Hoover's appointment of Benjamin Cardozo to the Court. Cardozo was a distinguished jurist widely admired in the legal community and a logical nominee to fill the court vacancy. Yet he was a liberal Democrat; he was a New Yorker when there were already two New Yorkers on the Court; and he was Jewish, and that "seat" was already occupied by Brandeis. Hoover compiled a short list of conservative, western Republicans to nominate and added Cardozo's name at the bottom of the list. Hoover handed Republican senator William E. Borah of Idaho the list and asked for his advice. Borah replied, "Your list is all right, but you handed it to me upside down" (Abraham 1993, 69). Hoover appointed Cardozo.

Confirmation Politics in the Senate

Deciding who will wield the power of judicial review is an enormously important decision. The careers of federal judges often go well beyond those of the presidents who nominated them and the senators who confirmed them. In other words, selecting someone to exercise judicial power has implications far beyond the next election or administration. Because the makeup of the federal bench is one of a president's biggest legacies, it is not surprising that the **confirmation process** for federal judges—that is, the period between when a presidential nomination is received in the Senate and when the nominee is either confirmed or defeated—is a political process. The process has become even more politicized in recent decades.

The Senate takes its power to confirm judicial appointments seriously. Of the 147 Supreme Court nominees forwarded to the Senate, about one-fifth have failed. During the nation's first century, the Senate blocked Supreme Court nominations with some regularity; in the 106 years from the founding to 1894, 22 Supreme Court nominees failed. Appointments came a little easier for presidents during much of the nation's second century, and "the confirmation process was distinguished by presidential prerogative to fill vacancies on the Supreme Court" (Silverstein 1994, 3). From 1895 to 1967, presidents made 45 nominations to the

confirmation process The period between when a presidential nomination of a federal judge is received in the Senate and when the nominee is either confirmed or defeated.

Supreme Court. Only one—John J. Parker in 1930—failed to gain confirmation. Since the late 1960s, the process of getting federal judges confirmed has become more politicized, and the Senate has once again become less deferential to presidents' preferences.

The shift from presidential prerogative to a more partisan and political process has its roots in procedural changes that took place in the mid-1950s. Before 1955, the only two Supreme Court nominees to testify before the Senate Judiciary Committee were Harlan Fiske Stone in 1925 and Felix Frankfurter in 1939. Nominees are now expected to go before the committee to answer questions about their judicial philosophies and their opinions on specific legal issues. This tradition has thrust Supreme Court nominees into controversial political issues as they are asked to publicly state their positions on, for example, the constitutionality of abortion or affirmative action.

Because the Supreme Court has played an increasingly significant role in American political life in the past several decades, the political stakes in Supreme Court nominations have increased. It was the Supreme Court that decided that abortion was a private decision subject to only limited regulation by the government, that law enforcement agencies had to inform people taken into custody of their rights, that school-sponsored prayer and Bible reading in public schools violated the constitutional requirement of separation of church and state, and that legislative districts must be equal in population. As the ideological stakes have increased, presidents have overtly politicized the nomination process. Both Ronald Reagan and the senior Bush made campaign promises to appoint conservative judges, particularly judges who opposed abortion. Reagan made good-faith efforts to deliver on his promise, even going to the extreme of screening judicial appointments for ideological consistency with his conservative agenda (Goldman 1985). Such openly political moves were justified on the grounds that they were needed to counter the liberal drift of the Court in the preceding two decades. But they invited an opposing political agenda from Democrats and from activists who wanted the Court to defend and uphold its rulings on civil rights, abortion rights, and similar issues. These two agendas clashed in a very public and partisan manner during confirmation hearings before the Senate Judiciary Committee from the 1980s to the 2000s.

The conflict became increasingly acrimonious during the second Clinton administration. As noted previously, during the Clinton administration, the Judiciary Committee changed the practice of senatorial courtesy to require approval of both home state senators, including Republicans, before it would hold confirmation hearings on judicial nominees. This change resulted in a lengthening of the confirmation process. The acrimony continued through the Bush administration as Democrats retaliated, and Republicans responded in kind to delay confirmation of Obama's judicial appointments. As Figure 15.5 shows, the average length of the confirmation process for Supreme Court and appellate court judges has increased exponentially since the 1960s. The average length of the confirmation process was about one-and-one-half months in the 1960s and 1970s (Johnson to Carter); it more than doubled to about four months during the 1980s and early 1990s (Carter to the first Clinton term); and

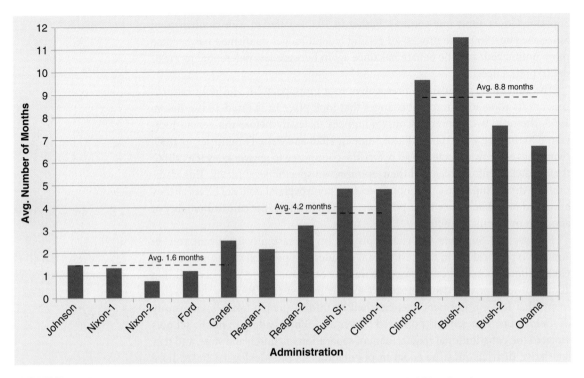

FIGURE 15.5 **Increasing Length of the Confirmation Process for Judicial Nominations**
Source: Bond, Fleisher, and Krutz (2009); Obama nominations updated by the authors.

it doubled yet again to nearly nine months in the period from Clinton's second term to Obama.

The longer confirmation process is symptomatic of other fundamental changes. Arguably the most important change is the increasing rate at which judicial nominees fail to be confirmed. Before the Reagan administration, the average failure rate for Supreme Court and Circuit Court nominations was about 7 percent. From the Reagan administration to Clinton's first term, the average failure rate for judicial nominations climbed to one in five, and it jumped to more than 40 percent from Clinton's second term to Obama (see Figure 15.6).

Moreover, the way nominations are defeated has changed. Traditionally, a nomination failed because the president withdrew it as controversy and opposition grew or because it was voted down in committee or on the Senate floor, though few nominations have been voted down (the last was Reagan's nomination of Judge Robert Bork to the Supreme Court in 1987). Most commonly, presidents have withdrawn controversial nominations before they are rejected by the Senate. This is what happened to President Bush's 2005 nomination of Harriet Miers. Although Miers was a highly respected lawyer and had served as the first female president of the Texas Bar Association, both Republicans and Democrats questioned whether she had the intellectual credentials and experience necessary to deal with the types of issues that come before the Supreme Court.

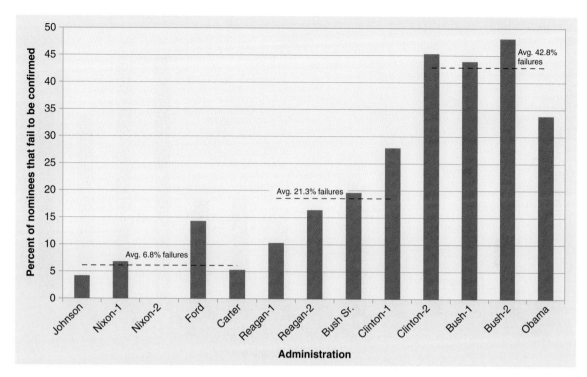

FIGURE 15.6 Increasing Failure Rates of Judicial Nominations

Source: Bond, Fleisher, and Krutz (2009); Obama nominations updated by the authors.

Nominations can also fail because the Senate does not act before Congress adjourns. Traditionally, such failures were rare, typically occurring when nominations were made late in an election year, when senators focus more on reelection than on Senate business. From 1965 to 1980, only nine nominations failed at the end of the session because of inaction, and seven of these were nominations made after the first quarter of a presidential election year. But the number of judicial nominations failing at the adjournment of Congress began increasing during the Reagan and senior Bush presidencies, and few of them were late election year nominations. During the Clinton years, such failures increased dramatically— Clinton had more nominees defeated by delay than the six preceding presidents combined. President Bush had similar numbers of judicial nominees defeated by stalling (see Figure 15.7). Delaying final action until Congress adjourns has become the most common way to defeat judicial nominations.

These changes seem to be the result of a political strategy in which opponents use Senate rules to block action on a nomination until Congress adjourns. The key to this strategy is the filibuster or the threat to filibuster by placing a "hold" on nominations. Recall from chapter 10 that a hold is a signal to party leaders that a senator has some concerns and wants to be notified before a bill or nomination comes to the floor. It is an implicit threat to filibuster if those concerns are not addressed. Holds are not explicitly authorized in Senate rules. Rather, the practice

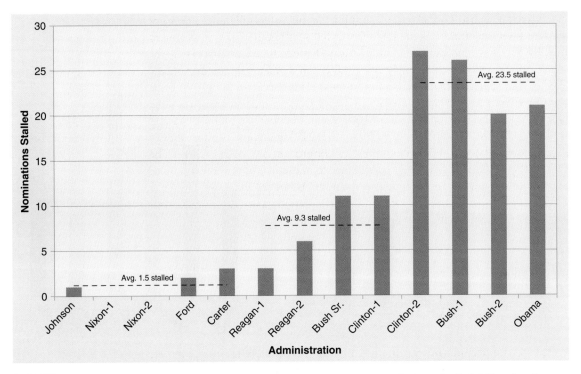

FIGURE 15.7 Increasing Use of Stalling the Confirmation Process to Defeat Judicial Nominations

Source: Bond, Fleisher, and Krutz (2009); Obama nominations updated by the authors.

is one aspect of senatorial courtesy that party leaders typically observe—but not always.

Whether party leaders honor a hold and whether a senator will actually have to make good on a filibuster threat depend on the configuration of party control of the presidency and the Senate. Holds on nominations are most likely to come from members of the opposition party. If the opposition party controls the Senate, an actual filibuster is unlikely to be necessary because the majority leader will honor a "hold" and not bring the nomination to the floor. This was the situation in the 106th Congress (1999–2000) when President Clinton was unable to get a vote on numerous judicial nominations because the Senate majority leader, Trent Lott (R-MS), would not schedule a vote if there was a hold on the nominee. But if the president's party has a majority, filibusters are more likely. Because he wants to help the president get his nominees confirmed, the majority leader is likely to ignore holds placed by opposition party senators, forcing them to make good on the threat to filibuster. This was the situation in the 108th Congress (2003–2004) when Senate Majority Leader Bill Frist (R-TN) brought a number of President Bush's nominations to the floor, forcing Democrats to make good on filibuster threats.

Unable to muster the 60 votes required to invoke cloture (a procedure to end debate), Senator Frist threatened to change Senate rules to require only a simple majority to invoke cloture on filibusters of nominations. Republicans called the procedure the "constitutional option," arguing that filibusters of judicial nominees violated the Constitution. Some Republicans felt so strongly that they promised never to filibuster a judicial nomination. Angry Democrats labeled Frist's tactic the "nuclear option" because the "explosive" conflict could potentially "incinerate" the Senate, fundamentally changing the institutional structure of the chamber. A compromise brokered by seven Republican and seven Democratic senators averted the crisis. The situation was similar in 2011, but the parties were on different sides of the debate. Senate Majority Leader Harry Reid (D-NV) ignored Republican threats to filibuster and brought President Obama's nomination of Goodwin Liu to the Court of Appeals to the floor. Democrats failed to muster the necessary 60 votes to invoke cloture, and Liu withdrew his nomination. Although he did not threaten a "nuclear option," a frustrated Reid read previous statements by Republican senators who had promised never to filibuster judicial appointments (Kane 2011).

JUDICIAL DECISION MAKING

Presidents are periodically disappointed by the decisions of their appointees. President Eisenhower, for example, was bitterly disappointed by his appointment of Earl Warren as chief justice in 1953 (White 1982), calling it the "biggest damned-fool mistake I ever made." There was little indication in Warren's background as a Republican and a prosecutor that he would become the leader of one of the most liberal, activist courts in the nation's history. Under his leadership, the Supreme Court compiled a long list of decisions that attracted the wrath of conservatives. But once a justice is appointed, there is little a president can do about that appointee's decisions. Years later, the Court's decision permitting a sexual harassment lawsuit to proceed against President Bill Clinton was unanimous, meaning that both of Clinton's appointees voted in favor of it. President Truman once observed that "packing the Supreme Court simply can't be done. . . . I've tried and it won't work. . . . Whenever you put a man on the Supreme Court, he ceases to be your friend" (quoted in Abraham 1993, 74).

Political scientists who study the courts have turned to several models to explain judicial decision making. The traditional approach is the **legal model**, adapted from the law school tradition. This model argues that judges set aside their own values and make decisions based solely on legal criteria: the evidence, the law, legal precedents, and the Constitution. One version of the legal model articulated by Justice Owen Roberts is referred to as the **slot machine theory** of judicial decision making. Justice Roberts argued that when faced with a case challenging the constitutionality of a law, all a judge does is lay the constitutional provision involved beside the statute being challenged and "decide whether the latter squares with the former" (*United States v. Butler* 1936). According to Roberts, judges don't "make" law, but rather they "find" the law. This perspective suggests

legal model A view of judicial decision making that argues that judges set aside their own values and make decisions based solely on legal criteria.

slot machine theory The view of judicial review that all judges do is lay the constitutional provision involved beside the statute being challenged and "decide whether the latter squares with the former."

that "finding" the law is a mechanistic process similar to putting coins in a slot machine and then picking up and reporting what comes out.

Others articulate a more nuanced and complex process in which considerations other than the law influence judicial decision making. The **legal realist model** argues that because judges are human beings, subject to human frailties, their own personal values and ideologies inevitably affect their decisions, no matter how hard they may try to set them aside. Legal realists believe that judges must reconcile conflicting principles and interests and balance the law and precedent with their judgment about the effect of their decision on society. Legal criteria may trump ideology in areas of law that are well settled—the fact that 35 to 40 percent of Supreme Court decisions are unanimous (see Figure 15.3) is clear evidence that legal criteria influence judicial decisions. But some areas are less well settled. In these gray areas of the law, judges' personal values inevitably influence decisions. Key words and phrases in the Constitution, such as "due process of law" and "necessary and proper," are so broad and general that they compel a judge to read his or her own views into them. According to this perspective, judges have no choice but to make law rather than merely find it.

Political scientists have extended the legal realist model with behavioral models that focus on attitudes. C. Hermann Pritchett (1948) pioneered the behavioral study of the courts with a statistical analysis of voting blocs on the Supreme Court from 1937 to 1947. He argued that analyzing nonunanimous decisions reveals "information about [justices'] attitudes and their values" (xii). Building on this important insight, Jeffrey Segal and Harold Spaeth (1993) developed the **attitudinal model**, suggesting that judges' decisions are largely, if not exclusively, determined by their personal ideological and policy preferences. Certain institutional features—life tenure, no ambition to seek higher office, and little or no chance of being impeached—free judges to use the judicial power to maximize their own ideological and policy goals. The attitudinal model assumes that judges' votes sincerely reflect their preferences.

Lee Epstein and Jack Knight (1998) challenge this assumption, arguing that judges behave strategically. The **strategic model** (based on a type of rational choice model called game theory) indicates that sincere voting—that is, voting for the most preferred alternative—does not always maximize utility. Why? Well, basically because judges—even Supreme Court justices at the apex of judicial power—cannot achieve their goals without help from other actors with competing preferences. A Supreme Court justice must get at least four other justices to join in a majority opinion. And after the Court hands down its decision, other institutional actors—for example, Congress, lower-court judges, and state legislatures—will have to take some action to implement the decision. To achieve their policy goals, therefore, judges must act strategically to get the help they need from other institutional actors. Thus, strategic behavior explains why, more than half the time, Supreme Court justices cast votes that do not reflect their personal preferences (Epstein and Knight 1998). In recent research, Epstein and her associates present evidence to support a view that the Supreme Court is a "mixed ideological–legalistic judicial institution" (Epstein, Landes, and Posner 2012).

legal realist model A model of judicial decision making that argues that personal values and ideologies affect a judge's decisions.

attitudinal model A model that suggests that judges' decisions are largely, if not exclusively, determined by their personal ideological and policy preferences.

strategic model The view that sincere voting does not always maximize utility.

If judicial decisions were politically neutral and not influenced by the political values of judges, all the political maneuvering in the appointment and confirmation process would be misdirected. Consistent with the legal model, judges invariably deny that their personal political values influence their decisions. Their legal training stresses that judges are supposed to be politically neutral and impartial. And most judges no doubt attempt to put aside their own personal values and biases when they decide cases. But the empirical evidence from analyzing judges' behavior supports the legal realist and attitudinal models of judicial behavior. Try as they may, the human beings who serve as judges do not become legal automatons when they put on their judicial robes. When gray areas of the law are involved, judges' backgrounds and personal values influence which arguments and which parts of the evidence they find most persuasive as they consider the facts, the evidence, and the meaning of the law. As a result, Democratic judges tend to make more liberal decisions, and Republican judges tend to make more conservative decisions. These differences, however, are tendencies; partisan and ideological differences in judicial behavior are not nearly as strong as they are among presidents and members of Congress.

Political scientists have found clear evidence that attitudes influence judicial decisions by analyzing how judges vote. This is not to say that a judge's vote is a direct indicator of his or her attitudes; nevertheless, if we find significant dif-

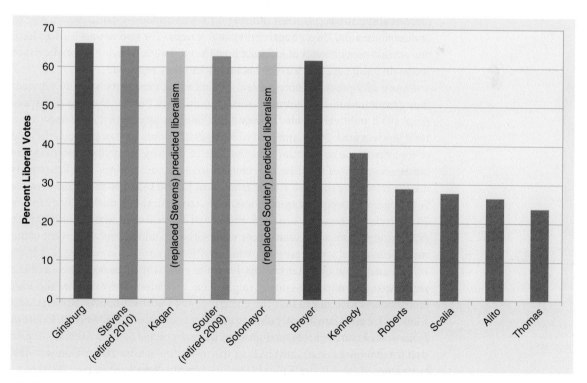

FIGURE 15.8 Civil Liberties Liberalism of Supreme Court Justices

Source: Constructed by the authors from data at Epstein et al. (2007).

ferences in how judges vote on controversial issues, then it is reasonable to infer that their personal values influence how they vote. Figure 15.8 shows how often members of the Supreme Court cast liberal votes on nonunanimous civil liberties cases. In recent years, the Court was divided into three distinct voting blocs:

- On the left were four justices (Ginsburg, Stevens, Souter, and Breyer) who voted on the liberal side of civil liberties questions more than 60 percent of the time.
- On the right were four justices (Thomas, Scalia, Roberts, and Alito) who cast liberal votes less than 30 percent of the time.
- In the middle was Justice Kennedy, who cast liberal votes slightly less than 40 percent of the time.

Because it takes five votes to decide a case, Kennedy often holds the balance of power to determine the outcome of controversial civil liberties cases.

President Truman's observation about not being able to "pack" the Court is partially correct. Consistent with Truman's view, there are some surprises among recent members of the Court. Republican presidents Gerald Ford and George H. W. Bush appointed fellow Republicans John Paul Stevens and David Souter to the Court, expecting that that they would be moderate conservatives; Stevens and Souter turned out to be two of the most liberal justices. Souter and Stevens retired in 2009 and 2010, respectively. President Obama appointed Sonia Sotomayor to replace Souter and Elena Kagan to replace Stevens. The two newest justices have not yet cast enough votes to estimate how liberal they will be, but the expectation is that they will vote much as the liberal justices they replaced.

Figure 15.9 provides more general evidence that presidents typically get what they expect from their Supreme Court appointments, but not always. For justices since 1937, political scientist Jeffrey Segal and his associates (Segal and Cover 1989; Epstein et al. 2007) analyzed newspaper editorials written between the date of the president's nomination and the date of the Senate's final action to determine perceptions of how liberal or conservative the nominee was. The figure plots the expected liberalism on a scale from most liberal (–1.0) to most conservative (+1.0) against the percentage of liberal votes the justices cast during their careers. The correlation between expected and actual liberalism is relatively high, with expectations expressed in newspaper editorials explaining about 46 percent of the variance in actual votes cast supporting civil liberties.

This analysis shows that justices generally vote as their backgrounds and the presidents who appointed them might have predicted. For example, the four most conservative justices on the current Court—Scalia, Thomas, Roberts, and Alito—were appointed by Republican presidents in hopes of moving the Court in a more conservative direction. President Bush appointed Samuel Alito, hoping he would vote more conservatively than the moderate Sandra Day O'Connor. And he appointed John Roberts to replace Chief Justice Rehnquist in part because he expected that Roberts would be a reliable conservative vote. These justices have voted as expected. Similarly, the most liberal justices from the Warren Court— Black, Douglas, Fortas, and Marshall—voted as expected. This analysis also

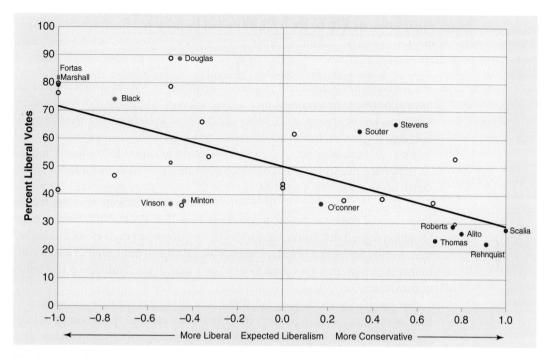

FIGURE 15.9 **Expected and Actual Liberalism of Supreme Court Justices**

Source: Constructed by the authors from data at Epstein et al. (2007).

reveals the justices who were surprises, including Stevens and Souter, who were more liberal than expected, and President Truman's appointments, Fred Vinson and Sherman Minton, who voted much more conservatively than expected.

Partisan differences also show up in the behavior of lower federal court judges. Political scientists have found evidence that Democratic judges are more likely to make liberal decisions than are Republican judges (Carp, Stidham, and Manning 2004, 158–163).

Interest groups also attempt to affect judicial decision making. Interest groups trying to advance their interests through the judicial process have become increasingly common in recent years. Political scientists Gregory Caldeira and John Wright (1990, 783) find that the Court is open to a wide range of interests, and the Court's continued willingness to permit this participation is "tacit recognition that most matters before the justices have vast social, political, and economic ramifications." As discussed in chapter 6, interest groups attempt to influence judicial decision making by filing amicus curiae briefs—that is, briefs filed by groups that are not actual parties to a case but that have an interest in the outcome. Political scientists have found evidence that amicus curiae briefs present new information not contained in the briefs of the actual parties in the case (i.e., the plaintiff and the defendant). The Court accepts arguments in these amicus curiae briefs fairly often, though not as often as it accepts the actual parties' arguments (Spriggs and Wahlbeck 1997).

JUDICIAL REVIEW IN A DEMOCRATIC SOCIETY

The Constitution is especially vague on the power of federal courts. It calls for judicial power to be exercised by a Supreme Court and lower courts created by Congress, and it sets up some basic jurisdictional guidelines. But the Constitution never specifies exactly what rights and responsibilities are encompassed by the term *judicial power*. The founders seemed to expect the judiciary to play an important role in the political system, but they provided only a rudimentary sketch of what that role should be.

In *Federalist* Number 78, Alexander Hamilton did indicate that the federal courts would have the power to overturn laws that violated the Constitution. Hamilton argued that neither majorities of the people nor their elected representatives could be trusted to always respect the principles embedded in the Constitution. Hamilton saw the courts as a bulwark against the "turbulence and follies of democracy."

But Hamilton's views were not universally held, and they are not explicit in the Constitution. Rather, the Supreme Court itself claimed the power of judicial review of lower-court decisions, laws, and the actions of elected officials. It is hard to overstate the importance of judicial review to the role of the courts in the American political system. Judicial review means that the judiciary has the power to decide who gets what, when, and how—that is, the judiciary is a policymaking institution in its own right.

In exercising judicial review, a court regards the Constitution as superior to ordinary laws or executive and judicial decrees. Article VI established the Constitution as the "supreme law of the land," and judges and legislators take an oath to uphold the Constitution. In determining that a law is unconstitutional and therefore invalid, the court must find that a legislature, an executive, or a judge has done something either prohibited or not authorized by the Constitution.

The power of a court to nullify actions of elected officials tends to concern students of democracy more than the power to invalidate the decisions of judges in a lower court. Very few nations grant courts the power of judicial review as it is exercised in the United States, and consequently, American courts have a much more prominent role in the political system than courts in other nations. Sooner or later, most important political conflicts end up in court, and the judicial branch in effect serves as the ultimate umpire to the democratic political process in the United States.

The Origins of Judicial Review

The power of judicial review was most famously asserted in the case of *Marbury v. Madison* in 1803. The conflict at the heart of this case was a by-product of the election of 1800, which decisively shifted political power from the Federalists to Jefferson's Democratic-Republicans. Having lost control of both the executive and legislative branches of government, the lame-duck Federalist president, John Adams, and the Federalist Congress rapidly began creating new judgeships and filling the vacancies with Federalist loyalists; the Federalists hoped to retain significant influence in the third branch of government. Caught in the middle of these machinations was John Marshall, Adams's secretary of state. Not only was it Marshall's job to sign and deliver the official commissions to the new judges after they had been appointed and duly confirmed by the Senate, but he was himself appointed chief justice of the Supreme Court as well. The Federalists' attempt to pack the judiciary infuriated incoming president Thomas Jefferson. Once in office, he told his secretary of state, James Madison, to withhold all the commissions Marshall had not yet delivered. Among these were commissions for 17 justices of the peace in the District of Columbia, one of whom was William Marbury. Without the commission, Marbury could not take his post, so along with several other disappointed Federalist appointees, he filed suit asking the Supreme Court to make Madison discharge his duty and deliver the commissions.

This suit, to put it mildly, put Marshall a bind. To begin with, he was being asked to rule on his own dereliction of duty.[8] And that was the least of his problems. If he and the other Federalist justices ruled that Marbury was entitled to the commission, Jefferson would simply order Madison not to deliver it, demonstrating that the judiciary could not enforce its mandates. As a Federalist, Marshall favored a strong national government, including a powerful judiciary. Having a Supreme Court decision ignored would undermine this goal. On the other hand, to rule that Marbury had no right to the commission would validate Jefferson's and Madison's claim that the so-called midnight appointments were improper and would undercut the standing of the Federalists who had just taken the bench. In short, either option could disastrously weaken the Court that Marshall had just been appointed to lead.

Marshall's response was a stroke of political genius—and a classic case of strategic behavior predicted by the strategic model. Technically, what Marbury had petitioned the court for was a **writ of mandamus**, a court order requiring a public official to perform an official duty over which he or she has no discretion. Speaking on behalf of a unanimous Federalist Court, Marshall ruled that Marbury had a right to the commission and that the writ of mandamus was indeed the proper remedy to obtain it. But he also argued that the Supreme Court was not the proper tribunal to issue the writ. In making the ruling, Marshall struck down part of the Judiciary Act of 1789 that in effect had granted the Supreme Court the power to issue writs of mandamus in cases under its original jurisdiction.

To understand this legal controversy, it is important to remember that the Supreme Court has both original and appellate jurisdiction. The Constitution

---

[8] Marshall probably should have recused himself from hearing this case. *Recuse* is from a Latin word meaning "to refuse." Judges usually refuse to participate in cases in which they have even the appearance of a conflict of interest or bias. Chief Justice Marshall was aware of this practice. He recused himself from participating in the decision in *Martin v. Hunter's Lessee* (1816) because he had appeared as counsel in an earlier phase of the case and had a financial interest in the property.

writ of mandamus A court order requiring a public official to perform an official duty over which he or she has no discretion.

© The Granger Collection, New York

John Marshall was the fourth Chief Justice. He is the author of the opinion in Marbury v. Madison (1803) establishing the power of judicial review. Because of his enormous influence on constitutional law and the development of an independent judiciary, he is generally considered the greatest Supreme Court Justice.

gives Congress authority to define the Court's appellate jurisdiction by statute. But the Court's original jurisdiction is specifically spelled out in the Constitution.[9] Because it is defined in the Constitution, the Court's original jurisdiction cannot be changed by ordinary statute; instead, changes can be made only by a constitutional amendment. Marshall said that the part of the Judicial Act that gave the Court the power to issue writs of mandamus was unconstitutional because it gave the Court powers of original jurisdiction beyond those set by the Constitution. In this ruling, Marshall officially claimed the power of judicial review for courts, saying that it is "the providence and duty of the judicial department to say what the law is." In effect, Marshall was saying that the meaning of the Constitution depends on how judges interpret the Constitution. Because the outcome (i.e., that Madison did not have to deliver the commissions) was the one Jefferson wanted, he did not challenge the ruling (Gunther 1980, 9–11), though Jefferson was surely outraged by this blatant judicial power grab.

The ruling had far-reaching effects. It raised the possibility that the Federalists could use the newfound power of judicial review to check the actions of the Democratic-Republican Congress and president. And most crucial of all, it established the power of the courts to declare acts of public officials invalid. *Marbury* did not settle all aspects of judicial review; for example, it was not until seven years later that the Court expanded this power to invalidate state laws. But it firmly planted the precedent, establishing the Court as a political institution of the highest order. The Supreme Court alone has the right to make final decisions about what the Constitution does and does not allow. This power means that the judiciary is a lawmaking institution, not simply a vehicle to resolve legal disputes.

Concepts of Judicial Review

How does a judge go about deciding whether a law or an executive order is unconstitutional? What role does the judge think judicial review should play in the political process? How do judges and how should judges interpret the Constitution?

There have been a number of famous answers to such questions. Roughly speaking, there are two primary perspectives on how judges should interpret the Constitution, and these lead to different views on the role of judicial review. **Originalism** is the idea that justices should interpret the Constitution in terms of the original intentions of the founders. This theory is based on the assumption

---

originalism The idea that Supreme Court justices should interpret the Constitution in terms of the original intentions of the framers.

[9] The Supreme Court can exercise original jurisdiction in cases affecting foreign ambassadors and consuls and those in which a state is a party. The Eleventh Amendment altered the provision that allows suits against a state by citizens of another state. This amendment overturned the decision in *Chisholm v. Georgia* (1793) that the Court had accepted and decided under its original jurisdiction.

that the meaning of the Constitution was fixed at the time of adoption, and the job of justices is to interpret the Constitution in terms of this original intent. In contrast to the theory of originalism is the theory of the **living Constitution**. This assumes that the Constitution was meant to be a dynamic document whose meaning has to account for contemporary social and political context. The basic argument of the living Constitution approach is that using the fixed ideas of a small seventeenth-century elite to decide key constitutional provisions as they relate to, say, freedom of speech or racial relations will lead to wildly inappropriate decisions that many would perceive to be at odds with the core principles of democracy. The living Constitution approach is viewed by many legal scholars as a practical approach that helps make the Constitution a meaningful and relevant guide for judicial decision making. Originalist critics, however, argue that the living Constitution approach leads justices down a dangerous path, one where the meaning of key constitutional provisions becomes nothing more and nothing less than the values of the judges making the decision.

Even if a judge concedes that personal values do play a role in judicial decision making, this does not solve the problem of deciding to what extent these values will affect rulings on constitutional issues. Justice Felix Frankfurter was one of the most articulate proponents of the "make law" perspective during the twentieth century, but he also hesitated to substitute his constitutional values for those of legislators and executives. For example, in a 1940 decision, *Minersville School District v. Gobitis,* Frankfurter upheld the right of a school board to expel students who refused to salute the flag, as required by Pennsylvania state law. Frankfurter took the position that the courts had no grounds to tell political authorities that they could not use this method to instill patriotism in children. Three years later, the Supreme Court overruled *Minersville,* with Frankfurter dissenting. In *West Virginia State Board of Education v. Barnette* (1943), Justice Robert Jackson argued that forcing students to salute the flag interfered with their right of free speech.

Although these cases may seem like little more than historical artifacts, they carry a modern lesson. In one case, the Supreme Court exercised **judicial restraint**, meaning that it deferred policymaking authority to other branches and levels of government. Restraint is often associated with the originalist perspective. In the other, the Court exercised **judicial activism**, taking a more forceful role in determining public policy through broad constitutional interpretation. Judicial activism is typically associated with the living Constitution perspective. The tension between judicial restraint and judicial activism is an important political issue. Those who favor restraint argue that making law is properly a legislative function and that judges should not be allowed to use the power of judicial review to legislate from the bench. Advocates of activism argue that legislatures sometimes pass bad laws that abrogate basic democratic values and constitutional rights. In such cases, the courts have not only a right but also an obligation to act.

When the Supreme Court established the power of judicial review, it introduced tensions over democratic values and over the roles of the different branches of government that remain unresolved today. One reason the battle over activism versus restraint is so hard to resolve is that it is a battle of political ideology rather

living Constitution The theory that assumes the Constitution was meant to be a dynamic document whose meaning has to account for contemporary social and political context.

judicial restraint A view of Supreme Court decision making that calls for the Court to defer policymaking to the other branches of government.

judicial activism A view of Supreme Court decision making that calls for the Court to take an active role in policymaking through its interpretation of the Constitution.

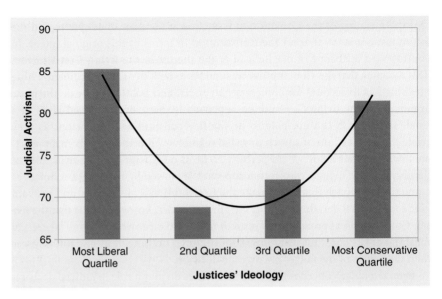

FIGURE 15.10 Supreme Court Justices' Ideology and Judicial Activism
Source: Constructed by the authors from data at Epstein et al. (2007).

than judicial philosophy. For the past quarter-century, the Supreme Court has largely been appointed by Republican presidents and is thus ideologically more conservative than some predecessors. Given that conservatives generally advocate an originalist perspective and often complain about liberal, activist judges "legislating" from the bench, one might expect the Supreme Court during this time period to have exercised restraint. Yet in many ways it has proven to be a highly activist Court, and it too has "thwarted the will of the majority." In *City of Boerne v. Flores* (1997), for example, it struck down the Religious Freedom Restoration Act, which passed unanimously in the House of Representatives and attracted only three dissenting votes in the Senate. And in *Citizens United v. Federal Election Commission* (2010), a conservative majority struck down a 70-year-old precedent banning corporate and labor contributions to political campaigns. Activism is not simply a trait of a liberal ideology or a living Constitution perspective on constitutional interpretation, any more than restraint is solely a trait of conservative ideology and an originalist perspective. Instead, as Figure 15.10 demonstrates, judicial activism tends to be supported by conservatives when it advances their ideological preferences and by liberals when it advances theirs; it is moderates who are more likely to exercise judicial restraint.

Patterns in the Exercise of Judicial Review

For the most part, the Supreme Court has used judicial review with considerable restraint. Fewer than 200 federal laws and about 1,300 state laws have been struck down. These numbers represent a tiny fraction of the hundreds of thousands of laws passed in more than two centuries.[10]

The Supreme Court's use of judicial review has not been uniform over the years. During some periods, the Court rarely used the power. For example, after the *Marbury v. Madison* (1803) decision, more than 50 years passed before the Supreme Court declared another federal law unconstitutional in *Dred Scott v. Sanford* (1857). In other periods of history, the Court has been much more active in its use of judicial review. For example, it declared 13 New Deal laws unconstitutional in the two years from 1934 to 1936. The Court was more restrained in the 1940s and 1950s and then became more activist in the 1960s and 1970s (see Figure 15.11).

The issues of concern to the Supreme Court have also changed over the years. Subject matter naturally varies from case to case, but different themes have occupied the Supreme Court's attention in different eras of constitutional history. The issues have reflected both the major problems of American society at the time and the justices' own conceptions of the values they should protect through the power of judicial review.

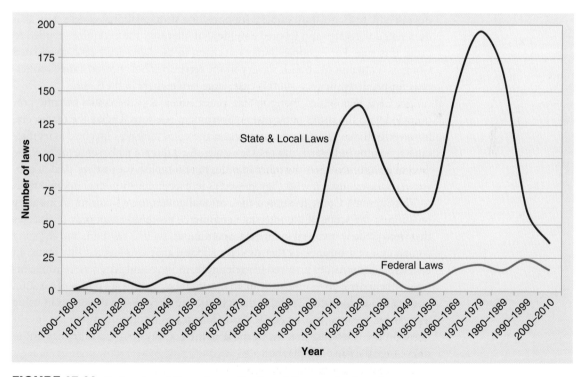

FIGURE 15.11 Federal and State Laws Declared Unconstitutional

Source: Adapted from Stanley and Niemi (2011), 285.

---

[10] All courts in the United States have the power of judicial review because all state and federal judges take an oath to uphold the Constitution. This discussion focuses on the U.S. Supreme Court because it has the most definitive say about what is constitutional.

The major issue facing the Supreme Court between 1789 and the Civil War was the relationship between the nation and the states. John Marshall, who was chief justice for much of this era, provided judicial support for a strong national government. The constitutional justification for the federal government's expansion during this time was a broad interpretation of the interstate commerce power and the "necessary and proper" clause. At the same time, state activities that restricted the powers of the national government were invalidated. Toward the end of this era, Marshall was replaced by Roger Taney, and under Taney's leadership the Court moderated its stand on the nation–state relationship. For example, it ruled that states could regulate interstate commerce if the regulation concerned local matters and did not affect a subject requiring uniform treatment throughout the United States. As a whole, however, this early era was a time of general support for the nation over the states in constitutional conflicts.

The pre–Civil War period was also characterized by judicial protection of private property. In fact, there was a connection between the nation–states and property rights issues. For the most part, the federal government was promoting business and commercial interests, whereas the states were more involved in trying to regulate them. Thus, judicial support for a strong national government that dominated the states also favored commercial interests. The exceptions tended to prove this rule. For example, Taney's decision in the *Dred Scott* case invalidated Congress's attempt to abolish slavery in the territories but showed Taney's solicitude for property owners—in this case, large landowners in the South.

The Civil War settled many nation–states issues, and the courts became preoccupied with the issues of business–government relations. Unlike the earlier era, however, both the national government and the states were now involved in regulating burgeoning industrial empires. Consequently, it did not make sense to favor one level of government over the other in order to accomplish the justices' goal of protecting business against what they viewed as improper governmental interference.

The Supreme Court frustrated the national government's control of industry by limiting the scope of the interstate commerce power to cover only businesses that were actually involved in interstate commerce, such as railroads and shipping companies, and businesses that directly affected that commerce. This focus, in effect, freed companies involved in agriculture, mining, and production from control by the federal government. Similarly, national government's power of taxation was restrained by judicial rulings that questioned congressional motives in using that power. For example, a special tax on businesses using child labor was invalidated on the reasoning that the purpose of the tax was not to raise money but to discourage the use of child labor.

State regulation of business was thwarted through a novel interpretation of the "due process" clause of Fourteenth Amendment. Historically, due process had referred to the procedures of public officials. The justices now held that unreasonable regulation of private interests deprived people of their property without due process of law.

This dual approach served to protect business against government regulation, and it dominated the Supreme Court's decision making up to the 1930s, when it was used to strike down many New Deal laws. Between the late 1930s and the early 1980s, the Supreme Court focused almost all of its attention on protecting the personal liberties of individuals against infringement by the national government and the states. During this time, the Supreme Court outlawed racial segregation and religious practices in public schools, provided constitutional protection for the choice to have an abortion, and significantly expanded the protections of the First, Fourth, Fifth, Sixth, Eighth, and Fourteenth Amendments (these issues are covered in more depth in chapters 4 and 5).

Between them, Presidents Reagan and Bush appointed five new justices to the nine-member Court, and it was widely anticipated that a new conservative majority would reverse the liberal trends of previous decades. By 2008, seven of the nine Supreme Court justices had been appointed by Republican presidents: two by Reagan, two by George H. W. Bush, two by George W. Bush, and one by Gerald Ford. With the Supreme Court becoming increasingly dominated by appointments from Republican presidents, most of whom had come to office promising to appoint conservative justices, a new conservative era on the Supreme Court was a reasonable expectation. And to some extent, this expectation has been met. From the late 1980s on, the Supreme Court has shifted focus, but in a relatively limited way that has sometimes disappointed conservatives. Court rulings have generally reflected the conservative backgrounds of the justices, but there has been a consistent level of support for liberal outcomes in civil liberties cases. In other words, the Supreme Court has been more likely to affirm than overturn the expansion of rights and liberties granted in earlier rulings (Lee, Sandstrum, and Weisert 1996). As we saw in Figure 15.8, two Republican appointees, Souter and Stevens, were relatively consistent liberal voters. These two justices have retired, and Sonia Sotomayor and Elena Kagan, appointed by President Obama, are expected to join with President Clinton's appointees, Ginsberg and Breyer, to keep the liberal bloc intact. The final Republican appointee, Kennedy, has established a record as a moderate conservative. Rather than a solidly conservative court, the current court is deeply divided—the number of 5–4 decisions has increased in recent years. The conservative side usually prevails, though there are periodic exceptions, as the ruling upholding the constitutionality of key parts of the health care reform law demonstrates. This decision is interesting because Kennedy, who was generally thought to be the most likely to side with the liberal bloc, voted to strike down the law. It was Chief Justice Roberts, usually a reliable conservative vote, who found a way to interpret the law to uphold the constitutionality of the individual mandate requiring everyone to have health insurance.

Constraints on the Exercise of Judicial Review

Giving unelected judges life tenure and the power to block actions that the popularly elected branches of government take on behalf of the majority challenges the basic democratic values of majority rule and popular sovereignty. Routine and frequent exercise of judicial review would pose a significant threat to democracy. But the limited exercise of judicial review suggests that there are constraints on its use. Several mechanisms keep the Court from straying too far from the popular will for too long.

IMPEACHMENT Federal judges are subject to removal through the impeachment process. As discussed in chapter 12, impeachment by the House and removal by a two-thirds vote in the Senate is both a legal and a political process. Article II, Section 4 of the Constitution establishes the grounds for impeachment and removal as "treason, bribery, or other high crimes and misdemeanors." Political considerations inevitably come into play. It is unlikely that Congress would impeach and remove judges only because of unpopular rulings; there would need to be some evidence of wrongdoing serious enough to merit impeachment. But if judges were to use the power of judicial review frequently and irresponsibly, Congress would be able to find grounds for impeachment and removal. Congress is the sole authority in impeachment; these decisions are not subject to review by the courts.

Removal through impeachment is an extreme and infrequently used tool. No Supreme Court justice has been removed through the impeachment process. One, Samuel Chase, was impeached by the House in 1804, but he was acquitted in the Senate. That impeachment was politically motivated; Chase was a strong Federalist who behaved obnoxiously toward the Jeffersonian Democratic-Republicans in control of Congress. Although he remained on the Court until his death in 1811, he served with more contrition after the impeachment (Abraham 1993, 44). A total of 14 federal judges have been impeached, most as a result of allegations of corruption. Two impeached judges resigned before their trials in the Senate. Of the twelve who went on trial in the Senate, seven were removed, and four were acquitted. On March 11, 2010, the House impeached Federal District Judge G. Thomas Porteous Jr. of Louisiana on charges of accepting bribes and perjury. The Senate voted to convict Porteous on December 8, thus removing him from office. (Federal Judicial Center n.d.).

AMENDMENTS TO THE CONSTITUTION When the Court exercises judicial review, this review may be based on either legislative or constitutional interpretation. In a decision based on **legislative interpretation**, the Court interprets a statute passed by Congress and rules on the meaning or intent of the disputed section. If Congress disagrees with the Court's legislative interpretation, it can overturn the faulty interpretation by passing another law by a simple majority vote in both chambers. In a **constitutional interpretation**, the Court declares a law unconstitutional based its interpretation of the Constitution. A constitutional interpretation cannot be overturned by a simple statute. But if the Court's interpretation of the meaning of the Constitution is contrary to the strongly held views of most Americans, the Constitution can be amended.

As discussed in chapter 2, amending the Constitution is cumbersome and difficult. Nonetheless, 7 of the 27 amendments overturned unpopular judicial inter-

legislative interpretation A ruling of the Supreme Court in which the Court interprets on the meaning and intent of statute passed by Congress. Congress can overturn a decision based on legislative interpretation by passing another law.

Constitutional interpretation A ruling of the Supreme Court that declares a law unconstitutional based the Court's interpretation of the Constitution. A constitutional interpretation cannot be overturned by a simple statute.

pretations of the Constitution. Four of these amendments reversed rulings that had declared federal laws unconstitutional:

- The Thirteenth Amendment prohibiting slavery and the Fourteenth Amendment giving African Americans rights of citizenship overturned *Dred Scott v. Sanford* (1857).
- The Sixteenth Amendment overturned the Court's decision in *Pollock v. Farmers' Loan and Trust* (1895) that declared an income tax unconstitutional.
- The Twenty-Sixth Amendment lowering the voting age to 18 overturned *Oregon v. Mitchell* (1970), in which the Court struck down part of the federal law trying to extend voting rights to 18-year-olds by statute.

Three other amendments changed practices that the Court had ruled were permitted under the Constitution:

- The Eleventh Amendment giving states immunity from suits in federal court overturned the decision in *Chisholm v. Georgia* (1793).
- The Nineteenth Amendment giving women the right to vote changed the ruling in *Minor v. Happersett* (1875) that held that the Fourteenth Amendment did not give women the right to vote.
- The Twenty-Fourth Amendment prohibiting poll taxes changed Court rulings that interpreted the Constitution to permit these practices.

APPOINTMENTS Federal judges have life tenure, but they are mortal. Periodic vacancies are created by death and retirement. On average, a new Supreme Court justice has been appointed about every two years. Only four presidents have been denied an opportunity to fill vacancies on the Court. William Henry Harrison and Zachary Taylor died early in their terms, and Congress eliminated a seat that became vacant to prevent Andrew Johnson from making the appointment. Jimmy Carter served a full term without getting a chance to appoint a Supreme Court justice. Most presidents get one or more opportunities to fill vacancies on the Supreme Court.

Because presidents and members of Congress are elected to office, their political values are likely to generally reflect those of society at a particular point in time. Presidents appoint individuals to the Court who share their political values, and the Senate is not likely to confirm individuals with views far out of the mainstream. Thus, through normal attrition, vacancies are filled with justices who better reflect contemporary views, and judicial interpretations of the Constitution are not likely to be greatly out of tune with the mainstream of American thought for too long.

There have been occasions, however, when the values represented on the Court have lagged behind contemporary thinking. Franklin Roosevelt, for example, was frustrated during his first term when the Supreme Court blocked his New Deal legislation. Justices serve life terms, and the salaries of sitting justices cannot be cut while they are in office. Thus, short of impeachment, there is not much elected officials can do to a sitting justice. But Congress and the president don't have sit idly by, waiting for vacancy to open up. The Constitution leaves it to Congress to decide the number of seats on the Supreme Court. By passing a statute expanding the number of seats on the Court, Congress could give a president some vacant seats to fill. Indeed, this was the basis of President Roosevelt's "court-packing plan" of 1937. Roosevelt proposed legislation that would create one new justice for every Supreme Court member who had reached the age of 70 and had not retired. This court-packing proposal provoked a storm of protest and was defeated in Congress. But Justice Owen Roberts, who had generally been aligned with four other justices who consistently voted to invalidate social and economic legislation, shifted loyalties and began voting with those who consistently voted to uphold these new laws. This shift—popularly known as the "switch in time that saved nine"—and a retirement in 1937 eliminated Roosevelt's political need to expand the Court.[11] Nonetheless, Congress has the power to give the president new seats to fill if the Court's exercise of judicial review comes to be viewed as illegitimate.

CONTROL OF THE COURT'S APPELLATE JURISDICTION As discussed earlier, Congress controls the Supreme Court's appellate jurisdiction by statute. Since almost all cases in which the Court exercises judicial review come under its appellate jurisdiction, Congress has the power to restrain the Court by altering its appellate jurisdiction. Following the outbreak of the Civil War, Congress passed legislation taking away the Supreme Court's appellate jurisdiction in certain habeas corpus proceedings— that is, legal proceedings in which a court orders government officials to bring a person being detained to court to determine whether that person is imprisoned lawfully. More recently, in response to a number of controversial rulings, members of Congress introduced bills intended to reduce the Court's jurisdiction to hear appeals of certain types of cases. In 2004, for example, the House passed bills to prevent federal courts from hearing cases involving "under God" in the Pledge of Allegiance and to strip federal courts of the ability to order states to recognize same-sex marriages permitted by other states. The Senate, however, did not pass the bill and it did not become law.

Efforts to restrict the Court's appellate jurisdiction usually fail. Even members of Congress who disagree with the Court's ruling may vote against such legislation because they respect the principle of separation of powers; they may not like the Court's interpretation, but they believe the Court has the legitimate right to make the ruling. But if the Court strikes down too many laws favored by the majority, members of Congress could come to view the Court's exercise of judicial review as illegitimate and pass legislation restricting its appellate jurisdiction.

NO POWER TO INITIATE POLICYMAKING Courts are most definitely policymaking institutions; they make authoritative decisions about who gets what, when, and how.

---

[11] Although some accounts attribute Justice Owen Roberts's switch to the court-packing plan, there is evidence that his change of philosophy occurred before the plan was proposed (Cushman 1998).

The language and the process through which courts make policy, however, differ from the way legislatures, executives, and bureaucrats make policy.

Among the most important procedural differences between judicial and other types of policymaking is that courts cannot initiate the policymaking process. If a member of Congress sees the need for a new policy, he or she can start the process by introducing a bill that frames the issue in a particular way. The president and federal bureaucrats can propose policy changes. Courts, by contrast, must wait for others to bring cases to them. It is the parties to the case who frame the issues posed to the Court. Moreover, the rules of the judicial process require cases to involve real people who have suffered real and substantial harm. Persons who cannot show that they have been harmed by some governmental action do not have standing to sue. Although the Court has considerable discretion to pick and choose the cases it wants to hear, it still must choose from among the cases filed and answer the questions posed. Lack of the power of initiative is a significant constraint on judicial policymaking through judicial review.

LACK OF ENFORCEMENT POWER The Court's exercise of judicial review is further limited because it must rely on other public officials to enforce its decisions. Although the first instance of judicial review in *Marbury v. Madison* (1803) was self-enforcing in that it required President Jefferson to do nothing, almost all the other cases have required action on the part of public officials in some other part of government. Take the case of school desegregation. In *Brown v. Board of Education* (1954, 1955), the Supreme Court ruled that segregated schools violated the equal protection clause of the Fourteenth Amendment and that the states must desegregate the schools "with all deliberate speed." But there was resistance in many parts of the South, and when the school doors opened in the fall of 1956, very little had changed. President Eisenhower called out federal troops in 1957 to enforce the ruling in Little Rock, Arkansas. But it was not until nearly a decade later, when President Lyndon Johnson ordered federal education funds withheld from schools that were still segregated—an action mandated by the Civil Rights Act of 1964—that significant progress was made toward integrating schools throughout the South.

When the Court declares a law unconstitutional, it is always controversial. By definition, the Court is telling representatives of the majority that they cannot do something that the majority wants them to do. Because the Court is generally respected, and its legitimacy is unquestioned, even those who disagree with a decision believe that they are obligated to obey it. Federal and state judges and elected officials take an oath to support the Constitution, so there is considerable voluntary compliance with the Court's decisions, even unpopular ones. But too-frequent use of judicial review would undermine the Court's legitimacy. The Court can do little if the president, members of Congress, and other public officials decide to ignore its rulings. The Court has the power of neither the sword nor the purse; the president is commander in chief of the armed forces, and Congress has the power to appropriate funds. Such considerations led legal scholar Alexander Bickel (1962) to label the judiciary "the least dangerous branch."

SELF-RESTRAINT Finally, the most common and effective constraint on the exercise of judicial review is the self-restraint of the justices themselves. Judges are taught in law school—and most of them sincerely believe—that it is not appropriate for them to routinely substitute their own views of good public policy for those of the elected branches of government. Justice Harlan Fiske Stone, who thought the Court was being too activist in *U.S. v. Butler* (1936), wrote,

> The only check on our own exercise of power is our own self-restraint. . . . Courts are not the only agency of government that must be assumed to have the capacity to govern. . . . For the removal of unwise laws from the statute books appeal lies not to the courts but to the ballot and to the process of democratic government.

The Court has adopted several self-imposed legal doctrines intended to restrain judicial power. These are the political question doctrine and the doctrines of standing to sue, ripeness, and mootness. The political question doctrine recognizes that courts do not have jurisdiction over certain issues that fall exclusively under the authority of the political branches (the president and Congress). The Court has modified the boundaries of issues reserved exclusively for other branches. In the case of *Baker v. Carr* (1962), for example, the Court held that federal courts had jurisdiction to hear disputes over reapportionment of congressional districts, a subject that had long been considered a political question to be resolved only by elected officials. Nonetheless, issues of foreign affairs and Congress's exclusive control over the impeachment and constitutional amendment processes continue to be beyond the Court's jurisdiction. Standing to sue (discussed previously) limits the Court by defining who can bring a case; the Court will hear cases brought only by someone who has suffered some actual harm. The remaining two doctrines deal with timing. The ripeness doctrine allows the Court to reject cases that are filed too early, before the issues and facts in question have clearly caused some real harm. The mootness doctrine means that the Court will not hear cases that are no longer a real controversy. Although they are sometimes ineffective, these doctrines are self-imposed limits on the Court's power.

CHAPTER FIFTEEN
Top Ten Takeaway Points

1 Most Americans want judges to be independent and to make decisions based on the rule of law rather than on partisan loyalty, ideological prejudice, or political pressure. But an independent judiciary is insulated from certain core democratic values, and Americans also want judges to be accountable for unpopular decisions.

❷ The judiciary is a political branch of government. Interpreting the law is an inherently political process, and judges make decisions that authoritatively allocate values.

....

❸ The jurisdiction of the federal courts is defined by the Constitution, by congressional statute, and by the courts themselves. Federal courts have jurisdiction over litigation involving the U.S. Constitution, federal law, treaties, and admiralty and maritime matters. They also have jurisdiction over cases affecting agents of foreign governments, suits that involve a state or U.S. citizen and a foreign citizen or government, and interstate litigation.

....

❹ The most important power of the federal courts is the power of judicial review, which is the authority to review lower-court decisions and to declare the laws and actions of public officials unconstitutional. This power is not explicitly spelled out in the Constitution but rather was originally claimed by the Supreme Court in *Marbury v. Madison* (1803).

....

❺ The organization and structure of the federal courts is largely determined by Congress. The federal court system, broadly speaking, consists of three tiers: district courts (courts of original jurisdiction); U.S. courts of appeals (which have only appellate jurisdiction); and the U.S. Supreme Court, which has both original and appellate jurisdiction and sits at the top of both the federal and state court systems.

....

❻ The Constitution does not specify any qualifications to be a federal judge. It simply mandates the nomination of all federal judges by the president and confirmation by the Senate. Once confirmed, federal judges serve for life.

....

❼ Although there are no formal qualifications, presidents, senators, and the general public expect that federal judges should have legal training. In nominating federal judges, presidents take into account a wide variety of considerations besides legal background. The most important political considerations are party affiliation and political philosophy. Other political considerations that sometimes come into play include geography, religion, ethnicity, gender, and judicial experience and merit.

....

❽ Although judges may strive to be politically neutral and impartial, there are many gray areas of the law, and it is virtually impossible for an individual's background and personal values not to play a role. Given the tenure of federal judges and the importance and wide-ranging effects of their decisions, the political stakes in the selection process are high.

⑨ The philosophy of judicial restraint emphasizes deferring policymaking authority to other branches and levels of government. Judicial activism promotes a more forceful role in determining public policy through constitutional interpretation. The tension between restraint and activism is a political conflict rather than a philosophical one. Ideologues on the left and the right are more likely than moderates to be activists. Whether liberals or conservatives advocate a philosophy of restraint or activism tends to depend heavily on their ideological preferences on a given issue.

⑩ Constraints on judicial power include the possibility of impeachment; amendments to the Constitution; turnover on the bench through death or voluntary retirement; Congress's power to set the jurisdiction of federal courts and to determine the number of justices; the Court's inability to initiate policymaking and its reliance on other branches of government to enforce its rulings; and the self-restraint of judges.

CHAPTER FIFTEEN

Key Terms and Cases

attitudinal model, 600
collegial courts, 579
concurring opinions, 583
conference, 582
confirmation process, 594
constitutional interpretation 612
courts of appellate
    jurisdiction, 575
courts of original
jurisdiction, 575
dissenting opinions, 583

en banc, 579
judicial activism, 607
Judicial Conference, 576
judicial power, 574
judicial restraint, 607
judicial review, 575
judiciary, 573
jurisdiction, 574
legal model, 599
legal realist model, 600
legislative interpretation, 612

living Constitution, 607
majority opinion, 583
Marbury v. Madison, 575
originalism, 606
plurality opinion, 583
rule of four, 581
senatorial courtesy, 586
slot machine theory, 599
strategic model, 600
writ of certiorari, 581
writ of mandamus, 605

MR. FRANKEN

KEY QUESTIONS

Why is public policy the ultimate test of how a political system upholds
the core principles of democracy?

What are the key stages of the policy process, and how are decisions
made in that process?

Does the American political system manage to uphold all three core
democratic principles in the process of policymaking?

WHEN CONGRESS IS IN SESSION, the average legislator has to juggle several hundred issues that might require his or her attention. Crammed onto the congressional calendar in a single week is everything from budgets to voter registration, civil service reform to national forests, war to science education, and immigration to cable television regulation. How do legislators make responsible policy decisions with so many issues demanding attention? Simple. They cheat.

Well, not cheat exactly, but many do employ voting cards—what most college students would call a crib sheet. Voting cards provide a brief synopsis of an issue and indications of whether party leaders, constituents, and special interest groups support whatever proposal is being made. They also include the answer to the political equivalent of a major pop quiz: whether to vote yea or nay on that proposal.

These answers, though, are not quite as clear as you might find on crib sheets smuggled into college exams. There is no true or false or multiple choice; in fact, there is no right answer. Whatever the proposal and whatever the vote, the answer is wrong to somebody and probably somebody important. Satirist P. J. O'Rourke (1991, 62–63) once spoofed a typical voting sheet like this:

Home: Constituents will murder you in November if you oppose [the bill].

Administration: President will kill you right now if you support it.

Remarks: A toughie.

Making public policy is like that: tough and not as simple as it seems. There are so many issues clamoring for the attention of government that it is a major task simply to sort them out into a rough list of priorities. Focus on any one of these, and you are likely to find a lively conflict, with different interests pushing for contradictory and mutually exclusive actions. Approving or rejecting any one of these actions may incur the heated displeasure of its supporters or opponents. If a policy decision actually emerges from this melee, it still has to be implemented, which likely will set off another round of argument and debate. Once it is implemented, someone somewhere will want it changed, and the clamor for government attention will rise again.

Making public policy is the ultimate test of the democratic process. Indeed, public policymaking can be viewed as a test of how well—or how poorly—core democratic principles are put into practice. Everything we have studied so far plays a part in making public policy—parties and interest groups, elections and legislatures, executives and judges, bureaucracies and the media, the Constitution and federalism, and all the rest of the machinery that makes up the political system.

As such, it is fitting to end this book with a chapter on how all these elements come together to tackle the fundamental undertaking of politics discussed in chapter 1. The study of public policy, in essence, is the study of how all these elements combine to produce the "authoritative allocation of values" (Easton 1953, 143) or decisions about what we ought to do.

Public policy can be defined as a relatively stable, purposive course of action pursued by government officials or agencies (Anderson 2000, 4). This definition implies several important things about the concept of public policy. First, it implies that public policy is goal-oriented (purposive). In other words, public policies are undertaken to achieve some objective; they are not random or happenstance. In democratic societies, public policies are not the product of the whims or fancies of arbitrary rulers. They are the product of problems, issues, or demands that citizens expect or want the government to address.

Second, what makes public policy "public" is that it represents a goal undertaken by government. Nongovernmental groups also make policy. All businesses, for example, engage in purposive courses of action. Specifically, they systematically and deliberately choose courses of action they believe will result in a profit. Thus, they have sales policies, return policies, and customer policies. Yet these policies are not public policy. The government is the only institution that has the authority to make decisions about who gets what and to use coercion to make those decisions binding on everyone. Public policy is just that: the government's decision about who is getting what.

Finally, this definition implies a time element and a process; public policy is not just an action, but a relatively stable course of action. Public policy is more than a declared intent to do something; it also must involve some action that attempts to achieve the goal expressed or implied in the statement of intent. A campaign promise or even an actual law is a necessary part of a public policymaking process. These represent declarations of intent. However, our definition of public policy requires more. There must be some consistent follow-through to implement and enforce that promise or law.

THE CONCEPT OF PUBLIC POLICY

Public policy is nothing less than the business of translating the promise of democracy into the performance of democracy. Public policy encompasses the demands and expectations that citizens place on government and the government's response to these demands and expectations in the form of laws and public programs. For the political system to be democratic in practice as well as in theory, the core principles must be upheld throughout the entire process that produces the public policy. That process includes citizens and groups making demands on government, government formulating courses of action to respond to those demands, and the substantive response itself.

Upholding those core democratic principles is an enormously difficult challenge because the key characteristic of public policymaking is conflict (Cobb and Elder 1983, 82–93). It is extraordinarily rare for the government to be faced with a demand, problem, or issue where there is a clear, universally approved response. Policymaking is easy if everyone knows what they want from government, and government can give everyone everything they want. Such consensus rarely happens.

Instead, public policy typically involves conflict between two or more groups over something they value. This can be something tangible such as budgets, tax cuts, health care benefits, or the war in Afghanistan; or it can be intangible and symbolic such as whether individuals have the right to burn the flag. Symbolic policies do not generate less conflict just because they deal with intangibles. Compared to conflicts involving tangible benefits, symbolic policies actually can generate more strife because they often involve fundamental beliefs about what is right and what is wrong (C. Mooney 2001). Conflict over tangible benefits can often be resolved by splitting the difference—that is, through compromise. It is hard to split the difference on fundamental moral values. Consider the conflict over flag burning: a compromise that says protesters can burn only half the flag will satisfy neither side.

The study of public policy is astonishingly broad. It not only encompasses all of the institutions and processes we have covered in individual chapters in this book; it also includes all the substantive issues at the heart of policy conflicts: educa-

public policy A relatively stable, purposive course of action pursued by government officials or agencies.

POLITICS IN PRACTICE

HOW EVOLUTIONARY BIOLOGY HELPS MAKE SENSE OF PUBLIC POLICY

Whether the public policy process is pluralist or elitist is a topic of endless debate among political scientists. Is policy disproportionately decided by and in favor of a small group of elites? Or does the system ensure that all interests are given a fair hearing in deciding questions of who gets what?

These questions have vexed some of the most brilliant democratic theorists studying the American political system. The sheer number of topics, actors, and decision makers allows pluralist and elitist points of view to muster at least some evidence to support their argument. Frustrated at the inability of democratic theory to provide clear answers to the hows and whys of the policy system in action, some political scientists have turned to another discipline for help: evolutionary biology.

One of the most important pieces of policy scholarship in the last 25 years is an extended study undertaken by Frank Baumgartner and Bryan Jones, two political scientists who took on the enormous challenge of making systematic sense of the entire policy system— how it works and, more importantly, why it changes.

Rather than simply relying on the standard models of the policy process produced by democratic theory, they borrowed a concept called "punctuated equilibrium," which is taken directly from evolutionary biology.

Originally developed by paleontologists Steven Jay Gould and Niles Eldredge, punctuated equilibrium argues that biological evolution is not a gradual process of incremental change; rather, it consists of long periods of stability interrupted—or punctuated— by rapid change.

Baumgartner and Jones noticed that the same general principle describes the policy system remarkably well. In most policy areas, and for most of the time, there is stability, with only incremental adjustments to the status quo. Occasionally, however, there is a fundamental shift, with a period of radical change. This eventually settles down to a new period of stability. It is hard to do justice to Baumgartner and Jones' thesis in a few words, but at the core of their argument is the notion that the political system spawns a lot of policy subsystems. Policy subsystems consist

tion, welfare, the environment, economic stimulus, and more. The list of issues, large and small, is virtually endless. How is it possible to encompass all of this and come to some general conclusion about whether public policy in the United States reflects the core values of democracy? (See the Politics in Practice feature "How Evolutionary Biology Helps Make Sense of Public Policy.")

THE STAGES OF POLICYMAKING

Political scientists who specialize in the study of public policy often impose order on their vast and sprawling topic by viewing public policymaking as a system made up of four distinct stages:

of the institutions and actors interested in particular issues such as the environment, education, nuclear energy, and so forth. These systems can become policy monopolies, which are issue areas where those outside the policy subsystem have little interest or influence in or over it, and those within the subsystem control the key policy decisions. Such policy monopolies, however, cannot be maintained indefinitely. Invariably something happens to attract the interest and attention of actors outside the subsystem. This creates pressure that can dissolve a policy monopoly by drawing decision-making power toward other actors and producing rapid changes in laws and regulations.

What drives this change? Policy image, or how a policy is understood and discussed. Dramatic changes in policy image can mobilize those outside the policy subsystem and create pressure for change. This pressure results in a shift away from the key actors in the policy monopoly. Once decision-making power is drawn out of the policy monopoly and into the hands of other actors and institutions, the monopoly collapses and rapid policy change is the result.

Baumgartner and Jones use nuclear power as an example. In the 1950s, nuclear power had a very positive image; it was viewed as a source of cheap, limitless, and clean energy. This positive image allowed the nuclear industry, the associated congressional committees, and the Atomic Energy Commission to create a policy monopoly (in effect, an iron triangle as discussed in Chapter 14).

This image, however, shifted dramatically in the 1970s. The dangers of radioactive waste and a high-profile (and potentially disastrous) accident at the Three Mile Island nuclear plant attracted media attention and turned public opinion negative. This created pressure to push decision making out of the original policy monopoly; other congressional committees, as well as state and local governments, began to enact new laws and regulations. The result was a significant policy shift—stricter laws and regulations and an enforcement bureaucracy that shifted from industry advocate to tough regulator. This created a new period of stability, but one in which nuclear energy is viewed negatively, fewer nuclear plants are authorized, and the costs rather than the benefits drive policy adjustments.

To a remarkable extent, Baumgartner and Jones provide a comprehensive explanation of the policy process—from agenda setting through policy adoption —that can help explain stability and change across a broad range of policy issues.

SOURCE Baumgartner, Frank, and Bryan Jones. 1993. *Agendas and Instability in American Politics.* Chicago: University of Chicago Press.

1. *Agenda setting,* which produces the list of issues and problems the government will pay attention to
2. *Policy formulation and adoption,* wherein the government considers the various alternatives to the issue at hand and formally approves a particular alternative
3. *Policy implementation,* in which the government translates the approved alternative into action
4. *Policy evaluation,* wherein government and nongovernment actors assess the successes and problems of public policies (Ripley 1988, 48–55)

The evaluation stage often leads to calls for changes in public policy, which takes the system back to the agenda-setting stage (see Figure 16.1).

This stages approach provides us with a systematic way to evaluate how well—or how poorly—the various actors, institutions, and processes we have studied in this book translate the theory of democracy into the practical push-and-pull of

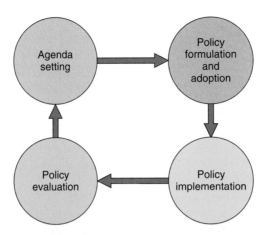

FIGURE 16.1 Stages of Policymaking

making public policy. Once we have a reasonable understanding of this process, we will have a basis for assessing how well it reflects the core democratic values in action.

Agenda Setting

Government cannot attend to all the possible issues, problems, and demands that exist. Somehow a manageable list of issues on which government can focus must be created. This list is known as the **public agenda**, and it consists of the issues and problems that the government is actually paying attention to. But even if an issue or problem makes it to the public agenda, this does not mean a public policy will result. The public agenda is simply a list of topics included in the national debate about what government should (or should not) do at a given point in time.

Political scientists have devoted considerable effort to explaining how and why some policy issues make it on to the public agenda and others do not. The reason for this interest is not hard to fathom; the ability of a political system to deliver on the promise of democracy critically depends on the list of policy issues and alternatives a government actively considers. If the government is paying attention to issues and alternatives that few people support, it seems unlikely that core democratic principles such as majority rule and popular sovereignty are going to be upheld. Connecting the actions of government to the will of the people presumes that the government is considering actions that actually represent the will of the people.

Yet political scientists have long known that no political mechanism—certainly not any form of democracy—can guarantee that government will consider, much less pursue, policies that reflect the will of the people. This surprising conclusion is one of the more important contributions of rational choice theory to an

public agenda All issues and problems that have the attention of the government at a particular point in time.

understanding of politics and public policy. **Arrow's impossibility theorem**, formulated by economist Kenneth Arrow (1963), is a formal proof that no decision-making system can guarantee that the rank-ordered preferences of a group will reflect the rank-ordered preferences of the individuals who make up that group. The startling implication of Arrow's theorem for democratic systems is that there is no way they can, for certain, determine exactly what policies people want.

How can this be? Well, imagine that you and two friends want to order ice cream. You have to make a group decision on what flavor to order (only one flavor can be ordered for all three of you). The alternatives on the agenda are strawberry, chocolate, and vanilla. All three of you rank-order those preferences differently; one prefers chocolate to strawberry to vanilla, another vanilla to chocolate to strawberry, and the third strawberry to vanilla to chocolate. There is no single preferred alternative here. So remembering the core democratic principles of majority rule, you all decide to take a vote on what flavor should be ordered by putting the flavors in direct, one-on-one electoral competition with each

The prestige, power, and visibility of the nation's chief executive give the president unrivaled ability to focus the public opinion and government on a particular set of issues. Here, President Barack Obama signs the health care reform bill he strongly advocated. Obama made the health care bill a top domestic priority of his first term.

© Ron Sachs/CNP/Corbis

other. Let's say chocolate and strawberry are voted on first. Assuming everyone votes rationally (i.e., to maximize their flavor preferences), in a vote of chocolate against strawberry, chocolate wins because two people prefer it over strawberry. Then you vote on chocolate over vanilla. Vanilla wins because two people prefer it over chocolate. The result of this voting is that the group has decided the following preference for ice cream flavor: vanilla over chocolate over strawberry. That vote, however, is not the will of the people in the group. Why? Well, let's retake the vote, but start by choosing between strawberry and vanilla. Now strawberry wins because two people prefer strawberry over vanilla. See what just happened? The group has the same set of alternatives, but because the choices were presented in a different order—in other words, because the agenda was framed differently—the preferences of the group were reversed by the voting process. Strawberry went from being ranked dead last in the original "flavor referendum" to being ranked first in the next vote. Arrow's theorem, in essence, demonstrates that this inability to aggregate individual preferences into group preferences is common to most mechanisms used to make group decisions. Those mechanisms, as the ice cream example demonstrates, include democratic processes.

Arrow's impossibility theorem A formal proof that no decision-making system can guarantee that the rank-ordered preferences of a group will reflect the rank-ordered preferences of the set of rational individuals who make up that group.

An obvious implication of this theorem is that the person setting the agenda can influence group decisions. If you can control which choices are presented to the group (think chocolate over vanilla versus strawberry over vanilla), you can influence the preferred outcome of the group. In short, if you can determine what is on the public agenda, you can influence what policy alternatives government will adopt. Regardless of how an issue is framed, however, getting it on the public agenda does not guarantee a public policy will be made. It is absolutely certain, though, that a policy will never be made if it does not gain the attention of public authorities in the first place. Getting on the public agenda therefore represents the first critical stage in public policymaking. But how is this accomplished? Perhaps more importantly, who gets to set the agenda? And how are topics chosen from among the thousands of possibilities?

AGENDA SETTERS There are a number of actors both inside and outside the government struggling to get their particular interests and issues on the public agenda, although they have varying abilities to do this. Inside the government, the most powerful agenda setter is the president. The prestige, power, and visibility of the nation's chief executive give the president unrivaled ability to focus public opinion and the government's attention on a particular set of issues.

Close behind the president is Congress. Individual members of Congress cannot command the attention or set the agenda in the same fashion as the president. Yet representatives and senators are in a unique position to influence the public agenda because of the legal authority of Congress (a member of Congress must introduce a specific bill, and majorities in the House and Senate must approve it) and the public nature of the institution (Kingdon 1995, 21–44).

The courts play less of a role in agenda setting because they cannot initiate the process—they can only respond to issues that are litigated. But court decisions do occasionally add topics to the national agenda. Abortion policy was being openly debated in only a handful of states until 1973, when the Supreme Court's decision in *Roe v. Wade* (1973) propelled it onto the national agenda, where it has remained for several decades; a decision by the Massachusetts Supreme Court saying that same-sex couples in Massachusetts had the same rights to marry as heterosexual couples thrust the issue of same-sex marriage onto the agenda in every state, in the halls of Congress, and in the 2004 presidential election.

Outside the government, the key forces in agenda setting are interest groups, the media, political parties, elections, and public opinion. Of these, interest groups play the most important role in agenda setting, primarily because they expend considerable effort and resources trying to focus the attention of lawmakers on their interests. As we learned in chapter 6, interest groups engage in a wide variety of lobbying efforts, all of them directed at gaining access to lawmakers so that their issue will be considered—that is, put on the agenda.

We also saw in chapter 8 that the media play a powerful role in agenda setting (McCombs and Shaw 1972). The media role in agenda setting, though, differs from that of interest groups. Interest groups bring a sustained effort to a narrow set of interests. In contrast, the media shift focus rapidly. Only a few issues (for example, the war in Afghanistan) are powerful enough to generate sustained attention from the media. The pressure of a daily news cycle drives constant turnover in the issues that get prominent play in the media.

Rational choice models view agenda setting as a competition between these various actors (the president, interest groups, etc.) to strategically frame the agenda so that it favors their policy preferences. For example, if the war in Afghanistan is framed as a choice between winning the war on terror and "cutting and running," this pushes policy action toward continuing the war. If it is framed as an expensive foreign entanglement that is propping up a corrupt government and benefiting war lords, this pushes policy action toward withdrawal.

GARBAGE CAN MODELS OF AGENDA SETTING Other theories of agenda setting rely less on rational choice and more on social-psychological approaches. One of the best-known theories of agenda setting is a so-called garbage can model, formulated by John Kingdon (1995).

Garbage can models were originally formulated by a trio of researchers seeking to explain why decision making in large complex institutions (they originally examined universities) seemed so, well, irrational (Cohen, March, and Olsen 1972). They called such systems "organized anarchies." In organized anarchies, decision making is not the product of a rational cost–benefit calculation based on a clearly defined problem with a clear set of preferred outcomes. Instead, preferences are unclear, and solutions and problems are viewed as the product of independent processes. Organized anarchies produce a lot of solutions that are not particularly well suited to any pressing problem of the moment, and these are tossed into the metaphorical garbage can. Many problems never gain the attention of decision makers, and these also get tossed into the garbage can. These garbage cans, jumbles of problems and solutions, become useful when they happen to mix together a useful—or at least handy—solution to a problem that does gain the attention of decision makers. This mixing, called a "choice opportunity" in the jargon of the garbage can model, is used to emphasize the difference from rational choice models. Rather than maximizing preferences, decision makers rake through the "garbage" to see if they can find a solution that will connect to the problem they are paying attention to.

Kingdon (1995) saw a similar garbage can process at work in agenda setting in the U.S. political system. For example, consider the domestic production of corn-based ethanol as a solution. Toss it in the garbage can. Then say government gets concerned about the rising cost of gasoline (a problem); ethanol production can be fished out of the garbage can as a way to make us less dependent on oil imports (a solution). Say government is concerned about the environment (a problem); then ethanol can be pitched as a carbon-neutral fuel (a solution). If government is concerned about a sagging agricultural sector, corn-based ethanol might be seen as a basis for a good cash crop (a solution). If government is now concerned about unemployment (a problem), new ethanol plants might be pitched as a source of new jobs (a solution). You get the idea—the solution here is not necessarily the result of a rational analysis of the problem; it is something

garbage can model A model that attempts to explain why decision making in large complex institutions often seems irrational.

in the garbage can that policymakers can "find" whenever a range of problems present themselves.

For any of this "finding" to happen, of course, policymakers must be paying attention to the problem. Kingdon sought to systematically explain exactly how this happens.

CHOOSING ISSUES In Kingdon's model, gaining a place on the public agenda means gaining the collective interest of policymakers. As a general rule of thumb, policymakers tend to focus on problems that they believe demand some sort of response or action on their part. This sort of focus is created when the various agenda-setting forces combine and produce one or more of the following: indicators, focusing events, and feedback.

Indicators are any measures that can be employed as systematic monitoring devices. A classic example is money. If gas prices spike, for example, the media pay attention, public opinion is aroused, sales of gas guzzlers fall, and policymakers are forced to pay attention to energy policy. Indicators are important because they send signals that a problem exists and that the government is expected to do something.

A **focusing event** is something that grabs attention immediately and puts an issue on the public agenda. The terrorist attacks on the World Trade Center on September 11, 2001, and Hurricane Katrina in 2005 are two classic examples. A comparable example is the BP oil spill of 2010. Prior to the spill, safety and environmental regulations for deep-sea drilling operations were not particularly high on the public agenda. Following the spill, they were the subject of sustained media coverage and congressional hearings.

Feedback consists of the information policymakers routinely receive through government reports, hearings, the news, casework, meetings with lobbyists and government officials, and contact with constituents. Much of this information is unlikely to push an issue onto the public agenda. An irate constituent complaining about taxes, for example, does not suggest a major problem; that is simply a normal part of the background noise of a democratic political system.

A focusing event is something that grabs attention immediately and puts an issue on the public agenda. Examples of focusing events include Hurricane Katrina, which put a national spotlight on state–federal relations and particularly on the abilities and competence of the Federal Emergency Management Agency (FEMA); the attacks of 9/11, which catapulted terrorism to the top of the public agenda; and the British Petroleum *Deepwater Horizon* oil well blowout in the Gulf of Mexico and subsequent spill, which focused attention on lax enforcement of federal safety and environmental regulations.

Feedback helps select an issue for the public agenda when it signals that something is seriously different from how policymakers expect it to be. For example, feedback from constituents and military officials that U.S. troops were buying their own body armor because of army shortages prompted congressional focus on what, until then, had been a backwater military logistical issue (Lenz 2004).

Policy Formulation and Adoption

Once a problem or issue has the focused attention of policymakers, the policy process shifts to the **policy formulation and adoption** stage. Here the government considers various alternatives to the issue or problem at hand and works to formally approve one of those alternatives. The alternatives now under consideration are those that are on an institutional agenda. In contrast to the public agenda, which includes all the issues that are part of the broad public debate about what the government should do, an **institutional agenda** is a short list of actionable items being given serious consideration by policymaking institutions (Theodoulou 1995, 87).

Once elevated to the institutional agenda, the policy problem shifts from one of deciding what issues to address to one of choosing among the competing alternatives. Again, making this choice represents a significant challenge for government. An issue's placement on the institutional agenda does not automatically suggest a solution (Baumgartner and Jones 1993, 28). Poor educational performance, for example, is a policy problem that has a near-permanent place on the institutional agendas of state and national governments. The range of possible responses to this problem includes more funding, tougher standards, a voucher system, and reform of teacher education. Each alternative has its champions and detractors. What alternative, or set of alternatives, should be chosen?

The garbage can model suggests that choices are a product of independently produced solutions and problems joining together at a particular point in time. Other decision-making models, however, not only suggest that there is more of an element of rational thought involved in making public policy; they actually prescribe how such rational decisions should be made. There are two general models of how rational decision makers should sort through policy alternatives and select the most appropriate response to the issue at hand. The first is based on classical rational choice theory and is known as **rational-comprehensive decision making**. In this model, a decision maker develops a comprehensive list of alternatives to the problem or issue, assesses the costs and benefits of each alternative, and then chooses the alternative that most effectively solves the problem or achieves the desired goal at the lowest cost (Chandler and Plano 1988, 127–131). The big advantage of the rational-comprehensive approach to policy formulation and adoption is that it considers all alternatives and is thus likely to hit on a policy that works to solve the problem at minimal cost. The big drawback is that it is not very practical. It assumes that policymakers have compatible objectives and complete information about the consequences of every potential alternative to achieving

policy formulation and adoption The stage in the policymaking process in which government considers various alternatives to the issue or problem at hand and formally approves one of those alternatives.

institutional agenda A short list of actionable items being given serious consideration by policymaking institutions.

rational-comprehensive decision making A decision-making approach characterized by consideration of all alternatives to a problem or issue, an analysis of the costs and benefits of each alternative, and selection of the alternative with the most benefits at the least cost.

POLITICS IN PRACTICE

INCREMENTALISM IN ACTION

The typical approach to public sector budgeting is to begin with the previous year's budget and make small incremental adjustments up or down. This is the classic example of incremental decision making. Figure 16.2 shows government spending from 1940 through 2015 in constant 2005 dollars so that spending can be compared across time. Changes in government expenditures from one year to the next are small (generally less than 5 percent), except during a major crisis such as the spike in spending during World War II in the 1940s or the massive economic stimulus package passed by the federal government in 2009.

There are a number of drawbacks to incremental budget making, and these problems periodically prompt calls for reform. Most of the reform proposals, in one way or another, call for injecting a measure of rational-comprehensive decision making into the budget-making process.

A good example is zero-based budgeting (ZBB). Consider that under incrementalism a public agency will use its previous funding level as a base and attempt to justify any increase (or decrease) to that base. This is how the budget will be framed for the public authorities who actually approve the budget (usually a legislature)—in terms of how much more or how much less the agency gets compared to the previous year.

Under ZBB, that same public agency will start with a base of zero and have to justify every dollar beyond that base. ZBB thus proposes a more rational-comprehensive approach to making budgeting decisions, forcing public authorities to consider alternatives for every expenditure.

While ZBB has much to recommend it in theory, in practice it simply is not practical. The federal budget today runs roughly $3.8 trillion in current dollars. If Congress were forced to set that to zero every year and painstakingly justify every one of those $3.84 trillion, it would undoubtedly save some money and put some unproductive programs out of business. But it would also be a highly impractical approach to making policy. Considering all of the potential alternatives to the expenditure of every dollar would require a massive amount of manpower. As an example, suppose that Congress worked 365 days a year, 7 days a week and managed to consider all potential alternatives

those objectives. This is very rarely the case. Policymakers often have different objectives for any given issue or policy problem, and they do not know all the possible consequences of every potential action. Even if they did, a comprehensive policy evaluation is enormously time-consuming; if the problem is to put out a raging forest fire, there is no time to collect and analyze information about all possible alternatives before the fire destroys the entire forest.

It is more practical for policymakers to engage in incremental decision making. **Incrementalism** describes an approach to the search for policy alternatives that involves looking at how similar problems or issues have been handled in the past, identifying a handful of alternative approaches to that issue or problem that are politically and financially feasible, and choosing the one that is the most "do-

incrementalism A decision-making approach characterized by making current decisions that are small adjustments to past decisions.

CHAPTER 16 **CORE DEMOCRATIC PRINCIPLES AND PUBLIC POLICY**

and still justify and approve $1 billion in expenditures per day. At that rate, it would take them about a decade to generate an annual budget. The result would certainly be comprehensive but ultimately not very rational.

The federal budget is a classic example of incremental decision making. This incremental approach makes federal budgets fairly predictable. Generally speaking, each year's budget is a little more than the previous year's budget, resulting in a linear trend over time.

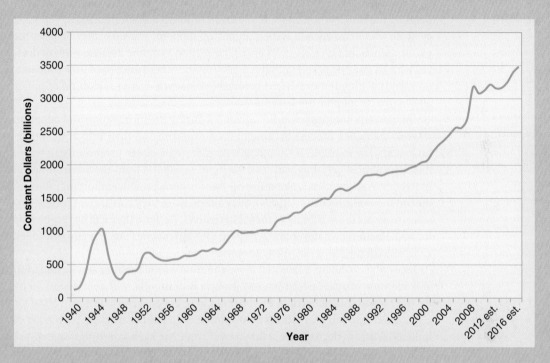

FIGURE 16.2 **Federal Government Spending, 1940–2017**
Source: Office of Management and Budget, "Historical Tables," http://www.whitehouse.gov/omb/budget/Historicals/.

able." Political scientist Charles Lindblom (1959) called this "the science of muddling through." (See the Politics in Practice feature "Incrementalism in Action.") Incrementalism reflects bounded rationality in action. As discussed in chapter 14, bounded rationality views humans as imperfectly rational. Their ability to make rational decisions is "bounded," or constrained, by lack of information. Rather than search through all possible solutions to find the one that maximizes utility, a boundedly rational decision maker selects the first solution that is "good enough"—in other words, one that works (Simon 1947). As a practical matter, then, decision makers typically begin with what worked last time and expand their search from there in small steps until they hit on something that looks like it will solve the problem.

The big drawback of the incremental approach is that the cheapest or most effective alternative may not be chosen for the simple reason that it was never considered. The big advantage of the incremental approach is its sheer practicality for policymaking bodies trying to cram lots of issues onto their institutional agendas. The alternatives chosen might be second-best, but for the most part, they work.

Regardless of the particular approach, the actors who are most influential in defining the range of solutions to any given problem are not necessarily the same as those who drive agenda setting. Public opinion, for example, may help set the public agenda, but it rarely gives enough direction to define detailed ways of dealing with an issue or problem. Bureaucrats, on the other hand, have little influence on agenda setting but exercise considerable influence over the selection of policy alternatives (Kingdon 1995).

Bureaucrats become powerful influences during the formulation and adoption stage of the policy process because of their expertise and their role in the political system. For example, if Congress is considering a law to promote clean water, members almost certainly will seek the input of experts from the Environmental Protection Agency (EPA). Not only will these experts provide important information on the impacts of the various policy alternatives; they also are in a unique position to assess the feasibility of these alternatives. Because they will be responsible for implementing whatever law is passed, EPA bureaucrats are best situated to tell Congress what is, or is not, likely to work.

Some actors remain influential throughout the agenda setting and formulation and adoption stages. Special interest groups, for example, will continue to lobby for their favored alternative. A member of Congress may consider how voting for a particular law will play with public opinion in his or her district. Yet the list of influential actors narrows as policy moves from the agenda-setting stage to the formulation and adoption stage, especially when the government actually moves to the point of selecting and formally approving a particular policy alternative.

The reason there is a limited range of actors at the formal adoption stage is simple: only government has the power to authoritatively allocate values and make those decisions binding on everyone. Congress can pass a law; the president can issue an executive order; a public agency can approve a rule; a judge can make a ruling or issue a court order. Special interest groups, political parties, the media, and public opinion may influence the official decision makers throughout the process, but these nongovernmental actors do not have the authority to formally make public policy. Whatever influence nongovernmental actors exert at the formal adoption stage is indirect (Kingdon 1995).

Policy Implementation

Laws, executive orders, rules, and judicial decisions are a formal pronouncement of the intent to take purposive action, not the action itself. **Policy implementation** is the process of translating that intent into action (Sabatier and Mazmanian 1980). As the policy process shifts from the selection and adoption stage to the implementation stage, the cast of important policy actors once again gets shuffled. Bureaucrats be-

policy implementation The process of translating government intent into government action.

come, by far, the most important actors in this stage of the policy process. The reason is simple: implementation is what public agencies are designed to do (Kerwin 1999).

Public agencies typically face a number of problems in translating the stated intent of the other institutions of government into action: laws with vague goals, laws with multiple or even contradicting goals, and inadequate resources to do the job. And though special interest groups, political parties, and governmental actors such as legislatures and executives play less of a role in implementation, they do not simply disappear from this stage of public policymaking. As the discussion on rulemaking in chapter 14 highlights, public agencies are often subject to varying degrees of lobbying and political pressure as they go about trying to implement policy decisions.

There is typically a considerable distance between a formal declaration of intent and the action actually taken by government. What happens between formal adoption and action determines to a large extent whether a public policy will achieve its desired objectives. Political scientists have discovered that the success or failure of public policy is often determined by what happens during the implementation stage.

The classic political science study of implementation was undertaken by Jeffrey Pressman and Aaron Wildavsky (1973). This was a case study of a federal policy program aimed at alleviating unemployment in inner-city Oakland. The policy, at least at first glance, had all the ingredients for success: there was a clear goal, there was just one federal agency running the program, the program was amply funded, and there was near-universal agreement that creating jobs in the inner city was a worthy policy goal. But although just about everyone wanted the program to work, it was a miserable failure.

Pressman and Wildavsky concluded that a primary reason for the program's failure was how the implementation process was shaped by the federal system. The city of Oakland is a municipality in the state of California, but this was a federal program using (mostly) federal dollars. There was only one federal agency involved, but there were three levels of government (national, state, and local). As discussed in chapter 3, the disadvantages of a federal system include a degree of inefficiency and complexity, and these disadvantages are particularly acute in attempts to implement a policy that requires the coordination of different levels of government.

Pressman and Wildavsky found that the multiple levels of government meant that a series of decision points had to be cleared before any action could be taken. In other words, before any money could be spent and before any action could be taken, it had to be approved by the federal, state, and local government units. The need to jump through these hoops had two major implications for implementation: (1) it made action—any action at all—much less likely; and (2) it made it difficult to hold any specific unit accountable for any particular action.

To see why implementation is so difficult, consider a hypothetical implementation scenario in which any action to implement a federal policy has to go through ten decision points at three levels of government (federal, state, and local). In other words, before there is any positive action to achieve the policy's objectives, ten groups or people have to approve that particular action. In our hypothetical scenario, we will make everything easy (and a little unrealistic) by assuming that all of the people at each of these ten decision points are more or less in agreement with the policy's goals and the actions that need to be taken in order to achieve them. Making it even easier, we will assume that whatever pressure is being applied from the political system—be it from legislators, public opinion, special interests, or whatever—this pressure is pushing for the same thing.

Surely under these ideal conditions, action will be undertaken and undertaken soon, right? Not necessarily. If the probability that an action is going to be approved is 90 percent at each of these decision points, the overall probability that the action will make it through all ten stages drops to about 35 percent (this is the product of multiplying 0.9 by 0.9 ten times). If it takes three days for a decision to be made by each group or person—a pretty reasonable time span if the action has to be carefully considered and meetings have to be scheduled—it will take a month for an action to be approved—that is, if it is approved. Even in ideal circumstances, that is no sure thing.

And if no action is taken, or an action turns out to be ineffective, inefficient, or just plain silly, who should be held accountable? Federal, state, or local authorities? The policy itself? Something else? Could the problem be not enough resources or vague or competing goals? Political pressure to take one particular action over another? All of these can be real obstacles to successful implementation of any single policy. Studying the implementation process leads not just to an understanding of why policies fail but also to an appreciation of the enormous effort that goes into making them work.

Implementation can founder not just on decision points or on practical considerations such as funding; one of the biggest challenges is the nature of the goal or the problem being addressed. A policy to lower noise disturbances in neighborhoods adjacent to a university campus, for example, is much more doable than a policy to safely produce electricity from nuclear power plants. In the first example, the action needed to achieve the goal is clear: reduce the number of fraternity parties, and you have less noise disturbance. What needs to be changed, whose behavior needs to change, and where they need to change it are all clear. Now consider the second policy. What needs to be changed? Whose behavior needs to be changed? What does it mean for nuclear energy to be "safe"? In this case, it is not clear what actions need to be taken or even how to define the goal that is to be achieved. Consequently, successfully addressing that problem is much less likely. Implementation is extraordinarily difficult—maybe even impossible—if overarching policy goals are unlikely to be achieved regardless of what course of action is pursued (Sabatier and Mazmanian 1980).

Policy Evaluation

Despite the difficulties inherent in policy implementation, once a policy is formally approved and adopted, some purposive course of action is likely to be undertaken. A whole range of actors within the political system will be interested in what those actions are and what, if anything, they achieve.

The process of examining the consequences of public policy is known as **policy evaluation**. Policy evaluation is undertaken for any number of reasons. The

policy evaluation The process of examining the consequences of public policy.

obvious reason is to assess whether the policy worked. This reason is far from the only one, however. If a policy is not achieving its objectives, we might want to know why. Is it because the problem is simply too complex and the solution difficult to achieve? Was the policy poorly implemented? Starved of resources? Poorly managed? Even if a policy worked and achieved its stated goals, we might still be interested in figuring out whether there is a way to achieve those goals more effectively and efficiently. If the policy goals were achieved effectively and efficiently, we might want to know why

Public education policies address what many consider intractable problems. Partly because the goals of education policy are so contradictory and so hard to achieve, education policy is being constantly evaluated to assess what outcomes are produced by particular programs and to try and figure out how—or if—things can be done more effectively and efficiently. One formal way to do this is through standardized testing. Much attention has been paid to the results of these tests, but many suggest that they are a more accurate reflection of how well students have been trained to take the tests rather than an accurate reflection of their knowledge base.

in order to apply these lessons to other policy areas. (See the Politics in Practice feature "Nerds, Sinners, and Perverts—Why Some Policies Fail.")

The various reasons for undertaking a policy evaluation serve the purposes of many different political actors. A special interest group might want to know how effectively a policy is serving its members' needs. The media might be interested in whether a program is wasting taxpayer dollars. The minority party may use evaluations to hold the majority party accountable for its policy failures, just as the majority party may use them to tout its policy successes.

For these reasons, public policies are constantly being evaluated. Evaluation can be done formally or informally and can be undertaken by a wide variety of actors, ranging from the public agency actually taking the actions to the media, interest groups, and academics. These actors all tend to use different approaches and have different goals for undertaking an evaluation, and they can come to very different conclusions about the same program or policy. Despite the wide variety of approaches, though, all policy evaluations can be classified into one of two broad categories: process evaluations and impact evaluations (Theodoulou 1995, 91).

Process evaluations assess whether a policy is being implemented according to its stated guidelines. If the policy is to reduce neighborhood noise by increasing police patrols, reducing response time to neighborhood complaints, and ticketing offenders for first offenses, then a process evaluation would look at the number of police patrols, the response time to noise complaints, and the ratio of tickets to warnings given to first offenders.

Impact evaluations assess policy outcomes. In other words, the goal in an impact evaluation is to see whether the policy has achieved its overall objectives. In the preceding example, an impact evaluation would assess whether the actions that are the focus of a process evaluation—increased police patrols, faster response times, and citations for first offenders—actually contribute to a reduction

process evaluation An evaluation undertaken with the goal of assessing whether a program or policy is being implemented according to its stated guidelines.

impact evaluations Evaluations undertaken to assess the outcomes or effects of a policy or program.

NERDS, SINNERS, AND PERVERTS—WHY SOME POLICIES FAIL

Political scientists have long noted that some public policies are more likely to achieve their goals than others. Policies that try to regulate morals, especially so-called "sin issues," are among the most notorious for failure.

Consider Prohibition: didn't work. The War on Drugs: well, just how hard is it to get drugs? Sodomy laws did not prevent homosexuality, and decency laws—even those that managed to squeeze past the First Amendment—have done little to stop online pornography.

Why do these sorts of policies fail? Political scientists have hit upon a simple answer to this question: We want them to fail.

Throughout the republic's history, different groups have demanded a government response to problems associated with things like booze or drugs or sex. Periodically they have been successful enough to push these issues onto the public agenda, swing public opinion behind their proposals, and actually get a policy adopted.

Yet, though public opinion might demand a clampdown on alcohol, drugs, sexually explicit materials, or particular sex acts, the public sometimes shows little inclination to obey the resulting laws. Why?

Scholars who study morality policies suggest there are two answers to this question. The first is that few people will speak out in favor of what is perceived as sinful, even if they commit the sinful act on a regular basis. For example, few people, and even fewer politicians, extol the virtues of drug use or pornography. This means when proposals to regulate drugs or pornography make it to the public agenda, few voices are raised in opposition.

Second, even if a law is passed, it will have, at best, mixed success in regulating people's behavior. Political scientist Kenneth Meier once illustrated this by dividing the population into three basic categories: nerds, sinners, and perverts. Nerds are those who have no interest in the behavior and will thus obey the law. Teetotalers, for example, had no problem obeying Prohibition.

Sinners are those who like engaging in the behavior but will only do so if the chances of getting caught are low. For example, a businessman who orders a hard-core pornographic film while in a hotel is unlikely to do the same at home.

Perverts are those who will not or cannot stop the behavior prohibited or regulated by policy. A drug addict, for example, may be psychologically or physiologically incapable of kicking his or her habit. Smokers will light up even if they have to go outside a building in the freezing cold or driving rain to do so.

The success of a morality policy, then, depends on the ratio of nerds, sinners, and perverts in the population. It is not necessarily the perverts that make the difference between success and failure.

If a large proportion of the public falls into what Meier labeled the category of sinners—that is, people who like to occasionally indulge in whatever is being regulated—the net result is policy failure because a big chunk of the public is ignoring the law on a semi-regular basis. Policy fails because, in effect, it does not turn sinners into nerds!

SOURCE Meier, Kenneth J. 1999. "Drugs, Sex, and Rock and Roll: A Theory of Morality Politics." *Policy Studies Journal*, 27 (4): 681–695.

in noise levels. Impact evaluations tend to come after process evaluations because it usually takes some time for a policy or program to produce a measurable change in outcomes. Process evaluations, on the other hand, can provide useful information on whether a policy is being implemented according to its guidelines as soon as the program gets underway.

Regardless of whether they are process or impact evaluations, reviews, reports, and analyses of public policy often lead to calls for change. Public policies that are adopted and implemented and that clearly achieve their stated goals do exist, but they are more the exception than the rule. A decision to build a bridge, for example, might fall into this category. The decision is made, funds are appropriated, plans are laid, contractors are hired, the bridge is built, and process and impact evaluations show an objective achieved in the time and manner expected.

A lot of public policy, however, is aimed at difficult or intractable problems. "Intractable" simply means the problem is complex, caused by many different factors, and hard to address within the confines of any single policy program—or even a whole group of them. Public education is a good example.

As already discussed, the underperformance or even outright failure of public schools is a staple of the public agenda. This is partially due to the intractable nature of the problems that public education policies address. It is hard enough just to define the goals of education policy. What constitutes a "quality education" or "equality of educational opportunity"? How do we know when these goals have been achieved? Some see tough academic standards as an education policy that will increase the quality of public education. Tough academic standards, though, may lead to higher dropout rates. Higher dropout rates may strike some as evidence of the failure of education policies.

Because the goals of education policy are so contradictory and so hard to achieve, education policy is being constantly evaluated to assess what outcomes are produced by particular programs and to figure out how or whether things can be done more effectively and efficiently. These evaluations are formal and informal, and they frequently lead to calls for policy change. Because public education affects so many people and because it consumes so many tax dollars, education issues are quick to get the attention of media, policymakers, special interest groups, and public opinion.

When this happens, evaluations shift the policy process back to the agenda-setting stage. What should we do about underperforming inner-city schools? A whole range of policy evaluations show that school voucher programs have not improved student achievement by much, if at all (Gill et al. 2001; Smith 2005). Does this mean vouchers do not work? Or does it mean that, to work, voucher programs should be expanded from relatively small-scale experiments involving small numbers of students? Should we expand the students eligible for vouchers? Scrap the voucher program and move back to neighborhood schools? What about setting tougher standards that will be more likely to increase achievement scores? What about after-school programs? Tougher teacher certification standards? Evaluations constantly raise such questions, and these questions are inevitably followed by the political conflict that breaks out over the proposed answers.

PUBLIC POLICY AND CORE DEMOCRATIC VALUES

Now that we have some idea of how the various institutions and actors that make up the political system interact to make public policy, let us assess how that process upholds the core principles of democracy. In this final section of the book, we examine each of the core principles and provide an appraisal of how well (or poorly) they are reflected in the policymaking process.

Majority Rule

The first core principle we encountered in chapter 1 was majority rule. Majority rule simply means that government follows the course of action preferred by most people. Majority rule can be defined (1) in terms of more than half of eligible citizens or voters preferring one particular policy or (2) as a plurality, which means no alternative has more than 50 percent support, but one alternative—the plurality choice—has more support than all the others.

Majority rule has a relatively good record in the policymaking process of the American political system. Large numbers of people express dissatisfaction with the policies of government, mostly saying they want middle-of-the-road government responses to problems. Yet political scientists find that government over the years has pretty consistently adopted a middle-of-the-road stance in making public policy. Americans often seem to be upset at government for giving them what they ask for (Hibbing and Theiss-Morse 2001). There are certainly people—sometimes even majorities—who disagree with specific substantive public policies. And most high-profile policy actions get varying levels of public support as they shift from adoption to implementation to evaluation. The wars in Iraq and Afghanistan, for example, began with high levels of public support that steadily dwindled with the expenditure of blood and treasure and a growing realization that many of the noble and idealistic goals justifying the conflicts were unlikely to be realized. Yet, overall, the evidence suggests that government does a pretty good job in addressing the policy preferences of its citizens. Given how divided public opinion is on most policy matters, an overall record indicating that there exists plurality, if not majority, support for government policies is no small feat.

For the system to remain true to core democratic values, though, majority rule needs to be balanced with minority rights. In this regard, the policymaking process in the United States has a much more mixed record. Historically, some public policies that were adopted and implemented were specifically aimed at robbing minorities of their rights as democratic citizens (for example, Jim Crow laws). Those sorts of egregious violations of minority rights are mostly a thing of the past. As we saw in the discussion on political equality, there remain some concerns about how minority groups are treated by the policymaking process. At a minimum, however, it is reasonable to conclude that the policy process has become much more attentive to minority rights during the past half-century or so.

Political Freedom

As we learned in chapter 1, government cannot respond to the will of the people if people are not free to express their wants and demands. The critical ingredients for this freedom are the right to criticize current governmental leaders and policies, the right to propose new courses of action for government to follow, the right to form and join interest groups, the right to discuss political issues free from government censorship, and the right of all citizens to seek and hold public office.

Of all the core democratic principles, political freedom is probably the easiest to recognize in the American policy process. From agenda setting to evaluation, the government's proposals and actions are discussed, analyzed, and criticized by just about everyone. Most people have an opinion on what the government should (or should not) do, and they are largely free to share that opinion as their means and abilities allow.

American citizens are free to speak in public places, write letters to the editor, contact public officials, join interest groups, circulate petitions, and start a blog or set up a Facebook page. Virtually all Americans, in short, have an opportunity and a venue to air their political views with little worry of government interference, restriction, or censorship. In some areas (states with ballot initiatives, for example), citizens even have the freedom to take public policy out of the government's hands entirely and make laws themselves. Americans also enjoy a free press and virtually unlimited access to information. Most government policy processes are, by law, transparent, meaning citizens can "see inside" government. In short, American citizens have all the necessary tools to enjoy a high degree of political freedom, and that freedom is widely exercised at every stage of the policy press.

However, as we learned in our discussion of the media in chapter 8, being free to express an opinion or criticize a policy does not necessarily mean those views will reach their intended audience. If there is a downside to political freedom, it is that in the marketplace of public opinions and ideas, some voices are always going to speak more loudly than others. The danger to political freedom in the policymaking process is not really that minority or dissenting opinions will be silenced. Relatively speaking, the policy process is largely free of censorship of any kind—people are pretty much free to say what they want about the government and what it should do. No, the real danger is that minority or dissenting opinions will not be heard. Just about anyone can put up a website, but that does not mean anyone will actually find and read it.

Political Equality

Chapter 1 pointed out that political equality is the most complex and difficult core principle of democracy because it can take many forms (social equality, economic equality, equality under the law, or equality of opportunity). Essentially, political equality means that individual preferences are given equal weight.

If political freedom is the core democratic principle most readily translated from theory into policymaking practice, political equality provides an interesting contrast. Political equality is the principle the American political system has had the hardest time putting into practice. This difficulty is clearly evident in historical terms, as indicated by our discussion of civil liberties and civil rights in chapters 4 and 5. For large parts of the republic's history, racial minorities, women, and other minority groups have been legally excluded from the policymaking process altogether.

Although such blatant inequalities are mostly a thing of the past, it is clear that some groups still enjoy more power and influence in the policymaking process. That power and influence translate into political inequality; in other words, the views and preferences of some count for more. The reasons for this are obvious. Economic inequality, for example, means different groups have different levels of influence in the policymaking process. Those with more money or more time or more organization are much better positioned to take advantage of the political freedoms the policymaking process affords. It is much easier (though far from guaranteed) to gain the attention of policy-makers if you can underwrite campaign donations and pay for television and newspaper ads.

Chapter 1 also discussed the pluralist ideal of a democracy, where government is used as a means to settle conflicts and reach compromise among competing group interests and where all groups have enough political resources to success-fully participate in the political process. In the pluralist ideal, groups are roughly equal, at least in the sense that they have the capability to defend their own inter-ests through the policymaking process.

A number of studies have shown that this pluralist ideal is far from the reality of policymaking. For example, in a wide-ranging study of how policy is made, po-litical scientists Anne Schneider and Helen Ingram (1997, 2005) argue that public policies always have target populations, or groups of people who will either re-ceive benefits or pay costs as a result of a policy decision. Schneider and Ingram found that some groups are consistently viewed as those who deserve to receive the benefits of policy, whereas others are consistently viewed as those who deserve to bear the costs. These differences break down along traditional social fault lines such as race and class. Thus, for example, middle-class, white-collar workers are typically viewed as deserving of policy benefits. Criminals are viewed as deserving of policy costs.

This is important because framing a policy in terms of its target population can have a powerful impact. For example, take the substantive issue of crime. It is no longer acceptable in mainstream American politics to promote policies that are blatantly racist. Yet it is perfectly acceptable to push a tough line on crime. Quick, think of a criminal—what does a criminal look like? For most people, it is a he, and he is a young black male. This group has been targeted as deserving to bear the costs of crime. Don't white people who commit crimes also go to jail? Yes, but not with the same probability. And crimes that are more associated with the middle-class suburbs (for example, use of powdered cocaine) are punished less—and less harshly—than crimes associated more with the inner cities (use of crack cocaine). A celebrity with a drug problem typically goes to rehab; an inner-city youth goes to jail. Crime, some political scientists argue, is a policy shot through with racist undertones all the way from agenda setting to evaluation (Beckett 1997).

There are numerous other substantive policies wherein scholars have found similar inequalities among groups. Tax policy tends to favor the middle class. For example, being able to deduct interest paid on your mortgage is a nice tax benefit—but you get this benefit only if you are a homeowner. State and federal higher-education policies tend to disproportionately favor middle-class students and private colleges rather than public colleges. The latter tend to have higher minority enrollments (Alexander 1998). Inequality is clearly still a fact of the policymaking process.

CONCLUSION

Popular sovereignty requires the policy process to abide by all three core principles of democracy simultaneously. As we have learned throughout this book, that is a tough balancing act; in some cases it is downright impossible. Unsurprisingly, then, the performance of American democracy falls short of its promise. The institutions and processes that make up the policymaking process struggle to put the core principles into practice, especially political equality. Judged by the standards of theoretical perfection, however, it is not just the United States but every democracy that ever existed that falls short. Compared to other democracies, America generally has a worse record on the core principle of political equality, a better record on political freedom, and a roughly similar record on majority rule.

In terms of putting core principles into action and resolving the conflicts that inevitably occur between these principles, and also in constructing and operating political institutions and processes that operate according to these values, America should get reasonably high marks. The American political system has not completely reflected the core principles of democracy and still does not—something that should always be remembered. However, taken as a whole, the American political system has consistently tried to measure itself by those same principles—something that should never be forgotten.

❶ Public policy is a relatively stable, purposive course of action undertaken by public authorities. The process of making public policy and the policies themselves are the ultimate test of how a political system implements the core principles of democracy.

❷ The public policy process can be systematically ordered into four stages: agenda setting, policy formulation and adoption, policy implementation, and policy evaluation.

❸ Agenda setting is the process of producing the list of issues and problems the government will address. Agenda setting can be viewed as a strategic game among rational actors or as a "garbage can" process where solutions and problems are produced independently and join together only when a particular problem has the focused attention of government.

❹ Policy formulation and adoption is the process government undertakes to consider various alternatives to the issue or problem at hand and to formally approve one of those alternatives. Policy adoption can be viewed as a garbage can process in which the independent problems and solutions actually join together, as the result of rational decision making, or as the result of boundedly rational decision making.

❺ Policy implementation is the process of attempting to translate the intent expressed in a formally approved policy into action.

❻ Policy evaluation is the process of assessing the impact, effectiveness, and problems of a public policy. Policy evaluations often lead back to the agenda-setting stage.

❼ With some important exceptions, the American political system has a fairly good record of upholding the core principle of majority rule. Though public opinion is mixed on most policy issues and is generally not positive about government performance, there is actually a high correlation between the policies people say they want from government and the policies government actually adopts and implements.

⑧ Political freedom is the core principle most easily observed in the policymaking process. Americans are free to express their views, share their opinions, and contact public authorities with relatively little censorship or restrictions.

⑨ Political equality is the core principle that the American political system has struggled the hardest to translate into practice. Even in the contemporary policymaking process, political scientists find that some groups are favored and others are not.

⑩ Overall, the American political system gets a mixed report card in its effort to sustain a policy process that is consistent with the core principles of democracy. Despite some failures and difficulties, however, it is clear that the core principles of democracy—especially the principle of political freedom—remain guiding goals of the American political system.

CHAPTER SIXTEEN
Key Terms and Cases

Arrow's impossibility theorem, 627
feedback, 630
focusing event, 630
garbage can model, 629
impact evaluations, 637

incrementalism, 634
indicators, 630
institutional agenda, 631
policy evaluation, 636
policy formation and adoption, 631

policy implementation, 634
process evaluations, 638
public agenda, 626
public policy, 623
rational-comprehensive decision making, 631

APPENDIX A

The Declaration of Independence

IN CONGRESS, July 4, 1776.

The unanimous Declaration of the thirteen united States of America, When in the Course of human events, it becomes necessary for one people to dissolve the political bands which have connected them with another, and to assume among the powers of the earth, the separate and equal station to which the Laws of Nature and of Nature's God entitle them, a decent respect to the opinions of mankind requires that they should declare the causes which impel them to the separation.

We hold these truths to be self-evident, that all men are created equal, that they are endowed by their Creator with certain unalienable Rights, that among these are Life, Liberty and the pursuit of Happiness.—That to secure these rights, Governments are instituted among Men, deriving their just powers from the consent of the governed.—That whenever any Form of Government becomes destructive of these ends, it is the Right of the People to alter or to abolish it, and to institute new Government, laying its foundation on such principles and organizing its powers in such form, as to them shall seem most likely to effect their Safety and Happiness. Prudence, indeed, will dictate that Governments long established should not be changed for light and transient causes; and accordingly all experience hath shewn, that mankind are more disposed to suffer, while evils are sufferable, than to right themselves by abolishing the forms to which they are accustomed. But when a long train of abuses and usurpations, pursuing invariably the same Object evinces a design to reduce them under absolute Despotism, it is their right, it is their duty, to throw off such Government, and to provide new Guards for their future security.— Such has been the patient sufferance of these Colonies; and such is now the necessity which constrains them to alter their former Systems of Government. The history of the present King of Great Britain is a history of repeated injuries and usurpations, all having in direct object the establishment of an absolute Tyranny over these States. To prove this, let Facts be submitted to a candid world.

He has refused his Assent to Laws, the most wholesome and necessary for the public good.

He has forbidden his Governors to pass Laws of immediate and pressing importance, unless suspended in their operation till his Assent should be obtained; and when so suspended, he has utterly neglected to attend to them.

He has refused to pass other Laws for the accommodation of large districts of people, unless those people would relinquish the right of Representation in the Legislature, a right inestimable to them and formidable to tyrants only.

He has called together legislative bodies at places unusual, uncomfortable, and distant from the depository of their public Records, for the sole purpose of fatiguing them into compliance with his measures.

He has dissolved Representative Houses repeatedly, for opposing with manly firmness his invasions on the rights of the people.

He has refused for a long time, after such dissolutions, to cause others to be elected; whereby the Legislative powers, incapable of Annihilation, have returned to the People at large for their exercise; the State remaining in the mean time exposed to all the dangers of invasion from without, and convulsions within.

He has endeavoured to prevent the population of these States; for that purpose obstructing the Laws for

Naturalization of Foreigners; refusing to pass others to encourage their migrations hither, and raising the conditions of new Appropriations of Lands.

He has obstructed the Administration of Justice, by refusing his Assent to Laws for establishing Judiciary powers.

He has made Judges dependent on his Will alone, for the tenure of their offices, and the amount and payment of their salaries.

He has erected a multitude of New Offices, and sent hither swarms of Officers to harrass our people, and eat out their substance.

He has kept among us, in times of peace, Standing Armies without the Consent of our legislatures.

He has affected to render the Military independent of and superior to the Civil power.

He has combined with others to subject us to a jurisdiction foreign to our constitution, and unacknowledged by our laws; giving his Assent to their Acts of pretended Legislation:

For Quartering large bodies of armed troops among us:

For protecting them, by a mock Trial, from punishment for any Murders which they should commit on the Inhabitants of these States:

For cutting off our Trade with all parts of the world:

For imposing Taxes on us without our Consent:

For depriving us in many cases, of the benefits of Trial by Jury:

For transporting us beyond Seas to be tried for pretended offences:

For abolishing the free System of English Laws in a neighbouring Province, establishing therein an Arbitrary government, and enlarging its Boundaries so as to render it at once an example and fit instrument for introducing the same absolute rule into these Colonies:

For taking away our Charters, abolishing our most valuable Laws, and altering fundamentally the Forms of our Governments:

For suspending our own Legislatures, and declaring themselves invested with power to legislate for us in all cases whatsoever.

He has abdicated Government here, by declaring us out of his Protection and waging War against us.

He has plundered our seas, ravaged our Coasts, burnt our towns, and destroyed the lives of our people.

He is at this time transporting large Armies of foreign Mercenaries to compleat the works of death, desolation and tyranny, already begun with circumstances of Cruelty & perfidy scarcely paralleled in the most barbarous ages, and totally unworthy of the Head of a civilized nation.

He has constrained our fellow Citizens taken Captive on the high Seas to bear Arms against their Country, to become the executioners of their friends and Brethren, or to fall themselves by their Hands.

He has excited domestic insurrections amongst us, and has endeavoured to bring on the inhabitants of our frontiers, the merciless Indian Savages, whose known rule of warfare, is an undistinguished destruction of all ages, sexes and conditions.

In every stage of these Oppressions We have Petitioned for Redress in the most humble terms: Our repeated Petitions have been answered only by repeated injury. A Prince whose character is thus marked by every act which may define a Tyrant, is unfit to be the ruler of a free people.

Nor have We been wanting in attentions to our British brethren. We have warned them from time to time of attempts by their legislature to extend an unwarrantable jurisdiction over us. We have reminded them of the circumstances of our emigration and settlement here. We have appealed to their native justice and magnanimity, and we have conjured them by the ties of our common kindred to disavow these usurpations, which, would inevitably interrupt our connections and correspondence. They too have been deaf to the voice of justice and of consanguinity. We must, therefore, acquiesce in the necessity, which denounces our Separation, and hold them, as we hold the rest of mankind, Enemies in War, in Peace Friends.

We, therefore, the Representatives of the united States of America, in General Congress, Assembled, appealing to the Supreme Judge of the world for the rectitude of our intentions, do, in the Name, and by Authority of the good People of these Colonies, solemnly publish and declare, That these United Colonies are, and of Right ought to be Free and Independent States; that they are Absolved from all Allegiance to the British Crown, and that all political connection between them and the State of Great Britain, is and ought to be totally dissolved; and that as Free and Independent States, they have full Power to levy War, conclude Peace, contract Alliances, establish Commerce, and to do all other Acts and Things which Independent States may of right do. And for the support of this Declaration, with a firm reliance on the protection of divine Providence, we mutually pledge to each other our Lives, our Fortunes and our sacred Honor.

Georgia:
Button Gwinnett
Lyman Hall
George Walton
North Carolina:
William Hooper
Joseph Hewes
John Penn
South Carolina:
Edward Rutledge
Thomas Heyward, Jr.
Thomas Lynch, Jr.
Arthur Middleton
Maryland:
Samuel Chase
William Paca
Thomas Stone
Charles Carroll of Carrollton

Virginia:
George Wythe
Richard Henry Lee
Thomas Jefferson
Benjamin Harrison
Thomas Nelson, Jr.
Francis Lightfoot Lee
Carter Braxton
Pennsylvania:
Robert Morris
Benjamin Rush
Benjamin Franklin
John Morton
George Clymer
James Smith
George Taylor
James Wilson
George Ross

Delaware:
Caesar Rodney
George Read
Thomas McKean
New York:
William Floyd
Philip Livingston
Francis Lewis
Lewis Morris
New Jersey:
Richard Stockton
John Witherspoon
Francis Hopkinson
John Hart
Abraham Clark
Rhode Island:
Stephen Hopkins
William Ellery

New Hampshire:
Josiah Bartlett
William Whipple
Matthew Thornton
Massachusetts:
John Hancock
Samuel Adams
John Adams
Robert Treat Paine
Elbridge Gerry
Thomas Lynch, Jr.
Roger Sherman
Samuel Huntington
William Williams
Oliver Wolcott

APPENDIX B

The Articles of the Confederation (1781)

TO ALL TO WHOM these Presents shall come, we the undersigned Delegates of the States affixed to our Names send greeting. Whereas the Delegates of the United States of America in Congress assembled did on the fifteenth day of November in the Year of our Lord One Thousand Seven Hundred and Seventy seven, and in the Second Year of the Independence of America agree to certain articles of Confederation and perpetual Union between the States of New Hampshire, Massachusetts bay, Rhode Island and Providence Plantations, Connecticut, New York, New Jersey, Pennsylvania, Delaware, Maryland, Virginia, North Carolina, South Carolina and Georgia in the Words following, viz. "Articles of Confederation and perpetual Union between the states of New Hampshire, Massachusetts bay, Rhode Island and Providence Plantations, Connecticut, New York, New Jersey, Pennsylvania, Delaware, Maryland, Virginia, North Carolina, South Carolina and Georgia.

ARTICLE I.

The Style of this confederacy shall be "The United States of America."

ARTICLE II.

Each state retains its sovereignty, freedom and independence, and every Power, Jurisdiction and right, which is not by this confederation expressly delegated to the United States, in Congress assembled.

ARTICLE III.

The said states hereby severally enter into a firm league of friendship with each other, for their common defence, the security of their Liberties, and their mutual and general welfare, binding themselves to assist each other, against all force offered to, or attacks made upon them, or any of them, on account of religion, sovereignty, trade, or any other pretence whatever.

ARTICLE IV.

The better to secure and perpetuate mutual friendship and intercourse among the people of the different states in this union, the free inhabitants of each of these states, paupers, vagbonds and fugitives from Justice excepted, shall be entitled to all privileges and immunities of free citizens in the several states; and the people of each state shall have free ingress and regress to and from any other state, and shall enjoy therein all the privileges of trade and commerce, subject to the same duties, impositions and restrictions as the inhabitants thereof respectively, provided that such restriction shall not extend so far as to prevent the removal of property imported into any state, to any other state of which the Owner is an inhabitant; provided also that no imposition, duties or restriction shall be laid by any state, on the property of the united states, or either of them.

If any Person guilty of, or charged with treason, felony, or other high misdemeanor in any state, shall flee from Justice, and be found in any of the united states, he shall upon demand of the Governor or executive power, of the state from which he fled, be delivered up and removed to the state having jurisdiction of his offence.

Full faith and credit shall be given in each of these states to the records, acts and judicial proceedings of the courts and magistrates of every other state.

ARTICLE V.

For the more convenient management of the general interests of the united states, delegates shall be annually appointed in such manner as the legislature of each state shall direct, to meet in Congress on the first Monday in November, in every year, with a power reserved to each state, to recall its delegates, or any of them, at any time within the year, and to send others in their stead, for the remainder of the Year.

No state shall be represented in Congress by less than two, nor by more than seven Members; and no person shall be capable of being a delegate for more than three years in any term of six years; nor shall any person, being a delegate, be capable of holding any office under the united states, for which he, or another for his benefit receives any salary, fees or emolument of any kind.

Each state shall maintain its own delegates in a meeting of the states, and while they act as members of the committee of the states.

In determining questions in the united states, in Congress assembled, each state shall have one vote.

Freedom of speech and debate in Congress shall not be impeached or questioned in any Court, or place out of Congress, and the members of congress shall be protected in their persons from arrests and imprisonments, during the time of their going to and from, and attendance on congress, except for treason, felony, or breach of the peace.

ARTICLE VI.

No state without the Consent of the united states in congress assembled, shall send any embassy to, or receive any embassy from, or enter into any conference, agreement, or alliance or treaty with any King prince or state; nor shall any person holding any office of profit or trust under the united states, or any of them, accept of any present, emolument, office or title of any kind whatever from any king, prince or foreign state; nor shall the united states in congress assembled, or any of them, grant any title of nobility.

No two or more states shall enter into any treaty, confederation or alliance whatever between them, without the consent of the united states in congress assembled, specifying accurately the purposes for which the same is to be entered into, and how long it shall continue.

No state shall lay any imposts or duties, which may interfere with any stipulations in treaties, entered into by the united states in congress assembled, with any king, prince or state, in pursuance of any treaties already proposed by congress, to the courts of France and Spain.

No vessels of war shall be kept up in time of peace by any state, except such number only, as shall be deemed necessary by the united states in congress assembled, for the defence of such state, or its trade; nor shall any body of forces be kept up by any state, in time of peace, except such number only, as in the judgment of the united states, in congress assembled, shall be deemed requisite to garrison the forts necessary for the defence of such state; but every state shall always keep up a well regulated and disciplined militia, sufficiently armed and accoutered, and shall provide and constantly have ready for use, in public stores, a due number of field pieces and tents, and a proper quantity of arms, ammunition and camp equipage.

No state shall engage in any war without the consent of the united states in congress assembled, unless such state be actually invaded by enemies, or shall have received certain advice of a resolution being formed by some nation of Indians to invade such state, and the danger is so imminent as not to admit of a delay, till the united states in congress assembled can be consulted: nor shall any state grant commissions to any ships or vessels of war, nor letters of marque or reprisal, except it be after a declaration of war by the united states in congress assembled, and then only against the kingdom or state and the subjects thereof, against which war has been so declared, and under such regulations as shall be established by the united states in congress assembled, unless such state be infested by pirates, in which case vessels of war may be fitted out for that occasion, and kept so long as the danger shall continue, or until the united states in congress assembled shall determine otherwise.

ARTICLE VII.

When land-forces are raised by any state for the common defence, all officers of or under the rank of colonel, shall be appointed by the legislature of each state respectively by whom such forces shall be raised, or in such manner as such state shall direct, and all vacancies shall be filled up by the state which first made the appointment.

ARTICLE VIII.

All charges of war, and all other expenses that shall be incurred for the common defence or general welfare, and allowed by the united states in congress assembled, shall be defrayed out of a common treasury, which shall be supplied by the several states, in proportion to the value of all land within each state, granted to or surveyed for any Person, as such land and the buildings and improvements thereon shall be estimated according to such mode as the united states in congress assembled, shall from time to time direct and appoint. The taxes for paying that proportion shall be laid and levied by the authority and direction of the legislatures of the several states within the time agreed upon by the united states in congress assembled.

ARTICLE IX.

The united states in congress assembled, shall have the sole and exclusive right and power of determining on peace and war, except in the cases mentioned in the sixth article—of sending and receiving ambassadors—entering into treaties and alliances, provided that no treaty of commerce shall be made whereby the legislative power of the respective states shall be restrained from imposing such imposts and duties on foreigners, as their own people are subjected to, or from prohibiting the exportation or importation of any species of goods or commodities whatsoever—of establishing rules for deciding in all cases, what captures on land or water shall be legal, and in what manner prizes taken by land or naval forces in the service of the united states shall be divided or appropriated—of granting letters of marque and reprisal in times of peace—appointing courts for the trial of piracies and felonies committed on the high seas and establishing courts for receiving and determining finally appeals in all cases of captures, provided that no member of congress shall be appointed a judge of any of the said courts.

The united states in congress assembled shall also be the last resort on appeal in all disputes and differences now subsisting or that hereafter may arise between two or more states concerning boundary, jurisdiction or any other cause whatever; which authority shall always be exercised in the manner following. Whenever the legislative or executive authority or lawful agent state in controversy with another shall present a petition to congress, stating the matter in question and praying for a hearing, notice thereof shall be given by order of congress to the legislative or executive authority of the other state in controversy, and a day assigned for the appearance of the parties by their lawful agents, who shall then be directed to appoint by joint consent, commissioners or judges to constitute a court for hearing and determining the matter in question; but if they cannot agree, congress shall name three persons out of each of the united states, and from the list of such persons each party shall alternately strike out one, the petitioners beginning, until the number shall be reduced to thirteen; and from that number not less than seven, nor more than nine names as congress shall direct, shall in the presence of congress be drawn out by lot, and the persons whose names shall be so drawn or any five of them, shall be commissioners or judges, to hear and finally determine the controversy, so always as a major part of the judges who shall hear the cause shall agree in the determination: and if either party shall neglect to attend at the day appointed, without showing reasons, which congress shall judge sufficient, or being present shall refuse to strike, the congress shall proceed to nominate three persons out of each state, and the secretary of congress shall strike in behalf of such party absent or refusing; and the judgment and sentence of the court to be appointed, in the manner before prescribed, shall be final and conclusive; and if any of the parties shall refuse to submit to the authority of such court, or to appear to defend their claim or cause, the court shall nevertheless proceed to pronounce sentence, or judgment, which shall in like manner be final and decisive, the judgment or sentence and other proceedings being in either case transmitted to congress, and lodged among the acts of congress for the security of the parties concerned: provided that every commissioner, before he sits in judgment, shall take an oath to be administered by one of the judges of the supreme or superior court of the state, where the cause shall be tried, "well and truly to hear and determine the matter in question, according to the best of his judgment, without favor, affection or hope of reward;" provided also that no state shall be deprived of territory for the benefit of the united states.

All controversies concerning the private right of soil claimed under different grants of two or more states, whose jurisdictions as they may respect such lands, and the states which passed such grants are adjusted, the said grants or either of them being at the same time claimed to have originated antecedent to such settlement of jurisdiction, shall on the petition of either party to the congress of the united states, be finally determined as near as may be in the same manner as is before prescribed for deciding disputes respecting territorial jurisdiction between different states.

The united states in congress assembled shall also have the sole and exclusive right and power of regulating the alloy and value of coin struck by their own authority, or by that of the respective states—fixing the standard of weights and measures throughout the united states—regulating the trade and managing all affairs with the Indians, not members of any of the states, provided that the legislative right of any state within its own limits be not infringed or violated—establishing and regulating post offices from one state to another, throughout all the united states, and exacting such postage on the pa-

pers passing through the same as may be requisite to defray the expenses of the said office—appointing all officers of the land forces, in the service of the united states, excepting regimental officers—appointing all the officers of the naval forces, and commissioning all officers whatever in the service of the united states—making rules for the government and regulation of the said land and naval forces, and directing their operations.

The united states in congress assembled shall have authority to appoint a committee, to sit in the recess of congress, to be denominated "A Committee of the States," and to consist of one delegate from each state; and to appoint such other committees and civil officers as may be necessary for managing the general affairs of the united states under their direction—to appoint one of their number to preside, provided that no person be allowed to serve in the office of president more than one year in any term of three years; to ascertain the necessary sums of Money to be raised for the service of the united states, and to appropriate and apply the same for defraying the public expenses—to borrow money, or emit bills on the credit of the united states, transmitting every half year to the respective states an account of the sums of money so borrowed or emitted,—to build and equip a navy—to agree upon the number of land forces, and to make requisitions from each state for its quota, in proportion to the number of white inhabitants in such state; which requisition shall be binding, and thereupon the legislature of each state shall appoint the regimental officers, raise the men and clothe, arm and equip them in a soldier like manner, at the expense of the united states, and the officers and men so clothed, armed and equipped shall march to the place appointed, and within the time agreed on by the united states in congress assembled. But if the united states in congress assembled shall, on consideration of circumstances judge proper that any state should not raise men, or should raise a smaller number than its quota, and that any other state should raise a greater number of men than the quota thereof, such extra number shall be raised, officered, clothed, armed and equipped in the same manner as the quota of such state, unless the legislature of such state shall judge that such extra number cannot be safely spared out of the same, in which case they shall raise officer, clothe, arm and equip as many of such extra number as they judge can be safely spared. And the officers and men so clothed, armed and equipped, shall march to the place appointed, and within the time agreed on by the united states in congress assembled.

The united states in congress assembled shall never engage in a war, nor grant letters of marque and reprisal in time of peace, nor enter into any treaties or alliances, nor coin money, nor regulate the value thereof, nor ascertain the sums and expenses necessary for the defence and welfare of the united states, or any of them, nor emit bills, nor borrow money on the credit of the united states, nor appropriate money, nor agree upon the number of vessels of war, to be built or purchased, or the number of land or sea forces to be raised, nor appoint a commander in chief of the army or navy, unless nine states assent to the same: nor shall a question on any other point, except for adjourning from day to day be determined, unless by the votes of a majority of the united states in congress assembled.

The congress of the united states shall have power to adjourn to any time within the year, and to any place within the united states, so that no period of adjournment be for a longer duration than the space of six Months, and shall publish the Journal of their proceedings monthly, except such parts thereof relating to treaties, alliances or military operations as in their judgment require secrecy; and the yeas and nays of the delegates of each state on any question shall be entered on the Journal, when it is desired by any delegate; and the delegates of a state, or any of them, at his or their request shall be furnished with a transcript of the said Journal, except such parts as are above excepted, to lay before the legislatures of the several states.

ARTICLE X.

The committee of the states, or any nine of them, shall be authorized to execute, in the recess of congress, such of the powers of congress as the united states in congress assembled, by the consent of nine states, shall from time to time think expedient to vest them with; provided that no power be delegated to the said committee, for the exercise of which, by the articles of confederation, the voice of nine states in the congress of the united states assembled is requisite.

ARTICLE XI.

Canada acceding to this confederation, and joining in the measures of the united states, shall be admitted into, and entitled to all the advantages of this union: but no other colony shall be admitted into the same, unless such admission be agreed to by nine states.

ARTICLE XII.

All bills of credit emitted, monies borrowed and debts contracted by, or under the authority of congress, before the assembling of the united states, in pursuance of the present confederation, shall be deemed and considered as a charge against the united states, for payment and satisfaction whereof the said united states, and the public faith are hereby solemnly pledged.

ARTICLE XIII.

Every state shall abide by the determinations of the united states in congress assembled, on all questions which by this confederation are submitted to them. And the Articles of this confederation shall be inviolably observed by every state, and the union shall be perpetual; nor shall any alteration at any time hereafter be made in any of them; unless such alteration be agreed to in a congress of the united states, and be afterwards confirmed by the legislatures of every state.

AND WHEREAS it hath pleased the Great Governor of the World to incline the hearts of the legislatures we respectively represent in congress, to approve of, and to authorize us to ratify the said articles of confederation and perpetual union. KNOW YE that we the undersigned delegates, by virtue of the power and authority to us given for that purpose, do by these presents, in the name and in behalf of our respective constituents, fully and entirely ratify and confirm each and every of the said articles of confederation and perpetual union, and all and singular the matters and things therein contained: And we do further solemnly plight and engage the faith of our respective constituents, that they shall abide by the determinations of the united states in congress assembled, on all questions, which by the said confederation are submitted to them. And that the articles thereof shall be inviolably observed by the states we respectively represent, and that the union shall be perpetual. In Witness whereof we have hereunto set our hands in Congress. Done at Philadelphia in the state of Pennsylvania the ninth Day of July in the Year of our Lord one Thousand seven Hundred and Seventy-eight, and in the third year of the independence of America.

On the part and behalf of the State of New Hampshire:
JOSIAH BARTLETT
JOHN WENTWORTH JUNR.
August 8th 1778

On the part and behalf of The State of
Massachusetts Bay:
JOHN HANCOCK
SAMUEL ADAMS
ELBRIDGE GERRY
FRANCIS DANA JAMES LOVELL
SAMUEL HOLTEN

On the part and behalf of the State of Rhode Island and Providence Plantations:
WILLIAM ELLERY
HENRY MARCHANT JOHN COLLINS

On the part and behalf of the State of Connecticut:
ROGER SHERMAN
SAMUEL HUNTINGTON
OLIVER WOLCOTT
TITUS HOSMER ANDREW ADAMS

On the part and behalf of the State of New York:
JAMES DUANE
FRANCIS LEWIS
WM DUER
GOUV MORRIS

On the part and in behalf of the State of New Jersey:
JNO WITHERSPOON
NATHANIEL SCUDDER
November 26, 1778

On the part and behalf of the State of Pennsylvania:
ROBT MORRIS
DANIEL ROBERDEAU
JOHN BAYARD SMITH
WILLIAM CLINGAN
JOSEPH REED
22nd July 1778

On the part and behalf of the State of Delaware:
THO McKEAN
February 12, 1779
JOHN DICKINSON
May 5th 1779
NICHOLAS VAN DYKE

On the part and behalf of the State of Maryland:
JOHN HANSON
March 1 1781
DANIEL CARROLL

On the part and behalf of the State of Virginia:
RICHARD HENRY LEE JOHN BANISTER
THOMAS ADAMS
JNo HARVIE
FRANCIS LIGHTFOOT LEE

On the part and behalf of the State of North Carolina:
JOHN PENN
July 21st 1778
CORNs HARNETT
JNo WILLIAMS

On the part & behalf of the State of South Carolina:
HENRY LAURENS
WILLIAM HENRY DRAYTON
JNo MATHEWS
RICHD HUTSON
THOs HEYWARD Junr

On the part and behalf of the State of Georgia:
JNo WALTON
24th July 1778
EDWD TELFAIR
EDWD LANGWORTHY

APPENDIX C

Constitution of the United States

WE THE PEOPLE of the United States, in order to form a more perfect union, establish justice, insure domestic tranquility, provide for the common defense, promote the general welfare, and secure the blessings of liberty to ourselves and our posterity, do ordain and establish this Constitution for the United States of America

ARTICLE I

Section 1.   All legislative powers herein granted shall be vested in a Congress of the United States, which shall consist of a Senate and House of Representatives.

Section 2.   The House of Representatives shall be composed of members chosen every second year by the people of the several states, and the electors in each state shall have the qualifications requisite for electors of the most numerous branch of the state legislature.

No person shall be a Representative who shall not have attained to the age of twenty five years, and been seven years a citizen of the United States, and who shall not, when elected, be an inhabitant of that state in which he shall be chosen.

Representatives and direct taxes shall be apportioned among the several states which may be included within this union, according to their respective numbers, which shall be determined by adding to the whole number of free persons, including those bound to service for a term of years, and excluding Indians not taxed, three fifths of all other persons. The actual enumeration shall be made within three years after the first meeting of the Congress of the United States, and within every subsequent term of ten years, in such manner as they shall by law direct. The number of Representatives shall not exceed one for every thirty thousand, but each state shall have at least one Representative; and until such enumeration shall be made, the state of New Hampshire shall be entitled to choose three, Massachusetts eight, Rhode Island and Providence Plantations one, Connecticut five, New York six, New Jersey four, Pennsylvania eight, Delaware one, Maryland six, Virginia ten, North Carolina five, South Carolina five, and Georgia three.

When vacancies happen in the representation from any state, the executive authority thereof shall issue writs of election to fill such vacancies.

The House of Representatives shall choose their speaker and other officers; and shall have the sole power of impeachment.

Section 3.   The Senate of the United States shall be composed of two Senators from each state, chosen by the legislature thereof, for six years; and each Senator shall have one vote.

Immediately after they shall be assembled in consequence of the first election, they shall be divided as equally as may be into three classes. The seats of the

Senators of the first class shall be vacated at the expiration of the second year, of the second class at the expiration of the fourth year, and the third class at the expiration of the sixth year, so that one third may be chosen every second year; and if vacancies happen by resignation, or otherwise, during the recess of the legislature of any state, the executive thereof may make temporary appointments until the next meeting of the legislature, which shall then fill such vacancies.

No person shall be a Senator who shall not have attained to the age of thirty years, and been nine years a citizen of the United States and who shall not, when elected, be an inhabitant of that state for which he shall be chosen.

The Vice President of the United States shall be President of the Senate, but shall have no vote, unless they be equally divided.

The Senate shall choose their other officers, and also a President pro tempore, in the absence of the Vice President, or when he shall exercise the office of President of the United States.

The Senate shall have the sole power to try all impeachments. When sitting for that purpose, they shall be on oath or affirmation. When the President of the United States is tried, the Chief Justice shall preside: And no person shall be convicted without the concurrence of two thirds of the members present.

Judgment in cases of impeachment shall not extend further than to removal from office, and disqualification to hold and enjoy any office of honor, trust or profit under the United States: but the party convicted shall nevertheless be liable and subject to indictment, trial, judgment and punishment, according to law.

Section 4. The times, places and manner of holding elections for Senators and Representatives, shall be prescribed in each state by the legislature thereof; but the Congress may at any time by law make or alter such regulations, except as to the places of choosing Senators.

The Congress shall assemble at least once in every year, and such meeting shall be on the first Monday in December, unless they shall by law appoint a different day.

Section 5. Each House shall be the judge of the elections, returns and qualifications of its own members, and a majority of each shall constitute a quorum to do business; but a smaller number may adjourn from day to day, and may be authorized to compel the attendance of absent members, in such manner, and under such penalties as each House may provide.

Each House may determine the rules of its proceedings, punish its members for disorderly behavior, and, with the concurrence of two thirds, expel a member.

Each House shall keep a journal of its proceedings, and from time to time publish the same, excepting such parts as may in their judgment require secrecy; and the yeas and nays of the members of either House on any question shall, at the desire of one fifth of those present, be entered on the journal.

Neither House, during the session of Congress, shall, without the consent of the other, adjourn for more than three days, nor to any other place than that in which the two Houses shall be sitting.

Section 6. The Senators and Representatives shall receive a compensation for their services, to be ascertained by law, and paid out of the treasury of the United States. They shall in all cases, except treason, felony and breach of the peace, be privileged from arrest during their attendance at the session of their respective houses, and in going to and returning from the same; and for any speech or debate in either house, they shall not be questioned in any other place.

No Senator or Representative shall, during the time for which he was elected, be appointed to any civil office under the authority of the United States, which shall have been created, or the emoluments whereof shall have been increased during such time: and no person holding any office under the United States, shall be a member of either House during his continuance in office.

Section 7. All bills for raising revenue shall originate in the House of Representatives; but the Senate may propose or concur with amendments as on other Bills.

Every bill which shall have passed the House of Representatives and the Senate, shall, before it become a law, be presented to the President of the United States;

if he approve he shall sign it, but if not he shall return it, with his objections to that house in which it shall have originated, who shall enter the objections at large on their journal, and proceed to reconsider it. If after such reconsideration two thirds of that house shall agree to pass the bill, it shall be sent, together with the objections, to the other house, by which it shall 1 ikewise be reconsidered, and if approved by two thirds of that house, it shall become a law. But in all such cases the votes of both houses shall be determined by yeas andnays, and the names of the persons voting for and against the bill shall be entered on the journal of each house respectively. If any bill shall not be returned by the President within ten days (Sundays excepted) after it shall have been presented to him, the same shall be a law, in like manner as if he had signed it, unless the Congress by their adjournment prevent its return, in which case it shall not be a law.

Every order, resolution, or vote to which the concurrence of the Senate and House of Representatives may be necessary (except on a question of adjournment) shall be presented to the President of the United States; and before the same shall take effect, shall be approved by him, or being disapproved by him, shall be repassed by two thirds of the Senate and House of Representatives, according to the rules and limitations prescribed in the case of a bill.

Section 8. The Congress shall have power to lay and collect taxes, duties, imposts and excises, to pay the debts and provide for the common defense and general welfare of the United States; but all duties, imposts and excises shall be uniform throughout the United States;

To borrow money on the credit of the United States;

To regulate commerce with foreign nations, and among the several states, and with the Indian tribes;

To establish a uniform rule of naturalization, and uniform laws on the subject of bankruptcies throughout the United States;

To coin money, regulate the value thereof, and of foreign coin, and fix the standard of weights and measures;

To provide for the punishment of counterfeiting the securities and current coin of the United States;

To establish post offices and post roads;

To promote the progress of science and useful arts, by securing for limited times to authors and inventors the exclusive right to their respective writings and discoveries;

To constitute tribunals inferior to the Supreme Court;

To define and punish piracies and felonies committed on the high seas, and offenses against the law of nations;

To declare war, grant letters of marque and reprisal, and make rules concerning captures on land and water;

To raise and support armies, but no appropriation of money to that use shall be for a longer term than two years;

To provide and maintain a navy;

To make rules for the government and regulation of the land and naval forces;

To provide for calling forth the militia to execute the laws of the union, suppress insurrections and repel invasions;

To provide for organizing, arming, and disciplining, the militia, and for governing such part of them as may be employed in the service of the United States, reserving to the states respectively, the appointment of the officers, and the authority of training the militia according to the discipline prescribed by Congress;

To exercise exclusive legislation in all cases whatsoever, over such District (not exceeding ten miles square) as may, by cession of particular states, and the acceptance of Congress, become the seat of the government of the United States, and to exercise like authority over all places purchased by the consent of the legislature of the state in which the same shall be, for the erection of forts, magazines, arsenals, dockyards, and other needful buildings;—and

To make all laws which shall be necessary and proper for carrying into execution the foregoing powers, and all other powers vested by this Constitution in the government of the United States, or in any department or officer thereof.

Section 9. The migration or importation of such persons as any of the states now existing shall think proper to admit, shall not be prohibited by the Congress prior to the year one thousand eight hundred and eight, but a tax or duty may be imposed on such importation, not exceeding ten dollars for each person.

The privilege of the writ of habeas corpus shall not be suspended, unless when in cases of rebellion or invasion the public safety may require it.

No bill of attainder or ex post facto Law shall be passed.

No capitation, or other direct, tax shall be laid, unless in proportion to the census or enumeration herein before directed to be taken.

No tax or duty shall be laid on articles exported from any state.

No preference shall be given by any regulation of commerce or revenue to the ports of one state over those of another: nor shall vessels bound to, or from, one state, be obliged to enter, clear or pay duties in another.

No money shall be drawn from the treasury, but in consequence of appropriations made by law; and a regular statement and account of receipts and expenditures of all public money shall be published from time to time.

No title of nobility shall be granted by the United States: and no person holding any office of profit or trust under them, shall, without the consent of the Congress, accept of any present, emolument, office, or title, of any kind whatever, from any king, prince, or foreign state.

Section 10. No state shall enter into any treaty, alliance, or confederation; grant letters of marque and reprisal; coin money; emit bills of credit; make anything but gold and silver coin a tender in payment of debts; pass any bill of attainder, ex post facto law, or law impairing the obligation of contracts, or grant any title of nobility.

No state shall, without the consent of the Congress, lay any imposts or duties on imports or exports, except what may be absolutely necessary for executing its inspection laws: and the net produce of all duties and imposts, laid by any state on imports or exports, shall be for the use of the treasury of the United States; and all such laws shall be subject to the revision and control of the Congress.

No state shall, without the consent of Congress, lay any duty of tonnage, keep troops, or ships of war in time of peace, enter into any agreement or compact with another state, or with a foreign power, or engage in war, unless actually invaded, or in such imminent danger as will not admit of delay.

ARTICLE II

Section 1. The executive power shall be vested in a President of the United States of America. He shall hold his office during the term of four years, and, together with the Vice President, chosen for the same term, be elected, as follows:

Each state shall appoint, in such manner as the Legislature thereof may direct, a number of electors, equal to the whole number of Senators and Representatives to which the state may be entitled in the Congress: but no Senator or Representative, or person holding an office of trust or profit under the United States, shall be appointed an elector.

The electors shall meet in their respective states, and vote by ballot for two persons, of whom one at least shall not be an inhabitant of the same state with themselves. And they shall make a list of all the persons voted for, and of the number of votes for each; which list they shall sign and certify, and transmit sealed to the seat of the government of the United States, directed to the President of the Senate. The President of the Senate shall, in the presence of the Senate and House of Representatives, open all the certificates, and the votes shall then be counted. The person having the greatest number of votes shall be the President, if such number be a majority of the whole number of electors appointed; and if there be more than one who have such majority, and have an equal number of votes, then the House of Representatives shall immediately choose by ballot one of them for President; and if no person have a majority, then from the five highest on the list the said House shall in like manner choose the President. But in choosing the President, the votes shall be taken by States, the representation from each state having one vote; a quorum for this purpose shall consist of a member or members from two thirds of the states, and a majority of all the states shall be necessary to a choice. In every case, after the choice of the President, the person having the greatest number of votes of the electors shall be the Vice President. But if there should remain two or more who have equal votes, the Senate shall choose from them by ballot the Vice President.

The Congress may determine the time of choosing the electors, and the day on which they shall give their votes; which day shall be the same throughout the United States.

No person except a natural-born citizen, or a citizen of the United States, at the time of the adoption of this Constitution, shall be eligible to the office of President; neither shall any person be eligible to that office who shall not have attained to the age of thirty five years, and been fourteen Years a resident within the United States.

In case of the removal of the President from office, or of his death, resignation, or inability to discharge the powers and duties of the said office, the same shall devolve on the Vice President, and the Congress may by law provide for the case of removal, de___ ___na-tion or inability, both of the P____ ___si-dent, declaring what offic____ ___t, and such officer shall act a____ ___ity be removed, or a Presid____

The President shall, at st____ services, a compensation, w____ creased nor diminished duri____ he shall have been elected, a____ within that period any other____ the United States, or any of them.

Before he enter on the execution of his office, he shall take the following oath or affirmation:—"I do solemnly swear (or affirm) that I will faithfully execute the office of President of the United States, and will to the best of my ability, preserve, protect and defend the Constitution of the United States."

Section 2. The President shall be commander in chief of the Army and Navy of the United States, and of the militia of the several states, when called into the actual service of the United States; he may require the opinion, in writing, of the principal officer in each of the executive departments, upon any subject relating to the duties of their respective offices, and he shall have power to grant reprieves and pardons for offenses against the United States, except in cases of impeachment.

He shall have power, by and with the advice and consent of the Senate, to make treaties, provided two thirds of the Senators present concur; and he shall nominate, and by and with the advice and consent of the Senate, shall appoint ambassadors, other public ministers and consuls, judges of the Supreme Court, and all other officers of the United States, whose appointments are not herein otherwise provided for, and which shall be by law: but the Congress may by law vest the appointment of such inferior officers, as they think proper, in the President alone, in the courts of law, or in the heads of departments.

The President shall have power to fill up all vacancies that may happen during the recess of the Senate, by granting commissions which shall expire at the end of their next session.

Section 3. He shall from time to time give to the Congress information of the state of the union, and recommend to their consideration such measures as he shall judge necessary and expedient; he may, on extraordinary occasions, convene both Houses, or either of them, and in case of disagreement between them, with respect to the time of adjournment, he may adjourn them to such time as he shall think proper; he shall receive ambassadors and other public ministers; he shall take care that the laws be faithfully executed, and shall commission all the officers of the United States.

Section 4. The President, Vice President and all civil officers of the United States, shall be removed from office on impeachment for, and conviction of, treason, bribery, or other high crimes and misdemeanors.

ARTICLE III

Section 1. The judicial power of the United States, shall be vested in one Supreme Court, and in such inferior courts as the Congress may from time to time ordain and establish. The judges, both of the supreme and inferior courts, shall hold their offices during good behaviour, and shall, at stated times, receive for their services, a compensation, which shall not be diminished during their continuance in office.

Section 2. The judicial power shall extend to all cases, in law and equity, arising under this Constitution, the laws of the United States, and treaties made, or which shall be made, under their authority;—to all cases affecting ambassadors, other public ministers and consuls;—to all cases of admiralty and maritime jurisdiction;—to controversies to which the United States shall be a party;—to controversies between two or more states;—between a state and citizens of another state;—between citizens of different states;—between citizens of the same state claiming lands under grants of different states, and between a state, or the citizens thereof, and foreign states, citizens or subjects.

In all cases affecting ambassadors, other public ministers and consuls, and those in which a state shall be party, the Supreme Court shall have original jurisdiction. In all the other cases before mentioned, the Supreme Court shall have appellate jurisdiction, both as to law and fact, with such exceptions, and under such regulations as the Congress shall make.

The trial of all crimes, except in cases of impeachment, shall be by jury; and such trial shall be held in the state where the said crimes shall have been committed; but when not committed within any state, the trial shall be at such place or places as the Congress may by law have directed.

Section 3. Treason against the United States, shall consist only in levying war against them, or in adhering to their enemies, giving them aid and comfort. No person shall be convicted of treason unless on the testimony of two witnesses to the same overt act, or on confession in open court.

The Congress shall have power to declare the punishment of treason, but no attainder of treason shall work corruption of blood, or forfeiture except during the life of the person attainted.

ARTICLE IV

Section 1. Full faith and credit shall be given in each state to the public acts, records, and judicial proceedings of every other state. And the Congress may by general laws prescribe the manner in which such acts, records, and proceedings shall be proved, and the effect thereof.

Section 2. The citizens of each state shall be entitled to all privileges and immunities of citizens in the several states.

A person charged in any state with treason, felony, or other crime, who shall flee from justice, and be found in another state, shall on demand of the executive authority of the state from which he fled, be delivered up, to be removed to the state having jurisdiction of the crime.

No person held to service or labor in one state, under the laws thereof, escaping into another, shall, in consequence of any law or regulation therein, be discharged from such service or labor, but shall be delivered up on claim of the party to whom such service or labor may be due.

Section 3. New states may be admitted by the Congress into this union; but no new states shall be formed or erected within the jurisdiction of any other state; nor any state be formed by the junction of two or more states, or parts of states, without the consent of the legislatures of the states concerned as well as of the Congress.

The Congress shall have power to dispose of and make all needful rules and regulations respecting the territory or other property belonging to the United States; and nothing in this Constitution shall be so construed as to prejudice any claims of the United States, or of any particular state.

Section 4. The United States shall guarantee to every state in this union a republican form of government, and shall protect each of them against invasion; and on application of the legislature, or of the executive (when the legislature cannot be convened) against domestic violence.

ARTICLE V

The Congress, whenever two thirds of both houses shall deem it necessary, shall propose amendments to this Constitution, or, on the application of the legislatures of two thirds of the several states, shall call a convention for proposing amendments, which, in either case, shall be valid to all intents and purposes, as part of this Constitution, when ratified by the legislatures of three fourths of the several states, or by conventions in three fourths thereof, as the one or the other mode of ratification may be proposed by the Congress; provided that no amendment which may be made prior to the year one thousand eight hundred and eight shall in any manner affect the first and fourth clauses in the ninth section of the first article; and that no state, without its consent, shall be deprived of its equal suffrage in the Senate.

ARTICLE VI

All debts contracted and engagements entered into, before the adoption of this Constitution, shall be as valid against the United States under this Constitution, as under the Confederation.

This Constitution, and the laws of the United States which shall be made in pursuance thereof; and alltreaties made, or which shall be made, under the authority of the United States, shall be the supreme law of the land; and the judges in every state shall be bound thereby, anything in the Constitution or laws of any State to the contrary notwithstanding.

The Senators and Representatives before mentioned, and the members of the several state legislatures, and all executive and judicial officers, both of the United States and of the several states, shall be bound by oath or affirmation, to support this Constitution; but no religious test shall ever be required as a qualification to any office or public trust under the United States.

ARTICLE VII

The ratification of the conventions of nine states, shall be sufficient for the establishment of this Constitution between the states so ratifying the same.

Done in convention by the unanimous consent of the states present the seventeenth day of September in the year of our Lord one thousand seven hundred and eighty seven and of the independence of the United States of America the twelfth. In witness whereof we have hereunto subscribed our Names,

---

Virginia
G. Washington—Presidt. and deputy from Virginia
New Hampshire
John Langdon, Nicholas Gilman
Massachusetts
Nathaniel Gorham, Rufus King
Connecticut
Wm. Saml. Johnson, Roger Sherman
New York
Alexander Hamilton
New Jersey
Wil. Livingston, David Brearly, Wm. Paterson, Jona. Dayton
Pennsylvania
B. Franklin, Thomas Mifflin, Robt. Morris, Geo. Clymer, Thos. FitzSimons, Jared Ingersoll, James

Wilson, Gouv Morris
Delaware
Geo. Read, Gunning Bedford jun, John Dickinson, Richard Bassett, Jaco. Broom
Maryland
James McHenry, Dan of St Thos. Jenifer, Danl Carroll
Virginia
John Blair—, James Madison Jr.
North Carolina
Wm. Blount, Richd. Dobbs Spaight, Hu Williamson
South Carolina
J. Rutledge, Charles Cotesworth Pinckney, Charles Pinckney, Pierce Butler
Georgia
William Few, Abr Baldwin

Bill of Rights

Amendments I through X of the Constitution

AMENDMENT I

Congress shall make no law respecting an establishment of religion, or prohibiting the free exercise thereof; or abridging the freedom of speech, or of the press; or the right of the people peaceably to assemble, and to petition the government for a redress of grievances.

AMENDMENT II

A well regulated militia, being necessary to the security of a free state, the right of the people to keep and bear arms, shall not be infringed.

AMENDMENT III

No soldier shall, in time of peace be quartered in any house, without the consent of the owner, nor in time of war, but in a manner to be prescribed by law.

AMENDMENT IV

The right of the people to be secure in their persons, houses, papers, and effects, against unreasonable searches and seizures, shall not be violated, and no warrants shall issue, but upon probable cause, supported by oath or affirmation, and particularly describing the place to be searched, and the persons or things to be seized.

AMENDMENT V

No person shall be held to answer for a capital, or otherwise infamous crime, unless on a presentment or indictment of a grand jury, except in cases arising in the land or naval forces, or in the militia, when in actual service in time of war or public danger; nor shall any person be subject for the same offense to be twice put in jeopardy of life or limb; nor shall be compelled in any criminal case to be a witness against himself, nor be deprived of life, liberty, or property, without due process of law; nor shall private property be taken for public use, without just compensation.

AMENDMENT VI

In all criminal prosecutions, the accused shall enjoy the right to a speedy and public trial, by an impartial jury of the state and district wherein the crime shall have been committed, which district shall have been previously ascertained by law, and to be informed of the nature and cause of the accusation; to be confronted with the witnesses against him; to have compulsory process for obtaining witnesses in his favor, and to have the assistance of counsel for his defense.

AMENDMENT VII

In suits at common law, where the value in controversy shall exceed twenty dollars, the right of trial by jury shall be preserved, and no fact tried by a jury, shall be otherwise reexamined in any court of the United States, than according to the rules of the common law.

AMENDMENT VIII

Excessive bail shall not be required, nor excessive fines imposed, nor cruel and unusual punishments inflicted.

AMENDMENT IX

The enumeration in the Constitution, of certain rights, shall not be construed to deny or disparage others retained by the people.

AMENDMENT X

The powers not delegated to the United States by the Constitution, nor prohibited by it to the states, are reserved to the states respectively, or to the people.

Additional Amendments

AMENDMENT XI

(1798)

The judicial power of the United States shall not be construed to extend to any suit in law or equity, commenced or prosecuted against one of the United States by citizens of another state, or by citizens or subjects of any foreign state.

AMENDMENT XII

(1804)

The electors shall meet in their respective states and vote by ballot for President and Vice President, one of whom, at least, shall not be an inhabitant of the same state with themselves; they shall name in their ballots the person voted for as President, and in distinct ballots the personvoted for as Vice President, and they shall make distinct lists of all persons voted for as President, and of all persons voted for as Vice President, and of the number of votes for each, which lists they shall sign and certify, and transmit sealed to the seat of the government of the United States, directed to the President of the Senate;—The President of the Senate shall, in the presence of the Senate and House of Representatives, open all the certificates and the votes shall then be counted;—the person having the greatest number of votes for President, shall be the President, if such number be a majority of the whole number of electors appointed; and if no person have such majority, then from the persons having the highest numbers not exceeding three on the list of those voted for as President, the House of Representatives shall choose immediately, by ballot, the President. But in choosing the President, the votes shall be taken by states, the representation from each state having one vote; a quorum for this purpose shall consist of a member or members from two-thirds of the states, and a majority of all the states shall be necessary to a choice. And if the House of Representatives shall not choose a President whenever the right of choice shall devolve upon them, before the fourth day of March next following, then the Vice President shall act as President, as in the case of the death or other constitutional disability of the President. The person having the greatest number of votes as Vice President, shall be the Vice President, if such number be a majority of the whole number of electors appointed, and if no person have a majority, then from the two highest numbers on the list, the

Senate shall choose the Vice President; a quorum for the purpose shall consist of two-thirds of the whole number of Senators, and a majority of the whole number shall be necessary to a choice. But no person constitutionally ineligible to the office of President shall be eligible to that of Vice President of the United States.

AMENDMENT XIII

(1865)

Section 1. Neither slavery nor involuntary servitude, except as a punishment for crime whereof the party shall have been duly convicted, shall exist within the United States, or any place subject to their jurisdiction.
Section 2. Congress shall have power to enforce this article by appropriate legislation.

AMENDMENT XIV

(1868)

Section 1. All persons born or naturalized in the United States, and subject to the jurisdiction thereof, are citizens of the United States and of the state wherein they reside. No state shall make or enforce any law which shall abridge the privileges or immunities of citizens of the United States; nor shall any state deprive any person of life, liberty, or property, without due process of law; nor deny to any person within its jurisdiction the equal protection of the laws.

Section 2. Representatives shall be apportioned among the several states according to their respective numbers, counting the whole number of persons in each state, excluding Indians not taxed. But when the right to vote at any election for the choice of electors for President and Vice President of the United States, Representatives in Congress, the executive and judicial officers of a state, or the members of the legislature thereof, is denied to any of the male inhabitants of such state, being twenty-one years of age, and citizens of the United States, or in any way abridged, except for

participation in rebellion, or other crime, the basis of representation therein shall be reduced in the proportion which the number of such male citizens shall bear to the whole number of male citizens twenty-one years of age in such state.

Section 3. No person shall be a Senator or Representative in Congress, or elector of President and Vice President, or hold any office, civil or military, under the United States, or under any state, who, having previously taken an oath, as a member of Congress, or as an officer of the United States, or as a member of any state legislature, or as an executive or judicial officer of any state, to support the Constitution of the United States, shall have engaged in insurrection or rebellion against the same, or given aid or comfort to the enemies thereof. But Congress may by a vote of two-thirds of each House, remove such disability.

Section 4. The validity of the public debt of the United States, authorized by law, including debts incurred for payment of pensions and bounties for services in suppressing insurrection or rebellion, shall not be questioned. But neither the United States nor any state shall assume or pay any debt or obligation incurred in aid of insurrection or rebellion against the United States, or any claim for the loss or emancipation of any slave; but all such debts, obligations and claims shall be held illegal and void.

Section 5. The Congress shall have power to enforce, by appropriate legislation, the provisions of this article.

AMENDMENT XV

(1870)

Section 1. The right of citizens of the United States to vote shall not be denied or abridged by the United States or by any state on account of race, color, or previous condition of servitude.

Section 2. The Congress shall have power to enforce this article by appropriate legislation.

AMENDMENT XVI

(1913)

The Congress shall have power to lay and collect taxes on incomes, from whatever source derived, without apportionment among the several states, and without regard to any census of enumeration.

AMENDMENT XVII

(1913)

The Senate of the United States shall be composed of two Senators from each state, elected by the people thereof, for six years; and each Senator shall have one vote. The electors in each state shall have the qualifications requisite for electors of the most numerous branch of the state legislatures.

When vacancies happen in the representation of any state in the Senate, the executive authority of such state shall issue writs of election to fill such vacancies: Provided, that the legislature of any state may empower the executive thereof to make temporary appointments until the people fill the vacancies by election as the legislature may direct.

This amendment shall not be so construed as to affect the election or term of any Senator chosen before it becomes valid as part of the Constitution.

AMENDMENT XVIII

(1919)

Section 1. After one year from the ratification of this article the manufacture, sale, or transportation of intoxicating liquors within, the importation thereof into, or the exportation thereof from the United States and all territory subject to the jurisdiction thereof for beverage purposes is hereby prohibited.

Section 2. The Congress and the several states shall have concurrent power to enforce this article by appropriate legislation.

Section 3. This article shall be inoperative unless it shall have been ratified as an amendment to the Constitution by the legislatures of the several states, as provided in the Constitution, within seven years from the date of the submission hereof to the states by the Congress.

AMENDMENT XIX

(1920)

The right of citizens of the United States to vote shall not be denied or abridged by the United States or by any state on account of sex.

Congress shall have power to enforce this article by appropriate legislation.

AMENDMENT XX

(1933)

Section 1. The terms of the President and Vice President shall end at noon on the 20th day of January, and the terms of Senators and Representatives at noon on the 3d day of January, of the years in which such terms would have ended if this article had not been ratified; and the terms of their successors shall then begin.

Section 2. The Congress shall assemble at least once in every year, and such meeting shall begin at noon on the 3d day of January, unless they shall by law appoint a different day.

Section 3. If, at the time fixed for the beginning of the term of the President, the President-elect shall have died, the Vice President-elect shall become President. If a President shall not have been chosen before the time fixed for the beginning of his term, or if the President-elect shall have failed to qualify, then the Vice President-elect shall act as President until a President shall have qualified; and the Congress may by law provide for the case wherein neither a President elect nor a Vice President-elect shall have qualified, declaring who shall then act as President, or the manner in which one who is to act shall be selected, and such person shall act accordingly until a President or Vice President shall have qualified.

Section 4. The Congress may by law provide for the case of the death of any of the persons from whom the House of Representatives may choose a President whenever the right of choice shall have devolved upon them, and for the case of the death of any of the persons from whom the Senate may choose a Vice President whenever the right of choice shall have devolved upon them.

Section 5. Sections 1 and 2 shall take effect on the 15th day of October following the ratification of this article.

Section 6. This article shall be inoperative unless it shall have been ratified as an amendment to the Constitution by the legislatures of three-fourths of the several states within seven years from the date of its submission.

AMENDMENT XXI

(1933)

Section 1. The eighteenth article of amendment to the Constitution of the United States is hereby repealed.

Section 2. The transportation or importation into any state, territory, or possession of the United States for delivery or use therein of intoxicating liquors, in violation of the laws thereof, is hereby prohibited.

Section 3. This article shall be inoperative unless it shall have been ratified as an amendment to the Constitution by conventions in the several states, as provided in the Constitution, within seven years from the date of the submission hereof to the states by the Congress.

AMENDMENT XXII

(1951)

Section 1. No person shall be elected to the office of the President more than twice, and no person who has held the office of President, or acted as President, for more than two years of a term to which some other person was elected President shall be elected to the office of the President more than once. But this article shall not apply to any person holding the office of President when this article was proposed by the Congress, and shall not prevent any person who may be holding the office of President, or acting as President, during the term within which this article becomes operative from holding the office of President or acting as President during the remainder of such term.

Section 2. This article shall be inoperative unless it shall have been ratified as an amendment to the Constitution by the legislatures of three-fourths of the several states within seven years from the date of its submission to the states by the Congress.

AMENDMENT XXIII

(1961)

Section 1. The District constituting the seat of government of the United States shall appoint in such manner as the Congress may direct:

A number of electors of President and Vice President equal to the whole number of Senators and Representatives in Congress to which the District would be entitled if it were a state, but in no event more than the least populous state; they shall be in addition to those appointed by the states, but they shall be considered, for the purposes of the election of President and Vice President, to be electors appointed by a state; and they shall meet in the District and perform such duties as provided by the twelfth article of amendment.

Section 2. The Congress shall have power to enforce this article by appropriate legislation.

AMENDMENT XXIV

(1964)

Section 1. The right of citizens of the United States to vote in any primary or other election for President or Vice President, for electors for President or Vice

President, or for Senator or Representative in Congress, shall not be denied or abridged by the United States or any state by reason of failure to pay any poll tax or other tax.

Section 2.   The Congress shall have power to enforce this article by appropriate legislation.

AMENDMENT XXV

(1967)

Section 1.   In case of the removal of the President from office or of his death or resignation, the Vice President shall become President.

Section 2.   Whenever there is a vacancy in the office of the Vice President, the President shall nominate a Vice President who shall take office upon confirmation by a majority vote of both Houses of Congress.

Section 3.   Whenever the President transmits to the President pro tempore of the Senate and the Speaker of the House of Representatives his written declaration that he is unable to discharge the powers and duties of his office, and until he transmits to them a written declaration to the contrary, such powers and duties shall be discharged by the Vice President as Acting President.

Section 4.   Whenever the Vice President and a majority of either the principal officers of the executive departments or of such other body as Congress may by law provide, transmit to the President pro tempore of the Senate and the Speaker of the House of Representatives their written declaration that the President is unable to discharge the powers and duties of his office, the Vice President shall immediately assume the powers and duties of the office as Acting President.

Thereafter, when the President transmits to the President pro tempore of the Senate and the Speaker of the House of Representatives his written declaration that no inability exists, he shall resume the powers and duties of his office unless the Vice President and a majority of either the principal officers of the executive department or of such other body as Congress may by law provide, transmit within four days to the President pro tempore of the Senate and the Speaker of the House of Representatives their written declaration that the President is unable to discharge the powers and duties of his office. Thereupon Congress shall decide the issue, assembling within forty-eight hours for that purpose if not in session. If the Congress, within twenty-one days after receipt of the latter written declaration, or, if Congress is not in session, within twenty-one days after Congress is required to assemble, determines by two-thirds vote of both Houses that the President is unable to discharge the powers and duties of his office, the Vice President shall continue to discharge the same as Acting President; otherwise, the President shall resume the powers and duties of his office.

AMENDMENT XXVI

(1971)

Section 1.   The right of citizens of the United States, who are 18 years of age or older, to vote, shall not be denied or abridged by the United States or any state on account of age.

Section 2.   The Congress shall have the power to enforce this article by appropriate legislation.

AMENDMENT XXVII

(1992)

No law varying the compensation for the services of the Senators and Representatives shall take effect until an election of Representatives shall have intervened.

APPENDIX D

Federalist Number 10

The Union as a Safeguard Against Domestic Faction and Insurrection

Author: James Madison

To the People of the State of New York:

AMONG the numerous advantages promised by a well-constructed Union, none deserves to be more accurately developed than its tendency to break and control the violence of faction. The friend of popular governments never finds himself so much alarmed for their character and fate, as when he contemplates their propensity to this dangerous vice. He will not fail, therefore, to set a due value on any plan which, without violating the principles to which he is attached, provides a proper cure for it. The instability, injustice, and confusion introduced into the public councils, have, in truth, been the mortal diseases under which popular governments have everywhere perished; as they continue to be the favorite and fruitful topics from which the adversaries to liberty derive their most specious declamations. The valuable improvements made by the American constitutions on the popular models, both ancient and modern, cannot certainly be too much admired; but it would be an unwarrantable partiality, to contend that they have as effectually obviated the danger on this side, as was wished and expected. Complaints are everywhere heard from our most considerate and virtuous citizens, equally the friends of public and private faith, and of public and personal liberty, that our governments are too unstable, that the public good is disregarded in the conflicts of rival parties, and that measures are too often decided, not according to the rules of justice and the rights of the minor party, but by the superior force of an interested and overbearing majority. However anxiously we may wish that these complaints had no foundation, the evidence, of known facts will not permit us to deny that they are in some degree true. It will be found, indeed, on a candid review of our situation, that some of the distresses under which we labor have been erroneously charged on the operation of our governments; but it will be found, at the same time, that other causes will not alone account for many of our heaviest misfortunes; and, particularly, for that prevailing and increasing distrust of public engagements, and alarm for private rights, which are echoed from one end of the continent to the other. These must be chiefly, if not wholly, effects of the unsteadiness and injustice with which a factious spirit has tainted our public administrations.

By a faction, I understand a number of citizens, whether amounting to a majority or a minority of the whole, who are united and actuated by some common impulse of passion, or of interest, adverse to the rights of other citizens, or to the permanent and aggregate interests of the community.

There are two methods of curing the mischiefs of faction: the one, by removing its causes; the other, by controlling its effects.

There are again two methods of removing the causes of faction: the one, by destroying the liberty which is essential to its existence; the other, by giving to every citizen the same opinions, the same passions, and the same interests.

It could never be more truly said than of the first remedy, that it was worse than the disease. Liberty is to faction what air is to fire, an aliment without which it instantly expires. But it could not be less folly to abolish liberty, which is essential to political life, because it nourishes faction, than it would be to wish theannihilation of air, which is essential to animal life, because it imparts to fire its destructive agency.

The second expedient is as impracticable as the first would be unwise. As long as the reason of man continues fallible, and he is at liberty to exercise it, different opinions will be formed. As long as the connection subsists between his reason and his self-love, his opinions and his passions will have a reciprocal influence on each other; and the former will be objects to which the latter will attach themselves. The diversity in the faculties of men, from which the rights of property originate, is not less an insuperable obstacle to a uniformity of interests. The protection of these faculties is the first object of government. From the protection of different and unequal faculties of acquiring property, the possession of different degrees and kinds of property immediately results; and from the influence of these on the sentiments and views of the respective proprietors, ensues a division of the society into different interests and parties.

The latent causes of faction are thus sown in the nature of man; and we see them everywhere brought into different degrees of activity, according to the different circumstances of civil society. A zeal for different opinions concerning religion, concerning government, and many other points, as well of speculation as of practice; an attachment to different leaders ambitiously contending for pre-eminence and power; or to persons of other descriptions whose fortunes have been inter-esting to the human passions, have, in turn, divided mankind into parties, inflamed them with mutual animosity, and rendered them much more disposed to vex and oppress each other than to co-operate for their common good. So strong is this propensity of mankind to fall into mutual animosities, that where no substantial occasion presents itself, the most frivolous and fanciful distinctions have been sufficient to kindle their unfriendly passions and excite their most violent conflicts. But the most common and durable source of factions has been the various and unequal distribution of property. Those who hold and those who are without property have ever formed distinct interests in society. Those who are creditors, and those who are debtors, fall under a like discrimination. A landed interest, a manufacturing interest, a mercantile interest, a moneyed interest, with many lesser interests, grow up of necessity in civilized nations, and divide them into different classes, actuated by different sentiments and views. The regulation of these various and interfering interests forms the principal task of modern legislation, and involves the spirit of party and faction in the necessary and ordinary operations of the government.

No man is allowed to be a judge in his own cause, because his interest would certainly bias his judgment, and, not improbably, corrupt his integrity. With equal, nay with greater reason, a body of men are unfit to be both judges and parties at the same time; yet what are many of the most important acts of legislation, but so many judicial determinations, not indeed concerning the rights of single persons, but concerning the rights of large bodies of citizens? And what are the different classes of legislators but advocates and parties to the causes which they determine? Is a law proposed concerning private debts? It is a question to which the creditors are parties on one side and the debtors on the other. Justice ought to hold the balance between them. Yet the parties are, and must be, themselves the judges; and the most numerous party, or, in other words, the most powerful faction must be expected to prevail. Shall domestic manufactures be encouraged, and in what degree, by restrictions on foreign manufactures? are questions which would be differently decided by the landed and the manufacturing classes, and probably by neither with a sole regard to justice and the public good. The apportionment of taxes on the various descriptions of property is an act which seems to require the most exact impartiality; yet there is, perhaps, no legislative act in which greater opportunity and temptation are given to a predominant party to trample on the rules of justice. Every shilling with which they overburden the inferior number, is a shilling saved to their own pockets.

It is in vain to say that enlightened statesmen will be able to adjust these clashing interests, and render them all subservient to the public good. Enlightened statesmen will not always be at the helm. Nor, in many cases, can such an adjustment be made at all without taking into view indirect and remote considerations, which will rarely prevail over the immediate interest which one party may find in disregarding the rights of another or the good of the whole.

The inference to which we are brought is, that the CAUSES of faction cannot be removed, and that reliefis only to be sought in the means of controlling its EFFECTS.

If a faction consists of less than a majority, relief is supplied by the republican principle, which enables the majority to defeat its sinister views by regular vote. It may clog the administration, it may convulse the society; but it will be unable to execute and mask its violence under the forms of the Constitution. When a majority is included in a faction, the form of popular government, on the other hand, enables it to sacrifice to its ruling passion or interest both the public good and the rights of other citizens. To secure the public good and private rights against the danger of such a faction, and at the same time to preserve the spirit and the form of popular government, is then the great object to which our inquiries are directed. Let me add that it is the great desideratum by which this form of government can be rescued from the opprobrium under which it has so long labored, and be recommended to the esteem and adoption of mankind.

By what means is this object attainable? Evidently by one of two only. Either the existence of the same passion or interest in a majority at the same time must be prevented, or the majority, having such coexistent passion or interest, must be rendered, by their number and local situation, unable to concert and carry into effect schemes of oppression. If the impulse and the opportunity be suffered to coincide, we well know that neither moral nor religious motives can be relied on as an adequate control. They are not found to be such on the injustice and violence of individuals, and lose their efficacy in proportion to the number combined together, that is, in proportion as their efficacy becomes needful.

From this view of the subject it may be concluded that a pure democracy, by which I mean a society consisting of a small number of citizens, who assemble and administer the government in person, can admit of no cure for the mischiefs of faction. A common passion or interest will, in almost every case, be felt by a majority of the whole; a communication and concert result from the form of government itself; and there is nothing to check the inducements to sacrifice the weaker party or an obnoxious individual. Hence it is that such democracies have ever been spectacles of turbulence and contention; have ever been found incompatible with personal security or the rights of property; and have in general been as short in their lives as they have been violent in their deaths. Theoretic politicians, who have patronized this species of government, have erroneously supposed that by reducing mankind to a perfect equality in their political rights, they would, at the same time, be perfectly equalized and assimilated in their possessions, their opinions, and their passions.

A republic, by which I mean a government in which the scheme of representation takes place, opens a different prospect, and promises the cure for which we are seeking. Let us examine the points in which it varies from pure democracy, and we shall comprehend both the nature of the cure and the efficacy which it must derive from the Union.

The two great points of difference between a democracy and a republic are: first, the delegation of the government, in the latter, to a small number of citizens elected by the rest; secondly, the greater number of citizens, and greater sphere of country, over which the latter may be extended.

The effect of the first difference is, on the one hand, to refine and enlarge the public views, by passing them through the medium of a chosen body of citizens, whose wisdom may best discern the true interest of their country, and whose patriotism and love of justice will be least likely to sacrifice it to temporary or partial considerations. Under such a regulation, it may well happen that the public voice, pronounced by the representatives of the people, will be more consonant to the public good than if pronounced by the people themselves, convened for the purpose. On the other hand, the effect may be inverted. Men of factious tempers, of local prejudices, or of sinister designs, may, by intrigue, by corruption, or by other means, first obtain the suffrages, and then betray the interests, of the people. The question resulting is, whether small or extensive republics are more favorable to the election of proper guardians of the public weal; and it is clearly decided in favor of the latter by two obvious considerations:

In the first place, it is to be remarked that, however small the republic may be, the representatives must be raised to a certain number, in order to guard against the cabals of a few; and that, however large it may be, they must be limited to a certain number, in order to guard against the confusion of a multitude. Hence, the number of representatives in the two cases not being in proportion to that of the two constituents, and being proportionally greater in the small republic, it follows that, if the proportion of fit characters be not less in the large than in the small republic, the former will present a greater option, and consequently a greater probability of a fit choice.

In the next place, as each representative will be chosen by a greater number of citizens in the large than in the small republic, it will be more difficult for unworthy candidates to practice with success the vicious arts by which elections are too often carried; and the suffrages of the people being more free, will be more likely to centre in men who possess the most attractive merit and the most diffusive and established characters.

It must be confessed that in this, as in most other cases, there is a mean, on both sides of which inconveniences will be found to lie. By enlarging too much the number of electors, you render the representatives too little acquainted with all their local circumstances and lesser interests; as by reducing it too much, you render him unduly attached to these, and too little fit

to comprehend and pursue great and national objects. The federal Constitution forms a happy combination in this respect; the great and aggregate interests being referred to the national, the local and particular to the State legislatures.

The other point of difference is, the greater number of citizens and extent of territory which may be brought within the compass of republican than of democratic government; and it is this circumstance principally which renders factious combinations less to be dreaded in the former than in the latter. The smaller the society, the fewer probably will be the distinct parties and interests composing it; the fewer the distinct parties and interests, the more frequently will a majority be found of the same party; and the smaller the number of individuals composing a majority, and the smaller the compass within which they are placed, the more easily will they concert and execute their plans of oppression. Extend the sphere, and you take in a greater variety of parties and interests; you make it less probable that a majority of the whole will have a common motive to invade the rights of other citizens; or if such a common motive exists, it will be more difficult for all who feel it to discover their own strength, and to act in unison with each other. Besides other impediments, it may be remarked that, where there is a consciousness of unjust or dishonorable purposes, communication is always checked by distrust in proportion to the number whose concurrence is necessary.

Hence, it clearly appears, that the same advantage which a republic has over a democracy, in controlling the effects of faction, is enjoyed by a large over a small republic,—is enjoyed by the Union over the States composing it. Does the advantage consist in the substitution of representatives whose enlightened views and virtuous sentiments render them superior to local prejudices and schemes of injustice? It will not be denied that the representation of the Union will be most likely to possess these requisite endowments. Does it consist in the greater security afforded by a greater variety of parties, against the event of any one party being able to outnumber and oppress the rest? In an equal degree does the increased variety of parties comprised within the Union, increase this security. Does it, in fine, consist in the greater obstacles opposed to the concert and accomplishment of the secret wishes of an unjust and interested majority? Here, again, the extent of the Union gives it the most palpable advantage.

The influence of factious leaders may kindle a flame within their particular States, but will be unable to spread a general conflagration through the other States. A religious sect may degenerate into a political faction in a part of the Confederacy; but the variety of sects dispersed over the entire face of it must secure the national councils against any danger from that source. A rage for paper money, for an abolition of debts, for an equal division of property, or for any other improper or wicked project, will be less apt to pervade the whole body of the Union than a particular member of it; in the same proportion as such a malady is more likely to taint a particular county or district, than an entire State.

In the extent and proper structure of the Union, therefore, we behold a republican remedy for the diseases most incident to republican government. And according to the degree of pleasure and pride we feel in being republicans, ought to be our zeal in cherishing the spirit and supporting the character of Federalists.

PUBLIUS.

Federalist Number 51

The Structure of the Government Must Furnish the Proper Checks and Balances Between the Different Departments

Author: James Madison

To the People of the State of New York:

TO WHAT expedient, then, shall we finally resort, for maintaining in practice the necessary partition of power among the several departments, as laid down in the Constitution? The only answer that can be given is, that as all these exterior provisions are found to be inadequate, the defect must be supplied, by so contriving the interior structure of the government as that its several constituent parts may, by their mutual relations, be the means of keeping each other in their proper places. Without presuming to undertake a full development of this important idea, I will hazard a few general observations, which may perhaps place it in a clearer light, and enable us to form a more correct judgment of the principles and structure of the government planned by the convention.

In order to lay a due foundation for that separate and distinct exercise of the different powers of government, which to a certain extent is admitted on all hands to be essential to the preservation of liberty, it is evident that each department should have a will of its own; and consequently should be so constituted that the members of each should have as little agency as possible in the appointment of the members of the others. Were this principle rigorously adhered to, it would require that all the appointments for the supreme executive, legislative, and judiciary magistracies should be drawn from the same fountain of authority, the people, through channels having no communication whatever with one another. Perhaps such a plan of constructing the several departments would be less difficult in practice than it may in contemplation appear. Some difficulties, however, and some additional expense would attend the execution of it. Some deviations, therefore, from the principle must be admitted. In the constitution of the judiciary department in particular, it might be inexpedient to insist rigorously on the principle: first, because peculiar qualifications being essential in the members, the primary consideration ought to be to select that mode of choice which best secures these qualifications; secondly, because the permanent tenure by which the appointments are held in that department, must soon destroy all sense of dependence on the authority conferring them.

It is equally evident, that the members of each department should be as little dependent as possible on those of the others, for the emoluments annexed to their offices. Were the executive magistrate, or the judges, not independent of the legislature in this particular, their independence in every other would be merely nominal.

But the great security against a gradual concentration of the several powers in the same department, consists in giving to those who administer each department the necessary constitutional means and personal motives to resist encroachments of the others. The provision for defense must in this, as in all other cases, be made commensurate to the danger of attack. Ambition must be made to counteract ambition. The interest of the man must be connected with the constitutional rights of the place. It may be a reflection on human nature, that such devices should be necessary to control the abuses of government. But what is government itself, but the greatest of all reflections on human nature? If men were angels, no government would be necessary. If angels were to govern men, neither external nor internal controls on government would be necessary. In framing a government which is to be administered by men over men, the great difficulty lies in this: you must first enable the government to control the governed; and in the next place oblige it to control itself. A dependence on the people is, no doubt, the primary control on the government; but experience has taught mankind the necessity of auxiliary precautions.

This policy of supplying, by opposite and rival interests, the defect of better motives, might be traced through the whole system of human affairs, private as well as public. We see it particularly displayed in allthe subordinate distributions of power, where the constant aim is to divide and arrange the several offices in such a manner as that each may be a check on the other that the private interest of every individual may be a sentinel over the public rights. These inventions of prudence cannot be less requisite in the distribution of the supreme powers of the State.

But it is not possible to give to each department an equal power of self-defense. In republican government, the legislative authority necessarily predominates. The remedy for this inconveniency is to divide the legislature into different branches; and to render them, by different modes of election and different principles of action, as little connected with each other as the nature of their common functions and their common dependence on the society will admit. It may even be necessary to guard against dangerous encroachments by still further precautions. As the weight of the legislative authority requires that it should be thus divided, the weakness of the executive may require, on the other hand, that it should be fortified. An absolute negative on the legislature appears, at first view, to be the natural defense with which the executive magistrate should be armed. But perhaps it would be neither altogether safe nor alone sufficient. On ordinary occasions it might not be exerted with the requisite firmness, and on extraordinary occasions it might be perfidiously abused. May not this defect of an absolute negative be supplied by some qualified connection between this weaker department and the weaker branch of the stronger department, by which the latter may be led to support the constitutional rights of the former, without being too much detached from the rights of its own department?

If the principles on which these observations are founded be just, as I persuade myself they are, and they be applied as a criterion to the several State constitutions, and to the federal Constitution it will be found that if the latter does not perfectly correspond with them, the former are infinitely less able to bear such a test. There are, moreover, two considerations particularly applicable to the federal system of America, which place that system in a very interesting point of view.

First. In a single republic, all the power surrendered by the people is submitted to the administration of a single government; and the usurpations are guarded against by a division of the government into distinct and separate departments. In the compound republic of America, the power surrendered by the people is first divided between two distinct governments, and then the portion allotted to each subdivided among distinct and separate departments. Hence a double security arises to the rights of the people. The different governments will control each other, at the same time that each will be controlled by itself.

Second. It is of great importance in a republic not only to guard the society against the oppression of its rulers, but to guard one part of the society against the injustice of the other part. Different interests necessarily exist in different classes of citizens. If a majority be united by a common interest, the rights of the minority will be insecure. There are but two methods of providing against this evil: the one by creating a will in the community independent of the majority that is, of the society itself; the other, by comprehending in the society so many separate descriptions of citizens as will render an unjust combination of a majority of the whole very improbable, if not impracticable. The first method prevails in all governments possessing an hereditary or self-appointed authority. This, at best, is but a precarious security; because a power independent of the society may as well espouse the unjust views of the major, as the rightful interests of the minor party, and may possibly be turned against both parties. The second method will be exemplified in the federal republic of the United States. Whilst all authority in it will be derived from and dependent on the society, the society itself will be broken into so many parts, interests, and classes of citizens, that the rights of individuals, or of the minority, will be in little danger from interested combinations of the majority. In a free government the security for civil rights must be the same as that for religious rights. It consists in the one case in the multiplicity of interests, and in the other in the multiplicity of sects. The degree of security in both cases will depend on the number of interests and sects; and this may be presumed to depend on the extent of country and number of people comprehended under the same government. This view of the subject must particularly recommend a proper federal system to all the sincere and considerate friends of republican government, since it shows that in exact proportion as the territory of the Union may be formed into more circumscribed Confederacies, or States oppressive combinations of a majority will be facilitated: the best security, under the republican forms, for the rights of every class of citizens, will be diminished: and consequently the stability and independence of some member of the government, the only other security, must be proportionately increased. Justice is the end of government. It is the end of civil society. It ever has been and ever will be pursued until it be obtained, or until liberty be lost in the pursuit. In a society under the forms of which the stronger faction can readily unite and oppress the weaker, anarchy may as truly be said to reign as in a state of nature, where the weaker individual is not secured against the violence of the stronger; and as, in the latter state, even the stronger individuals are prompted, by the uncertainty of their condition, to submit to a government which may protect the weak as well as themselves; so, in the former state, will the more powerful factions or parties be gradually induced, by a like motive, to wish for a government which will protect all parties, the weaker as well as the more powerful. It can be little doubted that if the State of Rhode Island was separated from the Confederacy and left to itself, the insecurity of rights under the popular form of government within such narrow limits would be displayed by such reiterated oppressions of factious majorities that some power altogether independent of the people would soon be called for by the voice of the very factions whose misrule had proved the necessity of it. In the extended republic of the United States, and among the great variety of interests, parties, and sects which it embraces, a coalition of a majority of the whole society could seldom take place on any other principles than those of justice and the general good; whilst there being thus less danger to a minor from the will of a major party, there must be less pretext, also, to provide for the security of the former, by introducing into the government a will not dependent on the latter, or, in other words, a will independent of the society itself. It is no less certain than it is important, notwithstanding the contrary opinions which have been entertained, that the larger the society, provided it lie within a practical sphere, the more duly capable it will be of self-government. And happily for the REPUBLICAN CAUSE, the practicable sphere may be carried to a very great extent, by a judicious modification and mixture of the FEDERAL PRINCIPLE.

PUBLIUS

APPENDIX E

Partisan Control of the Presidency, Congress, and the Supreme Court

Term	President	Party	Congress	Majority Party		Party of Appt. President
				House	Senate	Supreme Court
1789–1797	George Washington	Federalist	1st	(N/A)	(N/A)	6F
			2nd	(N/A)	(N/A)	
			3rd	(N/A)	(N/A)	
			4th	(N/A)	(N/A)	
1797–1801	John Adams	Federalist	5th	(N/A)	(N/A)	6F
			6th	Fed	Fed	
1801–1809	Thomas Jefferson	Democratic-	7th	Dem-Rep	Dem-Rep	5F	1DR
		Republican	8th	Dem-Rep	Dem-Rep	
			9th	Dem-Rep	Dem-Rep	
			10th	Dem-Rep	Dem-Rep	
1809–1817	James Madison	Democratic-	11th	Dem-Rep	Dem-Rep	3F	4DR
		Republican	12th	Dem-Rep	Dem-Rep	
			13th	Dem-Rep	Dem-Rep	
			14th	Dem-Rep	Dem-Rep	
1817–1825	James Monroe	Democratic-	15th	Dem-Rep	Dem-Rep	2F	5DR
		Republican	16th	Dem-Rep	Dem-Rep	
			17th	Dem-Rep	Dem-Rep	
			18th	Dem-Rep	Dem-Rep	
1825–1829	John Quincy Adams	Democratic-	19th	Admin	Admin	2F	5DR
		Republican	20th	Jack	Jack	
1829–1837	Andrew Jackson	Democratic-	21st	Dem	Dem	2D 1F	4DR
			22nd	Dem	Dem	

(Continued)

| Term | President | Party | Congress | Majority Party | | Party of Appt. President | |
				House	Senate	Supreme Court	
			23rd	Dem	Dem		
			24th	Dem	Dem		
1837–1841	Martin Van Buren	Democrat	25th	Dem	Dem	7D	2DR
			26th	Dem	Dem		
1841–1841	William Henry Harrison	Whig	27th	Whig	Whig	7D	2DR
1841–1845	John Tyler	Whig	27th	Whig	Whig	7D	2DR
			28th	Dem	Whig		
1845–1849	James K. Polk	Democrat	29th	Dem	Dem	8D	1W
			30th	Whig	Dem		
1849–1850	Zachary Taylor	Whig	31st	Dem	Dem	8D	1W
1850–1853	Millard Fillmore	Whig	32nd	Dem	Dem	7D	2W
1853–1857	Franklin Pierce	Democrat	33rd	Dem	Dem	7D	2W
			34th	Rep	Dem		
1857–1861	James Buchanan	Democrat	35th	Dem	Dem	8D	1W
			36th	Rep	Dem		
1861–1865	Abraham Lincoln	Republican	37th	Rep	Rep	5D 1W	3R
			38th	Rep	Rep		
1865–1869	Andrew Johnson	Republican	39th	Union	Union	2D 1W	6R
			40th	Rep	Rep		
1869–1877	Ulysses S. Grant	Republican	41st	Rep	Rep	2D	7R
			42nd	Rep	Rep		
			43rd	Rep	Rep		
			44th	Dem	Rep		
1877–1881	Rutherford B. Hayes	Republican	45th	Dem	Rep	1D	8R
1881	James A. Garfield	Republican	47th	Rep	Rep	1D	8R
1881–1885	Chester A. Arthur	Republican	48th	Dem	Rep		9R
1885–1889	Grover Cleveland	Democrat	49th	Dem	Rep		9R
			50th	Dem	Rep		
1889–1893	Benjamin Harrison	Republican	51st	Rep	Rep	2D	7R
			52nd	Dem	Rep		

(Continued)

| Term | President | Party | Congress | Majority Party | | Party of Appt. President |
				House	Senate	Supreme Court
1893–1897	Grover Cleveland	Democrat	53rd	Dem	Dem	2D 7R
			54th	Rep	Rep	
1897–1901	William McKinley	Republican	55th	Rep	Rep	3D 6R
			56th	Rep	Rep	
1901–1909	Theodore Roosevelt	Republican	57th	Rep	Rep	3D 6R
			58th	Rep	Rep	
			59th	Rep	Rep	
			60th	Rep	Rep	
1909–1913	William Howard Taft	Republican	61st	Rep	Rep	1D 8R
			62nd	Dem	Rep	
1913–1921	Woodrow Wilson	Democrat	63rd	Dem	Dem	2D 7R
			64th	Dem	Dem	
			65th	Dem	Dem	
			66th	Rep	Rep	
1921–1923	Warren G. Harding	Republican	67th	Rep	Rep	3D 6R
1923–1929	Calvin Coolidge	Republican	68th	Rep	Rep	2D 7R
			69th	Rep	Rep	
			70th	Rep	Rep	
1929–1933	Herbert Hoover	Republican	71st	Rep	Rep	2D 7R
			72nd	Dem	Rep	
1933–1945	Franklin D. Roosevelt	Democrat	73rd	Dem	Dem	5D 4R
			74th	Dem	Dem	
			75th	Dem	Dem	
			76th	Dem	Dem	
			77th	Dem	Dem	
			78th	Dem	Dem	
1945–1953	Harry S. Truman	Democrat	79th	Dem	Dem	9D
			80th	Rep		
			81st	Dem	Dem	
			82nd	Dem	Dem	
1953–1961	Dwight D. Eisenhower	Republican	83rd	Rep	Rep	6D 3R
			84th	Dem	Dem	

(Continued)

| Term | President | Party | Congress | Majority Party | | Party of Appt. President | |
				House	Senate	Supreme Court	
			85th	Dem	Dem		
			86th	Dem	Dem		
1961–1963	John F. Kennedy	Democrat	87th	Dem	Dem	4D	5R
1963–1969	Lyndon B. Johnson	Democrat	88th	Dem	Dem	5D	4R
			89th	Dem	Dem		
			90th	Dem	Dem		
1969–1974	Richard M. Nixon	Republican	91st	Dem	Dem	4D	5R
			92nd	Dem	Dem		
1974–1977	Gerald R. Ford	Republican	93rd	Dem	Dem	2D	7R
			94th	Dem	Dem		
1977–1981	Jimmy Carter	Democrat	95th	Dem	Dem	2D	7R
			96th	Dem	Dem		
1981–1989	Ronald Reagan	Republican	97th	Dem	Rep	2D	7R
			98th	Dem	Rep		
			99th	Dem	Rep		
			100th	Dem	Dem		
1989–1993	George Bush	Republican	101st	Dem	Dem	1D	8R
			102nd	Dem	Dem		
1993–2001	William Clinton	Democrat	103rd	Dem	Dem	2D	7R
			104th	Rep	Rep		
			105th	Rep	Rep		
			106th	Rep	Rep		
2001–2009	George W. Bush	Republican	107th	Rep	Dem	2D	7R
			108th	Rep	Rep		
			109th	Rep	Rep		
			110th	Dem	Dem		
2009–2017	Barack Obama	Democrat	111th	Dem	Dem	2D	7R
			112th	Rep	Dem	4D	5R
			113th	Rep	Dem		

REFERENCES

ABC News. 2008. "Obama Commends DNC for Cutting Lobbyist Contributions." ABC News, June 5. http://blogs.abcnews.com/politicalradar/2008/06/obama-commends.html (accessed September 19, 2010).

Abraham, Henry J. 1993. *The Judicial Process.* 6th ed. New York: Oxford University Press.

Abramowitz, Alan, and Kyle Saunders. 1998. "Ideological Realignment in the U.S. Electorate." *Journal of Politics* 60 (August): 634–652.

Abramson, Paul R., John H. Aldrich, and David W. Rohde. 1999. *Change and Continuity in the 1996 and 1998 Elections.* Washington, DC: CQ Press.

Abramson, Paul R., John H. Aldrich, and David W. Rohde. 2006. *Change and Continuity in the 2004 Elections.* Washington, DC: CQ Press.

Advisory Commission on Intergovernmental Relations. 1994. *Significant Features of Fiscal Federalism.* Washington, DC: Advisory Commission on Intergovernmental Relations.

Aftergood, Steven. 2008. "The Next President Should Open Up the Bush Administration's Record." *Nieman Watchdog,* February 7. http://www.niemanwatchdog.org/index.cfm?fuseaction=ask_this.view&askthisid=321 (accessed September 19, 2010).

Ainsworth, Scott H. 1997. "The Role of Legislators in the Determination of Interest Group Influence." *Legislative Studies Quarterly* 22 (November): 517–533.

Aldrich, John H. 1993. "Rational Choice and Turnout." *American Journal of Political Science* 37 (February): 246–278.

Aldrich, John H. 2011. *Why Parties? A Second Look.* Chicago: University of Chicago Press.

Alexander, F. King. 1998. "Private Institutions and Public Dollars: An Analysis of the Effect of Federal Direct Student Aid on Public and Private Institutions of Higher Education." *Journal of Education Finance* 23 (Winter): 390–416.

Alford, John R., Carolyn L. Funk, and John R. Hibbing. 2005. "Are Political Orientations Genetically Transmitted?" *American Political Science Review* 99 (May): 153–168.

Alger, David. 1996. *The Media and Politics.* 2nd ed. Belmont, CA: Wadsworth.

Allsop, Dee, and Herbert F. Weisberg. 1988. "Measuring Change in Party Identification in an Election Campaign." *American Journal of Political Science* 32 (November): 996–1017.

American National Election Studies. 2006. *The ANES Guide to Public Opinion and Electoral Behavior.* Ann Arbor: University of Michigan, Center for Political Studies. http://www.electionstudies.org/nesguide/nesguide.htm (accessed September 19, 2010).

Americans United for Affirmative Action. 1999. "Affirmative Action Timeline." http://www.aaua.org/timeline (accessed March 30, 1999).

Amnesty International. 2006. "The Death Penalty: Abolitionist and Retentionist Countries." Last updated May 15, 2006. http://web.amnesty.org/pages/deathpenalty--countries-eng (accessed June 13, 2006).

Anderson, James. 2000. *Public Policymaking.* 4th ed. New York: Houghton Mifflin.

Ansolabehere, S., S. Iyengar, A. Simon, and N. Valentino. 1994. "Does Attack Advertising Demobilize the Electorate?" *American Political Science Review* 88: 829–838.

Ansolabehere, Stephen. 2009. "Effects of Identification Requirements on Voting: Evidence from the Experiences of Voters on Elections Day." *PS: Political Science and Politics* 42: 127–130.

Appleman, Eric M. 2008. "Early Endorsements by Congressmen, Senators and Governors." *Democracy in Action: P2008.* http://www.gwu.edu/~action/2008/cands08/endorse08el.html.

Appleman, Eric M. 2012. "National Endorsements (pre-Iowa Caucuses)." *Democracy in Action: P2012.* http://www.p2012.org/candidates/natendorseprecaucus.html.

Arrow, Kenneth. 1963. *Social Choice and Individual Values.* New Haven, CT: Yale University Press.

Associated Press. 2009. "US Sen. Lindsey Graham Censured by SC County GOP." http://www.google.com/hostednews/ap/article/ALeqM5j5LOd06Q7MF-pkt9sNJ35kNoTM4wD9BTDPE81 (accessed November 30, 2009).

Associated Press. 2012. "What the Law Says about Campaigns and Super PACs at the Heart of the 2012 Election." *Washington Post,* May 15. http://www.washingtonpost.com/national/what-the-law-says-about-campaigns-and-super-pacs-at-the-heart-of-the-2012-election/2012/05/15/gIQA4ht7RU_story.html (accessed May 19, 2012).

Austin-Smith, David. 1995. "Campaign Contributions and Access." *American Political Science Review* 89 (September): 566–581.

Ayto, John. 1990. *Dictionary of Word Origins.* New York: Arcade Publishing, Little, Brown.

Baker, Ross. 2007. "In Defense of Lobbying," *USA Today,* September 27. http://blogs.usatoday.com/oped/2007/09/in-defense-of-l.html (accessed September 19, 2010).

Barber, Benjamin. 1996. *Jihad vs. McWorld: Terrorism's Challenge to Democracy.* New York: Ballantine Books.

Barber, James David. 1992. *The Presidential Character.* New York: Prentice-Hall.

Barone, Michael, and Richard E. Cohen. 2007. *Almanac of American Politics 2008.* Washington, DC: National Journal.

Barone, Michael, and Richard E. Cohen. 2009. *Almanac of American Politics 2010.* Washington, DC: National Journal.

Barone, Michael, and Chuck McCutcheon. 2011. *Almanac of American Politics 2012.* Washington, DC: National Journal.

Barr, Andy. 2010. "Poll: Majority of Republicans Believe Obama Is a Socialist." *Politico,* February 2. http://www.politico.com/news/stories/0210/32384.html (accessed September 19, 2010).

Barstow, David. 2010. "Tea Party Lights Fuse for Rebellion on Right." *New York Times,* February 15. http://www.nytimes.com/2010/02/16/us/politics/16teaparty.html (accessed February 26, 2010).

Bartels, Larry M. 1993. "Messages Received: The Political Impact of Media Exposure." *American Political Science Review* 87 (June): 267–285.

Bartels, Larry M. 2000. "Partisanship and Voting Behavior, 1952–1996." *American Journal of Political Science* 44 (January): 35–50.

Baum, Matthew, and Tim Groeling. 2008. "New Media and the Polarization of American Political Discourse." *Political Communication* 25: 345–365.

Baumgartner, Frank R., Jeffrey M. Berry, Marie Hojnacki, David C. Kimball, and Beth L. Leech. 2009. *Lobbying and Policy Change: Who Wins, Who Loses, and Why.* Chicago: University of Chicago Press.

Baumgartner, Frank R., and Bryan D. Jones. 1993. *Agendas and Instability in American Politics.* Chicago: University of Chicago Press.

Baumgartner, Frank R., and Beth L. Leech. 1998. *Basic Interests: The Importance of Groups in Politics and in Political Science.* Princeton, NJ: Princeton University Press.

Baumgartner, Frank R., and Beth L. Leech. 2001. "Interest Niches and Policy Bandwagons: Patterns of Interest Group Involvement in National Politics." *Journal of Politics* 63 (November): 1191–1213.

Baumgartner, Jody, and Jonathan Morris. 2006. "The Daily Show Effect: Candidates, Efficacy and American Youth." *American Politics Research* 34: 341–367.

Bawn, Kathleen. 1999. "Constructing 'Us': Ideology, Coalition Politics, and False Consciousness." *American Journal of Political Science* 43 (April): 303–334.

Baybeck, Brady, and William R. Lowry. 2000. "Federalism Outcomes and Ideological Preferences: The U.S. Supreme Court and Preemption Cases." *Publius* 30 (Summer): 73–97.

Bazelon, Emily. "Sounding Off: Judges Should Have the Right Not to Remain Silent." *Legal Affairs* (November–December 2002). http://www.legalaffairs.org/issues/November-December-2002/review_bazelon_novdec2002.html (accessed September 17, 2004).

Becker, Carl. 1922. *The Declaration of Independence: A Study in the History of Political Ideas.* New York: Harcourt, Brace.

Beckett, Katherine. 1997. *Making Crime Pay: Law and Order in Contemporary American Politics.* New York: Oxford University Press.

Beckmann, Matthew N. 2010. *Pushing the Agenda: Presidential Leadership in U.S. Lawmaking, 1943–2004.* Cambridge, UK: Cambridge University Press.

Bell, Roger. 1984. *Last among Equals.* Honolulu: University of Hawaii Press.

Bennett, Stephen Earl, and David Resnick. 1990. "The Implications of Nonvoting for Democracy in the United States." *American Journal of Political Science* 34 (August): 771–802.

Benson, T. 1996. "Rhetoric, Civility, and Community: Political Debate on Computer Bulletin Boards." *Communication Quarterly* 44: 359–378.

Benton, Wilbourne E., ed. 1986. *1787: Drafting the U.S. Constitution.* Vol. 2. College Station: Texas A&M University Press.

Berg-Andersson, Richard E. 2008. "Election 2008 Primary, Caucus, and Convention Phase." *The Green Papers*, http://www.thegreenpapers.com/P08/.

Berg-Andersson, Richard E. 2012. "Election 2012 Presidential Primaries, Caucuses, and Conventions." *The Green Papers*, http://www.thegreenpapers.com/P12/. Last accessed 3-2-13.

Berke, Richard L. 1999. "Weighing the Vice Presidential Factor in Gore's Feeble Showing in the Polls." *New York Times*, March 6, A7.

Berke, Richard L. 2001. "Bush Is Providing Corporate Model for White House." *New York Times*, March 11. http://www.nytimes.com/2001/03/11/politics/11GOVE.html (accessed October 23, 2004).

Berman, David R., and Tanis J. Salant. 1998. "Minority Representation, Resistance, and Public Policy: The Navajos and the Counties." *Publius* 28 (Autumn): 83–104.

Best, Judith A. 1996. *The Choice of the People: Debating the Electoral College*. Lanham, MD: Rowman & Littlefield.

Bibby, John F. 1996. *Politics, Parties, and Elections in America*. 3rd ed. Chicago: Nelson-Hall.

Bibby, John F., and L. Sandy Maisel. 1998. *Two Parties—Or More? The American Party System*. Boulder, CO: Westview Press.

Bickel, Alexander M. 1962. *The Least Dangerous Branch: The Supreme Court at the Bar of Politics*. Indianapolis, IN: Bobbs-Merrill.

Bickers, Kenneth N., and Robert M. Stein. 1996. "The Electoral Dynamics of the Federal Pork Barrel." *American Journal of Political Science* 40 (November): 1300–1326.

Binder, Sarah A., and Steven S. Smith. 1997. *Politics or Principle: Filibustering in the United States Senate*. Washington, DC: Brookings Institution.

Biskupic, Joan. 1999. "Disabled Pupils Win Right to Medical Aid." *Washington Post*, March 4, A1.

Biskupic, Joan. 2003. "Court Upholds Use of Race in University Admissions." *USA Today*, June 24, 1A.

Black, Charles, Jr. 1974. *Impeachment: A Handbook*. New Haven, CT: Yale University Press.

Bok, Derek, and William G. Bowen. 1998. *The Shape of the River*. Princeton, NJ: Princeton University Press.

Bond, Jon R. 1980. "The Politics of Court Structure: The Addition of New Federal Judges, 1949–1978." *Law and Politics Quarterly* 2 (April): 181–188.

Bond, Jon R., Cary Covington, and Richard Fleisher. 1985. "Explaining Challenger Quality in Congressional Elections." *Journal of Politics* 47 (May): 510–529.

Bond, Jon R., and Richard Fleisher. 1990. *The President in the Legislative Arena*. Chicago: University of Chicago Press.

Bond, Jon R., Richard Fleisher, and Glen S. Krutz. 2009. "Malign Neglect: Evidence That Delay Has Become the Primary Method of Defeating Presidential Appointments." *Congress and the Presidency* 36 (September–December): 226–243.

Boulard, Garry. 1999. "More News, Less Coverage?" *State Legislatures*, Vol. 25, No. 6. June, p.14(5).

Brady, David W., Joseph Cooper, and Patricia Hurley. 1979. "The Decline of Party in the U.S. House of Representatives, 1887–1968." *Legislative Studies Quarterly* 4 (August): 381–407.

Brands, H. W. 2003. "Founders Chic: Our Reverence for the Fathers Has Gotten Out of Hand." *Atlantic Monthly* 292 (September): 101–110.

Brehm, John, and Scott Gates. 1997. *Working, Shirking, and Sabotage*. Ann Arbor: University of Michigan Press.

Briffault, Robert. 1930. *Rational Evolution: The Making of Humanity*. New York: Macmillan.

Brinkley, Alan. 1993. *The Unfinished Nation*. New York: McGraw-Hill.

Broder, David S. 2000. *Democracy Derailed*. New York: Harcourt.

Browning, Graeme. 1996. "Please Hold for Election Results." *National Journal* 28 (November): 2517.

Brudnick, Ida A. 2008. "Salaries of Members of Congress: A List of Payable Rates and Effective Dates, 1789–2008." Congressional Research Service, February 21. Washington, DC: Library of Congress. http://www.senate.gov/reference/resources/pdf/97-1011.pdf (accessed May 21, 2010).

Budesheim, Thomas Lee, and Stephen J. DePaola. 1994. "Beauty or the Beast? The Effects of Appearance, Personality, and Issue Information on Evaluations of Candidates." *Personality and Social Psychology Bulletin* 20 (August): 339–349.

Byrne, Robert. 1988. *The 1,911 Best Things Anybody Ever Said*. New York: Fawcett Columbine.

Cain, Bruce, John Ferejohn, and Morris Fiorina. 1987. *The Personal Vote*. Cambridge, MA: Harvard University Press.

Caldeira, Gregory A., and John R. Wright. 1990. "Amici Curiae before the Supreme Court: Who Participates, When, and How Much?" *The Journal of Politics* 52 (August): 782–806.

Cameron, Charles M. 2000. *Veto Bargaining: Presidents and the Politics of Negative Power*. Cambridge, UK: Cambridge University Press.

Campaign Finance Institute. 2010a. "Campaign Funding Sources for House and Senate Candidates, 1984–2008." http://www.cfinst.org/pdf/vital/VitalStats_t8.pdf. (accessed June 25, 2010).

Campaign Finance Institute. 2010b. "How PACs Distributed Their Contributions to Congressional Candidates, 1978–

2008." http://www.cfinst.org/pdf/vital/VitalStats_t11.pdf. (accessed June 25, 2010).

Campbell, Angus, Philip Converse, Warren Miller, and Donald Stokes. 1960. *The American Voter*. New York: Wiley.

Campbell, Colin. 1986. *Managing the Presidency: Carter, Reagan, and the Search for Executive Harmony*. Pittsburgh: University of Pittsburgh Press.

Canon, David T. 1990. *Actors, Athletes, and Astronauts: Political Amateurs in the United States Congress*. Chicago: University of Chicago Press.

Capella, Joseph, and Kathleen Hall Jamieson. 1997. *Spiral of Cynicism: The Press and the Public Good*. New York: Oxford University Press.

Carlin, Diana Prentice. 1992. "Presidential Debates as Focal Points for Campaign Arguments." *Political Communication* 9 (January–March): 251–265.

Carp, Robert A., Ronald Stidham, and Kenneth L. Manning. 2004. *Judicial Process in America*. Washington, DC: CQ Press.

Carr, Robert K. 1947. *Federal Protection of Civil Rights: Quest for a Sword*. New York: Cornell University Press.

Center for Responsive Politics. 2008. "Banking on Becoming President." Politicians and Elections: 2008 Presidential Election, http://www.opensecrets.org/pres08/index.php?cycle=2008 (accessed September 22, 2008).

Center for Responsive Politics. 2010. "Totals by Sector Over Time", http://www.opensecrets.org/bigpicture/sectors.php?cycle=2010&bkdn=Source&sortBy=Rank. (accessed June 25, 2010).

Center for Responsive Politics. 2012a. "Super PACs." http://www.opensecrets.org/pacs/superpacs.php?cycle=2012 (accessed May 1, 2012).

Center for Responsive Politics. 2012b. "Types of Advocacy Groups." http://www.opensecrets.org/527s/types.php (accessed May 1, 2012).

Chaffee, Steven, and Stacey Frank. 1996. "How Americans Get Political Information: Print Versus Broadcast News." *Annals of the American Academy of Political and Social Science* 546: 48–58.

Chandler, Ralph C., and Jack C. Plano. 1988. *The Public Administration Dictionary*. Santa Barbara, CA: ABC-CLIO.

Chin, Michelle L., Jon R. Bond, and Nehemia Geva. 2000. "A Foot in the Door: An Experimental Study of PAC and Constituency Effects on Access." *Journal of Politics* 62 (May): 534–549.

Chong, Dennis, and James Druckman. 2007. "Framing Public Opinion in Competitive Democracies." *American Political Science Review* 101: 637–655.

Clark, Charles S. 1997. "Feminism's Future." *CQ Researcher* 7 (February): 169–192.

Clark, Peter, and James Q. Wilson. 1961. "Incentive Systems: A Theory of Organizations." *Administrative Science Quarterly* 6 (September): 129–166.

Cobb, Roger W., and Charles D. Elder. 1983. *Participation in American Politics: The Dynamics of Agenda Building*. Baltimore, MD: Johns Hopkins University Press.

Coffey, Brian, and Stephen Woolworth. 2003. "'Destroy the Scum, and Then Neuter Their Families.' The Web Forum as a Vehicle for Community Discourse?" *Social Science Journal* 41: 1–14.

Cohen, Bernard. 1963. *The Press and Foreign Policy*. Princeton, NJ: Princeton University Press.

Cohen, Jeffrey, Jon R. Bond, and Richard Fleisher. 2013. "Placing Presidential-Congressional Relations in Context: A Comparison of Barack Obama and His Predecessors." *Polity* 45 (January): 105–126.

Cohen, Marty, David Karol, Hans Noel, and John Zaller. 2001. "Beating Reform: The Resurgence of Parties in Presidential Nominations, 1980 to 2000." Paper presented at the annual meeting of the American Political Science Association, San Francisco, August 30–September 2.

Cohen, Marty, David Karol, Hans Noel, and John Zaller. 2008a. *The Party Decides: Presidential Nominations before and after Reform*. Chicago: University of Chicago Press.

Cohen, Marty, David Karol, Hans Noel, and John Zaller. 2008b. "Political Parties in Rough Weather." *The Forum* 5 (4): article 3. http://www.bepress.com/forum/vol5/iss4/art3.

Cohen, Michael D., James G. March, and Johan P. Olsen. 1972. "A Garbage Can Model of Organizational Choice." *Administrative Science Quarterly* 17 (March): 1–25.

Cohen, Richard E. 1995. *Washington at Work: Back Rooms and Clean Air*. Needham Heights, MA: Allyn & Bacon.

Coleman, John J. 1996. "Party Organizational Strength and Public Support for Parties." *American Journal of Political Science* 40 (August): 805–824.

Collier, Christopher, and James Lincoln Collier. 1986. *Decision in Philadelphia: The Constitutional Convention of 1787*. New York: Ballantine Books.

Colomer, Josep M. 2005. "It's Parties That Choose Electoral Systems (or, Duverger's Laws Upside Down)." *Political Studies* 53 (March): 1–21.

Committee on Standards of Official Conduct. n.d. "Members' Representational Allowance." U.S House of Representatives. http://ethics.house.gov/Subjects/Topics.aspx?Section=123 (accessed August 19, 2008).

Congressional Quarterly, Inc. 1993. *Congress A to Z: A Ready Reference Encyclopedia*. 2nd ed. Washington, DC: Congressional Quarterly, Inc.

Conley, Richard. 2011. "The Harbinger of the Unitary Executive? An Analysis of Presidential Signing Statements from Truman to Carter." *Presidential Studies Quarterly* 41 (September): 546–569.

Converse, Philip E. 1996. "The Advent of Polling and Political Representation." *PS: Political Science and Politics* 29 (December): 649–657.

Conway, Mike, Maria Elizabeth Grabe, and Kevin Grieves. 2007. "Villains, Victims and the Virtuous in Bill O'Reilly's 'No-Spin Zone'": Revisiting World War Propaganda Techniques." *Journalism Studies* 8: 197–223.

Cook, Timothy. 1998. *Governing with the News: The News Media as a Political Institution*. Chicago: University of Chicago Press.

Cooper, Phillip J. 2005. "George W. Bush, Edgar Allan Poe, and the Use and Abuse of Presidential Signing Statements." *Presidential Studies Quarterly* 35 (September): 515–532.

Cotter, Cornelius P., James L. Gibson, John F. Bibby, and Robert Huckshorn. 1989. *Party Organizations in American Politics*. Pittsburgh: University of Pittsburgh Press.

Cox, Gary W., and Mathew D. McCubbins. 1993. *Legislative Leviathan: Party Government in the House*. Berkeley: University of California Press.

Crispi, Irving. 1989. *Public Opinion, Polls, and Democracy*. Boulder, CO: Westview Press.

Cronin, Thomas E. 1975. *The State of the Presidency*. Boston: Little, Brown.

Crotty, William. 2003. "Presidential Policymaking in Crisis Situations: 9/11 and Its Aftermath." *Policy Studies Journal* 31: 451–464.

Cushman, Barry. 1998. *Rethinking the New Deal Court: The Structure of a Constitutional Revolution*. New York: Oxford University Press.

Dale, A., and A. Strauss. 2009. "Don't Forget to Vote: Text Message Reminders as a Mobilization Tool." *American Journal of Political Science* 5: 787–804.

Daniels, Jonathan. 1965. *They Will Be Heard: America's Crusading Newspaper Editors*. New York: McGraw-Hill.

Davis, James W. 1994. *The President as Party Leader*. New York: Praeger.

Death Penalty Information Center. 2012. *Facts about the Death Penalty*. Washington, DC: Death Penalty Information Center.

Deering, Christopher J., and Steven S. Smith. 1997. *Committees in Congress*. 3rd ed. Washington, DC: CQ Press.

Dinan, John. 2008. "The State of American Federalism 2007–2008: Resurgent State Influence in the National Policy Process and Continued State Policy Innovation." *Publius: The Journal of Federalism* 38: 381–415.

Dinan, John, and Shama Gamkhar. 2008. "The State of American Federalism 2008–2009: The Presidential Election, the Economic Downturn, and the Consequences for Federalism." *Publius: The Journal of Federalism* 39: 369–407.

Dionne, E. J., Jr. 2010. "So, Jindal, How's That Deregulation Workin' for Ya?" *Springfield News-Sun,* May 28. http://www.daytondailynews.com/news/lifestyles/philosophy/ej-dionne-jr-so-jindal-hows-that-deregulation-wo-1/nNDGB/ (accessed March 6, 2013).

Downie, Leonard, and Robert G. Kaiser. 2002. *The News about News*. New York: Knopf.

Downs, Anthony. 1957. *An Economic Theory of Democracy*. New York: Harper & Row.

Doyle, Arthur Conan. 1890. *The Sign of the Four*. Project Gutenberg, 2008. http://www.gutenberg.org/files/2097/2097-h/2097-h.htm#chap01 (accessed February 25, 2012).

Duverger, Maurice. 1972. *Party Politics and Pressure Groups*, translated by David Wagoner. New York: Thomas Y. Crowell.

Easton, David. 1953. *The Political System*. New York: Knopf.

The Economist. 2010. "What's Gone Wrong in Washington?" *The Economist* 394 (8670): 11.

Edmondson, Brad. 1996. "How to Spot a Bogus Poll." *American Demographics* 18 (October): 10–15.

Edsall, Thomas B. 2001. "Democrats Press Bush for Input on Judges: Court Nominees Concern Senators." *Washington Post,* April 28, A04.

Edwards, George C., III. 1989. *At the Margins: Presidential Leadership of Congress*. New Haven, CT: Yale University Press.

Edwards, George C., III. 2003. *On Deaf Ears: The Limits of the Bully Pulpit*. New Haven, CT: Yale University Press.

Edwards, George C., III. 2011. *Why the Electoral College Is Bad for America*. 2nd ed. New Haven, CT: Yale University Press.

Edwards, George C., III., and Andrew Barrett. 2000. "Presidential Agenda Setting in Congress." In *Polarized Politics: Congress and the President in a Partisan Era*, ed. Jon R. Bond and Richard Fleisher. Washington, DC: CQ Press.

Edwards, George C., III., and Stephen J. Wayne. 2003. *Presidential Leadership: Politics and Policy Making.* 6th ed. Belmont, CA: Thomson/Wadsworth.

Edwards, Keith M., and Charles Stewart III. 2006. "The Value of Committee Assignments in Congress since 1994." Presented at the annual meeting of the Southern Political Science Association, Atlanta, GA, January 5–7.

Ellsworth, Oliver. [1787] 1986. Letter to the *Connecticut Courant* (Hartford), December 17, 1787, signed "A Landholder" VII. In *The Debate on the Constitution: Federalist and Antifederalist Speeches, Articles, and Letters during the Struggle over Ratification,* part 1, ed. Bernard Bailyn 521–525. New York: Library of America.

Epstein, Lee, and Jack Knight. 1998. *The Choices Justices Make.* Washington, DC: CQ Press.

Epstein, Lee, William M. Landes, and Richard A. Posner. 2012. "Are Even Unanimous Decisions in the United States Supreme Court Ideological?" *Northwestern University Law Review* 106 (2): 699–713. http://www.law.northwestern.edu/journals/lawreview/v106/n2/699/LR106n2Epstein.pdf (accessed August 1, 2012).

Epstein, Lee, Jeffrey A. Segal, Harold J. Spaeth, and Thomas G. Walker. 2007. *The Supreme Court Compendium Online Edition.* CQ Press Electronic Library. http://library.cqpress.com/sccm/index.php (accessed July 28, 2012).

Erikson, Robert S., and Norman R. Luttbeg. 1973. *American Public Opinion: Its Origins, Content, and Impact.* New York: Wiley.

Erikson, Robert S., and Kent Tedin. 2002. *American Public Opinion: Its Origin, Contents, and Impact.* 6th ed. New York: Longman.

Erikson, Robert S., Gerald Wright, and John McIver. 1993. *Statehouse Democracy: Public Opinion and Policy in the American States.* New York: Cambridge University Press.

Erskine, H. 1970. "The Polls: Opinion of the News Media." *Public Opinion Quarterly* 34: 630–643.

Espenshade, Thomas, and Alexandria Walton Radford. 2009. *No Longer Separate, Not Yet Equal: Race and Class in Elite College Admission and Campus Life.* Princeton, NJ: Princeton University Press.

Eulau, Heinz. 1956. "The Politics of Happiness: A Prefatory Note to Political Perspectives 1956." *Antioch Review* 16 (Fall): 259–264.

Eulau, Heinz, and Paul D. Karps. 1977. "The Puzzle of Representation: Specifying Components of Responsiveness." *Legislative Studies Quarterly* 2 (August): 233–254.

Evans, Diana. 1996. "Before the Roll Call: Interest Group Lobbying and Public Policy Outcomes in House Committees." *Political Research Quarterly* 49 (June): 287–304.

Evans, Diana. 2004. *Greasing the Wheels: Using Pork Barrel Projects to Build Majority Coalitions in Congress.* New York: Cambridge University Press.

Federal Communications Commission. 2012. "Broadcast Station Totals as of December 31, 2011." http://hraunfoss.fcc.gov/edocs_public/attachmatch/DOC-311837A1.doc (accessed April 24, 2012).

Federal Election Commission. 2007. "Selected Presidential Reports For The 2007 October Quarterly." http://query.nictusa.com/pres/2007/Q3/.

Federal Election Commission. 2011a. "Coordinated Communications and Independent Expenditures." First published in June 2007, updated February 2011. http://www.fec.gov/pages/brochures/indexp.shtml (accessed May 1, 2012).

Federal Election Commission. 2011b. "Selected Presidential Reports For The 2011 October Quarterly." http://query.nictusa.com/pres/2011/Q3/.

Federal Judicial Center. n.d. "Impeachments of Federal Judges." http://www.fjc.gov/history/home.nsf/page/judges_impeachments.html (accessed June 17, 2010).

Federal Procurement Data system. 2011. "Top 100 Contractors Report Fiscal Year 2011." https://www.fpds.gov/fpdsng_cms/index.php/reports (accessed May 11, 2012).

Feldman, Paul, and James Jondrow. 1984. "Congressional Elections and Local Federal Spending." *American Journal of Political Science* 28 (February): 147–164.

Fenno, Richard. 1966. *The Power of the Purse: Appropriations Politics in Congress.* Boston: Little, Brown.

Fenno, Richard. 1978. *Home Style: House Members in Their Districts.* Boston: Little, Brown.

Fenno, Richard F., Jr. 1973. *Congressmen in Committees.* Boston: Little, Brown.

Ferguson, Andrew. 1995. "Disabling America." Excerpted in "Implementing the Disabilities Act," *CQ Researcher* 6 (December 1996): 1121.

Finifter, Ada W. 1970. "Dimensions of Political Alienation." *American Political Science Review* 64 (June): 389–410.

Fiorina, Morris. 1980. "The Decline of Collective Responsibility in American Politics." *Daedalus* 109 (Summer): 25–45.

Fiorina, Morris. 1981. *Retrospective Voting in American National Elections.* New Haven, CT: Yale University Press.

Fiorina, Morris. 1996. *Divided Government.* 2nd ed. Boston: Allyn & Bacon.

Fiorina, Morris. 2006. *Culture War? The Myth of a Polarized America.* New York: Longman.

Flanagan, Caitlin. 2004. "How Serfdom Saved the Women's Movement." *Atlantic Monthly* 293 (March): 109–128.

Fleisher, Richard. 1993. "Explaining the Change in Roll-Call Voting Behavior of Southern Democrats." *Journal of Politics* 55 (May): 327–341.

Fleisher, Richard, and Jon R. Bond. 2000a. "Congress and the President in a Partisan Era." In *Polarized Politics: Congress and the President in a Partisan Era,* ed. Jon R. Bond and Richard Fleisher, 1–8. Washington, DC: CQ Press.

Fleisher, Richard, and Jon R. Bond. 2000b. "Partisanship and the President's Quest for Votes on the Floor of Congress." In *Polarized Politics: Congress and the President in a Partisan Era,* ed. Jon R. Bond and Richard Fleisher, 154–185. Washington, DC: CQ Press.

Fleisher, Richard, and Jon R. Bond. 2004. "The Shrinking Middle in the US Congress." *British Journal of Political Science* 34 (July): 529–551.

Fletcher, Michael A. 2006. "Bush Starts 10-Day Texas Vacation: Shorter Summer Break Reflects Post-Katrina Criticism." *Washington Post,* August 4. http://www.washingtonpost.com/wp-dyn/content/article/2006/08/03/AR2006080300663.html (accessed September 25, 2006).

Fornell, Claes. 2010. "Citizen Satisfaction with Federal Government Services Dips Slightly." American Customer Satisfaction Index, January 26. http://www.theacsi.org/index.php?option=com_content&task=view&id=200&Itemid=62 (accessed June 1, 2010).

Fowler, James. 2008. "The Colbert Bump in Campaign Donations: More Truthful Than Truthy." *PS: Political Science & Politics* 41 (3): 533–539.

Frankfurter, Felix. 1957. "The Supreme Court in the Mirror of Justices." *University of Pennsylvania Law Review* 105 (April): 781–796.

Freedom House. 2006. "Freedom in the World 2006: Selected Data from Freedom House's Annual Global Survey of Political Rights and Civil Liberties." http://www.freedomhouse.org/uploads/pdf/Charts2006.pdf (accessed June 13, 2006).

Friedan, Betty. 1963. *The Feminine Mystique.* New York: Norton.

"From the Editors: The Times and Iraq." 2004. *New York Times,* May 26. http://www.nytimes.com/2004/05/26/international/middleeast/26FTE_NOTE.html?ei=500 (accessed August 5, 2006).

Gaines, Brian. 2001. "Popular Myths about Popular Vote–Electoral College Splits." *PS: Political Science and Politics* 34 (March): 71–75.

Gant, Michael M., and William Lyons. 1993. "Democratic Theory, Nonvoting, and Public Policy: The 1972–1988 Presidential Elections." *American Politics Quarterly* 21 (April): 185–204.

General Accounting Office. 2003. *Women's Earnings: Work Patterns Partially Explain Difference between Men's and Women's Earnings.* Washington, DC: U.S. Government Printing Office.

George, Alexander L., and Juliette L. George. 1998. *Presidential Personality and Performance.* Boulder, CO: Westview Press.

Gerring, John. 1997. "Ideology: A Definitional Analysis." *Political Research Quarterly* 50: 957–994.

Gerstein, Josh. 2009. "Obama: Ignore Signing Statements." *Politico,* March 9. http://www.politico.com/news/stories/0309/19795.html (accessed May 31, 2010).

Gerth, H. H., and C. Wright Mills. 1946. *Max Weber: Essays in Sociology.* New York: Oxford University Press.

Gettinger, Stephen. 1998. "When Congress Decides a President's 'High Crimes and Misdemeanors.'" *Congressional Quarterly Weekly Report* 56 (March): 565–568.

Gibson, James L., Cornelius P. Cotter, John F. Bibby, and Robert J. Huckshorn. 1989. "Whither the Local Parties? A Cross-Sectional and Longitudinal Analysis of the Strength of Party Organizations." *American Journal of Political Science* 29 (February): 139–160.

Gill, Brian, P. Michael Timpane, Karen E. Ross, and Dominic J. Brewer. 2001. *Rhetoric versus Reality.* Santa Monica, CA: RAND.

Gintis, Herbert. 2007. "A Framework for the Unification of the Behavioral Sciences." *Behavioral and Brain Sciences* 30: 1–16.

Goldmacher, Shane. 2009. "State Facing a $21-Billion Budget Gap." *Los Angeles Times,* November 18. http://www.latimes.com/news/local/la-me-budget-deficit18-2009nov18,0,7647152.story (accessed November 21, 2009).

Goldman, Sheldon. 1985. "Reaganizing the Judiciary: The First Term Appointments." *Judicature* 68 (April–May): 313.

Goldstein, Dana, and Ezra Klein. 2008. "It's His Party." *American Prospect,* August 18. http://www.prospect.org/cs/articles?article=its_his_party_08 (accessed May 29, 2010).

Goldstein, Joel K. 2008. "The Rising Power of the Modern Vice Presidency." *Presidential Studies Quarterly* 38 (September): 374–389.

Goodsell, Charles. 1994. *The Case for Bureaucracy.* Chatham, NJ: Chatham House.

Goren, Paul. 1997. "Gut-Level Emotion and the Presidential Vote." *American Politics Quarterly* 25 (April): 203–229.

Granat, Diane. 1984. "Parties' Schools for Politicians Grooming Troops for Election." *CQ Weekly Report* 42 (May): 1036.

Gray, Virginia, and David Lowery. 1996. *The Population Ecology of Interest Representation.* Ann Arbor: University of Michigan Press.

Greenblatt, Alan. 2008. "Recipe for Respect." *Governing* (February): 22–26.

Greenstein, Fred. 1965. *Children and Politics.* New Haven, CT: Yale University Press.

Grier, Kevin B., Michael C. Munger, and Brian E. Roberts. 1994. "The Determinants of Industry Political Activity, 1976–1986." *American Political Science Review* 88 (December): 911–926.

Groseclose, Tim. 2011. *Left Turn: How Liberal Media Bias Distorts the American Mind.* New York: St. Martin's Press.

Groseclose, Tim, and Jeffrey Milyo. 2005. "A Measure of Media Bias." *The Quarterly Journal of Economics* 120: 1191–1237.

Groseclose, Tim, and Charles Stewart III. 1998. "The Value of Committee Seats in the House, 1947–91." *American Journal of Political Science* 42 (April): 453–474.

Grunwald, Michael. 2007. "The New Action Heroes." *Time,* June 14. http://www.time.com/time/nation/article/0,8599,1632736,00.html (accessed October 26, 2009).

Gunther, Gerald. 1980. *Constitutional Law.* Mineola, NY: Fountain Press.

Gutin, Myra G. 1994. "Rosalynn Carter in the White House." In *The Presidency and Domestic Policies of Jimmy Carter,* ed. Herbert D. Rosenbaum and Alexej Ugrinsky. Westport, CT: Greenwood Press.

Habermas, Jürgen. 1991. *The Structural Transformation of the Public Sphere: An Inquiry into a Category of Bourgeois Society.* Cambridge, MA: MIT Press.

Hadley, Arthur T. 1976. *The Invisible Primary.* Englewood Cliffs, NJ: Prentice-Hall.

Haider-Markel, Donald P., and Kenneth J. Meier. 1996. "The Politics of Gay and Lesbian Rights: Expanding the Scope of the Conflict." *Journal of Politics* 58 (May): 332–349.

Hall, Richard L. 1996. *Participation in Congress.* New Haven, CT: Yale University Press.

Halloran, Liz. 2010. "Top Republicans: Yeah, We're Calling Obama Socialist." National Public Radio, March 5. http://www.npr.org/templates/story/story.php?storyId=124359632 (accessed September 19, 2010).

Halstead, T. J. 2007. "Presidential Signing Statements: Constitutional and Institutional Implications." Congressional Research Service, September 17.

Hamilton, James T. 2004. *All the News That's Fit to Sell.* Princeton, NJ: Princeton University Press.

Hargrove, Erwin C. 1974. *The Power of the Modern Presidency.* Philadelphia: Temple University Press.

Harris, Fred R. 1995. *In Defense of Congress.* New York: St. Martin's Press.

Hart, John. 1995. *The Presidential Branch: From Washington to Clinton.* 2nd ed. Chatham, NJ: Chatham House.

Hartranft, Dan. 2012. "Super PAC Spending Boosts Santorum." OpenSecrets.org. February 16. http://www.opensecrets.org/news/2012/02/super-pac-spending-boosts-santorum.html (accessed June 25, 2012).

Haskell, John. 1996. *Fundamentally Flawed: Understanding and Reforming Presidential Primaries.* Lanham, MD: Rowman & Littlefield.

Heldman, Carlin, Susan Carroll, and Stephanie Olson. 2005. "'She Brought Only a Skirt': Print Media Coverage of Elizabeth Dole's Bid for the Republican Presidential Nomination." *Political Communication* 22: 315–335.

Herman, Edward S., and Noam Chomsky. 2002. *Manufacturing Consent: The Political Economy of the Mass Media.* New York: Pantheon.

Herman, Edward S., and Robert W. McChesney. 1997. *The Global Media.* London: Cassell.

Herrnson, Paul S. 1995. *Congressional Elections: Campaigning at Home and in Washington.* Washington, DC: CQ Press.

Hibbing, John R. 1991. *Congressional Careers: Contours of Life in the U.S. House of Representatives.* Chapel Hill: University of North Carolina Press.

Hibbing, John R., and Elizabeth Theiss-Morse. 1995. *Congress as Public Enemy: Public Attitudes toward American Political Institutions.* New York: Cambridge University Press.

Hibbing, John R., and Elizabeth Theiss-Morse. 1998. "The Media's Role in Public Negativity towards Congress: Distinguishing Emotional Reactions and Cognitive Evaluation." *American Journal of Political Science* 42 (April): 475–498.

Hibbing, John R., and Elizabeth Theiss-Morse. 2001. "Process Preferences and American Politics: What People Want Government to Be." *American Political Science Review* 95 (March): 145–154.

Hibbing, John R., and Elizabeth Theiss-Morse. 2003. *Stealth Democracy.* New York: Cambridge University Press.

Hightower, Jim. 1998. *There's Nothing in the Middle of the Road But Yellow Stripes and Dead Armadillos.* New York: Harper Perennial.

Hill, Kevin A. 1995. "Does the Creation of Majority Black Districts Aid Republicans? An Analysis of the 1992 Congressional Elections in Eight Southern States." *Journal of Politics* 57 (May): 384–401.

Hill, Kevin A., and John E. Hughes. 1997. "Computer-Mediated Political Communication: The USENET and

Political Communities." *Political Communication* 14 (January–March): 3–27.

Hill, Kim Quaile, and Jan E. Leighley. 1992. "The Policy Consequences of Class Bias in State Electorates." *American Journal of Political Science* 36 (May): 351–365.

Hirsh, Michael. 2012. "Biden: Most Powerful VP Ever? Joltin' Joe Leads the Obama Attack on Romney." *National Journal,* April 26. http://www.nationaljournal.com/2012-presidential-campaign/biden-most-powerful-vp-ever-20120426 (accessed July 15, 2012).

Hofstetter, C. Richard, David Barker, James T. Smith, Gina M. Zari, and Thomas A. Ingrassia. 1999. "Information, Misinformation, and Political Talk Radio." *Political Research Quarterly* 52: 353–370.

Hojnacki, Marie, and David C. Kimball. 1998. "Organized Interests and the Decision of Whom to Lobby in Congress." *American Political Science Review* 92 (December): 775–790.

Holbrook, Thomas, and Brianne Heidbreder. 2010. "Does Measurement Matter? The Case of VAP and VEP in Models of Voter Turnout in the United States." *State Politics and Policy Quarterly* 10: 157–179.

Howell, William G. 2005. "Unilateral Powers: A Brief Overview." *Presidential Studies Quarterly* 35 (September): 417–439.

Huckfeldt, R. Robert, and John Sprague. 1995. *Citizens, Politics, and Social Communication: Information and Influence in an Election Campaign.* New York: Cambridge University Press.

Huckshorn, Robert J., James L. Gibson, Cornelius P. Cotter, John F. Bibby. 1986. "Party Integration and Party Organizational Strength." *Journal of Politics* 48 (November): 976–991.

Hull, Elizabeth. 2004. "Felons Deserve the Right to Vote." *USA Today Magazine* (January): 50–52.

Hulse, Carl. 2006. "House Assails Media Report on Tracking of Finances." *New York Times,* June 30. http://www.nytimes.com/2006/06/30/washington/30cong.html?ei=5088&en=88ca3feb069 (accessed August 5, 2006).

Humphries, Steve, and Pamela Wright. 1992. *Out of Sight: The Experience of Disability, 1900–1950.* London: Northcote House.

Hurley, Patricia A., and Brinck Kerr. 1997. "The Partisanship of New Members in the 103rd and 104th Houses." *Social Science Quarterly* 78 (December): 992–1000.

Hutchings, Vincent. 2003. *Public Opinion and Democratic Accountability: How Citizens Learn about Politics.* Princeton, NJ: Princeton University Press.

Institute for Women's Policy Research. 1996. *The Status of Women in the States.* Washington, DC: Institute for Women's Policy Research.

Isaak, Alan C. 1985. *Scope and Methods of Political Science.* 4th ed. Pacific Grove, CA: Brooks/Cole.

Iyengar, Shanto. 1997. "Media-Based Political Campaigns: Overview." In *Do the Media Govern?,* ed. Shanto Iyengar and Richard Reeves. Thousand Oaks, CA: Sage.

Iyengar, Shanto, and Donald Kinder. 1987. *News That Matters: Television and American Opinion.* Chicago: University of Chicago Press.

Jackson, John S., and William Crotty. 1996. *The Politics of Presidential Selection.* New York: HarperCollins.

Jackson, Robert A. 1997. "The Mobilization of U.S. State Electorates in the 1988 and 1990 Elections." *Journal of Politics* 59 (May): 520–537.

Jacobson, Gary C. 1989. "Strategic Politicians and the Dynamics of House Elections, 1946–1986." *American Political Science Review* 83 (September): 773–793.

Jacobson, Gary C. 1990. *The Electoral Origins of Divided Government: Competition in U.S. House Elections, 1946–1988.* Boulder, CO: Westview Press.

Jacobson, Gary C. 2001. *The Politics of Congressional Elections.* 5th ed. New York: Addison Wesley Longman.

Jacobson, Gary C. 2009. *The Politics of Congressional Elections.* 7th ed. New York: Pearson Longman.

Jacobson, Gary C. 2013. *The Politics of Congressional Elections.* 8th ed. New York: Pearson Longman.

Jacobson, Gary C., and Samuel Kernell. 1981. *Strategy and Choice in Congressional Elections.* New Haven, CT: Yale University Press.

Jacobson, Louis. 1995. "Tanks on the Roll." *National Journal* 27 (July): 1767–1771.

Jefferson, Thomas. 1823. "Letter to Lafayette." *Thomas Jefferson Digital Archive.* University of Virginia Library. http://etext.virginia.edu/jefferson/quotations/jeff1600.htm.

Jennings, M. Kent, and Richard Niemi. 1975. "Continuity and Change in Political Orientations: A Longitudinal Study of Two Generations." *American Political Science Review* 69 (December): 1316–1335.

Johnson, Peter. 2004. "Survey: Profit Pressures Worry Most Journalists." *USA Today,* May 24, 3D.

Jost, John T. 2006. "The End of the End of Ideology." *American Psychologist* 61 (October): 651–670.

Kahn, Kim Fridkin. 1992. "Does Being Male Help?" *Journal of Politics* 54 (May): 497–517.

Kahn, Kim Fridkin. 1996. *The Political Consequences of Being a Woman: How Stereotypes Influence the Content and*

Impact of Statewide Campaigns. New York: Columbia University Press.

Kaminer, Wendy. 1999. "Taking Liberties." *American Prospect.* http://www.prospect.org/cs/articles?article=taking_liberties (accessed September 19, 2010).

Kane, Paul. 2011. "Senate Republicans Block Judicial Nominee Goodwin Liu." *Washington Post,* May 19. http://www.washingtonpost.com/politics/judicial-nominee-goodwin-liu-faces-filibuster-showdown/2011/05/18/AF-6ak76G_story.html (accessed August 1, 2012).

Kaplan, Jonas, Joshua Freedman, and Marco Iacoboni. 2007. "Us versus Them: Political Attitudes and Party Affiliation Influence Neural Responses to Faces of Presidential Candidates." *Neuropsychologica* 45: 55–64.

Katz, Jeffrey. 1998. "Panel Drops Final Ethics Charges." *CQ Weekly Report* 56 (October): 2816.

Kern, Montague, and Marion Just. 1995. "The Focus Group Method, Political Advertising, and the Construction of Candidate Images." *Political Communication* 12: 127–145.

Kernell, Samuel. 1997. *Going Public: New Strategies of Presidential Leadership.* 3rd ed. Washington, DC: CQ Press.

Kerwin, Cornelius. 1994. *Rulemaking.* Washington, DC: CQ Press.

Kerwin, Cornelius. 1999. *Rulemaking.* 2nd ed. Washington, DC: CQ Press.

Kesler, Erin, David Vance, and Viveca Novak. 2012. "Double-Duty Donors, Part II: Large Numbers of Wealthy Donors Hit Legal Limit on Giving to Candidates, Turn to Presidential Super PACs in Continuing Trend." Open Secrets.org. February 21. http://www.opensecrets.org/news/2012/02/double-duty-donors-part-ii-large-nu.html (accessed May 19, 2012).

Kessel, John H. 1992. *Presidential Campaign Politics.* 4th ed. Pacific Grove, CA: Brooks/Cole.

Key, V. O., Jr. 1964. *Politics, Parties, and Pressure Groups.* 5th ed. New York: Crowell.

King, David C., and Jack L. Walker. 1992. "The Provision of Benefits by Interest Groups in the United States." *Journal of Politics* 54 (May): 394–426.

Kingdon, John W. 1995. *Agendas, Alternatives, and Public Policies.* 2nd ed. New York: HarperCollins.

Knack, Stephen, and James White. 1998. "Did State Motor Voter Programs Help the Democrats?" *American Politics Quarterly* 26 (July): 344–356.

Koger, Gregory. 2010. *Filibustering: A Political History of Obstruction in the House and Senate.* Chicago: University of Chicago Press.

Krane, Dale, and Heidi Koenig. 2005. "The State of American Federalism, 2004: Is Federalism Still a Core Value?" *Publius* 35 (Winter): 1–40.

Krehbiel, Keith. 1991. *Information and Legislative Organization.* Ann Arbor: University of Michigan Press.

Krueger, Brian. 2002. "Assessing the Potential of Internet Political Participation in the United States." *American Politics Research* 30: 476–498.

Krutz, Glen S., Richard Fleisher, and Jon R. Bond. 1998. "From Abe Fortas to Zoe Baird: Why Some Presidential Nominations Fail in the Senate." *American Political Science Review* 92 (December): 871–881.

Krutz, Glen S., and Jeffrey S. Peake. 2009. *Treaty Politics and the Rise of Executive Agreements: International Agreements in a System of Shared Powers.* Ann Arbor: University of Michigan Press.

Krutz, Glen S. and Jeffrey S. Peake. 2011. "President Obama, Congress and International Agreements: An Initial Assessment." Presented at the American Political Science Association annual meeting, Seattle, WA, August 31–September 4.

Kuhn, David P. 2004. "Blogs: New Medium, Old Politics." CBS News, December 8. http://www.cbsnews.com/stories/2004/12/08/politics/main659955.shtml?tag=mncol;lst;1 (accessed August 10, 2006).

Kuzenski, John C. 1997. "The Four—Yes Four—Types of State Primaries." *PS: Political Science and Politics* 30 (June): 207–208.

Lake, Celinda, and Jennifer Sosin. 1998. "Public Opinion Polling and the Future of Democracy." *National Civic Review* 87 (Spring): 65–70.

Lasswell, Harold D. 1938. *Politics: Who Gets What, When and How.* New York: McGraw-Hill.

Lazarsfeld, Paul F., Bernard Berelson, and Hazel Gaudet. 1944. *The People's Choice.* New York: Duell, Sloan and Pearce.

Lee, Emery G., III, Frances U. Sandstrum, and Thomas C. Weisert. 1996. "Context and the Court: Sources of Support for Civil Liberties on the Rehnquist Court." *American Politics Quarterly* 24 (July): 377–395.

Leech, Beth L. 2010. "Lobbying and Influence." In *The Oxford Handbook of American Political Parties and Interest Groups,* ed. L. Sandy Maisel and Jeffrey M. Berry, 534–551. Oxford, UK: Oxford University Press.

Lehigh, Scot. 2002. "President Needs OK by Congress for Iraq War." *Boston Globe,* August 23, A27.

Leighley, Jan E. 1995. "Attitudes, Opportunities and Incentives: A Field Essay on Political Participation." *Political Research Quarterly* 48 (March): 181–209.

Leighley, Jan E. 1996. "Group Membership and the Mobilization of Political Participation." *Journal of Politics* 58 (May): 447–463.

Leighley, Jan E., and Arnold Vedlitz. 1999. "Race, Ethnicity, and Political Participation: Competing Models and Contrasting Explanations." *Journal of Politics* 61 (November): 1092–1114.

Lenz, Ryan. 2004. "Soldiers in Iraq Buy Their Own Body Armor." *Guardian.* http://www.-guardian.co.uk/worldlatest/story/0,1280,-3904926,00.html (accessed June 1, 2004).

Levinthal, Dave. 2012. "How Super PACs Got Their Name." *Politico,* January 10. http://www.politico.com/news/stories/0112/71285.html#ixzz1q0eZYeTs (accessed May 1, 2012).

Lewis-Beck, Michael, William Jacoby, Helmut Norpoth, and Herbert Weisberg. 2008. *The American Voter Revisited.* Ann Arbor: University of Michigan Press.

Lichtblau, Eric, and James Risen. 2006. "Bank Data Sifted by U.S. in Secret Block to Terror." *New York Times,* June 23. http://www.nytimes.com/2006/06/23/washington/23intel.html?_r=1&ex130871520&en168d69d26685c26c&ei?5088&partner?rssnyt&emcrss (accessed June 26, 2010).

Light, Paul C. 1983. *The President's Agenda: Domestic Policy Choice from Kennedy to Carter (with Notes on Ronald Reagan).* Baltimore, MD: Johns Hopkins University Press.

Light, Paul C. 1999. *The True Size of Government.* Washington, DC: Brookings Institution.

Lijphart, Arend. 1984. *Democracies: Patterns of Majoritarian and Consensus Government in Twenty-One Countries.* New Haven, CT: Yale University Press.

Lindblom, Charles. 1959. "The Science of Muddling Through." *Public Administration Review* 19 (Spring): 79–88.

Lippmann, Walter. 1922. *Public Opinion.* New York: Macmillan.

Lippmann, Walter. 1949. *Public Opinion.* New York: Free Press.

Lipsky, Michael. 1980. *Street-Level Bureaucracy.* New York: Russell Sage Foundation.

Loveless, Tom. 1997. "The Structure of Public Confidence in Education." *American Journal of Education* 105 (February): 127–159.

Lowery, David, and Holly Brasher. 2004. *Organized Interests and American Government.* New York: McGraw-Hill.

Lowi, Theodore J. 1969. *The End of Liberalism: Ideology, Policy, and the Crisis of Public Authority.* New York: Norton.

Lowry, Robert C. 1997. "The Private Production of Public Goods: Organizational Maintenance, Managers' Objectives, and Collective Goals." *American Political Science Review* 91 (June): 308–323.

Luttbeg, Norman R., and Michael M. Gant. 1995. *American Electoral Behavior 1952–1992.* Itasca, IL: F. E. Peacock.

Lyman, Edward Leo. 1986. *Political Deliverance: The Mormon Quest for Utah Statehood.* Urbana: University of Illinois Press.

Lyons, William, and Robert Alexander. 2000. "A Tale of Two Electorates: Generational Replacement and the Decline of Voting in Presidential Elections." *Journal of Politics* 62 (November): 1014–1034.

Maguire, Robert. 2012. "The Ties That Bind: Romney and the Super PACs." OpenSecrets.org. April 6. http://www.opensecrets.org/news/2012/04/the-coordinated-non-coordination-of.html (accessed May 19, 2012).

Manheim, Jarol B., and Richard C. Rich. 1991. *Empirical Political Analysis: Research Methods in Political Science.* New York: Longman.

Manning, Jennifer E. 2010. "Membership of the 111th Congress: A Profile." Congressional Research Service, April 20. http://www.senate.gov/CRSReports/crs-publish.cfm?pid=%260BL%29PL%3B%3D%0A (accessed May 21, 2010).

Manning, Jennifer E. 2011. "Membership of the 112th Congress: A Profile." Congressional Research Service, March 1, 2011. http://www.senate.gov/reference/resources/pdf/R41647.pdf.

Marshall, Bob. 2010. "Oil Disaster Brought to You by Deregulation." *Times-Picayune,* May 23. http://www.nola.com/news/gulf-oil-spill/index.ssf/2010/05/oil_disaster_brought_to_you_by.html (accessed June 7, 2010).

Martin, N.G., L.J. Eaves, A.C. Heath, Rosemary Jardine, Lynn M. Feingold, and H.J. Eysenck. 1986. "Transmission of Social Attitudes." *Proceedings of the National Academy of Sciences* 15: 4364–4368.

Masket, Seth. 2011. *No Middle Ground.* Ann Arbor: University of Michigan Press.

Masters, Brooke A. 2001. "Judgeship Hinges on Politics, Practice: Md. Liberals Keep Bush Pick Off List." *Washington Post,* May 13, C05.

Matthews, Donald R. 1960. *U.S. Senators and Their World.* Chapel Hill: University of North Carolina Press.

Mayer, William G. 1996. "Forecasting Presidential Nominations." In *In Pursuit of the White House: How We Choose Our Presidential Nominees,* ed. William G. Mayer. Chatham, NJ: Chatham House.

Mayer, William G., and Andrew E. Busch. 2004. *The Frontloading Problem in Presidential Nominations.* Washington, DC: Brookings.

Mayhew, David. 1974. *Congress: The Electoral Connection.* New Haven, CT: Yale University Press.

McCombs, Maxwell, and Donald Shaw. 1972. "The Agenda-Setting Function of Mass Media." *Public Opinion Quarterly* 36 (Summer): 176–185.

McCool, Daniel. 1985. "Indian Voting." In *American Indian Policy in the Twentieth Century,* ed. Vine Deloria Jr., 105–134. Norman: University of Oklahoma Press, 1985.

McCubbins, Mathew D., and Thomas Schwartz. 1984. "Congressional Oversight Overlooked: Police Patrol versus Fire Alarms." *American Journal of Political Science* 28 (February): 165–179.

McCullough, David. 2001. *John Adams.* New York: Simon & Schster.

McDonald, Michael P. 2013. "2012 General Election Turnout Rates." United States Elections Project. http://elections.gmu.edu/Turnout_2012G.html, updated 2/9/13. (accessed March 5, 2013).

McDonald, Michael P., and Samuel L. Popkin. 2001. "The Myth of the Vanishing Voter." *American Political Science Review* 95 (December): 963–974.

McGlen, Nancy E., and Karen O'Connor. 1983. *Women's Rights: The Struggle for Equality in the Nineteenth and Twentieth Centuries.* New York: Praeger.

Meier, Kenneth J. 1993. *Politics and the Bureaucracy.* Pacific Grove, CA: Brooks/Cole.

Meier, Kenneth J. 1995. "The Policy Process." In *Regulation and Consumer Protection,* ed. Kenneth J. Meier and E. Thomas Garman. Houston, TX: Dame Publications.

Meier, Kenneth J. 1999. "Drugs, Sex, and Rock and Roll: A Theory of Morality Politics." *Policy Studies Journal* 27 (4): 681–695.

Mervin, David. 1995. "The Bully Pulpit, II." *Presidential Studies Quarterly* 25 (Winter): 19–23.

Milbrath, Lester W., and M.L. Goel. 1977. *Political Participation: How and Why Do People Get Involved in Politics?* 2nd ed. Chicago: Rand McNally.

Miller, Warren E. 1992. "The Puzzle Transformed: Explaining Declining Turnout." *Political Behavior* 14 (March): 1–43.

Miller, Warren E., and Teresa E. Levitin. 1976. *Leadership and Change: Presidential Elections from 1952 to 1976.* Cambridge, MA: Winthrop.

Mills, K. 1997. "What Difference Do Women Journalists Make?" In *Women, Media, and Politics,* ed. Pippa Norris. New York: Oxford University Press.

Moen, Matthew C., and Gary W. Copeland. 1999. *The Contemporary Congress: A Bicameral Approach.* Belmont, CA: Wadsworth.

Mondak, J. J., M. V. Hibbing, D. Canache, M. A. Seligson, and M. R. Anderson. 2010. "Personality and Civic Engagement: An Integrative Framework for the Study of trait Effects on Political Behavior." *American Political Science Review* 104: 85–110.

Mondak, Jeffery J. 1995. "Competence, Integrity, and the Electoral Success of Congressional Incumbents." *Journal of Politics* 57 (November): 1043–1069.

Mooney, Brian. 2008. "Lobbyists Are a Boon As Well As a Bane for McCain, Obama." *Boston Globe,* June 1. http://www.boston.com/news/nation/articles/2008/06/01/lobbyists_are_boon_as_well_as_bane_for_mccain_obama/ (accessed September 19, 2010).

Mooney, Christopher Z., ed. 2001. *The Public Clash of Private Values.* New York: Chatham House.

Morgan, Edmund S. 1992. *The Birth of the Republic.* Chicago: University of Chicago Press.

Morin, Richard. 2000. "The Big Picture Is Out of Focus." *Washington Post National Weekly Edition,* March 6–13, 21.

Mount, Steve. 2006a. "Comparing the Articles and the Constitution." March 15. http://www.usconstitution.net/constconart.html (accessed May 22, 2006).

Mount, Steve. 2006b. "Constitutional Topic: The Constitution and Religion." March 15. http://www.usconstitution.net/consttop_reli.html (accessed May 22, 2006).

Mueller, John. 1973. *War, Presidents, and Public Opinion.* New York: Wiley.

Mullainathan, Sendhil, and Andrei Schleifer. 2005. "The Market for News." *American Economic Review* 95 (4): 1031–1053.

National Conference of State Legislatures. 2010a. "Same Sex Marriage, Civil Unions and Domestic Partnerships." http://www.ncsl.org/programs/cyf/samesex.htm (accessed September 19, 2010).

National Conference of State Legislatures. 2010b. "State Laws Regarding Marriages between First Cousins." http://www.ncsl.org/programs/cyf/cousins.htm (accessed September 19, 2010).

National Public Radio. 2009. "The Watchmen." http://www.thisamericanlife.org/sites/default/files/382_transcript.pdf (accessed March 5, 2013).

Neustadt, Richard E. 1960. *Presidential Power.* New York: Wiley.

Newport, Frank. 1998. "History Shows Presidential Job Approval Ratings Can Plummet Rapidly." *Gallup Poll Monthly* 389 (February): 9–10.

Newspaper Association of America. 2010. "Total Paid Circulation." http://www.naa.org/TrendsandNumbers/Total-Paid-Circulation.aspx (accessed January 27, 2009).

Nie, Norman, Sidney Verba, and John Petrocik. 1979. *The Changing American Voter.* Cambridge, MA: Harvard University Press.

Niemi, Richard, and Herbert Weisberg. 1993. *Classics in Voting Behavior.* Washington, DC: CQ Press.

Niskanen, William. 1971. *Bureaucracy and Representative Government.* Hawthorne, NY: Aldine de Gruyter.

Niven, David. 2002. *Tilt?* New York: Praeger.

Numbers USA. 2002. "The 12 Top-Rated, Nationally Syndicated, Politically-Oriented Radio Talk Shows." June 2. http://www.numbersusa.com/text?ID_998 (accessed May 12, 2004).

O'Brien, David M. 1996. *Storm Center: The Supreme Court in American Politics.* 4th ed. New York: Norton.

Office of Management and Budget. 2012. "Historical Tables." http://www.whitehouse.gov/omb/budget/Historicals (accessed February 1, 2012).

Ohlemacher, Stephen. 2007. "Census Shows Early Primary States Are Far from 'Average.'" *Boston Globe,* May 17. http://www.boston.com/news/nation/washington/articles/2007/05/17/census_shows_early_primary_states_are_far_from_average/ (accessed September 19, 2010).

Oleszek, Walter J. 2008. "Senate Policy on 'Holds': Action in the 110th Congress." CRS Report for Congress, March 14. http://www.fas.org/sgp/crs/misc/RL34255.pdf (accessed May 24, 2010).

Olson, Mancur. 1965. *The Logic of Collective Action.* Cambridge, MA: Harvard University Press.

Ornstein, Norman J., Thomas E. Mann, and Michael J. Malbin. 2008. *Vital Statistics on Congress, 2008.* Washington, DC: Brookings Institution Press.

O'Rourke, P. J. 1991. *A Parliament of Whores.* New York: Atlantic Monthly Press.

Osborne, David, and Ted Gaebler. 1990. *Reinventing Government.* New York: Plume.

Overby, L. Marvin, and Kenneth M. Cosgrove. 1996. "Unintended Consequences? Racial Redistricting and the Representation of Minority Interests." *Journal of Politics* 58 (May): 540–550.

Parsons, Talcott. 1961. *Theories of Society: Foundations of Modern Sociological Theory.* New York: Free Press.

Patterson, Thomas E. 1984. *The Mass Media Election.* New York: Praeger.

Peltason, J. W. 1961. *Fifty-Eight Lonely Men: Southern Federal Judges and School Desegregation.* New York: Harcourt, Brace & World.

Peltason, J. W. 1982. *Corwin and Peltason's Understanding the Constitution.* 3rd ed. New York: Holt, Rinehart & Winston.

Percy, Stephen. 1989. *Disability, Civil Rights, and Public Policy.* Tuscaloosa: University of Alabama Press.

Peters, Gerhard. 1999–2012a. "Executive Orders." *The American Presidency Project,* ed. John T. Woolley and Gerhard Peters. http://www.presidency.ucsb.edu/executive_orders.php (accessed July 24, 2012).

Peters, Gerhard. 1999–2012b. "Presidential Signing Statements: Hoover-Obama." *The American Presidency Project,* ed. John T. Woolley and Gerhard Peters. http://www.presidency.ucsb.edu/signingstatements.php (accessed July 24, 2012).

Peters, John G., and Susan Welch. 1980. "The Effects of Charges of Corruption on Voting Behavior in Congressional Elections." *American Political Science Review* 74 (September): 697–708.

Peterson, Paul E. 1995. *The Price of Federalism.* Washington, DC: Brookings Institution.

Peterson, Paul E., and Mark C. Rom. 1990. *Welfare Magnets: A New Case for a National Standard.* Washington, DC: Brookings Institution.

Pew Research Center. 2001. "Terror Coverage Boost News Media's Images." November 28. http://people-press.org/report/143/terror-coverage-boost-news-medias-images (accessed August 9, 2004).

Pew Research Center. 2005. "Public More Critical of Press, but Goodwill Persists." June 26. http://people-press.org/report/?pageid=971 (accessed August 1, 2006).

Pew Research Center. 2006. "Online Newspapers Modestly Boost Newspaper Readership." July 30. http://people-press.org/report/282/online-papers-modestly-boost-newspaper-readership (accessed August 1, 2006).

Pew Research Center. 2007. "Internet News Audience Highly Critical of News Organizations." August 9. http://people-press.org/report/348/internet-news-audience-highly-critical-of-news-organizations (accessed November 28, 2008).

Pew Research Center. 2009. "Press Accuracy Rating Hits Two Decade Low." http://www.people-press.org/2009/09/13/press-accuracy-rating-hits-two-decade-low/ (accessed April 26, 2012).

Pew Research Center. 2011a. "The Internet and Campaign 2010." http://www.pewinternet.org/˜/media//Files/Reports/2011/Internet%20and%20Campaign%202010.pdf (accessed April 24, 2012).

Pew Research Center. 2011b. "Public Remains Divided over the Patriot Act." http://pewresearch.org/pubs/1893/poll-patriot-act-renewal (accessed February 13, 2012).

Pew Research Center. 2012. "Cable Leads the Pack as Campaign News Source." http://www.people-press.

org/2012/02/07/section-3-perceptions-of-bias-news-knowledge/ (accessed April 24, 2012).

Plano, Jack C., and Milton Greenberg. 2002. *The American Political Dictionary.* 11th ed. Belmont, CA: Thomson/Wadsworth.

Polsby, Nelson W. 1968. "The Institutionalization of the U.S. House of Representatives." *American Political Science Review* 62 (March): 144–168.

Polsby, Nelson, and Aaron Wildavsky. 2000. *Presidential Elections: Strategies and Structures of American Politics.* 10th ed. New York: Chatham House.

Posner, Paul. 2009. "The Next Federal Grant System." *Governing,* September 23. http://www.governing.com/column/next-federal-grant-system (accessed November 24, 2009).

Powell, G. Bingham. 1980. "Voting Turnout in Thirty Democracies: Partisan, Legal, and Socio-Economic Influences." In *Electoral Participation: A Comparative Analysis,* ed. Richard Rose. Beverly Hills, CA: Sage.

Pressman, Jeffrey L., and Aaron Wildavsky. 1973. *Implementation.* Berkeley: University of California Press.

Preuhs, Robert R. 2006. "The Conditional Effects of Minority Descriptive Representation: Black Legislatures and Policy Influence in the American States." *Journal of Politics* 69 (August): 585–599.

Prichard, Justin, Tamara Luch, and Holbrook Mohor. 2010. "BP Spill Response Plans Severely Flawed." *News Tribune,* June 9. http://www.newstribune.com/articles/2010/06/09/news_national/nt205nat02flawed10.txt (accessed June 9, 2010).

Pritchett, C. Herman. 1948. *The Roosevelt Court: A Study in Judicial Politics and Values, 1937–1946.* New York: Macmillan.

Pritchett, C. Herman. 1976. *The American Constitutional System.* New York: McGraw-Hill.

Puglisi, Riccardo. 2008. "Being the New York Times: The Political Behaviour of a Newspaper." Available at SSRN: http://ssrn.com/abstract=573801 or http://dx.doi.org/10.2139/ssrn.573801

Ragsdale, Lyn. 1996. *Vital Statistics on the Presidency: Washington to Clinton.* Washington, DC: CQ Press.

Ragsdale, Lyn, and John J. Theis, III. 1997. "The Institutionalization of the American Presidency 1924–92." *American Journal of Political Science* 41 (October): 1280–1318.

Rapoport, Ronald B. 1997. "Partisanship Change in a Candidate-Centered Era." *Journal of Politics* 59: 185–199.

Rasmussen Reports. 2012. "Partisan Trends." http://www.rasmussenreports.com/public_content/politics/mood_of_america/partisan_trends (accessed January 27, 2012).

Redford, Emmette S. 1969. *Democracy in the Administrative State.* New York: Oxford University Press.

Rees, Nigel. 1997. *Cassell Companion to Quotations.* London: Cassell.

Richardson, Richard J., and Kenneth N. Vines. 1970. *The Politics of Federal Courts.* Boston: Little, Brown.

Riker, William H., and Peter C. Ordeshook. 1968. "A Theory of the Calculus of Voting." *American Political Science Review* 62 (March): 25–42.

Ripley, Randall. 1988. *Policy Analysis in Political Science.* Chicago: Nelson-Hall.

Robson, William A. 1923. "Compulsory Voting." *Political Science Quarterly* 38 (December): 569–577.

Rogers, Will. 1974. *The Illiterate Digest.* Edited with an introduction by Joseph A. Stout Jr. Stillwater: Oklahoma State University Press.

Rohde, David W. 1991. *Parties and Leaders in the Post Reform House.* Chicago: University of Chicago Press.

Rom, Mark C., Paul E. Peterson, and Kenneth S. Scheve Jr. 1998. "Interstate Competition and Welfare Policy." *Publius* 28 (Summer): 17–37.

Rosenbloom, David H. 1998. *Public Administration: Understanding Management, Politics, and Law in the Public Sector.* 4th ed. New York: McGraw-Hill.

Rosenstone, Steven, and John Mark Hansen. 1993. *Mobilization, Participation, and Democracy in America.* New York: Macmillan.

Saad, Lydia. 2012. "Conservatives Remain the Largest Ideological Group in U.S." Gallup Politics, January 12, 2012. http://www.gallup.com/poll/152021/Conservatives-Remain-Largest-Ideological-Group.aspx.

Sabatier, Paul. 1988. "An Advocacy Coalition Framework of Policy Change and the Role of Policy-Oriented Learning Therein." *Policy Sciences* 21: 129–168.

Sabatier, Paul A., and Daniel Mazmanian. 1980. "The Implementation of Public Policy: A Framework for Analysis." *Policy Studies Journal* 8: 538–560.

Salisbury, Robert H. 1969. "An Exchange Theory of Interest Groups." *Midwest Journal of Political Science* 13 (February): 1–32.

Samuelson, Robert J. 2008. "Lobbying Is Democracy in Action." *Newsweek,* December 13. http://www.newsweek.com/id/174283 (accessed March 13, 2010).

Sanger, David E. 2001. "Look Sharp: Trying to Run a Country like a Corporation." *New York Times,* July 8. http://www.nytimes.com/2001/07/08/weekinreview/08SANG.html (accessed October 23, 2004).

Santiago, Chris. 2010. "The First Asian-American Supreme Court Justice?" Race in America, Change.org, June 8.

http://race.change.org/blog/view/the_first_asian-american_supreme_court_justice (accessed June 17, 2010).

Savage, Charlie. 2009. "Obama's Embrace of a Bush Tactic Riles Congress." *New York Times,* August 8. http://www.nytimes.com/2009/08/09/us/politics/09signing.html?_r=2&hpw (accessed May 31, 2010).

Sawyer, Diane. 2010. "Exclusive: Pelosi Defends Health Care Fight Tactics." *ABC World News with Diane Sawyer,* March 22. http://abcnews.go.com/WN/Politics/house-speaker-nancy-pelosis-exclusive-interview-diane-sawyer/story?id=10172685 (accessed May 22, 2010).

Schaefer, Todd M. 1997. "Persuading the Persuaders: Presidential Speeches and Editorial Opinion." *Political Communication* 14 (January–March): 97–111.

Schattschneider, E.E. 1942. *Party Government.* New York: Rinehart.

Schattschneider, E.E. 1960. *The Semisovereign People: A Realist View of Democracy in America.* New York: Holt, Rinehart & Winston.

Schlesinger, Arthur M., Jr. 1973. *The Imperial Presidency.* Boston: Houghton Mifflin.

Schlozman, Kay Lehman, and John T. Tierney. 1983. "More of the Same: Washington Pressure Group Activity in a Decade of Change." *Journal of Politics* 45 (May): 351–377.

Schneider, Anne, and Helen Ingram, eds. 2005. *Deserving and Entitled: Social Constructions and Public Policy.* Albany: SUNY Press.

Schneider, Anne Larson, and Helen Ingram. 1997. *Policy Design for Democracy.* Lawrence: University of Kansas Press.

Schneider, Judy. 2005. "House Committees: Categories and Rules for Committee Assignments." CRS Report for Congress, February 25. http://www.rules.house.gov/archives/98-151.pdf (accessed August 20, 2008).

Schneider, Judy. 2006a. "Committee Assignment Process in the U.S. Senate: Democratic and Republican Party Procedures." CRS Report for Congress, November 3. http://www.senate.gov/reference/resources/pdf/RL30743.pdf (accessed May 24, 2010).

Schneider, Judy. 2006b. "Senate Committees: Categories and Rules for Committee Assignments." CRS Report for Congress, October 26. http://www.rules.house.gov/Archives/98-183.pdf (accessed May 24, 2010).

Schneider, Judy. 2008. "House and Senate Rules of Procedure: A Comparison." Congressional Research Service, CRS Report for Congress (RL30945). Updated April 16, 2008. http://assets.opencrs.com/rpts/RL30945_20080416.pdf.

Schumpeter, Joseph. 1942. *Capitalism, Socialism and Democracy.* New York: Harper and Brothers.

Schutz, Astrid. 1995. "Entertainers, Experts, or Public Servants? Politicians' Self-Presentation on Television Talk Shows." *Political Communication* 12: 211–221.

Sclar, Elliott D. 2000. *You Don't Always Get What You Pay For.* Ithaca, NY: Cornell University Press.

Scott, Michael. 2012. "Portage County Veteran, 86, Doesn't Vote After VA Identification Card Rejected at Polls." *Plain Dealer.* http://www.cleveland.com/politics/index.ssf/2012/03/portage_county_veteran_86_turn.html (accessed May 24, 2012).

Sears, David, and Nicholas Valentino. 1997. "Politics Matters: Political Events as Catalysts for Preadult Socialization." *American Political Science Review* 91 (June): 45–65.

Seeman, Melvin. 1959. "On the Meaning of Alienation." *American Sociological Review* 24 (December): 783–791.

Segal, Jeffrey A., and Albert D. Cover. 1989. "Ideological Values and the Votes of U.S. Supreme Court Justices." *American Political Science Review* 83: 557–565.

Segal, Jeffrey A., and Harold J. Spaeth. 1993. *The Supreme Court and the Attitudinal Model.* New York: Cambridge University Press.

Sentencing Project. 2009. "Request for a Thematic Hearing on the Discriminatory Effects of Felony Disenfranchisement Laws, Policies and Practices in the Americas", http://www.sentencingproject.org/doc/publications/fd_IACHRHearingRequest.pdf (accessed March 3, 2013).

Shafer, Byron E. 1988. *Bifurcated Politics: Evolution and Reform in the National Convention.* Cambridge, MA: Harvard University Press.

Shepsle, Kenneth A., and Barry R. Weingast. 1987. "The Institutional Foundations of Committee Power." *American Political Science Review* 81 (March): 85–104.

Sherman, Mark. 2011. "U.S. Citizen Recalls 'Humiliating' Post-9/11 Arrest." Associated Press. http://www.msnbc.msn.com/id/41808706/ns/us_news-crime_and_courts/t/us-citizen-recalls-humiliating-post-arrest/ (accessed February 9, 2012).

Sifry, Micah. 1998. "Low Tide for the Angry Middle." *The Nation* 267 (July): 16–20.

Silverstein, Mark. 1994. *Judicious Choices: The New Politics of Supreme Court Confirmations.* New York: Norton.

Simon, Herbert. 1947. *Administrative Behavior.* New York: The Free Press.

Simonich, Milan. 2000. "Miranda's Life Ended with Warning, No Conviction." *Post-Gazette.com.* http://www.post-gazette.com/headlines/20000110mirandaside2.asp (accessed October 25, 2000).

Sinclair, Barbara. 2012. *Unorthodox Lawmaking: New Legislative Processes in the U.S. Congress.* 4th ed. Washington, DC: CQ Press.

Skocpol, Theda. 1999. "Associations without Members." *American Prospect* 45: 1–8.

Slater, Philip. 1991. *A Dream Deferred: America's Discontent and the Search for a New Democratic Ideal.* Boston: Beacon Press.

Smith, Aaron, Kay Lehman Schlozman, Sidney Verba, and Henry Brady. 2009. *The Internet and Civic Engagement.* Washington, DC: Pew Internet & American Life Project.

Smith, Kevin B. 1999. "Clean Thoughts and Dirty Minds: The Politics of Porn." *Policy Studies Journal* 27 (4): 723–734.

Smith, Kevin B. 2005. "Data Don't Matter? Academic Research and School Choice." *Perspectives on Politics* 3 (2): 285–299.

Smith, Kevin B., John Buntin, and Alan Greenblatt. 2004. *Governing States and Localities.* Washington, DC: CQ Press.

Smith, Richard A. 1995. "Interest Group Influence in the U.S. Congress." *Legislative Studies Quarterly* 20 (February): 89–139.

Sobieraj, Sarah, and Jeffrey Berry. 2011. "From Incivility to Outrage: Political Discourse in Blogs, Talk Radio, and Cable News." *Political Communication* 28: 19–41.

Sommers, Samuel, Evan Apfelbaum, Kirstin Dukes, Negin Toosi, and Elsie Wang. 2006. *Analysis of Social Issues and Public Policy* 6: 39–55.

Spitzer, Robert J. 1995. *The Politics of Gun Control.* Chatham, NJ: Chatham House.

Spitzer, Robert J. 1998. "Gun Control." In *Moral Controversies in American Politics: Cases in Social Regulatory Policy,* ed. Raymond Tatalovich and Byron W. Daynes. New York: Sharpe.

Spriggs, James F., II, and Paul J. Wahlbeck. 1997. "Amicus Curiae and the Role of Information at the Supreme Court." *Political Research Quarterly* 50 (June): 365–386.

Spring, Joe. 1998. *American Education.* 8th ed. New York: McGraw-Hill.

Stanley, Harold W., and Richard G. Niemi. 2011. *Vital Statistics on American Politics 2011–2012.* Washington, DC: CQ Press.

Starr, Paul. 2010. "Governing in the Age of Fox News." *The Atlantic* 305 (January): 95–98.

Stelter, Brian. 2009. "Fox's Volley with Obama Intensifying." *New York Times,* October 11. http://www.nytimes.com/2009/10/12/business/media/12fox.html (accessed January 20, 2010).

Sterling, Bryan B., ed. 1979. *The Best of Will Rogers.* New York: Crown Publishers.

Stewart, Charles, III. 2005. "Congress and the Constitutional System." In *The Legislative Branch,* ed. Paul J. Quirk and Sarah A. Binder. New York: Oxford University Press.

Stewart, Charles, III, and Tim Groseclose. 1999. "The Value of Committee Seats in the United States Senate, 1947–91." *American Journal of Political Science* 43 (July): 963–973.

Strickland, Rennard J. 1992. "Native Americans." In *The Oxford Companion to the Supreme Court of the United States,* ed. Kermit L. Hall. New York: Oxford University Press.

Svingen, Orlan J. 1987. "Jim Crow, Indian Style." *American Indian Quarterly* 11 (Autumn): 275–286.

Swain, Carol. 1995. *Black Faces, Black Interests: The Representation of African Americans in Congress.* Cambridge, MA: Harvard University Press.

Swanson, David L. 2000. "The Homologous Evolution of Political Communication and Civic Engagement: Good News, Bad News, and No News." *Political Communication* 17: 409–414.

Taber, Charles S., Damon Cann, and Simona Kucsova. 2009. "The Motivated Processing of Political Arguments." *Political Behavior* 31 (2): 137–155.

Tarr, G. Alan. 2000. *Understanding State Constitutions.* Princeton, NJ: Princeton University Press.

Tarr, G. Alan. 2003. *Judicial Process and Judicial Policymaking.* Belmont, CA: Thomson/Wadsworth.

Tesh, Sylvia. 1984. "In Support of 'Single-Issue' Politics." *Political Science Quarterly* 99 (Spring): 27–44.

Theodoulou, Stella. 1995. "Making Public Policy." In *Public Policy: The Essential Readings,* ed. Stella Z. Theodoulou and Matthew A. Cahn. New York: Prentice Hall.

Theriault, Sean, and David W. Rohde. 2011. "The Gingrich Senators and Party Polarization in the U.S. Senate." *Journal of Politics* 73 (October): 1011–1024.

Thomsett, Michael C., and Jean Freestone Thomsett. 1994. *Political Quotations: A Worldwide Dictionary of Thoughts and Pronouncements from Politicians, Literary Figures, Humorists, and Others.* Jefferson, NC: McFarland.

Tierney, John. 2004. "Using M.R.I.s to See Politics on the Brain." *New York Times.* http://www.nytimes.com/2004/04/20/science/20SCAN.html?ex=1095048000&en=2a2e7d3dd841d3ce&ei=5070&pagewanted=1 (accessed September 19, 2010).

Tocqueville, Alexis de. [1835] 1955. *Democracy in America.* Vol. 2. New York: Vintage Books.

Tolbert, Caroline J., and Romona S. McNeal. 2003. "Unraveling the Effects of the Internet on Political Participation?" *Political Research Quarterly* 56 (2): 175–185.

Tong, Lorraine H. 2009. "House Committee Party Ratios: 98th–111th Congresses." *Congressional Research Service*, March 30. http://www.fas.org/sgp/crs/misc/R40478.pdf (accessed May 21, 2010).

Tooby, John, and Leda Cosmides. 1992. "The Psychological Foundations of Culture." In *The Adapted Mind,* ed. Jerome H. Barkow, Leda Cosmides, and John Tooby. New York: Oxford University Press.

Traugott, Michael W., and Paul J. Lavrakas. 2000. *The Voter's Guide to Election Polls.* 2nd ed. New York: Seven Bridges Press.

Tribe, Laurence H. 2004. "*Lawrence v. Texas:* The 'Fundamental Right' That Dare Not Speak Its Name." *Harvard Law Review* 117: 1894–1895.

Truman, David B. 1951. *The Governmental Process: Political Interests and Public Opinion.* 2nd ed. New York: Knopf.

Tullock, Gordon. 1965. *The Politics of Bureaucracy.* Washington, DC: Public Affairs Press.

Tullock, Gordon. 1967. *Toward a Mathematics of Politics.* Ann Arbor: University of Michigan Press.

Turner, Joel. 2007. "The Messenger Overwhelming the Message: Ideological Cues and Perceptions of Bias in Television News." *Political Behavior* 29 (4): 441–464.

TV Turnoff Network. 2004 "Facts and Figures about our TV Habit." TV-Turnoff Network. http://www.tvturnoff.org/images/facts&figs/factsheets/Facts%20and%20Figures.pdf (accessed May 13, 2004).

Uhlaner, Carole J., Bruce E. Cain, and Roderick Kiewiet. 1989. "Political Participation of Ethnic Minorities in the 1980s." *Political Behavior* 11 (September): 195–231.

U.S. Census Bureau. 2001. Statistical Abstract of the United States. http://www.census.gov/prod/2002pubs/01statab/stat-ab01.html (accessed October 23, 2004).

U.S. Census Bureau. 2008. Statistical Abstract of the United States. http://www.census.gov/compendia/statab/cats/income_expenditures_poverty_wealth.html (accessed November 25, 2008).

U.S. Census Bureau. 2011. *The Hispanic Population: 2010.* http://www.census.gov/prod/cen2010/briefs/c2010br-04.pdf (accessed March 2, 2012).

U.S. Department of Justice. 2000. "Enforcing the ADA: Looking Back on a Decade of Progress." June 27. http://www.usdoj.gov/crt/ada/pubs/10thrpt.htm#anchor37661 (accessed October 26, 2000).

U.S. Government Customer Satisfaction Initiative. 2000. "Key Findings from the ACSI Report." http://www.customersurvey.gov/summary.htm (accessed May 3, 2000).

U.S. Senate. n.d. "Votes." Statistics and Lists. http://www.senate.gov/reference/common/generic/Votes.htm (accessed September 27, 2010).

Vedantam, Shankar. 2006. "How the Brain Helps Partisans Admit No Gray." *Washington Post,* July 31, A2.

Verba, Sidney, and Norman Nie. 1987. *Political Participation in America.* New York: Harper & Row.

Verba, Sidney, Kay Lehman Schlozman, and Henry E. Brady. 1995. *Voice and Equality: Civic Voluntarism in American Politics.* Cambridge, MA: Harvard University Press.

Verhulst, Brad, Lindon Eaves, and Peter Hatemi. 2011. "Correlation Not Causation: The Relationship between Personality Traits and Political Ideologies." *American Journal of Political Science* 56: 34–51.

Villalobos, Jose D. 2006. "When Made to Choose: Cross-Pressured Republican Senators and George W. Bush's Private Account Plan." In *A Dialogue on Presidential Challenges and Leadership,* ed. Thomas M. Kirlin and Jay M. Parker, 25–37. Washington, DC: Center for the Study of the Presidency.

Washington, George (1796). *Washington's Farewell Address 1796.* Retrieved from the Yale University Law School, Lillian Goldman Law Library, Avalon Project website: http://avalon.law.yale.edu/default.asp.

Wattenberg, Martin P. 1990. *The Decline of American Political Parties: 1952–1988.* Cambridge, MA: Harvard University Press.

Wattenberg, Martin P. 1998. "Politics: Should Election Day Be a Holiday?" *Atlantic Monthly* 1 (October): 42.

Wattenberg, Martin P. 2007. "Comments on Chapter 1." In *Red and Blue Nation? Volume 2: Consequences and Correction of America's Polarized Politics,* ed. Pietro S. Nivola and David W. Brady, 42. Washington, DC: Brookings Institution Press, 2007.

Wayne, Stephen. 2000. *The Road to the White House 2000.* Boston: Bedford/St. Martin's Press.

Wayne, Stephen. 2004. *The Road to the White House 2004.* Belmont, CA: Wadsworth/Thompson.

Weaver, David, Randal Beam, Bonnie Brownlee, Paul Voakes, and G. Cleveland Wilhoit. 2006. *The American Journalist in the 21st Century.* Mahwah, NJ: Lawrence Erlbaum.

Weber, Paul J., and Barbara A. Perry. 1989. *Unfounded Fears: Myths and Realities of a Constitutional Convention.* Westport, CT: Greenwood Press.

Weingast, Barry R., and William J. Marshall. 1988. "The Industrial Organization of Congress; or, Why Legislatures, like Firms, Are Not Organized as Markets." *Journal of Political Economy* 96 (February): 132–163.

Weiser, Wendy, and Lawrence Norden. 2011. "Voting Law Changes in 2012." New York: Brennan Center for Justice at NYU School of Law.

Welch, Susan, and John R. Hibbing. 1997. "The Effects of Charges of Corruption on Voting Behavior in Congressional Elections, 1982–1990." *Journal of Politics* 59 (February): 226–239.

White, G. Edward. 1982. *Earl Warren: A Public Life.* New York: Oxford University Press.

Wiecek, William. 1992. "Declaration of Independence." In *The Oxford Companion to the Supreme Court of the United States,* ed. Kermit L. Hall. New York: Oxford University Press.

Wildavsky, Aaron. 1965. "The Goldwater Phenomenon: Purists, Politicians, and the Two-Party System." *Review of Politics* 27 (July): 386–413.

Williams, David. 2003. *The Mythic Meanings of the Second Amendment.* New Haven, CT: Yale University Press.

Wilson, James Q. 1962. *The American Democrat.* Chicago: University of Chicago Press.

Wilson, Woodrow. 1885. *Congressional Government: A Study in American Politics.* Boston: Houghton Mifflin.

Wilson, Woodrow. 1887. "The Study of Administration." *Political Science Quarterly* 2 (March): 197–222.

Winter, Greg. 2003. "Change in Aid Formula Shifts More Costs to Students." *New York Times,* June 13. http://www.nytimes.com/2003/06/13/education/13COLL.html?pagewanted=all (accessed September 19, 2010).

Wolfinger, Raymond E. 1991. "The Politics of Voter Registration Reform." In *Registering Voters: Comparative Perspectives,* ed. John C. Courtney. Cambridge, MA: Harvard University Center for International Affairs.

Wolfley, Jeanette. 1991. "Jim Crow, Indian Style: The Disenfranchisement of Native Americans." *American Indian Law Review* 16 (Spring): 167–202.

Wood, B. Dan. 1992. "Modeling Federal Implementation as a System: The Clean Air Case." *American Journal of Political Science* 36 (February): 4–67.

Wood, B. Dan, and Richard W. Waterman. 1994. *Bureaucratic Dynamics: The Role of Bureaucracy in a Democracy.* Boulder, CO: Westview Press.

Woodward, Bob. 2002. *Bush at War.* New York: Simon & Schuster.

Worsnop, Richard L. 1996. "Implementing the Disabilities Act." *CQ Researcher* 6 (December): 1107–1127.

Wright, John R. 1990. "Contributions, Lobbying, and Committee Voting in the U.S. House of Representatives." *American Journal of Political Science* 84 (June): 417–438.

Younge, Gary. 2003. "A Supreme Showdown." *Guardian.* http://www.guardian.co.uk/weekend/story/0,3605,980731,00.html (accessed March 2, 2004).

Zaller, John R. 1992. *The Nature and Origins of Mass Opinion.* New York: Cambridge University Press.

Zelizer, Julian. 2010. "The Legacy of 'Drill, Baby, Drill.'" CNN.com, June 1. http://www.cnn.com/2010/OPINION/06/01/zelizer.deregulation.oil/index.html (accessed June 7, 2010).

Zhuravskaya, Ekaterina. 2010. "Federalism in Russia." Centre for Economic and Financial Research at New Economic School. http://www.cefir.ru/papers/WP141.pdf (accessed March 15, 2012).

Zink, James R. 2009. "The Language of Liberty and Law: James Wilson on America's Written Constitution." *American Political Science Review* 103 (August): 442–455.

GLOSSARY OF KEY TERMS

527 groups. Tax-exempt organizations that can raise and spend unlimited amounts of money to influence elections. They can engage in voter mobilization and issue advocacy, but they cannot expressly advocate the election or defeat of a federal candidate.

501(c) groups. Tax-exempt organizations that can raise and spend unlimited amounts of money to promote "social welfare." They may advocate for or against candidates, but political activities cannot become their primary purpose. They can keep their donors and names of members secret.

absolute majority. Fifty percent plus one of all members or all eligible voters.

absolutist approach. The view of the First Amendment that states that the founders wanted it to be interpreted literally so that Congress should make "no laws" about the expression of views.

ad hoc federalism. The process of adopting a state- or nation-centered view of federalism on the basis of political convenience.

adjudication. The process of determining whether a law or rule established by the bureaucracy has been broken.

adverse selection. Principal's lack of information about the abilities of an agent.

advertising. The activities of members of Congress (such as sending out newsletters or visiting the district) designed to familiarize the constituency with the member.

advisory committees. Temporary or permanent organizations created to provide information and technical expertise to the bureaucracy.

affirmative action. Governmental actions designed to help minorities compete on an equal basis and overcome the effects of discrimination in the past.

agency capture. A term used to describe when an agency seems to operate for the benefit of those whom it is supposed to regulate.

agenda setting. The process of selecting the issues or problems that government will pay attention to.

allegiant. Feeling great trust and support for the political system.

allocation responsiveness. Representation that takes the form of members of Congress ensuring that their district gets a share of federal benefits.

Americans with Disabilities Act (ADA). Specifically extended to citizens with disabilities, the civil rights and protections that were the cornerstone of the 1964 Civil Rights Act. It largely codified existing laws and regulations and extended them to the private sector.

amicus curiae brief. A legal brief filed by someone or some organization who holds an interest in a case but is not an actual party.

Anti-Federalists. The group of people who opposed a stronger national government than what existed under the Articles of Confederation and opposed the ratification of the Constitution.

appointment power. A power of the president that enables him or her to control the bureaucracy by selecting the people who will head its agencies.

Arrow's impossibility theorem. A formal proof that no decision-making system can guarantee that the rank-ordered preferences of a group will reflect the rank-ordered preferences of the set of rational individuals who make up that group.

Articles of Confederation. The first constitution of the United States.

attitudinal model. A model that suggests that judges' decisions are largely, if not exclusively, determined by their personal ideological and policy preferences.

autocracy. A form of government in which the power to make authoritative decisions and allocate resources is vested in one person.

bad tendency rule. An approach to determining whether an action should be protected under the First Amendment that considers whether the action would have a tendency to produce a negative consequence.

Baker v. Carr. The 1962 case in which the Supreme Court overturned the political question doctrine, holding that legislative apportionment was a justiciable issue that the courts had jurisdiction to hear and decide.

balancing test. The view of freedom of expression that states the obligation to protect rights must be balanced with the impact on society of the action in question.

Barron v. Baltimore. The 1833 Supreme Court case that explicitly confirmed that the Bill of Rights applied only to the national government.

biased sample. A group of poll respondents that does not accurately represent the target population and provides inaccurate estimates of the true opinions and attitudes of the target population.

bicameral. A legislature with two chambers.

Bipartisan Campaign Reform Act. A law that limits hard-money contributions during each election cycle to $2,000 from individuals and $5,000 from PACs.

block grants. A type of federal grant that provides funds for a general policy area but offers state and local governments discretion in designing the specific programs.

bounded rationality. Herbert Simon's theory that humans are not utility maximizers as suggested in classical rational choice models. Humans satisfice (see *satisficing*) rather than maximize.

Brandenburg v. Ohio. The 1969 case that upheld a KKK member's right to controversial speech, which supported lawbreaking in the abstract, because it contained no incitement to commit an "imminent or specific" crime, establishing the *imminent lawless action test.*

Brown v. Board of Education. The 1954 case in which a unanimous Court overturned the "separate but equal" precedent set by *Plessy v. Ferguson* and declared that separate educational facilities are inherently unequal.

bureaucracy. The term used to refer to the agencies of the federal government. It also refers to an organizational framework and has negative connotations.

by-product theory. The theory that most people will not engage in collective action with the sole aim of producing public goods. Instead, groups build membership by offering selective benefits available only to group members.

cabinet departments. The 15 largest and most influential agencies of the federal bureaucracy.

candidate image. Voters' perceptions of a candidate's qualities.

casework. Activities of members of Congress to act as intermediaries and help private individuals who are having problems with the administrative agencies in the executive branch.

categorical grant. A type of federal grant that provides money for a specific policy activity and details how the programs are to be carried out.

caucus. Party committees in the House and Senate composed of all members of the party in the chamber. Each party's caucus develops a policy agenda for the party, appoints committees to make committee assignments, and raises campaign money for House and Senate candidates.

caucus method. A method of selecting the delegates to a political party's national convention by permitting the state conventions to select representatives from their states.

censures and reprimands. Verbal condemnations of a member of Congress by the House or Senate, intended to punish bad behavior by expressing the public disapproval of the member's colleagues.

check and balance. The idea that each branch of the federal government should assert and protect its own rights but must also cooperate with the other branches. Each branch is to serve as a limit on the others' powers, balancing the overall distribution of power.

Citizens United v. Federal Election Commission. A 2010 Supreme Court case holding that a provision of the McCain-Feingold Act prohibiting corporations and unions from broadcasting "electioneering communications" within 60 days of a general election is an unconstitutional limitation on the First Amendment guarantee of free speech. It also held that corporations and labor unions can spend unlimited amounts of money in campaigns.

civil disobedience. Deliberately disobeying laws viewed as morally repugnant.

civil liberties. The freedoms and protections against arbitrary governmental actions given to the people in a democratic society.

Civil Rights Act of 1964. The landmark law that outlawed racial segregation in schools and public places and barred discrimination in employment based on sex.

civil rights. The obligations placed on government to protect the freedom of the people.

"clear and present danger" test. An approach to determining whether an action should be protected under the First Amendment that considers "whether the words used are used in such circumstances and are of such a nature as to create a clear and present danger that they will bring about the substantive evils that Congress has a right to prevent."

closed primaries. Elections to choose a party's nominees for the general election that are open only to party members.

closed rule. The rule that prohibits amending a bill when it is on the floor of Congress for consideration.

cloture. A procedure of the Senate to end a filibuster; invoking cloture requires votes of 60 senators.

coalition building. A means of expanding an interest group's influence that involves working with other groups.

collective action. Action in which a group of people work together for the provision of public goods.

collegial courts. Courts in which groups of judges decide cases based on a review of the record of the lower-court trial.

Committee of the Whole. A parliamentary action whereby the House of Representatives dissolves into a committee consisting of every member of the House. This procedure is used to facilitate consideration of legislation because it has less burdensome rules governing debate and requires a smaller quorum than the House itself.

concurrent powers. The powers listed in the Constitution as belonging to both the national and state governments.

concurring opinion. An opinion written by a Supreme Court justice who agrees with the ruling of the Court but not the reason behind it.

conditional party government. When members of the majority party caucus in Congress achieve consensus on policy issues, they adopt reforms that obligate congressional committee chairs and party leaders to try to enact the party's legislative agenda on which there is a consensus.

confederation. A political system in which the central government receives no direct grant of power from the people and can exercise only the power granted to it by the regional governments.

conference. The meeting of Supreme Court justices where they decide which cases they will hear.

conference committee. A temporary congressional committee made up of members of the House and Senate that meets to reconcile the differences in legislation that has passed both chambers.

confidence level. The chance, measured in percent, that the results of a survey will fall within the boundaries set by the margin of error.

confirmation process. The period between when a presidential nomination of a federal judge is received in the Senate and when the nominee is either confirmed or defeated.

Connecticut Compromise (Great Compromise). A proposal at the Constitutional Convention that called for a two-house legislature with a House of Representatives apportioned on the basis of population and a Senate representing each state on an equal basis.

constituency. The group of people served by an elected official or branch of government.

constitution. A document or unwritten set of basic rules that provides the basic principles that determine the conduct of political affairs.

constitutional interpretation. A ruling of the Supreme Court that declares a law unconstitutional based the Court's interpretation of the Constitution. A constitutional interpretation cannot be overturned by a simple statute.

contracting out. Hiring a private organization to deliver a public program or service.

cooperative federalism. The idea that the distinction between state and national responsibilities is unclear and that the different levels of government share responsibilities in many areas.

Council of Economic Advisers. An agency of the Executive Office of the President that is responsible for advising the president on the U.S. economy.

courts of appellate jurisdiction. Courts that review the decisions of lower courts.

courts of original jurisdiction. Trial courts that hear cases for the first time and determine issues of fact and law.

credit claiming. The efforts by members of Congress to get their constituents to believe they are responsible for positive government actions.

crossover sanctions. Conditions placed on grant money that have nothing to do with the original purpose of the grant.

custom and usage. The term used to describe constitutional change that occurs when the practices and institutions of government not specifically mentioned in the Constitution change over time through use and evolution.

de facto discrimination. Discrimination that exists in fact, in real life, or in practice.

de jure discrimination. Discrimination that is set forth in law.

Declaration of Independence. A document written by Thomas Jefferson that lays the foundation of American constitutional theory. In the document, Jefferson justifies the struggle for independence with a republican theory of government based on the concepts of natural rights and popular sovereignty.

delegate. A representative who makes legislative decisions based on the interests and views of his or her constituents, regardless of personal preference.

delegate model of representative democracy. The idea that the job of elected leaders is to make decisions solely based on the views of the majority of the people.

democracy. A form of government in which all the citizens have the opportunity to participate in the process of making authoritative decisions and allocating resources.

deregulation. The reduction or elimination of government rules and regulations that interfere with the efficient operation of market forces. It is often associated with conservatives who believe that government rules and regulations are a poor substitute for the natural discipline of free markets.

descriptive representation. The view of representation that calls for the racial and ethnic makeup of Congress to reflect that of the nation.

deviating election. An election in which the minority party is able to overcome the long-standing partisan orientation of the public based on temporary or short-term forces.

devolution. The return of policy power and responsibility to the states from the national government.

direct democracy. A form of democracy in which ordinary citizens, rather than representatives, collectively make government decisions.

direct lobbying. Direct contact by lobbyists with government officials in an effort to influence policy.

direct popular election plan. A proposal to abolish the electoral college and elect the president directly by national popular vote.

direct primary. The selection of a political party's candidate for the general election by vote of ordinary citizens.

direction. The idea of public opinion being either positive or negative (favorable or unfavorable) on an issue.

discharge petition. A procedure of the House of Representatives that permits a majority of the members of the House (218) to bring a bill out of committee for consideration on the floor.

dissenting opinion. An opinion written by a Supreme Court justice who is in the minority that presents the logic and thinking of the justices who opposed the majority opinion.

distributive benefits. Government expenditures and programs that concentrate benefits in specific geographical areas such as states or congressional districts for which the costs are spread across the entire population (see *pork-barrel benefits*).

District of Columbia v. Heller. The 2008 case in which the Supreme Court struck down the Washington, DC, ban on the possession of handguns and for the first time held that the Second Amendment protects an individual's right to possess a firearm for lawful purposes such as self-defense.

district plan. A plan to revise the electoral college that would distribute a state's electoral college votes by giving one vote to the candidate who wins a plurality in each House district and two votes to the winner statewide.

divided government. When one party controls the presidency and another controls Congress.

dual federalism. The idea that the national and state governments are sovereign, with separate and distinct jurisdictions.

Duverger's Law. The tendency for the single-member district plurality system to favor a two-party system, as documented by French sociologist Maurice Duverger.

economic equality. The idea that each individual should receive the same amount of material goods, regardless of his or her contribution to society.

election. A collective decision-making process in which citizens choose an individual to hold and exercise the powers of public office. Elections are the primary mechanism that representative democracies use to achieve popular sovereignty.

electoral college. The institution (whose members are selected by whatever means the state legislature chooses) that is responsible for selecting the president of the United States.

electronic media. Consists of television, radio, movies, video and audio recordings, and the Internet.

elite opinion. The attitudes or beliefs of those people with influential positions within society.

elitist. A term used to describe a society in which organized, influential minority interests dominate the political process.

en banc. A procedure in which all the members of a U.S. court of appeals hear and decide a case.

empirical. Questions and debates that can be answered by careful observation. Systematic empirical observation is the foundation of science and the scientific method.

enabling act. A resolution passed by Congress authorizing residents of a territory to draft a state constitution as part of the process of adding new states to the Union.

enumerated powers. The powers specifically listed in the Constitution as belonging to the national government.

equality under the law. The idea that the law is supposed to be applied impartially, without regard for the identity or status of the individual involved.

equality of opportunity. The idea that every individual has the right to develop to the fullest extent of his or her abilities.

establishment clause. A clause in the First Amendment of the Constitution that states that government cannot establish a religion.

Everson v. Board of Education. The 1947 case in which the Court for the first time directly articulated the principle of separation of church and state, concluding that transportation expenditures to parochial schools did not support any religious activity but rather assisted families and were therefore allowable.

exchange theory. The theory that interest groups form as a result of a deal—an exchange—between a group entrepreneur and an unorganized interest that may be underrepresented or not represented at all.

exclude. The refusal of Congress to seat any candidate who wins election but does not meet the constitutional requirements to hold congressional office.

exclusionary rule. The rule derived from the Fourth and Fourteenth Amendments that states that evidence obtained from an unreasonable search or seizure cannot be used in federal trials.

exclusive committees. Four House committees—Appropriations, Energy and Commerce, Rules, and Ways and Means—whose members typically typically receive no other committee assignments.

executive. A person or group that has administrative and supervisory responsibilities in an organization or government.

executive agreements. Agreements between the United States and other nations, negotiated by the president, that have the same weight as a treaty but do not require senatorial approval.

Executive Office of the President (EOP).
The organizational structure in the executive branch that houses the president's most influential advisors and agencies. The most important include the White House Office, the Office of Management and Budget (OMB), the National Security Council, and the Council of Economic Advisers.

executive orders. Directives of the president that have the same weight as law and are not voted on by Congress.

executive privilege. A prerogative power of the president to withhold information on matters of national security or personal privacy.

expulsion. The ejection of a member of Congress from office.

faction. In James Madison's terms, "a number of citizens, whether amounting to a majority or a minority of the whole, who are united and actuated by some common impulse of passion, or of interests, adverse to the right of other citizens, or to the permanent and aggregate interests of the community."

false consensus. The tendency of people to believe their views are normal or represent common sense and therefore are shared by most people.

Federal Election Campaign Act. A 1971 act that allowed unions and corporations to form political action committees to raise and contribute campaign funds to candidates.

federalism. A political system in which regional governments share power with a central or national government, but each level of government has legal powers that are independent of the other. This division of power between the national and state governments attempts to balance power by giving independent sources of authority to each and allowing one level of government to serve as a check on the other.

Federalist Papers. A series of 85 political essays written by James Madison, Alexander Hamilton, and John Jay with the intent of persuading New Yorkers to ratify the proposed Constitution. They remain the single best source for understanding the justifications for the political institutions and processes the Constitution established.

Federalists. The group of people who supported the adoption of the Constitution and favored a stronger national government.

feedback. The information policymakers routinely receive through government reports, hearings, the news, casework, meetings with lobbyists and government officials, and contact with constituents.

filibuster. The effort by a senator to delay the chamber's business by making long speeches.

fire alarm oversight. Oversight that becomes active only when there is evidence of bureaucratic wrongdoing.

focusing event. Something that grabs attention immediately and puts an issue on the public agenda.

framing. Emphasizing certain aspects of a story to make them more important.

franchise. The constitutional or statutory right to vote.

franking privilege. The ability of members of Congress to send mail to their constituents free of charge by substituting a facsimile of their signature in place of a stamp.

free exercise of religion. The First Amendment guarantee that individuals are free to choose religious beliefs and practice them as they see fit or not to practice any religion at all.

free rider. A person who makes the strictly rational choice to enjoy the benefits of public goods without incurring the costs of providing them, thus presenting a dilemma to the community as a whole.

frontloading. The tendency of states to move their primaries earlier in the season in order to gain more influence over the presidential selection process.

"full faith and credit." The provision in the Constitution that requires states to honor the civil obligations (wills, birth certificates, and other public documents) generated by other states. Note: states apparently are not required to recognize marriages under "full faith and credit."

garbage can model. A model that attempts to explain why decision making in large complex institutions often seems irrational.

gatekeeper. A person or institution that controls access to something.

general election. The process by which voters choose their representatives from among the parties' nominees.

general revenue sharing. A type of federal grant that returns money to state and local governments with no requirements as to how it is spent.

genocide. The killing of an entire race of people.

geographical constituency. Everyone and everything within the geographical boundaries of a congressional member's House district.

gerrymandering. The drawing of district lines in such a way as to help or hinder the electoral prospects of a specific political interest.

Gideon v. Wainwright. The 1963 case in which the Supreme Court ruled that state courts are required under the Sixth and Fourteenth Amendments of the Constitution to provide counsel in criminal cases for defendants who cannot afford to hire their own lawyer.

going public. A political strategy in which the president appeals to the public in an effort to persuade Congress to support his or her political goals.

good faith exception. An exception to the exclusionary rule that allows evidence obtained in a search with a flawed warrant to be admissible as long as the law officer believed the warrant was valid at the time of the search.

government. The institution that has the authority to make binding decisions for all of society.

government corporations. Federally established businesses that are narrow in focus and are in part self-supporting.

grandfather clause. A provision in election laws used in conjunction with literacy tests to prevent African Americans from voting. People whose ancestors were entitled to vote in 1866 (i.e., whites) were exempt from passing the literacy test, but African Americans, whose ancestors were slaves, had to pass the literacy test in order to vote. This clause was ruled unconstitutional in 1915.

grants-in-aid. A form of national subsidy to the states designed to help them pay for policies and programs that are the responsibility of states rather than the national government.

Griswold v. Connecticut. The 1965 case ruling that Connecticut could not prohibit the use of contraceptives by married couples, enumerating a right of privacy. Although the Constitution contains no explicit right of privacy, the Court argued that various guarantees in the First, Third, Fourth, Fifth, and Ninth Amendments create "zones of privacy" that the government has no right to invade.

group entrepreneur. Someone who invests resources (such as time, money, and organizational skill) to create and build an organization that offers various types of benefits (material, solidary, and purposive) to entice others to join the group.

hard money. Campaign contributions made directly to candidates and regulated by law.

hard news. Stories that focus on factual information about important decisions or events.

hierarchical model. A method of organizing the presidency that calls for clear lines of authority and that delegates responsibility from the president and through the chief of staff.

hold. The formal request by a member of the Senate to be notified before a specific bill or presidential nomination comes to the floor.

home style. The way a member of Congress behaves, explains his or her legislative actions, and presents himself or herself in the home district.

hyperdemocracy. The idea that policymakers have become so sensitive to public opinion that they are subservient to any brief shift in opinion.

ideology. A consistent set of values, attitudes, and beliefs about the appropriate role of government in society.

imminent lawless action test. As decided in *Brandenburg v. Ohio,* speech is protected if it contains no incitement to commit an "imminent or specific" crime. This test replaced the old "clear and present danger" test and protects a broader range of speech.

impact evaluations. Evaluations undertaken to assess the outcomes or effects of a policy or program.

impeach. To charge or accuse.

implied powers. Those powers belonging to the national government that are suggested in the Constitution's "necessary and proper" clause.

impoundment. The limited ability of the president to not spend money appropriated by Congress.

incorporation doctrine. The idea that the specific protections provided in the U.S. Bill of Rights are binding on the states through the "due process" clause of the Fourteenth Amendment.

incrementalism. A decision-making approach characterized by making current decisions that are small adjustments to past decisions.

incumbency advantage. The tendency for congressional incumbents to be overwhelmingly successful when they run for reelection due to the nature of congressional districts, resources, and relations with constituents, among other reasons.

independent agencies. Federal agencies that are not part of the cabinet-level executive departments. Members of these agencies serve fixed and overlapping terms and cannot be removed, which limits the president's control of them.

indicators. Any measures that can be employed as systematic monitoring devices.

indirect lobbying. The use of intermediaries by lobbyists to speak to government officials, with the intent to influence policy.

inevitable discovery exception. An exception to the exclusionary rule that states that evidence obtained from an illegal search may be used in court if the evidence eventually would have been discovered through legal means.

inherent powers (prerogative powers). Powers that are not listed or implied by the Constitution but that rather have been claimed as essential to the national government.

initiative. An election in which ordinary citizens circulate a petition to put a proposed law on the ballot for the voters to approve.

institutional agenda. A short list of actionable items being given serious consideration by policymaking institutions.

instrumentation. The process of designing survey questionnaires.

intensity. How strongly people hold the beliefs or attitudes that comprise public opinion.

interest group. A group organized around a set of views or preferences, and who seek to influence others in order to promote or protect those preferences.

interstate rendition. The obligation of states to return people accused of a crime to the state from which they fled.

invisible primary. The period of time between the election of one president and the first contest to nominate candidates to run in the general election to select the next president.

iron triangles. A term used to refer to the interdependent relationship among the bureaucracy, interest groups, and congressional committees.

issue public. A section of the public with a strong interest in a particular issue.

Jim Crow laws. Laws designed to prevent African Americans from voting.

judicial activism. A view of Supreme Court decision making that calls for the Court to take an active role in policymaking through its interpretation of the Constitution.

Judicial Conference. A committee of district and appellate judges that reviews the needs of the federal judiciary and makes recommendations to Congress.

judicial power. The authority of courts to interpret and apply the law in particular cases.

judicial restraint. A view of Supreme Court decision making that calls for the Court to defer policymaking to the other branches of government.

judicial review. The power to review decisions of the lower courts and to determine the constitutionality of laws and actions of public officials.

judiciary. A system of courts and judges concerned with administration of justice.

jurisdiction. The types of cases a given court is permitted to hear.

justiciable issue. An issue or topic over which the courts have jurisdiction or the power to make decisions.

lawmaking. A legislature's power to enact laws that address major problems and then to oversee government administration of those laws.

Lawrence v. Texas. The 2003 case ruling that the government had no right to regulate or control consensual personal relationships. This case overruled *Bowers v. Hardwick,* which had allowed states to make engaging in homosexual sex a crime.

leak. The revealing of information that officials want kept secret.

legal model. A view of judicial decision making that argues that judges set aside their own values and make decisions based solely on legal criteria.

legal realist model. A model of judicial decision making that argues that personal values and ideologies affect a judge's decisions.

legislative caucus. A method of selecting political party candidates that calls for party members in the state legislature to select candidates for statewide office and party members in the House of Representatives to select a party's candidates for president and vice president.

legislative intent. The intention of Congress when it passes laws.

legislative interpretation. A ruling of the Supreme Court in which the Court interprets the meaning and intent of a statute passed by Congress. Congress can overturn a decision based on legislative interpretation by passing another law.

legislative oversight of administration. A variety of tools Congress uses to control administrative agencies, including creating or abolishing agencies, assigning program responsibilities, providing funds, and confirming presidential appointments.

legislative veto. Measure that gives Congress the ability to reject an action or decision of the bureaucracy.

legislature. A deliberative council that has the authority to make and repeal laws. In representative democracies, ordinary citizens elect legislators to represent them.

libel. To make false or defaming statements about someone in print or the media.

liberal democracy. A representative democracy, such as Great Britain or the United States, that has a particular concern for individual liberty. The rule of law and a constitution constrain elected representatives and the will of the majority from using their power to take away the rights of minorities.

literacy tests. Reading or comprehension tests that citizens are required to pass to demonstrate their fitness to vote.

living Constitution. The theory that assumes the Constitution was meant to be a dynamic document whose meaning has to account for contemporary social and political context.

lobbying. Activity of a group or person that attempts to influence public policymaking on behalf of the individual or the group.

lobbyists. Individuals whose job it is to contact and attempt to influence governmental officials on behalf of others.

logrolling. The exchange of support on issues between individuals or groups in order to gain mutual advantage.

Madisonian dilemma. The problem of limiting self-interested individuals who administer stronger governmental powers from using those powers to destroy the freedoms that government is supposed to protect.

magic number. The number of delegates needed at a political party's national convention for a candidate to be nominated as the party's candidate for the presidency; this number equals 50 percent plus one of all delegates at the convention.

maintaining election. An election in which the traditional majority party maintains power based on the long-standing partisan orientation of the voters.

majority leader. The person, chosen by the members of the majority party in the House and Senate, who controls the legislative agenda. In the Senate, the majority leader is the most powerful person in the chamber.

majority opinion. A decision of the Supreme Court in which five or more of the justices are in agreement on the ruling on which party to the dispute should win a case and the reason that party should win.

majority rule. The principle under which government follows the course of action preferred by most people.

majority-minority districts. Districts in which the majority of the population is composed of ethnic or racial minorities.

malapportioned. A situation in which the distribution of legislative seats does not accurately reflect the distribution of the population.

Mapp v. Ohio. The 1961 case that extended the exclusionary rule to state trials.

Marbury v. Madison. The 1803 case in which the Court asserted the power of judicial review.

margin of error. The amount that sample responses are likely to differ from those of the population within very tight boundaries that are known as the confidence level.

mass media. All the means used to transmit information to masses of people.

material benefits. Tangible rewards gained from membership in an interest group.

McCulloch v. Maryland. An 1819 court case involving a dispute over whether the central government had the power to create a national bank.

McDonald v. Chicago. A 2010 case in which the Supreme Court ruled that the Second Amendment right of an individual to "keep and bear arms" applies to the states as well as the federal government.

media bias. The tendency to present an unbalanced perspective so that information is conveyed in a way that consistently favors one set of interests over another.

Members' Representational Allowance (MRA). An allowance of about $1 million per year that members of Congress receive to pay for official duties of representation and lawmaking (e.g., office functions, official travel, and staff). It cannot be used for personal or campaign expenses.

merit system. A system of governing in which jobs are given based on relevant technical expertise and the ability to perform.

midterm elections. The congressional and gubernatorial elections that occur in the middle of a presidential term.

minority leader. The leader of the minority party in the House or Senate. Works with majority leader to schedule legislation and leads opposition party.

minority rights. The full rights of democratic citizenship held by any group numerically inferior to the majority. These fundamental democratic rights cannot be taken away—even if a majority wishes to do so—without breaking the promise of democracy.

Miranda v. Arizona. The 1966 case that established a criminal suspect's right against self-incrimination and right to counsel during police interrogation.

misinformation. The belief that incorrect information is true.

mixed government. The idea that government should represent both property and the number of people.

mobilization. Efforts aimed at influencing people to vote in an election.

moral hazard. Principal's lack of information about the effort of an agent.

multimember district. A method of selecting representatives in which more than one person is chosen to represent a single constituency.

multiparty system. A political system in which three or more political parties effectively compete for political office, and no one party can win control of all.

national party convention. A nomination method in which delegates selected from each state attend a national party meeting to choose the party's candidates for president and vice president.

National Security Council. A group of presidential advisors made up of the vice president, the attorney general, and cabinet officers chosen by the president to advise the president on national security issues; it is part of the Executive Office of the President.

national security directive. A type of executive order with the force of law authorizing federal agencies or officials to take some action to protect national security.

neutral competence. The idea that agencies should make decisions based on expertise rather than political considerations.

new federalism. A movement to take power away from the federal government and return it to the states.

New Jersey plan. A proposal presented at the Constitutional Convention that called for a one-house legislature with equal representation for each state.

news. Accounts of timely and specific events.

news media. Organizations and journalists that cover the news.

nomination. The process through which political parties winnow down a field of candidates to a single one who will be the party's standard-bearer in the general election.

nongermane amendments. Amendments to a piece of legislation that are not related to the subject of the bill to which they are added.

nonpartisan primary. A type of election used in Louisiana in which candidates from all political parties run in the same primary, and the candidate who receives the majority of the vote obtains the office.

normative. Theories or statements that seek to prescribe how things should be valued, what should be, what is good or just, and what is better or worse.

null hypothesis. A statement positing that there is no relationship between the variables being observed. It is the opposite of the research hypothesis.

nullification. The act of declaring a national law null and void within a state's borders.

objective journalism. An approach to journalism that places emphasis on reporting facts rather than on analysis or a partisan point of view.

Office of Management and Budget (OMB). An agency of the Executive Office of the President that is responsible for assisting the president in creating the budget.

oligarchy. A form of government in which the power to make authoritative decisions and allocate resources is vested in a small group of people.

one-party system. A political system in which representatives of one political party hold all or almost all of the major offices in government.

one person, one vote. The idea, arising out of the 1964 Supreme Court decision of *Wesberry v. Sanders,* that legislative districts must contain about the same number of people.

open primaries. Elections to select a party's candidate for the general election that are open to independents and, in some cases, to member of other parties.

open rule. A rule formulated by the House Rules committee that permits any germane amendment to be considered on the floor.

open seats. Legislative seats for which there is no incumbent running for reelection.

originalism. The idea that Supreme Court justices should interpret the Constitution in terms of the original intentions of the framers.

overhead democracy. The idea that the bureaucracy is controlled through the oversight of elected officials, who are chosen by the people, thus giving the populace control over the bureaucracy.

parliamentary system. An electoral system in which the party holding the majority of seats in the legislature selects the chief executive.

partisanship. A psychological attachment to a political party.

party discipline. Requiring political party members in public office to promote or carry out the party's agenda and punishing those who do not.

party in the electorate. The component of a political party that is made up of the people in the public who identify with a political party.

party in government. The component of a political party that is made up of elected and appointed government officeholders who are associated with a political party.

party organization. The component of a political party that is composed of the party professionals who hold official positions in the party.

party polarization. Situation in which policy positions (or ideology) within political parties become more homogeneous, and policy positions across the parties move farther apart.

party professionals. Party activists whose incentives for participating in party activities are primarily material and social in nature.

party ratio. The proportion of the seats that each political party controls in the House and the Senate.

party vote. A vote in which a majority of Democrats vote on one side and a majority of Republicans vote on the other.

passive resistance. A nonviolent technique of protest that entails resisting government laws or practices that are believed to be unjust.

perquisites (perks). The benefits and support activities that members of Congress receive in order to help them perform their job.

personal constituency. A small number of intimate friends, advisors, and confidants who support a member of Congress.

Plessy v. Ferguson. An 1896 Supreme Court decision ruling that separate public facilities for people of different races satisfied the Fourteenth Amendment's equal protection clause, provided the facilities were "equal."

pluralist explanation (of interest groups). The idea that interest groups form in reaction to problems created by particular social or economic events.

pluralistic. A term used to describe a society in which power is widely distributed among diverse groups and interests.

plurality. The largest percentage of a vote, when no one has a majority.

plurality opinion. A decision of the Supreme Court in which a majority of the Court agrees on a decision, but there is no majority agreement on the reason for the decision.

pocket veto. The veto resulting from a president taking no action, before Congress adjourns, on legislation that has passed Congress.

police patrol oversight. The active oversight of the bureaucracy by elected officials to make sure that the bureaucracy is acting according to the wishes of the people.

police power. The authority of the states to pass laws for the health, safety, and morals of their citizens.

policy evaluation. The process of examining the consequences of public policy.

policy formulation and adoption. The stage in the policy-making process in which government considers various alternatives to the issue or problem at hand and formally approves one of those alternatives.

policy implementation. The process of translating government intent into government action.

policy-motivated activists. Party activists whose incentives for participating in party activities are primarily purposive and social. They are dedicated to implementing certain principles in public policies, and they are less willing to compromise those principles than are party professionals.

policy responsiveness. The amount of agreement between the people represented and their elected officials on policy issues.

policy subsystem. Networks of groups with an interest in a specific policy issue or area.

political action committees (PACs). Organizations specifically created to raise money and make political contributions on behalf of an interest group.

political alienation. The feeling of being isolated from or not part of the political process and system.

political bias. The tendency to favor a political party or ideological point of view.

political culture. A set of shared beliefs that includes broad agreement about basic political values, agreement about the legitimacy of political institutions, and general acceptance of the process government uses to make policy.

political efficacy. The belief that one's opinions are important and that government will respect and respond to one's views.

political equality. The idea that individual preferences should be given equal weight.

political machine. A political organization characterized by a reciprocal relationship between voters and officeholders. Political support is given in exchange for government jobs and services. Headed by a "party boss," political machines and party bosses maintain their power and control over government offices with techniques such as control over nominations, patronage, graft and bribery, vote buying, and election-rigging.

political participation. The translation of personal preference into a voluntary action designed to influence public policy.

political party. An organization that nominates and runs candidates for public office under its own label.

political patronage. The giving of government jobs to people based on their party affiliation and loyalty.

political science. The systematic study of government, political institutions, processes, and behavior.

political socialization. The process through which a younger generation learns political values from previous generations.

politico. A representative whose philosophy of representation is a mix of both delegate and trustee. See also *delegate* and *trustee*.

politics. The process of making binding decisions about who gets what or whose values everyone is going to live by.

poll taxes. A technique used to keep certain groups from voting by charging a fee to vote.

popular sovereignty. The idea that the highest political authority in a democracy is the will of the people.

pork-barrel benefits. Government-sponsored projects that bring economic benefits to a Congress member's state or district. This is a pejorative term first used in the mid-nineteenth century to describe projects viewed as a waste of tax dollars that serve no purpose other than to aid the reelection of a single incumbent (see *distributive benefits*).

position taking. Public statements made by members of Congress on issues of importance to the constituency.

positive government. The idea that government should play a major role in preventing or dealing with the crises that face the nation.

preemption. Congress expressly giving national laws precedence over state and local laws.

preferred freedoms doctrine. The idea that the rights provided in the First Amendment are fundamental and as such the courts have a greater obligation to protect those rights than others.

prerogative view of presidential power. A view of presidential power, promoted by Abraham Lincoln, that argues that the president is required to preserve the Constitution and take actions to do so that otherwise might be unconstitutional.

president of the Senate. The person who presides over the Senate and is responsible for many of the parliamentary duties such as recognizing speakers. The vice president of the United States holds this position.

president pro tempore. The person chosen by the members to preside over the Senate in the absence of the vice president.

presidential system. A political system in which the chief executive and the legislature are elected independently.

press. The print and electronic media that are partially or wholly devoted to collecting and reporting news in the United States.

prestige committees. Congressional committees that are highly prized and allow their members to wield tremendous power in Congress.

primary constituency. A member of Congress's strongest, mostly partisan supporters.

principal–agent model. A model explaining the relationship between Congress and the bureaucracy, which states that the relationship is similar to that between an employer who seeks to have work done (the principal) and an employee who does the work (the agent).

print media. Media consisting of newspapers, magazines, and books.

prior restraint. The prohibition or censoring of a news story prior to publication or broadcast.

process evaluation. An evaluation undertaken with the goal of assessing whether a program or policy is being implemented according to its stated guidelines.

propaganda model. The idea that mainstream media are biased toward corporate and conservative interests because most mainstream media are corporately owned.

proportional plan. A plan to revise the electoral college such that the number of electoral college votes given to candidates would be based on the proportion of the popular vote they obtained.

proportional representation. A method of selecting representatives in which representation is given to political parties based on the proportion of the vote obtained. This method has the effect of encouraging multiple parties.

prospective voting. Voting that is based on an individual's estimation of how well a candidate will perform duties in the future.

public agenda. All issues and problems that have the attention of the government at a particular point in time.

public good. A benefit that is provided to everyone and cannot be withheld from those who did not participate in its provision.

public opinion. The sum of individual attitudes or beliefs about an issue or question.

public policy. A relatively stable, purposive course of action pursued by government officials or agencies.

public sphere. A forum where information on matters important to civic life can be freely accessed and exchanged.

purposive benefits. Benefits that interest group members derive from feeling good about contributing to a worthy cause in an effort to improve the lot of society in general, not just the individual concerns of the group's members.

push poll. A type of public opinion poll that intentionally uses leading or biased questions in order to manipulate the responses.

racial segregation. The separation of people based on their race.

random sample. A method of selecting a sample (subset of the population) in which every person in the target population has an equal chance of being selected.

rational. Making choices that maximize benefits and minimize costs.

rational choice model. A model of voter choice that suggests that an individual will vote if the benefits of doing so outweigh the costs and will cast his or her ballot for candidates who are closest to sharing the individual's views on the issues.

rational-comprehensive decision making. A decision-making approach characterized by consideration of all alternatives to a problem or issue, an analysis of the costs and benefits of each alternative, and selection of the alternative with the most benefits at the least cost.

realigning election. An election in which the minority party is able to build a relatively stable coalition to win election, and this coalition endures over a series of elections.

reapportionment. The process of adjusting the number of House seats among the states based on population shifts.

redistricting. The process of redrawing congressional district lines after reapportionment.

reelection constituency. The people within a Congress member's House district who can be counted on for support.

reference groups. Groups that influence the political attitudes of non-group members.

referendum. An election in which a state legislature refers a proposed law to the voters for their approval.

regulatory agencies and commissions. Agencies that are independent of cabinet departments and are created by Congress to monitor and regulate specific areas of economic activity.

reinstating election. An election in which the majority party regains power after a deviating election.

representation. The relationship between elected officials and the people who put them in office, involving the extent to which officials are responsive to the people.

representative democracy. Defined as a system of government where ordinary citizens do not make governmental decisions themselves but choose public officials—representatives of the people—to make decisions for them.

republican form of government. A form of government in which the government operates with the consent of the governed through some type of representative institution.

responsible party model. A concept that describes democracies with competitive parties in which one party wins control of the government based on its policy proposals, enacts those proposals once it is in control, and stands or falls in the next election based on its performance in delivering on its promises.

restrictive view of presidential power. A view of presidential power that argues that the president can exercise only those powers listed in the Constitution.

retrospective voting. Voting that is based on an individual's evaluation of the past performance of a candidate.

rider. A nongermane amendment that is added to a popular bill in hopes that the desirability of the proposed legislation will help the amendment pass.

right to privacy. An individual's right to be free of government interference without due cause or due process.

Roe v. Wade. The 1973 case in which the Court reaffirmed the right of privacy enumerated in *Griswold,* balancing the mother's right to privacy against the state's interest in protecting an unborn fetus.

role theory. A behavioral model of politics based on the assumption that human beings have a psychological need for predictability in their relations with each other.

rule. A statement of the bureaucracy that interprets the law or prescribes a specific action. These rules have the force of law.

rule of four. Rule according to which four Supreme Court justices must agree to hear a case.

rulemaking. The process in which the bureaucracy decides what the laws passed by Congress mean and how they should be carried out.

runoff primary. A second primary election held between the top two candidates if no candidate received a majority of the votes in the first primary.

salience. The prominence or visibility of an issue or question and how important the issue is to the public.

satisficing. Considering possible alternatives until finding one that is good enough to solve the problem at hand even though it might not be the "best" possible solution.

Schenck v. United States. The 1919 case that articulated the "clear and present danger" test.

science. A method of acquiring knowledge through the formulation of hypotheses that can be tested through empirical observation in order to make claims about how the world works and why.

selective benefits. Benefits provided by interest groups that are available to members only.

senatorial courtesy. The practice that allows senators from states with federal district court vacancies to recommend individuals for the president to nominate. If the president fails to follow the home state senators' recommendations, a slighted senator may block the nomination from coming to the floor for a confirmation vote.

separation of church and state. The idea that neither national nor state governments may pass laws that support one religion or all religions or give preference to one religion over others.

separate but equal. A practice in southern states to comply with the Fourteenth Amendment's "equal protection" clause by passing laws requiring separate but equal accommodations for blacks and whites in public facilities. The Supreme Court ruled such laws unconstitutional in 1954.

separation of powers. The idea that each branch of government is authorized to carry out a separate part of the political process.

service responsiveness. Representation that takes the form of the tasks legislators perform based on the requests and needs of their constituents.

Shays's Rebellion. An armed revolt by farmers in western Massachusetts who were resisting state efforts to seize their property for failure to pay taxes and debts.

signing statements. Pronouncements of how the president intends to interpret and apply a law when he signs a bill into law.

simple majority. Fifty percent plus one of those participating or of those who vote.

single-issue groups. Groups that take positions and are active on only one specific issue (e.g., abortion, guns, LGBT rights, the environment).

single-member district. A method of selecting representatives in which the people in a district select a single representative.

single-member district plurality system. A method of selecting representatives in which a nation or state is divided into separate election districts and voters in each district choose one representative. The candidate in each district with a plurality of the vote wins the seat.

slander. To make false or defamatory oral statements about someone.

slot machine theory. The view of judicial review that all judges do is lay the constitutional provision involved beside the statute being challenged and "decide whether the latter squares with the former."

social equality. The idea that people should be free of class or social barriers and discrimination.

social-psychological model (Michigan model). A model explaining voter choice that focuses on individual attitudes.

socioeconomic status (SES). The social background and economic position of a person.

sociological model (Columbia model). A model explaining voter choice by considering factors such as religion, place of residence, and socioeconomic status.

soft money. Campaign contributions given to political parties rather than directly to candidates.

soft news. Stories characterized by opinion, human interest, and often entertainment value.

solidary benefits. Satisfaction gained from membership in interest groups such as friendship and a sense of belonging to a group or meeting people with similar interests.

sovereignty. The legitimate authority in a government to wield coercive power to authoritatively allocate values.

Speaker of the House of Representatives. The person who presides over the House. The Speaker is responsible for many of the parliamentary duties, such as recognizing speakers, and is the most powerful person in the chamber.

special rule. A rule formulated by the House Rules committee specifying the conditions under which a given bill will be considered on the House floor.

spoils system. A system of governing in which political positions and benefits are given to the friends of the winner.

spokes-of-the-wheel model. A method of organizing the presidency that calls for the president to be the center of activity, with numerous advisors reporting directly to the president.

stability. The likelihood of changes in the direction of public opinion.

standards of due process. The procedural guarantees provided to ensure fair treatment and constitutional rights.

standing committees. Permanent committees in Congress that are responsible for legislation in a specific policy area.

state presidential primary. A method of selecting delegates to a political party's national convention in which the voters directly elect delegates.

stewardship doctrine. A view of presidential power that states that the president is a steward of the people and should do anything the nation needs that is not prohibited by the Constitution.

straight-ticket voting. Voting for the same party's candidates for president and Congress.

strategic framing. Giving prominence in media stories to who is gaining or losing on an issue.

strategic model. The view that sincere voting does not always maximize utility.

straw polls. Unscientific polls based on nonrandom samples.

strong-executive model. A model of the presidency in which the powers of the executive office are significant and independent from Congress.

structured rule. A rule that permits only certain amendments to a bill.

substantive representation. The concept of representation that states that officeholders do not have to be minorities to accurately represent minority interests.

suffrage. The right to vote.

sunshine laws. Laws intended to keep the bureaucracy accountable to the people by requiring that agency meetings be open to the public.

Super PAC. A type of political committee that can raise unlimited sums of money from corporations, unions, associations, and wealthy individuals to independently support or oppose political candidates. Unlike traditional PACs, Super PACs may not contribute directly to or coordinate with political candidates' campaigns.

Super Tuesday. The day in early March when several states hold their primaries. These states choose a significant portion of delegates to the national convention.

"supreme law of the land." The idea that the U.S. Constitution, laws passed by Congress, and the treaties made by the federal government are supreme, and state constitutions and laws are subordinate to them.

swing states. States in which the outcome of a presidential race is unclear, and both candidates have a realistic chance of winning.

symbolic responsiveness. A congressional member's efforts to use political symbols to generate trust and support among the voters.

test case. A lawsuit filed to test the constitutionality of some government policy.

Texas v. Johnson. The 1989 case in which the Supreme Court ruled that burning the American flag was a form of expression that had constitutional protection.

third parties. Minor political parties that periodically appear but have little success in winning office.

trustee. A representative who uses his or her own judgment to make decisions promoting the best interests of the nation as a whole, with the particular interests of constituents remaining a secondary concern.

trustee system of democracy. The idea that the job of elected leaders is to make decisions based on their own expertise and judgment, and not just make decisions based on the wishes and preferences of constituents.

two-party system. A political system in which only two political parties have a realistic chance of controlling the major offices of government.

unanimous consent agreement (UCA). An agreement between majority and minority party leaders on the procedures and conditions under which a bill will be considered in the Senate.

unfunded mandates. Federal mandates for which the federal government does not pay any associated costs.

unicameral. A legislature with one chamber.

unilateral powers. Presidential directives that carry the weight of law even though they have not been formally endorsed by Congress.

unit rule. A rule that permitted a majority of a state's delegation to a political party's national convention to require that the entire state delegation vote the same way (or as a unit).

unitary system. A political system in which the power is concentrated in the national government, and the regional governments can exercise only those powers granted them by the central government.

utility. The amount of enjoyment an individual receives from a given situation or outcome.

Virginia plan. The first major proposal presented at the 1787 Constitutional Convention; the basis of the Constitution.

voter turnout. The percentage of eligible voters who cast votes in an election.

Voting Rights Act of 1965. Act authorizing the federal government to ensure that eligible voters were not denied access to the ballot, actively protecting the Fifteenth Amendment's promise of voting rights for African Americans.

weak-executive model. A model of the presidency in which the executive would have a limited term, would have no veto power, and would be allowed to exercise only the authority explicitly granted by Congress.

Weeks v. United States. The 1914 case that said that evidence obtained through an unreasonable search and seizure cannot be used in federal trials.

Wesberry v. Sanders. The 1964 case in which the Supreme Court invalidated unequal congressional districts, saying that all legislative districts must contain about equal numbers of people. The ruling is popularly known as the principle of one person, one vote.

whips. Assistants to the majority and minority party leaders in Congress who encourage rank-and-file members to support the party's positions. Whips make sure that rank-and-file members are present to vote on key legislative measures and that they know the party leader's desire.

White House Office. A section of the Executive Office of the President that houses many of the most influential advisors to the president, including the chief of staff; the White House legal counsel; presidential speechwriters; the president's press secretary; assistants for domestic, foreign, and economic policy; and liaisons with Congress, the public, and state and local governments.

writ of certiorari. An order from a higher court to a lower court ord ering the lower court to turn over transcripts and documents of a case for review. The U.S. Supreme Court formally exercises its discretionary powers over what cases to hear by issuing a writ of certiorari, which is granted according to the rule of four.

writ of mandamus. A court order requiring a public official to perform an official duty over which he or she has no discretion.

CASES INDEX

NAME INDEX

SUBJECT INDEX

475; purposive, 192–193, 227; rationality and, 192; selective, 195; solidary, 192, 226

Bertelsmann AG, 285

Biased mass media, 268, 286–293, 298. *See also* Mass media

Biased samples, 312–313

Bicameralism, in Congress, 451–463

Bicameral legislature, 46, 451–452

Big Four, 462

Bill of Rights, 52, 52n, 113–117. *See also* Civil liberties

Bills to law process, 464–473; bill introduction, 465–466; committee action, 465; 466–468; committee referral, 465–466; diagram, 465; enactment into law, 465, 473; floor action, 465, 467–472; resolving House-Senate differences, 472–473

Biological models: political science, 32; public opinion, 327–328

Bipartisan Campaign Reform Act (BCRA), 217–218, 375

Bisexuality. *See* Lesbian, gay, bisexual, and transgender citizens

Black Muslims, 153

Black Panthers, 153

Blacks. *See* African Americans

Blanket primary, 337n

Block grants, 98

Blogs, 296–297

Blue state-red state divide, 321–322, 421–422

Bounded rationality, 559

BP oil spill, 548–549, 560–562, 630

Brandenburg v. Ohio, 126

Breaking treaties, 486

Bribery, 440, 484, 612

British Parliament, 40, 433, 452, 455

Broadcast medium, Internet as, 284

Brookings Institution, 202

Brown v. Board of Education, 151, 210, 615

Budget: federal, incremental decision making, 632–633; Office of Management and Budget, 495; zero-based budgeting, 632–633

Bureaucracies, 534–569; behavior theories, 558–560; characteristics of, 538–543, 568; concept of, 537–538; controlling, 557–564; defined, 537; influencing, 562–564; introduction, 535–536; lobbying, 555–557; merit system, 540–541; monitoring, 560–562; power of, 552–557; purpose of, 537–538, 568; rational choice models, 558–559, 568; reforming, 565–567; stereotypes, 542; structure of, 544–552; takeaway points, 568–569; Weberian model, 539–540

Bureaucrats, 541–543

Bush doctrine, 482

Business, running government as, 565–567

Businesspeople, as Congress members, 444

By-product theory, of interest groups, 197–198

Cabinet, 492–494. *See also* Presidency

Cabinet departments, 544, 546

Cable television, 284, 290, 294, 295, 621

California: ballot initiatives, 11; blanket primary, 337n; electoral votes, 367; equal representation in Senate, 87; nonpartisan primary, 377; presidential campaign stops, 373; reapportionment and, 380; same-sex partnerships, 179; state party delegations, 338

Campaigns: BCRA and, 217–218, 375; FECA and, 217, 374; news sources, 273; support, interest groups, 209–210. *See also* Presidential campaigns; Presidential nomination campaigns

Canada: federalism, 79; NAFTA and, 503; political participation in, 401; two-party system, 235

Candidate image, 423–424

Capital punishment, 138–141

Career patterns, Congress members, 446–448

Cartel, legislative, 475

Casework, 436

Categorical grants, 97–98

Categorical groups, 189

Caucuses, 335, 336n. *See also* Iowa

Caucus method, 339

CBS News, 277, 278, 285

Censures and reprimands, 442

CEO presidency, 498

Chairs, committee, 461

Chamber of Commerce of the United States, 196, 208

Check and Balance, 58–59

Chief diplomat responsibilities, 502–504

Chief executive responsibilities, 499–501. *See also* Presidents

Chief justice, 576, 582, 586n. *See also* Supreme Court

Child pornography, 130

Christian Crusade, 173

Citizens for a Sound Economy, 203

Citizens United v. Federal Election Commission, 126–127, 128, 218, 375, 608

Civic engagement, public sphere, 295–297

Civil disobedience, 152, 153

Civil liberties, 108–143; Anti-Federalists and, 67; Bill of Rights, 113–117; civil rights *versus*, 147–148, 180–181; concept of, 111–113; corporations and, 128–129; criminal procedure and, 134–141; defined, 111; freedom of expression, 123–131; government authority and individual liberty, 112–113; al-Kidd case, 109–111; privacy rights, 131–134; religious freedom, 118–123; right to counsel, 136–137; state violations, 114–118; Supreme Court decisions, 601–602; takeaway points, 142–143

Civil rights, 144–182; African Americans, 157–160, 181; *Brown v. Board of Education*, 151, 210, 615; civil liberties *versus*, 147–148, 180–181; concept of, 147–149; defined, 147; disabilities, 175–178; Gratz case, 145–147; Latinos, 160–165, 181;

LGBT citizens, 178–180; Native Americans, 164–168, 181; takeaway points, 180–182; women, 168–175, 181–182

Civil Rights Act of 1964, 156, 615

Civil War: Confederate states after, 149; Reconstruction period, 95, 152, 235, 376, 382n; secession, 66, 80, 95, 442; slavery and, 47, 66, 89

Classical music interest group, 190

"Clear and present danger" test, 125

Closed primaries, 336–337

Closed rule, 469

Closed shop, 194

Cloture, 470–471

CNN, 277, 278, 291

Coalition building, 207–208

Coast Guard, 538, 546

Colbert bump, 276–277

The Colbert Report, 276–277

Collective action, 194

College education: African Americans, 160; Latinos, 162; political socialization and, 323–324; women, 174, 175

College students: activity fees, 196; politics and, 18–19

Collegial courts, 579

Colorado: electoral votes, 367; presidential campaign stops, 373; same-sex partnerships, 179; state party delegations, 338

Columbia Journalism Review, 285

Columbia model. *See* Sociological model

Commander-in-chief responsibilities, 501–502

Commerce, Energy and, 458, 462

Commission on the Status of Women, 171, 172

Committee action, bills to law process, 465, 466–468

Committee of the Whole, 470

Committee referral, bills to law process, 465–466

Committees: A, 459, 462; advisory, 550; Agriculture, 458, 459, 462, 463; Appropriations, 458, 459, 462, 474; Armed Services, 458, 459, 462; assigning to, 459–460; B, 459, 462; Big Four, 462; bills to law process, 465, 466–468; chairs, 461; conference, 472–473; Energy and Commerce, 458, 462; ethics, 458, 460n, 463; exclusive, 462; Finance, 459, 462; Foreign Relations, 459, 462; House Appropriations, 474; House of Representatives, 463–464; House Rules, 467–469; of 113th Congress, 458–459; Intelligence, 458, 459, 462, 463; prestige, 462–463; purpose of, 478; rankings, 461–462; Rules, 453, 458, 459, 460, 462, 467, 469; senate, 463–464; Standards of Official Conduct, 451, 462, 463; standing, 457–461; Super-A, 459, 462; system, 457–463; Veterans' Affairs, 458, 459, 463; Ways and Means, 458, 460, 462, 463

Commonwealth status, of Puerto Rico, 89

Communications Act, 283–284

Communications Decency Act, 130, 284
Communist Party, 243, 244
Competence, of public opinion, 308–309
Competitiveness, in elections, 333–334, 387–388
Concurrent powers, 86
Concurring opinions, 583
Conditional party government, 476
Confederate states, after Civil War, 149
Confederate States of America, 95
Confederation, 77–78. *See also* Federalism
Conferees, 473
Conference, 582
Conference committees, 472–473
Confidence levels, 313, 314
Confirmation process, in Senate, 594–599
Conflict resolution and stability, political parties, 251–252
Congress, 429–478; behavioral models, 473–476; bicameralism in, 451–463; bills to law process, 464–473; bureaucracy control, 562–563; concept of, 433; disapproval of, 431–432; distributive model, 474–475; First Congress, 65; First Continental Congress, 433; impeachment, 438–441; informational model, 475; interest group ratings for members, 208; lawmaking, 434–435; as legislature, 433; meaning of word, 433; misunderstandings about, 431–432; norms in, 474; 112th, 173, 377, 444, 445, 450; 113th, 455, 458–459, 460; partisan model, 475–476; party competition for, 236; party votes in, 260; pork-barrel benefits, 386, 387, 436, 437–438, 475; president and, 515–530, 531–532; presidential success in, 518–525; primary responsibilities, 433–438, 477; purpose of, 433; rational choice models, 474–476; responsibilities, 432–443; secondary responsibilities, 437–443, 477; Second Congress, 223; Second Continental Congress, 40, 433; takeaway points, 476–478; third house of, 473; women in, 173. *See also* Committees; Congress members; House of Representatives; Representation; Senate
Congressional apportionment periods, 237n
Congressional delegation of presidential power, 488
Congressional districts, 380–384; district plan, 370, 371, 372; gerrymandering, 380–383, 382n; majority-minority, 382, 383; multimember, 380; redistricting, 260, 379, 380, 382, 383, 388, 394; single-member, 380, 383n. *See also* Electoral college
Congressional elections, 379–393; candidate nomination process, 376–379, 394; competitiveness in, 333–334; distinguishing feature of, 394; financing, 389–392; incumbency advantage, 384–388, 394; president and, 507–508; presidential elections *versus*, 376
Congressional leaders, 454–455
Congressional Union, 169, 170

Congress members, 443–451; backgrounds of, 444–446; daily life of, 448–449; home styles, 437; pay for, 449–450; perks, 386–387, 450–451; seating and disciplining, 441–442; tenure and career patterns, 446–448
Connecticut: electoral votes, 367; *Griswold v. Connecticut*, 116, 132, 133; presidential campaign stops, 373; same-sex marriages, 179; state party delegations, 338
Connecticut Compromise (Great Compromise), 47, 72
Consent agreements, unanimous, 471–472
Conservatives, 23, 24, 320
Constituencies, 59, 60, 435, 437
Constituency committees, 462
Constitution, U.S., 36–73; Anti-Federalists, 43–44, 45, 46, 52, 53, 54, 71; Article II, 498, 525, 531; Articles of Confederation *versus*, 48–52, 49n, 71; authors of, 37–38; changes to, 61–71, 72; custom and usage, 68–69; economic conditions before, 42–43; elastic clause, 83; Federalist Papers, 33, 45, 54; full faith and credit, 51, 87–88, 106, 180; historical antecedents, 40–42; living Constitution, 607; Madisonian dilemma, 55–56; misunderstanding of, 37; mixed government, 60–61; powers of, 69–70; principles, 54–61; ratification campaign, 52–54; religion's role in, 47–48, 48n; representative government, 57; republican form of government, 56, 56n; separation of powers, 58–59; supreme law of the land, 49, 88, 91, 604; takeaway points, 71–72; as written document, 56–57. *See also* Amendments; Federalism
Constitutional Convention, 44–47
Constitutional option, filibuster, 599
Constitutional responsibilities, president and, 499–504
Constitutions: changes to, 61; defined, 38–39, 48, 56–57, 71; state, 41–42, 71; unwritten, 57
Consumer Financial Protection Bureau, 551
Consumer Product Safety Commission, 547, 553, 554
Contracting out, 566
"Contract with America", 261
Controlling bureaucracies, 557–564
Conventions, 336. *See also* Constitutional Convention; National conventions
Cooperative federalism, 95–99
Corporations: civil liberties and, 128–129; government, 549
Council of Economic Advisers, 495, 544
Courts, district, 576–578
Courts, federal: jurisdiction, 574–576; minorities in, 585; structure and organization, 576–583. *See also* Judges; Supreme Court
Courts of appeals, 578–579, 579n
Courts of appellate jurisdiction, 575, 614
Courts of original jurisdiction, 575
Credit claiming, 387

Criminal procedure, civil liberties and, 134–141
Crossover sanction, 98–99
Cuban missile crisis, 481
Culture, political, 317–318
Culture war, public opinion and, 321–322
Custom and usage, 68–69
Cycles, of party strength, 263

Daily Kos, 290, 296–297
Daily life, of Congress members, 448–449
Daily Show effect, 275
The Daily Show, 275, 276
D.C. *See* Washington, D.C.
Death penalty, 138–141
Decades, congressional apportionment periods, 237n
Declaration of Independence, 40, 71
De facto discrimination, 159
De jure discrimination, 157–158
Delaware: electoral votes, 367; presidential campaign stops, 373; state party delegations, 338
Delegate model of democracy, 307, 308, 317, 329
Delegates: accumulation of, 354–356; allocation of, 337–339; defined, 438; method and timing of selection, 339–342
Democracies: conflicting values in, 10; core principles, 7–10; death penalty and, 141; defined, 5, 10, 34; direct, 10–13; forms of, 10; idea of, 3–4; liberal, 13–14, 13n; misunderstanding of, 4; overhead, 560; popular sovereignty, 6, 7, 34; as process, 6; substance, 6–7; takeaway points, 34; trustee system of, 308–309. *See also* Democracy, in America; Representative democracies
Democracy, in America: case for, 25–26; central beliefs, 16–17; challenges, 20–25; college students' attitudes, 18–19; criticisms, 26–27; diversity and differences, 20–22; elitist view, 27, 34; fallacies, 17–20; false consensus, 24–25; ideological beliefs, 22–23, 24; partisanship, 23–24; pluralistic view, 25–26, 34; Washington, D.C., 90
Democratic invisible primary (2008), 348
Democratic Party. *See* Parties
Democratic presidential candidates' delegate accumulation, 355
Democratic-Republicans, Jeffersonian, 223, 231–232, 231n, 233, 234, 239, 239n, 365, 604
Department of Education, 555
Department of Homeland Security, 544
Department of Justice, 544, 546
Depression, Great, 92, 95, 101, 161, 313, 413, 426, 487. *See also* Great recession of 2008–2009
Deregulation, 547
Descriptive representation, 382–383
Desegregation, 88, 152, 615
Deviating elections, 425

The Federalist, 54–55; *Federalist* Number 10, 12, 33, 55, 59, 68, 81, 190, 211, 224; *Federalist* Number 51, 33, 59; *Federalist* Number 64, 363; *Federalist* Number 70, 485; *Federalist* Number 78, 604; *Federalist* Number 80, 584

Federal judges. *See* Judges

Federal judiciary. *See* Judiciary

Federal need analysis methodology, 555

Federal Register, 554

Federal Reserve, 229, 501, 550, 551

Federal stimulus money, 76, 92–93, 98, 325, 496, 632

Feedback, 630–631

Felony disenfranchisement, 245, 403–405

The Feminine Mystique (Friedan), 171

Fifteenth Amendment, 64, 67, 95, 115, 149, 157, 166, 169, 402, 403

Fifth Amendment, 115, 135, 135n, 137, 142

Files and records, bureaucracies, 539

Filibuster, 470–471, 523, 598, 599

Finance Committee, 459, 462

Financial crisis. *See* Great recession of 2008–2009

Financial Modernization Act, 547

Financing: congressional elections, 389–392; presidential elections, 374–376

"Finding" the law, 599–600

Fire alarm oversight, 560

First Amendment: essence, 302; freedom of expression, 123–131; freedom of religion, 118–123

First Congress, 65

First Continental Congress, 433

First gentlemen, 495n

First ladies, 495–496. *See also* Presidency

Fiscal federalism, 96

501(c) groups, 214

527 groups, 214, 218

Flag, U.S.: design, 526–527; "rally round the flag" effect, 324–325, 514

Floor action, bills to law process, 465, 467–472

Florida: death penalty laws, 140; electoral votes, 367; high-speed rail systems, 76; presidential campaign stops, 373; reapportionment and, 380; state party delegations, 338

Focus groups, 316. *See also* Public opinion polls

Focusing event, 630

Football teams example, 230

Foreign Intelligence Surveillance Act, 69

Foreign Relations Committee, 459, 462

Formal rules, bureaucracies, 539

Fourteenth Amendment, 52n, 64, 67, 70, 95, 115, 119, 135, 136, 142, 151, 158, 180, 210, 216, 381, 382, 610, 611, 613, 615

Fourth Amendment, 112, 133, 135, 136

Fox News, 267–268, 276, 277, 278, 281, 285, 289, 290, 291, 307

Framing, 279–280, 293

France: African Americans and, 152; political participation in, 401; unitary government, 80

Franchise, 402–416. *See also* Voting

Franking privilege, 451

Freedom. *See* Political freedom

Freedom of expression, 123–131

Freedom of Information Act, 283, 562

Freedom of religion, 118–123

Free exercise of religion, 119, 122–123

Free media, 276–277

Free press: concept of, 268, 269–270; defined, 269, 297; government control, 282–284, 298; private control, 284–286, 298; propaganda and, 290–291; role of, 298. *See also* Mass media

Free rider problem, 194, 195–196

Frontloading, 339, 341, 342

Full faith and credit, 51, 87–88, 106, 180

Functions of government, constitutions and, 38–39, 48, 56–57, 71

Funnel of causality, 418–419

Game theory, 600

Garbage can models, of agenda setting, 629–630

Gay citizens. *See* Lesbian, gay, bisexual, and transgender citizens

Gender bias, in mass media, 292. *See also* Women

General elections, 334, 334n, 393. *See also* Elections

General Electric, 285

General Federation of Women's Clubs, 199

General revenue sharing, 97

General schedule pay scale, 542, 543

Generational effect hypothesis, 413

Genocide, 165

Geographical constituency, 437

Georgia: abortions, 132; death penalty laws, 140; electoral votes, 367; illegal immigration policies, 163; presidential campaign stops, 373; state party delegations, 338; *Wesberry v. Sanders*, 382

Gerrymandering, 380–383, 382n

Gideon v. Wainwright, 116, 136–137

Going public, 509–513

Golden Rule, federalism and, 104–105

Good behavior, terms of, 584

Good faith exception, 136

Good losers, 251, 252

Government accountability, political parties and, 251

Government authority, individual liberty and, 112–113

Government control, free press and, 282–284, 298

Government corporations, 549

Government responsiveness, political parties and, 250–251

Governments: conditional party, 476; defined, 5; divided, 253, 258–259; mixed, 60–61; positive, 488; representative, 57; republican form, 56, 56n; running, as business, 565–567; structure-functions-procedures, 38–39, 48, 56–57, 71. *See also* Federal government; State governments

Grandfather clause, 151

Grants: block, 98; categorical, 97–98; crossover sanctions, 98–99; grants-in-aid, 96–100, 104–105

Gratz case, 145–147

Great Britain: African Americans and, 152–153; monarchs, 508; representative democracy, 13; responsible party model, 252; Revolutionary War and, 42, 43, 78, 118; two-party system, 235; unitary government, 80; unwritten constitution, 57

Great Compromise. *See* Connecticut Compromise

Great Depression, 92, 95, 101, 161, 313, 413, 426, 487

Great recession of 2008–2009: federal stimulus money, 76, 92–93, 98, 325, 496, 632; FMA and, 547; illegal immigration and, 165; salience and, 306–307; state-federal relations and, 75–76, 102–103, 106

Great Society programs, 96, 99

Greenhouse emissions, 102

Griswold v. Connecticut, 116, 132, 133

Group entrepreneur, 198

Groups: categorical, 189; 501(c), 214, 527, 214, 218; focus, 316; pressure, 215; reference, 324. *See also* Interest groups; Public opinion polls; Voting behavior models

Guadalupe Hidalgo, Treaty of, 161

Gulf of Mexico, 548, 560, 630

Handgun Control, Inc, 191, 215

Handicapped individuals. *See* Disabled individuals

Hard money, 217

Hard news, 285–286

Hard work norm, 474

Hastings impeachment, 441

Hawaii: American flag and, 526; electoral votes, 367; presidential campaign stops, 373; same-sex partnerships, 179; statehood, 89, 380n, 526; state party delegations, 338

Head Start, 96

Hierarchical model: bureaucracies, 539; presidency, 496–498

High crimes and misdemeanors, 440, 484, 612

Higher Education Act, 469, 555

Hispanics. *See* Latinos

Holds, 470

Home styles, 437

Homosexuality, 125–126, 133, 134

House Appropriations Committee, 474

House districts. *See* Congressional districts

House of Representatives: apportionment, 379–380; committees, 463–464; competitiveness in elections, 333, 387–388; leadership in, 455–457; reapportionment, 380, 394; Senate *versus*, 453; Speaker, 455–457, 477–478; women in, 173

House Rules Committee, 467–469

House-Senate differences, bills to law process, 472–473

Human aspect, judges, 571–572

Hurricane Katrina, 292, 325, 488, 630

Hypotheses, scientific method, 29

Lobbying: bureaucratic, 555–557; in court, 210; defined, 205; direct, 206–207; indirect, 206–207; presidential campaigns and, 188–189; regulations on, 216–217; spending on, 201. *See also* Interest groups

Lobbyists, 205–206, 219

Logrolling, 207–208

Louisiana: affirmative action and, 159; death penalty laws, 140; electoral votes, 367; nonpartisan primary, 337n, 377; presidential campaign stops, 373; state party delegations, 338

MADD. *See* Mothers Against Drunk Driving

Madisonian dilemma, 55–56, 111, 483

Magazines, as news source, 273, 274

Magic number, 343

Maine: electoral votes, 367; formation, 88n; presidential campaign stops, 373; same-sex partnerships, 179; state party delegations, 338

Maintaining election, 425

Majority: absolute, 7; simple, 7; supermajority, 49, 62, 440, 453, 518, 523; two-thirds, 49, 51, 359, 370, 439

Majority leader, 454

Majority-minority districts, 382, 383

Majority opinions, 583

Majority rule: apathy and, 31–32; defined, 7–8; direct democracy and, 13; Downs's theory and, 31; elections and, 15; electoral college and, 366; fallacy of, 17; public opinion and, 329; public policy and, 640, 644–645. *See also* Electoral college; Public opinion; Representative democracies

Malapportioned, 381

MALDEF (Mexican American Legal Defense and Educational Fund), 161, 162, 167

Mapp v. Ohio, 116, 136

Marbury v. Madison, 70, 575, 604, 606, 609, 615, 617

Margin of error, public opinion polls, 313–314, 512

Marriages: plural, 89, 122; same-sex, 11, 12, 179–180

Marshals Service, U.S., 546

Marxist parties, 244

Maryland: electoral votes, 367; *McCulloch v. Maryland*, 83; presidential campaign stops, 373; same-sex partnerships, 179; state party delegations, 338

Massachusetts: electoral votes, 367; presidential campaign stops, 373; same-sex marriages, 179; state party delegations, 338

Mass media, 266–299; agenda setting, 279–280; bias, 268, 286–293, 298; changes in public sphere, 293–297, 299; defined, 268, 297; differing information from, 272–275; electronic media, 268–269, 297; framing and, 279–280, 293; free, 276–277; free press, 269–270; gatekeepers, 294–295; gender bias, 292; information and education role, 270–272; misinformation, 275; negativity bias,

292–293; owners of, 285; political media bias, 287–291, 298; political parties and, 272; print media, 268, 284, 297; public advocate, 280–282; public opinion and, 326; public sphere, 269–270, 293–297, 298; racial bias, 292; roles, 298; strategic framing and, 293; takeaway points, 298–299; trusting, 276–279; watchdog function, 280–282. *See also* Free press; Information; News media; Press

Material benefits: interest groups, 192; political parties, 226

McCain-Feingold law, 375

McCulloch v. Maryland, 83

McDonald v. Chicago, 116, 117

Media. *See* Mass media

Media bias, 286–293, 298

Membership: interest groups, 190–191, 203; political parties, 226

Members' representational allowance (MRA), 450

Merit, judicial experience and, 592, 594

Merit system, 261–262, 540–541

Messages to Congress, president and, 516–517

Metros, 104

Mexican American Legal Defense and Educational Fund (MALDEF), 161, 162, 167

Mexican Americans, 160–161

Mexican-American War, 161

Mexico: Gulf of Mexico, 548, 560, 630; illegal immigration, 102, 163–165; Institutional Revolutionary Party, 235; NAFTA and, 503

Michigan: electoral votes, 367; presidential campaign stops, 373; state party delegations, 338; University of Michigan's admission policy, 145–147

Michigan Civil Rights Initiative, 147, 158

Michigan model. *See* Social-psychological model

Midterm elections, 405

Minerals Management Service, 548, 560–562

Minnesota: electoral votes, 367; presidential campaign stops, 373; state party delegations, 338

Minorities: in Congress, 445–446; federal court appointments, 585; rights, 7–8; women as, 26, 26n. *See also* Affirmative action

Minority leader, 454–455

Minor political parties, 234, 242–248, 242n

Miranda case, 138–139

Miranda v. Arizona, 137, 139

Misdemeanors, high crimes and, 440, 484, 612

Misinformation, 275

Mississippi: affirmative action and, 159; electoral votes, 367; presidential campaign stops, 373; state party delegations, 338

Missouri: electoral votes, 367; presidential campaign stops, 373; state party delegations, 338

Mist-clearing phase, presidential nomination campaigns, 354–357

Misunderstandings: Congress, 431–432; democracy, 4; U.S. Constitution, 37

Mixed government, 60–61

Mobilization, voting and, 413

Models, scientific method, 29. *See also specific models*

Moderates, 24, 320

Modified open rule, 469

Monarchs, 508

Money, interest groups and, 204

Money primary, 346–347, 362

Monitoring bureaucracies, 560–562

Monitoring of activities, terrorism, 113

Montana: electoral votes, 367; presidential campaign stops, 373; state party delegations, 338

Moral hazard, 567

Morality policy, 638

Mormon Church, 89, 122

Mothers Against Drunk Driving (MADD), 193

MRA. *See* Members' representational allowance

MSNBC, 278, 290, 291

Multimember district, 380

Multiparty systems, 235

Murray Hill Incorporated, 127–128

Muslims: Black, 153; al-Kidd case, 109–111

NAACP. *See* National Association for the Advancement of Colored People

NAFTA. *See* North American Free Trade Agreement

NARAL Pro-Choice America, 198, 202

National Academy of Sciences, 203

National American Woman Suffrage Association, 169

National Association for the Advancement of Colored People (NAACP), 150–152, 161, 163, 167, 210, 216, 324

National Association of Manufacturers, 196

National bank, *McCulloch v. Maryland*, 83

National Commission on Architectural Barriers, 176, 177

National conventions (national party conventions): accumulation of delegates, 354–356; allocation of delegates, 337–339; defined, 336, 393; delegate selection, method and timing, 339–342; functions of, 358–359; presidential nomination campaigns, 357–359

National Federation of Business and Professional Women's Clubs, 170, 171

National government. *See* Federal government

National Highway Traffic Safety Administration, 193, 554

National legislature. *See* Congress

National Organization for Women (NOW), 172, 199

National party conventions. *See* National conventions

National Public Radio (NPR), 278, 290, 294

National Rifle Association (NRA), 186, 191, 192, 198, 204, 209, 215, 218, 294

National Right to Life Committee, 197, 202
National Security Agency, 69
National Security and Homeland Security Presidential Directive, 530
National Security Council, 495
National security directives, 525, 530, 532
National Student Solidarity Protest, 18
National Women's Party, 170
Native Americans, 164–168, 181, 492
NBC News, 277, 278
Nebraska: affirmative action and, 158; electoral votes, 367; presidential campaign stops, 373
Need analysis methodology, federal, 555
Negative advertising, 127, 326
Negativity bias, in mass media, 292–293
Nerds, morality policy, 638
Netherlands, political participation in, 401
Netroots Nation, 297
Neutral competence, 541
Nevada: electoral votes, 367; presidential campaign stops, 373; same-sex partnerships, 179; state party delegations, 338
New Deal, 92, 96, 259, 426, 428, 488, 506, 609, 611, 613
New England town meeting, 12
New federalism, 99–102
New Hampshire: electoral votes, 367; presidential campaign stops, 373; primary, 339, 348, 350, 353, 354, 357, 362, 393; same-sex marriages, 179; state party delegations, 338
New Jersey: electoral votes, 367; presidential campaign stops, 373; same-sex partnerships, 179; state party delegations, 338
New Jersey plan, 46–47
New Mexico: electoral votes, 367; presidential campaign stops, 373
News, 269, 285–286
News Corporation, 284, 285, 294
News media: credibility, 277–278; defined, 269; entertainment and, 288; information and education role, 270–272; news sources, 273–275; primary role, 270. See also Mass media
Newspapers, as news source, 273–274
Newsweek, 278
New York: electoral votes, 367; presidential campaign stops, 373; reapportionment and, 380; same-sex marriages, 179; state party delegations, 338
New York Post, 285
New York Times, 274, 275, 281–282, 283, 287, 289, 290, 292
Niche theory, interest groups, 198–199
Nine, of thirteen states, 49, 49n
9/11 terrorist attacks, 110, 112, 481, 508, 512, 514, 577, 630
Nineteenth Amendment, 62, 64, 67, 166, 170, 403, 445, 613
No Child Left Behind law, 101, 102
Nominations: congressional candidates, 376–379, 394; defined, 334; methods, 335–337; presidential candidates,

337–362, 393. See also Congress; Elections; Presidency; Presidential nomination campaigns
Nongermane amendments, 464
Nonpartisan primary, 337n, 377
Normative theory, 28
Norms, in Congress, 474
North American Free Trade Agreement (NAFTA), 504
North Carolina: death penalty laws, 140; electoral votes, 367; presidential campaign stops, 373; state party delegations, 338
North Dakota: electoral votes, 367; presidential campaign stops, 373; state party delegations, 338
North Iowa Tea Party, 297
Northwest Ordinance of 1787, 95
No-Spin Zone, 290–291
NOW. See National Organization for Women
NPR. See National Public Radio
NRA. See National Rifle Association
Nuclear option, filibuster, 599
Null hypothesis, 29
Nullification, 94

Obamacare. See Patient Protection and Affordable Care Act of 2010
Objective journalism, 287
Obscenity, 127–130
Occupational Safety and Health Administration, 553–554
Occupy Wall Street, 18–19
Office of Management and Budget (OMB), 495
Office of president, 482, 489, 530. See also Presidency; Presidents
Office of Thrift Supervision, 552, 561
Ohio: Brandenburg v. Ohio, 126; electoral votes, 367; high-speed rail systems, 76; Mapp v. Ohio, 116, 136; presidential campaign stops, 373; state party delegations, 338
Oil spill, BP, 548–549, 560–562, 630
Oklahoma: electoral votes, 367; illegal immigration policies, 102; presidential campaign stops, 373; state party delegations, 338
Oligarchy, 5, 77
OMB. See Office of Management and Budget
112th Congress, 173, 377, 444, 445, 450
113th Congress, 455, 458–459, 460
One-party system, 233, 235
One person, one vote, 368, 382
Open primaries, 337
Open rule, 469
Open seats, 388
Opinion. See Public opinion; Public opinion polls
Opinions, Supreme Court, 583
Opportunity, equality of, 9–10
Oregon: electoral votes, 367; presidential campaign stops, 373; same-sex partnerships, 179; state party delegations, 338

O'Reilly's No-Spin Zone, 290–291
Originalism, 606–607
The O'Reilly Factor, 277
Overhead democracy, 560

PACs. See Political action committees
Panama Canal Treaty, 502
Parliament, British, 452, 455
Parliamentary systems, 240–241, 433
Participation: political parties and, 248–250; public opinion and, 328–329. See also Political participation
Parties (political parties), 222–265; concept of, 224–229; conflict resolution and, 251–252; constitutional change and, 68–69; contributions of, 248–253; defining, 224; divided government, 252–253; effective governance and, 244–245; facilitate participation, 248–250; factions versus, 225–226; football teams example, 230; government accountability and, 251; government responsiveness and, 250–251; incentives for associating with, 226–229; interest groups versus, 225; introduction, 223–224; list of, 234; mass media and, 272; membership in, 226; minor, 234, 242–248, 242n; need for, 223–224; paradox of, 223–224, 230; partisanship, 23–24; policy-motivated activists, 227–228; purpose, 24; rational choice explanation of, 231–233; reasons for, 230–233; representative democracy and, 15; responsible party model, 252–253; sociological explanation of, 230–231; stability and, 251–252; strength of, 253–263; takeaway points, 263–265; voter dissatisfaction with, 427. See also Tea Party movement; Two-party system
Partisan model, Congress, 475–476
Partisanship: described, 23–24; in electorate, 254; in news source credibility, 278
Party affiliation and philosophy, federal judges, 586–587
Party bosses, 227
Party discipline, 252–253
Party identification, 421–423
Party in government, 226, 258–261
Party in the electorate, 226, 253–257
Party leader, president as, 504–508, 531
Party organizations, 226, 228, 261–262
Party polarization, 476, 521–523
Party professionals, 227–228
Party ratio, 459–460
Party strength: cycles of, 263; in electorate, 254–257
Party votes, 259–260
Passive-negative presidents, 491
Passive-positive presidents, 491
Passive resistance, 153
Patient Protection and Affordable Care Act of 2010, 103, 515
Patriot Act, 112, 134
Patronage, political, 261
Paul Carroll case, 397–398. See also Voting

Texas v. Johnson, 125
Theoretical frameworks, in political science, 30–32, 34
Theories, scientific method, 29
Third house of Congress, 473
Third parties, 242, 242n. *See also* Minor political parties
Thirteen states, nine of, 49, 49n
Thirteenth Amendment, 64, 66, 67, 95, 115, 613
Threats, to free press, 282–286, 298
Three-fourths majority. *See* Supermajority
Time magazine, 278
Time Warner, 285
Town meetings, 12, 511
Transgender citizens. *See* Lesbian, gay, bisexual, and transgender citizens
Treason, 440, 484, 612
Treasury Department, 544, 550
Treaties, breaking, 486
Treaty of Guadalupe Hidalgo, 161
Trust, mass media and, 276–279
Trustee, 438
Trustee system, of democracy, 308–309
Truthiness, 276–277
Tuesday, elections on, 410
Twelfth Amendment, 64, 68, 69n, 364, 365, 366, 484
Twentieth Amendment, 64, 68, 484
Twenty-First Amendment, 64, 68
Twenty-Second Amendment, 64, 67, 68, 484
Twenty-Third Amendment, 64, 67, 67n, 89, 364
Twenty-Fourth Amendment, 64, 67, 156, 613
Twenty-Fifth Amendment, 68, 442, 443, 484
Twenty-Sixth Amendment, 64, 67, 149, 403, 613
Twenty-Seventh Amendment, 64, 67, 68, 450
Twins research, 327
Two-party system: competition at national level, 235–237; defined, 235; electoral rules, 239–242; reasons for, 237–242; voter turnout, 408–409
Two-thirds majority, 49, 51, 359, 370, 439

UAW. *See* United Automobile Workers
UN. *See* United Nations
Unanimous consent agreements, 471–472
Uncle Sugar example, 75–76
Undocumented immigration, 102, 163–165
Unfunded mandates, 101
Unicameral legislature, 40, 452
Unilateral powers, 525–530
Unintentional mobilization, 211
Union shop, 194
Unitary system, 78–79. *See also* Federalism
United Automobile Workers (UAW), 193, 207
United Kingdom: British Parliament, 40, 433, 452, 455; political participation in, 401
United Nations (UN), 78, 80
United States (U.S.): diversity and difference, 20–21; flag of, 526–527; political participation in, 401–402; population

growth, 21–22. *See also* Democracy, in America; Political participation; Voting
United States Postal Service, 537, 549
Unit rule, 359
University of Michigan, affirmative action and, 145–147
Unorthodox lawmaking, 464
Unprotected speech, 127–131
Unwritten constitution, 57
U.S. *See* United States
U.S. Constitution. *See* Constitution
Usage, custom and, 68–69
Utah: electoral votes, 367; illegal immigration policies, 163; presidential campaign stops, 373; statehood, 89; state party delegations, 338
Utility, 30

Vermont: electoral votes, 367; formation, 88n; presidential campaign stops, 373; same-sex marriages, 179; state party delegations, 338
Versailles peace treaty, 503, 510
Veterans' Affairs Committee, 458, 459, 463
Veto, 517–518, 562–563
Viacom, 285
Vice presidents, 491–492. *See also* Presidency
Vietnam War, 149, 283, 306, 403, 445, 485
Virginia: electoral votes, 367; presidential campaign stops, 373; state party delegations, 338
Virginia plan, 45, 46
Virginia Statute for Religious Freedom, 118
Vocational Rehabilitation Act, 176
Volunteer organizations: college students, 18–19; types, 191
Voter choice, 420–425; candidate image and, 423–424; issues and, 424–425; party identification and, 421–423
Voter ID law, 408
Voter registration, 407–408
Voter turnout, 405–411, 415
Voting, 396–428; college students' attitude, 18–19; dissatisfaction, with parties, 427; felony disenfranchisement, 245, 403–405; franchise, 402–416; issue votes, 257, 425; Jim Crow laws, 82, 156, 166–167, 640; laws, 406–407; literacy tests, 150, 151, 157, 403; mobilization hypothesis, 413; one person, one vote, 368, 382; party votes, 259–260; Paul Carroll case, 397–398; poll taxes, 64, 67, 154, 157, 403, 613; prospective, 425; resources and, 414–415; retrospective, 425; right to, 402–416; SES and, 411–413; straight-ticket voters, 257; suffrage, 169; takeaway points, 427–428; women's rights, 67, 169–170; write-in votes, 241n
Voting behavior models: rational choice model, 419–420; social-psychological model (Michigan model), 29, 31, 418–419, 420, 421, 424; sociological model (Columbia model), 416–418

Voting Rights Act of 1965, 156–157, 167, 260, 403, 476
Voucher system, 121, 631, 639

Wall Street Journal, 285
War on terror, 481, 487, 530, 536, 629
War Power Act of 1973, 501–502
Washington: blanket primary, 337n; electoral votes, 367; nonpartisan primary, 377; presidential campaign stops, 373; same-sex partnerships, 179; state party delegations, 338
Washington, D.C.: *District of Columbia v. Heller*, 117; electoral votes, 367; presidential campaign stops, 373; same-sex marriages, 179; statehood issues, 89; state party delegations, 338; state rights of, 90
Washington Times, 290
Watchdog, 280–282
Ways and Means Committee, 458, 460, 462, 463
Weak-executive model, 484
Weapons of mass destruction, 281, 511
Weberian model, of bureaucracy, 539–540
Weeks v. United States, 136
Welfare programs, 100, 101, 314–315
Wesberry v. Sanders, 382
Westboro Baptist Church, 125–126
Western Climate Initiative, 102
West Virginia, 88n, 367, 373
Whigs, 232, 233, 234
Whips, 455
White House Office, 494–495
Winnowing process, 343, 345. *See also* Presidential nomination campaigns
Wisconsin: electoral votes, 367; high-speed rail systems, 76; presidential campaign stops, 373; same-sex partnerships, 179; state party delegations, 338
Women: amendments and, 67; in Congress, 445–446; descriptive representation, 383; federal court appointments, 585; federal judges, 591–592; gender bias, mass media, 292; as minority, 26, 26n, 168; NOW, 172, 199; rights, 168–175, 181–182; voting rights, 67. *See also* Abortion
World Trade Center attacks. *See* 9/11 terrorist attacks
World War II, disabilities and, 176
Wounded Knee incident, 167
Write-in votes, 241n
Writ of appeal, 581n
Writ of certiorari, 581
Writ of habeas corpus, 166, 581n, 614
Writ of mandamus, 605
Written document, U.S. Constitution, 56–57
Wyoming: electoral votes, 367; equal representation in Senate, 87; presidential campaign stops, 373; state party delegations, 338

"Yes We Can" presidential campaign, 18
Young Americans for Freedom, 173

Zero-based budgeting, 632–633
Zones of privacy, 132, 143